C0 BPD-513

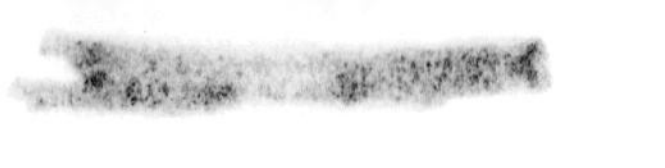

DIRECTORY

OF THE

ANCESTRAL HEADS

OF

NEW ENGLAND FAMILIES

1620 - 1700

COMPILED

BY

FRANK R. HOLMES

GENEALOGICAL PUBLISHING CO., INC.

Originally published: New York, 1923
Reprinted: Genealogical Publishing Co., Inc.
Baltimore, 1964, 1974, 1980, 1984, 1989
Library of Congress Catalogue Card Number 64-19755
International Standard Book Number 0-8063-0182-1
Made in the United States of America

FOREWORD

The study of names is of itself an absorbing subject. Their foundation and derivations are often of a mythical formation, others depending on occupation or place of residence. In the dim ages of the past there is no indication of kin, but only relation to the same stock, race, clan or tribe of people. The English had progressed beyond this, and their immigrants to the shores of the New World were able to trace back their forbears for several centuries before their exodus to the new country. The English parish registers contained a record of births, baptisms, marriages and deaths, which, with court records of wills and transfers of real estate, enabled lineage to be traced in many cases to the advent of William the Conqueror. Prior to this epoch in history, tribal or clan arrangements generally predominated, though in England this was more in the relations of tenantry. In Scotland, where the Gaelic was the language of the country prior to 1745, when the system of clans came to an end, there existed bodies of men all bearing the same surname and believing themselves to be related the one to the other and to be descended from the same stock. Thus the members of every clan were tied to another not only by the feudal but by the patriarchal bonds; for while the individuals composing it were vassals or tenants of their own hereditary chief, they were also descended from his family and could count exactly the degree of their descent.

The Western Indians had no family names; they used only descriptive cognomens which translated into English read something like this: "Long Time Sleeping," "Wipes his Eyes," besides a legion of other descriptive titles. Many of the white men derived their surnames in a similar manner, which had become necessary by the increase of population and for the purpose of identification. Therefore the place of birth or residence was often used; for example, James at-Wood, or John under-the-Hill. Then the occupation was used as a surname, hence the number of Smiths, derived from blacksmith, wagonsmith, tinsmith, goldsmith, etc. The physical characteristics, mental and moral qualities, were all turned into surnames, and families were named originally from their color as White, Black, Gray, Brown; others named for their height or strength, as Little, Long, Hardy, and Strong; while the moral attributes yielded Good, Gay, Moody, Wise, etc. The son of John, Peter and William in turn became Johnson, Peterson and Williamson, and this was also true of other given names; while in the language of the Russians, Paveloitch is the son of Paul; MacDonald in Scotch, is the son of Donald; and Fitzgerald in Irish, the son of Gerald. The prefix "O" signifies grandson, so that we have O'Brien, the grandson of Brien. In the Anglo-Saxon language the letters "ing" at the end of a name also stood for the same thing as Mac in Scotch and Fitz in Irish, hence Billing was the son of Bill, Harding the son of Hard, Birming the son of Birm. As an example, is the word Birmingham; the last syllable, "ham," meaning merely home in old English, became literally "the home of the sons of Birm." In these ways practically all English family nomenclatures have been constituted.

Though the custom is widespread for all males to bear the name of their parents, common law sanctions a change of name when made in good faith. There are no serious consequences growing out of an adoption of a new name, except the possibility of confounding the identity. Many who have become famous in history, arts, and literature, have adopted a new patronymic in whole or in part. Thomas W. Wilson on arriving at man's estate became Woodrow Wilson; and another incumbent of the presidential chair changed his name from Stephen G. Cleveland to Grover Cleveland. Brander Matthews and Bayard Taylor, well known authors, might have been lost amongst the mass of their competitors had they not dropped their plebeian given name James. The baptismal name of General Grant was Hiram Ulysses, but was changed when he was nominated for a cadetship to the Military Academy at West Point, when he was recorded as Ulysses S. Grant, in which form it ever since has remained. In literature and art there have been many radical changes from the original surname. The notable English actor, Henry Irving, was baptized John H. Broadribb; Maurice Barrymore was originally Herbert Lythe; the famous Mark Twain was Samuel L. Clemens; while O. Henry was Sidney Porter, and Charles H. Browne became Artemus Ward. The great explorer, Henry M. Stanley, was originally known as John Rowlands.

Similar illustrations are found among worthies in European literature and art. Melancthon's family name was Schwartzerde, meaning "black earth." As soon as his literary talents developed and began to forecast his future, he changed the name to the classic synonym by which he is known in history. Rembrandt's family name was Gerretz, which he changed to Van Ryn, on account of its greater dignity. Balzac was born a Guez, which means "beggar"; when he became conscious of his power as a writer, he selected the surname Balzac, from an estate he owned. Voltaire, Moliere, Dante Petrarch, Richelieu, Loyola, and Erasmus, were all assumed names. Even Bonaparte altered his name from Buonaparte to disguise his Italian origin; while his great opponent, the Duke of Wellington, was not by blood a Wellesley, but a Colley. His grandfather, Richard Colley, assumed the name of a relative named Wesley, which was afterwards expanded to Wellesley.

F. R. H.

Ancestral Heads of New England Families

ABBE, ABBEY, or ABBEL

JOHN, b. in England, 1615, was at Salem, Mass., in 1636-37, afterwards removed to Wenham, Mass., and in 1696-97 to Windham, Conn.

SAMUEL, brother of John, was also at Wenham, Mass.

ABBOT, ABBOTT

The name derived from the Hebrew word *Ab*, and the Syrian *Abba*, a father. It originated in the Monasteries of Syria from the chief ruler of an abbey.

ARTHUR, came from Totness in Devonshire, to N. E. in 1634, was identified with the settlement of Ipswich, Mass., afterwards removed to Marblehead, Mass.

DANIEL, admitted a freeman in Massachusetts in 1630, removed to Providence, R. I., in 1639.

GEORGE was at Windsor, Conn., in 1640, removed to Norwalk, Conn., in 1640.

GEORGE came from Yorkshire, Eng., in 1640, one of the first settlers of Andover, Mass., and was at Rowley, Mass., in 1647.

JOHN, an inhabitant of Saco, Maine, in 1680.

RICHARD was at Kittery, Maine, in 1663.

ROBERT, admitted a freeman at Watertown, Mass., in 1634, removed to Wethersfield, Conn., 1636-40, and removed to New Haven, Conn., in 1642.

WALTER, a vintner, b. in Eng., 1600, settled at Exeter, N. H., in 1640, removed to Portsmouth, N. H., in 1667.

ABBY

MATTHEW, fisherman, came from London, Eng., to Boston, Mass., in 1635.

ABELL, from a Hebrew word signifying vanity, breath.

BENJAMIN was at Norwich, Conn., in 1670.

ROBERT, made freeman at Weymouth, Mass., in 1631, removed to Rehoboth, Mass.

ABERNETHY, a local surname from a town in Strathern, Scotland, is of Gaelic and Celtic derivation.

WILLIAM, native of Scotland, came to Branford, Conn., was afterwards at Wallingford, Conn.

ABINGTON

WILLIAM was in Maine in 1642.

ABORN

SAMUEL, b. in 1611, one of the early settlers of Salem, Mass.

ACKERLY

HENRY was at New Haven, Conn., in 1640; at Stamford, Conn., from 1641-1653; Greenwich, Conn., in 1656.

ROBERT, at Brookhaven, L. I., admitted a freeman in Conn. in 1664.

SAMUEL, brother of the preceding, at Brookhaven, L. I., in 1655.

ACKLEY

NICHOLAS, at Hartford, Conn., in 1655, an early settler of Haddam, Conn.

ACKERMAN

Derived from the Saxon word *Acker*, oaken, made of oak, and man. The brave, firm, unyielding man.

STEPHEN, first colonial record, his marriage in 1684 at Newbury, Mass.

ACKERS or ACRES

The surname from Latin *Ager*, a field, in Saxon it signifies the place of oaks, *ac* and *ake* being terms for oak, the termination *ar* same as the Latin *vir*, a man.

HENRY, at Newbury, Mass., in 1764.

JOHN, in 1656 living in what is now Brookline, Mass.

ACTON

A place name from a town in Middlelesex, Eng.

JOHN, at North Yarmouth, Mass., in 1685.

ACY or ACIE

WILLIAM was at Rowley, Mass., in 1643, afterwards at Boston, Mass.

ADAMS

A surname of great antiquity in Scotland.

DUNCAN, son of Alexander Adam, lived in the reign of King Robert Bruce.

ANDREW was a school master at Hartford, Conn., in 1643.

CHARLES lived in 1648 at Dover, N. H.

CHRISTOPHER was at Braintree, Mass., in 1645, removed to Kittery, Maine.

DANIEL is recorded at Simsbury, Conn., in 1683.

EDWARD was at New Haven, Conn., in 1640, Milford, Conn., in 1646 and Fairfield, Conn., in 1650.

EDWARD is on record at Windsor, Conn., in 1660, left no male issue.

FERDINANDO, shoemaker at Dedham, Mass., in 1637.

GEORGE, b. in Eng., settled at Watertown, Mass., in 1645, removed to what is now Lexington, Mass.

HENRY came from Braintree, Essex, Eng., in 1632, to Braintree, Mass.

JEREMY was at Braintree, Mass., in 1632, made freeman at Cambridge, Mass., in 1635 and in 1636 removed to Hartford, Conn.

JOHN came to Plymouth, Mass., in 1621; he died in 1633.

JOHN, a millwright, came to Cambridge, Mass., in 1650.

JOHN was at Salem, Mass., in 1682.

JOHN was at Sudbury, Mass., in 1684.

NATHANIEL was at Newport, R. I., in 1639.

NATHANIEL, turner, was at Boston, Mass.

NATHANIEL, lockmaker, is on record at Boston, Mass., in 1653.

PHILIP, some authorities say brother of Henry of Braintree, Mass., settled in that town and in 1653 was at York, Maine.

RICHARD, a freeman at Weymouth, Mass., in 1635.

RICHARD, bricklayer, came from Northamptonshire, Eng., to Salem, Mass., in 1635.

ROBERT, tailor, came from Devonshire, Eng., to Ipswich, Mass., in 1635, removed to Salem, Mass., in 1638, and to Newbury, Mass., in 1640-41.

ROGER, was at Roxbury, Mass., in 1675.

THOMAS was at Charlestown, Mass., in 1654.

THOMAS took oath of fidelity at New Haven, Conn., in 1657.

THOMAS was a freeman at York, Maine, in 1680.

WALTER was at Charlestown, Mass., in 1657.

WILLIAM was at Cambridge, Mass., as early as 1635 and removed to Ipswich, Mass., in 1642.

WILLIAM was at Hartford, Conn., in 1650, afterwards at Farmington, Conn. No male issue.

WILLIAM was at Sudbury, Mass., in 1674.

ADDINGTON

ISAAC was at Boston in 1640, left an only son Isaac.

ADDIS

WILLIAM, brewer, was an inhabitant of Gloucester, Mass., in 1642. In 1658-62 was living at New London, Conn. No male issue.

ADGATE

THOMAS, first record at Saybrook, Conn., in 1651, afterwards removed to Norwich, Conn.

ADKINS or ATKINS

The surname derived from Little Adam, or the son of Adam, from *Ad* and *Kins,* a diminutive signifying child.

JOSIAH, an early settler of Middletown, Conn., in 1650.

THOMAS b. in Eng. in 1650, was at East Hartford, Conn., in 1682.

ADVERD or ADFORD

HENRY, inhabitant of Scituate, Mass., in 1640, left no male issue.

AGNEW

The surname from the town of Agneau in Normandy, where the family originated. They went from England into Ireland with Strongbow. *Agneau* in Norman French signifies a lamb.

NINIAN was at Kittery, Maine, in 1676.

AINSWORTH

A local surname from British and Welsh, from *Ains* a spring, a river and gwerth, a place, possession or court.

DANIEL b. in Eng., came to Roxbury, Mass., in 1647, later was at Dedham, Mass.

ALBEE, ALLBEE, or ALBY

BENJAMIN, carpenter and miller, inhabitant of Boston, Mass., in 1639, admitted a freeman at Braintree, Mass., in 1642, removed to Medfield in 1649, was at Mendon, Mass., in 1660 and Milford, Mass., in 1663.

ALBRO

JOHN, b. in Eng. in 1617, came to Boston, Mass., in 1634, in charge of William Freeborn, and removed to Portsmouth, R. I., in 1638.

ALCOCK

From *Hal* or *Al,* nickname for Henry, and cock a termination meaning little, a diminutive, the same as kin.

FRANCIS came in 1638 to N. E. in the employ of Richard Dummer, and was at Newbury, Mass.; no more known of him.

GEORGE, physician, came to N. E. in 1630, settled at Roxbury, Mass.

JOHN, admitted a freeman of Mass. in

1652, was at York and Kittery, Maine.

SAMUEL, admitted freeman at Kittery, Maine, in 1652; was at York, Maine, in 1659.

THOMAS, brother of Dr. George, came to N. E. in 1630, settled at Roxbury, Mass., afterwards at Dedham, Mass.

ALDEN

A local surname of Saxon origin from *Ald,* old and *Den* or *Dun,* a hill or town.

JOHN, *Mayflower* passenger, cooper by trade, born in Eng. 1599, resided most of his days at Duxbury, Mass.

ALDERMAN

Originally from German descent.

JOHN was at Dorchester, Mass., as early as 1634, admitted a freeman in 1639.

WILLIAM was an inhabitant of Windsor, Conn., in 1672 at Simsbury, Conn.

ALDIS

NATHAN came from Eng. to Dorchester, Mass., in 1640-41.

ALDRICH or ALDRIDGE

A corruption of Aldred from the Saxon language, originally from the German name Albert. *Bert* bright or famous, compounded with the old English word *All.*

GEORGE, tailor, born in Derbyshire, Eng., 1605, a freeman of Dorchester, Mass., in 1636, at Braintree, Mass., in 1640, and one of the first seven settlers of Mendon, Mass., 1663.

HENRY was at Dedham, Mass., in 1643.

ALEXANDER

The surname derived from two Greek words signifying to aid or help and a man, a powerful auxiliary.

GEORGE on record at Windsor, Conn., in 1644.

ROBERT, a native of Scotland, was an inhabitant of Boston, Mass., in 1684.

ALFORD or ALVORD

From Alford, a town in Lincolnshire, Eng., from the Saxon words *Ald,* old, and *Ford,* way or pass. The English seat of the family, Somersetshire, Eng.

BENEDICT, son of Thomas in the fifth generation from John Alvord, who resided in the parish of White Staunton, Somersetshire, was born in that parish 1615-18. Was at Windsor, Conn., in 1637, returned to Eng. in 1640, again was at Windsor, Conn. Was known as Sergeant Benedict Alford.

JOHN was at Salem, Mass., in 1668.

WILLIAM, merchant, came from London, Eng., to Salem, Mass., in 1634.

ALGER

From the Gaelic word signifying noble.

ANDREW, surveyor, came from Dunston, Norfolk, Eng., in 1640 to Saco, Maine, and settled in what is now Dunston, Maine, in 1658.

ARTHUR, brother of the preceding was at Scarborough, Maine, in 1658.

ROGER, of English descent, was an early settler of Lyme, Conn.

THOMAS was first at Roxbury, Mass., afterwards at Watertown, Mass., and in 1665 at Taunton, Mass.

ALLEN, ALLING, ALLYN

The name derived from British, a corruption of Latin, *Aelianus,* which signifies sunbright. The Slavonic Aland means wolf-dog, hound. The Gaelic *Aluinn* signifies handsome, elegant, lovely. The Irish *Alun,* fair, beautiful. The English Allan and Allen all running, all conquering. The name is a personal one and first borne by the Bard of Britain and came into prominence at the time of the Conquest, when the chief general of the Norman army was Allan, Duke of Brittany. The family seat, at the counties of Durham and Essex.

ABRAHAM was at Marblehead, Mass., in 1674.

ALEXANDER, a Scotchman, was at Windsor, Conn., in 1689.

ANDREW was on record at Lynn, Mass., in 1642.

ARNOLD was at Casco, Maine, in 1645.

BOZOUNE, a mercer or trader, came from Lynn, Norfolk, Eng., to Hingham, Mass., in 1638; removed to Boston, Mass., in 1650-52.

DANIEL, physician, was at Boston, Mass., in 1680.

DANIEL was at Swanzey, Mass., in 1673.

EDWARD came from Scotland in 1636, was at Ipswich and Dedham, Mass., also at Suffield, Conn.

EDWARD, b. in Eng. in 1670, settled in 1690 on Nantucket Island, Mass.

FRANCIS, was at Sandwich, Mass., in 1643.

GEORGE, b. in Thurcaston, Leicestershire, Eng., in 1568, settled at Saugus, Mass.; one of the purchasers of Sandwich, Mass., in 1637.

GEORGE, an inhabitant of Weymouth, Mass., in 1641, removed to Boston, Mass.

GIDEON was at Swanzey, Mass., in 1669,

removed to Boston in 1675, afterwards to Milford, Mass.

HENRY, joiner, was at Boston, Mass., in 1644, afterward at Rowley, Mass.

HENRY an inhabitant of Milford, Mass.

HOPE, currier, an inhabitant of Boston, Mass., in 1651.

JAMES, came from Colby, Norfolk, Eng., to Dedham, Mass., in 1637, one of the first thirteen settlers in 1652 of Medfield, Mass.

REV. JAMES, born in 1632, came from Hampshire to Boston, Mass., in 1662.

JEDEDIAH, was an inhabitant of Sandwich, Mass.

JOHN ALLIN, son of Robert of Horley, Oxford, Eng., b. in 1596, came to N. E. in 1637, was at Dedham, Mass.

JOHN was at Plymouth, Mass., in 1633 and at Scituate, Mass., in 1646.

JOHN b. in 1605, came from the county of Kent, Eng., to Charlestown, Mass., in 1635.

JOHN was taxed at Springfield, Mass., in 1639, removed to Rehoboth, Mass., in 1643, at Newport, R. I., in 1651, thence to Swanzey, Mass., in 1669.

JOHN was an inhabitant of Newbury, Mass., in 1656.

JOHN, a resident of Northampton, Mass., removed to Deerfield, Mass., where he was killed by the Indians in 1675.

JOHN of Barnstable, Mass., married in 1672-73.

JOHN was at Marblehead, Mass., in 1668.

JOHN, of Suffield, Conn., was married in 1682, removed to Deerfield, Mass., himself and wife killed by the Indians in 1704.

JONAH was at Taunton, Mass., in 1663.

JOSEPH of Newport, R. I., in 1662, may have been at Salem, Mass., previous to this date.

JOSEPH, blacksmith, was at Gloucester, Mass., in 1674.

JOSEPH of Rehoboth, Mass., where he was an inhabitant in 1673.

COL. MATTHEW ALLYN, son of Thomas of Chelmsford, Eng., was bap. in 1604-05, came from Brampton, Devonshire, Eng., to Charlestown, Mass., in 1632. He removed to Hartford, Conn., in 1637, thence in a few years to Windsor, Conn.

NICHOLAS was at Dorchester, Mass., in 1663.

ROBERT ALLYN, an inhabitant of Salem, Mass., in 1637, removed in 1651 to New London, Conn., and in 1659 to Norwich, Conn.

SAMUEL ALLYN, farmer, a brother of Col. Matthew, bapt. at Chelmsford, Essex, Eng., in 1586, came to Braintree, Mass., in 1632 and was at Windsor, Conn., in 1644.

SAMUEL was at Windsor, Conn., in 1636, died in 1648; his widow and family removed to Northampton, Mass.

SAMUEL was a resident of Newport, R. I., in 1639.

THOMAS ALLYN, a brother of Col. Matthew, was at Middletown, Conn.

THOMAS was at Barnstable, Mass., in 1644.

TIMOTHY at Marblehead, Mass., in 1648 removed to Norwich, Conn.

WALTER, b. in Eng., in 1615, was an inhabitant of Newbury, Mass., in 1640, removed to Watertown, Mass., in 1652.

WILLIAM, b. in Manchester, Eng., in 1602; was made freeman at Salem, Mass., in 1630; previous to this had resided at Gloucester, Mass., later he removed to Manchester, Mass.

WILLIAM, house carpenter, was at Newbury, Mass., in 1638, granted land at Salisbury, Mass., in 1639.

WILLIAM, a naitve of Wales, came to N. E. in 1660.

ALLERTON

The surname same as Alverton derived from Cornish British from *Al* high, *ver* green, and *ton*, hill, meaning a high green hill. The seat of the family being Suffolk, Eng.

ISAAC, *Mayflower* passenger, b. 1583-85, founded Marblehead, Mass. In 1636 removed to New Amsterdam; became a resident of New Haven, Conn., in 1635.

ALLEY

HUGH b. in Eng. 1608, settled at Lynn, Mass., in 1635.

ALLING

JOHN was a resident of New Haven, Conn., in 1652.

ROGER came from Bedfordshire, Eng., to New Haven, Conn., in 1639.

ALLISON

Ancient Scotch family; lineage traced to Alister or Alexander, son of Angus Nor of the clan of Donald.

JAMES was at Boston, Mass., in 1644.

LAWRENCE, first at Watertown, Mass., removed to Wethersfield, Conn., thence to Stamford, Conn., finally to Hempstead, L. I.

RALPH granted lands at Scarborough, Maine, in 1673.

ALLIS

WILLIAM was freeman at Boston, Mass., in 1640.

ALLISET or ALLESET

JOHN was at Boston, Mass., in 1684; left no male issue.

ALLT, or AULT, sometimes spelt OLT

JOHN sent to N. E. in 1631 by John Mason, patentee of N. H., was at Portsmouth, N. H., after 1640 lived at Dover, N. H.

ALLY

THOMAS was taxed at Rowley, Mass., in 1691.

ALMY

WILLIAM, b. in Eng. in 1601, was settled at Lynn, Mass., in 1631, was at Sandwich, Mass., in 1631, and Portsmouth, N. H. in 1644.

ALSOP

A place name from Alsop, Derbyshire, Eng.

RICHARD ALSOP was mayor of London in 1597.

JOSEPH came to Boston in 1635 at the age of fourteen years, took oath of fidelity at New Haven, Conn., in 1644.

THOMAS, brother of the preceding, came to N. E. in 1635, aged twenty years, was afterwards at Stratford, Conn., and before 1659 removed to Newtown, L. I.

ALVORD

From the Gaelic word *Amadon,* a numskull, a simpleton, may be so called by way of Antiphrasis because he was wise. Identical with Alford (see).

ALEXANDER, b. in Somersetshire, Eng., about 1620, was bap. in 1627 at Bridport, Dorsetshire, Eng., became a resident at Windsor, Conn., in 1645, removed to Northampton, Mass., in 1661.

BENEDICT b. in White Taunton, Eng., in 1615-18, brother of the preceding, was a soldier in the Pequot War and was at Windsor, Conn., in 1637.

AMADON or AMIDON

ROGER, a French Huguenot, was an inhabitant of Salem, Mass., in 1637, removed to Rehoboth, Mass., in 1648.

AMBLER

From a French word *Ambleur,* an officer of the King's stables, anciently *"le Amblour."*

RICHARD was at Weymouth, Mass., in 1637 removed to Boston, Mass., in 1650 to Stamford, Conn.

AMBROSE

From a Greek word signifying divine or immortal.

HENRY, carpenter, was at Hampton, N. H. earlier than 1641, was living at Boston, Mass., in 1654, and Charlestown, Mass., two years later.

AMBRY or AMBERY which often appears as EMRY or EMERY

ROBERT took oath of fidelity at New Haven, Conn., in 1644.

AMES (see Eames)

Derived from the French word *Amie,* a friend or beloved, or the Hebrew *Amos,* a burden.

HUGH was an inhabitant of Boston in 1667.

JOHN, son of Richard of Binton, Somersetshire, Eng., was born there in 1610, settled at Bridgewater, Mass., left no male issue.

WILLIAM, b. in 1605, brother of the preceding, came to Duxbury, Mass., in 1638, afterwards to Braintree, Mass., where he was admitted a freeman in 1647.

WILLIAM, son of Rev. William Ames, came to Cambridge, Mass., in 1637, removed in 1647 to Wrentham, Mass.

AMERY or AMEE

JOHN, ship carpenter, inhabitant of Woburn, Mass., in 1649, removed to Boston, Mass., in 1653.

WILLIAM was at Lynn, Mass., and settled at Sandwich, Mass., in 1637.

AMORY

The family is of French origin, descended from Montford L. Amaury.
The English ancestor in the sixteenth century was Hugh Amory.

JONATHAN, b. in Eng. 1653-54, was for a time at Boston, Mass., but in 1685 removed to Charleston, S. C. His son Thomas returned to Boston in 1719.

SIMON was a freeman at Boston, Mass., in 1672.

AMOS

HUGH, freeman at Boston, Mass., in 1666 removed to what is now Preston, Mass.

AMSBURY (see ORMSBRY)

AMSDEN

ISAAC was married at Cambridge, Mass., in 1654, he died in 1661 leaving male issue.

ANCHOR

THOMAS was an inhabitant of Boston, Mass., in 1646.

ANDERSON

(Means the son of Andrew).

JOHN, shipwright, was at Boston, Mass., in 1647.

JOHN was at Ipswich, Mass., in 1665.

JOHN, shipmaster, was at Boston in 1655 and at Salem, Mass., in 1673.

ANDREW

Derived from a Greek word meaning manly, courageous.

John was at Wickford, R. I, in 1674.

William, mariner, was a freeman at Cambridge, Mass., in 1634.

ANDREWS

Albert b. in Eng. in 1589 was at Ipswich, Mass., in 1634.

Edward was at Newport, R. I., in 1639, removed to Saco, Maine, where he was admitted a freeman in 1657.

Francis was of Hartford, Conn., in 1639, later removed to Fairfield, Conn.

Henry was an original purchaser at Taunton, Mass., in 1639.

Jedediah was at Dover, N. H., in 1657, removed to Salisbury, Mass.

John, b. in England in 1600, settled at Kittery, Maine, in 1640.

John, baker, was at Lynn, Mass., in 1650, and died at Ipswich, Mass., in 1662.

Lieut. John, b. in 1618, was at Ipswich, Mass., in 1642.

John, of Welsh descent, came from Berkshire, Eng., to Boston in 1656 and was one of the first settlers of Farmington, Conn.

Robert b. in Boxford, Eng., in 1600, came from Norwich, Norfolk, Eng., to Ipswich, Mass., in 1635, later at Boxford, Mass., in 1656.

Samuel, b. in 1598, came to Saco, Maine, in 1635 and died three years later.

Thomas was at Dorchester, Mass., in 1635.

Thomas was one of the founders of Watertown, Mass., later came to Cambridge, Mass., where he died before 1649.

William made freeman at Lynn, Mass., in 1634.

William, carpenter, came from Hampsworth, Eng., to Boston, Mass., in 1635, settled soon afterwards at New Haven, Conn.

William, schoolmaster, came from Cambridge, Mass., to Hartford, Conn., at the first settlement.

ANDROS

Jedediah, at Salisbury, Mass., in 1670.

ANGELL

The surname derived from a town in France, or from the Greek word signifying messenger.

Thomas, b. in Eng. in 1618, came to N. E. as an apprentice to Roger Williams in 1631; one of the first grantees of Providence, R. I.

Edmund, youngest son of John Angier of Dedham, Essex, Eng., where he was b. in 1612, made a freeman in Mass., in 1640.

John, was in Boston, Mass., in 1650, and died in 1657.

Jonathan was at Salem, Mass., in 1668.

Joseph was at Medford, Mass., in 1684, removed to Dorchester, Mass., finally to Framingham, Mass.

Sampson took the oath of allegiance to Mass., at York, Maine, in 1653.

ANNABLE

Anthony was an inhabitant of Plymouth, Mass., in 1623, one of the first settlers of Scituate, Mass., in 1630, removed in 1640 to Barnstable, Mass.

John, tailor, was at Ipswich, Mass., in 1642.

ANNIS

Charles (sometimes written Carmac) born in Enniskillen, Ireland, 1638, came to Newbury, Mass., in 1666.

ANTHONY

From the Greek, signifying a flower, flourishing, beautiful, graceful.

The English ancestor, Dr. Francis Anthony.

John, b. in Hempstead near London, Eng., in 1607, came to N. E. in 1634 and was resident of Portsmouth, R. I., in 1640.

ANTRAM

Thomas, weaver, came from Salisbury, Wiltshire, Eng., to Boston Mass., in 1635.

APPLEBY

Surname from a town in Westmoreland, Eng., called by Romans Aballaba. *By* signifies a town—the apple-town.

Thomas was at Rye, N. H., in 1662-72.

APPLETON

The name local, and town abounding in apples. It is of Saxon origin, *Apleton* meaning orchard. English ancestor in 1639, John Appleton.

Samuel, son of Thomas of Little Waldingfield, Suffolk, Eng., where he was b. 1586. Took oath of allegiance to Mass., in 1636; was a resident of Ipswich and Rowley, Mass.

APPLIN, name identical with APPLETON.

John, was married at Watertown, Mass., in 1671.

ARBUCKLE

William was a resident of Boston in 1694.

ARCHER

HENRY, was at Roxbury, Mass., in 1639, afterwards removed to Ipswich, Mass.

JOHN was a freeman at Portsmouth, R. I., in 1684.

JOHN was at Stamford, Conn., in 1660.

JOHN, cooper, was at Salem, Mass., in 1668, was granted lands in 1676.

SAMUEL, b. about 1608, was admitted freeman at Salem, Mass., in 1634.

ARMITAGE

The same as hermitage, the cell or habitation of a hermit, formerly a wilderness or solitary place.

ELEAZER married at Lynn, Mass., in 1669.

GODFREY, tailor, was at Lynn, Mass., in 1630, removed to Boston, Mass., and made a freeman in 1639.

JOSEPH, brother of the preceding, was at Lynn, Mass., in 1630.

THOMAS, came to Lynn, Mass., in 1635, two years later removed to Sandwich, Conn.

TIMOTHY was married at Boston, Mass., in 1677.

ARMS

WILLIAM was at Hatfield, Mass., before 1676, removed to Sunderland, Mass., afterward to Deerfield, Mass.

ARMSBEE or ARMSESBY

THOMAS was at Taunton, Mass., in 1668.

ARMSTRONG

A name given for strength in battle.

BENJAMIN was at Norwich, Conn., after 1670.

JONATHAN, b. about 1630, settled at Westerly, R. I., before 1670, afterwards removed to Roxbury, Mass.

ARNOLD

From the German *are* or *ehre,* honor, faithful to his honor. Ancient Welsh family. The English line is descended from Ynir, King of Gwentland 1100. The name Arnold was adopted by Roger in the twelfth generation from Ynir.

EDWARD was at Boston, Mass., in 1640.

ISAAC was at New Haven, Conn., in 1640, afterwards removed to Suffolk county, L. I.

JOHN, b. in Eng. in 1585, came to Cambridge, Mass., in 1634, and went to Hartford, Conn., in 1636.

JOHN was at Norwich, Conn., in 1680 removed to Boston, Mass., and was prison-keeper.

JOSEPH, b. in Eng. in 1625, was at Braintree, Mass., before 1648.

REV. SAMUEL was at Sandwich, Mass., in 1643, later at Yarmouth, Mass., 1658 ordained the third minister of Marshfield, Mass.

THOMAS, son of Thomas of Cheselbourne, Dorsetshire, Eng., of the sixth generation from Roger Arnold, born in Leamington, Eng., 1587, came to Hingham, Mass., in 1635, removed to Providence, R. I., in 1636, and was one of the first four settlers of Pawtucket, R. I.

WILLIAM, b. in Leamington, Eng., in 1589, brother of the preceding, came to Hingham, Mass., in 1635, removed to Providence, R. I., in 1636.

ASH

GEORGE was at Hartford, Conn., in 1682.

JOHN was at Dover, N. H., in 1659 and married at Salisbury, Mass., in 1667.

WILLIAM, mariner, was at Gloucester, Mass., in 1647, and at New London, Conn., in 1650.

ASHBURN or ASHBORN

JOSEPH was at Milford, Conn., 1675-1713.

ASHBY

The name is of Saxon origin. The house by the Ash; *by,* signifying a villa or habitation.

ANTHONY was at Salem, Mass., in 1665.

ASHCRAFT

JOHN was at Stonington, Conn., in 1662.

ASHLEY

In Saxon *leegh, ley* or *lea,* signifies uncultivated grounds. Therefore a lea or field abounding in ash-trees.

EDWARD, from Bristol, Eng., was in Maine in 1630.

EDWARD was a freeman at Boston, Mass., in 1677.

ROBERT came to Roxbury, Mass., and was at Springfield, Mass., in 1639.

THOMAS was in Maine in 1654.

THOMAS was a resident of Boston, Mass., in 1681.

WILLIAM was at Wells, Maine, in 1659.

ASHTON

From the Saxon word, the ash-hill or town.

HENRY was at Boston, Mass., in 1673, removed to Providence, R. I., in 1676.

JAMES was at Providence, R. I., in 1639, removed to N. J., about 1666.

THOMAS, brother of the preceding; he and his brother are mentioned as proprietors of R. I.

ASLETT or ARSLEBY

JOHN was at Newbury, Mass., prior to 1648, removed to Andover, Mass., 1652.

ASPINWALL

A local Saxon word signifying the Aspen-vale.

PETER came from Toxteth Park adjoining Liverpool, Lancastershire, Eng., at an early date to Boston and located in what is now Brookline, Mass.

WILLIAM came to Charlestown, Mass., in 1630; he went to R. I., but in 1641 was at New Haven, Conn., returned to Boston, Mass., but finally went to Eng. The male issue became extinct.

ASTWOOD

JAMES came to Roxbury, Mass., at an early date, removed to Boston, Mass., where his name is recorded as Ashwood.

JOHN, husbandman, b. in 1599, came to Roxbury, Mass., in 1635, from Stanstead Abbey, Herts, Eng.; removed to Milford, Mass., returned to London, Eng., in 1653, leaving no male issue.

ATCHISON

JOHN was at Hatfield, Mass., in 1672, killed by the Indians in 1671.

ATHERTON

A local saxon name from Atherstone, a town in Warwickshire, Eng. The family is seated at Atherton, ten miles northeast of Manchester, Gloucestershire, Eng. The earliest English ancestor recorded is Robert de Atherton.

GENERAL HUMPHREY, b. in 1607-8, came from the Parish of Winwick Preston, Lancashire, Eng., in 1636, to Dorchester, Mass.

JAMES, brother of the preceding, b. in Eng. in 1626, came to Dorchester, Mass., removed to Lancaster, Maine, in 1653, returned to Dorchester, then went to Milton and died at Sherburn, Mass.

ATKINS

The name derived from *At* an abbreviation of Arthur, *kins* signifying child i.e., the son of Arthur.

HENRY was at Yarmouth, Mass., in 1641 removed to Plymouth, Mass.

THOMAS, carpenter, was at Boston, Mass., in 1672.

ATKINSON

JOSEPH was at Exeter, N. H., admitted a freeman in 1657.

LUKE, signed the Compact at New Haven, Conn., in 1639, removed to Middletown, Conn.

THEODORE, feltmaker, came from Bury, Lancashire, Eng., to Boston, Mass., in 1636.

THOMAS, brother of the preceding, was at Concord, Mass., in 1636.

ATWATER

Local name at (the) Water. English ancestor in 1500, John Atwater of Royton, Eng.

DAVID, bapt. at Lenham, Eng., came to Boston, Mass., in 1637, removed to New Haven, Conn., in 1638.

JOSHUA, merchant at London, Eng., brother of the preceding, came to New Haven, Conn., in 1639, removed to Milford, Conn., in 1655.

ATWELL

Name local, at (the) well.

BENJAMIN was at New London, Conn., before 1670.

JOHN came to Casco, Maine, 1630-40, and was at Lynn, Mass., in 1650.

ATWOOD

Name local—at (the) wood.

ALEXANDER was a freeman at Northampton, Mass., in 1684.

HERMAN son of John Atwood, came from Sanderstead, Surrey, Eng., to Boston, Mass., in 1642.

JOHN came from London, Eng., to Plymouth, Mass., 1636; left no male issue.

JOSEPH was at Taunton, Mass., before 1679.

PHILIP came from London, Eng., to Malden, Mass., in 1635, aged twelve years; afterwards at Bradford, Mass.

STEPHEN b. in Eng., in 1620, was a resident of Eastham, Mass., in 1643.

THOMAS, physician, settled at Plymouth, Mass., in 1650, removed to Wethersfield, Conn., in 1663.

AUGER

JOHN was at Boston, Mass., in 1652.

WILLIAM, admitted freeman of Mass., in 1631, was at Salem, Mass., in 1636.

AUGUSTINE sometimes spelled Gastanor, Gastin.

JOHN came from the Isle of Jersey, Eng., in 1677, took a grant of land at Falmouth, now Portland, Maine, 1680; he removed to Lynn in 1690, but returned to Falmouth in 1719.

AUSTIN

A contraction from Augustine, from the Latin, *Augustinus,* imperial, royal, renowned.

ANTHONY was freeman at Rowley, Mass., in 1669, removed to Suffield, Conn., before 1681.

FRANCIS was at Dedham, Mass., removed to Hampton, N. H., in 1640.

JOHN was at New London, Conn., in 1647, removed in 1651 to Greenwich, Conn., later to Stamford, Conn.

JOHN settled at New Haven, Conn., about 1667.

JONAH came from Sandwich, Kent., Eng., in early days to Cambridge, Mass.; was at Hingham, Mass., in 1635 and at Taunton, Mass., in 1643.

JOSEPH was an inhabitant of Hampton, N. H., in 1642, and of Dover, N. H., in 1648.

RICHARD, tailor, b. about 1598, came in 1638 to Charlestown, Mass.

Robert, b. in Eng. in 1630 and was in 1661 one of the grantees of Westerly and Kingstown, R. I.

AVERILL

A corruption of Haverhill, the aspirate being dropped. Haverhill a town in Suffolk, Eng., named for Dutch *Hyver* and Teutonic *Haber,* oats and hill, the hill sown with oats.

WILLIAM b. in Eng., came to Ipswich, Mass., before 1638.

AVERY

From the Latin *Aviarius,* a bird-keeper or from *Avery* a grannary.

CHRISTOPHER, weaver, born in Cornwall, Eng., in 1590, came from Salisbury, Wiltshire, Eng., to Salem, Mass., in 1630. He was at Gloucester, Mass., in 1646 and removed to New London, Conn., in 1663.

JOHN was at Dorchester, Mass. in 1642, removed to Boston, Mass.

REV. JOSEPH came from Wiltshire, Eng., and was drowned, in 1635, off Marblehead, Mass.

THOMAS, blacksmith, made freeman at Salem, Mass., in 1643, afterwards removed to Portsmouth, N. H.

WILLIAM, physician, born in Eng., in 1622, came from Berkham, Berkshire, Eng., about 1650.

AVIS

In French, *Avis,* a projector, schemer, Latin *Avus* is grandfather, ancestor.

WILLIAM was at Boston, Mass., in 1664.

AVISTON or AVESSON

JOHN was a freeman at Reading, Mass., in 1685.

AWARDS

RICHARD was at Newport, R. I., in 1638, previous to this date had been at Boston, Mass.

AWKLEY

MILES was at Boston, Mass., in 1635.

AXEY

JAMES was at Lynn, Mass., in 1630.

AXTELL

THOMAS was at Sudbury, Mass., before 1646, the year of his death.

AYER or AYERS

A local surname derived from Ayr, a river, town and district in Scotland.

HENRY was a freeman at Portsmouth, N. H., in 1655.

JOHN, b. in Eng., settled at Salisbury, Mass., in 1640, removed to Ipswich, Mass., in 1646 and to Haverhill, Mass., in 1647.

RICHARD purchased land in Stamford, Conn., in 1666.

BABB

PHILIP was at Kittery, Maine, 1652.

BABBAGE, BABBIDGE or BABRIDGE

CHRISTOPHER, freeman at Salem, Mass., 1665; no male issue.

BABBITT or BOBBIT

EDWARD, came from Wales to Taunton, Mass., 1643.

BABCOCK

The name is from *Bab,* a nickname for Bartholomew; *cock,* small, little, a son; or from Bob, a nickname for Robert.

DAVID was at Dorchester, Mass., 1640.

JAMES, b. Essex, Eng., 1612, a resident of Portsmouth, R. I., 1642; settled at Westerly, R. I., 1662.

RETURN was at Dartmouth, Mass., before 1686.

CAPTAIN ROBERT, b. Eng., settled at Dorchester, Mass., 1648; was at Sherborn, Mass., 1674-75.

BABER

WILLIAM was at Boston, Mass., 1648.

BABSON

Name derived from an abbreviated personal name.

JAMES, cooper, sailed from Eng., previous to 1640; died on voyage; his widow Isabel granted lands at Gloucester, Mass., 1644; left only son James.

BACHELOR, BACHELDER or BATCHELDER

Name derived from Dutch word *Bock,* a book, and *leeraar,* a doctor of divinity, law, or physic.

HENRY, brewer, came from Dover, Kent, Eng., in 1636, to Ipswich, Mass.

JOHN, was at Watertown, Mass., and made a freeman at Dedham, Mass., 1635.

JOHN, tailor, from Canterbury, Kent, Eng., was granted land at Salem, Mass., 1638; a brother of Henry.

JOHN, freeman at Reading, Mass., 1666.

JOSEPH, tailor, brother of John and Henry, came from Canterbury, Kent, Eng., to Salem, Mass., 1636.

JOSHUA, brother of the preceding, came from County of Kent.

Rev. Stephen, b. Eng., 1561, came to Boston, Mass., in 1632; first minister at Lynn., Mass., 1633, 1636 went to Ipswich, Mass., in 1638 at Newbury, Mass.; the following year at Hampton, N. H.; finally at Saco, Maine. He returned to Eng., 1653-54, died at Hackney, near London, Eng., 1660.

William, a freeman at Charlestown, Mass., 1634.

BACKUS

Name from German *Back-haus,* a bake-house.

William, b. Norwich, Eng., was at Saybrook, Conn., 1637; removed to Norwich, Conn., 1659.

BACON

Name from Anglo-Saxon *bacan,* to bake. Some authorities derive it from Saxon *baccen* or *buccen,* a beech tree. It is a name of ancient seigniory in Normandy. William Bacon (1082) endowed the Abbey of Holy Trinity in Caen. Grimaldus Bacon was with William the Conqueror. The name is found in the Battle Rolls of the 11th century.

Andrew, b. Rutlandshire, Eng., was at Cambridge, Mass., and at Hartford, Conn., 1639; no male issue.

George, mason, b. Suffolk, Eng., 1592; settled at Hingham, Mass., 1635, coming from Ireland.

Michael or Mighill, b. Winsted, Suffolk, Eng., came from Ireland to Dedham, Mass., 1640.

Nathaniel was at Barnstable, Mass., 1642.

Nathaniel, son of William of Stretton, Rutlandshire, Eng., b. about 1630, came to N. E., 1649, settled at New Haven, Conn.; removed to Middletown, Conn., 1653.

Samuel was at Barnstable, Mass., 1659.

Thomas was at Roxbury, Mass., 1665.

William was at Salem, Mass., 1640.

BADCOCK or BABCOCK

George, a servant of Gov. Theophilus Eaton of New Haven, Conn., 1640, removed to Dorchester, Mass., 1646, and ten years later to Milton, Mass.

Robert, brother of the preceding, was at Dorchester, Mass., 1648; later at Milton, Mass.

BADGER

Name from a licensed dealer in grain, hawker, peddler, also a small animal.

Giles came from Eng., in 1635 and settled at Newbury; he died in 1647, leaving an only child, John.

Nathaniel, brother of preceding, was at Newbury, Mass., 1635, but of both he and another brother, Richard, there is no record.

BAGG

John, came from Plymouth, Eng., settled at Springfield, Mass., in 1659.

BAGLEY

A Saxon local name; the rising or swelling ground that lies untilled; from *boelge,* rising or swelling, and *leagh* or *ley,* plain or pasture land.

Orlando, b. Eng., about 1630, was living in 1658 at Boston, Mass.; in 1664 removed to that part of Salisbury that is now Amesbury, Mass.

Samuel was living at Weymouth, Mass., before 1688.

BAILEY

A name of office, a corruption of *Bailiff,* which is derived from French *bailler,* to deliver; a municipal office in Scotland corresponding to an alderman.

Henry was living before 1690 at Falmouth, Maine.

Hilkiah was at Scarborough, Maine, 1645.

James, b. Eng., 1612, settled at Rowley, Mass., 1663.

John came from Eng., to Hartford, Conn., before 1656; removed to Haddam, Conn., 1662.

Rev. John, b. Blackburn, Lancashire, Eng., 1644; came to Watertown, Mass., 1686, having been previously at Boston, Mass. No issue.

John, weaver, came from Chippenham, Wiltshire, Eng., to N. E., 1635, locating at Newbury, Mass., in 1637. In 1637 he removed to Colchester, now Salisbury, Mass.

John was at Scituate, Mass., in 1673.

John, an inhabitant of Marshfield, Mass., before 1677.

Richard, brother of James, came to Lynn, Mass., 1638, a servant of Richard Dummer. He came from Yorkshire, Eng.; was afterwards at Rowley, Mass., where he died 1648, leaving only child Joseph.

Samuel was at New Haven, Conn., 1643.

Theophilus was at Lynn, Mass., 1645.

Thomas, b. Eng., settled at Weymouth, Mass., 1640, and was at New London, Conn., 1651.

Rev. Thomas, brother of Rev. John, was at Watertown before 1688; died in 1689, only thirty-five years old.

William came from London, Eng., and was at Newport, R. I., as early as 1655.

BAKER

Occupation surname from the Saxon word *bacan,* to dry by heat.

ALEXANDER, ropemaker, came from Eng., to Boston, Mass., 1635.

CORNELIUS, blacksmith, was at Salem, Mass., 1658; removed to Beverly, Mass., 1668.

EDWARD, farmer, b. Eng., came to Winthrop's fleet, 1630; one of first settlers of Lynn, Mass., 1631.

FRANCIS, tailor, b. Eng., 1611, came from St. Albans, Hertfordshire, Eng., to Boston, Mass., 1635; removed 1641 to Yarmouth, Mass.

JEFFREY was at Windsor, Conn., as early as 1642.

JOHN, grocer, came from Norwich, Norfolk, Eng., in 1630, to Charlestown, Mass.

JOHN, made a freeman at Boston, Mass., 1642.

JOHN, blacksmith, was at Boston, Mass., 1644.

JOHN was at Hartford, Conn., as early as 1665.

LANCELOT was at Boston, Mass., as early as 1644, removed to New Haven, Conn.

MARK was at Hampton, N. H., 1678.

NATHANIEL was inhabitant of Hingham, Mass., 1635.

NICHOLAS, brother of preceding, resided at Hingham, Mass., 1635; the following year removed to Scituate, Mass.; was ordained third minister of the first church in that town.

RICHARD came from London, Eng., to Dorchester, Mass., 1635.

ROBERT was at Roxbury, Mass., as early as 1673.

SAMUEL, b. 1605, came from county of Kent, Eng., to Lynn in 1635.

SAMUEL, an inhabitant of Marshfield, Mass., before 1656.

SAMUEL a resident of Windsor, Conn., about 1669.

THOMAS was at Milford, Conn., 1639; removed in 1650 to Easthampton, L. I.

THOMAS was a freeman at Topsfield, Mass., 1665.

William, carpenter and pump-maker, was at Plymouth, Mass., removed to Boston, Mass., about 1650.

BALCH

JOHN, came from Bridgewater, Somersetshire, Eng., in 1623, to Salem, Mass.

BALCOM

The name was originally spelled Balkcom, and is derived from the Gaelic *bal,* a round body, a building, house, town, and *combe,* a valley.

ALEXANDER, b. Eng., 1630; settled at Portsmouth, R. I., afterwards lived at Providence, R. I., where he took the oath of allegiance, 1682.

HENRY, of Balcome, Sussex, Eng., was at Charlestown, Mass., 1664.

BALDWIN

The name from the old German or Scandinavian, the conqueror or victor; from *bald,* quick or speedy, and *win,* signifying victor or conqueror, as all win, all victorious. The name appears as early as 672 in records. One of the first names to appear in history is Baldwin, son of Gan, a young French knight, killed at the battle of Roncenvalles, 778. Baldwin of the Iron Arm was founder of Burges 837. His descendants ruled the Dukedom of Flanders. Matilda, daughter of the Duke of Flanders, married William the Conqueror. The name appears in the Roll of Battle Abbey; after the Conquest they became earls of Devonshire. The family is traced through earls of Flanders to Godfrey De Buillon, leader of the only successful crusade against Jerusalem.

HENRY came from Devonshire, Eng., to Charlestown, Mass., 1640; admitted freeman at Woburn, Mass., 1652.

JOHN settled at Guilford, Conn., removed to Norwich, Conn., 1660.

JOHN was at Stonington, Conn., removed to New London, Conn.

JOSEPH was a settler, 1639, at Milford, Conn.; removed to Hadley, Mass., in 1663.

NATHANIEL, cooper, brother of preceding, and son of Richard, of parish Cholesbury, Buckinghamshire, Eng., admitted freeman at Milford, Conn., 1639; removed to Fairfield, Conn., 1641.

SYLVESTER, son of Richard of St. Leonard's, in parish of Aston Clinton, near Wendover, Bucks, Eng.; he died on his voyage to America, 1638; his sons Richard and John were early settlers of New Haven and of the first planters of Milford, Conn.

TIMOTHY, brother of Joseph and Nathaniel, was an inhabitant of Milford, Conn., 1639.

BALKAM

ALEXANDER, b. 1635, was at Portsmouth, R. I., 1664, afterwards at Providence, R. I.

BALL

Cornish British and Gaelic; *Bal,* a mine, the top of a hill.

ALLEN or ALLING was an inhabitant of New Haven, Conn., 1643.

EDWARD was at Branford, Conn., 1667; in that year removed to N. J.

FRANCIS came from Eng., to Dorchester, Mass., 1639; removed to Springfield, Mass., the following year.

JOHN admitted freeman at Watertown, Mass., 1650; afterwards removed to what is now Bedford, Mass.

RICHARD was resident of Salisbury, Mass., 1651; removed to Dover, N. H., 1668.

BALLANTINE

A place where *Bal* or *Belus* were worshipped by the Celts; from *Bal* and *teine,* fire.

WILLIAM, cooper, was of Scotch descent; came to Boston, Mass., before 1652.

BALLARD

The name of Celtic and Gaelic origin; from *Ball,* a place, a round elevation, and *ard,* high. The Gaelic word *Ballart* signifies noisy, boasting.

SAMUEL, b. 1638, was a freeman at Charlestown, Mass., 1680.

WILLIAM, who came from Eng., to Lynn, Mass., 1634, and died in a few years.

WILLIAM came from Wales, was admitted freeman at Andover, Mass., 1635, afterwards resided at Salem, Mass.

BALLOU

Norman French descent. Queenbond Balou was a marshal in the army of William the Conqueror. The family is seated in the County of Sussex, Eng.

MATURIN, b. Devonshire, Eng., 1610-20, came to N. E., 1645; was a proprietor at Providence, R. I., 1646-47.

BALSER

RICHARD was a proprietor at Andover, Mass., 1643.

BALSTONE or BAULSTON

JOHN was a resident of Boston, Mass., 1653.

JOHN was an inhabitant of Boston, 1647.

JONATHAN, also a resident of Boston, Mass., 1645.

WILLIAM came to Boston in Winthrop's fleet, 1630, removed to Portsmouth, N. H., 1638.

BANCROFT

The name is from Cornish British *ban,* a mount; hill and croft, a green pasture.

JOHN came in 1632 from London, Eng., to Lynn, Mass., died 1637, leaving two sons, John and Thomas.

JOHN was at Windsor, Conn., before 1650.

NATHANIEL was at Westfield, Mass., before 1675.

ROGER was at Cambridge, Mass., 1636, made a freeman 1642.

BANGS

A corruption of Banks, or from the French *bain,* a bath, a hot-house.

WILLIAM DE BANC was living at Cambridge, Eng., 1130.

EDWARD, shipwright, afterwards licensed as a merchant, b. Chichester, Sussex, Eng., 1592; came to Plymouth, Mass., 1623; removed to Eastham, Mass., 1644.

BANKS

Identical with Bangs.

GEORGE was at New Haven, Conn., 1646.

JOHN, one of the first settlers of Windsor, Conn., settled at Fairfield, Conn., 1643.

RICHARD was at Kittery, Maine, 1649, living at York, Maine, 1673.

RICHARD, one of the founders of the first Episcopal Society in Boston, 1686.

BANISTER

The keeper of a bath, from the French word *bain,* a bath.

CHRISTOPHER was at Marlboro, Mass., 1657.

THOMAS, a resident of Boston, Mass., 1685.

BANNING

JOHN, settled at Lyme, Conn., 1695.

BARBER

Occupation surname.

EDWARD, an inhabitant at Dedham, Mass., 1644.

GEORGE, b. Eng., 1615, was a townsman in Dedham, Mass., 1635, one of the original proprietors of Medfield, Mass., 1656.

JAMES, tailor, at Dorchester, Mass., about 1683.

JOHN, carpenter, was at Salem, Mass., 1637.

JOSIAH, a resident of Simsbury, Conn., 1677.

RICHARD, a freeman at Dedham, Mass., 1640.

ROBERT, granted land at Exeter, N. H., 1690.

THOMAS was at Dorchester, Mass., 1634, removed to Windsor, Conn., the following year.

WILLIAM, granted land at Dorchester, Mass., 1638; was at Salem, Mass., 1639, and at Marblehead, Mass., 1648.

WILLIAM was at Killingworth, Conn., about 1667.

BARBRIDGE

CHRISTOPHER, b. Eng., settled at Salem, Mass., 1662.

BARDWELL

ROBERT, b. 1647, came from London, Eng., to Hatfield, Mass., 1676.

WILLIAM, b. Eng., 1624, came to Concord, Mass., 1638; afterwards settled at Duxbury, Mass.

BARKER

The name originated from the old English word barker, a stripper of bark from the trees. Where there was a tanner there was a barker. The family of County of Salop is descended from Randulp de Covgree, who, in 1200, changed his name to William le Barker.

EDWARD came to Boston, Mass., 1650.

FRANCIS was an inhabitant of Concord, Mass., 1655.

JAMES, tailor, b. Stragwell, Eng., 1605, was a freeman at Rowley, Mass., 1640.

JAMES, son of Rowland, son of Edward, son of John, b. Eng., in 1634, embarked for N. E., died on voyage. His son, James, b. Harwich, Essex, Eng., 1632, was left in charge of his aunt, Mrs. Thomas Beecher; in his boyhood he lived at Charlestown, Mass.; 1651 was at Newport, R. I., was identified with Westerly, R. I.

JOHN was at Duxbury, Mass., 1632; removed to Marshfield, Mass., 1638, and was drowned 1652.

JOSEPH was at Weymouth, Mass., 1652.

NICHOLAS, carpenter, was at Boston, Mass., 1655.

RICHARD, husbandman, b. Eng., was at Andover, Mass., 1643.

ROBERT, brother of James, b. Eng., 1616; came to Duxbury, Mass., 1641.

THOMAS, brother of James, b. Strongewell, Suffolk, Eng., settled at Rowley, Mass., 1638; no male issue.

THOMAS, freeman at Boston, Mass., 1678.

BARLOW

AARON was at Rochester, Mass., 1684.

BARTHOLOMEW, cooper, was an inhabitant of Boston, Mass., 1648-57.

EDWARD was at Malden, Mass., 1660.

GEORGE, minister and lawyer, was at Exeter, N. H., 1639, and Saco, Maine, 1652.

GEORGE was an inhabitant of Milford, Conn., before 1690.

JAMES was at Suffield, Conn., 1680.

THOMAS an inhabitant of Fairfield, Conn., 1653.

THOMAS was at Boston, Mass., as early as 1657.

BARNABY

JAMES was at Plymouth, Mass., 1647.

BARNARD

From the Saxon *Bearn* or *Bairn*, a child, and the Teutonic *ard*, nature, of a child-like disposition.

BARTHOLOMEW, carpenter, was at York, Maine, 1651, afterwards at Boston, Mass.

FRANCIS, an inhabitant of Hartford, Conn., 1644; removed to Hadley, Mass., 1650.

JOHN, b. Eng., 1604, settled at Watertown, Mass., 1634.

JOHN, b. Eng., 1598, came to Cambridge, Mass., 1634; removed to Hartford, Conn., 1636, and to Hadley, Mass., 1659.

MASSACHIEL was at Weymouth, Mass., 1637; no male issue.

NATHANIEL was at Boston, Mass., 1659; removed to Nantucket, Mass., 1663.

RICHARD died at Springfield, Mass., 1683.

ROBERT, yeoman, b. Eng., was at Salisbury, Mass., before 1640; at Andover, Mass., 1644; and Nantucket, Mass., 1663; had only son John.

ROBERT, one of the founders of the church at Andover, Mass., 1645.

THOMAS, husbandman, b. Eng., 1612; granted lands at Salisbury, Mass., 1640; brother of Robert who removed to Nantucket, Mass.; among the first settlers of Amesbury, Mass.

BARNES

A distinguished family of Sotterly, Suffolk, Eng.; *Bearn*, local, a city in France; Cornish British *Barnyz*, a judge. Traces of the family are found in England under Norman kings. The name may be also a corruption of the Norse *bjoin*, signifying warrior. The family seat for five hundred years has been in Surrey, Eng. Sir Hugo de Berners came from France with William the Conqueror. A clear pedigree of the family begins with John Berners of West Horsley, Surrey, in 1347.

DANIEL was at New Haven, Conn., 1644.

JAMES was a freeman at Boston, Mass., 1681.

JOHN, merchant and yeoman, b. near the town of Barnes, now a suburb of London, Eng., was at Plymouth, Mass., 1633, removed, 1639, to Yarmouth, Mass.

JOHN was an inhabitant at Concord, Mass., 1661.

MATTHEW, miller, was at Braintree, Mass., in 1641; removed to Boston, Mass., 1652.

RICHARD came to N. E., 1639; was afterwards at Marlboro, Mass.

THOMAS was resident of Hingham, Mass., 1637.

THOMAS was at Salem, Mass., about 1655.

THOMAS, a resident of Hartford, Conn., 1639; was one of the early settlers of Farmington, Conn.

THOMAS, b. Eng., 1636; came to N. E., 1656; settled at Marlboro, Mass., 1666; one of the original proprietors.

THOMAS, brother of Daniel, settled at New Haven, Conn., 1639; removed, 1660, to Middletown, Conn.

WILLIAM was a freeman at Salisbury, Mass., 1641; one of the first settlers of Amesbury, Mass., 1654.

BARNEY

A familiar abbreviation or corruption of Bernard or Barnard (see).

JACOB, son of Edward, b. Bradenham, Eng., 1601; came to Salem, Mass., 1634.

JACOB, one of the founders of the first Baptist church in Boston, Mass., 1668.

BARNUM

A corruption of Bearnham, the town in a wood or hill. The original family seat of the family was at Southwich, Hants, Eng.

THOMAS was at Fairfield, Conn., and in 1662 at Norwalk, Conn.; one of the first eight settlers at Danbury, Conn., 1684.

BARRELL

From the Gaelic *Barrail,* excellent, surpassing.

GEORGE, cooper, was at Boston, Mass., 1638.

JOHN, cooper, brother of preceding, b. Eng., came to Boston, Mass., 1643.

JOHN was at Watertown, Mass., before 1658; no male issue.

WILLIAM, brother of George, came to Boston, Mass., 1638, died the following year.

BARRET

From the old French word *barat,* strife, cunning.

HUMPHREY, b. Eng., 1592; came to Concord, Mass., 1640.

JAMES, b. Eng., 1615-19; was at Charlestown, Mass., 1643; removed to Malden, Mass.

JOHN was at Taunton, Mass., 1643.

JOHN, a resident of Malden, Mass., 1653.

JOHN, an inhabitant of Chelmsford, Mass., about 1659.

JOHN was at Charlestown, Mass.; afterwards removed to Chelmsford, Mass.

THOMAS came to N. E., 1635, made freeman at Braintree, Mass., 1645; granted lands at Chelmsford, Mass., 1660.

WILLIAM, brother of preceding, was at Cambridge, Mass., 1656.

BARROWS or BARRUS

The name of a river in Ireland; a circular earthen mound, marking the place of interment of some noted person, also a place of defense.

JAMES was taxed at Dover, N. H., 1670.

JOHN, b. Eng., sailed for N. E., and settled at Salem, Mass., 1637; removed to Plymouth, Mass.

BARSHAM

WILLIAM came in 1630 to Watertown, Mass., made freeman 1637.

BARSTOW

Barr, the top of a hill, and *stow,* a place or depository. *Bar* in Gaelic, Welch and Cornish British means the summit or top of anything. The Gaelic or Irish *aran* and *barr* signify bread, a crop of grain; Welch, *bar,* bread, an ear of corn; Saxon, *bar* and *bere,* corn, barley. *Barstow,* a place where grain is stored.

GEORGE, b. Eng., 1614; came from London, Eng., to Boston, Mass., 1635; granted land in Dedham, Mass., where he resided before 1642; removed to Scituate, Mass.

JOHN, youngest brother of preceding, b. Yorkshire, Eng., came to Cambridge, Mass., prior to 1650.

MICHAEL, or MILES, son of Matthew of Shelf near Halifax, Yorkshire, Eng., eldest brother of preceding, was at Charlestown, Mass., where his wife joined the church in 1635; removed in 1642 to Watertown, Mass.

WILLIAM, brother of preceding, came to Dedham, Mass., 1635; freeman at Scituate, Mass., 1649, and the first settler of Hanover, Mass.

BART

The family is descended from Sir Hamo de Burt of the Manor in the lordship of Homingtoft, Eng. The surname is derived from the Saxon *beart,* which signifies bright in sense of illustrious.

HENRY came from Eng., to Mass., 1631; was at Roxbury, Mass., 1638; removed to Springfield, Mass., 1640.

BARTHOLOMEW

Derived from Hebrew word *Bartholo-*

mew, the son of him who maketh the waters to mount, or a son that suspends the waters.

Henry was at Salem, Mass., 1635.

Richard, brother of the preceding, made freeman at Boston, Mass., 1641.

William, son of William, a mercer of Burford, Eng., and fourth generation from John of Warborough, Oxfordshire, Eng., b. Burford, Eng., 1602-03, came to Boston, Mass., with two brothers mentioned above; he was at Ipswich, Mass., 1634.

BARTLETT

A diminutive of Bartholomew—little Bart, originally spelled Barttelot; the family traced to Adam Barttelot, who came with William the Conqueror; granted lands in Stopham, Sussex.

Christopher was at Newbury, Mass., 1635.

George, an inhabitant of Guilford, Conn., 1641; removed to Branford, Conn., 1649; was known as Lieut. George.

Henry, b. Eng., 1600; settled at Braintree, Mass.; was afterwards at Marlboro, Mass.; was of Welsh descent.

John, son of Edward, came from Kent, Eng., to Newbury, Mass., 1635.

John, brother of George, was at Windsor, Conn., in 1640.

John was at Weymouth, Mass., before 1666; removed to Mendon, Mass.

Joseph settled in what is now Newton, Mass., 1668.

Richard, shoemaker, son of Edward, brother of John and Christopher, b. Wiltshire, Eng., 1575, settled at Newbury, Mass., 1634.

Robert, b. Eng., came to Plymouth, Mass., 1623; one of the first purchasers of land in Dartmouth, Mass.

Robert, an original proprietor of Cambridge, Mass., 1632; removed to Hartford, Conn., 1636.

Capt. Robert, yeoman and fisherman, b. Eng., 1638; was resident of Mass., 1666, settled at Marblehead, Mass., 1669.

Thomas was resident of Watertown, Mass., 1631.

BARTOL

John, bapt. Eng., 1601; came to Salem, Mass., short time afterward; in 1634, went to Marblehead, Mass.

BARTON

From a town in Lincolnshire, Eng., a corn or barley village from *bere,* barley, and *ton,* an enclosure, a house, a village. In Devonshire it is applied to any freehold estate not possessed of manorial privileges.

James, ropemaker, was at Newbury, Mass., 1688, previous to this at Boston, Mass.

Matthew was at Salem, Mass., before 1682.

Rufus was at Portsmouth, R. I., 1648.

Samuel located at Salem, Mass., 1693; afterwards resided at Oxford, Mass.

BARTRAM, BERTRAM

Norman ancestry. William Bartram in time of Henry I founded priory of Bunkham, County of Northumberland, Eng.

John came from Eng., to Stratford, Conn., an early settler, where he died 1676.

BASCOM

Thomas came from Eng., to Dorchester, Mass., 1633-34; removed to Windsor, Conn., 1639.

BASS

Samuel at Roxbury, Mass., 1632, removed to Braintree, Mass., 1640.

BASSETT

From French *Basset,* a little fat man with short legs and thighs.

John was resident of New Haven, Conn., 1647.

Joseph married in Hingham, Mass., 1677.

Thomas, b. Eng., 1604, came to Windsor, Conn., 1641; first sat down at Dorchester, Mass.; removed to Fairfield, Conn., before 1653.

William, son of Walter, came to Plymouth, Mass., 1621; original proprietor of Bridgewater, Mass.; lived at Sandwich, and Duxbury, Mass.

BASSOM or BASSUM (abbreviation for Bassamthwaite)

Thomas was at Windsor, Conn., 1642.

William was at Watertown, Mass., 1636; died early; his widow shared in lands at Watertown, Mass., and settled, in 1639, at Sudbury, Mass.

BASTON

Thomas settled at Saco, Maine, 1666.

BATEMAN

From Baitman, a keeper of a house of entertainment, and Bateman, a contentious man, from Saxon *bate*—strife, to beat, contention.

Eleazer was at Woburn, Mass., prior to 1686.

John, an inhabitant of Boston, Mass., 1644.

Thomas was a freeman at Concord, Mass., 1642.

William was at Charlestown, Mass., 1631; removed to Chelmsford, Mass.

BATES

From Anglo-Saxon *bate* meaning contention. The English ancestry is traced to Sir Gerard Bate, Yorkshire, Eng., Lord Mayor of London, 1248.

CLEMENT, tailor, son of Thomas, and direct descendant in fifth generation of Thomas Bate, of parish All Hallows, Kent, Eng., who died 1485, b. Hingham, Kent, Eng., 1598, settled at Hingham, Mass., in 1635.

EDWARD or EDMUND, b. Eng., 1605, brother of preceding, joined the first church at Boston, Mass., 1633; was a freeman at Weymouth, Mass., 1639.

FRANCIS was at Topsfield, Mass., 1661.

GEORGE, thatcher, freeman at Boston, 1636, lived in what is now Brookline, Mass.

JAMES, husbandman, brother of Clement and Edward, was at Dorchester, Mass., 1635.

BATRAM

JOHN came to Stratford, Conn., where he died 1675.

JOHN was resident of Weymouth, Mass., 1655.

JOHN lived at New London, Conn., 1677.

ROBERT was at Wethersfield, Conn., 1640.

ROBERT an inhabitant of Lynn, Mass., previous to 1672.

SAMUEL was at Saybrook, Conn., 1676.

BATSON

STEPHEN was at Saco, Maine, 1636, removed to Kennebunk, Maine, 1653.

BATT

CHRISTOPHER, tanner, came from Salisbury, Wiltshire, Eng., 1638, to Newbury, Mass.

NICHOLAS, brother of preceding, was at Boston, Mass., 1635; no male issue.

BATTELLE or BATTLE

A family name as early as 12th century, of Norwegian origin.

THOMAS, b. 1620, was at Dedham, Mass., 1648.

BATTEN

BENJAMIN, merchant, Boston, Mass., 1671.

HUGH, a resident of Dorchester, Mass., 1658.

BATTER

EDMUND, malster, came from Salisbury, Wiltshire, Eng., 1635; made a freeman at Salem, Mass., 1637.

NICHOLAS, was a freeman at Lynn, Mass., 1638.

BATTING or BATTENS

WILLIAM was at Saco, Maine, 1659 and moved to Scarborough, Maine, 1663.

BAXTER

Anglo-Saxon from *bagster,* a baker.

DANIEL was an inhabitant of Salem, Mass., 1639.

GEORGE was at Providence, R. I., 1650.

GREGORY came in Winthrop's fleet 1630, settled at Roxbury, Mass., next year removed to Braintree.

JAMES married at Charlestown, Mass., 1659.

JOHN, a resident of Salem, Mass., 1667.

NICHOLAS, mariner, was at Boston, Mass., 1639.

RICHARD came from Hingham, Eng., to Hingham, Mass., 1638.

WILLIAM was at Marblehead, Mass., 1674.

BAY or BAYES

MATTHEW was at Ipswich, Mass., 1659.

THOMAS was at Dedham, Mass., 1643, removed to Boston, Mass.

BAYLEY

BENJAMIN was a resident of Boston, Mass., 1673.

GUIDO was an inhabitant of Salem, Mass., as early as 1642.

JAMES was a resident of Roxbury, Mass., 1641.

JOHN, weaver, came from Chippenham, Wiltshire, Eng., to Salisbury, Mass., as early as 1634, removed, 1650, to Newbury, Mass.

JONAS swore allegiance to Mass., at Scarborough, Maine, 1658.

NICHOLAS, brother of preceding, was at Saco, Maine, 1663.

THOMAS was at New London, Conn., 1652.

BAYSEY

JOHN, weaver, an original proprietor of Hartford, Conn.; no male issue.

BEACH or BEECH

The shore of sea, lake or river.

JOHN, b. Eng., settled at Stratford, Conn.

RICHARD, brother of preceding, came from London, Eng.; settled in Watertown, Mass., 1635, at New Haven, Conn., 1639.

THOMAS, brother of preceding, was at New Haven, Conn.; in 1658 at Milford, Conn. He and his brothers were later at Wallingford, Conn.

BEACHEN

ROBERT was at Fairfield, Conn., 1669.

BEADLE

A name of office; a messenger or crier of a court; an officer belonging to a university or parish.

NATHANIEL was at Salem, Mass., 1670.

SAMUEL, resident of Charlestown, Mass., 1658; removed to Salem, Mass.

THOMAS, mariner, brother of Nathaniel, was resident of Salem, Mass., before 1679.

BEAL, BEALE or BEALS

Place name from Biel, a town in Switzerland. The Gaelic word *beul* signifies the mouth.

ABRAHAM, a resident of Charlestown, Mass., 1657.

BENJAMIN was at Dorchester, Mass., 1674; removed to Boston, 1676.

JOHN, shoemaker, came from parish of Hingham, Norfolk, Eng., where he was born 1588, to Hingham, Mass., 1638.

JOSEPH sent by Mason to Portsmouth, N. H., 1631.

SAMUEL was a resident of Salem, Mass., before 1682.

THOMAS at Cambridge, Mass., 1634; no issue.

COL. WILLIAM, spelled his name with a final "e," came from London, Eng., and in 1653 was at York, Maine; returned to Eng., and was succeeded by his son, Arthur, b. London, Eng., 1620, and came to York, Maine, 1655.

BEAMAN

GAMALIEL, b. Eng., 1623, came to N. E., as a minor 1635, lived at Dorchester, Mass., where he was proprietor 1649; one of the incorporators of Lancaster, Mass.

BEAMOND or BEAMAN

JOHN, b. Eng., 1612, came to N. E., 1635, was at Salem, Mass., 1640 and Scituate, Mass., 1643.

SIMON was at Springfield, Mass., in 1655.

WILLIAM, brother of John, b. Eng., 1608, came to N. E., 1635, located at Saybrook, Conn.

BEAMSLEY

WILLIAM was freeman at Boston, Mass., 1636, arrived from Eng., 1632.

BEAN, BEANE or BEANES

The surname comes from the Scotch clan Vean, the letters, *b* and *v* in Gaelic being interchangeable signify mountain; however, it may be derived from the fair complexion of the clan's progenitor, ***bean,*** **meaning white or fair, used by the** Highlanders to distinguish a man of fair complexion. The clan Vean or MacBean was one of the tribes of Clan Chattan, which occupied the Lochaber territory, 1300.

JOHN, b. Scotland, settled at Exeter, N. H., 1660-77.

LEWIS was at York, Maine, 1668.

MICHAEL was at Kittery, Maine, 1653.

PHILIP was granted lands at Salem, Mass., 1637.

BEARD

AARON swore fidelity to Mass., 1674 at Pemaquid.

JOHN was at Milford, Conn., 1642; came from Eng., with two brothers, James and Jeremy, of whom little is known.

THOMAS, shoemaker, was at Plymouth, Mass., 1629; removed to Portsmouth, N. H., 1644.

THOMAS, mariner, freeman at Boston, Mass., 1675.

WILLIAM, a resident of Dover, N. H., was killed by Indians 1675.

BEARDSLEY or BEADSLEY

THOMAS was a resident of Milford, Conn., 1647.

WILLIAM, mason, b. Stratford-on-Avon, Eng., 1605, came to N. E., 1635; located at Hartford, Conn., 1638; the following year was one of the first settlers at Stratford, Conn.

BEARSE, BEARCE or BEIRCE

AUSTIN, b. 1618, settled at Barnstable, Mass., 1638.

BEAUCHAMP

From Normandy French *De Beauchamp*, from the fair or beautiful field; in Latin *De Bello Campo.*

EDWARD was a resident of Salem, Mass., 1637.

JOHN, leather dresser, Huguenot descent; on record at Boston, Mass., 1687; removed to Hartford, Conn., 1711.

BECK

From Anglo-Saxon *becc,* a brook.

ALEXANDER, freeman at Boston, Mass., 1634.

HENRY came from Hertfordshire, Eng., to Portsmouth, N. H., 1635.

BECKETT

A little brook.

JOHN, shipwright, settled at Salem, Mass., 1649.

STEPHEN came as minor eleven years of age, 1634, under charge of Richard Pepper, to Roxbury, Mass. After a few years removed to Hartford, Conn.

BECKFORD or BICKFORD

GEORGE was at Dover, N. H., 1666, and lived at Marblehead, Mass., 1678.

JOHN, b. Eng., about 1612, settled, 1645, at what is now Durham, N. H.

SAMUEL lived at Salisbury, Mass., in 1678 purchased land and removed to Nantucket, Mass.

BECKLEY

The meadow or pasture by the brook, from *beck,* a brook, and *ley,* field or meadow.

RICHARD, b. Hampshire, Eng., 1618, on record at New Haven, Conn., 1639; removed to Wethersfield, Conn., 1660.

BECKWITH

The same as Beckworth, the farm or place by the brook, from *beck,* a brook, and *worth,* a farm. Hugh de Malebisse was a knight under William the Conqueror. His great-grandson, Sir Hercules, married Lady Beckwith Bruce, in 1226, and heiress of an estate named Beckwith, and Sir Hercules assumed the name of his wife's estate.

MATTHEW, b. Portefract, Yorkshire, Eng., 1610, came to Saybrook, Conn., 1635; three years later he was at Branford, Conn., and in 1645 lived at Hartford, Conn.; afterwards was at Lyme and New London, Conn.

STEPHEN was at Norwalk, Conn., 1654.

BEDLE, BEDEL or BEEDLE

ROBERT was at Wethersfield, Conn.; removed to New London, Conn., 1648.

BEDURTHA or BORDURTHA

RICE or REICE was a resident of Springfield, Mass., 1646.

BEEBE or BEEBY

The family is of Norman origin. Richard and William de Boebe were two knights in the Royal Guard of William the Conqueror.

JAMES was married at Hadley, Mass., 1668.

JAMES was a resident of Stratford, Conn., 1679; removed to Norwalk, Conn., thence to Danbury, Conn.

JOHN, son of John, grandson of Alexander of Great Addington, Eng., b. Broughton, Northampton, Eng., 1600, came to New London, Conn., 1650, with a family of five sons and two daughters.

BEECHER or BEACHER

From the French *Beau chere,* a fine entertainment; or from beech-wood.

HANNAH, widow of John of Kent, Eng., came to Boston, 1637, with her family, the only son being Isaac, who became identified with New Haven, Conn.

THOMAS, mariner, freeman at Charlestown, Mass., 1632, having come to N. E., 1630.

BEEDE

THOMAS was at Newport, R. I., 1639.

BEEFORD

RICHARD, an inhabitant of Gloucester, Mass., 1643.

BEERS or BEERE

Ancient English family; surname derived from Beer, a town in Dorsetshire, Eng. In Dutch, *beer* signifies a bear, a boar. The family existed as early as the 13th century, under the name of De Bere, in the parish of Westcliffe, Kent, Eng. There was a place called Bere's or Byer Court. William de Bere of Bere Court was bailiff of Dover, Eng., 1275. An unbroken line can be traced from Martin de Bere, living at Rochester, Kent, 1486, to the American progenitor.

ANTHONY, mariner, son of John of Gravesend, Eng., and fifth generation from Nicholas de Bere, who held the Manor of Bere's in the twentieth year of the reign of Henry III, came from Kent, Eng., 1635, settled with his uncle, Richard, and brother, James; removed to Fairfield, Conn., 1659, and was lost at sea 1676.

JAMES, brother of the preceding, was at Watertown, Mass., and in 1657 at Fairfield, Conn.

JOHN, son of Edward of Dorsetshire, Eng., was a resident of Newport, R. I., 1664.

JOHN was at Gloucester, Mass., 1675.

PHILIP, a resident of Salem, Mass., 1637.

RICHARD was inhabitant of Marshfield, Mass., 1636.

RICHARD, brother of John of Gravesend, Eng., b. 1607, came to Watertown, 1635, was killed in King Philip's War, ranking as captain.

ROBERT married at Rehoboth, Mass., 1673.

THOMAS, living at New Haven, Conn., 1654.

BEHONEY

PETER was living at Watertown, Mass., 1688.

BEIGHTON

SAMUEL, cooper, was at Boston, Mass., 1684.

BELCHER

From old French word *Bel-chere*—good cheer, fine entertainment.

ANDREW on record at Salisbury, Mass., 1639.

GREGORY, b. Eng., 1606, was at Boston, Mass., 1634; proprietor at Braintree, Mass., 1637.

JEREMY settled at Ipswich. Mass., 1635.

JOHN, resident of Braintree, Mass., before 1656.

BELCONGER

JOHN married at Newbury, Mass., 1666.

BELDEN or BELDING

From the Cornish British, the beautiful hill *Beildin,* the hill of Belus, a place of Druid worship; Bayldon or Buildon Common is a chapelry in the West Riding of Yorkshire, Eng. Walter Blaydon is the earliest English ancestor known in a direct line; lived in the 15th century.

HENRY was a resident of Woburn, Mass., 1641.

RICHARD, bapt. Kippax, Eng., 1591; was at Wethersfield, Conn., 1641.

WILLIAM was an inhabitant of Wethersfield, Conn., 1646.

BELKNAP

ABRAHAM, b. Eng., settled at Lynn, Mass., 1637, removed to Salem, where he died 1643.

BELL

A name taken from the sign of an inn or shop, a bell being frequently used.

ABRAHAM was at New Haven, Conn., 1639, removed to Charlestown, Mass., 1647.

FRANCIS was at Stamford, Conn., 1641, previously at Wethersfield, Conn.

JAMES took oath of fidelity at New Haven, Conn., 1644.

JOHN was at Sandwich, Mass., 1643; at Yarmouth, Mass., 1657.

PHILIP, at Boston, Mass., 1668.

RORERT, tailor, was resident of Hartford, Conn., before 1684.

SHADRACH, inhabitant of Portsmouth, N. H., 1685.

THOMAS, freeman at Roxbury, Mass., 1636.

THOMAS resided at Boston, Mass., 1637.

THOMAS resident of Stonington, Conn., 1667-79.

BELLAMY

From Bellesme, a town of France, or from the French *belami,* a dear friend; *bel* fair or beautiful, and *ami* friend or companion.

MATTHEW, schoolmaster, first at Fairfield, Conn., 1658 at Stamford, Conn.; married, 1671, at New Haven, Conn.; afterwards at Guilford and Killingworth, Conn.

BELLEW

Normandy French *De Bellew,* a corruption of *De Belle Eau,* from the beautiful water. The family originally came from Italy, went to England with William the Conqueror, afterwards settled at Meath, Ireland.

WILLIAM was at Dover, N. H., 1644.

BELLEFLOWER

HENRY was at Reading, Mass., 1656; no male issue.

BELLINGHAM

RICHARD came from Boston, Mass., 1634, afterwards removed to Ipswich, thence to Rowley, Mass.

WILLIAM, brother of the preceding, freeman at Rowley, Mass., 1650; no issue.

BELLOWS

JOHN, carpenter, b. Eng., 1623, came to N. E., 1635, at the age of 12 years; settled at Concord, Mass., 1645; later removed to Marlboro, Mass.

MATURIN was in Providence, R. I., 1645.

ROBERT, a resident of Boston, Mass., 1654.

BEMENT

JOHN, b. Eng., came to Salem, Mass., 1635.

SYMON, of French origin, was early resident of Springfield, Mass.

WILLIAM, brother of John, b. Eng., 1612, came to Salem, Mass., 1635.

BEMIS

JAMES, granted lands at New London, Conn., 1649; no male issue.

JOSEPH, blacksmith and farmer, b. Eng., 1619, came to Watertown, Mass., 1640.

BENDALL

EDWARD came in Winthrop's fleet, settled at Boston, Mass.

BENEDICT

From the Latin *Benedictus,* blessed, well spoken of, or a person wishing all good; the name in general use in the reign of Edward II; the ancient seat of the family was Norwich, Eng.

THOMAS, weaver, only son of William, b. Nottinghamshire, Eng., 1617, came to Mass., 1638; removed before 1650 to Southold, L. I.

BENHAM

JOHN came to Dorchester, Mass., 1630; removed to New Haven, Conn., 1640.

BENJAMIN

From Hebrew, the son of the right hand; the youngest of Jacob's twelve children.

JOHN came to Boston, Mass., 1632; proprietor at Cambridge, Mass., 1637; removed in that year to Watertown, Mass.

ROBERT, brother of preceding, came to N. E., 1632; located before 1663 at Southold, L. I.

BENMORE

CHARLES, resident of Boston, Mass., before 1677.

PHILIP was at Dover, N. H., before 1669.

BENNETT

A contraction or corruption of Benedict (see).

AMBROSE, a resident of Boston, Mass., 1653.

ANTHONY, Welsh descent, settled at Goose Creek, Gloucester, Mass., 1679, removed to Beverly, Mass.; later to Rowley, Mass.

DAVID, physician, was a resident of Rowley, Mass.

EDMUND or EDWARD, freeman at Weymouth, Mass., 1636; removed to Rehoboth, Mass., 1643, and 1676 was at Providence, R. I.

FRANCIS a resident of Boston, Mass., 1650; drowned at Noddle's Island the following year.

HENRY, b. Eng., 1629; settled at Ipswich, Mass., 1650; previous to this he was at Salem, Mass.

HENRY, an inhabitant of Lyme, Conn., 1673.

JAMES, b. Eng., freeman of Concord, Mass., 1639; in 1644 removed to Fairfield, Conn.

JOHN, weaver, b. Eng., 1632 was at Charlestown, Mass., 1650.

JOHN, a resident of Salem, Mass., 1633.

JOSEPH was a resident of Newport, R. I., 1674.

RICHARD was at Salem, Mass., 1636; removed to Boston, Mass., 1642.

ROBERT, freeman at Newport, R. I., 1655.

SAMUEL, carpenter, b. Eng., 1611, came to what is now Saugus, 1635; removed to what is now Chelsea, Mass., 1639.

SAMUEL was resident of Providence, R. I., prior to 1645, afterwards removed to East Greenwich, R. I.

THOMAS, a resident of Fairfield, Conn., 1664.

WILLIAM, b. Eng., 1602, came to Plymouth, Mass., 1631-33, and was at Salem, Mass., 1637.

BENNING

RALPH was an inhabitant of Boston, Mass., 1661.

BENSON

Ben's-son, the son of Benjamin. This large and ancient family identified with Masham, Eng., as early as 1300.

JOHN BENSON in 1348 held a croft from the Abbey of Fountains at Swenton by Masham.

JOHN, b. Caversham, Oxfordshire, Eng., 1608; came to Hingham, Mass., 1638.

JOHN, a resident of Rochester, Mass., before 1689.

BENT

A local name, a plain, a moor covered with bent grass.

JOHN, husbandman, son of Robert, grandson of John, b. Penton-Grafton, Eng., 1603, came to Sudbury, Mass., 1638.

JOSIAH, a resident of Marshfield, Mass., 1666.

ROBERT, died at Newbury, Mass., 1648.

BENTLEY

From *bent*, a moor, and *ley*, uncultivated ground. It is the name of a parish in the deanery of Doncaster, and south part of Yorkshire, Eng.

RICHARD was at Charlestown, Mass., 1690.

WILLIAM, b. 1588, came to Boston, Mass., 1635.

BENTON

ANDREW, bapt. at Eppong, Eng., 1620, settled at Milford, Conn., 1639, removed to Hartford, Conn., 1660.

DANIEL was at Guilford, Conn., 1669.

EDWARD, b. Wiltshire, Eng., settled at Guilford, Conn., 1650.

BERNON

GABRIEL, French Huguenot, son of Andre, b. Rochelle, France, 1644, came to Boston, Mass., and removed to Newport, R. I., after 1691, died at Providence, R. I., 1736; no male issue.

BERRY

A family of ancient English origin; the name derived from *bury* or *borough*, a place of safety, of defense. A province of France is named Berri.

AMBROSE was at Saco, Maine, 1636; no male issue.

ANTHONY was an inhabitant of Yarmouth, Mass., 1643; afterwards at Gloucester, Mass.

CHRISTOPHER was at Salem, Mass., 1640.

EDMUND resident of Sandwich, Mass., 1643.

EDWARD, weaver, was at Salem, Mass., about 1655.

JOHN was at Boston, Mass., 1664; afterwards, 1666, at Portsmouth, Mass.

JOHN married at Ipswich, Mass., 1671.

RICHARD was at Yarmouth, Mass., 1643.

THOMAS, mariner, was resident of Boston, Mass., 1668-73.

WILLIAM was at Portsmouth, N. H., 1631; removed to Newbury, Mass., 1635, and 1648-9 received land grants at Rye, N. H.

BESBEDGE, BESBITCH or BEESBEECH

THOMAS came from parish Hedcorn, Kent, Eng., to Scituate, Mass., 1635; removed to Duxbury, Mass., 1643; later to Sudbury, Mass.

BESSE or BESSEY

ANTHONY came from London, Eng., to Lynn, 1635, removed to Sandwich, Mass., 1637.

BEST

JOHN, tailor, came from parish St. George, city of Canterbury, Eng., 1630, to N. E.

ROBERT was at Sudbury, Mass., early date; no male issue.

BESWICK

GEORGE was at Wethersfield, Conn., where he died 1672.

BETSCOMBE or BETSHAM

RICHARD, freeman at Hingham, Mass., 1637.

BETTS

A contraction of the Latin *Beatus*—happy.

JOHN, b. Eng., 1594, came to N. E., 1634; was at Cambridge and Lexington, Mass.; no male issue.

JOHN, an inhabitant of Wethersfield, Conn., before 1648.

JOHN was at Charlestown, Mass., 1678.

RICHARD came from Hemel Hempstead, Herts, Eng., to Ipswich, Mass., 1648; removed, 1656, to Newtown, L. I.

ROGER took oath of fidelity at New Haven, Conn., 1644; two years later was at Branford, Conn.

SAMUEL, brother of preceding, was proprietor at Branford, Conn., 1679.

THOMAS, b. Eng., 1618, came to N. E., 1639; one of the founders of Guilford, Conn., 1650; resided at Milford, Conn., 1658; at Norwalk, Conn., 1664.

WILLIAM, turner, was at Barnstable, Mass., in 1635, joined church at Scituate, Mass., afterwards lived at Dorchester, Mass.

BETTY

JAMES was at Salem, Mass., 1661; no record of any male issue.

BEVANS or BEVENS

From Welch; a contraction of *Ap Evans* or *Ivan*, the son of John, from *ap* son, and *Ivan*, John.

ARTHUR died at Glastonbury, Conn., 1697.

BENJAMIN was at Farmington, Conn., before 1688.

ROWLAND, a resident of Boston, Mass., before 1660.

BEWETT, BUET, or BUITT

GEORGE was at Sandwich, Mass., 1643.

HUGH, banished from Mass., 1640; removed to Providence, R. I.

BIBBLE

JOHN, a resident of Boston, Mass., 1637, and of Malden, Mass., 1644; no record of any children.

BICKMORE

THOMAS, b. Eng., 1601, came to N. E., 1635.

BICKNELL

JOHN was at Weymouth, Mass., before 1651.

ZACHARY, b. Eng., 1590, came to N. E., with only son, John, 11 years of age, in 1635; he died following year at Weymouth, Mass.

BICKNOR or BICKNER

THOMAS was at Charlestown, Mass., before 1655.

WILLIAM was at Charlestown, 1658, and died following year.

BIDDLE

The same as Beadle, of which it is a corruption.

JOHN was resident of Hartford, Conn., 1639.

JOSEPH married at Marshfield, Mass., 1636, came to N. E., the previous year; no issue.

BIDFIELD, BEDFIELD or BETFIELD

SAMUEL, cooper, freeman at Boston, Mass., 1641.

BIDGOOD or BETGOOD

BOSTON, a merchant from Romsey, Hants, Eng., came 1638 to N. E., and was at Ipswich, Mass., 1642.

BIDWELL

From the Saxon word *Biddulph*, meaning a castle, same as *Botolph*, derived from *Boat* and *ulph;* a castle built in 1066 in County of Norfolk, Eng., was named Biddulph Castle.

RICHARD, an early settler of Windsor, Conn., where he died 1647.

BIGELOW

The name is from Anglo-Saxon *biggar*, big and *hlaew*, a hill or barrow. In

Cornish British *Bygel* is a herdsman, a shepherd, and the name may have been applied to a commander of an army. The American lineage is traced to Richard de Baguley, Lord of Baguley, Chestershire, Eng., 1243.

JOHN, blacksmith, son of Randle Baguley, of Wrentham, Suffolk, Eng., bapt. Eng., 1617, came to Watertown, Mass., 1642.

BIGGS or BIGG

JOHN came in Winthrop's fleet to Boston, Mass., 1630; removed, 1635, to Ipswich, Mass.; afterwards resided at Dorchester, Mass., and Exeter, N. H.

TIMOTHY, a resident of Boston, Mass., 1665.

WILLIAM died at Middletown, Conn., 1681.

BILL

Ancient English family, originally from Denmark. The name signifies a warlike weapon, called bill, an ancient battle axe, hence in warfare billman. Family is prominent in Shropshire, Wiltshire and Staffordshire. Dr. William Bill was prominent English ancestor of the family in 1490.

JOHN, the son of John, came to Boston, Mass., 1635, and died 1638.

THOMAS was a resident of Boston, Mass., 1657.

BILLINGS

Place name from the town of Billings, Lincolnshire, Eng., *Beilean* in Gaelic means loquacious, a prattling person.

NATHANIEL settled at Concord, Mass., before 1640.

RICHARD was resident of Hartford, Conn., 1640; removed to Hadley, Mass., 1661.

ROGER was at Dorchester, Mass., 1640; made freeman, 1643.

SAMUEL was at Newport, R. I., 1658.

WILLIAM, IX generation from John of Rowell, Eng., b. Taunton, Eng., came to Dorchester or Braintree, Mass., 1640; one of the original proprietors at Lancaster, Mass., 1654; four years later removed to Stonington, Conn.

BILLINGTON

JOHN, *Mayflower* passenger, hung for murder 1630.

THOMAS was at Exeter, N. H., 1650; removed to Taunton, Mass., where he died 1662.

BILLS or BILLES

MATTHEW was at Dover, N. H., 1654.

ROBERT, husbandman, b. Eng., 1602; came to Charlestown, Mass., 1635; died three years later; no issue.

BINGHAM

Place name from town of Bingham in Nottinghamshire, Eng., so named from Danish *Bing*, a place where provisions were deposited, and *ham*, a town or village.

THOMAS, son of Henry, a master cutler of Sheffield, Eng., bapt. parish of St. Peters and Holy Trinity, Sheffield, Eng., 1642. He came to N. E., with his mother and stepfather, William Backus, to Saybrook, Conn., 1658; resided at New London, Conn., 1660; afterwards at Norwich, Conn., and in 1693 to Windham, Conn.

BINGLEY

THOMAS married at Boston, Mass., 1665.

WILLIAM living at Newbury, Mass., 1659.

BINNEY

From Cornish British *bin*, a hill, and *ey* water. *Binneach* in Gaelic signifies hilly, mountains.

JOHN came from Worksop, Nottinghamshire, Eng., to Hull, Mass., before 1679.

BINNS

JONAS was at Dover, N. H., 1648.

BIRCH

A name given for residing at or near a birch tree.

SIMON was an inhabitant of Mass., 1635.

THOMAS died at Dorchester, Mass., 1657.

THOMAS married at Swanzey, Mass., 1684.

BIRCHARD, BURCHARD

THOMAS, b. Eng., 1595, settled first at Dorchester, Mass., 1635; removed to Hartford, Conn., and was original proprietor; in 1650 was at Saybrook, Conn.

BIRD

JATHIEL granted land at Ipswich, Mass., 1641.

SIMON, b. Eng., 1615, came to Boston, Mass., 1635; freeman at Chelsea, Mass., 1644; removed to Billerica, 1655; no issue.

THOMAS was at Hartford, Conn., before 1653.

THOMAS was at Scituate, Mass., before 1630.

THOMAS, b. Eng., 1613, was at Dorchester, Mass., 1640.

BIRDLEY

GILES was at Ipswich, Mass., 1648.

TYLER, brother of preceding, was at Ipswich, Mass., 1648. The name may have been Burley.

BIRDSEYE

JOHN came from Eng., to New Haven, Conn., 1636.

BIRGE

RICHARD settled at Dorchester, Mass., and in 1636 was among first settlers of Windsor, Conn.

BISBEE (see Besbedge)

EDWARD, husbandman and lawyer, settled in what is now Beverly, Mass., 1640.

HENRY, farmer, took oath of fidelity at New Haven, Conn., 1644.

HENRY, a resident of Ipswich, Mass., married at Boston, Mass., 1657.

JAMES was an inhabitant of New Haven, Conn., 1648.

JAMES was at Duxbury, Mass., 1679.

JOHN, carpenter, married at Newbury, Mass., 1647, removed to Nantucket, Mass., later to Woodbridge, N. J.

REV. JOHN was at Taunton, Mass., 1640; chosen minister at Stamford, Conn., 1644.

JOHN, b. Eng., 1600, one of the founders of Guilford, Conn., 1639.

NATHANIEL, currier, was at Ipswich, Mass., 1634, became freeman at Boston, Mass., 1645.

RICHARD was at Salem, Mass., 1635, made freeman 1642.

THOMAS, brother of Nathaniel, was a resident of Ipswich, Mass., 1636.

TOWNSEND was a freeman at Salem, Mass., 1635.

BISS

JAMES was living at Boston, Mass., 1668.

BISSELL

JOHN, French Huguenot descent, b. Somersetshire, Eng., 1591, arrived at Plymouth, Mass., 1628; removed to East Windsor, Conn., 1640.

BIXBY

The name is of Danish origin, signifying the house or village among the boxtrees. There is, however, a town in the eastern portion of England by this name; *by* signifies town, and Bixby was originally Biggsby—Bigg's town.

DANIEL married at Andover, Mass., 1674.

JOSEPH, carpenter, came from Assington, Suffolk, Eng., and was early settler, before 1647, at Salisbury, Mass. He was afterwards at Ipswich, Mass., 1649, and Rowley, Mass., 1667.

NATHANIEL was at Ipswich, Mass., 1636.

THOMAS, a resident of Salem, Mass., 1636.

BLACK

DANIEL, of Scotch descent, was at what is now Boxford, Mass., 1666.

GEORGE, a resident of Gloucester, Mass., before 1658.

JOHN was at Charlestown, Mass., 1634; made freeman 1644.

MILES, an inhabitant of Sandwich, Mass., 1643.

BLACKBURN or BLACKBURNE

The black brook or stream.

WALTER arrived Mass., 1638; freeman 1640; lived at Roxbury, and Boston, Mass.; returned to Eng., 1641.

BLACKFORD

NICHOLAS, freeman at Newport, R. I., 1655.

BLACKLEACH

BENJAMIN was resident of Cambridge, Mass., before 1650.

JOHN, merchant, freeman at Salem, Mass.; 1635, removed to Boston, thence Hartford, Conn.; died at Wethersfield, Conn., 1683.

RICHARD, b. 1655, was at Stratford, Conn., 1685.

BLACKLEY, BLAKESLEY or BLAKESLEE

SAMUEL, blacksmith, became resident of Hartford, Conn., 1641; removed to Branford, Conn., 1645; settled at Guilford, Conn., 1650; removed to New Haven, Conn., 1655.

THOMAS came to Mass., 1635, was at Hartford, Conn., 1641; removed to Branford, Conn., 1645.

BLACKMAN or BLAKEMAN

REV. ADAM, b. Staffordshire, Eng., 1598; came to N. E., 1638; was at Guilford, Conn., 1640; first minister at Stratford, Conn.

JOHN, b. Eng., 1625, was resident of Dorchester, Mass., before 1640.

BLACKMORE

JAMES purchased lands at Providence, R. I., 1690.

WILLIAM came from Eng., 1665, to Scituate, Mass.

BLACKWELL

JEREMY, aged 18 years, came to N. E., in 1635.

MICHAEL or MYLES, on record as able to bear arms at Sandwich, Mass., 1643.

BLAGGE

HENRY, brickburner, was at Braintree, Mass., 1643; removed to Boston, Mass., 1653.

BLAISDELL

Name derived from the Saxon words *Blas-del—val* signifying "a blazed path through the vale."

HENRY was resident of Salisbury, Mass., 1657.

RALPH, tailor, acted also as an attorney, b. Eng., 1600; was on record at York,

Maine, 1637; removed to Salisbury, Mass., 1640.

BLAKE

Ancient English family; the name is a corruption of British *Ap Lake,* from *Ap* signifying from or son, and *Lake*—the son of Lake. The name also has its origin in descriptive adjective of color, and was applied to one whose complexion was of dark color. The family went to Ireland with Strongbow. Ap Lake was one of the Knights of Arthur's Round Table. It is recorded in its present form in the Hundred Rolls of 1273, in which appears Hans le Blake. The name is also mentioned in the rolls of subsiders, 1286, in Wiltshire. Robert de Blake was a resident of Calne, adjoining the family estates in Blakeland, in the reign of Edward III. The American family traced their lineage from Robert de Blakeland, 1286.

CHRISTOPHER, tailor, was a resident of Boston, Mass., 1663.

GEORGE was selectman at Gloucester, Mass., 1644, where he had resided since 1640.

HENRY, inhabitant of Boston before 1652.

JASPER, b. Eng., settled at Hampton, N. H., 1650.

JEREMIAH purchased lands at New London, Conn., 1681.

JOHN, b. Malden, Eng., about 1652, came to N. E., 1660 with his mother and stepfather, George Durant; they were at Malden, Mass., and he settled at Middletown, Conn., 1673.

JOHN took oath of allegiance at Hampton, N. H., 1678.

JOHN, joiner, was at Boston, Mass., before 1692.

JOHN was at Wrentham, Mass., 1688.

NATHANIEL was at Boston, Mass., 1676.

PHILIP, a resident of Boston, Mass., 1676.

RICHARD, b. Eng., 1622, came to N. E., 1638, was at Dorchester, Mass., 1644.

WILLIAM, son of Giles of Little Braddow, Essex, Eng., and 11th generation from Robert de Blakeland, bapt. at Pitminster, Eng., 1594, settled at Dorchester, Mass., 1630.

BLANCHARD

From the French *Blanche,* meaning white—a white garment used by Monks and Nuns was called a *blanchard.*

PETER, resident of New London, Conn., 1662.

THOMAS, yeoman, came from Penton, Hampshire, Eng., to Braintree, Mass., 1640, and moved to Charlestown, Mass., 1651, where he lived previous to going to Braintree.

WILLIAM, a freeman at Salem, Mass., 1637.

BLANEY

From Welsh *Bluenae,* the inland extremity of a valley.

JOHN, b. about 1630, was at Lynn, Mass., 1659.

JOHN married at Charlestown, Mass., 1668; no male issue.

BLANTON or BLANDING

WILLIAM, carpenter, came from Upton, Worcestershire, Eng., to N. E., 1640; made a freeman at Boston, Mass., 1643.

BLATCHFORD

PETER granted lands at New London, Conn., for services in the Pequot war, 1637; removed, 1669, to Haddam, Conn.

BLATCHLEY

THOMAS was at Hartford, Conn., 1640; removed to New Haven, Conn., 1643.

BLAXTON

WILLIAM came to Boston, Mass., 1625-26; admitted freeman 1631, removed to near Providence, R. I.; the earliest settler in that part of the country.

BLIGH

THOMAS, sailmaker, was at Boston, Mass., 1652.

BLINMAN

Blin in Welsh signifies weary, troublesome.

REV. RICHARD came from Chepstow, Monmouth, Eng., 1641, to Marshfield, Mass., and in 1640 was at Plymouth, Mass.; in that year removed to Gloucester, Mass., where he was made freeman 1641; removed, 1650, to New London, Conn.; afterwards at New Haven, Conn.; returned to Eng., 1659.

BLISH or BLUSH

ABRAHAM was at Barnstable, Mass., before 1651.

BLISS

From Welsh *blys* signifying deserving, longing. The same as the Bolis family, of Normandy. The English family dates back to the Norman Conquest.

GEORGE, b. Belstone, Eng., 1591; came to Lynn, Mass., 1635; five years later removed to Sandwich, Mass., and in 1649 was at Newport, R. I.

THOMAS, son of Thomas of Belstone parish, Devonshire, Eng., brother of preceding, b. at Belstone, came to Braintree, Mass., 1635; settled at Hartford, Conn., 1639; died few years later.

THOMAS, freeman, Weymouth, Mass., 1642; removed to Rehoboth, Mass., 1649.

BLODGETT or BLODGET

ROBERT BLODGETT was appointed bishop of Lincoln, and one of the chancellors of William the Conqueror.

JONATHAN was married at Salisbury, Mass., 1689.

THOMAS, glover, b. Eng., 1605, came to Cambridge, Mass., 1635.

BLOIS or BLOYS

EDMUND, b. 1587, was freeman at Watertown, Mass., 1639.

FRANCIS, brother of preceding, made freeman at Cambridge, Mass., 1641.

BLOMFIELD, BLOOMFIELD or BLUMFIELD

HENRY was at Salem, Mass., 1638.

JOHN died in Mass., 1640, leaving two sons.

WILLIAM, b. Eng., 1604, came from Ipswich, Suffolk, Eng., in 1634, to Boston, Mass.; soon afterwards went to Newbury, Mass., and 1639, was a resident of Hartford, Conn.; removed to New London, Conn., 1650, and in 1663, to Newtown, L. I.

BLOOD

In the Dutch signifies timorous, cowardly.

JAMES came from Cheshire, Eng., to N. E., 1638, to Concord, Mass., where he was admitted freeman, 1641, accompanied by his four sons, James, John, Richard and Robert, all of whom married except John, and they were among the original proprietors of Groton, Mass.

BLOSSOM

THOMAS, b. Eng., 1580; an original passenger on the Speedwell in 1620; came later to Plymouth, Mass., removed, 1639, to Barnstable, Mass.

BLOTT

ROBERT was at Roxbury, Mass., 1632, two years later at Charlestown, Mass.; removed to Boston, Mass., 1644.

BLOUT or BLUNT

The name is from French word *blond,* referring to fair hair or complexion. Sir Robert and Sir William Le Blount, sons of Count of Guinis of France, came to England with William the Conqueror. The name has passed through many changes, but now is spelled Blount or Blunt, the latter form being more prevalent in England.

SAMUEL was at Charlestown, Mass., 1681.

WILLIAM settled at Andover, Mass., 1634.

BLOWERS

JOHN was at Barnstable, Mass., 1643, and at Boston, Mass., 1654.

PYAM married at Cambridge, Mass., 1668.

BLY or BLYE

JOHN, brickmaker, was resident of Salem, Mass., 1663.

SAMUEL was at Lynn, Mass., 1678.

BOADEN, BODEN or BOWDEN

AMBROSE was at Scarborough, Maine, 1658.

BENJAMIN, proprietor at New Haven, Conn., 1685.

JOHN, mason, was at Boston, Mass., 1668.

RICHARD, a resident of Boston, 1661.

THOMAS, resident of Marblehead, Mass., 1668.

WILLIAM was in Maine 1642.

BOARDMAN

One who keeps a boarding house. William Boreman of Banbury, Oxfordshire, Eng., living 1525, as the ancestor of the American family.

SAMUEL, cooper, son of Christopher, fifth generation of William, bapt. at Banbury, Eng., 1615, first resided at Ipswich, Mass., and in 1636 was one of the first settlers at Wethersfield, Conn.

THOMAS, carpenter, b. Eng., about 1601, granted land at Ipswich, Mass., 1635; previous to this was at Plymouth, Mass.; at Sandwich, Mass., 1638, and at Yarmouth, Mass., 1643.

MAJOR WILLIAM, b. Eng., came with his mother and stepfather to Cambridge, Mass., 1638.

BODMAN

JOHN, b. Eng., first appears on records of church at Boston, Mass., 1644.

WILLIAM was at Watertown, Mass., before 1643.

BODWELL

HENRY, b. Eng., 1654; made freeman 1678; resided at Newbury, Mass., later at Andover, Mass., finally removed to Haverhill, Mass.

BOHONION or BOHANNON

JOHN, an inhabitant of Boston, Mass., before 1658.

BOLLES

This family name existed in Eng., in the reign of Henry III.

JOSEPH came from Nottinghamshire, Eng., settled at Winter Harbor at the mouth of Saco river, Maine, in 1640; removed to Wells, Maine, 1653.

THOMAS was resident of New London, Conn., 1667.

BOLT

FRANCIS came to Boston, Mass., 1639, and the following year located at Milford, Conn.

BOLTON or BOULTON

Nicholas was at Dorchester, Mass., 1643.

William married at Newbury, Mass., 1655.

BOLTWOOD

Robert was an inhabitant of Hartford, Conn., 1648; removed to Hadley, Mass., 1659.

BOND

The father of a family, *"Pater familias,"* whence husband, that is—housebound. *Bonde* in Danish is a peasant, countryman, villager.

Grinstone was a resident of Boston, Mass., 1685.

John was at Newbury, Mass., 1642; removed 1660 to Rowley, Mass., thence to Haverhill, Mass.

Nicholas, freeman at York, Maine, 1652; removed to Hampton, N. H.

William, son of Thomas, grandson of James of Bury St. Edmunds, Suffolk, Eng., bapt. there 1625; brought in Winthrop's fleet, 1630, by his aunt, Eliza, wife of Ephraim Child; settled at Watertown, Mass., 1649.

BONDFIELD or BONFIELD

George was at Marblehead, Mass., 1676.

BONHAM or BONUM

George was at Plymouth, Mass., 1644.

Nicholas, brother of preceding, was at Barnstable, Mass., 1659.

BONNER

From French *bonheur*—happiness, prosperity.

John was inhabitant of Boston, Mass., 1678; removed to Cambridge, Mass., returned to Eng., with his children 1697.

BONNEY

From Scotch, genteel, spruce, the French *Bon, Bonne,* good, handsome.

Thomas, shoemaker, came from Sandwich, Kent, Eng., to Charlestown, Mass., 1635, one of the proprietors of Bridgewater, Mass., 1645, afterwards at Duxbury, Mass.

BONYTHON or BONIGHTON

Richard, captain and magistrate, was at Saco, Maine, 1636.

BOOBYAR

Joseph was at Marblehead, Mass., 1668.

BOOMER

Mathew, freeman at Newport, R. I., 1655.

BOODEY

This name in the Sanscrit language is supposed to have been *Buddha,* signifying divinity or divine knowledge.

Zachariah, b. France, 1677, came to Boston, Mass., 1695.

BOOSY

James was at Wethersfield, Conn., 1635.

BOOTFISH or BODFISH

Robert, freeman at Lynn, Mass., 1635, removed 1637 to Sandwich, Mass., later to Barnstable, Mass.

BOOTH

A small cottage. William de Boothe, son of Adam de Boothe, residing 1275 in county of Lancaster, Eng., is the ancestor of the American branch of the family.

George was resident of Lynn, Mass., 1674.

Humphrey, merchant, was resident of Charlestown, Mass.

John was at Scituate, Mass., 1655.

Richard, son of Richard, 14th generation from Sir William de Boothe, b. 1607, on record at Stratford, Conn., 1640.

Robert was at Exeter, N. H., 1645, removed to Saco, Maine, 1653.

BORDEN

The name came to Eng., from Normandy, appears in Battle Abbey as Bordoun. There is an ancient village in Normandy named Bourdenay, and Borden is a town, county of Kent, Eng. The family was represented in Eng., at the time of the Conquest, and were assigned estates in the county of Kent. Simon de Borden, in 1199, resided at Borden Court or Hall. The American branch is traced to Henry Borden of the parish Hedcorn, Kent, Eng., 1379-80.

Bryant was at Malden, Mass., before 1690.

John, b. 1607, came from Kent, Eng., to N. E., 1635; may have been at Stonington, Conn., 1650, removed to Lyme, Conn., 1660.

Richard, Quaker, surveyor, son of Matthew, 9th generation from Henry, was bapt. at Hedcorn, 1596, came to Boston, Mass., 1635, became one of the founders of Portsmouth, R. I., in 1637, whence he was admitted freeman 1641.

BORDMAN or BOREMAN

Daniel was at Ipswich, Mass., 1662.

Samuel was at Ipswich, Mass., 1639, removed to Wethersfield, Mass.

Thomas, brother of the preceding, was at Lynn, Mass., 1637, removed to Sandwich, Mass., one of the first purchasers of Middleboro, Mass.

Thomas, freeman at Ipswich, Mass., 1635, removed to Barnstable, Mass., before 1645.

WILLIAM was at Wethersfield, Conn., 1645, and at Guilford, Conn., 1650.

BOREL

SAMUEL was at Boston, Mass., 1691.

BORLAND

From Cornish British—the highland swelling or rising land; from *bor*, swelling or rising and *land*. In Saxon it signifies land belonging to common people. Bordlands were kept by the lords for the maintenance of their board or table.

FRANCIS was at Boston, Mass., in 1684.

BOSSON

WILLIAM, of French Huguenot descent, settled at Salem, Mass., 1630; afterwards went to Watertown, Mass., and 1636 was proprietor at Wethersfield, Conn.

BOSTWICK

Cornish British, the house near the haven or creek, from *bos*, a house, and *wick*, a haven or creek; also from the Dutch *bosch*, a wood, and *wick*, town in the wood.

ARTHUR, bapt. Tarporley, Cheshire, Eng., 1603, located as one of first seventeen settlers at Stratford, Conn., 1641-42.

BOSWELL

A corruption of *Bosseville*, from *bosch*, a wood, and *ville*, a village. *Bothel*, Gaelic, the house of the powerful.

SAMUEL was at Bradford, Mass., 1663, and Rowley, Mass., 1671.

BOSWORTH

EDWARD, b. Eng., died on voyage to America, 1634, leaving four sons—Edward, Jonathan, Benjamin and Nathaniel.

HANANIEL was at Ipswich, Mass., in 1648; removed to Haverhill, Mass., where he resided in 1674.

ZACCHEUS or ZECHERIAH was at Boston, Mass., 1630, made freeman 1636.

BOTHAM

ROBERT was at Ipswich, Mass., 1652.

BOTSFORD

Place name from town in Eng.

HENRY, inhabitant of Milford, Conn., 1639.

BOULTER

MATTHEW at Hampton, N. H., 1649.

NATHANIEL, brother of preceding, was resident of Hampton, N. H., 1644.

THOMAS was at Weymouth, Mass., 1661; one of first projectors of settlement of Mendon, Mass., 1660.

BOUND

WILLIAM, a freeman at Salem, Mass., 1637.

BOURNE

A place name from Bourne, Lincolnshire, Eng., which is named from old English *bourne*, a small river or spring-well.

GARRET or JARED came to Boston, 1630, in the employ of William Colbourne, 1630; afterwards resided in what is now Brookline, Mass.

HENRY came to Plymouth or Scituate, Mass., 1634, removed to Barnstable, Mass., 1639.

NEHEMIAH, ship builder, was at Charlestown, Mass., 1638; also at Dorchester, Mass.; removed to Boston, Mass., 1640.

RICHARD came from Devonshire, Eng., to Lynn, Mass., 1637; one of the early settlers of Sandwich, Mass.

THOMAS was at Plymouth, Mass., 1637; an early settler of Marshfield, Mass.

BOUTELL or BOUTWELL

HENRY was at New Haven, Conn., and married in Cambridge, Mass., 1657; died soon after; no issue.

JAMES was at Salem and Lynn, Mass., 1635.

JOHN, brother of preceding, was at Cambridge, Mass., before 1646.

BOUTINEAU

STEPHEN, Huguenot, merchant, came from La Rochelle, France, 1686, to Casco, Maine; removed to Boston, Mass.

BOUTON

JOHN, son of Count Nicholas Bouton, a French Huguenot, came to Boston, Mass., 1635; afterwards lived at Watertown, Mass., thence went to Hartford, Conn., and in 1651 became a resident of Norwalk, Conn.

BOWDITCH

JOHN, a resident of Boston, Mass., 1682.

WILLIAM came from Devonshire, Eng., to Salem, Mass., 1639.

BOWDOIN or BAUDOIN

MICHAEL was at Lynn, Mass., 1690.

PIERRE, physician, b. La Rochelle, France, of Huguenot descent, went to Ireland, 1685; two years later arrived at Casco Bay, now Portland, Maine, and in 1690 removed to Boston, Mass., where he became a merchant.

BOWE

ALEXANDER was at Charlestown, Mass., removed to Middletown, Conn., where he died 1678.

NICHOLAS married at Cambridge, Mass., 1684.

BOWEN

From Welsh, a corruption of *Ap Owen*, the son of Owen.

Griffith came from Llangeydd, Glamorganshire, Wales, to Boston, Mass., 1638; he was afterwards at Roxbury, Mass., returned to Eng., residing, 1670, at London.

Henry, a resident of Boston, Mass., 1657.

Obadiah was at Rehoboth, Mass., before 1657; removed to Swanzey, Mass.

Richard, brother of preceding, came from Wales to N. E., made freeman at Rehoboth, Mass., 1645; was at New London, Conn., 1657-60.

Thomas, brother of preceding, was at Salem, Mass., 1648; New London, Conn., 1657-60; removed to Rehoboth, Mass.

BOWERS

From Saxon *bur*, a chamber; a cottage; a shady recess.

George was at Plymouth, Mass., 1639; removed to Cambridge, Mass.

BOWKER

Edmund or Edward settled at Dorchester, Mass., 1635; removed to Sudbury, Mass., 1666.

James came from Sweden to Scituate, Mass., about 1675.

BOWLES

From Boel, a town in South Jutland; *boel* in Dutch an estate.

John, freeman at Roxbury, Mass., 1640.

Joseph was at Saco, Maine, 1640; afterwards at Wells, Maine.

Richard was at Dover, N. H., 1666.

BOWMAN

A military cognomen; an archer. English ancestor, 1544, Robert.

John was at Plymouth, Mass., 1633.

Nathaniel settled at Watertown, Mass., 1630, removed to Lexington, Mass.

BOWNE

From Cornish, British and Welsh, signifies ready, active, nimble.

Thomas of Norman French origin, bapt. Matlock, Derbyshire, 1595, came to Boston, Mass., 1648-49; early settler at Flushing, L. I.

BOYDEN

Thomas, b. Suffolk, Eng., came from Ipswich, Eng., in 1634, to Scituate, Mass., removed, 1650, to Boston, Mass., afterwards lived at Medfield, Watertown and Groton, Mass.

BOYES or BOYCE

The name is French origin from *bois*, meaning wood; the surname given to those who lived in or near woods or handled wood.

Antipas, merchant, was at Boston, Mass., 1659; his only son returned to Eng.

Joseph, tanner, b. Eng., 1609-15, was at Salem, Mass., 1639.

Matthew, freeman at Roxbury, Mass., 1639; removed to Rowley, Mass., before 1641; returned to Eng., before 1657.

Richard was in N. H., before 1677.

Samuel married at Saybrook, Conn., 1668.

BOYLSTON

Thomas, son of Thomas of London, Eng., grandson of Henry of Litchfield, Eng., b. Eng., 1615; came to Watertown, Mass., 1635.

BOYNTON

Name derived from the ancient village of Boynton in the eastern part of Yorkshire, Eng. Bartholomew de Boynton, in 1067, was seated at the Manor of Boynton.

John, b. Knapton, Wingham, in East Riding, Yorkshire, Eng., 1614, came to N. E., in 1635; settled at Rowley, Mass., 1643.

William, schoolmaster, brother of preceding, son of William, XXIII generation, from Bartholomew de Boynton, b. Knapton, Eng., 1606, came to N. E., 1635, settled at Rowley, Mass., 1638.

William lived at Salisbury, Mass., before 1670.

BRABROOK or BRAYBROOK

John was at Watertown, Mass., 1640; removed to Hampton, N. H., afterwards to Newbury, Mass.

Joseph was at Malden, lived at Concord, Mass., 1672.

Richard, b. 1613, was at Ipswich, Mass., at an early date.

William removed from Lynn, Mass., 1637, to Sandwich, Mass.

BRACE, BRACY or BRACIE

Place name from Bracy, a town in Normandy.

John was at New Haven, Conn., 1644; removed to Wethersfield, Conn., 1647.

Stephen, hatter, was at Swanzey, Mass., 1669; removed to Hartford, Conn., where he died 1692.

Thomas at Ipswich, Mass., 1635; afterwards removed to Branford, Conn.

Thomas, brother of John, was at Wethersfield, Conn.; removed to Hatfield, Mass., where he died 1704.

BRACKENBURY

John was at Charlestown, Mass., afterwards at Boston, where he married 1655.

WILLIAM, son of William, *Mayflower* passenger, b. Austerfield, Yorkshire, Eng., 1588.

RICHARD came with Gov. Endicott to Salem, Mass., 1628.

SAMUEL, physician, was at Boston, Mass., 1677.

WILLIAM, baker, came in Winthrop's fleet, 1630, afterwards removed to Malden, Mass.

BRACKETT

The ancient spelling of the name was Brockett; the family originated in Wales.

ANTHONY as early as 1623 was at the mouth of Piscataqua river, came to Portsmouth, N. H., before 1640.

PETER, freeman at Braintree, Mass., 1643, removed to Scarborough, Maine, 1673-74.

CAPT. RICHARD, brother of the preceding, b. 1612, was at Boston, Mass., 1632; removed, 1639, to what is now Quincy, Mass.

WILLIAM, one of employes of Mason, was at Portsmouth, N. H., 1624.

BRADBURY

Surname of local origin, a compound of *broad* and *bury,* the first signifying broad, the second a manor, hill or town. The English family traced on the maternal side to David I, King of Scotland, 1124, through Lady Jane Fitzwilliam of the XII generation from King David, who married Robert Bradbury, and their son Matthew was Lord of the Manor of Wicken Hall, parish of Wicken Bonant, Sussex, Eng., in 1557. The family is seated in Derbyshire, Eng. The earliest known ancestor of the American branch was Robert Bradbury, b. 1400, resided at Ollerset, Derbyshire, Eng.

CAPT. THOMAS, son of Wymond and great-grandson of Matthew, mentioned above, bapt. parish of Bonant, 1610-11, was at York, Maine, 1634; two years later was one of original proprietors of Salisbury, Mass., coming from Ipswich, Mass.

BRADE

JOSEPH was at Marblehead, Mass., 1638.

BRADFIELD

LESBY was an inhabitant of Wethersfield, Conn., as early as 1643.

BRADFORD

Place name, a town on the Avon, Wiltshire, Eng., signifying the broad ford, there being a ford across the river where the town is located.

ALEXANDER was at Dorchester, Mass., 1638; no issue.

ROBERT, tailor, b. Eng., 1626; freeman at Boston, Mass., 1642.

BRADHURST

RALPH was married at Roxbury, Mass., 1677; no male issue.

BRADING

JAMES was at Newbury, Mass., removed to Boston, Mass., 1659.

BRADISH

ROBERT was resident of Cambridge, Mass., 1635.

BRADLEY

The name is a compound of Anglo-Saxon words *brad,* broad, and *lea,* a field or meadow; there are numerous townships in England bearing the name. The earliest known ancestor bearing the name in England was Roger de Bradley, 1183, of Walsingham, who held forty acres at Bradley.

DANIEL took the oath of fidelity at New Haven, Conn., 1657.

DANIEL, b. Eng., 1615, came to Haverhill, Mass., 1635, and in 1662 was a taxpayer at Rowley, Mass.

FRANCIS came to Branford, Conn., 1660, removed to Fairfield, Conn., 1664.

ISAAC removed from Branford, Conn., where he located in 1667, to New Haven, Conn., 1683.

JOHN was at Dedham, Mass., 1642.

JOHN, a resident of Dover, N. H., 1667.

JOSEPH, b. London, Eng., 1649, located at Haverhill, Mass.

JOSHUA was at Rowley, Mass., 1663.

NATHAN was at Guilford, Conn., as early as 1669.

NATHANIEL was a resident of Dorchester, Mass., where he died 1701, aged 70 years.

PETER, mariner, was at New London, Conn., 1654.

RICHARD was at Boston, Mass., 1651.

STEPHEN, who took oath of fidelity 1660, was at Guilford, and New Haven, Conn.

WILLIAM, b. Eng., 1620, took oath of fidelity at New Haven, Conn., 1644.

BRADSHAW

HUMPHREY was at Cambridge, Mass., 1642.

BRADSTREET

HUMPHREY, b. Eng., 1594, came from Ipswich, Eng., to Ipswich, Mass., 1634; removed to Rowley, Mass., 1639.

SIMON, son of Rev. Simon, b. Hobling, Lincolnshire, Eng., 1603, came in Winthrop's fleet, 1630, to N. E., resided at Cambridge, Ipswich, Andover and Boston, Mass.

BRAGG

Brag among the Scandinavians was the god of eloquence; the word anciently used in the sense of eloquent, also accomplished, brave, daring.

EDMUND or EDWARD settled at Ipswich, Mass., 1646; no male issue.

BRAINERD or BRAINARD

Place name, originally spelled Brandewood or Brandewode. Tradition says the family came from Braine in France; the family founded in England 1350.
DANIEL, b. Braintree, Eng., 1641, lived as early as 1649 with Wadsworth family at Hartford, Conn.; removed to Haddam, Conn., prior to 1665.

BRALEY

ROGER, Welsh descent, settled at Portsmouth, R. I., 1696.

BRAMAN

From *Bramin,* a priest among the Hindoos, or from Bremen, a city of Germany.

THOMAS, b. about 1620-30; was a resident of Taunton, Mass., 1653.

BRAME, BRAM or BREAM

BENJAMIN, cooper, resided at Boston, Mass., 1668.

BRAMHALL

A place where goods are sold, from Danish *bram,* goods on sale.
GEORGE was at Dover, N. H., 1670, and Casco, Maine, 1678, where he was killed by Indians, 1689.

BRANCH

ARTHUR was at Saybrook, Conn., 1670.

PETER, carpenter, b. Eng., came from Holden, Kent, Eng., 1638, died on passage, leaving son, John, who was apprenticed to Thomas Wilburne, who settled at Duxbury, Mass.

WILLIAM, freeman at Springfield, Mass., 1648; no issue.

BRAND

In all Teutonic dialects *brand* signifies to burn; also a sword; the Welsh *bryn* is a steep, high hill.
GEORGE, baker, freeman at Roxbury, Mass.; no issue.

THOMAS, cooper, came to Salem, Mass., 1629.

BRANDEGEE

Name of German or Dutch origin.
JOHN was at Wethersfield, Conn., 1635.

BRATTLE

THOMAS was at Charlestown, Mass., 1656; removed following year to Boston, Mass.

WILLIAM, brother of preceding, was at Boston, Mass., 1677.

BRAWNE

MICHAEL was at Dover, N. H., 1655.

BRAY

JOHN, shipwright, was at Kittery, Maine, removed, 1674, to Gloucester, Mass.

ROBERT was at Salem, Mass., 1668.

THOMAS, shipwright, was at Gloucester, Mass., 1646.

WILLIAM resident of York, Maine, 1680.

BRAYDON

ARTHUR, b. Eng., 1598, settled at York, 1640.

BRAYTON

FRANCIS, b. Eng., 1611, was an inhabitant of Portsmouth, R. I., as early as 1642.

BRAZIER

EDWARD was at Charlestown, Mass., 1658.

BRECK

Old English word signifying broken, a gap; *brecca* is old Latin law term, used to denote a breach, decay or want of repair; *breck* in Gaelic is a wolf or wild savage.

EDWARD, b. Lancastershire, Eng., about 1595, came to Dorchester, Mass., 1635; removed to Lancaster, Mass., 1641.

JOHN was at Medfield, Mass., where he died 1660.

THOMAS, b. Lancaster, Eng., 1600, settled at Dorchester, Mass., 1650.

BREDANE

BYRON was at Malden, Mass., 1671.

BREED

From Dutch *Breed,* broad, large; Brede is a town in Sussex, Eng.; in Danish it signifies brim, margin; seaside, shore, river-side.

ALLEN, b. Eng., 1630; came to Lynn, Mass., 1630; removed to Southampton, L. I., 1640.

BRENTON

WILLIAM, b. Hammersmith, Eng., came in 1633 to Boston, Mass.; was in Portsmouth and Newport, R. I.; lived 1670-02 at Taunton, Mass.

BRETT

A contraction of Breton, which is from Bretton, a town in Flintshire, Wales.

WILLIAM, b. Kent, Eng., was at Duxbury, Mass., 1640; one of the first proprietors of Bridgewater, Mass., 1645.

BRETTON

PHILIP, rigger, a Huguenot, was at Falmouth, Maine, before 1700; removed to Boston, Mass.

BREWER

A brewer of malt liquor.

CHRISTOPHER, freeman at Lynn, Mass., 1684.

DANIEL, b. Eng., about 1600, settled at Roxbury, Mass., 1634.

REV. DANIEL ordained at Springfield, Mass., 1694.

JOHN, b. about 1620, came to Cambridge, Mass., 1642; removed to Sudbury, Mass., before 1647.

THOMAS, proprietor at Ipswich, Mass., 1639; removed, 1658, to Lynn, Mass.

THOMAS, an inhabitant of Lynn, Mass., 1682.

BREWSTER

Name derived same as Brewer.

FRANCIS came from London, Eng., to New Haven, Conn., 1640; lost at sea 1646.

JOHN was at Portsmouth, N. H., before 1664.

WILLIAM, *Mayflower* passenger, son of William, b. Scrooby, Nottinghamshire, Eng., 1560; came to Plymouth, Mass., 1620.

BRICE

A contraction of *Ap Rice,* the son of Rice, from Welsh *brys,* in that language, haste, lively.

THOMAS, ship carpenter, was at Gloucester, Mass., 1642.

BRICKETT

NATHANIEL was at Newbury, Mass., before 1673.

BRICKNALL

EDWARD was at Boston, Mass., 1681.

BRIDGE

EDWARD, freeman at Roxbury, Mass., 1639.

JOHN, brother of the preceding, freeman at Cambridge, Mass., 1635.

JOHN, a resident of Wickford, R. I., 1674.

SAMUEL, carpenter, freeman at Boston, Mass., 1671.

WILLIAM was at Watertown, Mass., 1636; removed to Boston, Mass., 1643.

WILLIAM, a resident of Charlestown, Mass., 1644.

BRIDGES

EDMUND, b. Eng., 1612, settled at Lynn, Mass., 1636; removed to Rowley, Mass, 1641; afterwards resided at Ipswich and Topsfield, Mass.

ROBERT, freeman at Lynn, Mass., 1641.

BRIDGHAM

HENRY, tanner, son of Henry, b. 1613, came from Teltain, Suffolk, Eng., to Dorchester, Mass., 1641; removed to Boston, Mass., 1644.

JAMES, carpenter, came from Winchester, Hants, Eng., to Hartford, Conn., 1641; was at Springfield, Mass., 1643-55; in latter year removed to Northampton, Mass.

BRIDGMAN

JAMES was at Hartford, Conn., before 1641; removed, 1645, to Springfield, Mass.

BRIGDEN or BRIDGEN

THOMAS came from Faversham, Kent, Eng., to Charlestown, Mass., 1635.

BRIGGS

Name from Anglo-Saxon *brigg*—a bridge; *brig* in Welsh—height, the top of anything. William atta Brigge of Salle is mentioned in records, 1270.

CLEMENT, felsmonger, came from Southwarke, Eng., to Plymouth, Mass., 1621; removed to Dorchester, Mass., 1631, and to Weymouth, Mass., 1633.

EDMUND was at Topsfield, Mass., 1667.

JAMES was in Mass., 1683.

JOHN, b. 1609, admitted an inhabitant of Newport, R. I., 1638; was at Portsmouth, R. I., 1650; lived at Kingstown, R. I., 1678.

JOSEPH was an inhabitant of Mass., 1679.

MATTHEW or MATTHIAS married at Hingham, Mass., 1648.

THOMAS, b. Eng., 1603; settled at Cambridge, Mass., 1637.

WALTER, early settler at Scituate, Mass.; on record, 1643, as able to bear arms.

WILLIAM, inhabitant of Boston, Mass., 1642.

BRIGHAM

SEBASTIAN was at Cambridge, Mass., 1636; removed to Rowley, Mass., before 1644.

THOMAS, b. 1603, freeman at Cambridge, Mass., 1636.

BRIGHT

HENRY, son of Henry of Bury St. Edmunds, Eng., came from Ipswich, Suffolk, Eng., b. 1602; was in Watertown, Mass., 1634.

BRIGHTMAN

Name derived from old Saxon word *bright* or *bricht.* John Brithman of Norfolkshire in records 1273.

HENRY was on record at Portsmouth, R. I., 1670.

THOMAS was at Watertown, Mass., 1640.

BRIGHTON

Place name from town on coast of Sussex, Eng., anciently called Brightelmstone, from Brithelm, *i. e.,* bright helmet, who was bishop of Bath and Wells, 955.

SAMUEL was at Boston, Mass., 1692.

BRIMBLECOME

JOHN, woolcomber, at Boston, Mass., 1654; removed to Marblehead, Mass., before 1674.

PHILIP, brother of preceding, was at Marblehead, Mass., 1668.

BRIMSDEN or BRIMSDELL

ROBERT, merchant, married at Lynn, Mass., 1667.

BRIMSMEAD or BRINSMADE

JOHN came from Eng., to Charlestown, Mass., 1637; removed to Stratford, Conn., 1650.

WILLIAM came to Dorchester, Mass., 1628-30.

BRINLEY

FRANCIS, son of Thomas of Datchett, Buckinghamshire, Eng., b. 1632; was at Newport, R. I., 1652.

BRINTNALL

THOMAS, resident of Boston, Mass., before 1655.

BRISCOE

BENJAMIN, shoemaker, was at Boston, Mass., where he married 1656.

NATHANIEL, tanner, known as the "Rich Tanner," a descendant of Edward Bisco, of Missenden, Buckinghamshire, Eng., who died 1653. Nathaniel was fourth generation from Edward, bapt. Little Missenden, Eng., 1595, came to N. E., 1639, then to Watertown, Mass. He returned to Eng., 1654, leaving two sons, Nathaniel and John, and two daughters, in N. E.

WILLIAM, tailor, freeman at Boston, Mass., 1640.

BRISTOL or BRISTOW

From Saxon *birhs*—pleasant, bright, and *stow*—the same as stead, a place.

HENRY, cooper, b. Eng. 1625, was at New Haven, Conn., 1647.

RICHARD, cooper, brother of the preceding, was at Guilford, Conn., 1640.

BRITTON

A native of Britain, from Welsh *Brydon* or *Prydyn*, the fair tribe or brave men, from Gaelic *Bridaione*, from *bri*, dignity, *daoine*, men, *Pryddain*, the fair and beautiful island, *Brait* or *Briand*, extensive, and *in* land. *Brit-tane*, the land of tin.

JAMES, b. Eng., 1610, subscribed to town orders at Woburn, Mass., 1637.

WILLIAM came from Bristol, Eng., to Newport, R. I. His family name was Summerill, but on leaving Eng., he assumed his mother's family name Britton.

BROADBRIDGE

RICHARD was at Casco, Maine, 1680.

BROCK

From Saxon *broc*, a badger, has same meaning in Cornish British, Gaelic, Irish and Welsh.

HENRY, at Dedham, Mass., 1642; no male issue.

RICHARD was at Watertown, Mass., 1635.

WILLIAM, resident of Salem, Mass., 1639.

BROCKETT

Family of Saxon origin. English ancestry is traced to 1201. Brockett Hall in Weatherhamstead, Herts, was the original ancestral home of the family.

JOHN signed first covenant at New Haven, Conn., 1639.

BROCKLEBANK

JOHN was at Rowley, Mass., before 1655

SAMUEL, brother of the preceding, was an inhabitant of Rowley, Mass., about 1655.

BROCKWAY

WOOLSTONE, b. Eng., 1638, purchased lands at Saybrook, Conn., 1659.

BRODBENT

JOSHUA married at Woburn, Mass., 1685.

BROMFIELD

The field abounding in broom.

EDWARD, merchant, son of Henry, grandson of Arthur, b. Haywood House, in the New Forest, Hants, 1649, came to Boston, Mass., 1675.

BROMLEY

Place name, a small town in Eng., so called from *brome* or *broom*, and *ley*—field.

LUKE was at Stonington, Conn., before 1692.

BRONSDEN

ROBERT, merchant, b. Eng., 1638-39; first mention colonial records 1667; freeman at Boston, Mass., 1690.

BRONSON or BRUNSON (see BROUNSON)

BROOKER

JOHN was at Guilford, Conn., 1695.

BROOKHAVEN

JOHN, citizen of London, Eng., came to R. I., 1681.

BROOKING or BROOKEN

JOHN, resident of Boston, Mass., 1658.

WILLIAM, sent over by Mason, 1631, to Portsmouth, N. H., removed to Charlestown, Mass.

BROOKS or BROOKES

A name signifying small river.

EBENEZER at Woburn, Mass., before 1688.

GILBERT, b. Eng., 1621; came, aged 14 years, with William Vassall; afterwards lived at Marshfield, Mass., 1645 at Scituate, Mass.

HENRY came to Boston, Mass., 1630; was at Concord, Mass., 1639, and Woburn, Mass., 1649.

HENRY came from Cheshire, Eng., to Wallingford, Conn., 1660; was at New Haven, Conn., 1670.

JOHN, brother of preceding, was at New Haven, Conn., 1649; removed to Wallingford, Conn., with his brother in 1685.

JOHN was at Windsor, Conn., where he married, 1652; removed to Simsbury, Conn.

RICHARD, b. 1621, was at Lynn, Mass., 1635, removed to Easthampton, L. I.

RICHARD, gunsmith, was at Boston, Mass., 1674.

ROBERT, a mercer of Maidstone, Kent, Eng., came to New London, Conn., 1635.

ROBERT married, at Plymouth, Mass., a daughter of Gov. Edward Winslow.

CAPT. THOMAS, b. 1613, came from Suffolk, Eng., assigned land at Watertown, Mass., 1631; removed to Concord, Mass., 1636.

THOMAS, brother of Richard of Lynn, b. Eng., 1617, came to N. E., 1635; one of the first settlers of Haddam, Conn.

THOMAS was at Kittery, Maine, 1640.

THOMAS, a freeman at Portsmouth, R. I., 1655.

TIMOTHY was at Billerica, Mass., 1679.

WILLIAM, b. Eng., 1615 (brother of Gilbert), came to Boston, Mass., 1635, then to Scituate, Mass.; was at Marshfield, Mass., 1643.

WILLIAM, b. Eng., came to Boston, Mass., 1635; settled at Springfield, Mass., 1649; removed to Deerfield, Mass., 1686.

WILLIAM, among early settlers of Milford, Conn., where he died 1684.

BROOMAN

JOSEPH married at Rehoboth, Mass., 1681.

BROUGH or BRUFF

EDWARD came to Marshfield, Mass., 1643.

WILLIAM, a resident of Boston, Mass., 1654.

BROUGHTON

A village in Flintshire, Eng., a town on the hill.

JOHN, among the early settlers of Northampton, Mass., 1650-60.

THOMAS, b. Eng., 1616, came from Gravesend, Eng., to Virginia, 1635; was resident of Watertown, Mass., 1643.

BROUNSMAYD

JOHN was at Stratford, Conn., 1650.

BROUNSON or BRONSON

The son of Brown.

JOHN, b. Eng., 1580, was at Hartford, Conn., 1636; removed to Farmington, Conn., 1641; afterwards settled at Waterbury, Conn.

RICHARD, brother of preceding, was resident of Farmington, Conn., 1641.

BROWN or BROWNE

A name derived from complexion, color of hair or garments. Among the English ancestors are Gamel fil Brun and John Broune of Stamford, Eng., 1377.

ABRAHAM, surveyor, son of Thomas, b. Swan Hall, Hawkendon parish, Suffolk, Eng., 1590; among first planters of Watertown, Mass.; made freeman 1632.

ABRAHAM, merchant, at Boston, Mass., 1650.

ALEXANDER was at Kennebeck, Maine, 1674.

ANDREW, resident of Scarborough, Maine, 1658.

ARTHUR, resident of Saco, Maine, 1636.

REV. CHAD, b. Eng., 1600, came to N. E., 1638; was at Boston, Mass.; settled at Providence, R. I., 1642.

CHARLES, b. Eng., settled at Rowley, Mass., 1647.

CHRISTIAN, one of the first settlers of Salisbury, Mass., 1640.

DANIEL, resident of Providence, R. I., 1646.

REV. EDMUND came to N. E., 1637; freeman 1640; first minister at Salisbury, Mass.; no issue.

EDWARD, early proprietor of Boston, Mass., came to N. E., in the employ of William Colborn before 1634; removed to Newport, R. I., 1639.

EDWARD, resident of Salem, Mass., 1638.

EDWARD, freeman at Ipswich, Mass, 1641.

FRANCIS, tailor, b. Eng., came from Stamford, Eng., to Boston, Mass., 1637; was at New Haven, Conn., 1639; removed to Stamford, Conn.

FRANCIS came as servant to Henry Walcott of Windsor, Conn.; went to Farmington, Conn., 1649, and to Stamford, Conn., 1660.

GEORGE, carpenter, one of the first settlers of Newbury, Mass., 1635.

GEORGE, resident of Stonington, Conn., 1680.

HENRY, shoemaker, b. Eng., 1615, granted land at Salisbury, Mass., 1639.

HENRY took oath of allegiance at Providence, R. I., 1652.

James, a resident of Boston, Mass., 1630.

James was at Charlestown, Mass., 1633.

James, b. Eng., came from Southampton, Eng., to Charlestown, 1635; removed to Newbury, Mass., 1637.

James was at Hatfield, Mass., 1678; removed to Deerfield, Mass., 1682, afterwards to Colchester, Mass.

James, landholder at Brandon, Conn., 1679, removed to Norwalk, Conn., 1687.

John, son of John of Hawkedon, Suffolk, Eng., bapt. 1601, was at Watertown, Mass., 1636; at Duxbury, Mass., and 1643 at Taunton, Mass.; died at Swanzey, Mass., 1662.

John, shipbuilder, b. Eng., 1595, came to Salem, Mass., 1629; in 1636 was at Duxbury, Mass.; in 1643 at Taunton, Mass.; following year, Rehoboth, Mass.

John, b. Eng., 1588-89, came to N. E., 1635; freeman at Salem, Mass., 1637; became permanent resident of Hampden, N. H., 1639.

John, mason, son of Richard of Barton Regis, Gloucestershire, Eng., was in Maine, 1641.

John, tailor from Badstow, Essex, Eng., came to N. E., 1635; was at Ipswich, Mass., 1641.

John, inhabitant of Milford, Conn., 1648.

John, Scotchman, was at Cambridge, Mass.; removed 1662 to Marlboro, Mass., 1678 to Falmouth, Maine; returned to Watertown, Mass.

John, married at Reading, Mass., 1659.

John, a resident of Duxbury, Mass., before 1673.

John, b. Eng., 1584, nephew of Peter, *Mayflower* passenger, came to Plymouth, Mass., before 1633; proprietor at Taunton, Mass., 1637; removed to Swanzey, Mass., 1643.

John, a resident of York, Maine, 1680.

John, married at Billerica, Mass., 1682.

John, a resident of Rowley, Mass., before 1686.

John, married at Stonington, Conn., 1692.

Capt. John, b. Eng., was at Marblehead, Mass., 1686.

Joseph was an inhabitant of Lynn, Mass., 1680.

Nathaniel was at Hartford, Conn., 1647, removed to Middletown, Conn., 1654, thence to Springfield, Mass.

Nathaniel, freeman at Ipswich, Mass., 1685.

Nicholas, mariner, son of Edward of Inkborrow, Worcestershire, Eng., was at Lynn, Mass., 1638; removed to Reading, Mass., 1663.

Nicholas, freeman at Portsmouth, R. I., 1655.

Peter, *Mayflower* passenger, came to Plymouth, Mass., 1620, afterwards removed to Duxbury, Mass.

Robert, b. 1611, came to Cambridge, Mass., 1635; no issue.

Stephen was at Newbury, Mass. before 1656.

Thomas, weaver, came from Malford, Wiltshire, Eng., to N. E. 1635; freeman at Newbury, Mass., 1639.

Thomas, b. Eng., 1609; came to Concord, Mass., 1632; an original proprietor of Salisbury, Mass., 1637.

Thomas, married at Cambridge, Mass., 1656.

Thomas, b. 1628, settled at Lynn, Mass., before 1656.

Thomas, resident of Stonington, Conn. before 1678.

William, employed in 1633 by Gov. Winthrop, at Boston, Mass.

William, son of Francis of Brandon, Suffolk, Eng., b. 1609, located 1635 at Salem, Mass.

William, one of the original settlers at Sudbury, 1639.

William, a selectman at Gloucester, Mass., 1644.

William, married in Plymouth, Mass., 1649.

William, brother of George the carpenter, was an early settler at Salisbury, Mass.

William, soapboiler, was at Salem and Boston, Mass. before 1650.

William, a resident of Boston, Mass., before 1655.

BROWNELL

Thomas, b. Eng., 1619, came from Derbyshire, Eng., 1636 to Portsmouth, R. I.

BROWNING

Henry, a resident of New Haven, Conn., 1639.

Joseph, printer and bookseller, of Dutch descent, was at Boston, Mass., 1683; spelled his name Brunning.

Nathaniel, b. London, Eng., about 1618; came to Portsmouth, R. I., 1640.

Thomas, freeman at Salem, Mass., 1637, no male issue.

BRUCE

From *De Bruys,* from Bruy or Bruys, a place in Normandy, where the family originated. De Bruys fought at the Battle of Hastings; from this ancestor King Robert Bruce was descended.

JAMES was at Haverhill, Mass., 1677.

JOHN, resident of Sudbury, Mass., before 1672.

PETER was at Haverhill, Mass., 1677.

ROGER, resident of Marlboro, Mass., before 1691.

BRUEN

OBADIAH came to Marshfield, Mass., 1640; removed to New London, Conn.; in 1667 went to N. J.

BRUNDISH

JOHN, freeman at Watertown, Mass., 1635; removed to Wethersfield, Conn.

BRUNETT

HENRY, merchant at Boston, died 1687.

BRUSH

GEORGE, Scotchman, married 1659 at Woburn, Mass.

BRYAN or BRYANT

From Gaelic, signifying the nobly descended from *bri*, dignity, honor, and a diminutive of that to which it is annexed, belonging to it. English family traced to Sir Guy De Briant of Edward III reign, seated in the Castle of Hereford, Wales.

ABRAHAM, blacksmith, b. Eng., settled at Reading, Mass., 1644.

ALEXANDER, b. Aylesburg, Eng., 1602; settled at Milford, Conn., 1639; removed to Meriden, Conn., finally located at Watertown, Conn.

JOHN was at Taunton, Mass., 1637.

JOHN, b. Eng., came from Kent, Eng., to Scituate, Mass., 1639, later removed to Barnstable, Mass.

STEPHEN, an inhabitant of Duxbury, Mass., 1643, removed to Plymouth, Mass., before 1650.

WILLIAM, taverner, was at Boston, Mass., before 1683.

BRYER or BRIARD

ELISHA, living at Portsmouth, N. H., 1689.

RICHARD settled at Newbury, Mass., before 1665.

BUBIER

JOSEPH, a resident of Marblehead, Mass., 1668.

BUCK

Surname borrowed from armorial bearings or shields and banners of war.

EMANUEL or ENOCH, resident of Wethersfield, Conn., before 1650.

EPHRAIM, married at Woburn, Mass., 1671.

HENRY was at Wethersfield, Conn., before 1660.

ISAAC was at Scituate, Mass., about 1643.

JAMES came from Hingham, Eng., to Hingham, Mass., 1638.

JOHN, brother of the preceding, came to Hingham, Mass., 1638; removed to Scituate, Mass., 1650.

WILLIAM, ploughwright, b. 1585, came from Eng., 1635, to Cambridge, Mass.; his only son, Roger, accompanied him.

BUCKINGHAM

From Saxon, a shire and town in England, so called from *bucen*, beechen, and *ham*, village, or from Saxon *bucca*, deer —the deer village.

THOMAS came from London, Eng., to Boston, Mass., 1637; the following year settled at New Haven, Conn., and 1639 removed to Milford, Conn.

BUCKLAND

BENJAMIN was at Braintree, Mass., removed 1675 to Rehoboth, Mass.

THOMAS, freeman at Dorchester, Mass., 1635; the following year removed to Windsor, Conn.

WILLIAM came from Weymouth, Eng., and was at Hingham, Mass., 1635, removed to Rehoboth, Mass., 1658.

BUCKMAN

WILLIAM came from Ipswich, Mass., to Salem, Mass., 1632; removed to Chelsea, Mass., and was, in 1664, at Malden, Mass.

BUCKMINSTER

From Saxon *bucen*, beecher, or *bugan*, to bend, a bow, a corner, round; and *minster*, a church or monastery. Ancient and noble English family.

JAMES, original proprietor of Sudbury, Mass., 1640.

THOMAS, a descendant of John of Northampton, Eng.; made a freeman at Sudbury, Mass., 1646. He settled at Scituate, Mass., 1639; afterwards at Boston, Mass.

BUCKNAM

WILLIAM located at what is now Malden, Mass., 1647.

BUDD

From Welsh, thrift, gain, riches, victory. *Bud* in Danish signifies a messenger, courier, a sergeant.

EDWARD, carver, resident of Boston, Mass., 1668.

JOHN was at Greenwich, Conn., 1664, and at Milford, Conn., 1677.

JONATHAN, a resident of New Haven, Conn., 1643.

BUDLEY

GILES was at Ipswich, Mass., 1648.

BUDLONG

FRANCIS, resident of Warwick, R. I., married in 1669.

BUELL

Place name from Bueil, a village of France. The name in Welsh signifies a herd of cattle; an ox. Branches of this family exist in England, France and Spain. The family of Bevilles, one of thirty-eight different ways of spelling the name, was ancient English family. Robert Beville was knight of shire for Huntingdonshire, 1410.

WILLIAM, b. Chesterton, Huntingdonshire, Eng., 1610, came to Dorchester, Mass., 1630, and was one of the first settlers at Windsor, Conn., 1635.

BUFFINGTON

THOMAS, Quaker, was at Salem, Mass., 1650.

BUFFUM

ROBERT came from Yorkshire, Eng., to Salem, Mass., 1638.

BUGBY

EDWARD, b. Eng., 1594, came from Stratford-le-Bow, near London, Eng., to Roxbury, Mass., 1634.

RICHARD, brother of preceding, came in Winthrop's fleet, 1630; located at Roxbury, Mass.

BULFINCH

JOHN, freeman at Salem, Mass., 1642.

BULGAR

RICHARD, bricklayer, came to Boston, Mass., 1630; went to Exeter, N. H., 1638, thence to R. I., where he died 1679.

BULKELEY or BUCKLEY

Name derived from the manor of Bulkeley in County of Palatine, of Chester, Eng. A corruption of *Bullockley*, the bullock-field or pasture. The English ancestor was Baron de Bulkeley, lord of the Manor of Bulkeley, 1199-1226.

REV. PETER, son of Rev. Edward of 13th generation from Baron Bulkeley, b. Odell, Bedfordshire, Eng., 1582-83, came to Cambridge, Mass., 1635; next year removed to Concord, Mass.

THOMAS, resident of Boston, Mass., before 1685.

WILLIAM was at Ipswich, Mass., 1648.

BULL

From well known armorial; *Bul* in Saxon is a brooch, a stud, a bracelet.

HENRY, b. 1610, came to Roxbury, Mass., 1635; two years later removed to Boston, Mass., 1638 to Portsmouth, R. I.

ISAAC married at Boston, Mass., 1653.

JOHN, feltmaker, resident of Boston, Mass., 1658.

ROBERT, a resident of Saybrook, Conn., 1653.

THOMAS, b. 1610, landed at Boston, Mass., 1635; next year removed to Hartford, Conn.

WILLIAM was inhabitant of Cambridge, Mass., 1644.

BULLARD

Having the disposition of a bull.

BENJAMIN was at Watertown, Mass., 1642.

GEORGE, freeman at Watertown, Mass., 1641.

ROBERT, b. Eng., 1599, came to Watertown, Mass., 1630, died 1634, leaving only son Benjamin, brought up by his uncle, William, of Dedham.

WILLIAM, brother of the preceding, b. Eng., 1601, came from Kent, Eng., and was granted land in Dedham, Mass., 1635.

BULLEN

JOHN was at Medfield, Mass., 1649.

SAMUEL, freeman at Dedham, Mass., 1641.

BULLIS

PHILIP, mariner, resident of Boston, Mass., 1663.

BULLOCK

A full grown ox. The members of families of Bulls, Bullards and Bullocks are noted for being firm and inflexible in their way.

DAVID, a resident of Rehoboth, Mass., 1668.

HENRY, husbandman, b. Eng., 1595, came from Essex, Eng., to Charlestown, Mass., 1635; was at Salem, Mass., 1643.

RICHARD, b. Essex Co., Eng., settled at Rehoboth, Mass., 1643.

SAMUEL married at Rehoboth, Mass., 1673; no male issue.

BULLY

NICHOLAS, a constable at Saco, Maine, 1664.

BUMPASS or BUMPUS

EDWARD came to Plymouth, Mass., 1621; removed to Duxbury, Mass., afterwards to Marshfield, Mass., and 1652 was one of the first proprietors of Dartmouth, Mass.

BUMSTEAD

EDWARD, freeman at Boston, Mass., 1640.

THOMAS came to Roxbury, Mass., 1640.

BUNCE

THOMAS, of Scotch descent, b. Eng.,

1612, proprietor at Hartford, Conn., 1636.

BUNDY

JOHN was at Plymouth, Mass., 1643, removed to Boston, Mass., afterwards was at Taunton, Mass.

BUNKER

Name derived from French *Bon Coeur*—a good heart.

GEORGE, son of William, a French Hugenot, b. Eng., came to Ipswich, Mass., removed to Topsfield, Mass., where he was drowned 1656.

GEORGE, freeman at Charlestown, Mass., 1634.

BUNN

In Gaelic a hill.

EDWARD was a resident of Hull, Mass., where he married 1673.

MATTHEW was at Hull, Mass., before 1659.

BUNNELL

A corruption of Bonhill, a parish in County of Dumbarton, Scotland. William La Bonnell came to Eng. with William the Conqueror.

BENJAMIN took oath of allegiance at New Haven, Conn., 1657.

SOLOMON, brother of preceding, was resident of New Haven, Conn., 1638.

WILLIAM, brother of preceding, came with his brothers from Cheshire, Eng., to New Haven, Conn., 1638.

BURBANK

The name of German origin; it is found just once in the Doomsday Book amongst 10,000 land owners.

JOHN, b. Eng., 1600, freeman at Rowley, Mass., 1640.

JOSEPH, b. Eng., 1611, came to Boston, Mass., 1635.

BURBEEN

JOHN, tailor, came from Scotland to Woburn, Mass., before 1660.

BURCHSTED

JOHN HENRY, a German physician, came from Silesia to Lynn, Mass., before 1690.

BURDEN

A corruption of *bourdon*—a pilgrim's staff.

FRANCIS, a freeman at Portsmouth, R. I., 1655.

GEORGE, shoemaker, b. Eng., 1615, came to Boston, Mass., 1635.

ROBERT, married at Lynn, Mass., 1650.

BURDETT or BURDITT

A little bird, *ett* signifying young, small and tender.

REV. GEORGE came from Yarmouth, Norfolk, Eng., to Salem, Mass., 1635; went to Dover, N. H., 1637-38; thence to York, Maine, afterwards returned to Eng.

ROBERT, b. Eng., 1633, was married at Malden, Mass., 1653.

BURDICK

ROBERT was at Newport, R. I., as early as 1652, removed to Westerly, R. I. before 1661.

BURDON

GEORGE came from Eng. to Boston, Mass., 1636.

BURDSALL

HENRY, freeman at Salem, Mass., 1638.

BURGE

In all Teutonic languages signifies a hill, a fortification, tower, etc.

GILES was at Dorchester, Mass., 1682.
THOMAS was at Lynn, Mass., removed 1637 to Sandwich, Mass.

BURGESS or BURGISS

An inhabitant of a borough, a freeman, citizen.

FRANCIS, a resident of Boston, Mass., before 1654.

JAMES, b. Eng., 1621, came to Boston, 1635, aged 14 years.

RICHARD was at Sandwich, Mass., 1643,
ROGER was at Boston, Mass., before 1664.

THOMAS came from Eng. to Duxbury, Mass., 1637; next year removed to Sandwich, Mass.

THOMAS, a resident of Concord, Mass., 1660.

BURKBY

THOMAS was at Rowley, Mass., 1643.

BURKE

A corruption of *De Burgo*, that is—from fort, castle, hill, etc. This family went to England with the Conqueror, afterwards into Ireland with Strongbow.

RICHARD, b. Eng., 1640, located at Sudbury, Mass., 1670; had land granted at Stow, Mass., 1686.

BURLEIGH

Place name from Burghley or Burleigh, i. e. the field belonging to the burgh.

GILES, an inhabitant of Ipswich, Mass., 1648.

BURLINGHAM or BURLINGAME

ROGER was at Stonington, Conn., 1654, and at Warwick, R. I., 1660; removed to Providence, R. I., before 1670.

BURLISSON

EDWARD was at Suffield, Conn., 1677.

BURMAN
THOMAS, resident of Barnstable, Mass., before 1663.

BURN or BURNS
EDWARD, freeman at Hingham, Mass., 1666.

JOHN, a resident of Plymouth, Mass., 1651.

LAWRENCE, resident of Marblehead, Mass., 1668.

RICHARD removed from Lynn, Mass., to Sandwich, Mass., 1637.

THOMAS was at Marshfield, Mass., 1648.

WILLIAM, a resident of Duxbury, Mass., 1638.

BURNAP
ROBERT, b. Eng., 1595, settled at Roxbury, Mass., removed to Reading, Mass. after 1642.

BURNELL
WILLIAM came from Yorkshire, Eng., to Boston, Mass., 1630.

BURNHAM
Place name derived from Burnham, a town in Norfolk, also Essex, Eng. In the old English *burn* signifies river, and *ham* village—the village by the river. In Cornish British Burnham means the house or town on rising ground. Walter le Ventre, a follower of William the Conqueror, was made lord of the Saxon village of Burnham; became known as De Burnham.

JOHN, carpenter, son of Robert, b. 1616, came to Ipswich, Mass., 1639.

ROBERT, brother of the preceding, b. Norwich, Norfolk, Eng.; 1635, to Boston, Mass., afterwards removed to Dover, N. H.

THOMAS, carpenter, brother of the preceding, b. Norwich, Eng., 1619; settled at Ipswich, Mass., 1639.

THOMAS, lawyer, b. Hatfield, Herefordshire, Eng., 1617, came to Barbadoes, 1635; first record in N. E. at Hartford, Conn., 1649.

BURPEE
THOMAS came from Eng. to Mass., about 1644, settled at Rowley, Mass., 1651.

BURR
From Gaelic *burt*—quizzing, joking; also in English, fish. *Burort*, Dutch, a hamlet, a neighborhood. The name was originally Beur, a district in Netherlands. The German *buer* means a rural district.

BENJAMIN, original settler of Hartford, Conn., 1635.

JEHU, b. Eng., came in Winthrop's fleet 1630 to Boston, Mass.; freeman at Rowley, Mass., 1632; pioneer at Springfield, Mass., 1636, and 1640, removed to Fairfield, Mass.

REV. JONATHAN, b. Redgrave, Suffolk, Eng., 1604, came to Dorchester, Mass., 1639, where he died of smallpox, 1641.

SIMON, brother of preceding, b. Eng., settled at Hingham, Mass., before 1645.

BURRAGE
The family was numerous in the 16th century. The American branch is traced to Robert Burrage of Seething, a small parish near Norton, Subcourse, 9 miles south of Norwich, Eng.

JOHN, son of John, of the 4th generation from Robert mentioned above, bapt. 1611; freeman at Charlestown, Mass., 1637.

THOMAS, married at Lynn, Mass., 1687.

BURRILL
GEORGE, a resident of Lynn, Mass., 1630.

JOHN was at Roxbury, Mass., prior to 1632.

JOHN settled at Weymouth, Mass., before 1659.

WILLIAM was resident of New Haven, Conn., 1650.

BURRITT
WILLIAM, b. Eng., early settler of Stratford, Conn., 1640.

BURROUGHS or BURROWS
The family seated near Barnstable, Devonshire, Eng.

FRANCIS, merchant, resident of Boston, Mass., 1685.

JEREMIAH was at Scituate, Mass., 1647.

JOHN, cooper, came from Yarmouth, Eng., to Salem, Mass., 1637.

JOHN, a resident of New Haven, Conn., 1644.

JOHN, resident of Enfield, Conn., 1684.

PETER was early settler of Wethersfield, Conn.; removed to New London, Conn.

ROBERT married at Wethersfield, Conn., 1645.

WILLIAM, b. 1616, came to N. E. 1635; was at Providence, R. I., 1641.

BURSLEY
JOHN, early settler at Weymouth, Mass.; afterwards removed to Dorchester, Mass., where he was admitted freeman 1630.

BURT (see BURR)
GEORGE, a resident of Lynn, Mass., 1635.

HENRY was at Roxbury, Mass., and in 1640 removed to Springfield, Mass.

JAMES came from Eng.; was at Newport, R. I., 1639; removed to Taunton, Mass., 1645.

RICHARD, one of the first purchasers at Taunton, Mass., 1639.

ROGER, resident of Cambridge, Mass., 1643.

BURTON

Place name from a town in Leicestershire, Eng. The name signifies Burtoun, from abundance of burs growing thereabout.

BONIFACE was at Lynn, Mass., 1630; made freeman at Salem, Mass., 1635; removed to Reading, Mass., 1644.

EDWARD was at Charlestown, Mass., 1633; removed to Hingham, Mass., where he was granted lands, 1647.

JOHN, tanner, was at Salem, Mass., 1637.

THOMAS, a resident of Hingham, Mass., 1640.

WILLIAM was at Warwick, R. I., removed to Providence, R. I., where he died 1714.

BURWELL

JOHN came from County Herts, Eng., to Milford, Conn., 1639.

BUSBY

NICHOLAS, b. Eng., 1587, weaver, came from Norwich, Eng., to Boston, Mass., 1637 removed to Watertown, Mass., returned to Boston, Mass., 1646.

BUSH

EDWARD was resident of Salem, Mass., 1665.

JOHN took oath of fidelity at Cambridge, Mass., 1652.

JOHN was at Wells, Maine, 1654.

RANDOLPH, RANDOLP or RENOLD was a resident of what is now Brighton, Mass., 1641.

SAMUEL was at Suffield, Conn., 1679.

BUSHELL

EDWARD, merchant, b. Eng., 1612, came to Boston, Mass., 1635.

BUSHNELL

From Dutch, *bossen-hall*, a fagot or wood market, or a hall or mansion in the wood.

FRANCIS, b. Eng., came to N. E., 1635, settled at Guilford, Conn., 1639.

JOHN, glazier, b. Eng., 1614, resided at Boston, Mass., coming to N. E. 1635.

BUSS, BUSSE or BUSSEY

Place name from town of Bussey in the province of Burgundy, France.

ISAAC, weaver, b. Eng., 1592, was at Salem, Mass., 1639; made freeman at Salisbury, Mass., 1640.

JOHN, brother of the preceding, was resident of Salisbury, Mass., 1640.

WILLIAM married at Portsmouth, N. H., 1687.

BUTCHER

JOHN, married at Boston, Mass., 1662.

BUTLER

The family derived their origin from the old counts of Briony or Biony in Normandy, a descendant of whom, Herveius Fitz Walter accompanied the Conqueror to Eng. The king conferred on him the office of Chief Butler of Ireland, hence his descendants took surname of De Boteler or Butler.

DANIEL, a resident of Wickford, R. I., 1674.

HENRY, schoolmaster, came from County of Kent, Eng., in 1642, to Dorchester, Mass., returned to Eng.

JAMES, resident of Lancaster, Mass., 1663, removed to Woburn, Mass., and to Billerica, Mass., where he died, 1681.

JOHN, physician, came to Boston, Mass., 1644, was at Hartford, Conn., 1666, removed to Branford, Conn., 1669.

JOHN, a resident of New London, Conn., before 1685.

NICHOLAS came from Eastwell, Kent, Eng., to Dorchester, Mass., 1637, removed 1651 to Martha's Vineyard, Mass., 1651.

PETER was resident of Boston, Mass., before 1655.

RICHARD came from Braintree, Eng., in 1632 to Cambridge, Mass., removed to Hartford, Conn., before 1643.

STEPHEN was at Boston, Mass., 1652.

THOMAS was at Lynn, Mass., removed to Lynn, Mass.; removed to Sandwich, Mass., 1637.

THOMAS, b. Eng., 1674, settled at Berwick, Maine, 1690.

WALTER was at Greenwich, Conn., 1672.

WILLIAM, brother of Richard, was at Cambridge, Mass., 1634; removed to Hartford, Conn., before 1641.

BUTMAN

A marksman.

JEREMIAH settled at Salem, Mass., before 1659.

BUTT or BUTTS

Butts were marks for archery in most parishes; places were set apart for this sport, which was called "the Butts," hence the name was given to a person residing near such a spot. Butt signifies a promontory, as the Butt of Lewis—an isle of Scotland.

RICHARD was a resident of Dorchester, Mass., before 1675.

BUTTER or BUTTERS

Isaac, freeman at Medfield, Mass., 1666.

William, b. Scotland, 1630, was at Woburn, Mass., before 1689.

BUTTERFIELD

Benjamin was at Charlestown, Mass., 1638; went to Woburn, 1640; one of the original proprietors of Chelmsford, Mass., 1654.

BUTTERWORTH

John was at Rehoboth, Mass., 1643; was at Swanzey, Mass., before 1663.

Samuel, freeman at Weymouth, Mass., 1640; removed to Rehoboth, Mass., 1645.

BUTTOLPH

Thomas, glover, b. Eng., 1603, came to Boston, Mass., 1635.

BUTTON

John, miller, freeman at Boston, Mass., 1634.

Matthias, a Dutchman, was at Boston, Mass., as early as 1634.

Robert, freeman at Salem, Mass., 1642.

BUTTRICK

William, b. Eng., about 1617, came from Kingston on the Thames to Concord, Mass., 1635, removed to Chelmsford, Mass.

BUTTRY or BUTTERY

Nicholas, b. Eng., 1602, came from London, Eng., to Cambridge, Mass., 1635.

BUXTON

Place name—a village in Derbyshire, Eng. From Saxon *boc,* a beech, and German *buche* and *ton*—the beech town.

Anthony, b. Eng., about 1601, came to Salem, Mass., 1637.

BUZZELL or BUSWELL

Isaac, b. Eng., about 1593, proprietor at Salisbury, Mass., 1639; removed to Hampton, N. H., in that year; returned to Salisbury.

BYAM

George, freeman at Salem, Mass., 1642; removed to Wenham, Mass., from there to Chelmsford, Mass., about 1653.

BYFIELD

Nathaniel, son of Rev. Richard, b. Long Ditton, Surrey, Eng., 1653; was a proprietor at Bristol county, Mass., 1679.

BYLES

Josiah, sadler, came from Winchester, Hants, Eng., to Boston, Mass., 1695.

BYLEY

Henry, tanner, b. Eng., 1612, original settler at Salisbury, Mass., 1639.

BYNNS

Jonas was at Dover, N. H., 1654.

BYRAM

Nicholas, physician, was at Weymouth, Mass., 1638, removed to Bridgewater, Mass., 1662.

CABELL

George, merchant, Boston, Mass., 1695.

John came to N. E., 1631, was at Springfield, Mass., 1636, removed to Fairfield, Conn., was on list of freeman 1669.

CABOT

Family of Norman origin.

George, son of Francis of St. Trinity, Island of Jersey, Eng., came to Boston, Mass., 1670.

Jean, brother of the preceding, was an inhabitant of Boston, Mass., 1670.

CADMAN

George was at Dartmouth, Mass., 1685.

CADOGAN

From Welsh *cad,* battle, *gwg,* fierce, terrible in battle.

Rice or Richard, freeman at Kittery, Maine.

CADWELL

Thomas, a resident of Hartford, Conn., 1632.

CADY or CADE

From Gaelic *cadia,* the house of God. There is a community in Switzerland called *Casdee,* i. e., the house of God; *Cadie* in Scotch, errand boy, messenger.

Benjamin, married at Andover, Mass., 1664.

James came from Wales to Hingham, Mass., 1635; removed to Boston, Mass.; 1640 to Yarmouth, Mass.

Jonathan was at Rowley, Mass., before 1667; removed to Killingly, Conn.

Nicholas, b. Eng., was at Watertown, Mass., 1645; removed to Groton, Mass., 1668.

Richard was an inhabitant of Mass., 1652.

CAFFINGE or CAFFINS

John, an original proprietor at Guilford, Conn., 1639; was at New Haven, Conn., 1643.

Samuel, brother of the preceding, freeman 1649 at New Haven, Conn.

Thomas, brother of the preceding, died at New Haven, Conn., 1647.

CAHOON

William was at Swanzey, Mass., 1669.

CAINE or CAIN

In Welsh and Gaelic, *chaste,* beloved, fair, beautiful.

Christopher, freeman at Cambridge, Mass.

CAKEHEAD

THOMAS, freeman at Watertown, Mass., 1634, was a resident of Dedham and Sudbury, Mass.

CALDWELL

From *cold* meaning cold, and *well*, spring; became known as Coldwell, finally Caldwell.

JOHN, weaver, b. Eng., 1624, was at Boston, Mass., 1643, removed to Ipswich, Mass., 1654.

CALEF or CALFE

JAMES was at Rowley, Mass., 1644.

ROBERT, b. Eng., about 1648, settled at Boston, Mass., 1688, removed to Roxbury, Mass., 1707.

CALKINS

DEACON HUGH, Welsh descent, b. Wales, 1600, settled in Marshfield, Mass., 1638-40, later at Gloucester, Mass.

CALL

From Welsh, prudent, discerning, trickish; *Caill* and *Cuil*, same in Gaelic.

JOHN was at Charlestown, Mass., 1637.

THOMAS, tilemaker or husbandman, was at Charlestown, Mass., 1636.

CALLENDER

ELIAS, cooper, one of the founders of the First Baptist Church at Boston, Mass., 1669.

CALLOWAY or CALLOWE

OLIVER, mariner at Watertown, Mass., 1642, removed to Boston, Mass., 1656.

CALLUM

JOHN took oath of fidelity at Haverhill, Mass., 1677.

CALVERLY

EDMUND at Warwick, 1661, removed to Newport, R. I.; no record of any issue.

CAMP

EDWARD, a resident of New Haven, Conn., 1643.

JOHN, freeman at Hartford, Conn., 1669.

NICHOLAS, b. Eng., before 1630, came from Nasing, Essex, Eng., to Watertown, Mass., 1638, removed to Guilford, 1639, granted land at Milford, Conn., 1646.

WILLIAM married at New London, Conn., 1683.

CAMPBELL

From Celtic and Gaelic, Wry-mouth, the man whose mouth is inclined a little on one side; from *cam*, crooked, distorted, *bevl*, the mouth. The family is traced to the beginning of the fifth century, was possessed of Lochore in Argyleshire, Scotland, as early as the time of Fergus II.

DUNCAN, bookseller, was at Boston, Mass., 1685.

JOHN, proprietor at Boston New's Letter, resident of Boston, Mass., 1695.

CAMFIELD or CANFIELD

JOHN, freeman at Portsmouth, R. I., 1655.

MATTHEW, a resident of New Haven, Conn., 1644, removed to N. J., 1665.

THOMAS, brother of the preceding, b. Yorkshire, Eng., was at New Haven, in 1646 at Milford, Conn.

CAMPION

CLEMENT at Portsmouth, N. H., 1647.

CANADA

JAMES, a resident of Rowley, Mass., 1671.

CANDE

ZACCHEUS, proprietor at New Haven, Conn., 1685.

CANN

From Gaelic *Ceann* and *Kin*, and Welsh *Ken* or *Cen*, the head; projection.

JOHN, married at Boston, Mass., 1661.

CANNEY

THOMAS, sent over by Mason, 1631 to Portsmouth, N. H., removed to Dover, N. H., 1644.

CANNIN or CANON

From Welsh; the river *Taf* is called in the interior, *Canon*, or the singing river; a rule, a law, a dignitary of the church.

JOHN, came to Plymouth, Mass., 1621.

CANTERBURY

CORNELIUS, settler at Hingham, Mass., 1639, no male issue.

WILLIAM, b. Eng., settled at Salem, Mass., 1638; removed to Lynn, Mass., 1641.

CAPEN

BERNARD, b. Eng., came to Mass., 1630; proprietor at Dedham, Mass., 1633; had only son John who may have preceded his father to N. E.

CAPRON

BANFIELD or BENFIELD, b. Chester, Eng., about 1660, came to N. E. 1680, settled at what is now Barrington, R. I., was later a resident of Attleboro, Mass.

CARD

A word used in some parts of Scotland to denote a traveling tinker; *Cleairde*, Gaelic, a tradesman.

RICHARD, freeman at Newport, R. I., 1665.

CARDER

RICHARD was at Roxbury, Mass., freeman, Boston, Mass., 1636, removed the following year to Warwick, R. I.

CARLETON

From the Saxon word *coere,* husbandman and *town.* The English family is traced to Baldwin de Carleton of Carleton near Penrith, Eng., 1066.

EDWARD, son of Eramas, mercer of London, Eng., of the XIX generation from Baldwin de Carleton, b. Eng., 1605, one of founders of Rowley, Mass., 1638-39, returned to Eng., 1651, where he died that year; his son John came to N. E. after the death of his father.

CARLILE, CARLEY or CARLISLE

BARTHOLOMEW, married at Sudbury, Mass., 1686.

WILLIAM came from Eng., was proprietor 1637, at Hingham, Mass., one of the first planters of Hull, Mass., 1642; a founder of Lancaster, Mass., 1653; later resided at Marlboro, Mass.

CARMAN

JOHN was at Roxbury, Mass., 1631, removed to L. I., a patentee of Hempstead.

CARNES

From Welsh *Carne,* a rock, a heap of stones. This family claims descent from *Ithel,* King of Ghent, now Monmouthshire, through his son Thomas o'r Gare, who was brought up at one of his father's seats called *Pencarne* (from *pen,* the head, and *carne,* a rock, a heap of stones), whence he was named *Carne.*

JOHN, resident of Boston, Mass., 1649.

THOMAS was at New Haven, Conn., 1684.

CARNEY

JAMES, surgeon, at Boston, Mass., 1686.

CARPENTER

Occupation surname; ancient English family seated in Hertfordshire and other parts of Eng. The English family has been traced to John, b. 1303, who was a member of Parliament in 1323.

DAVID was at Farmington, Conn., where he died 1651.

JOHN was at Ipswich, Mass., 1678.

THOMAS, carpenter, came from Amesbury, Wiltshire, Eng., to Boston, Mass., 1536.

WILLIAM, in the ninth generation from John, b. Eng., 1576, came with his son, William, b. 1605, to N. E. 1637, returned on the same ship leaving his son William in America; the latter made a freeman at Weymouth, Mass., 1640; was one of the founders of Rehoboth, Mass.; a carpenter by trade.

WILLIAM, carpenter, son of Richard, Amesbury, Wiltshire, Eng., and of the tenth generation from John, mentioned above, settled in Providence, R. I., 1637, and was founder of the R. I. branch of the family.

CARR

This surname has several significations; *Caer,* Cornish British, a city, a town, a fort, a castle. *Carre,* French, a stout, broad-shouldered man. *Cawr,* Welsh, a giant. The family is of Norman and French origin; William Karrie was a noble in the train of William the Conqueror.

CALEB, son of Benjamin, b. London, Eng., 1616, came to Newport, R. I., 1638.

GEORGE, shipwright, was at Ipswich, Mass., 1633, removed to Salisbury, Mass., 1640, and 1662 was at Amesbury, Mass.

RICHARD, b. 1606, came to N. E., 1635, on record 1640, at Hampton, N. H., and at Ipswich, Mass., 1678.

ROBERT, tailor, brother of Caleb, b. London, Eng., 1614, settled at Bristol, R. I., 1635, became a resident of Portsmouth, R. I., 1639, removed to Newport, R. I., one of the original purchasers of Island of Conanicut in Narragansett Bay.

CARRIER

THOMAS, b. Wales about 1630, was at Billerica, Mass., 1674, later at Andover, Mass., and Colchester, Conn.

CARRINGTON

EDWARD, a resident of Charlestown, Mass., 1633.

JOHN, inhabitant of Wethersfield, Conn., 1644.

CARROLL

ANTHONY was at Topsfield, Mass., 1661.

NATHANIEL an inhabitant of Mass., 1672.

CARTER

Occupation surname, one who drives a cart. *Cairtear,* Gaelic, a tourist, a sojourner.

CALEB married at Charlestown, Mass., 1678.

JOHN was at Charlestown, Mass., 1640, one of the early settlers of Woburn, Mass.

JOSHUA, freeman at Dorchester, Mass., 1634, removed to Windsor, Conn., before 1647.

LAWRENCE was at Hadley, Mass., 1686.

PHILIP took oath of allegiance at Exeter, N. H., 1677.

RALPH was at Boston, Mass., 1676.

RICHARD, broadweaver, was at Boston, Mass., 1640; no male issue.

ROBERT was at Malden, Mass., 1674.

SAMUEL, freeman at Charlestown, Mass., 1647.

THOMAS, freeman at Charlestown, Mass., 1637.

REV. THOMAS, b. Hertfordshire, Eng., 1608, came from St. Albans, Hertfordshire, Eng., to Dedham, Mass., in 1641; first minister at Woburn, Mass., 1642.

THOMAS, planter, b. Eng., settled in Ipswich, Mass., 1638, the following year was amongst first settlers at Salisbury, Mass.

THOMAS was at York, Maine, 1663.

WILLIAM was at Marblehead, Mass., 1668.

CARTHRICK or CARTRACK

MICHAEL, carpenter, was at Ipswich, Mass., 1635.

CARTWRIGHT

ARTHUR, a resident of Dorchester, Mass., 1666.

EDWARD, mariner, was at Boston, Mass., 1662.

EDWARD was at Nantucket, Mass., before 1678.

NICHOLAS, was at Nantucket, Mass., before 1706.

CARVEATH

EZEKIEL, resident of Boston, Mass., 1674.

CARVER

Occupation name from wood carver. The name appears in the Hundred Rolls as Adam C. Karver and Richard C. Kerver.

JOHN, *Mayflower* passenger, first governor of Plymouth Colony; left no male issue.

RICHARD, b. 1578, came from Cratly, Norfolk, Eng., to Watertown, Mass., 1638, he died 1641-43; no record of any issue.

ROBERT, planter, son of Isaac, nephew of Gov. John, b. Boston, Lincolnshire, Eng., 1594, settled at Marshfield, Mass., 1638.

CARRWITHEN, CARWITHEN

DAVID was at Salem, Mass., 1644.

JOSHUA, mariner, married at Boston, Mass., 1657.

PHILIP was at New London, Conn., 1650.

CARY

Place name from the manor of Cary or *Kari*, in parish of St. Giles, near Launceston, Eng., *Cary* in the British signified beloved, dear. English ancestor, Adam de Karry, 1198.

JAMES came from Bristol, Eng., to Charlestown, Mass., 1639.

JOHN, brother of the preceding, son of William, b. 1609, came from Bristol, Eng., to Plymouth Colony. Among the first settlers at Duxbury and Bridgewater, Mass.

NATHANIEL, resident of Salem, Mass., 1637.

CASE

From Latin meaning a house or a cottage. French *case*, a hut, a hovel; Gaelic *cass, caise*, steep, quick, hasty, passionate. The name is found in the Hundred Rolls in the thirteenth century.

EBENEZER, married at Roxbury, Mass., 1690.

EDWARD came to Watertown, Mass., 1638, one of the incorporators of Taunton, Mass.

JOHN, farmer and landowner, b. Aylesham, Eng., 1616, came to N. E., 1635, settled at Hartford, Conn., removed to Newtown, L. I., returned 1656 to Windsor, Conn., and in 1667 settled in what is now Simsbury, Conn.

RICHARD, brother of the preceding, was at Hartford, Conn., 1660.

WILLIAM, freeman at Newport, R. I., 1655.

CASELEY or CASLEY

EDWARD was at Scituate, Mass., 1638, removed to Barnstable, Mass., 1639.

WILLIAM was at Lynn, Mass., removed to Sandwich, Mass.

CASEY

THOMAS, resident of Newport, R. I., 1658.

CASH

WILLIAM, mariner, was at Salem, Mass., before 1667.

CASKIN

WILLIAM, a resident of Concord, Mass., before 1642.

CASS

From Gaelic *cas*, a verb, to turn against, to thwart, oppose.

JAMES was at Westerly, R. I., 1669.

JOHN, resident of Hampton, N. H., 1644.

CASSELL or CASSILEY

GEORGE was inhabitant of Mass., 1657.

ROBERT was at Ipswich, Mass., 1637, and at Hampton, N. H., 1639.

CASTLE

HENRY, b. Eng., an early settler of Woodbury, Conn.

MATTHEW, married at Charlestown, Mass., 1687.

WILLIAM, mariner, was a resident of Boston, Mass., 1673.

CAWLY

Thomas was at Marblehead, Mass., 1671.

CAYME

Arthur took oath of allegiance at York, Maine, 1680.

CENTER

John was a resident of Boston, Mass., before 1682.

CHADBOURNE

Humphrey, sent over by Mason to Portsmouth, N. H., 1631.

James was at Kittery, Maine, 1677.

William was at Kittery, Maine, 1631.

CHADSEY

William, b. Wales, came to Newport, R. I., 1692.

CHADWELL

Richard was at Lynn, Mass., 1636, removed next year to Sandwich, Mass.

CHADWELL

Richard was at Lynn, Mass., 1636, removed next year to Sandwich, Mass.

Thomas, brother of the preceding, b. Eng., 1611, came to Salem, Mass., 1636, removed to Lynn, Mass., thence to Sandwich, Mass., was living at Charlestown, Mass., 1670; finally returned to Lynn, Mass.

CHADWICK

From Saxon *Cyte* and *wick; Cyte* signifies cottage, and *wick,* harbor, a sheltered place.

Charles, b. Eng., 1596, freeman at Charlestown, Mass., 1630.

John, brother of the preceding, b. Eng., was at Watertown, freeman 1656; removed early to Malden, Mass.

Samuel, married at Reading, Mass., 1685.

Thomas, brother of John, b. Eng., 1655, settled in Newbury, Mass., 1679, removed to Watertown, Mass.

CHAFFEE or CHAFFIN

From French *Chafe,* to heat, to grow warm or angry; *chauffer,* to warm, to cannonade, attack briskly.

Ebenezer, was at Boston, Mass., before 1690.

Matthew, ship carpenter, freeman at Boston, Mass., 1636.

Thomas came to Hingham, Mass., 1635, on record at Nantasket, Mass., 1642, afterwards resided at Hull and Rehoboth, Mass.

CHALCROFT

Richard, a resident of Salem, Mass., 1668.

CHALLIS or CHALICE

A cup or bowl; taken from the sign of a house or shop.

Philip, b. Eng., 1617, was at Ipswich, Mass., 1637.

CHALKER

Alexander, married at Saybrook, Conn., 1637.

CHALKLEY or CHAUKLEY

Robert, freeman at Charlestown, Mass., 1646.

CHAMBERLAIN or CHAMBERLIN

John de Tankerville, son of Count Tankerville of Tankerville Castle in Normandy came to England with William the Conqueror. His son, John de Tankerville, was Lord Chamberlain to Henry I, and his son, John, held the same position at the court of Stephen I, and assumed the surname of Chamberlain.

Edward or Edmund, was resident of Woburn, Mass., married at Roxbury, Mass., 1647, removed to Chelmsford, Mass., 1655.

Henry, shoemaker, came from Hingham, Norfolk, Eng., 1638, settled at Hingham, Mass., removed to Hull, Mass., 1660.

John, currier, was resident of Boston, Mass., 1651.

John was a resident of Charlestown and Woburn, Mass., before 1652.

John, freeman at Malden, Mass., 1690.

John was at Cambridge, Mass., 1635.

Joseph, freeman at Cambridge, Mass., 1654, removed to Billerica, Mass.

Richard, b. Eng., settled in Braintree, Mass., 1642, removed to Roxbury, later to Sudbury, Mass.

Thomas, brother of Edmund and William, freeman at Woburn, Mass., 1644, removed to Chelmsford, Mass.

William was at Boston, Mass., 1647, removed two years later to Hingham or Hull, Mass.

William, brother of Edmund and Thomas, b. Eng., 1620, settled at Woburn, Mass., 1648, removed to Billerica, Mass., 1654.

CHAMBERS or CHALMERS

One of the clan Cameron of Scotland, going thence to France, put his name in Latin dress, styling himself *De Cameraria,* which was called in French *De La Chambre.* Upon his return to Scotland he was again, according to their dialect, called Chambers. Chalmers is a corruption of same.

Thomas was at Scituate, Mass., 1640, removed to Charlestown, Mass., 1658.

CHAMBERNOON

Francis was at Kittery, Maine, 1639; at Portsmouth, N. H., 1646, and York, Maine, 1665.

CHAMPION

A soldier, one who fought in public combat, in his own or another man's quarrel.

HENRY came from Eng. to Saybrook, Conn., 1647; removed to Lyme, Conn.

CHAMPLIN

A flat, open country, from *champ* an open, level field or plain, and *lean,* a meadow. The family of Norman-French origin.

GEOFFREY or JEFFREY, b. Eng., 1621, was at Portsmouth, N. H., 1638, soon afterwards became a resident of Newport, R. I.

CHAMPNEY

From French *champ,* a field, and *ey,* water—the wet country—country near the water. Sir Henry de Champney was in the train of William the Conqueror.

CHRISTOPHER was at Cambridge, Mass., 1644.

JOHN, a resident of Cambridge, Mass., 1635.

JOSEPH, freeman at Cambridge, Mass., 1654; removed to Billerica, Mass.

RICHARD, brother of John, came from Lincolnshire, Eng. to Cambridge, Mass., where he was a freeman in 1636.

CHANDLER

Occupation surname, a maker or seller of various wares, originally of candles.

EDMUND settled at Plymouth, Mass., 1633; granted land at Duxbury, Mass., was at Scituate, Mass., 1650; returned to Duxbury, Mass., 1662.

JOHN, freeman at Concord, Mass., 1640.

JOHN, shoemaker at Portsmouth, N. H., 1658.

NATHANIEL was at Duxbury, Mass., 1643.

ROGER, a resident of Plymouth, Mass., 1633.

ROGER married at Concord, Mass., 1671.

SAMUEL was at Plymouth, Mass., 1633, removed to Dorchester, Mass., where he married 1664.

WILLIAM, b. Eng., came to Roxbury, Mass., 1637, an original proprietor of Andover, Mass.

WILLIAM was a resident of Newbury, Mass., before 1652.

CHAPIN

A corruption of Chapman, a trader, a shopman. The family of French origin.

SAMUEL came from Eng. to Roxbury, Mass., settled permanently at Springfield, Mass; freeman in 1641.

CHAPLEMAN

MICHAEL at Salem, Mass., 1668.

CHAPLIN or CHAPLAIN

CLEMENT, chandler, b. Eng., 1587; came from Bury St. Edmunds, Suffolk, Eng., in 1635 to Cambridge, Mass.; in 1636 removed to Hartford, Conn., and in or sell. Saxon *ceap,* a bargain, a price, 1643 was at Wethersfield, Conn.

HUGH, son of Ebenezer, grandson of Jeremiah of Bradford, Eng., b. 1603, came to Rowley, Mass., 1638.

CHAPMAN

From Saxon *ceapan* or *cypan,* to buy or sell. Saxon *ceap* a bargain, a price, a trader, a shopman.

EDWARD was at Windsor, Conn., 1662.

EDWARD came from Yorkshire, Eng., to Boston, Mass., 1639; was at Ipswich, Mass., 1642, afterwards at Rowley, Mass.

JOHN, weaver, freeman at Charlestown, Mass., 1634; was at New Haven, Conn., 1639; removed to Fairfield, thence to Stamford, Conn.

RALPH, ship carpenter, b. Eng., 1615, came from Southwark, Surrey, Eng., 1636, to Duxbury, Mass., afterwards removed to Marshfield, Mass.

RICHARD was at Braintree, Mass., 1649.

ROBERT came from Hull, Eng. to Boston, Mass., 1635, the same year removed to Saybrook, Conn.

ROBERT was at Dover, N. H., 1663.

SIMON, freeman at Ipswich, Mass., 1675.

WILLIAM came from Eng., to New London, Conn., 1656.

CHAPPELL

GEORGE, b. Eng., 1615, came to N. E., 1635, and in 1637 was a resident of Wethersfield, Conn.; removed to New London, Conn., 1650.

NATHANIEL, freeman, Boston, Mass., 1634, where he had resided since 1634.

WILLIAM settled at New London, Conn., 1653.

CHARD

WILLIAM, a freeman at Weymouth, Mass., 1654.

CHARLES

From German *carl,* stout, strong, courageous and valiant.

JOHN at Charlestown, Mass., 1636; removed to New Haven, Conn., before 1640.

WILLIAM was resident of Salem, Mass., 1637.

CHARLETT

NICHOLAS was at Boston, Mass., 1642, in the employ of John Mylam, made freeman 1645.

CHASE or CHACE

The family is of Norman origin, the

name formerly being La Chassie. The seat of the English family is at Chesham, Buckinghamshire, Eng.

AQUILLA, mariner, son of Richard of the parish of Hundrich, Chesham, Eng., of fourth generation of Thomas, b. 1618, settled at Hampton, N. H., 1640; removed to Newbury, Mass., 1646.

BARTHOLOMEW was at Providence, R. I., 1645.

THOMAS, brother of Aquilla, settled at Hampton, N. H., about 1640.

WILLIAM came to Roxbury, Mass., 1630; in 1645 removed to Scituate, Mass., thence to Yarmouth, Mass.

CHATFIELD

FRANCIS one of the first settlers of Guilford, Conn., 1639.

GEORGE, brother of the preceding, was at Guilford, Conn., 1640; removed to Killingworth, Conn., 1663.

THOMAS, brother of preceding, was a resident of Guilford, Conn.; removed to Easthampton, L. I. No male issue.

CHAUNCEY

The family of Norman French origin. Chauncy de Chauncy came with William the Conqueror to England.

REV. CHARLES, son of George of Yardley, Hertfordshire, Eng., bapt. 1592, came to Plymouth, Mass., 1637; in 1641 removed to Scituate, Mass.; became first president of Harvard College, 1654.

CHECKLEY

ANTHONY, merchant, son of William of parish Preston Capes, near Daventry, Northamptonshire, Eng., bapt. 1636.

JOHN was at Boston, Mass., 1645.

JOHN, cooper, came from St. Saviour, Southwark, Eng., 1670, to Boston, Mass.

SAMUEL, brother of Anthony, was at Boston, Mass., 1670.

CHEDSEY or CHIDSEY

Place name from Chertsay, a town in Surrey, Eng., near the Thames.

JOHN was at New Haven, Conn., 1644.

CHEEVER

From French *Chevir,* signifying to master or overcome.

BARTHOLOMEW, cordwainer, b. Canterbury, Kent, Eng., 1608, freeman at Boston, Mass., 1637.

DANIEL, brother of preceding, was at Cambridge, Mass., 1646.

EZEKIEL, schoolmaster, b. London, Eng., 1616, arrived at Boston, 1637; next year removed to New Haven, Conn.; came to Ipswich, Mass., 1650, and in 1660 to Charlestown, Mass.; 1670 to Boston, Mass.

PETER was at Salem, Mass., 1668.

CHELSON

ROBERT was at Ipswich, Mass., 1644.

WILLIAM, a resident of Scarborough, Maine, 1676.

CHENEY

From French *Chene,* an oak; *Chenaie,* a grove, a plantation of oaks. The name has appeared in English records since 1066. Sir Nicholas Chenney acquired the manor of Up Ottery, Devonshire, Eng., 1207.

JOHN, shoemaker, b. Eng., was at Roxbury, Mass., 1635; resided at Newbury, Mass., 1636.

JOHN, early settler of Watertown, Mass., died 1675.

LAMBERT, b. Eng., 1593, arrived at Salem, Mass., 1630; was at Watertown, Mass., and in 1635 at Dedham, Mass.

THOMAS, b. Eng., 1604, early resident of Roxbury, Mass., where he died 1667.

WILLIAM, brother of John, was at Roxbury, Mass., as early as 1639.

CHEREY

DAVID was at Wickford, R. I., 1674.

CHESEBOROUGH or CHESSEBOROUGH

Place name from *Chessbro,* the hill or town on the river Chess.

WILLIAM, b. 1594, came from near Boston, Lincolnshire, Eng., in 1630, to Boston, Mass., removed to Braintree, Mass., in 1643 to Rehoboth, Mass.; one of the founders of Stonington, Conn., 1650.

CHESHOLME or CHISHOLM

THOMAS, freeman at Cambridge, Mass., 1636; no issue.

CHESLEY

PHILIP at Dover, N. H., 1642.

CHESTER

Place name from Chester, the capital of Cheshire, Eng. From the Latin *Castrum;* the Saxon *ceaster,* a fortified place, a castle or camp.

LEONARD, son of Balby, of Leicester, Eng., was at Watertown, Mass., 1635, removed to Wethersfield, Conn., 1636.

SAMUEL, engineer and navigator, b. Eng., about 1625, resident of Boston, Mass., 1663; removed in that year to New London, Conn.

SAMUEL, merchant, at Boston, Mass., 1676.

CHICHESTER

Place name from city of Chichester, Sussex, from Saxon *ceaster* or chester, a city, from *castrum,* a Roman station.

JAMES was at Taunton, Mass., 1643, and Salem, Mass., 1650; removed to Huntington, L. I., 1664.

WILLIAM, brother of preceding, at Marblehead, Mass., 1648.

CHICK

RICHARD, a resident of Roxbury, Mass., 1678.

THOMAS at Dover, N. H., 1671.

CHICKERING

From Cornish British *chi*, a house and *cairne*, a rock or stones, i. e. stone house; a house on a rock; a fortress.

FRANCIS came from Suffolk, Eng., to N. E., 1637; freeman at Dedham, Mass., 1640.

HENRY, physician, brother of preceding, son of Stephen, grandson of Thomas, of Wymondham, Eng., came from Ringsford, Eng., proprietor at Salem, Mass., 1630, removed to Dedham, Mass.

CHILD or CHILDS

A name given to youths from seven to fourteen years of age while receiving their education for knighthood. It is derived from *Hildr*, of the Norse mythology. The Domesday book mentions Edward Child as part proprietor of the Archbishop of York's church at Wynn, Eng.

ALWIN, merchant at Boston, Mass., 1673.

BENJAMIN, son of Benjamin, was first at Roxbury, Mass., 1630, afterwards at Boston, Mass.

EPHRAIM, freeman at Watertown, Mass., 1631, came from Nayland, Suffolk, Eng.

JEREMIAH, a resident of Swanzey, Mass., 1669.

JOHN, resident of Watertown, Mass., before 1664.

RICHARD, brother of preceding, b. Eng., was at Watertown, Mass., afterwards settled at Barnstable, Mass., before 1663.

RICHARD married at Marshfield, Mass., 1665.

ROBERT, physician, came from Northfleet, Kent, Eng., was at Watertown, Mass., granted land at Lancaster, Mass. He was a bachelor.

SAMUEL came to Plymouth, Mass.; killed by Indians, 1675.

WILLIAM, brother of Ephraim, b. Eng. about 1600, freeman at Watertown, Mass., 1634.

CHILLINGWORTH or CHILLINGSWORTH

THOMAS was at Lynn, Mass.; removed to Sandwich, Mass., 1637, thence to Marshfield, Mass., before 1648.

CHILSON

JOHN, married at Lynn, Mass., 1667.

WALSINGHAM came from Kent, Eng. to Marblehead, Mass., before 1647.

CHILTON

Place name from a town in Wiltshire, Eng., signifying the chalk-hills, from the Saxon *cylt*, clay or chalk.

JAMES, *Mayflower* passenger, was at Plymouth, Mass., 1620; no male issue.

CHINN or CHINE

GEORGE, an inhabitant of Salem, Mass., 1638; removed to Marblehead, Mass., 1648.

CHIPMAN

The same as Chapman (see).

JOHN, son of Thomas, of near Dorchester, Dorsetshire, was b. Eng., 1613, came to N. E., 1631. He was at Plymouth, Mass., before 1650 at Yarmouth, Mass.

CHIPPERFIELD

EDMUND, brickmaker, b. Eng., 1615, came to N. E., 1635, was a resident of New Haven, Conn., 1639; died 1648.

CHISHOLME

THOMAS came from Eng. to N. E., before 1653.

CHITTENDEN

From Cornish British and Welsh, from *Chy-tane-din*, *Chy* a house; *tane* lower, and *din*, a hill, i. e. the lower house on the rising or fortified ground.

JOHN, son of Robert of Cranbrook, Kent, Eng., bapt. 1594. He was a major in the English army; arrived at New Haven, Conn., 1639, and one of the first settlers of Guilford, Conn.

THOMAS, linen weaver, came from Kent county, b. Eng., 1585, came to Scituate, Mass., 1635.

WILLIAM, brother of John, settled in New Haven, Conn., 1639; afterwards a resident of Guilford, Conn.

CHOATE

In the Netherlands the name bore the prefix Van. The first seat of the family was in Essex and Suffolk counties, Eng.

JOHN, b. Eng., 1624, came from Sudbury, Suffolk, Eng. and is on record at Ipswich, Mass., 1648.

CHRISTOPHERS

CHRISTOPHER, mariner, came from Devonshire, Eng., to New London, Conn., 1667.

JEFFREY, brother of the preceding, was at New London, Conn., 1667.

RICHARD was at Boston, Mass., before 1685.

CHUBB

From Saxon *cob*, a great-headed, full-cheeked fellow.

Thomas, b. Crewkerne, Somerset, Eng., 1609, came to Boston, Mass., before 1630; removed to Dorchester, Mass., thence to Salem, Mass., 1636, later lived at Beverly, Mass.

CHUBBUCK

Thomas was at Charlestown, Mass., 1634, removed next year to Hingham, Mass.

CHURCH

A house of Christian worship, derived from old English *chirch* and Scottish *Kirk,* from Latin *circus,* the Gaelic *cearcal,* a temple, a round building. The root of church is from the Gaelic *car,* roundness, from which we have *cirke* or *kirke.*

Cornelius, married at Groton, Mass., 1670.

Garrett or Jared, b. 1611, was at Watertown, Mass., 1637.

John, at Dover, N. H., 1662, at Salisbury, Mass., 1666.

Richard, carpenter, b. Eng., came to N. E., 1630, in Winthrop's fleet; was at Weymouth, Mass.; removed to Plymouth, Mass., 1633; was at Charlestown, Mass., 1653; Hingham, Mass., 1657; Sandwich, Mass., 1664.

Richard, an original proprietor at Hartford, Conn., 1637; removed to Hadley, Mass., 1660.

CHURCHILL

This family is of ancient French lineage. In the 11th century Wandril de Leon became Lord of Coureil (now Courcelles) in the province of Lorraine, and adopted Corcil as his family name. His sons accompanied William the Conqueror to England; were granted lands in Dorsetshire, Somersetshire, Wiltshire and Shropshire.

Jeremiah married at Wethersfield, Mass., 1638.

John, b. Eng., about 1620, was resident of Plymouth, Mass., 1643.

CHURCHMAN

Humphrey was at Kittery, Maine, 1677.

Josiah married at Wethersfield, Conn., 1667.

CHUTE

Lionel, schoolmaster, was at Ipswich, Mass., 1639.

CLAFLIN

Scotch ancestry, sometimes spelled Macklotham or Maclachen.

Robert, freeman at Wenham, Mass., 1661.

CLAP or CLAPP

From Cornish British *clap*—prating, full of chat. The origin of the surname is from the personal name of Osgood Clapa, a Danish noble at the court of King Canute, 1017-36. The ancient seat of the family was Salcombe, Devonshire, Eng.

Ambrose came to Dorchester, Mass., 1636.

Edward came to N. E., 1633, made freeman, 1636.

Increase married at Barnstable, Mass., 1675.

Nicholas, brother of Ambrose, son of Richard Clap, of Dorchester, Eng., b. 1612, came to Dorchester, Mass., 1636.

Robert came from Littenham, Devonshire, Eng., to Dorchester, Mass., 1660, was at Boston, Mass., 1687.

Capt. Roger, son of William, brother of Edward, b. Salcombe Regis, 1609, came to Dorchester, Mass., 1630, removed to Boston, Mass., 1686.

Thomas, b. Eng., 1597, came to Dorchester, Mass., 1634, removed to Weymouth, Mass., 1638, later to Scituate, Mass.

CLAPHAM

Arthur was in N. H. before 1676.

Peter was at Fairfield, Conn., 1670; two years later at Norwalk, Conn.

CLARK or CLARKE

The name signifies a learned man, who could read and write ancient and medieval lore.

Arthur settled at Hampton, N. H., before 1640; made freeman in that year in Salem, Mass.; removed 1643 to Boston, Mass.

Benjamin, freeman at Medfield, Mass., 1682.

Carew, b. Bedfordshire, Eng., 1603, came to Newport, R. I., 1638; no issue.

Christopher, mariner, was at Boston, Mass., 1646.

Daniel on records of Ipswich, Mass., 1634; was at Topsfield, Mass., 1661.

Daniel, son of Joseph, b. Eng., 1622, came to N. E., 1639, with his uncle, Rev. Ephraim Hunt, settled at Windsor, Conn.

Edmund was at Gloucester, Mass., 1650.

Edward, carpenter, was at Haverhill, Mass., 1646; at Kennebunk, Maine, 1652; later at Wells, Maine.

Ephraim, freeman at Medfield, Mass., 1673.

George, carpenter and builder, came from Surrey or Kent, Eng., to N. E., 1637, settled at Milford, Conn., 1639.

George, husbandman, settled at Milford, Conn., 1639.

HENRY was at Windsor, Conn., 1640; removed to Hadley, Mass.

HUGH, b. Eng., 1613, came to Watertown, Mass., 1640; removed, 1657, to Roxbury, Mass.

JAMES, one of the first settlers at New Haven, Conn., 1637, removed before 1669 to Stratford, Conn.

JAMES, a resident of Boston, Mass., before 1646.

JEREMIAH, b. Eng., was at Portsmouth, R. I., 1640.

JOHN, freeman at Cambridge, Mass., 1632; removed, 1636, to Hartford, Conn.; later at Farmington, Conn. and in 1645 removed to Saybrook, Conn.

JOHN, b. Eng., 1612, came from Ipswich, Suffolk, Eng., 1634, to N. E.; was at New Haven, Conn., 1639; was afterwards in N. H.

JOHN, author and physician, son of Thomas of Bedfordshire, brother of Carew, came to Boston, Mass., 1637; removed following year to Newport, R. I.; no issue.

JOHN, physician, freeman at Newbury, Mass., 1639; removed to Boston, Mass., 1649.

JOHN, married at Springfield, Mass., 1647.

JOHN, a resident of Saybrook, Conn., 1640; previous to this date was at Wethersfield, Conn., later at Milford, Conn.

JOHN, carpenter at New London, Conn., removed to Norwich, Conn., 1656.

JONAS, shipmaster, b. Eng., 1619-20, was at Cambridge, Mass., 1642.

JOSEPH was at Cambridge, Mass., where he was made freeman in 1635; later removed to Windsor, Conn.

JOSEPH, b. Suffolk, Eng., settled at Dorchester, Mass., afterwards was at Dedham, Mass., where he was made freeman 1653.

JOSEPH, youngest brother of Dr. John, came to N. E., 1637, located at Boston, Mass., 1638; removed to Newport, R. I.

MALACHI was at Ipswich, Mass., 1648.

MATTHEW, mariner, was at Boston, Mass., 1656, removed, 1661, to Marblehead, Mass.

NATHANIEL, b. Eng., 1638, freeman at Newbury, Mass., 1668.

NICHOLAS arrived at Boston, Mass., 1632, removed to Hartford, Conn., 1635.

PERCY or PERCIVAL freeman at Boston, Mass., 1675.

RICHARD, early settler at Rowley, Mass., 1642.

ROBERT located at Lynn, Mass., about 1636, removed to Sandwich, Mass.

ROBERT, freeman at Stratford, Conn., 1669.

SAMUEL was at Wethersfield, Conn., removed to Stamford, Conn.; at Milford, Conn., 1669, thence he removed to Hempstead, L. I.

THADDEUS, married at Falmouth, Maine, 1663.

THOMAS, carpenter, b. Eng., 1599, came to Plymouth, Mass., 1623; was at Harwich, Mass., 1670.

THOMAS, elder brother of Dr. John, was at Newport, R. I., 1638.

THOMAS, merchant, was first at Dorchester, Mass., 1636, and in 1653 at Boston, Mass.

THOMAS, blacksmith, freeman at Boston, 1641.

THOMAS, resident of Lynn, Mass., 1640, removed to Reading, Mass., where he died 1693.

THOMAS, merchant, resident of Dorchester, Mass., before 1644.

TRISTRAM or THURSTON, b. Eng. 1594, came from Ipswich, Suffolk, Eng., to Plymouth, Mass., 1634.

WILLIAM, freeman at Ipswich, Mass., 1630.

WILLIAM, freeman at Watertown, Mass., 1631, removed to Woburn, Mass., before 1646.

LIEUT. WILLIAM, b. Plymouth, Dorsetshire, Eng., 1609, came to N. E. 1630, settled at Dorchester, Mass., before 1635; removed to Northampton, Mass., 1659.

WILLIAM, admitted freeman at Salem, Mass., 1630; kept a hotel at that place 1634.

WILLIAM, a servant of John Crow; was at Hartford, Conn., 1639; one of the first settlers of Haddam, Conn., 1662.

WILLIAM died at Yarmouth, Mass., 1668.

WILLIAM was at Boston, Mass., 1659.

WILLIAM, resident of Boston, Mass., 1661.

WILLIAM, married at Saybrook, 1678.

CLARY

JOHN, b. Eng., settled at Watertown, Mass., where he was married, 1644.

CLAWKIN

THOMAS, resident of Providence, R. I., 1645.

CLAUS or CLAWSON

Place name from a town in Germany, near Posen, from *Klause,* a mountain defile.

JOHN, resident of Providence, R. I., 1646.

STEPHEN, inhabitant of Stamford, Conn., 1670.

CLAY

Place name from town in France, also a lake on the Isle of Lewis, Scotland. *Clee* in Welsh means hills, *Cledh, cloid* and *cladd* in Gaelic, Welsh, British, signifies a ditch, a trench, a wall.

HUMPHREY, innholder in New London, Conn., 1651.

JOSEPH, married at Guilford, Conn., 1670.

THOMAS was inhabitant of Scituate, Mass., 1643.

CLAYTON

The clay-hill.

THOMAS, resident of Dover, N. H., 1650; removed to R. I. No male issue.

CLEAR

GEORGE was at Newport, R. I., 1639.

JOHN, shoemaker, resident of Boston, Mass., 1674.

CLEAVELAND or CLEVELAND

Place name from Cleveland, Yorkshire, Eng.; a corruption of Cliff-lane, so-called from it being steep and almost impassable with cliffs and rocks.

The family is descended from Thorkill, a Saxon who, at the time of the Conquest, assumed the name De Cliveland from the ancient seat of the family in Yorkshire.

MOSES, b. Ipswich, Suffolk, Eng., 1624, came as youth to N. E. 1635; admitted freeman at Woburn, Mass., 1643.

SAMUEL, brother of the preceding, was at Chelmsford, Mass., before 1681; removed to Canterbury, Conn., 1693.

CLEAVES or CLEVES

Place name; parishes of this name are found in the counties of Gloucester, Somerset and Worcester.

GEORGE, b. Eng., 1576, came from Plymouth, Devonshire, Eng., 1630, to Scarborough, Maine; two years later removed to Falmouth, Maine.

WILLIAM married at Roxbury, Mass., 1659.

WILLIAM located at Beverly, Mass., before 1676.

CLEMENT, CLEMENS

From Latin *clemens,* mild, meek, gentle.

ABRAHAM married at Newbury, Mass., 1683.

AUSTIN or AUGUSTINE, painter, came from Southampton, Eng., to N. E. 1635; located at Dorchester, Mass.

GODFREY, freeman at Watertown, Mass., 1634.

JOHN, resident of Haverhill, Mass., 1645.

ROBERT, brother of the preceding, b. Eng. about 1590; freeman at Haverhill, Mass., 1643.

SALMON married at Boston, Mass., 1660.

THOMAS, a resident of Providence, R. I., 1645.

CLEVERTON

THOMAS, freeman at Newport, R. I., 1655.

CLIFFORD

Place name, originally the name of a ford, later a town which grew up by the ford.

GEORGE, b. parish of Arnold, Nottinghamshire, Eng., resident of Boston, Mass., 1644; removed to Hampton, N. H.

JOHN, brother of the preceding, was a resident of Hampton, N. H., 1658.

CLIFT or CLIFF

Place name, a small village in Eng.; the town of the cliff.

THOMAS, Quaker, freeman of Mass., 1641; an early settler of Rehoboth, Mass., 1643; later a resident of R. I.

CLISBY or CLESBY

EZEKIEL, freeman at Boston, Mass., 1690.

JOHN, resident of Charlestown, Mass., before 1669.

CLOADE

ANDREW, wine-cooper, married at Boston, Mass., 1653.

CLOSE

THOMAS was at Greenwich, Conn., 1672.

CLOUGH or CLUFF

From Anglo-Saxon, a small valley between hills, a breach; from the participle *cleofian,* to cleave, divide.

EBENEZER was at Boston, Mass., 1690.

JOHN, tailor, b. Eng. 1613, came to Watertown, Mass., 1635; removed to Salisbury, Mass., 1639.

JOHN, resident of Charlestown, Mass., 1652.

JOHN, freeman at Hartford, Conn., 1654.

RICHARD was at Plymouth, Mass., 1634.

WILLIAM, resident of Charlestown, Mass., before 1659.

CLOUTMAN or CLOUDMAN

JOHN came from Hingham, Aberdeenshire, Scotland, to Plymouth, Mass., 1690, removed to Marblehead, Mass.

THOMAS, brother of preceding, came at same time and located as above.

CLOYES

JOHN married, resident of Watertown, Mass., 1637.

COALBORNE

NATHANIEL, freeman at Dedham, Mass., 1641.

COATES

The side, the shore, coast, border.

ROBERT, b. Eng., 1627, was at Lynn, Mass., before 1663.

THOMAS, inhabitant of Lynn, Mass., 1658.

COBB

A harbor; as the Cobb of Lyme-Regis, Dorsetshire, Eng.

AUSTIN or AUGUSTINE, inhabitant of Taunton, Mass., 1670.

EDWARD, brother of preceding, took oath of fidelity at Taunton, Mass., 1657.

HENRY, b. Kent, Eng., 1596, came to Plymouth, Mass., 1629; settled at Scituate, Mass., 1633; removed to Barnstable, Mass., 1639.

JOHN, brother of preceding, was an inhabitant of Taunton, Mass., 1659.

COBBETT

JOSIAH, b. Eng., 1614, came to N. E., 1635, settled at Cambridge, Mass., removed, 1637, to Hingham, Mass.; proprietor at Salisbury, Mass., 1640.

REV. THOMAS, b. Newbury, Bucks, Eng., 1608, came to N. E., 1637, located at Lynn, Mass.; in 1656, removed to Ipswich, Mass.

COBBLE

EDWARD, a resident of Salisbury, Mass., before 1652.

COBHAM

JOSIAH was at Salisbury, Mass., 1640; removed to Boston, Mass., 1659.

COBLEIGH

The name of Saxon origin; the first syllable is derived from the word meaning head or chief of tribe.

JOHN, shoemaker, came to Swanzey, Mass., and was an early settler of N. H.

COCHRAN

From Gaelic *cocrinn,* a point or promontory in open sight; from *Coc,* manifest, plain, and *rim,* a cape or promontory.

WILLIAM was a resident of Boston, Mass., 1684.

COCKERILL

WILLIAM was at Hingham, Mass., 1635, removed to Salem, Mass., where he died 1661.

COCKERUM

WILLIAM, mercer, b. Eng., 1609, came to Hingham, Mass., 1637.

CODDINGTON

JOHN was at Boston, Mass., 1650.

WILLIAM from Boston, Lincolnshire, Eng., came in Winthrop's fleet, 1630, to Boston, Mass.; returned to Eng. and in 1633 again came to Boston; in 1636 removed to R. I., locating at Newport.

CODMAN

ROBERT, granted land at Salem, Mass., 1637.

WILLIAM was at Portsmouth, N. H., before 1661.

CODNER

CHRISTOPHER was at Marblehead, Mass., before 1660.

EDWARD, resident of New London, 1651, removed to Saybrook, Conn., 1669.

PETER, mariner, was at Boston, Mass., before 1674.

Richard married at Swanzey, Mass., 1671.

COE

The primitive word *Co* is an elevation, exalted; *Koh* in the Coptic is a rock; *Coey,* Gaelic, a hero. John Coe, the English ancestor, b. 1340.

MATTHEW, fisherman, was at Portsmouth, N. H., 1645; removed to Gloucester, Mass., afterwards to Casco, Maine.

ROBERT, son of Henry, VIIIth generation from John, mentioned above, b. Thorpe-Morieux, Suffolk, Eng., 1596; came to Watertown, Mass., 1634; the following year removed to Wethersfield, Conn.; one of the founders of Stamford, Conn., 1640; went to Hempstead, L. I., 1652; afterwards to Newtown, L. I.; one of the founders of Jamaica, L. I., 1658.

COFFIN

In Welsh, *Cyffin,* signifies a boundary, a limit, a hill; *cefyn* the ridge of a hill. The name has its origin from *Co,* high, exalted, and *fin,* a head, extremity, boundary.

TRISTRAM, b. Buxton, Dorsetshire, Eng., came with his mother, Joanna, widow of Peter, in 1643, to Newbury, Mass.; afterwards resided at Salisbury, Mass., and in 1660 settled at Nantucket, Mass.

COGGAN or COGAN

HENRY was at Barnstable, Mass., 1639.

JOHN, merchant, was at Dorchester, Mass., 1632; later removed to Boston, Mass.

JOHN, son of Humphrey, was admitted freeman at Boston, Mass., 1642.

JOHN married at Charlestown, Mass., 1664.

COGGESHALL

An ancient English surname, derived

from town of Coggeshall, Essex, Eng. *Cog,* a small boat, and *shoal,* a place where the water is shallow. Thomas de Coggeshall was of Essex and Suffolk, Eng., 1135-54.

JOHN, mercer, b. Eng., 1581, came from Essex, Eng., in 1632, to Roxbury, Mass.; two years later he removed to Boston, Mass., and in 1637 settled at Providence, R. I.; became one of the founders of Newport, R. I.

COGSWELL (see Coggeshall)

JOHN, son of Edward, grandson of Robert, a manufacturer of woolen cloths at Westbury, Lehigh, Wiltshire, Eng., b. Westbury, 1592, came to N. E. 1635, freeman at Ipswich, Mass., 1636.

JOHN, b. Trowbridge, Eng.; was at Pascoag, R. I., 1652.

ROBERT was at New Haven, Conn., 1643, from where he removed soon after. Samuel married at Saybrook, Conn., 1668.

COIT or COYTE

A local word meaning wood.

JOHN, shipwright, b. Glamorganshire, Wales; granted land at Salem, Mass., 1638; removed to Gloucester, Mass., 1644; to New London, Conn., in 1650.

COKER

RICHARD was a resident of Hartford, Conn., 1640.

Robert came to Newbury, Mass., 1634.

COLBRON, COLBURN, COULBORNE

From Cornish-British, the dry well, or the well on the neck of the hill.

EDWARD, b. Eng., 1618, arrived at Boston, Mass., 1635; settled at Ipswich, Mass., became a pioneer settler at Chelmsford, Mass.

JOHN married at Dedham, Mass., 1672.

NATHANIEL, a proprietor at Dedham, Mass., 1637.

RICHARD was at Dorchester, Mass., 1641.

ROBERT, brother of Edward, b. Eng., 1607, came to Ipswich, Mass., 1635.

WILLIAM came to Boston, Mass., in Winthrop's fleet, and admitted freeman 1630.

COLBY

Place name from Kolbye, a town in Denmark; Coe, with or near, the *by*—town.

ANTHONY came with Winthrop from the eastern coast of Eng. to Boston, 1630; removed to Cambridge, Mass., 1632, and to Salisbury, Mass., 1634, finally to Amesbury, Mass., 1647.

ARTHUR, a brother of the preceding, was at Ipswich, Mass., 1637.

COLCORD

EDWARD, planter, b. Eng. 1617, came to Mass., 1631; removed to Dover, N. H., 1640, to Hampton, N. H., 1644, and to Saco, Maine, 1668, returning to Hampton, N. H., 1673.

COLDAM or COLDHAM

CLEMENT, miller, was at Lynn, Mass., 1630.

THOMAS, brother of the preceding, was resident of Lynn, Mass., 1630.

COLE, COALE or COALES

An abbreviation of Nicholas, common among the Dutch. Coal was an early king of Britain; gave his name to Colchester. Justice Cole lived in the reign of King Alfred.

ALEXANDER, Scotchman, was a resident of Salem, Mass., 1685.

ARTHUR died at Cambridge, Mass., 1676.

CLEMENT, b. Eng., 1615, came from London, Eng., to Boston, Mass., 1635, was granted lands at Braintree, Mass.

DANIEL, tailor, b. Eng., 1614, came to Plymouth, Mass., 1637, removed to Yarmouth, Mass., a resident of Eastham, Mass., 1643.

EDWARD was at Penaquid, Maine, 1674.

FRANCIS was at Boston, Mass., 1689.

GEORGE was at Lynn, Mass., 1637, removed to Sandwich, Mass.

GREGORY was at Portsmouth, R. I., 1655.

HENRY was at Sandwich, Mass., 1643, removed, 1646, to Middletown, Conn.

HENRY was a resident of Boston, Mass., before 1687.

ISAAC came from Sandwich, Kent, Eng., 1635, settled at Charlestown, Mass.

JACOB was a resident of Charlestown, Mass., 1669.

JAMES, tavern-keeper, b. Highgate, a suburb of London, Eng., 1600, came to Saco, Maine, 1632, following year located at Plymouth, Mass.

JAMES was at Hartford, Mass., as early as 1636.

JOB, brother of Daniel, located at Plymouth, Mass., afterwards was at Duxbury, Mass., went to Yarmouth, Mass., finally joined his brother at Eastham, Mass.

JOHN, brother of preceding, came to Mass. with brothers, but died 1637.

JOHN was resident of Boston, Mass., before 1642.

JOHN, carpenter, was at Hartford, Conn., as early as 1647.

JOHN married at Boston, Mass., 1659.

JOHN, freeman at Hadley, Mass., 1666.

JOHN, a resident of Gloucester, Mass., 1669.

JOHN, an inhabitant of Pemaquid, Maine, 1674.

NICHOLAS was a resident of Wells, Maine, 1658.

RICE or RISE, a member of the church at Boston, Mass., 1630.

ROBERT made freeman at Roxbury, Mass., 1630, removed to Salem, Mass.

SAMPSON married at Boston, Mass., 1673.

SAMUEL came in Winthrop's fleet, 1630, to Boston, Mass.; opened the first hotel of entertainment at that place.

THOMAS settled at Salem, Mass., 1634; an original proprietor of Hampton, N. H., 1638.

WILLIAM, b. Eng., 1580, was at Exeter, N. H., 1639; removed following year to Wells, Maine.

WILLIAM, a resident of Boston, Mass., before 1687.

COLEMAN

A dealer or workman in coals. Gaelic *colman*—a dove.

THOMAS came from Marlborough, Wiltshire, Eng., in 1635; made a freeman at Newbury, Mass., 1637; removed to Nantucket, Mass., 1663.

THOMAS, a resident of Wethersfield, Conn., 1639; removed, 1656, to Hadley, Mass.

COLEY or COLLEY

From Welsh *Coll-lle,* signifying the place of hazel. The Gaelic *Coille* means a wood.

SAMUEL, one of the original settlers at Milford, Conn., 1639.

COLFAX

WILLIAM, a resident of Wethersfield, Conn., 1645.

COLLAMORE or COLLEMORE

Place name from *Coulommier,* a town in France. The family came to England with William the Conqueror. *Colmar* in Gaelic—a brave man; *Collmor,* the great wood.

ANTHONY, shipmaster, b. Eng., married at Scituate, Mass., 1666; wrecked at sea 1693.

ISAAC, shipwright, granted lands at Braintree, Mass., 1638; was at Boston, Mass., two years earlier.

JAMES, resident of Salem, Mass., 1668.

PETER, uncle of Anthony, was at Scituate, Mass., 1643; no issue.

COLLAR or COLLER

JOHN, b. Eng., 1633, a resident of Cambridge, Mass., before 1661.

COLLICOTT or COLLACOT

EDWARD was at Hampton, N. H., 1642.

RICHARD, freeman at Dorchester, Mass., 1633, removed to Boston, Mass., 1656, and to Falmouth, Maine, 1669, finally to Saco, Maine.

COLLIER or COLLYER

Occupation name, a dealer or workman in coals.

JOSEPH was at Salisbury, Mass., before 1662.

THOMAS, b. Eng., 1575-76, settled at Hingham, Mass., 1635.

COLLINS

From Gaelic *Cuilein*—darling, a term of endearment applied to young animals. The Welsh word, *Collen,* signifies hazel —a hazel grove.

ABRAHAM was at Dover, N. H., 1666.

BENJAMIN was householder at Salisbury, Mass., 1668.

BENJAMIN, freeman at Lynn, Mass., 1691.

CHRISTOPHER, b. Eng., 1606, was at Boston, Mass., granted lands at Braintree, Mass., 1640, was at Saco, Maine, 1660, at Scarborough, Maine, 1664.

DANIEL, b. Eng., 1648, settled at Enfield, Conn., about 1680.

EBENEZER married at New Haven, Conn., 1683.

EDWARD, b. Eng., 1603, located at Cambridge, Mass., 1638; afterwards removed to Medford, Mass.

FRANCIS was at Salem, Mass., 1637.

HENRY, b. Eng., 1606, came to Lynn, Mass., 1635.

JOHN, shoemaker and tanner, brother of Edward, son of John of Suffolk, Eng., b. 1616, came to N. E. before 1638; was at Boston, Mass.; member of church at Braintree, Mass., 1646.

JOHN settled first at Cambridge and Watertown, Mass., afterwards at Sudbury, Mass., and was at Farmington, Mass., 1687.

SAMUEL was at New London, Conn., 1680-83; removed to Lyme, Conn.

THOMAS, merchant, at Boston, Mass., 1677.

COLMAN

EDWARD married at Boston, Mass., 1648.

JOHN, a resident of Dover, N. H., 1661.

JOSEPH, shoemaker, came from Sandwich, Kent, Eng., in 1635, to Charlestown, Mass., in 1638 was at Scituate, Mass.

WILLIAM came from Satterly, Norfolk, Eng., to Boston, Mass., 1671.

COLSON

The son of Cole (see).

ADAM, an early settler of Reading, Mass., before 1668.

NATHANIEL, resident of Newport, R. I., before 1678.

COLT or COULT

A name given to one of a sportive disposition. Sir Peter Colt, the English ancestor.

JOHN of the 5th generation from Sir Peter, b. Colchester, Essex, Eng., came to Dorchester, Mass., at the age of eleven years in 1625; removed to Hartford, Conn., 1638; afterwards resided in Windsor, Conn.

COLTMAN or COULTMAN

JOHN, schoolmaster, was a resident of Wethersfield, Conn., 1645.

COLTON

GEORGE came from Sutton, Coldfield, Warwickshire, Eng., in 1644 to Springfield, Mass., later was at Long Meadow, Mass.

COLWELL

The village on the neck of a hill, or near the hazel-wood. *Coe* Gaelic, hazel, and *ville,* a village, changed into *well.* Coldwell denotes the quality of the water. *Colwold,* the hazel-wild, or bushy place of hazels.

ROBERT, first on record at Providence, R. I., 1654, removed to L. I., 1667.

COBY, COLIE, COLEY

A little river in Devonshire, Eng.

PETER, a resident of Fairfield, Conn., 1668.

SAMUEL at Milford, Conn., 1639.

COMBS or COOMBS

The "Norman People" mentions Theobald Combs 1180-95. The name is from the Welsh *cromb,* a narrow valley.

ALLISTER was in Maine, 1665.

ANTHONY, seafaring man, French Huguenot, b. France about 1656, came to Plymouth, Mass., 1674, removed to Berwick, Maine.

HENRY was at Marblehead, Mass., 1648.

JOHN, freeman at Plymouth, Mass., 1630.

JOHN, cooper, married at Boston, Mass., 1662.

JOHN was at Northampton, Mass., before 1690, removed to Springfield, Mass., before 1714.

JOHN was resident of Sherborn, Mass., 1676.

THOMAS, inhabitant of Maine, 1665.

COMBY or COMBEE

ROBERT, resident of Boston, 1681.

COMEE, COMEY or COMEYN

The name was anciently written De Cominges; it is from Cominges, a town in France, situated on the hills near the banks of the river Garonne. De Cominges came to England with William the Conqueror.

DAVID, b. in Scotland, was at Woburn, Mass., 1663; the following year removed to Concord, Mass.

COMER

ISAAC or JOHN, resident of Weymouth, Mass., 1662.

JOHN, Baptist preacher, inhabitant of Newport, R. I., 1656.

JOHN, a resident of Boston, Mass., before 1674.

RICHARD was at Ipswich, Mass., 1651.

COMPTON

JOHN, freeman at Roxbury, Mass., 1634.

WILLIAM, bought land in Ipswich, Mass., 1662.

COMSTOCK

From Danish *kom*—a dock or harbor, and *stock,* a stick of timber. Maybe place name from Colstock or Colmstock, an ancient town of Eng., mentioned in the Domesday Book.

CHRISTOPHER was at Fairfield, Conn., 1661.

JOHN was at Weymouth, Mass., afterwards at Saybrook, Conn.

SAMUEL, a resident of Wethersfield, Conn., 1648.

WILLIAM came from Eng. to Wethersfield, Conn., 1637; later was at New London, Conn.

CONANT

Etymological research indicates the name is of Celtic origin, and is equivalent of the Welsh *Cun,* the Irish *Cean,* the Saxon *Cying,* the German *konig,* the Swedish *Konang,* the Oriental *Kahn,* all signifying head, chief, leader, or king. The family was seated at Devonshire, Eng., as early as the 14th century. The English family is traced to John Conant, who resided, in 1520, in the parish of East Budleigh, Devonshire, Eng.

CHRISTOPHER came to Plymouth, Mass., 1623, removed to Cape Ann, Mass., 1627.

ROGER, brother of Christopher, son of Richard, grandson of John, bapt. 1592, came to Plymouth, Mass., 1623; soon after removed to Nantasket (Hull), afterwards to Gloucester and Salem, Mass.

CONCKLIN or CONKLIN

From Dutch *Con*, bold, wise, knowing, and *klein*, little or son. *Konkelen*, in Dutch, signifies to plot, intrigue, conspire. *Ceangleann*, Gaelic, the head of the valley.

JOHN granted land at Salem, Mass., 1640.

CONDY or CANDY

SAMUEL was at Marblehead, Mass., 1668.

WILLIAM, shipmaster, granted land at New London, Conn., 1664, removed to Boston; captured by the Algerines, 1679.

CONE

In the Hebrew a bishop or priest; *Koen*, in Dutch, signifies bold, daring, intrepid.

DANIEL resident of Haddam, Conn., 1662.

CONEY

JAMES, inhabitant of Braintree, Mass., before 1640.

JEREMY took oath of allegiance at Exeter, N. H., 1677.

JOHN, cooper, b. Eng., was at Boston, Mass., 1633.

CONGDON

BENJAMIN came from Pembrokeshire, Wales, and is recorded at Portsmouth, R. I., 1671.

JOHN accompanied his brother, Benjamin, to N. E.

CONIGRAVE

WALTER, freeman at Warwick, R. I., 1655; afterwards a resident of Newport, R. I.

CONNER or CONNOR

The Celtic and Gaelic word *conal* signifies love, friendship.

CORNELIUS settled at Salisbury, Mass., in 1637; removed to Exeter, N. H., returned to Salisbury, 1659.

WILLIAM came to Plymouth, Mass., 1621; died before 1627.

CONNOWAY

JEREMIAH, b. 1634, was at Charlestown, Mass., 1678.

CONSTABLE

A name of office. Roger de Lacey first assumed this surname from being constable of Chester, Eng.; a commander of cavalry.

THOMAS came from Ipswich, Mass., to Boston, Mass., where he died 1650.

CONVERSE

The original seat of the family was in Navarre, France. Roger de Corgniers removed to Eng. at the close of the reign of William the Conqueror. Conyers of Horden, Durham, was knighted in 1548.

ALLEN, granted land in Salem, Mass., 1639.

DEACON EDWARD, b. Wakeley, Northamptonshire, Eng., 1590, came with Winthrop in 1630 to N. E., settled at Salem, Mass., granted land in Charlestown, Mass., 1631; one of the founders of Woburn, Mass., before 1667.

COOK or COOKE

Occupation surname.

AARON, b. Eng., 1610, settled at Dorchester, Mass., 1634; removed to Windsor, Conn., 1636, and to Northampton, Mass., 1661; was proprietor at Westfield, Mass., 1667.

CALEB married at Watertown, Mass., 1685.

ELKANAH, resident of Boston, Mass., 1658.

FRANCIS, "Mayflower" passenger, one of the first purchasers at Dartmouth, Mass., 1652, and of Middleboro, Mass., 1662.

GEORGE, b. Eng., 1610, came to Cambridge, Mass., 1635; returned to Eng., 1645.

GREGORY, shoemaker, came from Stannaway, Essex, Eng., to Cambridge, Mass., 1640, also resided at Watertown and Mendon, Mass.

HENRY, b. Eng., 1615, settled at Salem, Mass., 1638.

ISAAC married at Salem, Mass., 1664.

JOHN was at Plymouth, Mass., 1633, removed 1643 to Rehoboth, Mass., later to Warwick, R. I.

JOHN came to Salem, Mass., 1637.

JOHN, a resident of Ipswich, Mass., 1664.

JOHN, a resident of Portsmouth, R. I., 1655.

JOHN, inhabitant of Middletown, Conn.

JOHN, resident of Hampton, N. H., 1686.

JOSEPH, brother of George, b. 1608, came from Earl's Colne, Essex, to Cambridge, Mass., 1635; returned to Eng., 1658, conveying his real estate to his son, John.

JOSEPH swore allegiance at Wells, Maine, 1680.

NATHANIEL married at Windsor, Conn., 1649.

PHILIP, a freeman at Cambridge, Mass., 1647.

RALPH, a resident of Charlestown, Mass., 1640.

RICHARD, b. Eng., 1608, came to Charlestown, Mass., 1639.

RICHARD, tailor, came from Gloucestershire, Eng., to Boston, Mass., 1635.

RICHARD granted land at Norwich, Conn., 1680.

RICHARD, b. Eng., 1610, freeman at Gloucester, Mass., 1635; removed to Maine, afterwards to Dover, N. H.

ROBERT married at Portsmouth, N. H., 1678.

ROGER was at Marshfield, Mass., 1643.

SAMSON died at Gloucester, Mass., 1674.

SAMUEL, of English descent, came from Dublin, Ireland, to Cambridge, Mass., 1640.

SAMUEL, b. Yorkshire, Eng., emigrated to N. E. before reaching manhood, and was at New Haven, Conn., 1661.

STEPHEN, brother of Gregory, freeman at Mendon, Mass., 1673, removed to Watertown, Mass.

CAPT. THOMAS came from Essex, Eng., to N. E. 1635-36, locating at Boston, Mass. Original proprietor at Taunton, Mass., 1639; removed to Providence, R. I.

THOMAS, b. Eng., settled at Guilford, Conn., 1639; removed later to Hartford, Conn.

THOMAS, inhabitant of Portsmouth, R. I., 1643.

THOMAS, resident of Windsor, Conn., where he died 1697; no male issue.

WALTER settled at Weymouth, Mass., 1643, removed to Mendon, Mass., 1664.

WILLIAM, resident of Maine, 1665.

COOLEDGE or COOLIDGE

The English ancestor, Thomas Coulynge, 1495.

JOHN, son of William, of Cottenham, Cambridge, bapt. 1604, settled at Watertown, Mass., where he became freeman, 1636.

COOLEY

BENJAMIN, resident of Springfield, Mass., 1646.

HENRY, cooper, was at Boston, Mass., 1670.

JOHN settled at Ipswich, Mass., 1638, removed to Salem, Mass., where he died 1654.

PETER, freeman at Fairfield, Conn., 1664.

WILLIAM, mariner, b. 1604, came to Mass. 1634, was at New London, Conn., 1652.

COOPER

Occupation surname. The name is also local, from *Cupar*, a town in Fifeshire, Scotland, which is derived from *Cupyre*, the inclosed fire, or *Co*, high, a beacon fire; *Pyre*, a beacon fire on high, which is the origin of the word *pier*.

ANTHONY was at Hingham, Mass., 1635.

BENJAMIN, b. 1587, came from Brampton, Suffolk, Eng., to Salem, Mass., 1637

JOHN, b. Eng., 1594, came from Olney, Bucks, Eng., 1637, to Lynn, Mass., removed to Southampton, L. I., 1664.

JOHN, b. Eng., 1618, came with his stepfather, Gregory Stone, to Cambridge, Mass., about 1636.

JOHN married at Scituate, Mass., 1634.

JOHN, agent for iron works, came to New Haven, Conn., 1639.

JOHN, resident of Duxbury, Mass., 1666.

NATHANIEL, a resident of Rehoboth, Mass., 1676.

PETER, b. Eng., 1617, came to N. E. 1635, was at Rowley, Mass., 1643, afterwards at Rehoboth, Mass.

SIMON, physician, at Newport, R. I., 1663.

THOMAS came from Hingham, Eng., to Hingham, Mass., 1638; removed to Rehoboth, Mass., 1643.

THOMAS, b. Eng., 1617, came to Boston, Mass., 1635; removed to Windsor, Conn., in 1641; was at Springfield, Mass.

TIMOTHY, an inhabitant of Lynn, Mass., 1637.

TIMOTHY married at Groton, Mass., 1669.

WILLIAM sent by Mason to N. H., 1631.

COPELAND

This Scotch family has been seated at Dumfrieshire, Scotland, since the 14th century.

LAWRENCE, b. Scotland, 1599, settled at Braintree, Mass., where he was on record 1651.

COPP

From the Saxon, a hill.

WILLIAM, shoemaker, b. Eng., 1609, came to Boston, Mass., 1635, accompanied by his brother Richard.

CORBEE or CORBY

WILLIAM, early settler of Haddam, Conn,. in 1640.

CORBIN or CORBYN

Name derived from the Latin *corvus*, meaning raven or crow; it also is the name of a place in Glenceran, Scotland, signifying a steep hill; from the Gaelic *Cor-beann* or *Cor-beinn*. The family is of French-Norman descent, and the name appears in the Battle Abbey Roll at the time of the Norman Conquest.

Clement, b. Eng., 1626, came to N. E. and settled at Roxbury, Mass. He was at Woodstock, Conn., 1687.

Robert was at Casco, Maine, 1663.

COREY or CORY

From *Correy,* a town in Scotland. The word conveys the idea of roundness, bending, turning, the winding of a stream. From Gaelic *car,* Welsh *cor,* a circle, a dell, a glen; *caire,* a circular hollow, surmounted by hills.

Giles, resident of Salem, Mass., 1649.

John, resident of Chelmsford, Mass., 1691.

Thomas was at Chelmsford, Mass., 1691.

William, freeman at Portsmouth, R. I., 1658.

CORLESS or CORLISS

George, son of Thomas, b. Devonshire, Eng., about 1617, came to N. E. 1639; settled at Newbury, Mass., 1645; removed to Haverhill, Mass.

CORLET

Elijah, schoolmaster, son of Henry of London, Eng., freeman at Cambridge, Mass., 1645.

CORNELL

In the British it signifies a corner, a place shaped like a horn; from the Latin *Cornu; Corneille,* in the French, sigfies a crow.

Samuel took oath of fidelity at Dartmouth, Mass., 1684.

Thomas, b. Essex, Eng., about 1595, located at Boston, Mass., 1638; later removed to Portsmouth, R. I.

CORNELLY

William was at Duxbury, Mass., 1637.

CORNEY or CURNEY

John at Falmouth, Maine, before 1668, afterwards removed to Salem, or Gloucester, Mass.

CORNING or CORNHILL

From Welsh *Cornyn,* a small horn, or the place of winding or turning.

Samuel was at Salem, Mass., 1638, afterwards at Beverly.

Thomas, innholder at Boston, Mass., 1638; removed to R. I. thence to L. I.

CORNISH

A local name, belonging to Cornwell, Eng.

James, schoolmaster, was at Saybrook, Conn., 1659; two years later at Windsor, Conn.; in 1664 at Northampton, Mass.; removed to Westfield, Mass., and in 1678 was at Norwalk, Conn.; in 1695 finally settled at Simsbury, Conn.

Richard was in Mass., 1634, removed from Weymouth, Mass., to York, Maine, 1644.

Samuel was at Salem, Mass., 1637.

Thomas, inhabitant of Gloucester, Mass., 1641.

CORNWELL

William was at Roxbury, Mass., 1634; removed to Hartford, Conn., 1639, thence to Middletown, Conn.

CORRINGTON

John came to Mass., 1635, aged 33 years.

CORSE

From Welsh, a fen, a wet meadow; *Carse,* Armoric and Gaelic, a level tract of land.

James was at Deerfield, Mass., before 1690.

CORT

John, ship carpenter of Glamorganshire, Wales, came to N. E., 1630-38, resided at Salem, Mass., 1644; removed to Gloucester, Mass., later to New London, Conn.

CORWIN or CURWIN

George came to Salem, Mass., 1638.

Matthias, b. Eng., was at Ipswich, Mass., 1634; removed to Southold, L. I.

COSIN, COZENS or COUSINS

Abraham married at Woburn, Mass., 1684.

Edmund, resident of Boston, Mass., 1656.

Francis was at Boston, Mass., 1640.

George came from Southampton, Eng., to Boston, Mass., 1635.

Isaac from Marlborough, Wiltshire, Eng., arrived at Rowley, Mass., 1650.

John, b. Eng., 1596, was at what is now North Yarmouth, Maine, 1645; removed to York, Maine, 1675.

Richard married at Saybrook, Conn., 1678.

COSTIN or COSTING

William was at Concord, Mass., 1642; at Boston, Mass., 1654.

COTTA, COTTY or COTTEY

John, freeman at Boston, Mass., 1671.

Robert, freeman at Salem, Mass., 1635.

COTTER

William, inhabitant of New London, Conn., 1660-68.

COTTERILL or COTTRELL

A cottage or cottager.

Francis was at Wells, Maine, 1668.

Nicholas, a resident of Newport, R. I.,

1639; removed to Westerly, R. I., 1669.

ROBERT, an inhabitant of Providence, R. I., 1645.

COTTLE

EDWARD was at Nantucket, Mass., before 1670; previous to this he had lived at Salisbury, Mass.

WILLIAM, son of Edward of Salisbury, Wiltshire, Eng., b. Eng., 1626, came at age of 12 years, in 1638, to Newbury, Mass., as servant of John Saunders.

COTTON

This name affords several derivations. Welsh *Coedton,* the woody hill; *Coiton, Cuiton,* Cornish British; *Cwthen,* Welsh, the cottage hill; *Cotden,* Saxon, the cot in the valley; *Cwthen,* Welsh, the ancient cottage or dwelling.

REV. JOHN, son of Rowland, b. 1588, came to Boston, Mass., 1633.

THOMAS was at Roxbury, Mass., 1664.

WILLIAM, butcher, joined church at Gloucester, Mass., 1647; and owned lands as early as 1641.

WILLIAM was at Portsmouth, N. H., 1640.

COUCH

JOHN, freeman at York, Maine, 1652.

JOSEPH, son of William of Cornwall, Eng., came to Kittery, Maine, 1662.

ROBERT was in N. H., 1656-69.

SIMON, freeman of Fairfield, Conn., 1664.

THOMAS, resident of Wethersfield, Conn., 1666.

COUNTER

EDWARD, a resident of Salem, Mass, 1668.

COUNTS

EDWARD married at Charlestown, Mass., 1663; afterwards became a resident of Malden, Mass.

COURSER

The name is derived from the Latin *Currsr,* to run, hence runner. In middle English the word means warhorse or horse dealer. The family is of Norman origin.

ARCHELAUS was at Charlestown, Mass., 1658; afterwards at Lancaster, Mass.

WILLIAM, b. 1609, shoemaker, came to Boston, Mass., 1635.

COURTEOUS

THOMAS, freeman at York, Maine, 1652.

WILLIAM died at Newbury, Mass., 1654.

COVE

FRANCIS, a resident of Salisbury, Mass., 1650.

COVEL or COVELL

JOHN, resident of Marblehead, Mass., 1668.

PHILIP married at Malden, Mass., 1688.

COVENTRY

Place name, from city in Warwickshire, Eng.; from *Coven,* a convent, and *tre,* British, a town, the town of the convent; Welsh *Cyfaint-tre.*

JONATHAN, a resident of Marshfield, Mass., 1651.

COVEY

JAMES, granted land at Braintree, Mass., 1640.

COVINGTON

JOHN, resident of Ipswich, Mass., 1644.

COWDALL

JOHN was at Boston, Mass., 1644; freeman at Newport, R. I., 1655, and was at New London, Conn., 1659.

COWDRY

WILLIAM, b. Eng., 1602, came to Lynn, Mass., 1630; was at Weymouth, Mass., 1640; removed to Reading, Mass., 1642.

COWELL

EDWARD, cordwainer, b. Eng., 1620, resident of Boston, Mass., 1645.

EZRA, able to bear arms at Plymouth, Mass., 1643.

COWEN or COWAN

From Gaelic *Gobhainn,* a smith; *Gowan,* a Scottish word for wild flower.

JOHN, Scotchman, purchased land at Scituate, Mass., 1656.

COWLAND

RALPH, freeman at Portsmouth, R. I., 1655.

COWLES

A monk's hood or habit.

JOHN, b. Eng., 1598, settled at Hartford, Conn., 1635; removed to Farmington, Conn., 1640, and 1664 to Hadley, Mass.

ROBERT, a resident of Plymouth, Mass., 1633.

COWLEY

ABRAHAM was resident of Maine, 1656.

AMBROSE was at Boston, Mass., 1660.

HENRY, brother of preceding, inhabitant of Marblehead, Mass., 1660.

JOHN was at Ipswich, Mass., 1641.

WILLIAM, a resident of Newport, R. I., 1639.

COX or COXE

Cock, little, a term of endearment, a diminutive; the same as *at* or *kin,* used as a termination, as *Willcox,* little Will. The word is often used to denote a leader or chief man.

Edward, mariner, was at Boston, Mass., 1672.

George married at Salem, Mass., 1671.

John, resident of Boston, Mass., 1674.

John took oath of fidelity at Pemaquid, Maine, 1674.

Joseph, freeman at Boston, Mass., 1673.
Moses was at Hampton, N. H., 1639.

Richard, resident of Salem, Mass., 1645.
Robert, mariner, freeman at Boston, Mass., 1666.

COY

James was a resident of Boston, Mass., 1696.

Matthew came to Boston, Mass., 1638, aged 15 years.

Richard, brother of preceding, aged 13 years, arrived at Boston, Mass., 1638, and 1650 was a resident of Salisbury, Mass.

William, one of the first settlers at Taunton, Mass., 1637.

COYTEMORE

Thomas, merchant, was at Charlestown, Mass., 1636; freeman 1640, and was lost at sea 1645, on the coast of Spain.

CRABB

Henry married at Boston, Mass., 1658.

Richard was at Wethersfield, Conn., 1639, removed to Stamford, Conn., 1643, and 1655 to Greenwich, Conn.

CRACKBONE

Gilbert, freeman, Dorchester, Mass., 1636, removed to Cambridge, Mass., soon after.

CRADDING

William was at Taunton, Mass., 1638.

CRAFORD or CRAFFORD

John was at Dover, N. H., 1671.

Mordecai, resident of Salem, Mass., 1663.

Mungo, Scotchman, was at Boston, Mass., 1686.

Stephen, an inhabitant of Kittery, Maine, 1640.

CRAFTS

Griffin came to Roxbury, Mass., 1630.

Thomas, resident of Hadley, Mass., 1678.

CRAGGAN

John married at Woburn, Mass., 1661.

CRAM

From German *kram,* a retail dealer.

John, son of Burkhart, of New Castle-on-Tyne, Eng., b. 1607; was a proprietor at Boston, Mass., 1635; early proprietor of Exeter, N. H., 1639; removed to Hampton, N. H., 1650.

CRAMPTON or CRAMTON

Dennis married at Guilford, Conn., 1656.

John came to Norwalk, Conn., 1672; had lived at Fairfield, Conn., 1661.

CRANDALL

From Welsh *kren,* round, or *cran,* wood; and *dal* or *dol,* a vale—the round or woody vale. Crandal, in Irish, signifies the woody vale.

Rev. John, b. Eng., came to Boston, Mass., 1634-35, settled at Providence, R. I., 1637, was at Newport, R. I., 1655; removed to Westerly, R. I., 1667.

CRANE

The name dates back to the Hundred Rolls in the 13th century, when on the records William de Crane's name appears in 1272. The name is derived from town of Crannes, in Maine, a province in northern France; its root is from the Gaelic *Cran,* meaning water.

Benjamin, b. Eng., 1630, was at Medfield, Mass., 1649; removed to Wethersfield, Conn., 1655; may have lived later in life at Taunton, Mass.

Henry, tanner and currier, b. Eng., 1635, settled at Dorchester, Mass., 1658, and in Milton, Mass., 1667.

Henry, ironmaker, brother of Benjamin, b. Eng. 1621; settled at Wethersfield, Conn., 1655; was at Guilford, Conn., 1664, one of the first planters of what is now Clinton, Conn.

Jasper came to New Haven, Conn., 1639; removed to Branford, Conn., 1668.

Jonathan married at Norwich, Conn., 1680.

CRANIVER

Place name from the town of *Crans;* name of Danish leader who invaded Eng. The English ancestor Lord William Cranston. A parish in Edinburgshire, Scotland.

Gov. John, physician, first on the records of Portsmouth, R. I., 1644; removed to Newport, R. I., 1655.

Walter married at Woburn, Mass., 1683.

CRANWELL

John, freeman at Boston, Mass., 1630.

CRAPO

From French *crapaud,* a toad, an ugly man.

Peter, French descent, came to N. E., 1680; first record at Rehoboth, Mass.

CRARY

Peter settled in New London, Conn. 1663.

CRAW

ROBERT, resident of Newport, R. I., 1651.

CRAWLEY

THOMAS was at Exeter, N. H., 1651.

CREHORE

TEAGUE, of Irish origin, was at Dorchester, Mass., as early as 1650.

CRESSY or CRISSEY

From a town in France by that name.

MIGHILL, known as Michael, was at Salem, Mass., 1649; removed to Ipswich, Mass., 1660.

WILLIAM, brother of the preceding, b. Eng., 1630; settled at Stamford, Conn., 1649.

CRICK or CREEK

ANDREW died at Topsfield, Mass., 1658.

EDWARD was at Boston, Mass., 1674.

CRISP

BENJAMIN, freeman at Watertown, Mass., 1630; late in life removed to Groton, Mass.

RICHARD, merchant, married at Boston, Mass., 1666.

CRITCHLEY or CRUTCHLEY

RICHARD, blacksmith, freeman at Boston, Mass., 1642; afterwards lived at Chelsea, Mass.

CRITTENDEN

ABRAHAM came from Eng. and was one of the first settlers of Guilford, Conn.

CROADE

JOHN married at Salem, Mass., 1659.

RICHARD, merchant, son of Richard of Frampton, Dorsetshire, Eng., came to Hingham, Mass., and was at Boston, Mass., 1664.

CROCKER

A maker of coarse pottery; *Crock* signifies a large barrel shaped jar.

DANIEL married at Boston, Mass., 1660.

FRANCIS was, in 1643, at Barnstable, Mass.; of age to bear arms.

JOHN, brother of the preceding, was at Scituate, Mass., 1636, and at Braintree, Mass., 1638; removed to Barnstable, Mass.

THOMAS was at New London, Conn., 1660.

WILLIAM, brother of Francis and John, was at Scituate, Mass.; removed to Barnstable, Mass.

CROCKETT

From Danish *Kroget*—crooked, bowed, bent.

THOMAS, b. 1611, was at Little Harbor (Piscataqua), N. H., 1633-34; in 1648 was at Kittery, Maine; 1652 at York, Maine.

CROFT

Place name from a town in Eng.; a small field near a dwelling.

GEORGE was at Wickford, R. I., 1674.

THOMAS married at Hadley, Mass., 1683.

WILLIAM, a resident of Lynn, Mass., 1650.

CROMWELL

From British *crom,* crooked, and *hal* or *hayle,* low, level land bordering on the river or sea; lowlands on the bend of a river.

GILES an early settler of Newbury, Mass., before 1648.

JOHN, a resident of Boston, Mass., 1654.

PHILIP was at Dover, N. H., 1657.

SAMUEL, a freeman in Mass., 1634.

THOMAS, mariner, resident of Boston, Mass., 1646.

CROOKER

FRANCIS married at Scituate, Mass., 1647.

CROSBY

Name signifies cross-town, or town built by the cross. Ode de Crosseby was constable at Tikehall, Yorkshire, 1204. John Crosby, the English ancestor.

ANTHONY, surgeon, was at Rowley, Mass., 1643.

SIMON, b. Eng., 1608-09, came to N. E., 1634; settled at Cambridge, Mass.

THOMAS, the 5th generation from John, mentioned above, came to Cambridge, Mass., 1640; removed the next year to Rowley, Mass.

CROSCUM

GEORGE, fisherman, at Marblehead, Mass., 1653.

CROSS

A place where a cross was erected, or where two ways, roads, or streets intersected each other.

HENRY, carpenter, b. Eng., 1615, came to Mass., 1635.

JOHN, b. Eng., 1584, came to Watertown, Mass., 1634; he died 1640; left no male issue.

JOHN came to Ipswich, Mass., 1635; removed to Hampton, N. H., 1639; was at Dover, N. H., 1642; returned to Ipswich, Mass., 1652.

JOHN was at Windsor, Conn., 1645; removed to Stamford, Conn.

JOHN was resident of Wells, Maine, 1647.

JOHN, brewer, resident of Boston, Mass. 1663.

JOSEPH was at Plymouth, Mass., 1638; removed to Maine; was at Wells 1670.

ROBERT, brother of John of Ipswich, was at Ipswich, Mass., 1639.

SAMUEL was at Windsor, Conn., 1677, previously at Stamford, Conn.

WILLIAM, seafaring man, was at Wethersfield, Conn., before 1637; removed to Windsor and Fairfield, Conn., in 1649.

CROSSMAN

JOHN, b. Somersetshire, Eng., one of the early purchasers of Taunton, Mass., 1639.

CROSSTHWAYTE or CROSWAIT

CHARLES was resident of Boston, Mass., before 1671.

CROSWELL

THOMAS, a resident of Charlestown, Mass., before 1680.

CROUTCH or CROUCH

A cross from the Latin *crux.*

WILLIAM was at Charlestown, Mass., 1654.

CROW

CHRISTOPHER, freeman at Windsor, Conn., 1658.

JOHN was at Charlestown, Mass., 1635; removed, 1638, to Yarmouth, Mass.

JOHN, an original proprietor at Hartford, Conn., in 1637.

WILLIAM, came from Coventry, Eng.; was able to bear arms at Plymouth, Mass., 1643.

YELVERTON or ELVERTON was at Plymouth, Mass., and as early as 1643 had been to Yarmouth, Mass.

CROWELL (see CROW)

Place name from a town in Eng.

CROWFOOT

JOSEPH was at Springfield, Mass., 1658.

CROWTHER

JOHN sent by Mason to Portsmouth, N. H., 1631.

CUDWORTH

From *Cud* or *Coit,* a wood, and *worth,* a place, a dwelling—the farm or dwelling in the wood.

JAMES came to N. E., 1632; two years later was in Scituate, Mass., and for a few years was at Barnstable, Mass.

JONATHAN, brother of the preceding, was at Scituate, Mass., before 1667.

CULLICK

JOHN came from Felstead, Essex, Eng.; was a resident of Hartford, Conn., 1639; removed to Boston, Mass., 1659.

CULLIVER

JOHN, mariner, an inhabitant of Boston, Mass., 1655.

CULVER

The name signifies a pigeon, a dove.

EDWARD, wheelwright, was at Dedham, Mass., before 1640; removed to Roxbury, Mass.; in 1650 went to New London, Conn., and in 1662 to Mystic, Conn.

CUMMINGS

A corruption of *Comeyn,* anciently written *De Comminges.* The family is Scottish, dating back to 1080. Red Comyn or Cumin was the east lord of Badenock in Inverness-shire, Scotland.

DAVID, a resident of Dorchester, Mass., 1664.

ISAAC, b. Eng., 1601; proprietor at Ipswich, Mass., 1639; also was at Topsfield and Salem, Mass.

RICHARD was at Isle of Shoals, N. H., purchased land in Portsmouth, N. H., 1645; freeman in Mass., 1669; died at Scarborough, Maine, 1676.

CUNDY

SAMUEL was at Marblehead, Mass., 1674

CUNLIFF or CUNLITH

HENRY, freeman at Dorchester, Mass., 1644; removed to Northampton, Mass., 1659.

CUNNINGHAM

Place name from a district in Ayrshire, Scotland, signifying the dwelling of a chief or king, from the Saxon, *cyning,* Dutch *konig*—a leader or chief, and *ham,* a house or town.

ANDREW, a resident of Boston, Mass., 1684.

PATRICK, inhabitant of Springfield, Mass., before 1685.

CURNEY or CORNEY

JOHN married at Gloucester, Mass., 1670.

CURRIER

RICHARD, millwright and planter, b. Eng. or Scotland, 1616; a resident of Salisbury, Mass., 1640; removed to Amesbury, Mass., 1651.

CURTIS or CURTICE

An abbreviation of courteous. It may be for *Curthose,* a name given for wearing of short hose; or Courtors, a district in France; maybe for the polite address on whom the name was bestowed. Ancient English family appearing in the records of Kent, Eng., 1450, when Stephen Curtis and sons are mentioned.

DEODATE was at Braintree, Mass., 1643.

FRANCIS married at Plymouth, Mass., 1671.

GEORGE, freeman at Boston, Mass., 1640.

HENRY, b, Eng., 1607-08, was at Watertown, Mass., 1635; an original proprietor at Sudbury, Mass., in 1636.

HENRY, family seated in Kent, Eng., granted land at Windsor, Conn., 1645.

HENRY, a resident of Boston, Mass., 1657.

HENRY was an inhabitant of Marblehead, Mass.; went before 1674 to Pemaquid, Maine.

JOHN, from County of Sussex, Eng.; on the list of inhabitants at Roxbury, Mass., 1638; was at Wethersfield, Mass., 1639; his widow, Elizabeth, removed to Stratford, Conn., with her two sons, John and William.

JOHN settled at Scituate, Mass.; afterwards was resident of Topsfield, Mass.; no issue.

RICHARD, brother of preceding, was at Marblehead, 1648; following year removed to Scituate, Mass.

RICHARD, freeman at Dorchester, Mass., 1642.

RICHARD, resident of Salem, Mass., before 1646.

RICHARD, resident of Boston, Mass., 1657.

SAMUEL was at Northampton, Mass., 1668.

THEOPHILUS, freeman at Woburn, Mass., 1684.

THOMAS, brother of John and Richard of Scituate, Mass., was at Scituate, Mass.; removed to York, Maine.

THOMAS, an early settler of Wethersfield, Conn., before 1639; removed to Wallingford, Conn., 1670.

WILLIAM came to Roxbury, Mass., 1632.

WILLIAM, brother of John, Richard and Thomas of Scituate, Mass., came to that town, 1643.

WILLIAM, a resident of Salem, Mass., before 1658.

ZACCHEUS came from Dounton, Wiltshire, Eng., to Salem, Mass., 1635; later removed to Gloucester, Mass.

CUSHING

This patronymic is derived from the Anglo-Saxon designation of Cousin or Cussyn. The name was used in the Domesday Book in connection with the land title of Cossey, a part of a landed estate possessed by the Cushings for several generations. The family was seated at Norfolk. William Cussyn appears on the records of that county 1327. Galfudus Cushing was an early English ancestor.

DAVID was at Exeter, N. H., 1655.

MATTHEW, son of Peter of Hardingham, Eng., bapt. 1589; came from Hingham, Eng., to Hingham, Mass., 1638.

THEOPHILUS, brother of the preceding, came to Hingham, Mass., 1633; no issue.

CUSHMAN

JAMES was an inhabitant of Scituate, Mass., 1639 to 1648.

ROBERT, b. Canterbury, Eng., 1580, came to Plymouth, Mass., 1621; returned to Eng. 1625, leaving one son, Thomas, in the care of Gov. Bradford.

CUTHBERTSON

CUTHBERT, a Dutchman, came to Plymouth, Mass., 1623; died before 1633.

CUTLER

Occupation surname.

JAMES, b. Eng., 1606, came from Sprowston, a suburb of Norwich, Eng., and was one of the original grantees of land at Watertown, Mass., 1634, afterwards was at Cambridge, Mass.; 1651 at Lexington, Mass.

JOHN came from Sprowston, Eng., to Hingham, Mass., 1637; died following year, leaving 4 sons, Henry, John, Samuel and Thomas.

JOHN married at Woburn, Mass., 1650.

SAMUEL, b. 1629, was a resident of Marblehead, Mass., 1654.

Samuel, a resident of Charlestown, Mass., 1683.

CUTT or CUTTS

JOHN, merchant, son of Richard, came from Wales to Portsmouth, N. H., about 1660.

RICHARD, mariner, brother of the preceding, was at Portsmouth, N. H., as early as 1647; freeman of Mass., 1665.

ROBERT, brother of the preceding, lived at Great Island, Portsmouth, N. H.; went to Barbadoes, and in 1663 came to Kittery, Maine.

CUTTER

A boat; *Coutier,* French, a weaver, a seller of ticking.

RICHARD came with his mother Elizabeth from Newcastle-on-the-Tyne; freeman at Cambridge, Mass., 1641.

WILLIAM, brother of the preceding, freeman at Cambridge, Mass., 1637; returned to England 1648.

CUTTING

From Saxon *Cuth,* well known, famous, and *ing,* equivalent to the Latin *ens,* expressing the existence of the quality or action of the word to which it is affixed, as *Cuthing,* the son of Cuth.

JOHN was at Watertown, Mass., 1636, afterwards at Charlestown, Mass., thence removed to Newbury, Mass., 1642.

RICHARD, b. Eng., 1623, came a youth of 11 years, under care of Henry Kimball, in 1634, to Ipswich, Mass., settled in 1640 at Watertown, Mass.

DADE, DAVY, DADY or DAWDY

WILLIAM, butcher, came to Charlestown, Mass., freeman in 1633.

DAFFORNE or DAFFERN

JOHN was at Boston, Mass., in 1677.

DAGAN

RICHARD was at Scituate, Mass., in 1690.

DAGGETT or DOGGETT

Local surname, a corruption of Dowgate, one of the Roman gateways of London, from British *dow*, water, the water-gate.

JOHN, bapt. at Boxford, Suffolk, 1602, came to N. E. in 1630, made freeman at Watertown 1631, removed to Martha's Vineyard and was at Rehoboth, Mass., in 1645.

THOMAS, b. Eng., 1607, came from Norwich, Eng., 1637, as servant to Thomas Oliver, settled at Concord, Mass., removed to Marshfield, thence to Weymouth, Mass.

DAILLE

PETER, first minister of the Huguenots, was at Boston, Mass., in 1686.

DAKIN

Name of French derivation from *De Acquignay*, pronounced Akeny, Baldwin Dakeny fought at the Battle of Hastings.

THOMAS, son of John, b. Eng., 1624, was at Concord, Mass., before 1650.

DALE, DEAL, DELL

Nearly synonymous; a bushy Vale; low ground, with ground ascending around it.

JOHN was at Salem, Mass., in 1682.

ROBERT was a resident of Woburn, Mass., in 1680.

DALISSON or DALISON

GILBERT was at Milford, Mass., in 1647.

DALTON or DOLTON

This surname originally signified a farm-stead or hamlet in Eng. It means enclosure in the dale or valley. It may, however, be a corruption from Daleton, the town in the dale.

PHILEMON, linen-weaver, b. Eng., 1577, came to Watertown, Mass., 1635, removed to Dedham, Mass., in 1637 and to Hampton, N. H., in 1644, later was an inhabitant of Ipswich, Mass.

REV. TIMOTHY, elder brother of the preceding, made freeman at Dedham, Mass., 1637, removed to Hampton, N. H., 1639, descent extinct.

DAME, DAMME or DAM

JOHN came from Cheshire, Eng., in 1633 to Dover, N. H.

DAMRILL

HUMPHREY, master marine, was at Boston, Mass., in 1654.

DAMON, DAMMAN, DAMAN or DAMING

Name of French origin.

EDWARD was at Marblehead, Mass., in 1674.

JOHN came from Kent, Eng., a minor, in care of uncle, William Gilson, to Scituate, Mass., in 1643.

JOHN, bapt. in 1621, came from Reading, Berkshire, Eng., to Reading, Mass., in 1633 and was admitted freeman in 1645.

DANA

The surname from Celtic word *Dana*, bold, daring. The chosen successor of a king among the Celts was so called; a poet. Family of French descent.

RICHARD, builder, b. France in 1612, came to Cambridge, Mass., 1640.

DANE

JOHN came from Berkhamsted, Bishop's Stortford, Herts, Eng., to Roxbury, Mass., in 1636; was for a short time at Ipswich, Mass.

DANFORTH

A place name, the way or ford of the Danes, the seat of the English family is Suffolk, Eng.

NICHOLAS, son of Thomas, and of the fifth generation of William Danforth who died at Framlingham, Suffolk, Eng., in 1512, was bapt. at Framlingham in 1589, settled at Cambridge, Mass., 1634.

DANIELS

In the Hebrew language Daniel signifies the judgment of God, the *s* added being a contraction of *son*—the son of Daniel.

DANIEL was at Dover, N. H., 1661-72.

JAMES took the oath of allegiance at Exeter, N. H., 1661.

JOSEPH was at Falmouth, Maine, in 1680.

JOHN was at New London, Conn., in 1663.

RICHARD was at Billerica, Mass., in 1675, also was at Andover, Mass.

ROBERT, b. Eng., about 1590, settled at Watertown, Mass., in 1636, removed to Cambridge, Mass., in 1651.

STEPHEN was at Saybrook, Conn., 1655, removed to New Haven, Conn.

THOMAS was at Kittery, Maine, in 1652, removed to Portsmouth, N. H.

WILLIAM, b. Eng., settled in Dorchester, Mass., in 1646.

DANIELSON

SERG. JAMES, of Scotch ancestry, settled at Block Island now Shoreham, R. I., in 1688.

DARLING

A name of endearment, *ing* denoting child, progeny, offspring.

DENNIS, b. Eng., about 1640, is recorded at Braintree, Mass., in 1660, removed to Mendon, Mass., in 1677.

GEORGE, brother of the preceding, b. Eng., 1615 or 1620, settled at Salem, Mass., in 1647, afterwards lived at Lynn, 1650, and Marblehead, Mass., in 1674.

JOHN, b. about 1640, was at Braintree, Mass., 1660-70.

DARMAN

JOHN was at Braintree, Mass., before 1644.

DARROW or DARRAH

GEORGE was at New London, Conn., in 1676.

DART

A place name from a river in Eng., and a town in Scotland.

AMBROSE was at Boston, Mass., 1653.

RICHARD, b. Eng., settled in 1664 at New London, Conn.

DARVALL, DARVILL or DARVELL

ROBERT an original proprietor of Sudbury, Mass., where he died in 1662, no male issue.

WILLIAM, merchant, Boston, Mass., 1674.

DASSETT

JOHN admitted freeman at Braintree, Mass., in 1640.

DAVENPORT

A place name from Davenport, Cheshire, Eng., so called from *Dan* or *Daven,* signifying river and *port,* a haven or harbor. The family is of French lineage.

FRANCIS, mariner, was at Boston, Mass., in 1675.

HUMPHREY came from Barbadoes to Dorchester, Mass., removed to Hartford, Conn., and in 1667 to New York.

REV. JOHN, son of John, b. Coventry, Warwickshire, Eng., 1597. Came to Boston, Mass., in 1637, following year settled at New Haven, Conn.; removed to Boston, Mass., in 1669.

RICHARD came from Weymouth, Dorsetshire, Eng., in 1628 to Salem, Mass.

THOMAS was admitted to the church at Dorchester, Mass., in 1640.

DAVIES

Name of Welsh origin, first known in 1581, when Robert ap David of Grugsany assumed it.

HUMPHREY, merchant, son of Sir John Davies came from London, Eng., to Boston, Mass., was made a freeman at Billerica, Mass., in 1665, afterwards at Woburn, Mass.

JOHN was made a freeman at Boston, Mass., in 1636.

SAMUEL was at Boston, Mass., in 1668.

DAVIS or DAVIES

The name is a corruption of Davids, the son of David.

AARON resided at Newport, R. I., in 1650, was one of the proprietors at Dartmouth, Mass., in 1694.

ANTHONY, a resident of Boston, Mass., where he died in 1674.

BARNABAS, tallow chandler, b. Tewksbury, Eng., 1599, settled at Cambridge, Mass., 1635.

DANIEL, a freeman at Kittery, Maine, 1652.

DOLOR, DOLLARD or DOLLAR, master builder, came from Kent, Eng., to Cambridge, Mass., 1634, removed to Duxbury, Mass., in 1640, and was a resident of Barnstable, Mass., 1643.

EDWARD was at Boston, Mass., where he married in 1657.

EPHRAIM was at Haverhill, Mass., as early as 1660.

FRANCIS, son of Philip of Wales, b. Eng., 1620, settled at Salisbury, Mass., 1638, afterwards at Amesbury, Mass.

GEORGE, weaver and shop owner, b. Eng., name first on record in Salem, Mass., 1641, removed to Reading, Mass., in 1644.

GEORGE, blacksmith, was at Weymouth, Mass., in 1654.

GERSHOM was at Cambridge, Mass., about 1665.

HOPEWELL was at Charlestown, Mass., in 1686.

ISAAC was at Salem, Mass., in 1637, at Beverly, Mass., 1650, afterwards at Casco, Maine.

JAMES, b. Eng., 1583-88, freeman at Newbury, Mass., 1635, removed to Haverhill, Mass., in 1640.

JAMES, a freeman at Hampton, N. H., in 1638.

JAMES, mariner, was at Boston, Mass., 1634.

JAMES, tailor, was at Plymouth, Mass., in 1639.

JAMES was at Boston, Mass., in 1647.

JAMES was at Charlestown, Mass., 1658.

JAMES was at Gloucester, Mass., 1666.

JAMES was at Scituate, Mass., 1673; removed to Boston, Mass.

JOHN, joiner, was at Boston, Mass., 1635.

JOHN was at Newbury, Mass., in 1641.

JOHN was on record at Watertown, Mass., in 1642.

JOHN was at York, Maine, and made a freeman, 1652.

JOHN, tailor, was at Roxbury, Mass., in 1653.

JOHN was a resident of New London, Conn., 1651-64.

JOHN was at Charlestown, Mass., in 1668, a year later removed to Westerly, R. I.

JOHN was a resident of Lynn, Mass., in 1664.

JOHN, yeoman, b. 1612, was a resident of Newbury, Mass., in 1662.

JOHN, shoemaker and herdsman, settled at Ipswich, Mass., 1638, removed to Gloucester, Mass., afterwards returned to Ipswich.

LAWRENCE was at Falmouth, Maine, 1662, removed to Ipswich, Mass., returned to Falmouth, 1681.

NATHANIEL was at Charlestown, Mass., in 1677.

NICHOLAS, b. 1595, came to Charlestown, Mass., 1635, and settled at Woburn, Mass., in 1640.

PHILIP came as a minor from Southampton, Eng., to Newbury, Mass., afterwards removed to Hartford, Conn.; no male issue.

PHILIP was at Plymouth, Mass., in 1638; removed to Duxbury, Mass.

RICHARD was at Ipswich, Mass., in 1642.

RICHARD was married at Roxbury, Mass., about 1654.

ROBERT, b. 1608, came to Sudbury, Mass., in 1638, as servant to Peter Noyes. No male issue.

ROBERT came to Yarmouth, Mass., in 1638, recorded as able to bear arms at Barnstable, Mass., in 1643.

SAMUEL was at Watertown, Mass., removed in 1646 to Boston, Mass.

SAMUEL was a resident of Groton, Mass., as early as 1662.

SAMUEL was at Salisbury, Mass., in 1663.

STEPHEN was at Hartford, Conn., in 1646, admitted freeman of Conn., 1658.

THOMAS, sawyer, came from Marlborough, Wiltshire, Eng., in 1635 to Boston, Mass., removed to Haverhill, Mass., 1642.

TOBIAS, brother of Richard, of the same town, was at Roxbury, Mass., 1647.

TOBIAS was a freeman at Dover, N. H., 1666.

WILLIAM, apothecary, was at Boston, Mass., 1644, was at Springfield, Mass., 1645, removed to Haverhill, Mass., 1668.

WILLIAM, a brother of Tobias, of Welsh descent, b. in Wales or Eng., 1617, settled at Roxbury, Mass., 1635.

DAVOL

The name of French origin derived from Deyville, a village or district in France, anglicised form of the name David.

WILLIAM was at Duxbury, Mass., 1640, later at Braintree, Mass., in 1645 at Rehoboth, Mass., and 1650 at Newport, R. I.

DAWES

A local name from D'Awes from the river, fountain or water.

FRANCIS was at Boston, Mass., about 1659.

JOHN was an inhabitant of Windsor, Conn., 1647.

WILLIAM, bricklayer, b. Sudbury, Suffolk, Eng., came to Braintree, Mass., 1635, removed to Boston, Mass., 1652.

DAWSON

A corruption of Normandy French D'Ossone, from the town of that name in Normandy, some authoress claims it a contraction of Davison, the son of David.

DANIEL was at Ipswich, Mass., before 1693.

GEORGE, a Quaker, was at Boston, Mass., 1679.

ROBERT was at New Haven, Conn., in 1677.

DAY

Celtic and Gaelic word *deag* or *dagh*, signifies good, same meaning as *Da*, in Welsh *Dai*, *Du* in Welsh signifies dark, an allusion to complexion or color of hair. *Dhu* in Gaelic, dark color, black *Deah*, Anglo-Saxon, dark, obscure. *Dee* is the name of a small river in Wales and the name was transferred to the people living along its banks.

ANTHONY, b. Eng., 1616, was as a minor at Salem, Mass., as early as 1630. He was afterwards at Ipswich, Mass., and 1645 was a proprietor at Gloucester, Mass.

NATHANIEL was at Ipswich, Mass., 1637.

RALPH, mason, b. Eng., settled at Dedham, Mass., about 1640.

ROBERT of Welsh descent, b. Eng., 1604, came from Ipswich, Eng., to Cambridge, Mass., 1634; removed to Hartford, Conn., 1636.

ROBERT, b. Eng., 1605, came to Ipswich, Mass, 1635.

STEPHEN, originally a locksmith, became the first printer in America, came to Cambridge, Mass., 1638, in 1643 settled at Lancaster, Mass.

DAYNES, DEANS or DAINES

ABRAHAM was at New London, Conn., 1664, coming from Casco, Maine.

DAYTON

RALPH signed the Covenant at New Haven, Conn., 1639, removed to East-hampton, L. I.

SAMUEL was for a short time a resident of New Haven, Conn., 1646-55.

DEAN

Name from Latin word *Decanus* a term applied to a Roman military officer of minor rank, often spelled with a final *e*.

LIEUT. DANIEL was at Concord, Mass.

GEORGE, cord-weaver, was at Salem, Mass., 1660-86.

JAMES, blacksmith, was at Stonington, Conn., 1674.

JOHN, son of William of Chard, Somersetshire, Eng., came to Dorchester, Mass., 1636, was a proprietor at Taunton, Mass., 1639.

JONAS came from Taunton, Eng., to Scituate, Mass., 1690.

SAMUEL was at Stamford, Conn., 1650.

SAMUEL was an inhabitant of Lancaster, Mass., 1653.

STEPHEN came to Plymouth, Mass., in 1621. Built the first corn mill in N. E., 1632.

THOMAS, carpenter, b. 1603, came to Concord, Mass., 1635.

THOMAS, merchant, came from Hampshire, Eng., in 1640; returned to Eng.

THOMAS, mariner, was at Charlestown, Mass., as early as 1668.

WALTER, tanner, known as Deacon Walter, brother of John, b. Chard, near Taunton, Somersetshire, Eng., 1615-17, came to Dorchester, Mass., and was a freeman at Taunton, Mass., 1638.

DEAR or DEARE

EDWARD was at Ipswich, Mass., 1683.

PHILIP was an inhabitant of Salem, Mass., 1638.

DEARBORN

The name from the Saxon *Dear-boren,* well born.

GODFREY, b. Exeter, Devonshire, Eng., 1600, came to Mass., about 1638, and was at Exeter, N. H., in 1639, later at Hampton, N. H., 1651.

DEERING

GEORGE, planter, came to province of Maine, 1635, and was at Scarborough, Maine, 1639.

SAMUEL was at Braintree, Mass., as early as 1649.

DEATH

JOHN was at Sudbury, Mass., 1672, removed in 1678 to Sherborn, Mass.

DECKER

Name from German Decker, the quantity of ten, probably the name given to the tenth child.

JOHN was a resident of Exeter, N. H., 1672.

DELAND

JOHN was a resident of Beverly, Mass., before 1680.

DELANO

The name is derived from Lannoy, a village situated seven miles from Little France. The family is traced to Hugues de Lannoy, a knight of "Tournia d' Auelin," 1096.

PHILIP, son of Jean de Launey, b. Leyden, Holland, 1602, came to Plymouth, Mass., 1621, had land granted in Duxbury, Mass., 1624; later he removed to Bridgewater, Mass.

DELL or DILL

GEORGE, merchant, was a resident of Salem, Mass., 1639, removed to Boston, Mass., where he was admitted a freeman, 1651.

DEMING

JOHN, one of the earliest settlers at Wethersfield, Conn., 1635.

THOMAS, brother of the preceding, was at Wethersfield, Conn., at an early date, was one of the early proprietors of Farmington, Conn., 1645, finally removed to L. I.

DENISON or DENYSON

ROBERT was at Milford, Conn., 1645, went to Newark, N. J., 1667.

THOMAS was at Kittery, Maine, 1652.

WILLIAM, son of John Denyson, b. Bishop's Stortford, Hertfordshire, Eng., about 1586, came to Mass., 1631, settled at Roxbury, Mass.

DENMAN

Name derived from Welsh *Dinman,* the place of a fortress, from *din,* a fortress, and *man,* a place. The Saxon word *Denman* meant the man of the valley.

ALEXANDER was at Hampton, N. H., 1678.

JOHN was at Dorchester, Mass., 1639.

DENMARK.

PATRICK was at Dover, N. H., 1663, afterwards at Saco, Maine.

DENNEN

NICHOLAS, b. Eng., 1645, was an inhabitant of Gloucester, Mass.

WILLIAM was a proprietor at Boston, Mass., 1635.

DENNETT

The family of Norman origin. Hugh D'Anet, came to Eng. with William the Conqueror.

ALEXANDER, b. 1639, was at Portsmouth, N. H., 1670.

JOHN, carpenter, brother of the preceding, was at Portsmouth, N. H., 1670.

DENNIS

A corruption of the Greek name *Dionysius,* which is derived from two words signifying divine and mind. *Dinas,* in Welsh, a fort, a stronghold.

EDWARD was a resident of Boston, Mass., 1636.

JAMES, an inhabitant of Boston, Mass., as early as 1653.

LAWRENCE was in the Province of Maine in 1665.

ROBERT was at Yarmouth, Mass., 1643-59.

THOMAS came to Mass. in 1630, removed to N. J.

WILLIAM was at Scituate, Mass., at an early date, left no male issue.

DENSLOW

HENRY came from Dorchester, Mass., to Windsor, Conn., 1644.

JOHN resided at Windsor, Conn., was made freeman 1657.

NICHOLAS was at Dorchester, Mass., 1630, removed in 1640 to Windsor, Conn.

DENTON

A Saxon place name from a town in Buckingham, Eng., derived from *den,* a valley, and *ton,* a town.

REV. RICHARD came to N. E. 1638, was at Wethersfield, Conn., 1640, removed in 1644 to Stamford, Conn., later to Hempstead, L. I.

DERBY, DARBY or DORBY

From Derby, Eng., name derived from *Deer-by,* town or country abounding with deer.

EDWARD came from Bisley, Surrey, Eng., 1650, was at Weymouth, Mass., 1650, afterwards at Braintree, Mass., finally removing to Boston, Mass.

FRANCIS was at Warwick, R. I., before 1663.

JOHN, son of Christopher, came from Dorsetshire, Eng., proprietor at Plymouth, Mass., 1647, removed to Yarmouth, Mass., before 1643.

RICHARD, brother of the preceding, was at Plymouth, Mass., 1637.

ROGER, shopkeeper, came from Topsham, Devonshire, Eng., accompanied by his brother, John, to Ipswich, Mass.

DERING or DEERING

The name from a Saxon word *Dearran* or *Darran,* to dare, bold, daring, a name given to an old Saxon chieftain.

HENRY was at Boston, Mass., 1663.

DESHON or DESHORN

A local name from *Dijon,* a French town. The family is of French Huguenot descent.

DANIEL came from France to Oxford, Mass., 1686, soon afterwards removed to New London, Conn.

DEVELL or DEVILLE

From the French *De Ville,* from the village or town.

WILLIAM was at Braintree, Mass., in 1643, a freeman at Newport, R. I., 1655.

DEVEREAUX

A place name from *Evereaux,* a town in Normandy, France.

JOHN came to Salem, Mass., 1630, a youth of sixteen; was at Marblehead, Mass., 1648.

DEVOTION

EDWARD joined the church at what is now Brookline, Mass., 1645.

DEW or DUE

AMBROSE, cord-weaver, was at Boston, Mass., 1645.

THOMAS was an inhabitant of Marblehead, Mass., 1668.

DEWER

THOMAS, tailor, was a resident of Boston, Mass., 1652.

DEWEY

In the Welsh language *Dewi* is a corruption of David.

THOMAS came from Sandwich, Kent, Eng., and was one of the original grantees of Dorchester, Mass., 1633. He removed to Windsor, Conn., 1635.

DEWING or DEWON

ANDREW b. Eng., was at Dedham, Mass., 1644.

DE WOLF

The family originally Scotch, immigrated to Germany.

Balthazar is on record at Hartford, Conn., 1656; removed to Lyme, Conn., 1668.

DEXTER

Place name from Exeter, Eng., a contraction of *De Exeter,* from *Exe,* a name of a river, and *cester,* a camp, a town, anciently written Excester.

Family descended from Richard de Excester, Lord Justice of Ireland.

Rev. Gregory, b. Olney, Northamptonshire, Eng., 1610, came to N. E. in 1644, locating at Providence and Warwick, R. I.

Richard b. Eng., about 1606, from the county of Meath, Ireland, and admitted freeman at Boston, Mass., 1642, two years later removed to Charlestown, Mass.

Thomas came to Lynn, Mass., 1630 and 1637 removed to Sandwich, Mass., and 1646 to Barnstable, Mass.

DIBBLE, DEEBLE

John was at Springfield, Mass., in 1641.

Robert came from Weymouth, Eng., to Dorchester, Mass., 1634.

DICKERMAN

Name of German origin compounded of two words, *dick* or *dicker,* and *mann,* meaning "stout man."

Thomas, tailor, settled in Dorchester, Mass., 1636.

DICKERSON

The family of Norwegian origin, the early known ancestor Ivar in 725, Walter De Caen, later De Kenson was a follower of William the Conqueror.

John was a resident of Salisbury, Mass., 1640.

Nathaniel, son of William of the XVth generation from Walter De Kenson anglicized to Dickerson, b. Ely, Cambridge, Eng., 1600, came to Watertown, Mass., 1634, removed to Wethersfield, Conn., 1636-37 and 1659 to Hadley, Mass.

Philemon, tanner, granted lands at Salem, Mass., 1639, removed to Southhold, L. I., recorded as a freeman of Conn., 1662.

Thomas was an inhabitant of New Haven, Conn., in 1642, later removed to Fairfield, Conn.

Thomas was on record at Rowley, Mass., 1643.

DICKSON

The son of Dick or Richard.

William, of Scotch ancestry, was made a freeman at Cambridge, Mass., 1642.

DIKE

Abraham was an inhabitant of Dorchester, Mass., before 1656.

Anthony b. in Eng., settled at Plymouth, Mass., 1623.

Richard married at Gloucester, Mass., 1667.

DILLINGHAM

A place name in Cambridge, Eng., from the Saxon *Daelan,* to divide, separate, and *ham,* a village. Ancient English family.

Edward came from Bitteswell, Leicestershire, Eng., to Lynn, Mass., 1630, removed to Sandwich, Mass., 1637.

John, brother of the preceding, came to Boston, Mass., 1630, shortly afterwards to Ipswich, Mass.

DIMAN

John, ropemaker, was at Lynn, Mass., 1647, removed to Kittery, Maine, 1652.

John was at New London, Conn., 1674.

Thomas was at Fairfield, Conn., where he died 1658.

DIMOCK

The name originates with the Welsh, a corruption of Dia Madoc, that is David, the son of Madoc. Dia being the diminutive of David; Madoc is derived from Mad, good, with the termination oc affixed.

Elder Thomas b. Eng., settled at Dorchester, Mass., 1635, removed to Hingham, Mass., 1638, the next year to Scituate, Mass., and in 1640 was one of the founders of Barnstable, Mass.

DINELY or DYNELEY

William, barber surgeon, was a resident of Boston, Mass., 1635.

DINGLEY

John was at Lynn, Mass., removed to Sandwich, Mass., 1637, thence 1644 to Marshfield, Mass.

DINMAN, DIMAN or DIMOND

Thomas was an early settler at Farmington, Conn., removed to Easthampton, L. I.

DISBROW

Peter came from Eng., 1660, one of the first and principal proprietors of Rye, N. Y. in 1665, removed to Stamford, Conn.

DIVEN

John was an inhabitant of Lynn, Mass., 1643.

DIX

The name as Dicks or Dickens, the S being a contraction of son—the son of Dick or Richard.

ANTHONY was one of the first comers being at Plymouth, Mass., in 1623, afterwards at Charlestown and Salem, Mass.

EDWARD came in Winthrop's fleet to Boston, Mass., in 1630.

JOHN an inhabitant of Taunton, Mass., in 1669.

LEONARD b. 1624 was at Wethersfield, Conn., in 1645, granted land at Branford, Conn., 1648; his brother John settled at Hartford, Conn.

RALPH, fisherman, was at Ipswich, Mass., 1647.

RALPH was a freeman at Malden, Mass., 1685; previous to this he was living at Reading, Mass.

SAMUEL b. Eng., 1594, came from Norwich, Eng., to Boston, Mass., 1637.

DIXIE or DIXEY

From the Saxon *Dic,* a ditch, dike, and *ea,* water, or *ig,* an island.

JOHN was at Salem, Mass., 1639.

THOMAS was a resident of Salem, 1637, and was at Marblehead, Mass., 1674.

WILLIAM came to Cape Ann, 1629, afterwards at Lynn, Mass.

DIXON

JEREMIAH was one of the seven founders of the Church at New Haven, Conn., 1639.

WILLIAM was a resident of Charlestown, Mass., 1633-38, a freeman at Kittery, Maine, 1649, afterwards at York, Maine.

DIXWELL

JOHN, one of the regicides, came to New Haven, Conn., 1664.

DOANE

HENRY was at Watertown, Mass., 1643.

DEACON JOHN came from Eng., to Plymouth, Mass., 1630, removed to Eastham, Mass., 1644.

DOBLE

TOBIAS was a resident of Boston, Mass., where he died 1670.

DODD OR DOD

In Gaelic the word *Dod* signifies "the pet;" peevishness; in German, a godfather.

DANIEL was at Bradford, Conn., 1644.

GEORGE, mariner, was an inhabitant of Boston, Mass., 1645.

THOMAS was at Marblehead, Mass., 1674.

WILLIAM was a resident of Salem, Mass., 1644.

DODGE

To evade by a sudden shift of place; one who evades, or quibbles. The family is of Ancient English origin, in 1306 Peter Dodge of Stockworth, County of Chester, Eng., was granted a coat of arms.

RICHARD, son of John of East Coker, Somersetshire, Eng., b. 1602, settled at Salem, Mass., 1638, in 1667 was one of the founders of Beverly, Mass.

TRISTRAM came from Suffolk, Eng., to Newfoundland in 1647, later to Mass., was one of the original settlers in 1661 of Block Island, R. I.

WILLIAM, husbandman, brother of Richard, settled at Salem, Mass., 1629; he resided in Beverly, Mass., 1637.

DODSON

The son of Dod.

ANTHONY was at Scituate, Mass., 1650.

DOE

An ancient English surname.

NICHOLAS came from Eng., to Oyster Bay, now Durham, N. H., where he was a taxpayer in 1667.

DOLE

The name is of French origin, written De Dole, a town in France.

Dowyll in Welsh signifies shady, dark.

GEORGE was at Lynn, Mass., removed to Sandwich, Mass., 1637.

RICHARD, son of William, a tanner and grandson of Richard in Thornbury, Gloucestershire, Eng., was bapt. at Ringworth, Gloucestershire, in 1622, he came in 1639 to Newbury, Mass., apprenticed to John Towle, a glover, he late in life removed to Rowley, Mass.

DOLIBER or DOLIVER

The name is of Welsh origin from *Dollyr,* the short vale; from *dol,* a dell, a valley, and *lyr,* short. Dalbyr is a town in Jutland, where the family may have originated.

JOSEPH was an inhabitant of Salem, Mass., 1648.

SAMUEL, yeoman, son of Robert, bapt. at Stoke Abbott, Dorsetshire, Eng., 1608, was at Marblehead, Mass., 1642, removed to Gloucester, Mass., 1652.

DONNELL or DUNNELL

HENRY was a freeman at Kittery, Maine, 1652, removed to Falmouth, Maine.

DOOLITTLE

ABRAHAM b. Eng., 1619, was at Boston, Mass., 1640, settled at New Haven, 1644, removed to Wallingford, Conn., 1670.

JOHN was at Lynn, Mass., 1643, removed to what is now Chelsea, Mass., where he was constable in 1653.

DORCHESTER

ANTHONY settled at Hingham, Mass., removed to Windsor, Conn., and was at Springfield, Mass., in 1649.

DORMAN

EDWARD was at New Haven, Conn., 1657.

THOMAS was a freeman at Ipswich, Mass., 1635, removed to Rowley, Mass., and died at Topsfield, Mass.

DORR

In Gaelic, *Dorr* is difficult, easily vexed, and in the same language, persevering, earnest, obstinate. In Icelandic, *Dorr* signifies a spear, in Cornish British, *dor* is earth; also *dorre* to break; in Welsh, *dar* is oak.

EDWARD was at Roxbury, Mass., prior to 1674.

DORYFALL or DORIFIELD

BARNABY came to Boston, Mass., 1633, admitted freeman 1636, afterwards lived at Braintree, Mass.

DOTEY or DOTEN

From the Welsh *Diotty,* an ale house.

EDWARD, "Mayflower" passenger, a London youth, b. Eng., came to America as a servant of Stephen Hopkins, afterwards removed to Yarmouth, Mass.

DOUBLEDAY

ROGER, currier, was at Boston, Mass., 1674.

DOUGHTY

FRANCIS was at Taunton, Mass., 1639, removed to L. I. 1641.

JAMES was at Scituate, Mass., 1649.

DOUGLAS or DOUGLASS

A river of Scotland, town of Lanarkshire, from the Gaelic word *Dhu,* black, dark, and glass.

DEACON WILLIAM, son of Robert, cooper, b. Scotland, 1610, located in 1640 at Gloucester, Mass., in 1645 at Boston, Mass., and 1659 removed to New London, Conn.

DOVE

MATTHEW was at Salem, Mass., 1654.

DOW

The name first appears in the Hundred Roll of the 13th century.

John Dow was the English ancestor in 1584.

FRANCIS came from Salisbury, Wiltshire, Eng., to Salisbury, Mass., before 1650.

HENRY, husbandman, son of Henry and of the fourth generation from John Dow of Tylner, Norfolk, Eng., where he died in 1651, b. Runham, Eng., 1608, settled at Watertown, Mass., 1637, removed to Hampden, N. H., 1644.

JOHN was a freeman at Haverhill, Mass., 1668.

ROBERT was at Salisbury, Mass., before 1676.

SAMUEL was at Hartford, Conn., prior to 1665.

THOMAS a freeman at Newbury, Mass. 1642, removed to Haverhill, Mass. 1654.

DOWD, DOWDE, DOWDY

HENRY came from Surrey or Kent Eng., in 1639 to Guilford, Conn.

DOWDEN

LEONARD was at Boston, Mass., 1679.

DOWNAM

DEERMAN was at Braintree, Mass., 1646.

JOHN, brother of the preceding, was at Boston, Mass., 1645.

DOWNE or DOWNES

A term applied in Eng., to a tract of poor, sandy hill land, used only for pasturing sheep.

JOHN, was a miner at New Haven, Conn., 1648, became a freeman in 1654.

JOHN was at Boston, Mass., before 1657.

ROBERT was an inhabitant of Milford, Conn., 1660.

THOMAS b. Eng., 1610, came to Boston, Mass., 1635, was at Dover, N. H., 1657.

WILLIAM was in Mass., 1635.

DOWNER

JOSEPH was at Newbury, Mass., 1660.

DOWNING

BENJAMIN took oath of allegiance at Hatfield, Mass., 1679.

DENNIS settled at Kittery, Maine, 1652.

EMANUEL, son of Rev. Emanuel of Ireland, lawyer, came from London, Eng., to Salem, Mass., made freeman 1639.

JOHN was at Charlestown, Mass., before 1659.

MALEDON of Scotch descent, resided in Lynn, Mass., 1642.

THEOPHILUS, fisherman, granted lands at Salem, Mass., 1642.

DOWNTON

WILLIAM was a freeman at Salem, Mass., 1668.

DOWSE

FRANCIS in the employment of George Burden came to Boston, Mass. in 1640, next year made freeman, removed to Charlestown, Mass.

LAWRENCE, carpenter, was an inhabitant of Boston, Mass., 1644, afterwards lived at Charlestown, Mass.

LODORWICK was at Sherborn, Mass., prior to 1683.

SAMUEL was at Portsmouth, N. H., 1689.

DOXY

THOMAS was among the early planters in 1650 at New London, Conn.

DRAKE

From the Gaelic *drak,* a drake, *drac,* a route, a way, a foot-step; one who draws or leads, a leader.

A Saxon family established before the Conquest and was located in what is now the Manor of Masbury, Axminster, Devonshire, Eng.; the location became known as Mount Drake. In the Dooms Day Book, six places are in the possession of persons of this name. John Drake lived at Exmouth, Eng., in 1360.

FRANCIS, surveyor, was at Portsmouth, R. I. in 1661, soon afterwards removed to N. J.

JOHN, son of William, 9th generation from John, mentioned, b. Wiscomb, Eng., 1600, came to Boston, Mass., in 1630, removed to Windsor, Conn., before 1639.

ROBERT, b. Devonshire, Eng., 1580, came to Exeter, N. H. before 1643, removed to Hampton, N. H., 1651.

SAMUEL was at Fairfield, Conn., 1650, removed to East Chester, Conn., 1665.

THOMAS, bapt. 1635 at St. Andrew's Church, Colyton, Devonshire, Eng., came for Weymouth, Mass., about 1654.

DRAKELEY

THOMAS came from Stratford, Conn. to Woodbury, Conn., 1682.

DRAPER

One who sells cloth.

JAMES, son of Thomas, b. Heptinstall, Yorkshire, Eng., 1618, was a proprietor at Roxbury, Mass., 1640, was at Lancaster, Mass., 1654, and a resident of Dedham, Mass., 1683.

ROGER, b. Eng., was a freeman at Concord, Mass., 1639.

DRAYTON

HENRY is recorded as able to bear arms at Marshfield, Mass., 1643.

JOHN was a farmer in Maine in 1642.

DRECKAN

NICHOLAS came to Salem, Mass., 1660.

DRESSER

JOHN was an inhabitant of Rowley, Mass., 1643.

SAMUEL was at Salem, Mass., in 1638.

DREW or DRUCE

JOHN, son of William, grandson of Sir Edward Drew, who was knighted 1589 by Queen Elizabeth, appears on records of Plymouth, Mass., 1660-73.

DRING

THOMAS first recorded at Little Compton, R. I., 1696.

DRINKER

PHILIP b. 1596, came from Eng., to Charlestown, Mass.

DRIVER

One who compels or urges anything else to move.

ROBERT came to Lynn, Mass., 1630, made a freeman in 1635.

DROWNE

LEONARD, shipwright, came from West of Eng., as early as 1680 to Kittery, Maine, removed to Boston, Mass., 1692.

DRUMMOND

JOHN was a resident of Boston, Mass., 1661.

DRURY

GEORGE b. 1616, came to N. E. in 1635.

HUGH, carpenter, b. Eng., was at Salisbury, Mass., 1641, removed to Boston, Mass., 1646.

DUDLEY

Place name from a town in Worcestershire, Eng., so called from the old English *Dode-ley,* the place of the dead, a burying ground. *Dodelig* in Danish signifies pale, death-like, mortal, so also the Dutch *Doodelijk* and German *Todlich: Duv-da-lethe* in the Gaelic and Celtic has the same signification.

Hugh de Suttin was the progenitor of the barons of Dudley.

FRANCIS b. about 1640, settled at Concord, Mass., 1663.

HUGH was in the employ of William Pynchon at Springfield, Mass., 1656.

THOMAS, son of Capt. Roger, b. Northamptonshire, Eng., 1575, came in Winthrop's fleet in 1630, after living a short time at Cambridge and Ipswich, settled at Roxbury, Mass.

WILLIAM, b. Richmond, Surrey, Eng., came to Guilford, Conn., 1639.

DUDSON

FRANCIS was resident of Boston, Mass., 1675.

JOSEPH was at Boston, Mass., 1669.

DUGALL or DOUGALL

ALISTER, a Scotch prisoner, sent over by Cromwell in 1650.

DUMBLETON

JOHN, a servant of William Whiting,

of Hartford, Conn., was at Springfield, Mass., in 1649.

DUMMER

From the Danish *Dommer,* an arbiter or judge.

RICHARD b. Bishopstoke, Hants, Eng., came to Boston, Mass., 1632, settled at Roxbury, Mass., 1636 and later removed to Newbury, Mass.

STEPHEN, brother of the preceding, came to Mass., 1638, returned to Eng., 1647, leaving in America no male issue.

THOMAS, brother of the preceding, came to Mass., 1638, settled at Salisbury, Mass., left no male issue.

DUNBAR

Place name from Danbar at the mouth of Firth of Forth, Scotland; *Dunabar,* Gaelic, signifies castle, town, or fort on the height or summit. The family traces its Scotch lineage to George, earl of Danbar. The Danbars of George Hill of Scotland were founded in 1575.

PETER was at Hingham, Mass., before 1691.

ROBERT, son of Ninian of George Hill, Scotland, was b. 1630, settled at Hingham, Mass., before 1655.

DUNCAN

A powerful chieftain; from the Gaelic *Dun,* a fortress, and *ceann,* head or chief. *Duncean* or Duncan, strong-headed.

CAPT. NATHANIEL, b. Eng., came to Dorchester, Mass., 1630.

DUNCKLEE

ELNATHAN was resident of Dedham, Mass., where he died in 1669.

DUNHAM

A place name from a small village in Eng., *dun,* a hill, and *ham* a village. Rychet Dunham is on record at Devonshire, Eng., 1294, owning a large estate at Beaminster, Somersetshire, Eng.

BENAIAH was an inhabitant of Eastham, Mass., 1660.

BENJAMIN, brother of the preceding, was also a resident of Eastham, Mass., in 1660.

JOHN, b. Eng., 1589, came from Lancashire, Eng., to Plymouth, Mass., 1630-31.

JONATHAN was at Barnstable, Mass., about 1655.

JOSEPH was at Plymouth, Mass., in 1659.

DUNK or DUNCK

THOMAS came from Kent, Eng., in 1645 to Guilford, Conn., was at Saybrook, Conn., 1662.

DUNKIN

JOHN was at Billerica, Mass., 1675.

SAMUEL a resident of Newbury, Mass., 1638, afterwards removed to Boston, Mass.

DUNN

From Gaelic *Dun,* a heap, a hill mount, a castle, tower, also Saxon *Dunn,* brown, of a dark color, swarthy.

RICHARD was a freeman at Newport, R. I. 1655, removed to Westerly, R. I., 1661.

THOMAS, freeman of Mass., 1647, removed to Rehoboth, Mass., at New Haven, Conn., 1648, afterwards at Fairfield, Conn., left no male issue.

DUNNING

The brown offspring; from the Saxon *Dunn,* brown; termination *ing* means offspring. *Dunning* has retained its original orthography since the days of the Saxon.

GEORGE was for a short time in 1644 at New Haven, Conn.

HICKS was an inhabitant of Hingham, Mass., prior to 1669.

DUNSTER

The name is of Saxon origin, signifying a dweller upon a *dun,* down, or little hill. There is a market-town and castle by the name in Somersetshire, Eng. The parish records of Middleston record in 1543, Hugh Dunster.

REV. HENRY, son of Henry of Barry Lancashire, Eng., came to Boston, Mass., 1640, afterwards removed to Scituate, Mass.

RICHARD, brother of the preceding, was at Cambridge, Mass., 1642.

DUNTON

NATHANIEL was at Reading, Mass., 1647.

SAMUEL, brother of the preceding, b. Eng., 1620, settled at Reading, Mass., before 1644.

DURAND

JOHN was at Scituate, Mass., 1659.

JOHN, physician, of Huguenot descent, settled at Derby, Conn., 1685; he was for a time at Stratford, Conn.

DURANT

From the Latin word *Durandus,* enduring, strong, from *duro,* to harden, to inure to hardships.

GEORGE was at Malden, Mass., 1662, removed in 1666 to Middletown, Conn.

DUREN

ANDREW was at Dedham, Mass.
GEORGE was at Lyme, Conn., 1685.

DURFEE

THOMAS b. Eng., 1643, came to Portsmouth, R. I., 1660.

DURGIN

JOHN was at Ipswich, Mass., prior to 1689.

WILLIAM was at Dover, N. H., 1664, was for a time at Ipswich, Mass.

DURHAM

A local name derived from the Saxon *Dun* and *holm,* a town in a wood, or from the British *Dour,* water, *holm,* land surrounded mostly by water.

HUMPHREY was at Casco, Maine, 1658, killed by the Indians in 1676.

THOMAS was at Marshfield, Mass., 1659.

DURREN or DURRUM

EPHRAIM was at Guilford, Conn., 1672.

DURRELL

PHILIP, of French descent, came from Isle of Guernsey, Eng., to Exeter, N. H., 1675, removed to Kennebunkport, Maine, 1700.

DUSTON

For Welsh *Dysdain,* a steward of a feast.

JOSIAH was at Reading, Mass., 1647.

THOMAS was at Dover, N. H., 1640, removed to Kittery, Maine.

DUTCH

Osman or Osmyn was admitted an inhabitant of Newport, R. I., 1638, was at Gloucester, Mass., 1646.

ROBERT was at Gloucester, Mass., prior 1646.

THOMAS was at Edgartown, Mass., 1654.

DUTTON

Place name from a village in Cheshire, Eng., has several derivations. *Dut-ton,* Dutch-town. *Duton* from *Du,* Cornish British, side, and *ton,* the same as *dun,* a hill, *Dhu-ton,* Gaelic and Welsh, the black hill. Hodard was the progenitor of the family in reign of William the Conqueror.

JOHN b. Eng., came to N. E. 1630, became identified with Reading, Mass.

DUTY

WILLIAM was at Rowley, Mass., 1691.

DWELLEY

RICHARD was first at Watertown, Mass., lived some years at Hingham, Mass., was at Lancaster, Mass., 1654 and at Scituate, Mass., 1663.

DWIGHT

A place name from Saxon word *thwarte,* meaning a clearing in the forest.

JOHN b. Eng., came from Dedham, Eng., to Dedham, Mass., 1635.

TIMOTHY, brother of the preceding, b. Eng., came as a young man to Dedham, Mass., was at Hampton, N. H., 1640, resided many years at Medfield, Mass.

DWINNELL

MICHAEL, of Scotch ancestry of French origin, was at Topsfield, Mass., 1668.

DYER

Occupation name, one who dyes cloth.

GEORGE settled at Dorchester, Mass., 1630.

GILES was a resident of Boston, Mass., 1680.

JOHN b. 1607, came to N. E., 1635, was at New London, Conn., before 1650, soon afterwards went to L. I.

DEACON THOMAS, cloth-worker, b. Eng., 1611-12, came to Weymouth, Mass., 1632.

WILLIAM, milliner from London, Eng., came to Boston, Mass., 1635. He removed to Portsmouth, R. I., 1638, and was one of the eight signers to the Compact of Newport, R. I. in 1639.

WILLIAM was in 1665 an early settler of Sheepscott, Maine.

WILLIAM was at Barnstable, Mass., as early as 1686.

WILLIAM was an inhabitant of Lynn, Mass., prior to 1673.

DYMOKE

ELDER THOMAS Dymoke, came from Pinchback, Eng., to Dorchester, Mass., 1635, removed to Hingham, Mass., 1638, and a year later to Barnstable, Mass.

EAMES or EMMES

CAPT. ANTHONY, b. Dorsetshire, Eng., 1595, was a proprietor of Charlestown, Mass., 1634, two years later removed to Hingham, Mass., and 1650 to Marshfield, Mass.

GERSHAM was at Marlborough, Mass., before 1671, died at Watertown, Mass., 1676. No male issue.

HENRY was a freeman at Boston, Mass., 1684.

JOHN was a resident of Woburn, Mass., before 1690.

ROBERT was at Charlestown, Mass., 1651, taxed at Woburn, Mass., 1666.

THOMAS, brickmaker and Mason, b. Eng., about 1618, came from Stratford-on-Avon, Eng., 1630, resided at Dedham, Mass., 1630. Afterwards at Medford, Cambridge, Sudbury, and what is now Framingham, Mass.

EARLE

RALPH b. Eng., 1606, was at Newport, R. I., 1638, at Portsmouth, R. I., 1649, in 1686 was one of the townsmen of Dartmouth, Mass.

ROBERT came to N. E. in 1634, located at Newport, R. I.

EAST

FRANKLIN, carpenter, freeman at Boston, Mass., 1637.

WILLIAM was at Milford, Conn., 1639, no male issue.

EASTMAN

The surname is synonymous with Easterling. A native of Hansetown of the east of Germany was known as "easterling."

ROGER, house carpenter, son of John of Romsey, Hampshire, Eng., b. Wales, 1611, came from Langford, Wiltshire, Eng., 1638, granted lands at Salisbury, Mass., 1640-43.

EASTERBROOK

THOMAS b. Enfield, Middlesex, Eng., settled at Concord, Mass., 1660.

EASTON

JOSEPH b. Eng., about 1602, came to N. E. 1634, made freeman at Cambridge, Mass., 1635, removed to Hartford, Conn., with Hooker's colony in 1636.

NICHOLAS, tanner, came from Wales in 1634, was one of the earliest settlers of Ipswich, Mass., the next year removed to Newbury, Mass., and 1638 to R. I.

WILLIAM made freeman in Newbury, 1633, in that year removed to Hampton, N. H., no male issue.

EASTY or ESTY

JEFFREY, land granted at Salem, Mass., 1637.

EATON

Surname of Welsh and Saxon origin, in Welsh *au* means water, *tayn* a small hill. *Autyn* called Eyton, a small hillock near the water. In Saxon *ea* means water and *ton*, town. There are several parishes of that name in Eng. The English family trace their ancestry to Bangue Thane of Lochabar, 1000.

FRANCIS, Mayflower passenger, carpenter, removed to Duxbury, Mass., 1633.

JOHN, bapt. Eng., 1611, came to N. E., 1635, made freeman at Watertown, Mass., 1636, same year removed to Dedham, Mass.

JOHN, manufacturer of stoves, on record at Salisbury, Mass., 1639, removed to Haverhill, Mass., 1646.

JONAS, son of Peter, brother of William, settled as early as 1637 at Watertown, Mass., removed to Reading, Mass., 1647.

PETER, son of William, XX generation from Bangue, settled at Watertown, Mass., 1637, removed to Reading, Mass., 1644.

THEOPHILUS, son of Richard, vicar of Great Badworth, Cheshire, b. Stony Stratford, Bucks, Eng., came in 1637 to Boston, Mass., and in 1638 removed to New Haven, Conn.

THOMAS was at Haverhill, Mass., before 1659.

THOMAS, an inhabitant of Reading, Mass., 1659.

THOMAS, a freeman at Dedham, Mass., 1681.

WILLIAM, husbandman, b. Eng., 1604, brother of Peter, came from Staples, Kent, Eng., to Watertown, Mass., 1637, removed to Reading, Mass., 1644.

EAYRS

MOSES, b. Eng., about 1640, lived at Boston and Dorchester, Mass., supposed to be a relative of Rev. Simon Eayrs, who settled at Watertown, Mass., 1635.

EBORNE or EBURNE

THOMAS, tanner, was a freeman at Salem, Mass., 1634.

ECCLES

A church from a Greek word signifying an assembly, a church.

RICHARD, freeman at Cambridge, Mass., 1642.

EDDY

In the Gaelic *Eddee* signifies an instructor, or from the Saxon *Ed* backwards and *ea* water, a current of water running back, a whirlpool; *Edd* in Welsh signifies motion, *Eddu* to go, to move.

JOHN, son of Rev. William Eddy of Cranbrock, Kent, Eng., b. Eng. about 1595, came to Plymouth, Mass., 1634, removed to Watertown, Mass., 1634.

SAMUEL, brother of the preceding, came to Plymouth, Mass., 1630.

EDENDON, EDDINGTON

EDMUND was at Scituate, Mass., 1641, removed to Boston, Mass., 1642.

EDES

JOHN, son of John, grandson of John, b. Lawford, Essex, Eng., settled at Charleston, Mass., before 1674.

WILLIAM came to Salem, Mass., 1629.

EDGARTON or EGERTON

RICHARD settled at Saybrook, Conn., in 1653, was at Norwich, Conn.

EDGECOMB

A place name from the Manor of Edgecomb, Devonshire, Eng., signifies the "edge of the valley."

JOHN was at New London, Conn., 1670.

NICHOLAS came from Devonshire, Eng., as early as 1639, settled at Scarborough, Maine, removed to Saco, Maine, 1660.

EDGERLY

THOMAS was a resident of Oyster river, now Durham, N. H., 1665.

EDMASTER

JOHN was an inhabitant of Charlestown, Mass., 1678.

EDMONSON

WILLIAM was in R. I., in 1672.

EDMUNDS or EDMONDS

From the Saxon word meaning happy peace.

ANDREW, b. Eng., 1639, was at Providence, R. I., 1675, afterwards at Warwick, R. I.

JAMES, merchant, was a resident of Boston, Mass.; had been before this located at Salem, Mass.

JOHN was at Hartford, Conn., 1639.

JOHN, a freeman at Charlestown, Mass., 1631.

ROBERT swore fidelity to Mass., in Maine, 1674.

SAMUEL was at Concord, Mass., 1645.

WALTER, b. Eng., settled in Concord, Mass., 1638, removed to Charlestown, Mass.

WILLIAM, tailor, a freeman at Lynn, Mass., 1635.

EDSALL or EDSELL

THOMAS, turner, was at Boston, Mass., 1652.

EDISON

DEACON SAMUEL, bapt. Fillongley, Eng., 1613, admitted inhabitant in 1639 at Salem, Mass., removed to Bridgewater, Mass., 1650.

EDWARDS

From the Saxon meaning happy keeper.

ALEXANDER came from Wales to Springfield, Mass., 1642, removed to Northampton, Mass., 1654.

JOHN inhabitant of Wethersfield, 1640, previous to this was at Watertown, Mass.

JOHN was at Ipswich, Mass., before 1660.

JOHN was a resident of Charlestown, Mass., prior to 1687.

MATTHEW came from London, Eng., to Reading, Mass.

RICE, joiner, b. Eng., about 1615, was a resident of Salem, Mass., 1642, removed to Boston, Mass., 1646.

ROBERT, b. 1613, came from London, Eng., to Concord, Mass., in 1635.

THOMAS, shoemaker, was at Salem, Mass., 1637, removed to Lynn or Watertown, Mass.

THOMAS was a resident of Wethersfield, Conn., 1648.

WILLIAM, son of Rev. Richard Edwards of Wales, came with his stepfather, William Coles, in 1630 to Boston, Mass., settled at Hartford, Conn., 1636.

WILLIAM was at Taunton, Mass., 1643, afterwards removed to Lynn, Mass., thence to Easthampton, L. I. 1650.

WILLIAM was at Marblehead, Mass., 1668.

EELLS, ELLS, EELS, or EALES

JOHN, came from Eng., and was made a freeman at Dorchester, Mass., 1634, removed to Hingham, Mass., and in 1645 was at Newbury, Mass., there called "beehive maker."

EGERTON

JOHN, son of John, Earl of Bridgewater, came to Saybrook, Conn., 1632; he returned to Eng., to succeed to his father's title.

RICHARD, brother of the preceding, founder of the family in America, came to Saybrook, Conn., 1632, is on record at Norwich, Conn., 1655.

EGGLESTON

From the Welsh or British *Egles*, a church, and *tun* or *dun*, a hill—the church on the hill.

BEGAT b. Eng., about 1590, came to Dorchester, Mass., 1630, removed to Windsor, Conn., 1636.

EGLIN

WILLIAM was at Boston, Mass., about 1667.

ELA

DANIEL, tanner, was a resident of Haverhill, Mass., in 1675.

ELCOCK

DANIEL, resided at New Haven, Conn., in 1657.

ELDER

DANIEL, inhabitant of Dorchester, Mass., 1667.

ELDERKIN

JOHN settled at Lynn, Mass., 1637; was at Dedham, Mass., 1641; Reading, Mass., 1646, two years later Providence, R. I., at New London, Conn., 1651, finally settled at Norwich, Conn., 1664.

ELDERTON
JOHN was at Providence, R. I. in 1645.

ELDRED
The name of several Saxon kings. From Saxon, signifying all reverent fear.

JOHN an inhabitant of Hampton, N. H., 1640.

SGT. SAMUEL, b. Eng., 1620, a resident of Cambridge, Mass., 1646, afterwards at Medford and Chelsea, Mass., later Kingstown, R. I., 1668 at Wickford, R. I.

THOMAS, ship carpenter, was a resident of Boston, Mass., 1670.

ELDRIDGE
The family of Scotch origin.

JAMES an inhabitant of Stonington, Conn., 1670.

NATHANIEL, resided at Windsor, Conn., 1642.

ROBERT settled at Yarmouth, Mass., 1657.

SAMUEL, brother of the preceding, was of Cambridge, Mass., removed to Stonington, Mass., 1670.

WILLIAM, brother of the preceding, settled at Yarmouth, Mass., 1657.

ELIOT, ELLIOT, or ELLIOTT
Surname signifies the son of *Elias; Heliat* in Welsh and Cornish British, a huntsman, a pursuer. English line traces to time of William the Conqueror.

ANDREW, son of William, came from Somersetshire, Eng., to Beverly, Mass., 1670.

DANIEL was at Sudbury or Marlboro, Mass., 1687.

EDMUND, planter, was at Salisbury, Mass., 1652, removed to Amesbury, Mass., 1659.

FRANCIS, youngest brother of the Apostle.

JOHN b. Eng., made freeman at Braintree, Mass., 1641.

JACOB, elder brother of Rev. John, came to Boston, Mass., 1631.

REV. JOHN, son of Bennett of Widford, Herefordshire, Eng., b. Nazing, Essex, Eng., 1603, came to Boston, Mass., 1631, afterwards settled in Natick and Roxbury, Mass.

JOHN was resident of Watertown, Mass., 1633.

JOHN took oath of allegiance at Amesbury, Mass., 1677.

JOSEPH was at New London, Conn., 1667, removed to Stonington, Conn.

PHILIP, brother of Rev. John, made a freeman at Roxbury, Mass., 1636.

ROBERT was at Casco, Maine, 1670, removed to Scarborough, Maine, 1685, afterwards at Portsmouth, N. H.

WILLIAM in 1634 came to Ipswich, Mass., from Salisbury, Wiltshire, Eng., was drowned the following year, no male issue.

ELISTONE or ELLISTON
GEORGE was a freeman in Boston, Mass., 1690.

ELITHORP or ELITHROP
NATHANIEL was at Ipswich, Mass., before 1663.

ELKINS
CHRISTOPHER was at Scarborough, Maine, 1663.

ELEAZER was an inhabitant of Exeter, N. H. in 1677.

GERSHOM took the oath of allegiance at Hampton, N. H., 1677.

HENRY, tailor, b. Eng., came to Boston, Mass., 1634.

ELLERY
WILLIAM first appears on record at Gloucester, Mass., 1663.

ELLINGWOOD
RALPH came to Salem, Mass., 1637, and was one of the founders of a church at Beverly, Mass., 1667.

ELLINS or ELLINGS
ANTHONY sent to Portsmouth, N. H. by Mason the patentee, made freeman of Mass., 1674.

ELLIS
A contraction from Elias, William Alis was a renowned Norman Lord, a member of a family of upper Normandy which had its seat at Alis or Alisay near Pont de L'Arche, Normandy.

JOHN, Welsh descent, was made freeman at Dedham, Mass., 1641, one of the founders of Medfield, Mass.

JOHN was at Sandwich, Mass., 1641.

JOSEPH made freeman of Mass., 1663.

RICHARD an inhabitant of Dedham, Mass., 1650.

ROGER was at Yarmouth, Mass., prior to 1648.

THOMAS bapt. Wrenham, Eng., 1629, was at Medfield, Mass., 1649.

ELLISON or ELLISSON
LAWRENCE b. Eng., about 1590, settled at Watertown, Mass., removed to Wethersfield, Conn., and 1644 to Hempstead, L. I.

ELLMES

RHODOLPHUS came at the age of fifteen to Scituate, Mass., 1635.

ELLSWORTH

Place name from a small village, a few miles from Cambridge, Eng.

JEREMIAH was at Rowley, Mass., 1650. SGT. JOSIAH, son of John of Cambridge, Eng., a merchant of London, b. 1629, was in Conn. as early as 1646, settled at Windsor, Conn., 1654.

ELMER or ELMORE

In the Domesday Book in 1086, the earliest record of land titles in Eng., the name appears as "Elmer habet."

EDWARD, b. Quinton, Northamptonshire, Eng., 1604, came from Braintree, Essex, Eng., to Boston, Mass., 1632. He removed to Cambridge, Mass., and 1636 to Hartford, Conn. One of the first settlers at Northampton, Mass., 1654, returned 1660 and purchased lands in what is now South Windsor.

ELSE or ELZIE

ELISHA was freeman at Newbury, Mass., 1673.

NICHOLAS was an inhabitant of New Haven, Conn., 1639.

Roger came to Yarmouth, Mass., 1643.

ELSON, ELSEN or ELSING

ABRAHAM was at Wethersfield, Conn., 1638; no male issue.

JOHN, brother of the preceding was an inhabitant of Wethersfield as early as 1638.

ELTHAN

WILLIAM, inhabitant of Woburn, Mass., 1690.

ELTON

Place name, the derivation from Saxon words *ael* an *eel,* and *ton,* town, a town abounding in eels. Family seat in Wiltshire, Eng.

JOHN came from Bristol, Eng., and was at Middletown, Conn., prior to 1672.

ELWELL

ROBERT was a resident of Dorchester, Mass., 1634, afterwards removed to Salem, Mass., and was at Gloucester, Mass., 1648.

ELY

A place name from Ely, Cambridgeshire, Eng., signifies the place of willows from Cornish British, and Welsh *Helig,* Latin *Salix.*

NATHANIEL b. Tenterden, Kent, 1605, located at Cambridge, Mass., 1632, an original settler at Hartford, Conn., 1636, one of the founders of Norwalk, Conn., and in 1659 went to Springfield, Mass.

RICHARD, merchant, b. Hampshire, Eng., 1610, came from Plymouth, Eng.; 1660-63 to Boston, Mass., afterwards located at Lyme, Conn.

EMERSON

From Saxon *Emar,* from *Ethelmar,* noble, son of the noble. The family traces back to Armeric, archdeacon of Carlisle and Durham, 1196-1214. The first to use the name was Johannes Emeryson of Branelpeth parish, county of Durham, Eng., who was born before 1300. In the thirteenth century appears the name of Richardus fil Emerici.

JOHN, baker, was at Ipswich, Mass., 1635, removed to Scituate, Mass., and was married in 1638 at Duxbury, Mass. ROBERT was at Rowley, Mass., as early as 1655, made freeman at Haverhill, Mass., 1668.

THOMAS, baker, son of Robert, son of Thomas, a resident of Great Dunmow, Essex, b. Bishop Stortford, Eng., 1584, settled at Ipswich, Mass., 1638.

EMERY

The surname was borne in France before the twelfth century.

Gilbert D. Amory of Tours was a follower of William the Conqueror.

ANTHONY, carpenter, son of John, b. Romsey, Hants, Eng., 1600, came to N. E. 1635, locating at Newbury, Mass., in 1644 removed to Dover, N. H., afterwards Kittery, Maine, in 1662 was a resident of Portsmouth, N. H.

JAMES was made a freeman at Kittery, Maine, in 1652.

JOHN, brother of Anthony, b. Romsey, Hants, Eng., 1598, settled at Newbury, Mass., in 1635.

EMMONS

HENRY, a resident of Boston, Mass., 1690.

THOMAS on record at Newport, R. I., 1639, a freeman at Boston, Mass., 1652.

ENDICOTT

GILBERT, b. Eng., 1648, Kennebunk, Maine, 1677.

JOHN, b. Dorchester, Eng., 1589, came to Salem, Mass., 1628.

WILLIAM was an inhabitant of Boston, Mass., 1686.

ENGLAND

JOHN was a resident of New Haven, Conn., 1647 removed to Branford, Conn., where he died 1655. No male issue.

ENGLISH or ENGLES

CLEMENT was at Salem, Mass., 1667.

MAUDETT was an inhabitant of Boston, Mass., as early as 1639.

WILLIAM, shoemaker, a resident of Ipswich, Mass., 1638, was admitted an inhabitant of Boston, Mass., 1652.

ENO or ENNOE

JAMES was at Windsor, Conn., 1646.

ENSIGN

Family seated in Norfolk, Essex, and other counties as early as 1395.

JAMES was made a freeman at Cambridge, Mass., 1635, removed in 1639 to Hartford, Conn.

THOMAS was married at Scituate, Mass., 1639, and was resident of Duxbury, Mass., 1656.

EPES or EPPES

DANIEL, son of Daniel came from Kent, Eng., 1637 to Ipswich, Mass.

ERRINGTON

ABRAHAM an inhabitant of Cambridge, Mass., 1649.

THOMAS was at Lynn, Mass., 1642, afterwards at Charlestown, Mass., made freeman at Warwick, R. I., 1655.

ERWIN

from Welsh *Erwyn,* very fair, white, Gaelic *Urfiom,* beautiful, fair.

EDWARD was a resident of Dover, N. H., 1658.

ESSET

WILLIAM died at Boston, Mass., 1697.

ESTERBROOK or EASTERBROOK

REV. JOSEPH, b. Enfield, Middlesex, Eng., 1640, came to Concord, Mass., 1660, was ordained 1664.

THOMAS, brother of the preceding, b. Eng., 1629, settled at Concord, Mass., and in 1669 settled at Swanzey, Mass.

ESTEN

THOMAS swore allegiance to Providence, R. I., 1682.

ESTES

The surname is derived from a colony planted by Rome, fifteen miles south of Padua, named *Ateste* or *Este,* the latter plural used to represent the whole family.

MATTHEW, son of Robert, of Dover, Eng., b. 1645, came to N. E. before 1676, was at Dover, N. H., afterwards at Portsmouth, N. H.

RICHARD, weaver, brother of the preceding, b. Eng., 1647, joined his brother at Portsmouth, N. H.

ESTON

WILLIAM was at Hampton, N. H., 1639.

ETHEREDGE

EDWARD was in Mass., 1646.

EUSTIS

WILLIAM was at Charlestown, Mass., resided at Malden, Mass., and at Boston, Mass., 1695.

EVANCE

DAVID, merchant, was at Boston, Mass., 1654.

EVANS

The Welsh for John; Evan, *eofn,* fearless, bold.

DAVID, merchant, at Boston, Mass., 1654.

HENRY, husbandman, made a freeman at Boston, Mass., 1645.

JOHN was at Wethersfield, Conn., 1640, afterwards at Hatfield, Mass., 1678.

JOHN was an inhabitant of Roxbury, Mass., before 1671.

NICHOLAS b. Wales, came to Windsor, Conn., about 1680, afterwards removed to Simsbury, Conn.

PHILIP was at Newbury, Mass., before 1689.

RICHARD was freeman at Dorchester, Mass., 1643.

RICHARD was at Rehoboth, Mass., before 1681.

ROBERT was a resident of Dover, N. H., 1665.

THOMAS was at Dorchester, Mass., 1640.

THOMAS resided at Salisbury, Mass., 1686.

WILLIAM was at Taunton, Mass., 1643, afterwards at Gloucester, and Ipswich, Mass.

EVARTS

JOHN admitted freeman at Concord, Mass., 1637-38.

EVELETH

JOHN was a resident of Ipswich, Mass., 1683.

SYLVESTER, baker, at Boston, Mass., 1642, removed to Gloucester, Mass., 1647.

EVERDEN

ANTHONY took oath of allegiance at Providence, R. I., 1666.

THOMAS, a Quaker preacher, was at Salem, Mass., 1682.

EVERED or EVEREST

ANDREW b. Eng., settled at York, Maine, 1646.

JOHN, with a prefix of Webb for surname, came from Marlborough, Wiltshire, Eng., 1635 to Boston, Mass., was at Chelmsford, Mass., 1663. No male issue.

EVEREST

ISAAC was at Guilford, Conn., before 1677.

EVERETT or EVERTS

A corruption of *Everard* from the Saxon, also the Greek signifying well reputed, ever honored.

FRANCIS was an inhabitant of Reading, Mass., 1675.

RICHARD came from Eng., to N. E. and settled at Watertown, Mass., was at Cambridge, Mass., 1636, afterward removed to Dedham, Mass.

EVERILL

ABIEL was a resident of Boston, Mass., 1655.

JAMES admitted freeman at Boston, Mass., 1634.

EVERSON

RICHARD settled in what is now Plympton, Mass., before 1700.

EVERTON

WILLIAM was at Manchester, Mass., 1658 and was at Charlestown, Mass., 1674.

EWELL

Place name from a town in Eng., Cornish British *Ewhill,* signifying high, tall.

HENRY, shoemaker, came from Sandwich, Kent, to Scituate, Mass., removed to Barnstable, Mass., 1640.

EWER

HENRY was at Sandwich, Mass., 1637.

THOMAS b. Eng., about 1595, came to Charlestown, Mass., 1635, removed to Barnstable, Mass., 1641.

EWINGTON or EUINGTON

THOMAS was at Lynn, Mass., 1642, a freeman of R. I., 1655.

EWSTEAD

RICHARD came to Salem, Mass., with Higginson, 1629.

EXELL or EXILE

RICHARD was at Springfield, Mass., 1646.

EYRE or EYERS

The same as Ayers (see).

SIMON, surgeon, came to Watertown, Mass., 1635, soon removed to Boston, Mass.

FABENS or FABINS

Surname derived from Latin *Fabius, Faba,* a bean, the bean, the bean-man so called for his success in cultivating beans.

FABER

From Latin, a workman, a smith.

JOSEPH, cooper, b. 1611, came to Boston, Mass., 1635.

FACE

ROBERT, carpenter, at Boston, Mass., 1657.

FAIRBANKS

JONATHAN, of English descent, b. Yorkshire, Eng., about 1600, came from Sowerby, West Riding, Yorkshire, Eng., to Boston, Mass., 1633, and three years later removed to Dedham, Mass.

RICHARD came to Boston, 1633, no male issue.

FAIRCHILD

The name originally Fairbairn, a fair, handsome bairn or child.

The family of Scotch origin was seated in Eng., in the fifteenth century.

THOMAS b. Eng., among the first settlers of New Haven, Conn., in 1646, was at Stratford, Conn.

FAIRFIELD

DANIEL was at Boston, Mass., before 1639.

DANIEL resided at Weymouth, Mass., 1666.

JOHN came from Ireland to Eng., was resident of Charlestown, Mass., 1638, removed to Wenham, Mass., no issue.

FAIRMAN or FIRMAN

JOHN came from Suffolk, Eng., was at Watertown, Mass., 1630.

JOSIAH, freeman at Boston, Mass., 1640.

THOMAS, freeman at Ipswich, Mass., 1641.

FAIRWEATHER or FAYERWEATHER

THOMAS came in Winthrop's fleet, made freeman at Boston, Mass., 1634.

FALCONER

DAVID at Boston, Mass., 1656.

FALES

From Fale, a river at Cornwall, Eng., also a rough, rocky place.

JAMES, b. Eng., about 1600, came from Cheshire, Eng., to Dedham, Mass., 1630.

JOHN was at Wrentham, Mass., before 1684.

FALLAND

THOMAS, freeman at Yarmouth, Mass., 1641.

FALLOWAY or FALLOWELL

GABRIEL admitted freeman at Plymouth, Mass., 1640.

FANE

HENRY, turner, was at Boston, Mass., 1648.

FANNING

EDMUND came from Ireland, settled at New London, Conn., 1653, afterwards resided at Groton, Conn.

THOMAS married at Watertown, Mass., 1655.

WILLIAM was at Newbury, Mass., where he married, 1668.

FARGO

MOSES was at New London, Conn., 1680.

FARLEY

GEORGE, son of Fabian, b. 1619, settled at Woburn, Mass., one of the proprietors of Billerica, Mass., 1640.

MICHAEL, brother of the preceding, was at Ipswich, Mass., 1675.

FARMAN

From German *Fahr-mann,* master of a ferry-boat.

RALPH, barber-surgeon, came from London, Eng., one of the first settlers of Andover, Mass.

FARMER

EDWARD, son of John Ansley, near Atherstone, Warwickshire, Eng., came to Billerica, Mass., 1671.

FARNHAM or FARNUM.

Surname from a town in Surrey, Eng., so called from Saxon *Fearn,* fern, and *ham,* a habitation or village—the village in the place overgrown with fern. Robert de Farnham was a companion of William the Conqueror. The family was seated at Querndon House, Gloucestershire, Eng., line of Henry III.

HENRY, joiner, was at Roxbury, Mass., 1644, was an inhabitant of Killingworth, Conn., 1666.

JOHN, freeman at Dorchester, Mass., 1640.

JOHN married in Andover, Mass., 1667.

JOHN, inhabitant of Boston, Mass., 1654.

PETER, early settler of Killingworth, Conn.

RALPH, a descendant of Robert, b. Eng., 1603, came from Surrey, Eng., to Boston, Mass., 1635, was proprietor at Ipswich, Mass., 1639, removed to Andover, Mass.

FARNSWORTH

A place name from two places in Eng., one in the parish of Prescott near Liverpool, the other in the parish of Dean in the Hundred of Salford near Manchester, Eng. It is Anglo-Saxon from *fearn,* fern, and *worth,* a place signifying place of ferns. The English records as early as 1297 record the name of Roger de Farnworth.

JOSEPH, freeman at Dorchester, Mass., 1639.

MATTHIAS, weaver, b. 1612 was resident of Lynn, Mass., 1657, a proprietor at Groton, Mass., 1661.

FARR

From Gaelic and Welsh *Fawr* same as *Mawr,* Gaelic and Welsh.

GEORGE, shipwright, b. Eng., 1594, came to Salem, Mass., 1629, removed to Lynn, Mass., finally to Ipswich, Mass.

JAMES was at Newport, R. I., 1638.

THOMAS was a resident of Boston, Mass., 1645.

FARRABAS

DANIEL was a resident of Cambridge, Concord, and Marlboro, Mass.

FARRAND

NATHANIEL was at Milford, Conn., 1645.

FARRAR

The name is a corruption of *Farrier,* name of a trade from old French word *fenier,* a horse-shoer; *Pfarrer* in German is a minister. Gualkeline or Walkeline de Farraris was a Norman of distinction attached to William, Duke of Normandy before the invasion of Eng.

JACOB came from Lancashire, one of the incorporators of Lancaster, Mass., 1653, killed by Indians, 1675.

JOHN, brother of the preceding was at Woburn, Mass., and at Lancaster, Mass., 1653.

THOMAS, a resident of Lynn, Mass., 1639.

FARRINGTON

An old Saxon name same as Ferndon, signifying fernhill. There are parishes and towns in Eng., named Farrington. The ancient family of Farringtons lived at the time of the Conquest at Shaw Hall in Lancashire.

EDMUND b. Eng., 1587-88, came from Olney, Buckinghamshire, Eng., and was proprietor at Lynn, Mass., as early as 1638, having arrived in N. E., 1635.

JOHN, son of Edmund Farrington, b. Olney, Buckinghamshire, came to Mass., 1635, was proprietor at Dedham, Mass., 1646.

FARROW

GEORGE was an inhabitant of Ipswich, Mass., 1637.

JOHN came from Hingham, Eng., to Hingham, Mass., 1635.

FARWELL

The English ancestor in 1280 was Richard Farwell.

HENRY, son of John, of Hill Bishop, Eng., was in 1639, among the first settlers of Concord, Mass.

THOMAS was at Taunton, Mass., 1639; his son John, the only one of the children there is any record of, returned to Eng.

FASSETT or FASSELL

From French *Fausette,* falsehood, cheat.

JOHN was a freeman at Dedham, Mass., 1654.

FAULKNER

From the German, signifying a catcher or trainer of hawks.

EDMUND b. Eng., 1625, came first to Salem, Mass., settled at Andover, Mass., 1648.

FAUNCE

JOHN came as young man to Plymouth, Mass., 1623.

FAVOR or FEAVER

PHILIP was married at Salisbury, Mass., 1689.

FAWER or FOWER

BARNABAS came from Eng. to Dorchester, Mass., 1635.

FAWNE

JOHN was freeman at Ipswich, Mass., 1635.

FAXON or FAXSON

PHILIP, b. 1660, was a resident of Sudbury, Mass., 1688.

THOMAS, b. Eng., 1601, settled at Dedham, Mass., 1647, removed to Braintree, Mass., where he was made freeman 1657.

FAY

From Spanish word *Fe,* faith. In Normandy, plantations of beech were called *Faye* or Fayel. It first appears as patronymic in 1173, was originally identified with *Foy.*

HENRY, weaver, died at Newbury, Mass., 1655.

JOHN, son of John, b. Eng., 1648, came a youth of eight years to N. E., first resided at Watertown, Mass., afterwards settled at Sudbury, Mass., was at Marlboro, Mass., 1675.

FEAKE

HENRY was at Lynn, Mass., 1630, a freeman in 1634, removed to Sandwich, Mass., before 1643.

ROBERT came with Winthrop, 1630, settled at Watertown, Mass.

FEARING

JOHN came from Cambridge, Eng., to Hingham, Mass., 1638, in the employ of Matthew Hawke.

FELAH

A corruption of Welsh.

HENRY, b. Wales, 1585, was at Gloucester, Mas before 1642, at that time settled at Watertown, Mass.

FELLOWS

More commonly spelled in Eng. Fellowes; the word *fellow* in some dialects signified a young unmarried man —a servant engaged in husbandry. The name dates back to the twelfth century on the Hundred Rolls appearing as *Le Felove, Le Felawes, Fellowe.*

RICHARD was at Hartford, Conn., 1643, removed to Springfield, Mass., 1659. soon after to Northampton, Mass., in 1661 to Hatfield, Mass.

SAMUEL, b. England, 1619, settled at Salisbury, Mass., 1639.

WILLIAM, shoemaker, brother of the preceding, son of William Fellowes, London, Eng., b. St. Albans, Hertfordshire, Eng., 1609, came to Ipswich, Mass., 1635.

FELMINGHAM or FILLINGHAM

FRANCIS, b. 1605, came from Brampton, Suffolk, Eng., 1637 to Salem, Mass., the following year granted land at Wenham, Mass.

FELT

Fel in the Dutch signifies fierce, violent, also local, a rock place, barren and stonyhills, uninclosed place, a moor, a valley.

GEORGE, Welsh descent, b. 1601, came to N. E. with Gov. Endicott, 1628, on record at Charlestown, Mass., 1633, removed to Casco, Maine, 1663, died at Malden, 1693, where he had resided since 1689.

FELTON

Place name from a small town in Eng., a rocky or stony hill.

BENJAMIN came to Salem, Mass., 1635, made a freeman in 1639.

NATHANIEL, brother of the preceding, b. Eng., 1615, settled at Salem, Mass., 1633.

FENN

BENJAMIN b. Eng., 1612, came from the parish of Whittington, Masworth, Eng., to Dorchester, Mass., 1630, where he was a proprietor, in 1637 removed to New Haven, Conn., thence to Milford, Conn.

ROBERT came from London, Eng., to Boston, Mass., was also resident of Salem, Mass., before 1644.

FENNER

ARTHUR b. Eng., 1622, settled as early as 1650 at Providence, R. I.

JOHN a resident of Saybrook, Conn.

ROBERT was a resident of Stamford, Conn., 1641.

THOMAS, b. Eng., died at Branford, Conn., 1647.

WILLIAM, brother of Arthur, was at Providence, R. I., 1645.

WILLIAM was a proprietor at Saybrook, Conn., before 1673.

FENNO

JOHN came from Lancashire, Eng., was a resident of Milton, Mass., 1660.

FENTON

From Welsh or British, a well.

ROBERT was at Woburn, Mass., before 1688.

FERGUSON

The name simply means son of Fergus; an ancient Scotch personal name; it was prominent throughout Scotland as early as 1466. Fergus was first King of Scotland; the plaid of the clan is green and black with red and white lines through it, the badge a sunflower or foxglove.

DANIEL, an early settler of Maine, was living in 1659 in Upper Eliot in that province.

FERNALD

The English ancestor in 1497 was John Fernol.

REGINALD, surgeon, son of Capt. William, b. Eng., 1595, came to Portsmouth, N. H., 1630.

THOMAS, brother of the preceding, was at Portsmouth, N. H., 1631.

FERNESIDE, FERNISIDE or FARNYSEEDE

JOHN was married at Duxbury, Mass., 1643, removed to Boston, Mass.

FERRIS

A corruption of Ferrers, from *Ferorieres,* a small town of Gastinors, France, so called from the iron mines in which the country abounded. In Welsh *fferis* signifies steel.

JEFFREY, freeman at Watertown, Mass., 1635, one of the first settlers of Wethersfield, Conn., removed to Stamford, Conn.

ZACHARIAH came from Reading, Eng., to Charlestown, Mass., 1673, afterwards went to Stamford, Conn.

FERRY

CHARLES b. Eng., 1635, came to Springfield, Mass., 1661.

FESSENDEN

JOHN, b. Kent, Eng., about 1600, came from Canterbury, Eng., to Cambridge, Mass., 1636.

NICHOLAS, b. Eng., 1650, came to Cambridge, Mass., 1674.

FEVERYEAR

EDWARD was married at Salem, Mass., 1664.

FIELD

The name correctly written is De la Field or De La Feld. Sir Hubertus De la Feld settled in the counties of Lancashire and Kent, Eng. Roger del Feld was the English ancestor, 1240.

ALEXANDER, shoemaker, was at Charlestown, Mass., 1640, removed to Salem, Mass., 1642, was at New Haven, Conn., 1649.

DANIEL took oath of allegiance at Providence, R. I., 1671.

DARBY, son of John, tenth generation from Roger del Feld, b. Boston, Eng., 1610, came to Boston, Mass., 1636, removed to Exeter, N. H., 1638, and ten years later was at Dover, N. H.

GEORGE was at Boston, Mass., before 1655, removed to Salisbury, Mass.

JAMES, freeman at Dedham Mass., 1683.

JOHN, b. Eng., appears on record at Providence, R. I., as early as 1637; was at Bridgewater, Mass., 1655.

ROBERT, tailor, brother of Darby, Berkshire, Eng., came to N. E. in 1635, was at Providence, R. I., 1638, removed to Boston, Mass., 1650, was at Saco, Maine, 1653.

WILLIAM was at Providence, R. I., before 1643.

ZACHARIAH, b. East Ardsley, Yorkshire, Eng., 1596, came to N. E. 1629, later settled at Dorchester, Mass., in 1636, removed to Hartford, Conn., in 1659 to Northampton, Mass., was one of the original settlers at Hatfield, Mass., 1666.

FIFIELD

Has the same signification as Mannfield, lands held in *fee* or *fief* for which individual pays service or owes rent. The family is of Scotch descent, and some authorities say that the name is a union of the county of Fife in Scotland with the name of Field.

GILES married at Charlestown, Mass., 1652, removed to Hampton, N. H., returned 1663 to Charlestown.

WILLIAM came from Eng., to Ipswich, Mass., 1634, removed to Newbury, Mass., and 1639 to Hampton, N. H.

FILER or FYLER

WALTER came from Eng., to Dorchester, Mass., 1634, removed to Windsor, Conn., 1636.

FILLEBROWN

THOMAS was at Charlestown, Mass., 1658, freeman at Cambridge, Mass., 1666.

FILLEY

From a town in Eng., by that name. *Filid,* in Gaelic, a poet, a bard.

WILLIAM was at Windsor, Conn., before 1640.

FINCH

ABRAHAM made freeman at Watertown, Mass., 1634, removed the following year to Wethersfield, Conn.

DANIEL, brother of the preceding, came to N. E. in Winthrop's fleet, located at Watertown, Mass., among the first settlers of Wethersfield, Conn., thence to Stamford, Conn., one of the original proprietors of Fairfield, Conn., 1653.

JOHN, brother of the preceding, was at Watertown, Mass., 1630, removed in 1637 to Wethersfield, Conn.

JOSEPH was at Greenwich, Conn., 1672.

SAMUEL, freeman at Roxbury, Mass., 1634.

FINNEY

From Gaelic *Finne,* genitive of *Fionn,* fair, sincere, true; bringing to an end, a head chief. The name may be also local from *Fines,* a place in France. The more common spelling of this name is Phinney.

JOHN was at Plymouth, Mass., as early as 1643.

ROBERT an inhabitant of Plymouth, Mass., 1643.

FISH

GABRIEL an early inhabitant of Boston, Mass., removed 1638 to Exeter, N. H. Returned to Boston, Mass.

JOHN was at Lynn, Mass., removed 1637 to Sandwich, Mass.

JOHN was freeman at Portsmouth, R. I., 1655, afterwards at Stonington, Conn., about 1670.

JONATHAN, brother of John and Nathaniel, b. Eng., about 1610, came to N. E., 1635, settled at Lynn, Mass., 1637, removed to Salisbury, Mass., before 1659, finally removed to Middleburg or Newtown, L. I.

NATHANIEL was at Sandwich, Mass., 1643.

ROBERT married at Portsmouth, R. I., 1686.

THOMAS was at Portsmouth, R. I., 1655.

WILLIAM was at Windsor, Conn., 1647, made a freeman 1669.

FISHER

ANTHONY, son of Anthony of Syleham, Suffolk, Eng., was bapt. at that place 1591, settled at Dedham, Mass., 1637.

ANTHONY was a freeman at Dorchester, Mass., 1645.

DANIEL settled at Taunton, Mass., amongst the early settlers, where he married in 1666.

EDWARD freeman at Portsmouth, R. I., 1655.

ELEAZER was married at Wrentham, Mass., 1688.

JOSHUA, brother of the first Anthony, came to N. E., 1640, settled at Dedham, Mass., afterwards at Medfield, Mass.

OLIVER was at Wrentham, Mass., 1689.

SAMUEL was married at Boston, Mass., 1659.

SAMUEL, a resident of Wrentham, Mass., as early as 1670.

THOMAS came from Winston, Eng., to Cambridge, Mass., 1634, removed to Dedham, Mass., 1637.

WILLIAM was married at Marshfield, Mass., 1684.

FISKE

The surname is from the French word *Fisc,* revenue, public funds. Daniel Fisc of Laxfield, Suffolk in 1208, received a grant of lands. Lord Symond Fiske was Lord of the Manor of Standhough, parish of Laxfield, Suffolk, 1399-1422.

BENJAMIN married at Medfield, Mass., 1674.

DAVID was at Watertown, Mass., 1637.

JAMES, son of Thomas of Suffolk, Eng., was at Salem, Mass., 1641, removed to Haverhill, Mass.

REV. JOHN, eighth generation from Lord Symond Fiske, brother of David, was proprietor at Dedham, Mass., 1638, afterward removed to Watertown, Mass.

NATHAN, brother of David and John was freeman at Watertown, Mass., 1643, soon after removed to Wrentham, Mass.

FITCH

JAMES, tailor, b. 1605, came to Boston, Mass., 1635, was at what is now Brookline, Mass., 1638.

REV. JAMES, b. Bocking, Essex, Eng., 1622, came to N. E., 1638, was at Saybrook, Conn., settled at Norwich, Conn., 1660, and 1696 was a resident of Lebanon, Conn.

JEREMIAH was at Lynn, Mass., 1634, removed to Reading, Mass., 1644.

JOHN a resident of Windsor, Conn., before 1676.

JOHN married at Gloucester, Mass., 1667.

JOSEPH, brother of Rev. James, son of Thomas, came from Braintree, Eng., to N. E., with his mother, 1638, was at

Norwalk, Conn., 1652, removed to Northampton, Mass., 1655 and 1660 Hartford, Conn., finally to Windsor, Conn.

RICHARD, brother of James, came N. E., 1635, was at what is now Brookline, Mass., 1638.

SAMUEL, schoolmaster, was at Milford, Conn., 1644, at Hartford, 1650, two years later was living at Wethersfield, Conn.

THOMAS, brother of Rev. John, came to N. E., 1638, was at Norwalk, Conn., 1652.

THOMAS, cordwainer, was at Boston, Mass., prior to 1656.

ZECHARY, brother of Rev. John, came to N. E., 1638 to Reading, Mass., where he was made a freeman.

FITTS or FITZ

The English ancestor John Fitts, 1428.

RICHARD, son of Walter of Taverstock, Devonshire, Eng., settled at Ipswich, Mass., 1635, removed to Newbury, Mass.

ROBERT, brother of the preceding, b. Eng., 1600, was property owner at Salisbury, Mass., 1639, afterwards removed to Ipswich, Mass.

FITZRANDLE

EDWARD was at Scituate, Mass., 1637, was resident of Barnstable, 1639.

FLACK

From Dutch *Vlak,* flat, low ground.

COTTON was at Boston, Mass., 1634, afterward was a resident of what is now Brookline, Mass.

FLAGG or FLEGG

THOMAS, yeoman, b. Scratly, one of the hundred of East Flegg, Norfolk, Eng., came to N. E. as servant of Richard Carver, 1637, proprietor of Watertown, Mass., 1641.

FLANDERS

A native of Flanders, which took its name from *Flandrina,* wife of Liderick II, Prince of Buc, or from *Flambert,* the nephew of Clodion, King of France.

STEPHEN b. Eng., about 1620, was at Salisbury, Mass., 1640.

FLATMAN or FLACKMAN

THOMAS was a freeman at Braintree, Mass., 1640; previous to this was at Salem, Mass.

FLEMING

A native or inhabitant of Flanders (see).

ABRAHAM, husbandman, b. 1595 came to N. E., 1635.

JOHN was resident of Watertown, Mass., about 1639.

ROBERT, granted lands at Stonington, Conn., 1669.

FLETCHER

A maker of arrows or superintendent of archery, from the French *flèche,* an arrow.

EDWARD, cutler, afterwards minister, admitted as a townsman in Boston, 1640. No issue.

HENRY was at Reading, Mass., about 1662.

JOHN was resident of Wethersfield, Mass., before 1641, removed to Milford, Conn., where he died 1662.

ROBERT, Welsh and English descent, b. Eng., 1592, came from Yorkshire, Eng., to Concord, Mass., 1630, was one of the founders of Chelmsford, Mass., afterwards resided at Middletown, Conn.

FLINT

Place name from a market town near the sea in Flintshire, Wales.

REV. HENRY b. Matlock, Derbyshire, Eng., came to Boston, Mass., 1635, freeman at Braintree, Mass., 1636.

THOMAS, brother of Rev. Henry, came to Boston, Mass., and 1637 settled at Concord, Mass.

THOMAS b. Wales, mentioned in town records of Salem, Mass., 1650, he died 1663.

WILLIAM, brother of the preceding, was at Salem, Mass., 1645.

FLOOD or FLOYD

From Welsh *Fludd* or *Floyd,* same meaning as *Llwyd,* brown, gray, hoary.

HENRY was at Boston, Mass., before 1666.

JAMES, inhabitant of Boston, as early as 1668.

JOHN, merchant, was at Scituate, Mass., 1640, at Boston, Mass., 1653.

CAPT. JOHN resided at Lynn, Mass., 1680, removed to what is now Chelsea, Mass.

JOSEPH resided at Dorchester, Mass., 1635.

PHILIP, originally from the Isle of Guernsey, Eng., came from N. J. to Newbury, Mass., 1680.

RICHARD was at Boston, Mass., 1642.

ROBERT b. 1620, was resident of Wethersfield, Mass., 1646.

FLOWER or FLOWERS

LAMROCK was inhabitant of Hartford, Conn., 1686.

FOBES

JOHN was at Duxbury, Mass., 1636, was early at Bridgewater, Mass.

FOGG

RALPH was at Plymouth, Mass., 1633, removed to Salem, Mass., where he was made freeman 1634, returned to Eng., before 1652.

SAMUEL b. Eng., 1600, came in Winthrop's Fleet 1630 to N. E., 1638, settled at Hampton, N. H.

FOLGER

Place name *Fougeres,* town in France near the frontiers of Normandy.

JOHN came from Norwich, Norfolk, Eng., 1635, settled at Martha's Vineyard, Mass.

FOLLANSBEE

THOMAS b. Eng., 1640, came to Portsmouth, N. H., and 1667 removed to Newbury, Mass.

FOLLET

From French; frolicsome, merry, gay. JOHN was at Dover, N. H., 1640.

PHILIP was at Dover, N. H., 1671-5.

ROBERT was an inhabitant of Salem, Mass., 1671.

WILLIAM resided at Dover, N. H., 1651.

FOLSOM

The name is derived from seat of the family Foulsham, Warwickshire, Eng., which took its name from being the home of many *foutes* (birds). The American branch is traced to Roger Foulsham of Nestin, Norfolk, Eng., whose will is dated 1534.

ADAM, son of Adam, grandson of Roger, came from Hingham, Eng., to Boston, Mass.

JOHN b. Eng., 1617, brother of the preceding, came in 1638 to Hingham, Mass., removed to Exeter, N. H., 1655.

NATHANIEL was at Rehoboth, Mass., 1676.

FONES

The English ancestor of the family, William Fones, lived at Saxbie, Devonshire, Eng., in the early part of the 15th century.

CAPT. JOHN settled at Newport, R. I., 1659, afterwards lived at Jamestown and Kingstown, R. I.

FOOTE or FOOT

A place at the bottom of a hill or mountain, the base.

NATHANIEL, son of Nathaniel, b. Eng., 1593, came from Shalford, Colchester, Eng., and was made freeman at Watertown, Mass., 1634, removed to Wethersfield, Conn., 1636.

PASCO was granted land at Salem, Mass., 1637.

FOOTMAN

THOMAS a resident of Dover, N. H., 1648.

FOP

DANIEL was at Hingham, Mass., 1635.

FORBES

From *Saor Forba,* lands free from military service, name of parish in Aberdeenshire, Scotland, granted by Alexander II, 1249 to the progenitor of the family, John De Forbes on record in 1214.

JOHN b. Scotland, proprietor at Sudbury, Mass., 1636, removed to Bridgewater, Mass., 1645.

DANIEL, of Scotch descent, b. 1620, was at Cambridge, Mass., 1656-60, afterwards removed to Concord, Mass., thence to Marlboro, Mass.

FORBUSH, FORBISH or FORBAS

ALEXANDER married at Charlestown, Mass., 1674.

DANIEL b. about 1620, came from Kinellar, Scotland, and is recorded at Cambridge, Mass., 1662, settled at Marlboro, Mass., 1681.

FORD

ANDREW, freeman in 1654 at Weymouth, Mass., afterwards at Abington, Mass.

JOHN came with his mother to Plymouth, Mass., 1621, removed late in life to Marshfield, Mass.

MARTIN married at Bradford, Mass., 1685.

MATTHEW a proprietor at New Haven, Conn., 1685.

THOMAS came in 1630 to Dorchester, Mass.

THOMAS resided at Milford, Conn., 1646.

THOMAS was at Boston, Mass., 1690.

TIMOTHY b. Eng., came to Charlestown, Mass., 1637, removed to New Haven, Conn., 1639.

WILLIAM, brother of John, settled in Duxbury, Mass., where his name appears 1643 as able to bear arms.

FORDHAM

Place name a town in England, the house or village at the ford.

REV. ROBERT came to N. E. 1640, was at Cambridge and Sudbury, Mass., removed to Southampton, R. I.

FORT

ABRAHAM was at Boston, Mass., 1656.

FORTUNE
ELIAS resident of Marblehead, Mass., 1674

FORWARD
SAMUEL came from Devonshire, Eng., about 1666 to Windsor, Conn.

FOSDICK
STEPHEN came from Lincolnshire, Eng., to Charlestown, Mass., 1635.

FOSKETT
JOHN was householder at Charlestown, Mass., 1678, having been resident since 1658.

FOSS
In Cornish British signifies entrenchment, moat or ditch. *Fos* in Danish a waterfall, cataract.

JOHN settled at Dover, N. H., 1665.

FOSTER
A corruption of *Forrester* or *forster*. The first known of the name was in 1065 when Sir Richard Forrester went with his brother-in-law William the Conqueror to Eng.

ANDREW b. Eng., 1579, made a freeman at Andover, Mass., 1669.

BARTHOLOMEW married at Gloucester, Mass., 1669.

CHRISTOPHER b. Eng., 1603, settled at Lynn, Mass., 1635, removed to Southampton, L. I.

EDWARD, son of Timothy, b. Eng., 1610, came with his uncle Timothy Hatherty to Plymouth, Mass., 1623, settled at Scituate, Mass., 1633.

EDWARD resident of Marblehead, Mass., 1668.

EDWARD married at Springfield, Mass., 1661.

EDWARD inhabitant of Middletown, Conn., 1670.

HOPESTILL, brewer, son of Hopestill, came with mother at the age of fourteen to N. E., locating at Dorchester, Mass.

JOHN b. Eng., 1618, admitted freeman at Salem, Mass., 1649.

REGINALD b. Bramton, Eng., 1595, settled at Ipswich, Mass., 1638.

SAMUEL b. Eng., 1619, was at Dedham, Mass., 1647, removed to Wenham, Mass., 1650 to Chelmsford, Mass., 1655.

THOMAS was at Boston, Mass., 1641.

THOMAS, freeman at Weymouth, Mass., 1647, afterwards at Braintree and Billerica, Mass.

THOMAS, son of John of Kingsware, Eng., was a resident of New London, Conn., 1666.

TIMOTHY b. Devonshire, Eng., came to Plymouth, Mass., 1623, returned to Eng., and came again to N. E., locating in 1633 at Scituate, Mass.

WILLIAM a resident of Newport, R. I., 1638.

WILLIAM, merchant, a resident of Boston, Mass., 1644.

FOUNTAIN
Originally de Fonte or De Fontibus from the springs or fountains near which they reside.

AARON married at New London, Conn., 1680.

FOWKES or FOOKS
HENRY freeman at Dorchester, Mass., 1635, removed to Windsor, Conn., where he died in 1640, no issue.

FOWLE, FOWLER or FOWLAR
Occupation name from bird hunter, a sportsman who pursues wild-fowl. English ancestor Sir Richard Fowler.

AMBROSE resident of Windsor, Conn., 1640, removed to Westfield, Mass., 1671.

GEORGE, Scotch descent, came to Mass., 1638, locating at Concord, Mass., removed to Charlestown, Mass., spelled his name with the final *r*.

HENRY swore allegiance at Providence, R. I., 1655.

PHILIP, clothworker, b. Eng., 1591-98, settled at Ipswich, Mass., 1634, coming from Marlborough, Wiltshire, Eng.

PHILIP married at Malden, Mass., 1688.

SAMUEL was at Salisbury, Mass., 1665.

THOMAS, merchant, came to Boston, Mass., before 1635, returned to Eng., 1646.

WILLIAM came in party of Rev. John Davenport from Eng., to Boston, Mass., 1637, removed to New Haven, Conn., next year; 1661 settled at Milford, Conn.

FOWNELL
JOHN, miller, made freeman at Charlestown, Mass., 1645, removed to Cambridge, Mass., 1655.

FOX
Name taken from the cunning animal; in 1333 the *Shanachs* in Ireland anglicized their name to Fox.

DAVID was married at Woburn, Mass., 1678.

ISAAC inhabitant of Medford, Mass., 1679.

NICHOLAS was at Marblehead, Mass., 1674.

THOMAS, son of Samuel, grandson of

John of Boston, Lincolnshire, Eng., b. 1608, freeman at Concord, Mass., 1638, removed to Cambridge, Mass., 1649.

THOMAS, a descendant of the author of the "Book of Martyrs," freeman at Cambridge, Mass., 1644.

FOXCRAFT or FOXCROFT

FRANCIS, son of Daniel, mayor of Leeds, Yorkshire, Eng., in 1665, came to Boston, Mass., 1679.

FOXWELL

JOHN was at Braintree, Mass., 1643.

RICHARD, freeman at Salem or Boston, Mass., 1630; removed to Scituate, Mass., 1634; to Barnstable, Mass., 1646.

RICHARD at Piscataqua, N. H., before 1631, removed to Scarborough, Maine, in 1636.

FOY

JEFFREY, mariner, at Boston, Mass., 1676, no issue.

JOHN, mariner, a resident of Boston, Mass., 1671.

FRAILE

GEORGE was at Lynn, Mass., 1637, previously at Charlestown, Mass.

FRAME

THOMAS, tailor, took oath of allegiance at Amesbury, Mass., 1677.

FRANCIS

From Saxon *Frank,* free. The ancient Franks inhabited part of Germany, conquered Gaul, changed the name to France.

FRANCIS was at Reading, Mass., 1657.

JOHN resident of Braintree, Mass., 1650.

RICHARD, bricklayer, b. Eng., proprietor at Cambridge, Mass., 1640, previous to this date was at Dorchester, Mass.

ROBERT, resident of Wethersfield, Conn., 1651.

FRANKLIN

In ancient Eng., a superior freeholder, next below gentlemen in dignity, now called squires.

JOHN, cooper, was at Boston, Mass., 1652.

JOHN was at Roxbury, Mass., 1664.

JONATHAN an inhabitant of Hadley, Mass., 1678.

WILLIAM, blacksmith, came to Ipswich, Mass., 1634, next year was at Newbury, Mass.

FRARY

JOHN came from Eng., to Dedham, Mass., before 1640, was afterwards at Medford, Mass.

FRAZER or FRASER

From French *Fraischeur,* freshness, coolness, bloom, *Friseur,* a hairdresser, *fusier* to curl.

COLIN was at Newbury, Mass., removed to Rowley, Mass., before 1685.

WILLIAM was at Portsmouth, N. H., 1645.

FREAKE

JOHN, merchant, at Boston, Mass., 1660.

FREATHY

WILLIAM, freeman at York, Maine, 1652.

FREEBORN or FREEBORNE

WILLIAM b. Eng., 1594, came to Boston, Mass., 1634, settled in R. I. in 1637 and in that year signed the Covenant at Newport, R. I.

FREELY

NICHOLAS at Casco, Maine, 1680.

FREELOVE

MORRIS married at Portsmouth, R. I., 1681.

FREEMAN

One who enjoys liberty, or is entitled to a franchise, or peculiar privilege. The family is believed to be descendants of natives of Firesea or Fireslend, a Teutonic race occupying the country about Zuyder Zee. In the fifth century a band of *Frisir,* the Latin name, joined the Saxons and Angles in their invasion of England.

EDMUND b. Eng., 1590, settled at Lynn, Mass., 1637, later resided at Duxbury, Mass.

JOHN was original proprietor at Salisbury, Mass., 1639.

JONATHAN, freeman at Hampton, N. H., 1678.

JOSEPH married at Sudbury, Mass., 1680.

RALPH b. Eng., 1630, signed Dedham Covenant, 1651.

SAMUEL b. Kent, Eng., came in Winthrop's fleet 1630, was original proprietor at Watertown, Mass.

FREEZE or FRIEZE

JAMES, builder of ships, b. Eng., 1641-42, settled at Salisbury, Mass., removed 1667 to Amesbury, Mass.

FRENCH

Originally coming from or belonging to France. Tradition states there were three brothers called French armourers in train of William the Conqueror.

EDWARD, tailor, b. Eng., 1590, settled at Ipswich, Mass., 1636, removed to Salisbury, Mass., 1640.

EPHRAIM, early settler of Enfield, Conn., before 1674.

FRANCIS, b. Eng., came at the age of ten years, 1635, with his uncle William, to Cambridge, Mass., settled at Derby, Conn., 1654.

JOHN b. Dorset, Eng., 1612, came to Dorchester, Mass., 1639, the following year removed to Braintree.

JOHN was at Northampton, Mass., 1676, coming from Rehoboth, Mass.

RICHARD was at Cambridge, Mass., 1652, was one of the grantees of Billerica, Mass.

STEPHEN came to Dorchester, Mass., 1630, soon after removed to Weymouth, Mass., made freeman 1634.

THOMAS at Boston, Mass., 1631, removed to Ipswich, Mass., 1639.

THOMAS resident of Charlestown, Mass., removed to Guilford, Conn., 1650.

LIEUT. WILLIAM, brother of John, b. Halstead, Essex, Eng., 1603, settled at Cambridge, Mass., 1635, one of the first settlers of Billerica, Mass., 1652.

FRIEND

JOHN, carpenter, at Saybrook, Conn., removed to Salem, Mass., 1637.

FRIESE

JAMES was at Salisbury, Mass., 1667, afterwards at Newbury, Mass.

FRINK

JOHN a resident of Stonington, Conn., 1666.

JOHN, early settler of Ipswich, Mass., about 1640.

FRISBIE or FRISBY

In Danish, a new or fresh town, Welsh *fies,* French *Frais,* fresh, new, recently built.

EDWARD was a resident of Brandon, Conn., 1668.

JOHN signed plantation Covenant at Brandon, Conn., 1668.

FRISK

JOHN a proprietor at Bridgewater, Mass., 1645.

FUSSELL or FUZILL

JAMES, Scotch descent, was inhabitant of Roxbury, Mass., 1656.

JOHN came from Scotland to Braintree, Mass., before 1664.

WILLIAM, a Scotchman, married at Concord, Mass., 1667.

FROST

From Welsh *Ffrost,* a brag, a popular Scandinavian personal name.

EDMUND, son of Rev. John, b. Eng., 1610, freeman at Cambridge, Mass., 1635.

GEORGE was at Saco, Maine, 1636-40.

JASPER was inhabitant of Boston, Mass., where he married 1660.

JOHN, merchant at Boston, Mass., 1677, proprietor at New Haven, Conn., 1685.

JOSEPH married at Boston, Mass., 1660.

NICHOLAS, brother of Edmund, b. Tiverton, Devonshire, Eng., 1595, came before 1632 to N. E., was at Cambridge, Mass., 1635, afterwards was at Portsmouth, N. H.

THOMAS married at Sudbury, Mass., 1678.

WILLIAM came from Nottinghamshire to Fairfield, Conn., 1639.

FROTHINGHAM

A house or village situated near a strait or arm of the sea. *Frithingham,* the house or village among the hawthorns; *Frith,* Cornish British, a hawthorn, white thorn. *Frith,* Gaelic, a forest, a place of deer.

WILLIAM, Scottish descent, b. near Holderness, Yorkshire, Eng., about 1600, came to N. E. with Winthrop's fleet; one of the original proprietors of Charlestown, Mass., 1630.

FRYE

Cornish British, a hill, a town, a house on most prominent part of a hill or eminence. German *Frie,* free. Dutch *Vry* or *Fry,* free.

GEORGE, weaver, freeman at Weymouth, Mass., 1651.

JOHN, wheelwright, b. Eng., 1601, came from Baringstoke, Hampshire, Eng., to Newbury, Mass., 1638, removed to Andover, Mass.

FRYER or FRIER

JAMES was at Cambridge, Mass., before 1640.

THOMAS granted lands at Salem, Mass., 1639, removed to Gloucester, Mass., 1642.

FULHAM

Place name, a village on the Thames, Eng., derives its name from Saxon *Fullen,* fowl, and *ham,* the house or village of fowl.

FRANCIS married at Watertown, Mass., before 1693.

FULLER

Occupation surname dating from the twelfth century; one who fulls cloth. The ancient seat of the family was in the parish Redenhall in Harleston, near the center of the Hundreds of Eastham, Norfolk, Eng. The English ancestor, John Fuller, lived in this parish.

EDWARD, "Mayflower" passenger, bapt. parish of Redenhall, Norfolk, Eng., 1575, came to Plymouth, Mass., 1620, died following year.

GILES was at Hampton, N. H., 1640.

JACOB, freeman in what is now Danvers, Mass., 1690.

JAMES was at Ipswich, Mass., before 1673.

JOHN b. Eng., 1620, came to Ipswich, Mass., 1634.

JOHN, farmer and malster, b. Eng., settled at Cambridge, Mass., 1635.

LANCELOT was at New Haven, Conn., 1643.

ROBERT, freeman at Dorchester, Mass., 1641, removed to Dedham, Mass., 1643.

ROBERT, bricklayer, freeman at Salem, Mass., 1658, where he had resided since 1639, removed to Rehoboth, Mass.

SAMUEL, physician, "Mayflower" passenger, brother of Edward, settled at Plymouth, Mass., 1620.

SAMUEL married at Rehoboth, Mass., 1673.

THOMAS was resident of what is now Middleton, Mass., in 1638.

THOMAS, proprietor at Woburn, Mass, 1640.

THOMAS an inhabitant of Dedham, Mass., 1643.

WILLIAM, brother of John, came to Ipswich, Mass., 1635, a minor fifteen years of age.

WILLIAM, gunsmith and miller, was at Concord, Mass., 1637.

FURBER

LIEUT. WILLIAM, b. London, Eng., 1614, was at Dover, N. H., 1637.

FURBISH

JOHN was resident at Marblehead, Mass., 1668.

FURNELL

JOHN b. 1607, was at Cambridge, Mass., 1638.

STRONG, soapboiler, freeman at Boston, Mass., 1643.

WILLIAM, brother of the preceding, was a resident of Boston, Mass., before 1652.

FURNESS

DAVID b. 1667, was at Marblehead, Mass., 1692.

FUSSELL or FUZZELL

JOHN, Scotch descent, came to Weymouth, Mass., 1640, recorded at Braintree, Mass., 1664.

JOSHUA a resident of Medfield, Mass., 1649.

FYLER

LIEUT. WALTER, b. Eng., settled at Dorchester, Mass., 1634, removed to Windsor, Conn., 1636.

GAGE

The family is of Norman descent and dates back to 1498 to the English ancestor John Gage.

JOHN of the ninth generation from the above came from Stoneham, County of Suffolk, Eng., in 1630, settling at Boston, Mass. He was one of the proprietors of Ipswich, Mass., removed to Rowley, Mass., 1660.

THOMAS, born Eng., 1625, settled at Yarmouth, Mass., in 1649, died at sea the following year.

GAGER

WILLIAM, surgeon, came in Winthrop's fleet in 1630 from County of Suffolk, Eng., was deacon of the first church of Mass. He died Sept. 20, 1630, leaving a son John who became identified with New London, Conn.

GAINES, GAYNES

HENRY, a freeman at Lynn, Mass., in 1639.

THOMAS was at Lynn, Mass., in 1640.

GALE

The root of Gall or Gaul is *Hal,* the sun, from which is derived *Gal, Gel, Gl,* brilliant, bright, glorious. In Gaelic or Scotch, a stranger, Fingal the white stranger, Dugal the black stranger, alluding to the complexion or color of hair. Gaul the ancient name of France signifying *"Sunny France."*

AMBROSE was at Salem, Mass., before 1663.

BARTHOLOMEW, married at Salem, Mass., 1662.

EDMUND, resident of Cambridge, Mass., where he died 1642.

EDMUND, freeman at Salisbury, Mass., 1666, removed to Marblehead, Mass., afterward to Falmouth, Me.

HUGH, a freeman at Kittery, Me., 1652.

RICHARD was at Watertown, Mass., in 1640.

GALLOP, GALLUP

The name is derived from the German, a corruption of *Gottlieb,* from *Gott,* God, and *lieb,* love or praise—God's praise.

The English family was connected with the parish of Mosterne in Dorsetshire.

JOHN, a fisherman and pilot, settled at Dorcester, Mass., 1630, removed two years later to Boston, Mass.; father of Capt. John Gallup of the Pequot War.

GALLY

JOHN, granted land on Beverly side of Salem, Mass., in 1637.

GALPIN

PHILIP, b. Somersetshire, Eng., settled at New Haven, Conn., 1646, removed to Fairfield, Conn., 1657, later to Rye, N. Y.

GALUSHA

The name of Dutch origin.

DANIEL was at Chelmsford, Mass., before 1691, removed to Dunstable, Mass., where his house was burned by the Indians in 1706.

GAMLYN, GAMLYNE, GAMLIN, GAMBLIN

ROBERT, son of Robert, came to N. E. in the ship William and Francis in 1632 with Rev. Thomas Welde. He located at Roxbury, Mass.

GAMMON

PHILIP, fisherman at Casco, Maine, before 1690.

ROBERT took the oath of allegiance in 1674 at Pemaquid, Me.

GANNETT

MATTHEW came from Eng. in 1638, settled at Hingham, Mass., removed to Scituate, Mass., 1651.

THOMAS, brother of preceding was a proprietor at Duxbury, Mass., removed to Bridgewater, Mass., 1645.

GARDE, GARD, GARRARD

JOHN was at Warwick, R. I., in 1655, removed to New Londonn, Conn., in 1667.

GARDINER

The name derived from the same roots as *Gairden* which is Gaelic origin signifying an enclosed or fortified place, the beacon hill, from *gair,* an outcry, an alarm, and *din,* a hill or fortress. Some authorities claim the derivation of the name is from two Saxon words, *gar,* signifying weapon, and *dyn,* sound, alarm.

CHRISTOPHER, a knight of holy order, came from Bristol, Eng., in 1630, and lived for awhile at Mount Wollaston, near Boston, Mass.

GEORGE, son of Sir Thomas Gardiner, born in Eng. 1601, admitted an inhabitant of R. I., 1638.

LION, a Scotchman, came to Saybrook, Conn., 1635. He built a fort at that place and his son David was the first white child born in Conn. He later removed to Easthampton, Long Island.

RICHARD, *Mayflower* passenger, left no issue.

GARDNER

EDMUND, a freeman at Ipswich, Mass., in 1640.

JACOB took the oath of allegiance at Hatfield, Mass., in 1679.

JAMES married at Gloucester, Mass., in 1662.

JOHN was at Hingham, Mass., as early as 1652.

JOHN, a freeman at Woburn, Mass., 1680.

NATHANIEL, a merchant at Boston, Mass., 1649, afterwards removed to London, Eng.

PETER, b. in Eng. in 1617, embarked on the ship *Elizabeth* at London, Eng., 1635, and settled at Roxbury, Mass.

RICHARD, married at Woburn, Mass., 1651.

SAMUEL was at Wethersfield, Conn., 1641, removed to Hadley, Mass., 1663.

THOMAS, b. Eng. 1592, located at Cape Ann, Mass., 1624, was admitted freeman in 1637 while resident of Salem, Mass.

THOMAS, brother of Peter, died at Roxbury, Mass., 1638.

GARFIELD

From the Saxon *Garwain,* to prepare, German and Dutch *gar,* dressed, done, ready, prepared, and *field,* a place where everything is furnished necessary for an army.

EDWARD, b. Eng. 1575, was a proprietor of Watertown, Mass., in 1635.

GARFORD

JARVIS, freeman at Salem, Mass., in 1639.

GARLAND

GEORGE was a resident of Maine in 1659.

JABEZ was at Dover, N. H., before 1690.

JOHN, b. Eng. 1621, was at Hampton, N. H., 1650.

PETER resided at Charlestown, Mass., as early as 1637.

GARLICK

JOSEPH was at New London, Conn., 1651, removed in a few years to Brookhaven or Easthampton, Long Island, where his wife was charged with witchcraft.

GARNER, GARNIER

From the French *Garnir,* to summons, warn, call out; the Italian *Gvarnier;*

Norman *Garner,* to warn, to summon, to fortify.

Edmund was at Cambridge, Mass., 1635.

Thomas, merchant at Boston, Mass., in 1648.

GARNET, GARNETT

From the Welsh word *Garnedd,* a tumulus, an ancient place of worship. *Garnet,* a precious stone.

John, came from Ipswich, Eng., and became identified with Hingham, Mass., before 1650.

GARNSEY

Henry was at Dorchester, Mass., as early as 1655.

Joseph was at New Haven, Conn., 1647, removed to Stamford, Conn., where he married in 1659.

Joseph, married at Milford, Conn., in 1673.

William, freeman at York, Maine, 1652.

GARRETT, GARRAD, GARRARD

Daniel was prison keeper for many years at Hartford, Conn., where he located in 1640.

Hiram or Herman lived at Concord, Mass., and became a resident of Charlestown, Mass., in 1638.

James was made a freeman at Charlestown, Mass., in 1639; as master of the ship he was lost at sea 1657; his widow returned to England, disposing of his lands.

Richard, a shoemaker, came to N. E. with Winthrop's fleet in 1630, admitted freeman at Charlestown, Mass., in that year. Lost in wreck at sea leaving no issue.

Richard, first town clerk of Scituate, Mass., in 1636.

Robert, a mariner, married at Boston, Mass., before 1643.

GASCOYNE, GASKIN, GASKELL

An ancient English family. The name derived from the Gaelic word *Gaisgell,* valorous.

Edward, shipwright, granted land at Salem, Mass., 1637.

GATCHELL, GETCHELL, GITCHELL

John, b. 1611, was at Salem, Mass., 1637, removed to Marblehead, Mass., 1648.

Samuel, a resident of Salem, Mass., removed to Hampton, N. H., 1641. Hence to Salisbury, N. H., 1648.

GATES

The word *Gate* in Scotland means a road or way.

George, known as captain, b. in Eng. 1634, came to N. E. 1651, was an original proprietor at Haddam, Conn., 1661.

Stephen, the son of Thomas, was of the tenth generation from Thomas Gates, of Higheaster and Thurstebic, County of Essex, Eng.; the latter was born in 1327. Stephen came from Hingham, County of Norfolk, Eng., to Hingham, Mass., in 1638. He removed to Cambridge, Mass., thence in 1654 to Lancaster, Mass. Two years later he returned to Cambridge.

GATLINE or GATTLIFFE

Thomas, a miller, was at Braintree, Mass., 1650.

GAUNT

Peter, was at Lynn, Mass., and removed to Sandwich, Mass., 1637.

GAY

John came to N. E. in 1630 and was admitted freeman at Watertown, Mass., 1635; removed to Dedham, Mass., and became one of the petitioners for establishing the town in 1636.

GAYER

The name signifies a greyhound, a swift dog.

Samuel was a resident of Nantucket, Mass., previous to 1691.

William, brother of the preceding, married at Nantucket, Mass., before 1673.

GAYLORD, GAYLOR, GAYLER, GALLARD, GALLERD

From the word Geller, loud-voiced. The surname is of Norman-French extraction. A place name from Gaillard. It was a personal name in Eng. as early as 1248.

John was a resident of Dorchester, Mass., 1632.

William, brother of the preceding, known as deacon, b. Exeter, Devonshire, Eng., arrived at Boston, Mass., 1630. One of the founders of Dorchester, Mass., 1633; removed to Windsor, Conn., 1636.

GEARS, GEER, GEERS

This surname signifies all sort of wearing apparel and equipments for horses and men. From the Saxon word *gearrian,* to make ready; the name was given to one who took charge of and superintended the gear, as John of the Gear, John O' Gear.

George, b. Eng., 1621, came with his uncle during his boyhood. He was in Boston, Mass., 1635; granted land at New London, Conn., 1651.

Thomas, brother of the preceding, came

to N. E. at the same time. He was located at Enfield, Conn., 1682.

GEARY, GERY, GERRY, GARY

A corruption of Gerard, which see.

ARTHUR, made freeman at Roxbury, Mass., 1639.

DENIS, b. Eng. 1605, came from London, Eng., to Lynn, Mass., 1635.

HENRY was at Salem, Mass., 1648.

THOMAS, b. in Eng. or Ireland, 1638; settled at Charlestown, Mass., (now Stoneham) 1668.

WILLIAM, a freeman at Salem, Mass., 1641.

GEDNEY, GIDNEY

JAMES, b. Eng. 1603; came from Norwich, County of Norfolk, Eng.; admitted freeman at Salem, Mass., 1638.

GEE

PETER, fisherman, was resident of Boston, Mass., 1667.

GENERY or CHENERIE

LAMBERT, was at Watertown, Mass., and 1636 at Dedham, Mass.

GEORGE

Derived from two Greek words signifying earth-workers; a husbandman, farmer.

ELEAZER was at Salem, Mass., 1668.

GIDEON came from Yorkshire, Eng., to Salem, Mass., 1680.

JAMES, on record at Haverhill, Mass., 1652; became a resident of Salisbury, Mass., 1653.

JOHN, apprentice to Gov. Winthrop, 1641, resident Charlestown, Mass., 1657, later at Boston, Mass.

NICHOLAS, innholder, freeman at Dorchester, Mass., 1666.

PETER, at Braintree, Mass., before 1643; removed to Block Island, R. I., 1670.

RICHARD, married at Boston, Mass., 1655.

GERARD, GERAERD, GARRIARD, GERAERDI

Surname of Teutonic origin from *Gar,* all, and *ard,* nature, signifying apt, docile, one ready to do or learn, amiable.

JOHN, of Holland descent, came to Narragansett country in 1651, freeman at Warwick, R. I., 1655.

GERRISH

WILLIAM, b. Bristol, Eng., 1617 or 1620; settled at Newbury, Mass., 1639; removed to Boston, Mass., 1678.

GERRY

HENRY was a resident of Salem, Mass., 1648.

GIBBARD

See Gilbert.

GIBBONS or GIBBINS

The surname from the Welsh word *Guiban,* a fly; *Gibean* in Gaelic signifies a hunch-back; *Gibb-ing,* the son of Gilbert.

AMBROSE, factor for the Company of Laconia came to Portsmouth, N. H., 1630; he afterwards lived in what was called Oyster river.

EDWARD was early at Mount Wollaston, Mass.; became a freeman at Charlestown, Mass., 1631; soon after removed to Boston, Mass.

HENRY was at New Haven, Conn., in 1644; afterwards returned to Eng.

JAMES, b. Eng. 1614; came to Saco, Maine, in 1635.

WILLIAM came to Hartford, Conn., 1639; signer of the compact of 1639, at New Haven, Conn.; no male issue.

GIBBS

Surname from *Gib,* a nickname for Gilbert.

FRANCIS was a resident of Windsor, Conn., 1640.

GILES, came from County of Devon, Eng., 1630; granted land at Dorchester, Mass., 1633; removed to Windsor, Conn., 1635.

JOHN, early settler of Wethersfield, Conn.; representative of General Court of Conn., in 1638.

JOHN came to Cambridge, Mass., 1637; removed later to New Haven, Conn., where he was a freeman in the earlier lists.

MATTHEW was at Charlestown, Mass., before 1650; removed 1654 to Sudbury, Mass.

ROBERT, b. Eng., 1636 or 1639; merchant; descended from an ancient family in Warwickshire, Eng., of the eighth generation from Thomas, from his eldest son of the same name, the line was continued to Sir Henry, father of Robert, who settled at Boston, Mass., before 1660.

SAMUEL, a resident of Sandwich, Mass., before 1649.

THOMAS, brother of the preceding; an early settler of Sandwich, Mass., where his name appears amongst those able to bear arms in 1643.

WILLIAM, hatter, took the oath of fidelity at New Haven, Conn., 1654.

GIBSON

The son of Gib or Gilbert.

CHRISTOPHER, soap-boiler, came to N. E. in 1630; settled at Dorchester, Mass.

JOHN, b. Eng. 1601; came to N. E. 1631; was at Cambridge, Mass., 1634; became a freeman 1637.

RICHARD, clergyman, was at Portsmouth, N. H., 1637; returned to Eng., 1642.

WILLIAM was at Boston, or Lynn, Mass., 1665.

GIDDINGS

A place name from Little Giddings in Huntingdon; also a parish in County of Suffolk, Eng. Some authorities claim the name is derived from the Hebrew word Gideon, signifying a brave soldier. The family is of Scotch and Welsh descent. The earliest English ancestor of the American family is Edmund Giddings, 1334.

GEORGE, born St. Albans, Hertfordshire, Eng., in 1610; came to Ipswich, Mass., 1635.

JOHN, a brother of the preceding, was representative to the General Court for Ipswich, Mass., 1653.

GIFFORD

Ancient English family; the first ancestor known being Sire Randolph de Gifford 1066. The surname is derived from a Saxon word signifying liberal disposition, the giver. It is also a place name from a town on the water of Gifford, Huddington County, Scotland; from the Celtic word *Gaf,* a hook, a bend, and ford.

JOHN, as agent for a company in London, Eng., for iron works; came to Lynn, Mass., 1653.

STEPHEN, b. Eng., 1641; was at Norwich, Conn., 1659; an original proprietor.

WILLIAM, on record at Stamford, Conn., 1647; afterwards at Sandwich, Mass.

GILBERT

From the German word *Gisle,* a pledge or gold-like, bright; also from the Saxon word *Geele,* yellow. The early English ancestor was Gilbert, of Compton, parish of Marldon, County of Devon, in the thirteenth century.

HUMPHREY, b. Eng. 1615; was at Ipswich, Mass., before 1648.

JOHN, b. Devonshire, Eng., came in Winthrop's fleet in 1630; settled at Dorchester, Mass., and 1637 removed to Taunton, Mass.

JOHN, married at Boston, Mass., 1653.

JONATHAN, son of Thomas of the manor of Waldcote, Eng.; on record at Hartford, Conn., 1645.

MATTHEW, one of seven pillars for foundation of the church at New Haven, Conn., 1638; came to Boston, Mass., 1637.

THOMAS, b. Eng., 1600; settled in Windsor, Conn., 1644; removed to Springfield, Mass., 1655.

THOMAS, clergyman, arrived at Boston, Mass., 1661; two years later became the first minister of Topsfield, Mass; removed to Charlestown, Mass., where he died, 1673.

WILLIAM, wrote his name Gibbard; came from Warwickshire, Eng., to New Haven, Conn., 1647. Secretary of the colony of New Haven, 1657.

WILLIAM, made a freeman of Windsor, Conn., 1640.

WILLIAM, cordwainer and merchant; was a resident of Boston, Mass., 1675.

GILDERSLEEVE

Surname no doubt from gilded sleeves, an insignia of office at the Court of Flanders before the Norman Conquest. Roger Gyldersleeve, County of Norfolk, Eng., name appears in the Hundred Rolls in 1273.

RICHARD, b. Hempstead, Hertfordshire, Eng., 1601; came to Boston, Mass., 1635; one of the first settlers of Wethersfield, Conn.; also of Stamford, Conn., 1641; four years later removed to Hempstead, Long Island.

GILE, GUILE, GYLES, GILES

DANIEL, a fisherman at Salem, Mass., 1689.

EDWARD, a freeman at Salem, Mass., 1634.

JOHN was at Dedham, Mass., 1636; made freeman 1643.

JOHN, schoolmaster, was at Salem, Mass., 1690; removed to Boston, Mass.

SAMUEL, brother of the first John, was early settler of Newbury, Mass.; removed in 1640 to Haverhill, Mass.

GILL

A local surname, a valley or woody glen, a narrow dell with a brook running through it, a small stream.

ARTHUR, ship-wright, was at Dorchester, Mass., before 1639, removed to Boston, Mass., made a freeman 1641, returned to Eng., 1654, where he died the following year.

JOHN was in Dorchester, Mass., 1640, in that part of the town that afterwards became Milton; removed to Boston, Mass., where he died 1678.

JOHN, married at Salisbury, Mass., 1645.

JOHN, mariner and merchant at Boston, Mass., 1649-77.

THOMAS was at Hingham, Mass., 1635.

WILLIAM, married at Salem, Mass., 1668.

GILLAM, GILLIAN, GILHAM

A local surname for a town in Scotland.

BENJAMIN, ship carpenter, freeman at Boston, Mass., 1635.

ROBERT was in R. I., in 1638.

GILLETT, GILLETTE

From Guillot, the French diminutive for William; the family came from Gillette, a town in Piedmonte, France, with William the Conqueror, to England.

JONATHAN came to N. E. 1630, freeman at Dorchester, Mass., 1635, removed the next year to Windsor, Conn.

MATTHEW came to Dorchester, Mass., 1634, removed to Windsor, Conn., 1636.

NATHAN, brother of Jonathan, resident of Dorchester, Mass., 1630, removed to Windsor, Conn., 1636.

SAMUEL, married at Hatfield, Mass., 1668.

GILLIGAN

ALEXANDER, at Marblehead, Mass., 1674.

GILLINGHAM

JAMES was at Salem, Mass., before 1692.

GILLON

JOHN, resident of Lynn, Mass., 1637.

THOMAS, brother of the preceding, was at Salem, Mass., 1639.

GILMAN

This family came to Eng. with William the Conqueror, from the province of Maine, France. The family seat was in County of Essex. It is a place name from gill, a brook, hence a *brookman* became gill-man.

EDWARD, grandson of Edward, son of Robert, b. Caston, Eng., came to Boston, Mass., 1638, from Hingham, Eng., made freeman at Hingham, Mass., in that year, removed to Rehoboth, Mass., 1643, and to Ipswich, Mass., soon after, and 1652 to Exeter, N. H.

RICHARD, b. Eng., settled at Hartford, Conn., admitted freeman 1672.

GILSON

Authorities on nomenclature state that the surname is derived from Gill or Giles.

JAMES was a resident of Rehoboth, Mass., 1668.

JOSEPH, first mentioned on record in 1660, when he was married. An original proprietor of Groton, Mass., 1661, he removed to Chelmsford, Mass., 1674, became a resident of Concord, Mass.

THOMAS, b. Eng. 1614, early settler of Chelmsford, Mass.

WILLIAM, at Scituate, Mass., 1631.

GILVIN

THOMAS was at Ipswich, Mass., 1639.

GINGELL, GINGLE, GENGILL, GINGEN

JOHN, at Taunton, Mass., 1639, removed to Dorchester, Mass., thence to Salem, Mass.

WILLIAM, at Westerly, R. I., 1661.

GIRDLER

FRANCIS, freeman at Salem, 1678.

GIVAN

JOHN, Scotch descent, resident of Boston, Mass., 1684.

GLADING, GLADDING

JOHN, married at Newbury, Mass., 1666.

JOHN came from England to Plymouth, Mass., 1640, removed the same year to Bristol, R. I.

GLANFIELD

ROBERT, mariner, married, at Salem, Mass., 1665.

GLASS

From the Welsh word *glas,* meaning green, in the Gaelic, gray, pale, wan.

JAMES was at Plymouth, Mass., 1638.

JAMES, married at Boston, Mass., before 1688.

ROGER, brother of first James, was at Duxbury, Mass., 1639, freeman 1657.

GLAZIER

JOHN, b. Eng. 1640, a resident of Woburn, Mass., 1663.

GLEASON

THOMAS, b. Sulgrave, County of Northampton, Eng., 1607, settled at Watertown, Mass., 1652, on town records of Cambridge, Mass., 1657, removed to Charlestown, Mass., 1666.

GLENN

CHARLES, printer at Boston, Mass., 1682.

GLIDDEN

CHARLES, b. Hampshire, Eng., 1630, settled at Portsmouth, N. H., 1665, took oath of fidelity at Exeter, N. H., 1677, granted land at New Market, N. H., 1697.

GLOVER

The name is of Saxon origin; the family was seated in the counties of Warwick and Kent, Eng., in the fourteenth century.

CHARLES, shipwright, was at Salem, Mass., 1632, freeman 1641, removed to Gloucester, Mass., 1644.

HENRY, b. Eng. 1603, came to N. E. from Ipswich, Eng., 1634, freeman at Dedham, Mass., 1642, located at Boston, Mass., afterwards at New Haven, Conn., about 1645.

JOHN, bapt. at Rainhill, Prescott, Lancashire, Eng., 1600, son of Thomas G., settled at Dorchester, Mass., 1631, removed to Boston, Mass., 1652.

RALPH came in Winthrop's fleet 1630, but died before July, 1633.

STEPHEN, married at Gloucester, Mass., 1658.

GOAD, GOARD

RICHARD, b. Eng. 1618, came to Roxbury, Mass., 1635.

GOBLE

JOHN was at Concord, Mass., removed to Fairfield, Conn., 1644.

GODARD, GODDARD

Surname from the German, signifying God-like disposition. The name may be also local from *Goddard*, a mountain in Switzerland. An early English ancestor Goddardus, 1241, also John Goddard, of Poulton, near Marlborough, Wiltshire, Eng., 1453.

THOMAS came from Marlborough, Wiltshire, Eng., to Boston, Mass., 1635.

WILLIAM came from London, Eng., in 1635, to Watertown, Mass.

GODFREY

Name from the German signifying God's peace, godlike peace, from *God*, and *frid* or *frede*, peace, or from *Gad-fred*, joyful peace.

CHRISTOPHER, resident of Fairfield, Conn., before 1685.

FRANCIS, carpenter, b. Eng., 1600, settled at Duxbury, Mass., 1638, removed to Marshfield, Mass., later to Bridgewater, Mass.

GEORGE was at Eastham, Mass., before 1663.

GEORGE, resident of Marblehead, Mass., 1668-74.

JOHN, b. Eng. 1622, was at Ipswich, Mass., 1634, later at Andover, Mass., and at New London, Conn., 1667.

PETER, married at Newbury, Mass., 1656.

RICHARD, settled at Taunton, Mass., as early at 1650.

WILLIAM, freeman at Watertown, 1640, removed to Hampton, N. H.

GODING, GODDING, GODWIN

GEORGE, resident of Fairfield, Conn., 1651.

HENRY, married at Watertown, Mass., 1663.

RICHARD was at Gloucester, Mass., 1666.

SAMUEL, a resident of Fairfield, Conn., 1670.

GOFF, GOFFE

The name is from the Welsh word *Gof*, a smith.

EDWARD came from Ipswich, County of Suffolk, Eng., in 1634, to Watertown, Mass.

JOHN, freeman at Newbury, Mass., 1639, died two years later, no male issue.

JOHN, freeman at Boston, Mass., 1678.

GOLDHAM

HENRY was at New Haven, Conn., 1645, later at Guilford, Conn., no male issue.

GOLDSMITH

A name of a trade; formerly in England, a banker.

JOSHUA, married at Salisbury, Mass., 1667.

RALPH was an inhabitant of Mass., 1661.

THOMAS, granted land at Salem, Mass., 1643, soon afterward removed to Southampton, Long Island.

ZACCHEUS, freeman at Wenham, Mass., 1685; his brother Richard, unmarried, was killed by lightning in that town 1673.

GOLDTHWAIT

A Yorkshire family.

THOMAS, b. Eng. 1610, came in Winthrop's fleet in 1630, a resident of Roxbury, Mass., 1631.

GOLT, GAULT

WILLIAM, cordwainer, b. 1608, came from Yarmouth, County of Norfolk, to Salem, Mass., 1637.

GOOCH, GOUCH, GUTCH

EDWARD, resident of Boston, Mass., 1685, warden of King's Chapel, 1692.

JOHN, freeman at York, Maine, 1652.

ROBERT was at Salem, Mass., 1638, removed to near the mouth of Kennebec river, Maine.

GOODALE, GOODELL

Name derived from *Good-hall* or *Goodale*.

JOSEPH, married before 1681 at Boston, Mass.

NEHEMIAH, resident of Lynn, Mass., 1673.

RICHARD came from Yarmouth, County of Norfolk, Eng., to Newbury, Mass., 1638, removed to Salisbury, Mass., 1639.

RICHARD, mariner, resident of Boston, Mass., 1665.

ROBERT, planter, b. Eng. 1604, came from Ipswich, Eng., to Salem, Mass., 1637.

GOODE or GOOD

ROBERT, inhabitant of Mass., 1646.

THOMAS, b. Eng. 1614, came from Southampton, Eng., to N. E., 1638, was at Salem, Mass., 1640.

GOODENHOUSE

See Vangoodenhousen.

GOODENOW, GOODNOW, GOODENOUGH

Name from the French *Godenot* or *Godeno,* a jack in the box, a little ugly man. It may be, however, local from Gudenow, a town on the Lower Rhine, Germany.

EDMUND, b. Shaftsbury, Borough of Dorset, Wiltshire, Eng., 1611, came from Dunhead, Wiltshire, Eng., settled at Sudbury, Mass., 1638.

JOHN, husbandman, eldest brother of the preceding, b. Eng. 1596, settled at Sudbury, Mass., 1638.

THOMAS, brother of the preceding, b. Eng. 1608, settled with his brothers at Sudbury, Mass., 1638, afterwards removed to Marlboro, Mass.

GOODHEART

ISBRAND, servant of Caspar Varleet at Hartford, Conn., 1658.

GOODHUE

A compound name of good and Hugh, Good-Hugh; Will and Robert Goodhewan were English ancestors 1280.

NICHOLAS, cloth-worker, b. Eng. 1675, came from London, Eng., 1635, to Ipswich, Mass.

WILLIAM, b. Eng. 1612-13, immigrated to N. E.; was a freeman at Ipswich, Mass., 1636, first of the name in America.

GOODING

DANIEL was at Kittery, Maine, 1659.

GOODMAN

JOHN, *Mayflower* passenger, unmarried.

JOHN, married at Sudbury, Mass., 1656.

RICHARD, came from England to Cambridge, Mass., where he was a proprietor 1632. Removed to Hartford, Conn., later to Hadley, Mass.

GOODRICH

Surname of Saxon origin. God suffix *ric,* meaning rich, signifying rich in God or in Goodness. The Domesday Book indicates the family was of standing at the time of the Norman Conquest. A Father Godric was elected Abbott of the Abbey Croyland 870. Reference is made to Goodrich Castle 1204.

BARTHOLOMEW, signer of the plantation and church covenant at Branford, Conn., 1667.

JOHN was at Wethersfield, 1643.

WILLIAM, brother of the preceding, born Bury St. Edwards, County of Suffolk, Eng., came to Wethersfield, Conn., 1643.

GOODRIDGE, GUTTERIDGE

JOHN was at Watertown, Mass., 1637.

JOHN, tailor, freeman at Boston, Mass., 1642.

RICHARD, resident of Guilford, Conn., 1639.

ROBERT, innkeeper, in Boston, Mass., before 1677.

THOMAS, mariner, resident of Boston, Mass., before 1691.

WILLIAM came from Eng., settled at Watertown, Mass., 1636.

GOODSELL

THOMAS, on record at Branford, Conn., 1667.

GOODSPEED

ROGER, married at Barnstable, Mass., 1641.

GOODWIN, GOODWYN

The surname derived from the Saxon *God,* or *good,* and *win,* conqueror that is, a conqueror in God, converted or victorious in God. The family is of ancient English origin seated at Braintree and Bocking, County of Essex; the first English ancestor is Robert Goodwin, living in Norwich, 1238.

ADAM, b. 1617, came to N. E. 1637, as servant to John Moulton, of Ormsby, County of Norfolk, Eng., was at Providence, R. I., 1641.

CHRISTOPHER, mason, b. Eng., 1618, on record in 1647 at Charlestown, Mass.

DANIEL, b. Eng., came from Torrington near Plymouth, Eng., settled at Kittery, Maine, 1652, kept an inn at Berwick, Maine, 1662.

EDWARD, shipwright, was at Salisbury, Mass., 1667.

EDWARD, freeman at Boston, Mass., 1641.

JOHN, married at Charlestown, Mass., 1669, removed to Boston, Mass.

JOHN, an early settler of Reading, Mass.

NATHANIEL, brother of the preceding, freeman at Reading, Mass., 1679.

OZIAS, b. County of Essex, Eng., 1596, came to N. E. from Braintree, County of Essex, 1632, settled at Cambridge, Mass., removed to Hartford, Conn., with the first settlers, 1636.

RICHARD, married at Gloucester, Mass., 1666.

RICHARD, married at Amesbury, Mass., 1677.

WILLIAM, known as Elder William, brother of Ozias, came to Cambridge, Mass., 1632, removed to Hartford, Conn., 1636, and in 1654 to Hadley, Mass., left no male issue.

GOODWRIGHT

ISAAC was at Kittery, Maine, 1686.

GOODYEAR

STEPHEN, resident of New Haven, Conn., 1638, Deputy Governor of New Haven Colony, 1643-58, lost at sea on his return to Eng., 1658.

GOOKIN, GOOGINS

From the Gaelic word *Gugan,* a bud, flower, a daisy.

DANIEL, b. County of Kent, Eng., 1612, went with his father Daniel, of the fourth generation from Arnold Gookin, to Virginia, and came to Boston, Mass., 1644, soon after settled in Roxbury, Mass., removed to Cambridge, Mass., 1648. In the Indian Wars he attained the rank of Major-General.

GOOLE

FRANCIS was at Duxbury, Mass., 1643, removed to Braintree, Mass.

GOOSE

WILLIAM, resident of Salem, Mass., 1637, was at Charlestown, Mass., 1658.

GORDON

The Gordon clan has a record that extends to the days of Malcolm III, King of Scotland. The head of the clan is the Marquis of Huntley, one of whose ancestors raised the famous regiment the Gordon Highlanders. Gordon Castle is the family seat, the badge is the Ivy, the war cry A Gordon! A Gordon! The ancient family is of Norman origin. Richard de Gordon was Knight bannert, 1150. The surname is from the Gaelic word *Gurtduine,* a fierce man; the Welsh word *Gurddyn,* a strong man; *Cawrdyn,* a hero, a giant.

ALEXANDER, husbandman, native of Scotland, soldier in the Royalist army, sent by Cromwell to Watertown, Mass., 1651, as a prisoner, released in 1654, he went to Exeter, N. H.

JOHN was at Bridgewater, Mass., 1682.

NICHOLAS, an inhabitant of N. H., 1689.

GORE

JOHN, freeman at Roxbury, Mass., 1637.

GORHAM, GORUM, GORAM

The family traced to the De Gorrams of La Tanniere on the borders of Brittany, France. William, the son of Ralph de Gorham, built a castle in 1128.

RALPH, son of James, b. Benefield, Northamptonshire, Eng., 1575, came to N. E. 1635, to Plymouth, Mass., returned to Eng., where he died 1643, leaving one son Captain John, b. at Benefield, Eng., a land owner at Yarmouth, Maine, 1652, died at Swansea, Mass., 1675.

GORNELL

JOHN, tanner, came in Winthrop's fleet 1630 to N. E. from Devonshire or County of Suffolk, Eng., located at Dorchester, Mass., left no issue.

GORTON

From the Gaelic word *Gairtean,* a garden, a small piece of enclosed arable land.

JOHN was at Roxbury, Mass., before 1636.

SAMUEL, b. Groton, parish of Manchester, County of Lancaster, Eng., 1592. Came to Boston, Mass., 1636, soon after went to Plymouth, Mass., thence in 1638 to R. I., and 1641 settled at Warwick, R. I.

THOMAS, freeman at Portsmouth, R. I., 1655.

GOSNALL

HENRY, resident of Boston, Mass., 1634.

GOSS

From the Saxon word *Gos,* a goose.

EDWARD, a resident of Marblehead, Mass., 1668.

JAMES, came to N. E. in Winthrop's fleet 1630, freeman at Watertown, Mass., 1631.

PHILIP lived at Roxbury, Mass., purchased estate in Lancaster, Mass., 1687.

RICHARD, an inhabitant of N. H. 1689.

GOTT

CHARLES came with Endicott from Eng. 1628, settled at Salem, Mass., removed to Wenham, Mass., 1654.

GOULD, GOOLD

The English family traced to Thomas Goold, of Bovington, parish of Hemel Hempstead, Hertfordshire, Eng., born about 1455.

ADAM was at Gorton, Mass., before 1683; removed to Woburn, Mass.

CHRISTOPHER, at Hampton, N. H., 1660.

DANIEL, freeman at Newport, R. I., 1655.

EDWARD, pailmaker, b. Hawkhurst, County of Kent, Eng., 1607, came to Hingham, Mass., 1635.

FRANCIS, resident of Braintree, Mass., before 1655.

HENRY was at Ipswich, Mass., 1675.

JAMES, took the oath of fidelity Haverhill, Mass., 1677.

JARVIS or JARVICE, cordwainer, came to N. E. with family of Clement Bates from the parish of All Hallows, Lydd,

County of Kent, Eng., granted land at Hingham, Mass., 1636, removed to Boston, Mass., 1646.

JEREMIAH, freeman, Newport, R. I., 1638.

JOHN, husbandman, b. Eng., 1610, came from Towcester, Northamptonshire, Eng., 1635, to Stoneham, Mass.

JOHN, resident of Charlestown, Mass., 1636.

JOHN was at Newport, R. I., 1655.

JOHN, married at Taunton,' Mass., 1673.

NATHAN, son of Nathan, came from St. Edmundsbury in South Britain. He was at Milford, Conn., 1647, three years later removed to Fairfield, Conn.

NATHAN, a resident of Salisbury, Mass., 1660.

ROBERT, married at Hull, Mass., 1666.

THOMAS, b. Eng., 1607, came to Boston, Mass., 1639, where he was admitted freeman 1641.

THOMAS, married at Newport, R. I., 1655.

THOMAS, member of the Church of Charlestown, Mass., 1640, later removed to Boston, Mass.

THOMAS, married at Boston., Mass., 1656.

ZACCHUS, b. Eng., 1589, son of Richard Golde, was of the sixth generation from Thomas Goold, who resided at Great Monerden, County of Bucks, Eng., Zaccheus came from Hants Green, near Potter's Row, County of Bucks in 1638, to N. E.; he located at Weymouth, Mass., removed to Lynn, Mass., and 1644 to Ipswich, Mass., being that part known as Topsfield.

GOULDER

FRANCIS was at Plymouth, Mass., 1643.

GOULDING, GOULDEN, GOLDEN

The ancient spelling of the name was Gouldingham, the surname being derived from *goal,* a bound, and *ham,* a hamlet or town. Alanus de Gouldingham is mentioned in 1302 in the Foldera and an early roll of Parliament.

PETER, saddler, b. Eng., 1635, came from Shipman, six miles from Norwich, Eng.; was in Virginia 1667, afterwards came to Boston, Mass., and in 1693 was at Worcester, Mass.; died at Salisbury, Mass., 1703.

ROGER, mariner, brother of the preceding, known as Captain Roger, was inhabitant of R. I., 1676.

WILLIAM, clergyman, was resident of Boston, Mass., 1646.

GOURDING

ABRAHAM, mariner, Boston, Mass., 1672.

GOVE

EDWARD was first at Salisbury, Mass., removed to Hampton, N. H.; representative in first assembly of N. H., 1680.

JOHN, dealer and worker in brass, settled in Charlestown, Mass., where he was freeman, 1631.

JOHN, brother of Edward, married at Cambridge, Mass., 1658.

GOWING or GOWEN

From the Gaelic, signifying a smith. The gowan or smith of a Highland clan was held in high estimation. His skill in the manufacture of military weapons was usually united with great dexterity in using them and with the strength of body which his profession required. The Gowan ranked as third officer in the Chief's household.

JOHN was at Lynn, Mass., 1682.

NATHANIEL, freeman at Reading, Mass., 1691.

RICHARD or ROBERT, b. Scotland, 1618, resided at Dedham, Mass., 1634, afterwards at Wenham, Lynn, Watertown, and was at Lynnfield, Mass., 1660.

GOYT

JOHN was at Dorchester, Mass., 1635, removed to Salem, Mass., 1642.

GOZZARD

DANIEL came from Eng. to Hartford, Conn., 1646.

NICHOLAS, a resident of Windsor, Conn., where he died 1693.

GRAFTON

JOSEPH, mariner and merchant, freeman at Salem, Mass., 1637.

THOMAS, inhabitant of N. H., 1689.

GRAHAM

This surname is used interchangeably with Graeme in Scotland. It is also spelled Grahames, Graems and Grimes. The patronymic is derived from Greme, who was regent of Scotland during the minority of Eugene II, 419. The derivation of the name is from the Anglo Saxon *grim,* Dutch *germ,* Welsh *grem,* Gaelic *guiam,* surly, sullen, dark, having a fierce and stern look, courageous. There is no record of the family earlier than King David of Scotland, 1123, and was of local origin from a place called Graham or Graeme. The only place now, however, is near Kestoven, Lincolnshire, Eng. The name is found in the Hundred Rolls of Eng., in the twelfth century, where the family was established in Linlithgowshire, Forfurshire, Perth-stone, Shirlingshire, Dumfriesshire. The family possesses the dukedom marquisate and earldom of Montrose, the marquisate of Graham and Buchanan, earldoms of Airth Kincardine, Menteith and Strathen, Viscountcies of Dundas, Dundee and Preston, lordships of Abevithven, Kilpoint and barony of Esk, etc.

BENJAMIN was resident of Hartford, Conn.

JAMES was attorney-general for Andros at Boston, Mass.

GRAME

SAMUEL, pewterer, joined church at Boston, 1642.

GRANGER

From the Saxon, one who superintended a large farm or grange.

BYRAN was at Salem, Mass., 1637.

LAUNCELOT came from Eng., to Ipswich, Mass., 1648; removed to Newbury, Mass.

GRANNIS

EDWARD, married at Hartford, Conn., 1655, removed to Hadley, Mass., 1670, afterwards was at New Haven, Conn.

JOHN, brother of the preceding, was at New Haven, Conn., 1677.

GRANT

The surname either from Saxon word *grant,* that signifies crooked or bowed; in old Irish, *Grant* and *Ciar,* signifies much the same thing. In French, *grand* signifies great, brave, valorous; in Irish the letter d is sounded short and thereby changed to t. Richard Grant was made Archbishop of Canterbury in 1229.

ALEXANDER, one of the founders of the Scots Charitable Society at Boston, Mass., 1657.

CALEB, mason, located at Watertown, Mass., 1670.

CHRISTOPHER, glover, b. Eng., 1608, settled at Watertown, Mass., 1634.

EDWARD, shipwright, married at Boston, Mass., 1658.

JAMES, one of the founders of the Scots Charitable Society at Boston, Mass., 1657.

JAMES was at Charlestown, Mass., 1658, took oath of allegiance at York, Maine, 1681.

JAMES, resident of Dedham, Mass., 1664.

JOHN, living at Newbury, Mass., 1690, taxed at Rowley, Mass., 1691.

MATTHEW, b. Eng., 1601, came from Devonshire, Eng., to Dorchester, Mass., 1630, removed to Windsor, Conn., 1636.

PETER, one of the founders of Scots Charitable Society at Boston, 1657, later removed to Hartford, Conn.

ROBERT, at Ipswich, Mass., 1685.

SETH came to Cambridge, Mass., 1632, removed to Hartford, Conn., where he died 1647.

GRAVES

Ancient English family living in counties of Lincoln, Nottingham, Derby and York. In the first records the name is spelt Greves or Greaves, appearing in the parish of Beeley near Cholsworth, Derbyshire. The first progenitor reported is John de la Greves in the twelfth century.

FRANCIS was resident of Salisbury, Mass., before 1690.

GEORGE, original progenitor of Hartford, Conn., where he was representative 1657.

JOHN, b. Eng., before 1585, was at Concord, Mass., 1643.

JOHN, b. Eng., came to Roxbury, Mass., 1633, died 1644.

JOHN, cordwainer, freeman at Ipswich, Mass., 1685.

MARK was at Lynn, Mass., before 1657.

RICHARD was at Boston, Mass., 1656.

ROBERT, a resident of Ipswich, Mass., 1638.

SAMUEL, b. Eng., settled at Lynn, Mass., 1630, was at Hartford, Conn., 1645.

SAMUEL, feltmaker, married at Ipswich, Mass., 1658.

THOMAS, engineer, laid out Charlestown, Mass., 1629, returned to Eng., 1632-33.

THOMAS, b. Eng., 1585, settled at New Haven, Conn., 1637, came to Hartford, Conn.; one of the founders of Hadley, Mass., 1645.

THOMAS, known as Admiral Thomas, b. Radcliffe, Eng., in 1605, admitted to membership in church at Charlestown, Mass., 1639.

WILLIAM was at Dover, N. H., 1659.

GRAY

A place name from a town in Burgundy, France, on the banks of the Saone. Rollo, chamberlain to Robert, Duke of Normandy, received from him the castle and honor of Croy in Picardy; his family assumed the name of De Croy afterwards changed to De Gray.

EBENEZER, resident of Hartford, Conn., 1638.

EDWARD, merchant, came in his youth from Eng.; in 1643, at Plymouth, Mass.

EDWARD, from Lancashire, Eng., was an apprentice at Boston, Mass., 1686.

HENRY married at Fairfield, Conn., 1643.

JAMES took oath of allegiance at Providence, R. I., 1671.

JOHN, brother of Henry, was at Fairfield, Conn., 1643.

JOHN married at Yarmouth, Mass., 1643.

JOSEPH married at Taunton, Mass., 1668.

ROBERT, b Eng., 1634, settled at Salem, Mass., 1669.

SAMUEL married at Boston, Mass., before 1684.

SAMUEL married at Salem, Mass., 1671.

SAMUEL, goldsmith, was at Boston, Mass., removed to New London, Conn., where he died 1713, under twenty-nine years of age; no issue.

THOMAS purchased Nantucket Island from the Indians, 1622; was also at Salem and Marblehead, at the latter place in 1648; bachelor.

THOMAS, eldest brother of Edward of Plymouth, came to Plymouth, Mass., 1643, where he died 1652.

WALTER a resident of Hartford, Conn., 1644.

GREELEY, GREELY, GRELE

A place name same as Grelley or De Grelley from Greilly, France. *Grele* in French, slender, slim, delicate. In the Roll of Battle Abbey the name is included as coming to England with William the Conqueror.

ANDREW, miller, b. Eng., 1617, on records of Salisbury, Mass., 1640, was at Haverhill, Mass., 1669.

NATHANIEL, brother of the preceding, was at Salisbury, Mass., 1649.

GREEN, GREENE

The family is of great antiquity being connected with the Grene or Greene of Northamptonshire, Eng. The earliest on record was Alexander de Boketon in 1336 took the name of Att Grene or de la Grene. The Boketon Manor House was known as an estate before the Conquest, situated as a parish in the southern division of Northamptonshire, now known as Broughton. The ancient manor seat, the residence of the Grenes, was at Greene's Norton, formerly Norton Davey, and in the Doomesday Book, Nortone, a large village two miles west by north from Towcester.

ABRAHAM was at Hampton, N. H., 1678.

BARTHOLOMEW freeman at Cambridge, Mass., 1634, removed to Hartford, Conn., 1636.

CHARLES, a resident of Marblehead, Mass., 1668.

DANIEL was at Wickford, R. I., 1671.

HENRY, clergyman, ordained as first minister at Reading, Mass., 1645, died three years later.

HENRY freeman at Ipswich, Mass., 1640.

HENRY b. Eng., 1620, was at Hampton, N. H., 1644.

HENRY was at Wickford, R. I., 1674.

ISAAC was a resident of Salisbury, Mass., 1678.

JACOB a resident of Salisbury, Mass., 1678.

JAMES b. Eng., about 1620, freeman at Charlestown, Mass., 1647, removed later to Malden, Mass.

JAMES lived at Romney Marsh now Chelsea, Mass., married at Dorchester, Mass., 1661.

JAMES, mariner, sold lands at Portsmouth, R. I., 1669.

JOHN came from London, Eng., to Charlestown, Mass., 1632.

JOHN, surgeon, grandson of Richard, son of Richard, b. Bowridge Hill, parish of Gillingham, Dorsetshire, Eng., about 1590; first settled at Salem, Mass., 1635, the following year went to Providence, R. I., and in 1639 was at Wickford, R. I.

JOHN a resident of Sandwich, Mass., 1643.

JOHN a resident of Kittery, Maine, 1652.

JOHN located at Fairfield, Conn., 1648, made freeman 1662.

JOHN b. Eng., 1630, settled at Stamford, Conn., 1657.

JOHN, mariner, brother of James of Chelsea, Mass., was at Malden, Mass., 1673.

JOHN, inhabitant of Newport, R. I., 1655.

JOHN married at Woburn, Mass., 1671.

JOSEPH was at Plymouth, Mass., 1643.

JOSEPH resident of Weymouth, Mass., 1632.

NATHANIEL married at Boston, Mass., 1657.

NICHOLAS died at York, Maine, 1663.

PERCIVAL, brother of Bartholomew, b. Eng., 1603, freeman at Cambridge, Mass., 1636.

RALPH was at Boston, Mass., before 1642, removed to Malden, Mass., before 1654.

RICHARD came to N. E., 1622 was at Weston's plantation at Weymouth, Mass.

RICHARD, mariner, inhabitant of Boston, Mass., 1654.

ROBERT married at Hingham, Mass., 1666.

THOMAS, b. Eng., 1600, came from St. Albans, Hertfordshire, Eng., to Lynn, Mass., 1635, afterwards was at Ipswich, Mass.; about 1655 removed to Malden, Mass.

TOBIAS was at Hull, Mass., 1675.

WILLIAM, freeman at Charlestown, Mass., 1644, resided in that part that became Woburn, Mass.

WILLIAM, mariner, kept hotel at Boston, Mass., 1659-77.

WILLIAM took oath of allegiance in Providence, R. I., 1671.

WILLIAM original proprietor of Groton, Mass., 1660.

GREENFIELD

SAMUEL, weaver, b. Eng., 1610, came from Norwich, County of Norfolk, Eng., to Salem, Mass., 1637, removed to Hampton, N. H., thence to Exeter, N. H., 1645.

THOMAS was at Sandwich, Mass., 1643.

GREENHILL

SAMUEL came from Staplehurst, County of Kent, Eng., to Cambridge, Mass., 1634, removed to Hartford, Conn., 1636.

GREENLAND

HENRY, physician, b. Eng., 1628, resident of Newbury, Mass., 1662-75.

JOHN was at Charlestown, Mass., 1644.

GREENLEAF

The family is of Huguenot origin, the name being translated from the French word *Feuillvert.* The family located at Ipswich, County of Suffolk, Eng.

EDMUND, dyer, son of John, bapt. parish of St. Mary's La Tour, Ipswich, County of Suffolk, Eng., 1574. Settled at Newbury, Mass., 1639, removed to Boston, Mass., 1650.

JOHN, shipwright, married at Boston, Mass., 1666.

GREENMAN, GRENMAN

DAVID early proprietor of Taunton, Mass., freeman at Newport, R. I., 1655.

JOHN inhabitant of R. I., 1638.

GREENOUGH

Local name, the green hill.

WILLIAM b. Eng., 1639, sea captain, freeman at Boston, Mass., 1669; no male issue.

WILLIAM, shipwright, cousin of the preceding, born Eng., freeman at Boston, Mass., 1673.

GREENSMITH

STEPHEN was resident of Boston, Mass., 1636.

THOMAS was at Hartford, Conn., 1660.

GREENWAY, GRINWAY

CLEMENT was at Saco, Maine, 1636.

JOHN, freeman at Dorchester, Mass., 1630.

RICHARD lived at Salem, Mass., 1637.

GREENWOOD

The family in Eng., in the County of York, 1154; the name originating with Richard Greenwode in the reign of Richard III.

NATHANIEL, son of Miles, b. Norwich, Eng., came to Boston, Mass., married at Weymouth, Mass., 1660.

SAMUEL was at Boston, Mass., 1670.

THOMAS, weaver, son of Miles of Norwich, Eng., b. 1643, was at Cambridge, Mass., 1665, removed to Newton, Mass., 1667.

GREGORY

Derived from Gregor, some of the Clan McGregor changed their name to Gregory when the clan was prosecuted and outlawed. The English family traced to Adam Gregory of Lancashire, Eng., 1450.

ELIZAPHAL, was at Windsor, Conn., 1641.

HENRY, son of John, sixth generation from Adam, settled at Boston, Mass., 1633, removed to Springfield, Mass., 1639, later to Stratford, Conn.

JOHN was at New Haven, Conn., removed to Norwalk, Conn., 1653.

JOHN was at Weymouth, Mass., before 1669.

JONAS married at Ipswich, Mass., 1653.

GRENNELL

MATTHEW, freeman at Portsmouth, R. I., 1655.

GRICE, GRISE

CHARLES, freeman at Braintree, Mass., 1651.

JOSIAH, brother of the preceding, freeman at Boston, Mass., 1690.

SAMUEL, freeman at Boston, Mass., 1690.

GRIDLEY

RICHARD resident of Boston, Mass., 1631.

THOMAS b. County of Essex, Eng., settled at Cambridge, Mass., about 1635; removed to Hartford, Conn., later to Farmington, Conn., thence to Northampton, Mass.

GRIFFIN, GRIFFING

In Welsh *Griffwn*, a man having a crooked nose, like a hawk's beak.

Griffyn, Cornish British signifies to give.

HUGH, freeman at Sudbury, Mass,. 1645.

HUGH at Stratford, Conn., 1654.

HUMPHREY, b. Eng., 1605, at Ipswich, Mass., 1641.

JASPER at Marblehead, Mass., 1674.

JOHN resident of Windsor, Conn., 1646, one of the first settlers of Simsbury, Conn., granted land for introduction of manufacture of pitch and tar.

JOHN, caulker, married at Boston, Mass., 1655.

MATTHEW at Saybrook, Conn., 1645, removed to Charlestown, Mass., where he married 1654.

PHILIP at Salisbury, Mass., 1657.

PHILIP died at Scarborough, Maine, 1668.

RICHARD, freeman at Concord, Mass., 1635.

RICHARD, resident of Roxbury, Mass., before 1657.

ROBERT, freeman at Newport, R. I., 1653.

ROBERT, Welsh descent, b. 1590, settled at Concord, Mass., 1639.

THOMAS at New London, Conn., 1651, removed 1654 to Stonington, Conn.

GRIFFITH

Surname from Welsh *cryf*, strong, and *ffyd*, faith, one who has strong faith.

JOSHUA b. Eng., 1610, came to Cambridge, Mass., from London, Eng., 1635.

WILLIAM at Boston, Mass., 1676.

GRIGGS

GEORGE, b. Eng., 1593, came from London, Eng., to Boston, Mass., 1635; no male issue.

HUMPHREY died Braintree, Mass., 1657.

STEPHEN at Marblehead, Mass., 1674.

THOMAS b. Eng., at Roxbury, Mass., 1639, where he died 1646.

WILLIAM, cooper, freeman at Boston, Mass., 1672.

GRIGSON, GREGSON

Surname, a son of Greer or Gregor, same as McGregor.

THOMAS, merchant, came to Boston, Mass., 1637, same year went to New Haven, Conn.; lost at sea in 1646.

GRIMES

GEORGE, of Scotch descent, born 1650, lived at Charlestown, Billerica and Lexington, Mass.

HENRY at Hartford, Conn., where he died 1684.

Samuel, pewterer, freeman at Boston, Mass., 1642, removed to Plymouth, Mass., about 1657.

WILLIAM died at Greenwich, Conn., leaving no male issue.

GRINNELL

Place name from Grenelle, a town in France.

DANIEL, inhabitant of Portsmouth, R. I.

MATTHEW, French Huguenot, b. Macon, France, 1602, freeman at Newport, R. I., 1638, removed to Portsmouth, R. I., 1655.

GRISWOLD, GRESWOLD

Place name; family established at Solehull, Warwickshire, Eng., prior to 1400.

EDWARD, attorney, son of George, b. Eng., 1607, came from Kenilworth, Eng., to Windsor, Conn., 1639, removed 1667 to Killingworth, now Clinton, Conn.

FRANCIS at Cambridge, Mass., 1639, lived at Charlestown, Mass., 1649.

MATTHEW, younger brother of Edward, b. Kenilworth, Warwickshire, Eng., settled at Windsor, Conn., 1639, removed to Saybrook, Conn., 1644, instrumental in settling Lyme, Conn.

GROOM

NICHOLAS inhabitant of Mass., 1651.

SAMUEL, mariner, at Salisbury, Mass., 1650, returned to London, Eng., before 1658.

GROSS, GROSSE

ISAAC, husbandman, b. Cornwall, Eng., admitted to church at Boston, Mass., 1636, granted land at Muddy River, now Brookline, Mass.

GROSVENOR

Name signifies a great hunter or the grand huntsman, from the French *Gros Veneur*. The ancestor of the family assumed the name from holding the office of grand huntsman to the Duke of Normandy. English family traced to Gilbert Le Grosvenor, related to William the Conqueror.

JOHN, son of Sir Richard G of the sixteenth generation from Gilbert Le Grosvenor, b. Eng., 1641, came from Cheshire, Eng., to N. E., 1670, settled at Roxbury, Mass., 1673, removed to Pomfret, Conn., 1686.

GROUT

Family originated in Germany where they bore the name of Grotioux or Grout alias Grote; descended from

Guidic or the Great, a courageous and daring tribe of Belgic Gaul fifty years before the Christian Era. The English lineage is traced to Sir Richard Groutte of Walton, Derbyshire, Eng., knighted 1587.

JOHN, son of Sir Richard, b. Eng., settled at Watertown, Mass., 1640, removed to Sudbury, Mass., 1643, was known as Captain John.

WILLIAM resident of Charlestown, Mass., 1664.

GROVE

EDWARD, soldier, of Salem and Boston, Mass., 1636; no male issue.

GROVER

From Groover, Graver, one who carves or engraves.

ANDREW, married at Malden, Mass., 1674.

EDMUND, resident of Salem, Mass., 1633.

JOHN was at Charlestown, Mass., 1634, removed to Boston, Mass., the part now known as Chelsea.

THOMAS was at Malden, Mass., 1642.

GROVES

JOHN was at Kittery, Maine, removed to Little Compton, R. I.

PHILIP was representative to General Court from Hartford, Conn., 1642, removed to Stratford, Conn., before 1650.

GROW

JOHN b. Eng., 1642, settled at Ipswich, Mass., where he married 1669.

GRUBB

GABRIEL at Isle of Shoals, N. H., before 1677.

THOMAS, leather dresser, freeman at Boston, Mass., 1634.

GRUMAN, GRUMMAN, GOWMAN

JOHN, freeman at Fairfield, Conn., 1664.

GRUNDY

ROBERT resident of Roxbury, Mass., before 1679.

GUERNSEY

JOHN married at Suffield, Conn., 1693.

JOHN came from Isle of Guernsey, Eng., settled at Milford, Conn., 1640.

GUILD, GUILE

JOHN, weaver, born Eng., 1616, came to N. E. 1636, admitted church at Dedham, Mass., 1640.

GULL

WILLIAM at Wethersfield, Conn., 1649.

GULLIFORD, GULLIFER, GULLIVER

ANTHONY at Dorchester, Mass., 1656, in that part of the town now Milton, freeman 1666.

GULLY

JACOB, resident of Boston, Mass., 1677.

GULTHROP

RALPH admitted inhabitant of Boston, Mass., 1643.

GUNN

From Cornish British *Gun*, a plain, a down, a common.

JASPER, physician, b. Eng., 1606, came to Roxbury, Mass., 1635, removed to Hartford, Conn., 1645 and 1657 to Milford, Conn.

THOMAS, freeman at Dorchester, Mass., 1635, removed to Windsor, Conn., the following year.

GUNNISON

HUGH b. Eng., 1610, freeman at Boston, Mass., 1636, removed to Kittery, Maine, 1646, hence to Wells, Maine, 1654.

GUPPIE, GUPPY, GUPPEY

JOHN, freeman at Weymouth, Mass., 1653, removed to Charlestown, Mass.

REUBEN at Salem, Mass., 1648.

ROBERT, resident of Salem, Mass., 1647.

GURLEY

WILLIAM at Northampton, Mass., 1679.

GURNEY

Place name from the town of Gournay in Normandy.

EDWARD resident of Cambridge, Mass., 1636.

JOHN b. Eng., 1615, settled at Braintree, Mass., 1635.

RICHARD resident of Weymouth, Mass., before 1665.

GUSTIN

Huguenot ancestry; Edmund de la Tacq, of St. Owens Isle of Jersey, Eng., progenitor of the family.

Augustine Jean Le Rossignot, son of the above of St. Owens, 1647, changed his name to the present spelling. The name gradually changed to Guston or Gustin, and the scrivener turned it into Augustine.

JOHN, (see Augustine).

GUTTERSON

JOHN married at Andover, Mass., 1689.

WILLIAM, resident of Ipswich, Mass., 1648.

GUY

A term given in Gaul to the mistletoe or cure-all; also a guide, a leader, or director, from Spanish word *Guia*.

HENRY, merchant, Charlestown, Mass., 1652.

JOHN, tenant, Casco, Maine, 1663-75.

NICHOLAS b. Eng., 1588, came to Watertown, Mass., 1638, coming from the County of Hants, Eng.

GWIN

JOHN at Charlestown, Mass., 1646.

THOMAS married at Boston, Mass., 1660.

GYLES

THOMAS, early resident of Salem, Mass.

HABBERFIELD

WILLIAM, clothier, Boston, Mass., 1683; freeman at Lynn, Mass., 1691.

HACK

WILLIAM, b. Eng., Plymouth, Mass., 1662, afterwards at Taunton, Mass., 1660.

HACKER

From the Dutch; a chopper, cleaver, hewer, figuratively a brave soldier. Danish *hakker,* to cut in pieces, to chop, to hoe. *Hekker,* a hedge from *hekhe,* a protection, place of security.

WILLIAM settled at Lynn, Mass., 1650.

HACKETT

Surname a corruption from the Anglo-Saxon word *Hacket,* which appears in the Hundred Rolls of Battle Abbey, 1273.

JABEZ, Lynn, Mass., 1644, removed to Taunton, Mass., 1654.

WILLIAM, mariner, Salisbury, Mass.; in 1657 at Dover, N. H., took oath of allegiance Exeter, N. H., 1667. Known as Captain William.

HADDEN, HADDON

JARED or GERARD came Winthrop's fleet to N. E. 1630, proprietor at Salisbury, Mass., 1640.

HADLEY

A place name; a town in Counties of Suffolk and Essex, Eng., from *houdt,* a wood, and *ley,* a place or field.

DENNIS b. Eng., 1650, settled at Sudbury, Mass.

GEORGE, b. Eng., 1600, settled at Ipswich, Mass., 1639, removed to Rowley, Mass., 1665, returned to Ipswich, Mass.

HADLOCK

JAMES, b. Eng.; at Salem, Mass., before 1669, afterwards at Roxbury, Mass.

JOHN died at Concord, Mass., 1675.

NATHANIEL at Charlestown, Mass., 1643, freeman 1646, removed to Lancaster, Mass., 1658.

HAFFELL, HAFFIELD

RICHARD b. Eng., 1581, came to Ipswich, Mass., 1635; no male issue.

HAGAR

From Hebrew *hagar,* a stranger, one fearing. *Hygar* in Welsh is amiable, pleasing. *Hegar* in Cornish British, lovely, also a bondsman, a slave; in Gaelic, *argher,* gladness, joy, mirth.

WILLIAM, b. Eng., 1625, at Watertown, Mass., 1645, where he died 1683-84.

HAGBORNE, HACKBORNE

ABRAHAM, shoemaker, at Boston, Mass., as early as 1639.

SAMUEL, first record at Roxbury, Mass., 1635.

HAGGETT

HENRY at Salem, Mass., 1642, freeman 1676, resided afterwards at Wenham, Mass.

HAILSTONE

WILLIAM, original proprietor, Taunton, Mass., 1640, acquired estate at Boston, Mass., 1646.

HALBRIDGE, HOLBRIDGE

ARTHUR at Boston, Mass., 1635, removed to New Haven, Conn., 1639.

HALE

Hal from the Welsh, signifying a moor, *hayle,* a salt-water river. The Hales of Kent have existed in that locality since the reign of Edward III. They were numerous in Hertfordshire early in the thirteenth century.

GERSHOM, inhabitant of Springfield, Mass., 1698.

JOHN from Berwick on the Tweed, Eng., came to N. E., 1631. Lived at Roxbury and Cambridge, Mass., before becoming one of the first settlers of Concord, Mass.

ROBERT b. Eng., 1609, came from County of Kent, Eng., to Charlestown, Mass., 1632.

SAMUEL b. Eng., 1610, was at Hartford, Conn., 1640, removed to Wethersfield, Conn., two years later; one of the first proprietors of Norwalk, Conn., 1654, returned to Westersfield, that part now known as Glastonbury, 1660.

THOMAS, brother of the preceding, bachelor, freeman Roxbury, Mass., 1634; removed 1636 to Hartford, Conn., and was one of the first settlers at Norwalk, Conn., 1656.

THOMAS, glover, only son of Thomas H. of the parish of Walton-at-Stone, Hertfordshire, Eng., b. 1606, settled at Newbury, Mass., 1635, removed to Haverhill, Mass., 1649, returned to Newbury, Mass., 1652, and 1659 became resident of Salem, Mass.

THOMAS freeman at Saco, Maine, 1653.

THOMAS married at Charlestown, Mass., 1659.

THOMAS married at Hadley, Mass., 1676.

TIMOTHY married at Windsor, Conn., 1663, removed to Suffield, Conn., 1680.

WILLIAM died at Billerica, Mass., 1668.

HALEY

Family of Irish origin.

ANDREW, fisherman, was at Isle of Shoals, N. H., purchased land at York, Maine, 1684.

JOHN married at Hadley, Mass., 1681.

THOMAS an inhabitant of Wells or Saco, Maine, before 1650.

HALL

The Norman or Anglo-Saxon usage of de la Hall is without doubt the foundation of this surname. Some authorities claim it is the Welsh word for salt, others from the Norwegian word *hallo*.

ANDREW, mariner, married at Boston, Mass., 1677.

BENJAMIN, a Quaker, was at Dover, N. H., 1659, removed to Portsmouth, R. I., where he married 1676.

BENJAMIN, married, Wrentham, Mass., 1692.

CHRISTOPHER resident of Groton, Mass., 1672.

Daniel, merchant at New Haven, Conn., 1670, died at Barbadoes, 1675.

EDWARD, freeman at Cambridge, Mass., 1636.

EDWARD, son of Francis H. of Hinborough, Eng., was at Duxbury, Mass., 1636, removed to Taunton, Mass., 1641, settled at Bridgewater, Mass., 1645, hence to Rehoboth, Mass., 1652.

FRANCIS, attorney, son of Gilbert H. of Kent, Eng., came to N. E. in Rev. Henry Whitfield's company from Milford, County of Surrey, Eng., settled at New Haven, Conn., 1639, the next year went to Fairfield, Conn., and 1659 to Stratford, Conn.

GEORGE came from Devonshire, Eng.; recorded as a proprietor at Duxbury, Mass., 1637, one of the original proprietors of Taunton, Mass., 1643-64.

HENRY resident of Westerly, R. I., 1664.

JOB resident of New Haven, Conn., 1646.

JOHN b. Eng., 1605, came from Coventry, Eng., in Winthrop's fleet 1630, locating at Charlestown, Mass.; removed to Barnstable, Mass., 1640, thence in 1653 to Yarmouth, Mass.

JOHN inhabitant of Kittery, Maine, 1640.

JOHN b. Eng., 1617, freeman at Charlestown, Mass., 1635; removed to Dover, N. H., on tax list of 1648.

JOHN b. County of Kent, Eng., 1584, freeman at Boston, Mass., 1635, at Hartford, Conn., 1636, removed to Middletown, Conn., 1654.

JOHN a selectman of Boston, Mass., 1657.

JOHN a resident of Newport, R. I., 1638, freeman there 1655.

JOHN b. Eng., 1605, came to Boston, Mass., 1633, thence to Hartford, Conn., was one of the free planters of New Haven, Conn., 1639, removed to Wallingford, Conn., 1670.

JOHN married at Taunton, Mass., 1671.

JOHN freeman at Roxbury, Mass., 1684.

JOHN, inhabitant of Wethersfield, died there 1692.

JOHN b. Eng., 1627, granted land in Billerica, Mass., 1652; was at Concord, Cambridge and Medford, Mass.

MARY, widow, at Cambridge, Mass., 1653; had three sons, John, William and Stephen.

NATHANIEL, resident of Dorchester, Mass., 1633.

RALPH, brother of John of Dover, b. Eng., 1619, was at Charlestown, Mass., 1647, removed to Dover, N. H., 1650, thence in 1664 to Exeter, N. H.

RICHARD, freeman Dorchester, Mass., 1644.

RICHARD came from Stratford on the Avon, Eng., to Dorchester, Mass., settled Bradford, Mass., 1672, made freeman 1676.

SAMUEL, resident of Salisbury, Mass., 1640.

SAMUEL on record at Taunton, Mass., 1666.

SAMUEL, freeman at Dorchester, Mass., 1670.

THOMAS, brother of Edward of Cambridge, Mass., resident of that town, 1648.

TRISTAM at Barnstable, Mass., 1645.

WILLIAM, living at Portsmouth, R. I., 1638, freeman there 1655.

WILLIAM, brother of Francis, came with him to N. E., settled at Guilford, Conn., 1640.

HALLADAY, HALLIDAY

This name originated from Holy-day, the slogan or war cry of a Gaelic clan residing in Annandale, who made frequent raids on the English border. On these occasions they employed the war-cry of *"A holy-day,"* every day being holy that was spent in ravaging the enemy's country.

WALTER settled at Springfield, Mass., 1673.

HALLAM

From *hall,* Welsh, salt, and *ham,* a house or village from its manufacture at that place or being situated near salt water. Also from *hal* or *hayle,* a moor, and *ham,* the house on the moor. *Halham,* the house on the hill, from *hal* Cornish British, a hill.

JOHN came from Barbadoes to Stonington, Conn., 1677.

NICHOLAS, brother of the preceding, married at New London, Conn., 1686.

HALLETT, HOLLETT

Little Hal or Henry, the diminutive termination *ett* being added as Willett, Ellett.

ANDREW came to Plymouth Colony, 1637, proprietor at Dorchester, Mass., 1638, removed to Sandwich, Mass., afterwards to Yarmouth, Mass.

HALLOCK, HALLECK

DAVID at Dorchester, Mass., 1640, removed to Boston, Mass., 1644.

PETER at New Haven, Conn., 1640, same year settled at Southold, L. I.

HALLOWELL, HOLLOWAY

Signification of the surname Holy well.

ANDREW, New Haven, Conn., 1654.

TIMOTHY, Taunton, Mass., 1643.

WILLIAM, Marshfield or Taunton, Mass., 1643, removed to Boston, Mass., 1650.

HALSEY

From the Saxon *hals* and *ey* or *ig,* an island, water, the sea; the neck on the water or running into the sea, the island neck.

GEORGE, blacksmith, b. Eng., 1614, first settled at Dorchester, Mass., removed to Boston, Mass., 1642.

JAMES, mathematician, freeman at Boston, Mass., 1690.

THOMAS, b. Eng., 1591-92, at Lynn, Mass., 1637, removed in a few years to Southampton, L. I.

WILLIAM, living at Boston, Mass., 1654.

HALSTEAD

HENRY, Concord, Mass., 1648.

NATHANIEL, freeman Dedham, Mass., 1641.

HAM

A house, borough or village, the termination of many places in England. German *heim,* a home.

JOHN, b. Eng., 1640, at Dover, N. H., 1665, afterwards at Casco, Maine.

WILLIAM, Scotch ancestry, came to N. E. in 1645 to Exeter, N. H., removed to Portsmouth, N. H., 1652.

HAMILTON

Originally from the manor of the Hambleton in Buckinghamshire, Eng. William the third son of Robert, third Earl of Leicester, took the surname from the place of his birth as above. He was the founder of the family in Scotland, whither he went in 1215. The name of Norman origin is derived from *Hamell,* a mansion, the seat of a freeholder, and *dun,* an enclosure, a fortified place, a town. The family was firmly established in Lanarkshire, Renfrewshire and Ayrshire, Scotland, before the fourteenth century.

DAVID, descendant of Lanarkshire family, came from Hamilton near Glasgow, Scotland, to Charlestown, Mass., 1652, one of the prisoners sent by Cromwell, after the battle of Worcester. After working for his liberty settled at Dover, N. H., what is now known as Rollinsford.

JOHN, first recorded at Charlestown, Mass., 1658, removed to Concord, Mass., 1667 and in 1671 to Marlboro, Mass.

WILLIAM married at Boston, Mass., 1654.

HAMLET

WILLIAM, b. Eng., 1614, settled at Watertown, Mass., 1642, removed to Cambridge, Mass., 1645, granted land at Billerica, Mass., 1656.

HAMLIN, HAMBLIN

A corruption of Hammeline, which was taken from Hamelin, a town on the river Weser, Lower Saxony, Germany. Hamelin, a town in Scotland so called from *ham,* a house or village, and *lin,* a waterfall, a small lake or pond. The family was brought into England by a follower of William the Conqueror.

EZEKIEL married at Boston, Mass., 1654.

GILES, engaged in foreign commerce, known as captain, b. Eng., 1622, settled at Middletown, Conn., 1654.

JAMES, son of Giles, grandson of John Hamelyn, living at Cornwall, Eng., 1570, came from parish of St. Lawrence, Reading, Berkshire, Eng., to Barnstable, Mass., 1639.

JOHN, brother of the preceding, at Barnstable, Mass., 1639.

HAMMANT

FRANCIS, settled before 1650 in that part of Dedham, Mass., that afterwards became Medfield.

HAMMATT, HAMMETT

THOMAS took oath of allegiance to Mass., 1658, while residing at Scarborough, Maine.

HAMMOND

Ham-mount, the town or house on the elevation. It may, however, come from the Hebrew word *hamon,* faithful.

BENJAMIN, son of William, came from London, Eng., to Yarmouth, Mass., 1643, was at Sandwich, Mass., 1650, removed to Rochester, Mass., where he was living 1663.

EDWARD, b. Eng., 1640, settled in R. I.

GEORGE, freeman at Newport, R. I., 1655.

JOHN, twin brother of Thomas, grandson of John, son of John, b. at Milford, County of Suffolk, Eng., 1603, settled at Hingham, Mass., where land was granted him 1636.

LAWRENCE, freeman Charlestown, Mass., 1666, a captain and representative, removed to Boston, Mass., 1677.

THOMAS, twin brother of John, settled at Hingham, Mass., 1636, removed to Cambridge, the part now known as Newton, 1650.

WILLIAM, only son of Thomas H., b. Lavenham, County of Suffolk, Eng., 1575. First record in 1636 at Scituate, Mass., the same year admitted freeman at Watertown, Mass.

WILLIAM, b. Eng., 1597, came from Slymbridge, Eng., settled at Wells, Maine, 1653. He died in 1702 being one hundred and five years of age.

HANBURY

DANIEL, b. Eng., 1606, came to N. E., 1635.

LUKE, inhabitant of Mass., 1637.

PETER at Sandwich, Mass., 1643.

WILLIAM, living at Duxbury, Mass., 1639, where he married 1641, removed to Boston, Mass., 1649.

HANCOCK

ANTHONY, living at Wrentham, Mass., 1681, had been a domestic of William Sumner of Dorchester, Mass.

JOHN, proprietor at New Haven, Conn., 1679.

NATHANIEL at Cambridge, Mass., 1634.

THOMAS at Hadley, Mass., 1678.

HANCOX

THOMAS, b. 1645, living at Farmington, Conn., 1670, keeper of the goal at Hartford, Conn., 1691.

HAND

JOSEPH, one of the first settlers of Killingworth, Conn., 1663.

HANDFORTH

NATHANIEL came from London, Eng., to Lynn, Mass., 1637.

HANDS

MARK, nailer, b. 1619, came to Boston, Mass., 1639.

HANFORD

From Welsh *hen,* old, and *ford* a way, "the old way."

THOMAS, clergyman, came to Scituate, Mass., 1643, freeman of Mass., 1650, two years later became minister at Norwalk, Conn.

HANMER, HANMORE

JOHN at Scituate, Mass., 1639, next year at Duxbury, Mass, lived at Marshfield, Mass., 1663.

HANNADOWN

ROGER, ship carpenter, was at Weymouth, Mass., removed to Boston, Mass., 1643.

HANNAH

ROBERT, married at Wickford, R. I., before 1690.

HANNIFORD, HANNIFALL

JOHN, mariner at Boston, Mass., 1647.

RICHARD, inhabitant of Marblehead, Mass., 1674.

HANNUM

WILLIAM, came from Eng., to Dorchester, Mass., 1630, removed to Windsor, Conn., 1637, and to Springfield, Mass., 1655.

HANOVER

RICHARD settled at Marblehead, Mass., 1660.

HANSCOM, HANSON

Family traced in England to Roger de Rastrick, living in 1251 at Wapentake, Morley, Yorkshire; of the sixth generation from him. Henry, son of John de Rastrick, became known as Henry's son then Hanson, thus the foundation of the name.

ISAAC, resident of Portsmouth, N. H., 1679.

JAMES, inhabitant of Mass., 1666.

THOMAS, b. Eng., 1623, came from Sutton parish, Bedfordshire, Eng., 1629, with his relations; to Salem, Mass., granted lands near Salmon Falls, N. H., 1658, afterwards lived at Dover, N. H., and at Kittery, Maine, 1678.

HANSETT, HANCHET

JOHN, admitted church at Boston, Mass., 1634, removed to Braintree, Mass., afterwards to Roxbury, Mass.

THOMAS, brother of the preceding, was at Wethersfield, Conn., removed to New

London, Conn., 1651, was at Northampton, Mass., 1660, removed to Westfield, Mass., thence to Suffield, Conn., where he died 1686.

HANWELL

AMBROSE took oath of fidelity to Mass., at Pemaquid, Maine, 1674.

HAPGOOD

SHADRACH, b. Eng., 1642, came to Sudbury, Mass., 1656, was killed King Philip's War, leaving male issue.

HARCUTT, HARKER

RICHARD, freeman Warwick, R. I., 1655.

HARDEN, HARDIN

EDWARD at Gloucester, Mass., 1675.

RICHARD, resident of Boston, Mass., 1671.

HARDIER

RICHARD, freeman at Braintree, Mass., 1648.

HARDING

Har from *here,* an army, and *ing,* a meadow or common. The place where an army was encamped. The surname is derived from the ancient personal name of Hardin, used in Germany, Scandinavia and Britain before the Feudal system. The name is mentioned 1086 in the Doomesday Book.

ABRAHAM, glover and planter, son of John H. of Boram, County of Essex, Eng., b. 1620. Came to N. E., settled at Boston, Mass., 1640, freeman 1645, removed to Braintree 1648, hence 1653 to Medfield, Mass.

GEORGE, Marblehead, 1649.

JOHN, freeman at Weymouth, Mass., 1640.

MARTHA, widow, resident of Plymouth, Mass., 1632, died the following year leaving two sons.

PHILIP, married, Boston, Mass., 1659.

ROBERT, came with Winthrop 1630, freeman 1631 at Boston, Mass., removed to R. I., returned to Eng., 1645, leaving no issue in this country.

THOMAS, admitted inhabitant Boston, Mass., 1656.

HARDISON

STEPHEN, English descent, settled at Berwick, Maine, 1691.

HARDMAN

JOHN, at Lynn, Mass., 1647.

HARDY, HARDIE

From French, bold, free, noble.

GEORGE, resident of Newbury, Mass, before 1693.

JOHN, freeman at Salem, Mass., 1634.

RICHARD, at Concord, Mass., 1639, removed to Stamford, Conn.; no male issue.

SAMUEL, town clerk, Beverly, Mass., 1674.

THOMAS, brother of John, b. Eng., 1606, at Ipswich, Mass., 1633, removed to Rowley, Mass., and in 1653 to Bradford, Mass.

HARLOW

WILLIAM, known as Sergeant William, a youth with an unknown father came from Eng., to Lynn, Mass., where he appeared in list of inhabitants 1629-30, one of the settlers of Sandwich, Mass., 1637, was living at Portsmouth, Mass., 1662.

HARMON, HARMAN, HERMAN

The surname same as *Heartman* to wit, a man of heart and courage or like *Herman* from *here,* an army, and *man,* a soldier.

FRANCIS, came to N. E. from London, Eng., 1635, settled at Braintree, Mass., 1640.

JAMES, Saco, Maine, 1655.

JOHN, b. Eng., 1617, came to N. E., 1640, proprietor at Springfield, Mass., 1644.

JOHN at Plymouth, Mass., 1643, Duxbury 1659, removed to Saco, Maine, 1680.

JOSEPH, resident of Kittery, Maine, 1674.

NATHANIEL, brother of first John, settled at Braintree, Mass., 1640.

SAMUEL at Boston, Mass., 1689.

HARNDEN, HARNDALE

BENJAMIN, at Lynn, Mass., 1647, prominent in the settlement of Reading, Mass.

HARNETT

EDWARD, granted land Salem, Mass., 1640.

HARPER

JOSEPH was at Braintree, Mass., at early period.

ROBERT, Quaker, at Sandwich, Mass., resident of Boston, Mass., 1659.

HARRADEN, HARRIDIN

EDWARD at Ipswich, Mass., 1651, removed to Gloucester, Mass., 1658.

HARRIMAN, HERRIMAN

AUGUSTINE at Saybrook, Conn., 1651.

JOHN, an innholder at New Haven, Conn., 1646.

LEONARD, brother of the preceding, b. Rowley, Yorkshire, Eng., 1622, came as a minor in 1640, settled at Rowley, Mass.

HARRINGTON

Place name from parish of Harrington, County of Cumberland, Eng., corrupted from Haverington so called from *haver,* Dutch, *haber,* Teutonic, oats, *ing* a field, and *ton.* The town in or surrounded by oat fields.

EDWARD, resident of Charlestown, Mass., 1643.

RICHARD, freeman at Charlestown, Mass., 1647.

ROBERT, b. Eng., 1616, settled at Watertown, Mass., 1634, proprietor 1642.

SAMUEL, at Hatfield, Mass., 1679.

HARRIS

The Welsh in order to distinguish between the bearers of the same Christian names used as follows: Williams, son of Harry: this eventually became William Harris.

ANTHONY, arrived N. E., 1644, lived at Ipswich, Mass., 1648, afterwards removed to Boston, Mass.

ARTHUR at Duxbury, Mass., 1640, amongst first settlers of Bridgewater, Mass., later removed to Boston, Mass.

BENJAMIN, bookseller, Boston, Mass., 1687, returned to London, Eng., 1694.

BERNARD, resident of Boston, Mass., 1666.

DANIEL, brother of Anthony, at Rowley, Mass., 1643, removed to Middletown, Conn., 1652, there became innholder and captain in militia.

DANIEL, resident of Boston, Mass., 1695.

DAVID, mariner, at Boston, Mass., 1676.

EXPERIENCE, resident of Boston, Mass., 1676.

GEORGE, b. Eng., proprietor at Salem, Mass., 1636.

GEORGE married at Concord, Mass., 1669.

GEORGE died at Boston, Mass., 1686.

JAMES, resident of Boston, Mass., before 1668.

JOHN, son of Thomas, grandson of John of Ottery, St. Mary's, Devonshire, Eng., b. Eng., 1607, came to N. E. 1635, freeman 1647, became identified with Rowley, Mass.

JOHN, married at Boston, Mass., 1671.

JOHN, resident of Charlestown, Mass., 1658.

JOHN, freeman at Ipswich, Mass., 1685.

JOHN, fisherman, at Marblehead, Mass., 1673.

JOHN, weaver, resided at Marblehead, Mass., 1674.

JOSEPH, resident Charlestown, Mass., 1672.

RICHARD at Braintree, Mass., 1663.

RICHARD, merchant, at Boston, Mass., 1680.

RICHARD, living at Charlestown, Mass., 1682.

ROBERT, resident of Boston, in the part now known as Brookline, Mass., 1643.

SAMUEL, mariner, Salem, Mass., afterwards at Manchester, Mass., 1667, removed to Beverly, Mass.

THOMAS, b. Deal, County of Kent, Eng., came with Winthrop to N. E., 1630, one of the twelve that signed the compact with Roger Williams, and became proprietor of Providence, R. I.

THOMAS at Ipswich, Mass., 1636, granted land Rowley, Mass., 1644.

THOMAS, butcher, at Boston, Mass., before 1679.

THOMAS at Concord, Mass., 1688.

WALTER came to N. E., 1632, freeman Weymouth, Mass., 1641, was at Dorchester, Mass., 1649, removed to New London, Conn., 1653.

WILLIAM, brother of Thomas of Providence, b. Eng., 1609-10, came to Boston, 1636, with Roger Williams, among the first settlers of Providence, R. I. Sold into slavery by Algerines, 1679, ransomed, reached London, Eng., 1680, where he died in that year.

WILLIAM, brother of Anthony, came with his mother in his youth to N. E., removed to Rowley, Mass., thence to Charlestown, Mass., again in a few years to Middletown, Conn.

WILLIAM, resident of Boston, Mass., before 1672.

WILLIAM, merchant, died before 1684 at Boston, Mass.

HARRISON

The same as Harris.

ISAAC married at Hadley, Mass., 1671.

JOHN, ropemaker, at Salisbury, Mass., 1640, removed to Boston, Mass., 1643.

MARK, signed memorial to General Court of Mass., 1654.

NICHOLAS, resident of Dover, N. H., 1673-1707.

RICHARD, New Haven, 1644; descendants removed to Newark, N. J.

THOMAS, clergyman, brother of the preceding, b. Eng., settled 1654, New Haven, Conn., afterwards removed to Branford, Conn.

HARROD

JOHN, resident of Boston. Mass.. 1651.

HART

EDMUND came to N. E. with Winthrop 1630, removed to Weymouth, Mass.; freeman, 1634.

EPHRAIM, brother of the preceding, resided at Weymouth, Mass., 1634.

ISAAC, b. Scratby, Eng., 1614, settled at Watertown, Mass., 1637.

JOHN, shipwright, b. Eng., 1595, came to N. E. 1635, at Salem, Mass., 1637, at Marblehead, Mass., 1648, and removed to Boston, Mass., 1651.

JOHN, at Portsmouth, N. H., 1665.

JOSEPH married at Lynn, Mass., 1684.

LAWRENCE at Newbury, Mass., 1679.

NATHANIEL, resident of Ipswich, Mass., 1636.

NICHOLAS came to Taunton, Mass., 1642, afterwards to Boston, Mass.

RICHARD living at Portsmouth, R. I., 1687.

SAMUEL, b. Eng., 1622, was at Lynn, Mass., 1640.

STEPHEN, b. Braintree, County of Essex, Eng., 1605, came to N. E., 1632, freeman at Cambridge, Mass., 1634, removed with Rev. Thomas Hooker's company to Hartford, Conn., one of the original proprietors of Farmington, Conn.

THOMAS, tanner, came to Boston, Mass., 1635, proprietor Ipswich, Mass., 1639, at New Haven, Conn., 1645.

HARTSHORN

The horn of the hart or male deer, an emblem or sign over shop or inn, hence the name "Will at the Hartshorn." It is also a place name from a parish in the Litchfield diocese, Derbyshire, Eng. The early English records mentioned Henry de Hartshorn living in the thirteenth century.

THOMAS, b. Reading, Eng., 1614, freeman at Reading, Mass., 1648.

HARTUT, HARTOPP

WILLIAM at Duxbury, Mass., 1643.

HARTWELL

Place name from a village in Buckinghamshire, Eng. The well or spring frequented by deer. Decannarius de Hertwell recorded in the Hundred Rolls 1273 as living in Northamptonshire.

WILLIAM, b. Eng., 1613, settled at Concord, Mass., 1636, in the part now known as Lincoln. Granted land at Chelmsford, Mass., 1663.

HARVEY

From Saxon *here*, an army, and *wie*, a fort. The progenitor of the family was Herveus de Bourges, who came with William the Conqueror according to the Doomesday Book. He was a baron in 1086 in the County of Suffolk, and a grandson of Geoffrey, third viscount of Bourges, an ancient city of Berry, a former province of France.

EDMUND, merchant, Milford, Conn., 1639, removed to Fairfield, Conn., 1642.

JOACHIM, freeman Newcastle or Great Isle, N. H., 1669.

JOHN, resident of Lyme or New London, Conn., 1682.

PETER, shipbuilder, at Salem, Mass., 1692.

THOMAS, son of Thomas, sixth generation from Humphrey Harvey, born 1485, a noted archer in the reign of Henry VIII.

THOMAS, American immigrant, b. Ashill, Somersetshire, Eng., 1617, came to Dorchester, Mass., 1636, proprietor Taunton, Mass., 1639.

THOMAS married at Amesbury, Mass., 1643.

WILLIAM, brother of the first Thomas, was at Plymouth, Mass., proprietor at Taunton, Mass., 1639.

WILLIAM, resident of Boston, Mass., 1644.

HARWOOD

The ancient spelling of the name is Hereward and is of Saxon origin. According to the Doomesday Book the family held lands in Lincoln and Warwick before the Conquest. Hereward was the son of Leofric, Earl of Mercia, and Lord of Bourne of Lincolnshire.

ANDREW, b. Eng., came from Devonshire to Boston, Mass., 1640.

EDWARD at New Haven, Conn., 1641.

GEORGE, carpenter, resident of Boston, Mass., 1639, removed to New London, Conn., 1651.

HENRY, came to N. E. with Winthrop, 1630, freeman at Charlestown, Mass., 1633.

HENRY at Salem, Mass., 1638, freeman 1643.

HENRY, shoemaker, resident at Boston, Mass., 1665, removed to Casco, Maine, 1675, returned to Boston, Mass., before 1683.

JOHN, tailor, freeman at Boston, Mass., 1649, returned to Eng., 1657.

NATHANIEL, cordwainer, brother of Henry of Charlestown, came to N. E. 1630, settled at Boston, Mass., was at Concord, Mass., 1665, afterwards at Charlestown, Mass.

ROBERT, baker, at Boston, Mass., 1674.

THOMAS married at Boston, Mass., 1654.

HASEMAN

NATHANIEL, at Braintree, Mass., 1662.

HASEY, HAZZEY

WILLIAM, lived at Rumsey Marsh, now Chelsea, Mass., 1652, freeman 1665.

HASKELL, HASCALL

From Welsh *hasg,* a place of rushes or sedgy place, and *hall* or *hayle* a moor, "The sedgy place." *Asgall* in the Gaelic signifies a sheltered place, a retreat, with addition of the asperate H might mean the name.

ROGER, of Norman French descent, b. 1613, came to Mass., 1637, settled at Salem, Mass., removed to Beverly, Mass.

TOBIAS, resident of Lynn, Mass., 1645.

WILLIAM, brother of Roger, b. 1617, first on record Gloucester, Mass., 1642, held the title of captain.

WILLIAM, resident of Salem, Mass., 1679.

HASKETT

STEPHEN, soap-boiler, at Salem, Mass., 1664.

HASKINS, HOSKINS

ANDREW, freeman at Windsor, Conn., 1654.

JOHN, b. Eng., came to N. E., 1630, settled at Dorchester, Mass., where he was a freeman 1631; one of the pioneers of Windsor, Conn.

SAMUEL married at New Haven, Conn., 1642.

THOMAS, at Barnstable, Mass., 1668.

WILLIAM, at New Haven, Conn., 1643.

WILLIAM, b. Eng., settled at Plymouth, 1633, afterwards at Scituate and Middleboro, Mass.

HASSELL

JOHN, freeman, Ipswich, Mass., 1637, removed Rehoboth, Mass., 1642, returned to Ipswich, 1648.

RICHARD, freeman Cambridge, Mass., 1647, removed Watertown, Mass.

HASTINGS

The name is of Danish origin and has been in existence in England, since Alfred the Great reign, when a Danish chief named Hastings took possession of a portion of County of Sussex. At the time of the Norman Invasion the family held the castle and seaport of Hastings at which place William the Conqueror landed and gave battle to the Saxons under Harold II., who was defeated, dying on the field of battle. The first of the family to be elevated to the peerage was Henry. Lord Hastings, son of William de Hastings, steward of Henry III, 1154-89.

JOHN, tanner, freeman Braintree, Mass., 1643.

ROBERT took oath of fidelity, Haverhill, Mass., 1677.

THOMAS, farmer, b. Eng., 1605, came to N. E., 1634, settled at Watertown, Mass.

HATCH

The ancient stops, or hatches consisted of sundry great stakes and piles erected by fishermen in rivers and other streams for their better convenience of securing fish. Also a term for gates leading to deer-parks or forests.

CHARLES, fisherman, at York, Maine, before 1655.

JOSEPH, located at Falmouth, Maine, 1630.

PHILIP, b. Eng., 1600, became inhabitant of Maine, 1638, proprietor of York, Maine, 1648.

THOMAS, freeman Dorchester, Mass., 1634, removed to Scituate, Mass., where he died 1646.

WILLIAM, merchant, brother of the preceding, b. Sandwich, County of Kent, Eng., came to N. E., 1630, returned to Eng., and again returned to N. E., locating 1635 at Scituate, Mass.

WILLIAM, resident of New London, Conn., 1690.

HATHAWAY

Place name from Port Haethwy in Wales.

ARTHUR, married Marshfield, Mass., 1643.

JOHN, b. Eng., 1617, came to Barnstable, Mass., 1635, removed to Taunton, Mass., 1649.

JOSEPH, brother of the preceding, freeman Taunton, Mass., 1657.

HATHERLY, HETHERLY

ARTHUR, Plymouth, Mass., 1660.

GEORGE, first record Boston, Mass., 1676.

THOMAS was at Boston, Mass., 1668.

TIMOTHY, merchant, came to Plymouth, Mass., 1623, returned to Eng. next year, arrived second time in N. E. at Boston, Mass., 1632, coming from Barnstable, Devonshire, Eng., where there is a parish of Hatherly.

HATHORNE, HAWTHORNE

A dwelling near haw thorns.

EBENEZER, Salem, Mass., 1669.

JOHN, farmer, son of William H., b. Binfield, Berkshire, Eng., 1615, located at Salem, Mass., 1635, removed to Lynn, Mass., 1650.

WILLIAM, brother of the preceding, b. Binfield, Berkshire, Eng., 1607, came in Winthrop's fleet to N. E., 1630, settled at Dorchester, Mass., removed to Salem, Mass., 1636.

HAUGHTON

HENRY, came to Salem, Mass., 1629, in fleet of Higginson, made ruling elder, died same year.

RICHARD, shipwright, at Boston, Mass., removed New London, Conn., 1642.

HAVEN or HAVENS

From *haven,* a harbor.

RICHARD came from west of England, to Lynn, Mass., 1645.

WILLIAM in list of inhabitants Portsmouth, R. I., 1639.

HAVILAND

EDWARD was at Boston, Mass., before 1657.

WILLIAM, freeman Newport, R. I., 1653.

HAW, HAWES

From Saxon word *haeg,* a small inclosure near a house, a haugh, a close. The name of a town in Eng.; Alen del Hawes on record in the Hundred Rolls 1273.

DANIEL, resident of Wrentham, Mass., before 1681.

EDMUND, cutler, came from London, Eng., to Boston, Mass., 1635, removed to Yarmouth, Mass.

EDWARD, mason, b. Eng., 1620, settled at Dedham, Mass., 1648.

RICHARD, b. Eng., 1606, came to Dorchester, Mass., 1635, freeman, 1638.

ROBERT, soap-boiler, came from London, Eng., 1635, to Salem, Mass.

ROBERT joined the church at Roxbury, Mass., 1665.

THOMAS, b. Eng., 1590, settled at Salem, Mass., 1637, removed 1639, Yarmouth, Mass.; had the title of captain.

WILLIAM, resident of Boston, Mass., 1652.

HAWKE, HAWKES, HAWKS

ADAM, b. Eng., 1608, came to N. E. with Gov. Winthrop, located at Charlestown, Mass., proprietor in Lynn, Mass., 1638, what is now North Saugus, Mass.

JOHN, b. Eng., freeman Dorchester, Mass., 1634, settled at Windsor, Conn., 1640.

MATTHEW came from Cambridge, Eng., to Hingham, Mass., 1638.

HAWKEHURST, HAWXHURST

CHRISTOPHER, freeman Warwick, R. I., 1655.

HAWKESWORTH

THOMAS, b. Eng., 1612, came to N. E. 1635, original proprietor of Salisbury, Mass., 1640.

HAWKINS

The early English records mention Capt. John Hawkins in the reign of Henry VIII.

ABRAHAM, freeman Charlestown, Mass., 1642.

ANTHONY, resident Windsor, Conn., 1644.

GAMALIEL, mariner, at Salem, Mass., 1688.

GEORGE, shipwright, at Boston, Mass., 1644.

JAMES at Boston, Mass., 1635.

JOHN, mariner, married at Boston, Mass., 1654.

RICHARD at Boston, Mass., 1637, afterwards at Portsmouth, R. I.

ROBERT, son of Sir John H., b. Eng., 1610, settled at Charlestown, Mass., 1635, removed to Fairfield, Conn.

ROBERT, freeman, Boston, Mass., 1690.

THOMAS, merchant, granted lot Charlestown, Mass., 1636, lived at Dorchester, Mass., removed to Boston, Mass.

THOMAS, baker, brother of Abraham, arrived N. E., 1649; in his latter days he kept an inn.

TIMOTHY, resident of Watertown, Mass., 1635.

WILLIAM, butcher, resident of Boston, Mass., 1666.

WILLIAM, b. Eng., 1609, freeman at Providence, R. I., 1655.

HAWLEY

From *haw,* a hedge, Saxon *haeg,* a small piece of ground near a house, and *ley,* a field or meadow. The name appears in the Battle Abbey, at time of the Conquest and it was prominently identified in Derbyshire 1200.

JOSEPH, yeoman, born Parwich, Derbyshire, Eng., 1603, came to N. E. 1639, on record at Stratford, Conn., 1650.

SAMUEL at Norwalk, Conn., 1657, among the first settlers at Stratford, Conn., 1666.

THOMAS, resident of Roxbury, Mass., before 1651.

HAWTHORNE—see HATHORNE

HAXIE, HAUKSIE, HOXIE

LODOWICK, married at Sandwich, Mass., 1664.

HAY

In Dutch *hoag,* Saxon *hege,* German *heck,* Danish *hekke,* Swedish *hayn*

French *haie,* Welsh *car,* Gaelic *ca,* Cornish British *hay.*

James, among the early settlers of Reading, Mass.

HAYDEN, HAYDON, HEYDON

Surname derived from the town of Heyden, Denmark; a place built, made, inclosed or cultivated, from Danish *daene,* to form, to fashion, to make, cultivate. In the County of Norfolk, Eng., is the town of Heyden, where Thomas de Heyden was a resident 1221.

James, freeman, Charlestown, Mass., 1637.

John, son of Gideon H., XVIIth generation from Sir Thomas de Heyden, came to Boston, Mass., 1630, proprietor Dorchester, Mass., 1632, removed to Braintree, Mass.

William, came to Dorchester, Mass., 1630, removed to Hartford, Conn., later, 1637 to Windsor, Conn., in 1666, at Killingworth, Conn., and at Fairfield, Conn., 1662.

HAYES

Same derivation as Hay.

George came from Scotland to N. E., 1680, settled at Windsor, Conn., 1682, removed to Simsbury, Conn.

John at Dover, N. H., 1680.

Nathaniel, inhabitant of Norwalk, Conn., 1652.

Thomas at Milford, Conn., 1645.

HAYMAN, HEYMAN

Same as Hayward.

John, ropemaker, had liberty to spin in Boston, Mass., 1662, freeman 1668, had the title of major.

HAYNES, HAINES

Derived from the Saxon word *ainulpp* and that from *ana,* alone, *ulpp,* help, that is, one that needs not the assistance of others. Haine, a river in Belgium. *Haine,* French, signifies malicious, full of hatred; *hain,* German, a wood, forest, thicket, grove.

Charles, resident of New London, Conn., 1664.

Edmund, was at Springfield, Mass., 1645; no male issue.

James, freeman Salem, Mass., 1637.

John, b. Copford Hall, County of Essex, Eng., 1594, came to N. E., with Rev. Thomas Hooker; freeman at Cambridge, Mass., 1634, removed to Hartford, Conn., 1637; first governor of Colony of Conn.

Mark, resident of Boston, Mass., 1665.

Richard at Beverly, Mass., 1671.

Samuel, b. Eng., 1611, came from Bristol, Eng., to N. E., 1635, settled at Pemaquid, now Bristol, Maine, removed to Dover, N. H., 1640, and to Portsmouth, N. H., 1646.

Thomas in Maine, 1658-65, removed to Amesbury, Mass., married 1667.

Walter, linen weaver, b. Sutton, Manderfield, Wiltshire, Eng., 1583, came to Boston, Mass., 1638, removed to Watertown, Mass.; one of the first proprietors of Sudbury, Mass., 1639.

HAYNOR

William, tailor, came from Virginia to Salem, Mass., 1660.

HAYWARD, HEAWARD, HAILWARD

In ancient England, the keeper of the common herd or cattle of a town, from Saxon *hieg,* hay and ward, a keeper.

George, early settler Concord, Mass., 1635, freeman 1638.

James, b. Eng., 1613, came to Charlestown, Mass., 1635; removed to Woburn, Mass.

John at Watertown, Mass., 1632, freeman 1634, removed to Dedham, Mass.

John, resident Plymouth, Mass., 1643.

John, scrivener, at Boston, Mass., 1671, postmaster of the colony, 1673.

Nicholas at Salem, Mass., 1643, removed to Boston, Mass., before 1665.

Richard, came from Bedfordshire, Eng., with Higginson, in 1629 to Salem, Mass.

Robert, miller, married Windsor, Conn., before 1647, removed to Northampton, Mass., 1659, returned to Windsor, Conn.

Samuel on record at Gloucester, Mass., 1641.

Samuel, resident of Boston, Mass., 1645.

Samuel, b. Eng., 1613, came to Charlestown, Mass., 1635, settled at that part of the town afterwards Malden, Mass.

Thomas, tailor, came from Aylesford, County of Kent, Eng., settled at Cambridge, Mass., 1635, removed Duxbury, Mass., 1638, one of first settlers Bridgewater, Mass., 1651.

Thomas, resident Enfield, Conn., before 1686.

William at Charlestown, Mass., 1637, freeman Hampton, N. H., 1640.

William, grandson of Sir Robert Hayward, Lord Mayor of London 1570, settled at Bridgewater, Mass., 1646.

William, inhabitant of Braintree, Mass, 1648.

William was at Swanzey, Mass., before 1672.

HAYWOOD

ANTHONY, inhabitant of Boston, Mass., 1671, one of the founders of the first Episcopal Church.

HAZARD

From Cornish British *ard,* nature, and *has,* high—of high disposition, proud, independent.

THOMAS, ship carpenter, on record at Boston, Mass., 1635, freeman 1636, removed in a few years to R. I., signed the covenant of cities 1639, was at Newtown, Long Island, 1656, he died 1669. One of the first founders of Newport, R. I.

HAZELTINE, HAZELTON

Place name from Hazelton, signifying where hazel bushes grew.

CHARLES, inhabitant of Ipswich, Mass., 1661-66.

DANIEL, freeman at Bradford, Mass., 1676.

JOHN, b. Eng., 1620, came from Bideford, Devonshire, Eng., church member Boston, Mass., settled at Rowley, Mass., 1640, later resided at Haverhill, Mass.

ROBERT, brother of the preceding, came from Bradford, Yorkshire, Eng.; first at Salem, Mass., 1636, freeman at Rowley, Mass., 1640, lived in that part of the town that afterwards became Bradford, Mass.

HAZELWOOD

FRANCIS, resident of Boston, Mass.. where he died 1674.

HAZEN

From Danish word *hasen,* a hare.

EDWARD, settled at Rowley, Mass., before 1649.

HEAD

Anciently written *Hede* or *Hide.* From place written in Doomesday Book, now Hithe in County of Kent, Eng., where the earliest trace of the Head family are found. The surname is from Anglo-Saxon *hithe,* harbor, a shelter for boats.

ARTHUR, on record at Portsmouth, N. H., 1671.

HENRY, identified with Little Compton, R. I., representative to Plymouth Council 1683.

RICHARD, inhabitant of Marblehead, Mass., 1674.

HEALD

JOHN, came from Berwick on the Tweed, County of Northumberland, Eng., settled at Concord, Mass., 1635.

HEALEY, HALEY

DENNIS, married at Watertown, Mass., 1682.

NICHOLAS, took oath of fidelity, Pemaquid, Maine, 1674.

SAMUEL, married at Salisbury, Mass., 1685.

WILLIAM, early settler Lynn, Mass., removed to Roxbury, Mass., finally to Cambridge, Mass.

HEARD

BENJAMIN, inhabitant of Salisbury, Mass., 1691.

JAMES, was at Kittery, Maine, ensign 1659.

JOHN, brother of the preceding, was at Kittery, Maine, before 1643.

LUKE, son of Edmund H. of Claxton, County of Norfolk, Eng., came to Newbury, Mass., went to Salisbury, Mass., 1640, removed to Ipswich, Mass., where he died 1647.

THOMAS, was at Portsmouth, N. H., 1630, sent by Mason the patentee.

WILLIAM, came to Plymouth, Mass., 1623, from Devonshire, Eng.

HEATH

BARTHOLOMEW, b. Eng., 1615, settled at Newbury, Mass., removed to Haverhill, Mass., 1645.

CHARLES, inhabitant of Boston, Mass., 1683.

ISAAC, b. Eng., 1585, came to Roxbury, Mass., 1635.

JOHN, brother of Bartholomew, was at Haverhill, Mass., left no male issue.

JOSEPH, brother of Charles, inhabitant of Boston, Mass.

THOMAS, brother of preceding, was at Boston, Mass., 1676.

WILLIAM, brother of Isaac, settled at Roxbury, Mass., 1632, freeman 1633, resident of Dover, N. H., 1645.

HEATHFIELD, HITHFIELD

MATTHIAS, took oath of fidelity, New Haven, Conn., 1660.

HEATON

From the Saxon word *hea,* high town or hill, and *ton.*

JAMES, inhabitant of New Haven, Conn., 1661-85.

NATHANIEL, b. Eng., came to Boston, Mass., 1634, freeman 1636.

HEBARD, HEBBERD

ROBERT, b. Eng., 1612, was at Salem, Mass., 1646.

HEDGE, HEDGES

A fence of thorn-bushes; a thicket of shrubs; an inclosure of shrubs or small trees.

JOHN, b. Eng., 1610, inhabitant of Lynn, Mass., 1634.

STEPHEN, resident of Fairfield, Conn., 1670.

TRISTRAM, married, Boston, Mass., 1657.

WILLIAM, freeman Lynn, Mass., 1634, removed to Sandwich, Mass., thence to Yarmouth, Mass.

WILLIAM, freeman, Taunton, Mass., 1652, where he had resided since 1648.

HEDLEY

JOHN, was at Newport, R. I., before 1676.

HEFERMAN

WILLIAM, inhabitant of Wickford, R. I., 1674.

HEIFOR

ANDREW, was at Kittery, Mass., 1640.

HELMAN

JOHN, was at Nantucket, R. I., before 1682.

HELME

CHRISTOPHER, inhabitant of Exeter, N. H., 1639, removed to Mass., 1643, thence to Warwick, R. I., 1644.

HELSON

JOHN, married at Saco, Maine, 1658.

HEMAN

FRANCIS, freeman of Mass., 1646.

HEMMENWAY, HEMINGWAY

RALPH, b. Eng., was at Roxbury, Mass., 1633, proprietor and freeman, 1634.

SAMUEL, b. Eng., 1636, settled at East Haven, Conn., 1662.

HEMPSTEAD

ROBERT, one of the four inhabitants to assist Winthrop in settlement New London, Conn., 1645.

HENBURY

ARTHUR, resident of Windsor and Simsbury, Conn., died Hartford, Conn., 1697.

HENCHMAN, HINCHMAN

DANIEL, school master, Boston, Mass., 1666, removed to Worcester, Mass.

EDMUND, at Marshfield, Mass., 1652, removed to Chelmsford, Mass., 1657.

JOSEPH, living at Scituate, Mass., 1680.

THOMAS, settled Concord, Mass., removed to Chelmsford, Mass., where he became freeman 1654.

WILLIAM, married, Boston, Mass., 1653.

HENDEE, HANDY, HENDY

RICHARD, b. Eng., original proprietor Norwich, Conn., 1660.

HENDERSON

The name is derived from Henry's son or from Hendrick's son, and is of Scotch origin.

JOHN, took oath of allegiance, Dover, N. H., 1655, later was at Springfield, Mass., and Hartford, Conn.; removed Haddam, Conn., 1663.

WILLIAM, ship carpenter and builder, came from Glasgow, Scotland, and was at Dover, N. H., 1650.

HENDRICK

DANIEL, at Hampton, N. H., 1639, removed Haverhill, Mass., 1645.

PETER, lived Windsor, Conn., 1675, removed to Wallingford, Conn., 1712.

HENDRICKSON

PETER, living Boston, Mass., 1643.

HENFIELD

EDMUND, master mariner, lived Salem, Mass., 1669.

JOSEPH, married, living at Salem, Mass.

HENING, HENNEN

RICHARD, at Newbury, Mass., before 1671.

HENLEY, HANLEY

From *hen*, old, and *ley*, a field or common; place name from a market town in Oxfordshire and Warwickshire, Eng.

ELIAS, married Boston, Mass., 1657, living at Marblehead, Mass., 1668-74.

JOSEPH, resident of Chelmsford, Mass., 1680.

HENRY

The name derived from *Einrick*, ever rich, from Latin *Honoricus*, honorable; also written Heynrich i. e. rich at home.

ISAAC, at Medfield, Mass., 1675.

JOHN, freeman Topsfield, Mass., 1690.

HENRYSON

JOHN, at Springfield, Mass., 1661, removed to Haddam, Conn., thence to Hartford, Conn.

HENSHAW, HINSHAW, HINSHEW

From *hein*, a kind of fowl, and *shaw*, a shady inclosure.

DANIEL, son of Sir Joshua H. of Liverpool, Eng., came in his youth to Dorchester, Mass., 1652, where he married, had one son Daniel, who died unmarried.

JOSHUA, brother of the preceding, b. Liverpool, Eng., 1644, came to Dorchester, Mass., 1652, when only eight years of age, married, returned to Eng., 1688, where he died, leaving four sons in Mass.

HENSHER, HEINSHER

THOMAS, married, Woburn, Mass., 1677.

HEPBURN, HEPBOURNE

GEORGE, leather dresser, freeman, Charlestown, Mass., 1636.

Patrick, Scotch descent, inhabitant of Conn., 1680.

HERBERT, HARBERT

From Saxon *here*, a soldier, and *beorht*, bright, famous in war.

HENRY, married at Charlestown, Mass., 1653.

JOHN, shoemaker, came from Northampton, Eng., to N. E., 1637, granted land Salem, Mass., 1637.

JOHN, merchant, freeman Braintree, Mass., 1641.

JOHN, captain of militia, married Reading, Mass., 1680.

SYLVESTER, inhabitant of Boston, Mass., 1652.

HERNDALE

BENJAMIN, was at Lynn, Mass., in 1647 swore allegiance Providence, R. I.

HERRICK

The ancient family of the Ericks or Herricks derive their lineage from Erick, the Forrester, a great Scandinavian commander who raised an army to oppose the invasion of William the Conqueror. Erick is derived from German *ehr* honor, and *rick*, rich, rich in honor. The name had undergone many modifications, from Eiriks, Eric to the form of Herrick, which is assumed in the middle of the seventeenth century. The English family is traced from Eric or Eyryk of Great Streton and of Houghton, Leicestershire, Eng.

GEORGE, shopkeeper, inhabitant of Salem, Mass., 1686-96.

HENRY, son of Sir William H. of Beau Manor Park, parish of Loughborough, Leicestershire, Eng., the tenth generation from Eyryk of Great Streton, b. Beau Manor, 1604, came first to Virginia, and was member of Church at Salem, Mass., 1629. He removed to Wenham, Mass., finally to Beverly, Mass.

HERRING

From Hirring, town in the Diocese of Alburg, Denmark.

JAMES, inhabitant at Dedham, Mass., 1642.

THOMAS, freeman at Dedham, Mass., 1654.

HERRINGBORNE

GEORGE, living at Boston, Mass., 1664.

HERSEY

From the Village of Herseaux in West Flanders, Belgium, Hughe de Hersey was governor of Frau Normandy, 1204.

WILLIAM, husbandman, son of Nathaniel H. of Reading, Berkshire, Eng., b. Eng., 1596, came to N. E. 1635, freeman Hingham, Mass., 1638.

HETHERSAY, HITHERSEA

ROBERT, living at Charlestown, Mass., 1640, Dover, N. H., 1648, and at York, Maine, 1651.

HETT

THOMAS, cooper, proprietor Cambridge, Mass., 1632, removed Hingham, Mass., 1637, Rehoboth, Mass., 1645, and that part of Charlestown, now Malden, Mass., 1658.

HEWES, HEWS

CHRISTOPHER, inhabitant, Haverhill, Mass., 1646.

GEORGE, resident Salisbury, Mass., 1672.

JAMES, was at Boston, Mass., 1669.

JOHN, called Welshman, was at Plymouth, Mass., and living 1632 at Scituate, Mass.

JOHN, b. Eng., 1621, proprietor at Watertown, Mass., 1642.

JOSHUA, merchant, came to Roxbury, Mass., 1633, removed to Wickford, R. I., 1662, returned Boston, Mass., 1657.

ROBERT, inhabitant Lynn, Mass., 1642.

HEWETT see HUET

HEWINS, HEWENS

JACOB, settled at Boston, Mass., proprietor Dorchester, Mass., 1660.

HEWLET, HEWLETT

LEWIS, came from Buckinghamshire, Eng., to Charlestown, Mass., 1636, was a resident of Hempstead, Long Island, 1647.

HEYWOOD

JAMES, settled in Charlestown, Mass., where he died 1642.

JOHN, b. Eng., 1620, settled at Concord, Mass., 1650.

HIBBARD, HIBBERT

Same as Hubbard, q. v.

ROBERT, saltmaker and brickmaker, b. Salisbury, Eng., 1613, settled Salem, Mass., 1635-39.

HIBBINS, HIBBENS

GILES, married at Saco, Maine, 1670.

WILLIAM, merchant, came Boston, Mass., 1634, freeman 1640, no issue.

HIBBS

DAVID, resident Watertown, Mass., 1686.

JOSEPH, brother of preceding, resident Watertown, Mass., 1686.

HICHBORN

DAVID, b. Eng., settled Boston, Mass., 1650.

HICKCOX, HICOX, HICKOX

The son of Hig or Hugh; *cock*, signifying little.

WILLIAM, among New Haven people 1643, returned to Eng., 1643, leaving two sons, Joseph and Samuel, identified with Farmington, Conn.

HICKENS

THOMAS, inhabitant of Stamford, Conn.

HICKS

The son of Hugh. Hig or Hick being a common nick-name for Hugh. *Hick* in Dutch signifies a simpleton. Sir Ellis H. was knighted by Edward, the Black Prince, 1356.

JOHN, resident of Newport, R. I., 1639, removed to Newtown and Hempstead, Long Island.

RICHARD, at Boston, Mass., 1649.

ROBERT, leather-dresser, b. Eng., 1580, came to Plymouth, Mass., 1621.

THOMAS, brother of preceding, inhabitant of Scituate, Mass., 1630.

TIMOTHY, shipwright, Boston, Mass., removed 1673 to Salem, Mass.

HICKSON

ROBERT, married Eastham, Mass., 1679.

WALTER, soldier from Hatfield, Mass., 1676.

HIDDEN

ANDREW, b. Eng., 1626, came to Rowley, Mass., 1655, where he died 1729, aged 103 years.

HIGBEE, HIGBY

EDWARD, b. Eng., settled New London, Conn., 1647, removed to Middletown, Conn., and 1675 to Jamacia, Long Island.

HIGGINBOTTOM

RICHARD, tailor, inhabitant New Haven, Conn., 1682, afterwards at Stamford, Conn., where his name appears 1701.

HIGGINS

Name of Celtic origin, anglicized from Hugonis; has existed in England, as early as reign of Richard II.

ALEXANDER, granted land Salem, Mass., 1637.

JOHN, resident Boston, Mass., 1656.

JONATHAN, brother of preceding, married Eastham, Mass., 1661.

RICHARD, tailor, came from north of Ireland; name appears in records of Plymouth, Mass., 1633. One of seven original settlers at Eastham, Mass., 1654.

ROBERT, resident of Eastham, Mass., 1654.

HIGGINSON

FRANCIS, clergyman, son of Rev. John H., a descendant of John H., living at Berkswell, Eng., 1518, b. Eng., 1588, came to Salem, Mass., 1629.

WILLIAM, proprietor Farmington, Conn., 1673.

HIGLEY

JOHN, came from Frimley in County of Surrey, Eng., and was proprietor at Farmington, Conn., 1671.

HILDRETH

RICHARD, b. Eng., 1615, freeman Cambridge, Mass., 1643, removed to Woburn, Mass.; one of grantees Chelmsford, Mass., 1653.

HILL, HILLS

ABRAHAM, b. Eng., 1615, at Charlestown, Mass., 1636.

BENJAMIN, was at New Haven, Conn., 1646.

CHARLES, merchant, son of George H., b. Barlow near Chesterfield, Derbyshire, Eng., came from Maryland to New London, Conn., 1665.

EBENEZER, took oath of allegiance, Newbury, Mass., 1678.

ELIPHALET, resident of Boston, Mass., 1670.

FRANCIS, at Boston, Mass., 1664.

HERCULES, soldier, at Scituate, Mass., 1636, returned to Eng., living at Rochester, County of Kent, 1666.

IGNATIUS, inhabitant of Boston, Mass., 1658.

JAMES, married at Boston, Mass., 1662.

JOHN, first record, Plymouth, 1630, next year removed to Boston, Mass.; was at Dover, N. H., 1649.

JOHN, blacksmith at Boston, Mass., 1641.

JOHN, blacksmith, came from vicinity of Chard, Somersetshire, Eng., to Dorchester, Mass., 1633.

JOHN, inhabitant of New Haven, Conn., 1643, no issue.

JOHN, living at Rowley, Mass., 1641.

JOHN, came from Northamptonshire, Eng., to Branford, Conn., 1646, was at Guilford, Conn., 1654.

JOHN, merchant, inhabitant Boston, Mass., 1668.

JONATHAN, came to N. E. before 1660, lived at Warwick and Portsmouth, R. I.

JOSEPH, woolen draper, son of George H., bapt. parish of Great Barsted Billericay, County of Essex, Eng., 1602, settled Charlestown, Mass., 1638; one of founders of Malden, Mass., removed 1664 to Newbury, Mass.

LUKE, at Windsor, Conn., 1651.

PETER, planter and sailor, b. Eng., settled at Biddeford, Maine, and in 1648 lived near the mouth of the Saco river.

RALPH, b. Eng., came from Billericay, Eng., to Plymouth, Mass., 1638, at Woburn, Mass., 1643, and ten years later one of first settlers of Billerica, Mass.

RICHARD, cooper, brother of Abraham, came to Charlestown, Mass., 1638, died unmarried following year.

ROBERT, signer of original compact, New Haven, Conn., 1639, came from Eng., to Boston, Mass., 1635.

THOMAS, at Middletown, Conn., 1678, removed to Hartford, Conn., 1692.

VALENTINE, mercer, came from London, Eng., to Boston, Mass., 1636.

WILLIAM, came to N. E., 1630, freeman Dorchester, Mass., 1633, removed to Windsor, Conn., 1636, and to Fairfield, Conn., 1645.

WILLIAM, came from County of Essex, Eng., to Roxbury, Mass., 1632, removed to Hartford, Conn., with Rev. Thomas Hooker's party, later went to Hadley Mass.

ZEBULON, came from Bristol, Eng., granted land Gloucester, Mass., 1652, removed to Salem, Mass., 1662.

HILLIARD

ANTHONY, was at Hingham, Mass., 1638.

EDWARD, resident Salem, Mass., 1658.

EMANUEL, b. Eng., 1620, settled Hampton, N. H., 1649, drowned 1657.

HUGH, freeman Salem, Mass., 1634.

WILLIAM, carpenter, b. Eng., 1614, came to Boston, Mass., 1635.

WILLIAM, b. Eng., 1642, lived at Little Compton, R. I.

HILLIER, HELYER, HILLER

HUGH, at Yarmouth, Mass., afterwards at Braintree, Mass., where he died 1647.

JOHN, inhabitant Windsor, Conn., 1637.

ROGER, married at Charlestown, Mass., 1691.

WILLIAM, carpenter, at Duxbury, Mass., 1639-43.

HILLMAN

JOHN, worsted comber, came from Eng., 1670, settled at Martha's Vineyard, Mass.

HILTON

EDWARD, fishmonger, settled at Dover Neck, N. H., 1623, removed to Exeter, N. H., 1643.

WILLIAM, fishmonger, brother of preceding, came from London, Eng., to Plymouth, Mass., 1621, removed to Dover Neck, N. H., before 1627, freeman Newbury, Mass., 1643, later returned to Dover, N. H.

HINCKES, HINCKS

JOHN, came from Chester, Eng., settled at Portsmouth, N. H., 1670.

HINCKLEY, HINKLEY

SAMUEL, b. Tenterden, County of Kent, Eng., 1595, settled in Plymouth Colony, Mass., 1634, removed to Scituate, Mass., 1635, removed Barnstable, Mass., 1639.

HINCKSON, HINKSMAN

JOHN, inhabitant of Charlestown, Mass., 1683.

PETER, at Scarborough, Maine, 1671-76.

PHILIP, freeman Saco, Maine, 1653.

SIMON, brother of Peter, resident of Scarborough, Maine, 1671-76.

HINDS

Name derived from Scotch word *hyne* or *hine,* a tiller of the ground—a farmer, or from the Anglo-Saxon word *hind,* the female of the red deer.

JAMES, cooper, came to Salem, Mass., 1637, removed to Southold, L. I.

RICHARD, brother of preceding, settled at Salem, Mass., 1644.

WILLIAM, brother of the above, was resident of Salem, Mass., 1644, later removed to Marblehead, Mass.

HINE

THOMAS, first of the name in N. E., had a home lot in Milford, Conn., 1646.

HINMAN, HINDMAN

A domestic, a servant; one who has the care of herds.

EDWARD, farmer, settled Stamford, Conn., before 1650, removed to Windsor, Conn., later Stratford, Conn., where he died 1681.

HINSDALE

This family originated in the district of Loos, County of Leige, now Belgium, where it settled early in twelfth century. The name, however, is French as well as Dutch, in the former language *dal* or *dale* means valley and corresponds with the Dutch *dael,* and English *dale.*

ROBERT, came from Dedham, County of Essex, Eng., to Dedham, Mass., where he was a proprietor, 1637, one of original thirteen settlers Medfield, Mass., 1651, removed to Hadley, Mass., 1667.

HINTON

Place name from a borough in Wiltshire, Eng. In Welsh *henton,* the old town, from *hen,* old.

BENJAMIN, resident Springfield, Mass., 1678.

HIRST

WILLIAM, married Salem, Mass., 1674.

HITCHCOCK, HISCOCK

EDWARD, inhabitant of New Haven, Conn., 1643.

LUKE, b. Fenny Compton, Warwickshire, Eng., settled New Haven, Conn., 1644, removed to Wethersfield, Conn., 1646, a resident of Hartford, Conn., 1647.

MATTHEW or MATHIAS, b. Eng., 1610 came to Boston, Mass., 1635, removed New Haven, Conn., 1639.

RICHARD, b. Eng., 1608, assessed Saco, Maine, 1636.

SAMUEL, resident of Hartford, Conn., 1669.

HITCHENS, HITCHINGS

Place name a town in Hertfordshire, Eng.

DANIEL, freeman, Lynn, Mass., 1691.

EDWARD, resident Boston, Mass., 1634.

JOSEPH, living at Lynn, Mass., 1662.

HOADLEY, HODLEY

Plame name from two parishes in County of Sussex, Eng.

WILLIAM, merchant, b. Eng., 1630, at Saybrook, Conn., 1663, covenant planter, Branford, Conn., 1667.

HOAG

From the Welsh, signifying low in stature, small.

JOHN, weaver, b. Eng., 1643, married Newbury, Mass., 1669.

HOAR

Definition of name white, hoar, gray.

CHARLES, prominent citizen of Gloucestershire, Eng., his widow Joanna came to N. E., 1643, with four sons: John, Hezekiah, Daniel and Lawrence settled at Scituate, Mass., she died at Braintree, Mass., 1661.

RICHARD, representative to General Court from Yarmouth, Mass., 1641.

SAMUEL, freeman Concord, Mass., removed Boston, Mass., 1669.

WILLIAM, baker, Salem, Mass., removed Boston, Mass., 1669.

HOBART

From the Saxon *hiewe,* color, form, beauty; *beart* bright.

EDMUND, b. Hingham, County of Norfolk, Eng., 1574, came to N. E., 1633, first recorded at Charlestown, Mass., 1633, removed to Hingham, Mass., 1635.

HOBBS

From *Hob,* nickname for Robert.

CHRISTOPHER, freeman at Saco, Maine, 1653.

HENRY, married, Dover, N. H., 1657.

JOSIAH, came from London, Eng., to Woburn, Mass., 1671, removed to Lexington, Mass., 1690.

MAURICE or MORRIS, b. Eng., 1615, inhabitant of Newbury, Mass., removed to Hampton, N. H., 1640-45, later went to Rollinsford, N. H.

THOMAS, settled at Salem, Mass., 1648, freeman Topsfield, Mass., 1671, died at Boston, Mass., 1690.

HOBBY

From *hob,* a herd and *by* a town—the town of herds and flocks.

JOHN, resident of Greenwich, Conn., 1666.

WILLIAM, merchant, inhabitant of Boston, Mass., 1669.

HOBSON, HOPSON

The son of Hob or Robert.

JOHN, b. Eng., came to N. E. 1635, resident of Guilford, Conn., 1664.

WILLIAM, son of Henry H. of Usflete near Whitgift, in the southern part of West Riding, Yorkshire, Eng., came to Rowley, Mass., 1652.

HOCKADAY

NATHANIEL, died Isle of Shoals, 1664.

HODDY

JOHN, resident in N. H,. 1675.

HODGDON, HODGSON, HODSDON

The son of Hod or Hodge.

BENONI, resident of Kittery, Maine, 1675.

GEORGE, came to Cambridge, Mass., before 1645.

JEREMIAH, lived at Dover, N. H., 1666.

JOHN, merchant, married New Haven, Conn., 1651.

JOSEPH, brother of Benoni at Casco, Maine, removed 1686 to York, Maine.

NICHOLAS, at Hingham, Mass., 1635, removed to Newton, Mass., 1650, and six years later became a resident of Kittery, Maine.

ROBERT, married at Warwick, R. I., about 1657.

WILLIAM, b. Eng., 1600, came to N. E., 1634, locating at Plymouth, Mass., removed to Salisbury, Mass., 1641.

HODGE, HODGES

The same as Roger, which signifies quiet or strong counsel. Hodges is a nickname for Roger the "s" being added for son.

ANDREW, at Ipswich, Mass., 1639, where he became a freeman, 1641.

GEORGE, married at Salem, Mass., 1663.

Humphrey, Quaker, at Boston, Mass., 1671.

John, original settler Salisbury, Mass., returned to London, Eng., 1647.

John, at Charlestown, Mass., 1633.

John, married at Killingworth, Conn., 1664.

Nicholas, resident of Plymouth, Mass., 1643.

Nicholas, inhabitant Little Harbor, N. H., 1684.

Thomas, married Charlestown, Mass., 1663.

William, b. Eng., came to Salem, Mass., 1638, removed to Taunton, Mass., 1643.

HODGKIN, HODGKINS

John, resident of Guilford, Conn., 1665.

Samuel, brother of preceding, living at New Haven, Conn., 1651.

William, b. Eng., 1590, settled at Plymouth, Mass., 1634, one of first purchasers of Middleboro, Mass.

William, resident of Ipswich, Mass., 1665.

HODGMAN

Thomas, resident of Reading, Mass., 1663.

HOGG

Same as Hoag, see.

Richard, tailor resident Boston, Mass., 1637.

Thomas, inhabitant of New Haven, Conn., 1646.

HOGGRIDGE, HOGGERIDGE

Abel, took oath of fidelity, Pemaquid, Maine, 1674.

HOIT, HOITT

John, b. Eng., 1610, settled in Charlestown, Mass., as early as 1630.

Simon, b. Eng., 1595, came to Salem, Mass., 1628, one first settlers Charlestown, Mass., in 1633 removed to Dorchester, Mass., in 1635 to Scituate, Mass., became a resident of Windsor, Conn., 1639, thence to Fairfield, Conn., before 1657 living at Stamford, Conn.

HOLBEECH, HOLBRIDGE

Arthur, was at Boston, Mass., 1635, removed to New Haven, Conn., 1638.

HOLBROOK

John, freeman Dorchester, Mass., 1640, lived a short time Rehoboth, Mass., and 1643 went to Weymouth, Mass.

Richard, freeman Dorchester, Mass., 1648, resident of Milford, Conn., 1658, one first settlers Huntington, Long Island, N. Y. where he died 1670.

Thomas, of Weymouth, Eng., came to Weymouth, Mass., before 1643.

HOLCOMB, HOLCOMBE

From Saxon *holt* or *hultz,* a woody vale, and *combe,* a valley.

Thomas, freeman Dorchester, Mass., 1634, removed 1636 Windsor, Conn.

HOLDEN

In Danish language indicating safe, entire, wealthy; a safe place held, protected, defended.

Justinian, b. Eng., 1611, came from Ipswich, Eng., to Watertown, Mass., 1634.

Randall, came from Salisbury, Wiltshire, Eng., and in 1638 a resident of Portsmouth, R. I., thence he removed to Warwick, R. I., before 1643.

Richard, brother of Justinian, b. Eng., 1609, came to N. E., 1634, resided at Cambridge, Mass., removed to Woburn, Mass., one of first proprietors Groton, Mass.

HOLDER

The earliest record of the name is an ancient account of a Saxon Chief, called Holder, who in 500 A. D. obtained jurisdiction over a district which became known as Holderness.

Christopher, Quaker and clergyman, b. Winterburne, Alverton, Gloucestershire, Eng., 1631, located Boston, Mass., 1656, banished from Massachusetts Colony, 1659, returned to N. E.; a freeman at Newport, R. I., 1673

Nathaniel, resident Dorchester, Mass., 1634.

HOLDRIDGE, HOLDRED

John, resident of Roxbury, Mass., 1665.

William, tanner, b. Eng., 1610, parish of St. Alphage, Cripplegate, London, Eng., came to N. E., 1635. He was first at Salisbury, Mass., removed Haverhill, Mass., 1646.

HOLDSWORTH

Joshua, mariner, married at Boston, Mass., 1669.

HOLGAVE, HALGRAVE

John, freeman Salem, Mass., 1633, resident of Gloucester, 1640.

Joshua, inhabitant of Salem, Mass., 1636.

HOLLAND

A name given to a native of that country which was called *Hollowland* because it abounds with ditches full of water.

Christopher, was at Boston, Mass., 1652.

John, freeman Dorchester, Mass., 1636.

Thomas, resident of Yarmouth, Mass., 1641.

HOLLARD

ANGEL, shoemaker, freeman Boston, Mass., 1636, removed to Weymouth, Mass.

GEORGE, mariner, resident of Boston, Mass., 1664.

HOLLEY, HOLLY

JOHN, b. Eng., 1618, settled at Stamford, Conn., 1642.

JOSEPH, at Dorchester, Mass., 1634, removed to Weymouth, Mass., 1639, thence 1643 Sandwich, Mass.

SAMUEL, inhabitant Cambridge, Mass., 1636.

HOLLIDAY

WALTER, married, Springfield, Mass., 1673.

HOLLIDGE

RICHARD, freeman Boston, Mass., 1639.

HOLLINGSHEAD

RICHARD, fisherman, Boston, Mass., 1674.

HOLLINGSWORTH

RICHARD, shipwright, b. Eng., 1595, came from London, Eng., to Salem, Mass., 1635.

HOLLIS

JOHN, b. Eng., 1612, came from Weymouth, Eng., locating Weymouth, Mass., 1642, removed to Wethersfield, Conn., 1644.

HOLLOWAY, HOLWAY

HENRY, inhabitant Dover, N. H., 1662.

JOHN, b. Eng., 1614, came from London, Eng., to Boston, Mass., 1635. No issue.

JOSEPH, was at Lynn, Mass., 1636, removed the next year to Sandwich, Mass.

MALACHI, resident of Taunton, Mass., 1668.

SAMUEL, married Taunton, Mass., 1666.

TIMOTHY, at Taunton, Mass., 1643-59.

WILLIAM, at Taunton, Mass., 1639-1643, removed to Boston, Mass., 1650.

HOLMAN, HOMAN, HOLLMAN

A corruption of *Allemand*, a German, that is, a mixture of all men *Alle-Mann*.

EDWARD, came Plymouth, Mass., 1623, returned to Eng., 1627, again N. E., 1632, one of the purchasers of Dartmouth, Mass., 1652.

EDWARD, inhabitant of Marblehead, Mass., 1674.

EZEKIEL, first record Dedham, Mass., at Salem, Mass., 1637; one of the founders of First Baptist Church, Providence, R. I., 1638, later removed to Warwick, R. I.

GABRIEL, brother of second Edward, at Marblehead, Mass., 1674.

JOHN, resident of Dorchester, Mass., 1634.

SOLOMON, living at Newbury, Mass., 1694.

WILLIAM, b. Eng., 1595, came from Northampton, Eng., to Cambridge, Mass., 1635.

HOLMES, HOLME

Family of ancient English origin, the name is of local derivation. Meadow lands near or surrounded by water, grassy plains, sometimes an island. The Saxon word *holm* means a flat ground in or near water. John Holmes was in the army of William the Conquerer.

DAVID, resident of Dorchester, Mass., 1666.

FRANCIS, resided at Stamford, Conn., 1648.

GEORGE, came from County of Essex, Eng., to Roxbury, Mass., where he became freeman, 1639.

JOHN, was at Plymouth, Mass., 1632.

JOHN, b. Eng., 1644, settled at Dorchester, Mass.; became one of original proprietors of Woodstock, Conn.

JOHN, resident of Northampton, Mass., 1678.

JOHN, married Duxbury, Mass., 1661.

JOHN, resident of Roxbury, Mass., 1690.

JOSEPH, married Roxbury, Mass., 1651.

JOSEPH, tailor, at Boston, Mass., 1677.

JOSHUA, living at Westerly, R. I., 1678.

JOSIAH, married Duxbury, Mass., 1666.

NATHANIEL, married at Plymouth, Mass., 1667.

OBADIAH, clergyman, came from Preston, Lancashire, Eng., to Salem, Mass., 1639, removed to Rehoboth, Mass., thence to Newport, R. I., and took part in the settlement of New Jersey, 1664.

RICHARD, b. Eng., 1610, was at Rowley, Mass., 1643.

RICHARD, resident of Norwalk, Conn., 1654.

ROBERT, freeman Cambridge, Mass., 1641, where he had resided since 1636.

ROBERT, married Newbury, Mass., 1669.

ROBERT, resident of Stonington, Conn., 1670.

SAMUEL, living Rehoboth, Mass., before 1674.

THOMAS, b. London, Eng., 1625, came from Virginia, to New York, 1665, thence to New London, Conn.

WILLIAM, b. near Holme, East Riding, Yorkshire, Eng., 1592, came to N. E., 1636, was at Scituate, Mass., in that year. He was one of the Conihasset planters in 1646, afterwards at Marshfield, Mass.

WILLIAM, was at Plymouth, Mass., 1632, returned to Eng., was major in great rebellion; returned to Boston, where he died 1649, leaving no issue.

HOLT

From Dutch word *hultz*, a wood; a peaked hill covered with wood, a grove of trees around a house.

NICHOLAS, tanner, came from Romsey, County of Hants, Eng., to Boston, Mass., 1635, one first settlers of Newbury, Mass, removed to Andover, Mass., 1644.

WILLIAM, inhabitant of New Haven, Conn., 1643.

HOLTON, HOLTEN

JOHN, freeman at Dedham, Mass., 1671.

NATHANIEL, at Salem, Mass., 1668.

ROBERT, slater, freeman at Boston, Mass., 1634.

WILLIAM, b. Eng., 1611, came from Ipswich, Eng., 1635, to Cambridge, Mass., with Thomas Hooker's party, he went to Hartford, Conn., returned to Eng., where he remained three years, and joined the colonists at Northampton, Mass., before 1663.

HOLYOKE

EDWARD, clergyman, b. Tamworth, County of Stafford, Eng., freeman Lynn, Mass., 1639, resided at Rumney Marsh, now Chelsea, Mass.

HOMAN, HOMANS

EDWARD, at Marblehead, Mass., 1674.

JOHN, inhabitant of Salem, Mass., 1668.

HOMER

The name derived from Greek signifying a hostage, a pledge or security. The old Saxon name is from the Manor Homer which now bears the name of Hummer in County of Somerset, Eng. In that language *hob* means high, and *mere*, a pool or lake, therefore meaning "the high lake." The first of the name was Thomas de Homere, lord of the manor in Dorsetshire, 1338.

MICHAEL, son of Edward H., living at Ettingshall, parish of Bilston, County of Stafford, Eng., was at Boston, Mass., 1676.

HOOD

From Saxon word *houdt*, the wood.

JOHN, weaver, b. Eng., 1600, son of John H. of Halstead, County of Essex, Eng., settled at Cambridge, Mass., 1638, removed to Lynn, Mass., was living at Kittery, Maine, 1652.

RICHARD, came from Lynn, Regis, County of Norfolk, Eng., 1650, to Lynn, Mass.

HOOKE

FRANCIS, son of Humphrey H. alderman city of Bristol, Eng., married at Boston, Mass., 1660, removed to Kittery, Maine, 1666.

JOHN, Mayflower passenger, died shortly after arrival, no issue.

WILLIAM, clergyman, b. County of Hants, Eng., was at Taunton, Mass., 1639, removed to New Haven, Conn., 1644, returned to Eng., leaving no issue in N. E.

WILLIAM, brother of Francis, at York, Maine, 1633.

HOOKER

NICHOLAS, resident of Charlestown, Mass., 1678.

THOMAS, clergyman, grandson of John H., son of Thomas H., of Devonshire, b. Marfield, Leicestershire, Eng., 1586. Arrived Boston, Mass., 1633, settling at Cambridge, Mass., in 1636, led the party of colonists that settled Connecticut at Hartford.

HOOPER

From Saxon word *hoppere*, a dancer. The surname first used in Eng., 1275, William H. in that year possessing land in Dorsetshire, Eng.

GEORGE, mariner, Boston, Mass., 1674.

JOHN, brother of preceding, Marblehead, Mass., 1674.

JOHN, married Marblehead, Mass., 1691.

RICHARD, surgeon, first at Hampton, N. H., removed to Watertown, Mass., before 1684.

ROBERT, brother of second John, b. Eng., 1607, at Marblehead, Mass., 1663.

SAMUEL, married Marblehead, Mass., 1694.

WILLIAM, b. Eng., 1617, came from London, Eng., to N. E., 1635, resided 1660 Reading, Mass., what is now Wakefield.

HOPEWELL

THOMAS, at Fairfield, Conn., 1670.

HOPKINS

Little Robert, or the child of Robert, the surname originally spelled Hopkyns is one of the earliest of purely English surnames; it is baptismal signifying the son of Robert and is derived from Hob or Hothe, nicknames for Robert. The seat of the family is Oxfordshire, Eng.

EDWARD, merchant, came to Boston, Mass., 1637, went to Hartford, Conn., same year, returned to Eng., 1652; no issue.

JOHN, proprietor Cambridge, Mass., 1634, removed to Hartford, Conn., 1636.

SAMUEL, at Milford, Conn., 1658, married, New Haven, Conn., 1667.

STEPHEN, Mayflower passenger.

THOMAS, son of William, b. Chelselbourne, Eng., 1616, name appears on records at Providence, R. I., 1640, removed 1676, to what is now Oyster Bay, Long Island.

WILLIAM, at Stratford, Conn., 1640.

WILLIAM, inhabitant of Roxbury, Mass., 1660.

HOPKINSON

MICHAEL, b. Eng., 1610, came Boston, Mass., 1635, freeman Rowley, Mass., 1640.

HOPPER

DANIEL, freeman New Haven, Conn., 1654.

HOPPIN

STEPHEN, living Dorchester, Mass., 1653, afterwards Roxbury, Mass.

HORN, HORNE

JOHN, b. Eng., 1603, came with Winthrop to N. E., 1630, freeman Salem, Mass., 1631, on tax list at Dover, N. H., 1659.

WILLIAM, Dover, N. H., 1659.

HORNER

EPHRAIM, inhabitant of Rehoboth, Mass., before 1684.

HORSLEY

JAMES, resident of Newton, Mass.

JOSEPH, at Rowley, Mass., 1672.

HORTON

Place name from a town in Yorkshire, Eng., from *horr,* a ravine, or town in the ravine.

BARNABAS, resident of Hampton, N. H., 1640, removed to Southold, Long Island, 1662.

BENJAMIN, brother of preceding, at Hampton, N. H., 1640.

CALEB, brother of preceding, inhabitant of Hampton, N. H., 1640.

JOHN, freeman Guilford, Conn., 1669.

JOSEPH, brother of Barnabas at Southhold, Long Island, 1662, when he was made a freeman of Conn.

THOMAS, b. 1620. At Charlestown, Mass,. 1655, removed to Milton, Mass., before 1669, but finally returned to Charlestown.

THOMAS, an inhabitant of Windsor, Conn., removed to Springfield, Mass., 1638, where he died 1641.

HOSFORD, HORSFORD

From Ouseford, in England, the "O" being aspirated—that is, the ford or the way of the river Ouse.

WILLIAM, clergyman, b. Eng., settled Dorchester, Mass., 1630, removed to Windsor, Conn., 1636, at Springfield, Mass., 1652, returned to Eng., 1656, leaving in N. E. an only son John.

HOSIER

SAMUEL, came Watertown, Mass., 1630, where he died 1665, leaving no issue.

HOSMER

JAMES, b. Eng., 1607, came from Hawkhurst, County of Kent, Eng., 1635 to Cambridge, Mass., was at Concord, Mass., went to Hartford, Conn., 1636.

THOMAS, brother of preceding, freeman at Cambridge, Mass., 1635, removed with Hooker to Hartford, Conn., in his later days lived at Northampton, Mass.

HOTCHKISS

DANIEL, resident New Haven, Conn., 1688.

JOSHUA, married, New Haven, Conn., 1677.

SAMUEL, b. County of Essex, Eng., was at New Haven, Conn., 1641.

HOUCHIN, HOUTCHIN

JEREMY, tanner, was at Dorchester, Mass., freeman Boston, Mass., 1640.

ROBERT, inhabitant of Newport, R. I., 1666.

HOUGH

Place name from village in County of Lincoln, Eng., from Saxon and Dutch, *hoch, hoog,* and *hou,* high. The name still exists in Flanders as De la Hooghe and is of Gaelic Flemish origin. Representatives of the family were in Cheshire, Eng., at the time of the Conquest.

ATHERTON, mayor of Boston, county of Lincoln, Eng., 1628, made a freeman at Boston, Mass., 1634, died at Boston, 1646.

WILLIAM, housewright, son of Edward H., b. Cheshire, Eng., came to Gloucester, Mass., 1640, removed to Saybrook, Conn., thence New London, Conn., where he died 1670.

HOUGHTON

Surname from a town in Lancashire, Eng., from the Saxon *hoog* or *hock,* high and *ton,* a hill, castle or town. The family is of great antiquity dating back to Sir Roger de Bresli, who came to England with William the Conqueror and was given large estate in Lancashire on which was De Hocton Castle.

JOHN, son of John, b. Eaton Bray, Lancashire, Eng., 1620, came to N. E., 1647-50, lived for a short time at Dedham, Mass., removing in 1652 to Lancaster, Mass.

JOHN, resident of Woburn, Mass., before 1676.

RALPH, cousin of first John, inhabitant Lancaster, Mass., 1654.

WILLIAM, butcher, b. 1613, came from London, Eng., to N. E., 1635, was an early inhabitant of Connecticut.

HOUNSLOW

EDWARD, at Scarborough, Maine, 1676.

HOUSE

A covering, a dwelling place, a mansion.

SAMUEL, one of founders of Church Scituate, Mass., 1635, removed to Cambridge, Mass.

WALTER, inhabitant New London, Conn., where he died 1670.

HOUSING

PETER, Casco, Maine, 1666-73.

HOUSLEY

JOSEPH, Rowley, Mass., 1691.

HOVEY

DANIEL, b. Eng., 1618, proprietor Ipswich, Mass., 1636, removed to Brookfield, Mass., 1668, hence Hadley, Mass., returned to Ipswich, Mass., where he died 1692.

THOMAS, inhabitant Hadley, Mass., 1677.

HOWARD

WILLIAM, son of Roger Fitz Valvine, took the name of Howard from being born in the Castle of Howard in Henry I. reign. The word is derived from *hafward,* keeper of a hall or *hold-ward,* keeper of stronghold; also *hoch-ward,* the high keeper.

EDWARD, married Boston, Mass., 1661.

HENRY, early inhabitant at Hartford, Conn., married at Wethersfield, Conn., 1648.

JAMES, came to Charlestown, Mass., 1634-35.

JOHN, resident of Dedham, Mass., 1636-60.

JOHN, carpenter, came from England to Plymouth, Mass., 1635, about fifteen years of age was brought in the family of Captain Myles Standish, on record 1645, as one of original proprietors Bridgewater, Mass.

JONATHAN, brother of preceding, was at Bridgewater, Mass., and had the title of major.

NATHANIEL, from County of Suffolk, Eng., became freeman Dorchester, Mass., 1643.

NATHANIEL, married at Charlestown, Mass., 1666.

ROBERT, proprietor of Dorchester, Mass., 1639, removed to Boston, Mass., 1668.

SAMUEL, resident of Malden, Mass., 1666.

THOMAS, married Lynn, Mass., 1667.

THOMAS, inhabitant of Norwich, Conn., 1660.

THOMAS, b. Eng., 1643, at Lynn, Mass., and Enfield, Conn.

WILLIAM, Topfield, Mass., 1650.

WILLIAM, resident of Swanzey, Mass., 1671.

WILLIAM, at Malden, Mass., 1686.

WILLIAM, brother of Robert, b. Eng., 1609, came Braintree, Mass., 1635, settled at Salem, Mass., at Boston, Mass., 1666.

HOWD

ANTHONY, early settler of Branford, Conn., where he died 1676.

HOWE, HOW, HOWES

From French De La Howe, original name of the family; a hill, critically a hill in the valley. The name came with William the Conqueror to England.

ABRAHAM, freeman, Roxbury, Mass., 1638, at Dorchester, Mass., 1636.

ABRAHAM, married Watertown, Mass., 1658 at Charlestown, Mass., removed 1660, Marlboro, Mass.

DANIEL, at Lynn, Mass., 1630, freeman 1634, removed to Southampton, L. I., 1640.

EDWARD, freeman, Watertown, Mass., 1634.

EDWARD, b. Eng., settled Lynn, Mass., 1660.

JAMES, brother first Abraham, b. Eng., 1606, came from Hatfield, County of Essex, Eng., freeman Roxbury, Mass., 1637, removed to Ipswich, Mass., 1648.

JOHN, son of John of Warwickshire, Eng., brother second Abraham, on record Watertown, Mass., 1638, the following year removed to Sudbury, Mass., and in 1657 Marlboro, Mass.

JOHN, married Yarmouth, Mass., 1689.

JOSEPH, cooper, freeman Boston, Mass., 1657.

NATHANIEL, took oath of fidelity New Haven, Conn., 1660.

SAMUEL, freeman at Yarmouth, Mass., 1635.

THOMAS, one grantees Yarmouth, Mass., 1638.

WILLIAM, inhabitant Concord, Mass., before 1657.

ZECHARIAH, took oath of fidelity New Haven, Conn., 1660.

HOWELL

From Cornish British *houl,* the sun, from the Greek signifying *euhill,* high, exalted.

EDWARD, freeman Lyme, 1639, one of grantees Southampton, Long Island, 1640.

MORGAN, at Cape Porpoise, Maine, 1636.

HOWEN, HOWING, HOWYN

ISRAEL, tailor, Cambridge, Mass.

JOHN, shoemaker, Boston, Mass.

ROBERT, cutler, Boston, Mass., 1639, freeman 1642.

HOWLAND

ARTHUR, settler Marshfield, Mass., before 1643, where he was proprietor 1647.

HENRY, inhabitant Duxbury, Mass., 1633.

JABEZ, married Duxbury, Mass., before 1669.

JOHN, Mayflower passenger.

ZOAR, inhabitant Newport, R. I., 1656.

HOWLETT

A night-bird, an owl.

JOHN, mariner, Boston, Mass., where he died before 1676.

THOMAS, came in Winthrop's fleet 1630, one first settlers Ipswich, Mass., 1633.

HOYLE

JOHN, Marblehead, Mass., 1674.

HOYT

JOHN, b. Eng., 1610-15, one early settlers Salisbury, Mass., 1639, removed Amesbury, Mass., 1668.

JOHN, Fairfield, Conn., 1650, freeman 1664.

SIMON, Salem, Mass., 1629, removed Dorchester, 1633, located Scituate, Mass., 1635, afterwards Windsor, Conn., 1639, and Stamford, Conn., 1659.

WILLIAM, took oath of fidelity Amesbury, Mass., 1677.

HUATT

DANIEL, Guilford, Conn., 1669.

HUBBARD

A corruption of Hubert from Anglo-Saxon *hiewe,* color, form, beauty, and *beort,* bright. The name dates back from the first invasion of the Danes into England, in 866, when King Hubba, the Danish King landed on the coast of Kent.

ANTHONY, Dedham, Mass., 1648.

BENJAMIN, came with mother Elizabeth to Charlestown, Mass., 1633, returned to Eng., 1644.

GEORGE, b. Eng., 1600-01, came from Glastenbury, Somersetshire, Eng., to Watertown, Mass., 1633, removed to Wethersfield, Conn., 1636, thence three years later to Milford, Conn., and 1648 became a resident of Guilford, Conn.

GEORGE, Indian trader and agent, b. Eng., 1601, settled at Dorchester, and Charlestown, Mass., removed Hartford, Conn., 1639, thence 1654 to Middletown, Conn.

HUGH, from Derbyshire, Eng., at New London, Conn., 1670.

JAMES, Lynn, 1637, removed to Long Island, N. Y., 1641.

JOHN, came from Boston, Mass., before 1670, also lived at Roxbury, Mass., original proprietor of Woodstock, Conn., 1686.

RICHARD, mariner, Boston, Mass., 1690.

ROBERT, married Boston, Mass., 1654.

SAMUEL, came to Salem, Mass., 1633, in his youth, removed to Watertown, Mass., thence to Wethersfield, Conn., thence to Springfield, Mass., finally locating at Newport, R. I., his only son Samuel died without issue.

THOMAS, died Billerica, Mass., 1656.

WILLIAM, husbandman and historian, b. Eng., 1595, came to Ipswich, Mass., 1635, freeman 1638.

HUBBELL

From Danish chief Hubba, Hubba's hill, or Hubbill. Hub means a heap or a lump, indicating a small round hill on the summit of another. Hubba's hill is situated near Milford Haven in Pembrokeshire, Wales. The English ancestry traced to Hubba the Dane, 867 A. D.

RICHARD, son of Francis H., b. Plymouth, Eng., 1627, came to N. E., 1645, took oath of allegiance New Haven, Conn., 1647, removed to Fairfield, Conn., 1664.

HUBBS, HUBS

ROBERT, freeman Newport, R. I., 1655.

HUCKINS

ROBERT, Dover, N. H., 1640.

THOMAS, b. Eng., 1617, resident Boston, Mass., 1637, removed to Barnstable, Mass.

HUCKLEY

THOMAS, took oath of fidelity, 1660.

HUDDLESTONE

Place name from a small parish in the West Riding of Yorkshire, Eng.

VALENTINE, resident of Newport, R. I., 1673.

HUDSON

The son of Hud or Roger.

DANIEL, arrived Watertown, Mass., 1640, removed Lancaster, Mass., 1664.

FRANCIS, son of William, fisherman, came from Chatham, County of Kent to Boston, Mass., Gov. Winthrop's fleet.

JAMES, settled Boston, Mass., as early as 1641.

JOHN, resident New Haven, Conn., 1654.

JOHN, inhabitant Duxbury, Mass., before 1683, no male issue.

JONATHAN, married Lyme, Conn., 1686.

NICHOLAS, freeman Hingham, Mass., 1637.

RALPH, woolen draper, b. Eng., 1593, came from London, Eng., to Boston, Mass., 1635.

THOMAS, resident Lynn, Mass., 1637.

WILLIAM, baker, came Winthrop's fleet, to Boston, Mass., 1630, returned to Eng., 1656.

HUESTED, HUSTED

ROBERT, granted land at Mount Wollaston, now Braintree, Mass., 1640, soon after removed to Stamford, Conn.

HUET, HEWITT

The son of Hugh.

EPHRAIM, clergyman, came from Wraxall near Kenilworth, Eng., arrived Boston, Mass., 1639, next year went to Windsor, Conn., died 1642, no male issue.

NICHOLAS, resident Boston, Mass., 1643.

ROBERT, came to N. E., 1632, was at Hartford, Conn., 1646.

THOMAS, brother of Rev. Ephraim, proprietor Hingham, Mass., 1647, among the pioneers of Oxbridge, Mass.

THOMAS, mariner, Stonington, Conn., 1651, lost at sea.

WILLIAM, resident of Marblehead, Mass., 1668.

HUGGINS

The same as Higgins, see.

JOHN, Hampton, N. H., 1640.

JOHN, took oath of allegiance Newbury, Mass., 1678.

ROBERT, Dover, N. H., 1642.

HUGHES

The son of Hugh, which is derived from *Hougen,* slasher, cutter. Alfred the Great used Hugh to denote comfort, in Gaelic it is *Aoidh,* signifying affability, a guest, a stranger. Hu suggests the idea of elevation; *Ho Hu,* highness.

ARTHUR, Salem, Mass., 1676.

JAMES, resident Gloucester, Mass., 1670.

RICHARD, living Guilford, Conn., 1640-50.

HULBERT, HULBURD

WILLIAM, came to N. E., 1630, locating Dorchester, Mass., freeman 1632, removed Windsor, Conn., 1636, thence 1655, Northampton, Mass.

HULING

JAMES, b. Eng., 1635, died Newport, R. I., 1697.

HULL

Place name from city of Hull, Yorkshire, Eng., it is derived from the Teutonic or Saxon *Hulen,* or *Heulen,* to howl, from the river Hull, when its mouth meets the sea. Hull is an old word for a hill; Hull Welsh, a rough uneven place.

ANDREW, b. Eng., 1610, came New Haven, Conn., 1639, where he died shortly afterward.

BENJAMIN, clergyman, Weymouth, Mass., 1635, soon after at Bass river, now Beverly, Mass., in 1643, at York, Maine, at Dover, N. H., 1659-61, returned to Eng.

GEORGE, son of Thomas, b. Krewkerne, Somersetshire, Eng., 1590, at Plymouth, Mass., 1629, lived at Boston, and Dorchester, Mass., 1630, Windsor, Conn., in 1636, afterwards Killingworth, Conn. and in 1646, Fairfield, Conn.

JOHN, blacksmith, freeman Dorchester, Mass., 1632, removed to Boston, Mass., 1638.

JOHN, mint-master, son of Robert, b. Market Harborough, County of Leicester, Eng., 1624, freeman Boston, Mass., 1649; no male issue.

JOHN, merchant, resident of Boston, Mass., where he died 1673.

JOHN, Stratford, Conn., 1661-70.

JOSEPH, freeman Hingham, Mass., 1635.

JOSEPH, clergyman, b. Somersetshire, Eng., 1594, came to Boston, Mass., 1635, afterwards at Weymouth, Mass., and York, Maine, 1642; also at Barnstable and Yarmouth, Mass. Returned to Eng., 1652, ten years later settling Dover, N. H., where he died 1665.

RICHARD, of Derbyshire, Eng., freeman Mass., 1634, removed New Haven, Conn., 1640.

ROBERT, blacksmith, came from Bristol, Eng., to Boston, Mass., 1635.

THOMAS, cooper, married Boston, Mass., 1660.

TRISTRAM, Yarmouth, Mass., 1643.

WILLIAM, inhabitant of R. I., 1654.

HULTON

RICHARD, Salisbury, Mass., 1673.

HUMBER

EDWARD, freeman Salem, Mass., 1665.

HUMMERSTON, Henry, resident of New Haven, Conn., 1644.

HUMPHREY, inhabitant Hampton, N. H., 1645.

HUMPHREY, HUMFREY

From Anglo-Saxon *Humfred*, house-peace.

JEREMIAH, Saco, Maine, 1653.

JOHN, first major-general of the colony, came to Boston, 1634, from Sandwich, County of Kent, Eng., returned to Eng., 1641.

JONAS, tanner, came from Wendover, County of Bucks, Eng., to Dorchester, Mass., freeman of Conn., 1657.

MICHAEL, was at Dedham, Mass.; freeman of Conn., 1657.

NATHANIEL, freeman Ipswich, Mass., 1680.

THOMAS, married Dover, N. H., 1660.

HUNGERFORD

Place name a market town in Berkshire, Eng. Hunger's pass or way so called from Hunger, a celebrated Danish leader who invaded England. The lineage traced to Sir Thomas H. first speaker of the House of Commons, 1377. Farley Castle, the home of Sir Thomas located Blark, Bouton, County of Oxford.

THOMAS, mariner, proprietor of Hartford, Conn., 1639, shortly after removed to New London, Conn.

HUNKIN, HUNKINS

JOHN, Portsmouth, N. H., 1660.

MARK, brother of preceding, died Portsmouth, N. H., 1667.

HUNLOCK, HUNLOKE

EDWARD, attorney, came from Derbyshire, Eng., to Boston, Mass., before 1682, removed to Burlington, N. J.

HUNN

A native of Hungary or from the German *Hune*, a giant; a Scythian.

GEORGE, tanner, freeman Boston, Mass., 1637, had estates Braintree, Mass., and Long Island, N. Y.

HUNNIWELL

JOHN, surveyor of roads, Wethersfield, Conn., 1682.

ROGER, died at Saco, Maine, 1654.

HUNT

Mention in Chaucer for Huntsman. The Saxon word Hunter, a wolf used in connection with the animal to mean the pursuit of all game. The family took its name from their prowess in the hunting-field. Adam le Hunt lived in Nottinghamshire, Eng., as early as 1275.

BARTHOLOMEW on record at Dover, N. H., 1640, removed Newport, R. I., 1655.

EDMUND, settled Cambridge, Mass., 1634, at Duxbury, Mass., 1637.

EDWARD, died at Duxbury, Mass., 1665.

ENOCH, blacksmith, b. Titenden, parish Lee, County of Bucks, Eng., freeman Newport, R. I., 1638, removed Weymouth, Mass., 1640.

JONATHAN, malster, b. Sudburrow, Thrapstone, Northamptonshire, Eng., 1637, came to Hartford, Conn., 1658, shortly after removed to Northampton, Mass.

PETER, inhabitant Rehoboth, Mass., 1644.

RICHARD, resident Boston, Mass., 1676.

ROBERT, first on record, Charlestown, Mass., 1638, original proprietor Sudbury, Mass.

SAMUEL, inhabitant Duxbury, Mass., 1663-90.

THOMAS, at Boston, Mass., 1654.

THOMAS, resident Boston, Mass., 1677.

THOMAS, freeman Northampton, Mass., 1684.

WILLIAM, b. Halifax, Yorkshire, Eng., 1605, one of founders of Concord, Mass., 1641, removed Marlboro, Mass., 1664.

WILLIAM, resident Boston, Mass., 1682.

WILLIAM, living at Weymouth, Mass., 1688.

ZACCHEUS, freeman Hull, Mass., 1680.

HUNTER

ROBERT, freeman Ipswich, Mass., 1640.

WILLIAM, married Boston, Mass., 1657.

WILLIAM, resident Springfield, Mass., 1662.

WILLIAM, married at Barnstable, Mass., 1671.

HUNTING

JOHN, b. Eng., 1597. One of the founders of Church at Dedham, Mass., 1638.

HUNTINGTON, HUNTINGDON

From Saxon *Hunter's don*, the mount of hunters, the name of a shire and town in England.

CHRISTOPHER, son of Simon who died of small pox on passage to N. E., 1633. The widow Margaret settled Roxbury, Mass., in 1636, married Thomas Stoughton with her four sons removed to Windsor, Conn. Christopher later settled at Norwich, Conn.

SIMON, brother of the preceding, freeman of Conn., 1657, lived at Branford, Conn., one founders of Newark, N. J.

WILLIAM, came to N. E., 1640, at Hampton, N. H., 1643, rated at Salisbury, Mass., 1650.

WILLIAM, took oath of fidelity Amesbury, Mass., 1677.

HUNTLEY

Place name from a town in Aberdeenshire, Scotland; the hunting field.

JOHN, resident of Boston, Mass., 1652, removed Roxbury, Mass., 1659, two years later Lyme, Conn.

HUNTON

Family of Saxon origin. Thomas and William de Hunton lived in Eng., 1272.

WILLIAM, at Hampton, N. H., 1644.

HUNTRESS

GEORGE, inhabitant Portsmouth, N. H., 1688.

HURD

From Welsh word ***hurdh,*** a ram.

ADAM, living Stratford, Conn., 1650-69.

JOHN, brother of preceding, among first settlers Windsor, Conn., removed to Stratford, Conn., 1639.

JOHN, tailor, resident Boston, Mass., 1639, freeman 1640.

JOHN, weaver, freeman of Mass., 1652, was at Lynn, Mass.

JOHN, freeman Stratford, Conn., 1669.

JOHN, located at Dover, N. H., 1648, at Marblehead, Mass., 1669.

HURLBURT, HULBERT

THOMAS, blacksmith, b. Scotland, 1610, at Saybrook, Conn., a soldier in the Pequot War in 1638, settled Wethersfield, Conn.

THOMAS, resident Woodbury, Conn., 1680.

WILLIAM, Dorchester, Mass., 1635, removed to Windsor, Conn., as early as 1640.

HURRY

WILLIAM, Charlestown, Mass., 1664.

HURST

From Saxon word signifying a wood, a grove.

JAMES, tanner, erected first tannery at Plymouth, Mass., 1640, one of original purchasers Dartmouth, Mass.

JOHN, resident Boston, Mass., 1653.

THOMAS, living 1678 Hadley, Mass., removed Deerfield, Mass., about 1685.

WILLIAM, married at Sandwich, Mass., 1640.

HUSE

ABEL, of Welsh ancestry, came from London, Eng., to Newbury, Mass., 1635.

EDWARD, freeman, Gloucester, Mass., 1690.

HUSSEY, HUZZEY

The name came into England at the time of William the Conqueror. Hugh or Hubert, Holse or Husey, married in 1014 a daughter of the third Duke of Normandy, therefore the name changed from a German form to French and afterward anglicized to Hussey. The family after the Conquest was seated in counties of Kent and Dorset.

CHRISTOPHER, son of John H., of Dorking, County of Suffolk, Eng., b. in that place 1598-99, came to N. E., settling Charlestown, Mass., 1630, shortly after removed to Lynn, Mass., thence to Newbury, Mass., in 1635 was one of first settlers Hampton, N. H., removed 1650 to Hampton Falls, N. H., and 1659 became one proprietors Nantucket Island, Mass.

JOSEPH, brother preceding, resident Hampden, N. H., 1672, bore the title of captain.

ROBERT, resident Duxbury, Mass., 1643-55.

ROBERT, taxed at Dover, N. H., 1657.

ROBERT, freeman Boston, Mass., 1690.

HUSTING

JOHN, Manchester, Mass., 1649.

HUTCHINS, HUTCHINGS

The child of Hugh, see Hitchins.

ENOCH, married in N. H., 1667.

GEORGE, freeman Cambridge, Mass., 1638.

JOHN, resident Newbury, Mass., 1640.

JOHN, died Wethersfield, Conn., 1681.

JOSEPH, married Boston, Mass., 1657.

NICHOLAS, resident Lynn, Mass., 1666.

HUTCHINSON

The son of Hitchins or Hutchins. The origin of the family has been assigned to one Urtchensis, a Norwegian who came with William the Conqueror. The first English record is in 1282, when Barnard Hutchinson lived at Crowland, Yorkshire, Eng.

EDWARD, son of Susanna, a widow, came to Boston, Mass., from Alford, Lincolnshire, Eng., 1633, he removed R. I., 1637, soon after returned to Eng.

FRANCIS, died Concord, Mass., 1661.

FRANCIS, b. Eng., 1630, married at Lynn, Mass., 1661.

GEORGE, came in Winthrop's fleet, 1630,

early connected with church at Boston, Mass.

JOHN, inhabitant Salem, Mass., 1643.

RALPH, married Boston, Mass., 1656, removed to Northampton, Mass., 1662.

RICHARD, son of Thomas, tenth generation from Bernard, b. Eng., 1602-03, settled what is now Danvers, Mass., 1634.

SAMUEL, bachelor, brother of William, came to Boston, Mass., granted land R. I., 1638.

SAMUEL, resident of Reading, Mass., 1670.

SAMUEL, married Andover, Mass., 1686.

THOMAS, Lynn, Mass., 1637, removed Long Island, N. Y., freeman Conn., 1664.

WILLIAM, husband of the noted Ann H., came to N. E., from Alford, Lincolnshire, Eng., to Boston, Mass., 1634, freeman 1635, removed to R. I., 1638, died 1642.

HUTTON

Hutain in French, haughty, proud. A town in England; the high town.

JOHN, Wenham, Mass., 1675.

RICHARD, brother of preceding, b. Eng., 1621, freeman Wenham, Mass., 1672.

HUXLY, HUXLEY

THOMAS, married Hartford, Conn., 1668, removed Suffield, Conn., 1680.

HUXSTABLE

CHRISTOPHER, inhabitant Marblehead, Mass., 1668.

HYATT, HYETT

THOMAS, resident Dorchester, Mass., 1633, moved Stamford, Conn., 1641.

HYDE

From Saxon *hyd* or *hithe,* a landing place, a haven, harbor, also locally a farm, as much land as can be cultivated with one plow. A town of Cheshire, Eng.

GEORGE, ship-carpenter, at Boston, Mass., 1642.

ISAAC, married, Salem, Mass., 1665.

JOHN, resident Stratford, Conn., 1668.

JONATHAN, b. London, Eng., 1626, settled Newton, Mass., 1647, removed following year Cambridge, Mass.

RICHARD, living Salem, Mass., 1642.

SAMUEL, elder brother of Jonathan, b. Eng., 1610, settled Cambridge, Mass., 1640, proprietor Billerica, Mass., 1652.

WILLIAM, came to N. E., 1633, located at Newton, Mass., went with Hooker's colony to Conn., 1636, locating at Hartford, Conn., removed Saybrook, Conn., 1652, thence 1660 Norwich, Conn.

HYLAND

GEORGE, resident Guilford, Conn., 1662, no male issue.

THOMAS, from Tenterden, County of Kent, Eng., located Scituate, Mass., 1637.

IBROOK

RICHARD, Hingham, Mass., 1643.

IDE

The same as Hyde, (see); the "H" being dropped in the pronunciation. Iden, a town in England.

NICHOLAS, son of Nicholas, came with his mother, who married Thomas Bliss, to N. E., 1636, located Rehoboth, Mass., 1643.

IGGLEDEN, EGGLEDEN

RICHARD, son of Stephen, came to N. E., 1638, married Boston, Mass., 1660.

ILSLEY

Isle's-ley, the place on the island.

JOHN, barber, original proprietor and freeman Salisbury, Mass., 1639.

WILLIAM, shoemaker, brother of the preceding, b. Eng., 1612, came to N. E. from Wiltshire, Eng., 1638, located Newbury, Mass.

INCE

JONATHAN, original proprietor Hartford, Conn., removed Boston, Mass., before 1640.

INDICUTT, INDICUT

JOHN, resident Boston, Mass., 1670.

JOHN, cooper, warden King's Chapel, Boston, Mass., 1698.

INES, INNES

The name of Celtic or Gaelic origin, an island or peninsular made by a fresh water river or the sea. The family is of great antiquity in Scotland, where it derives its surname from the lands of *Innis,* from the Gaelic *Inch,* a part of that barony being an island formed by two branches of a stream running through the estate.

MATTHEW or MATTHIAS, in the employment of William Colburn, when 1634 admitted to the church, Boston, Mass.

INGALL, INGALLS

The name of Scandinavian origin. In the Doomsday Book the form of the name is Ingaldus, and this authority gives a Baron Ingald, a tenant of King William in Leicestershire, 1080. The earliest record of the present spelling is Henry Ingalls, 1480.

BENJAMIN, married Portsmouth, R. I., 1682.

EDMUND, grandson Henry, son of Robert, b. Lincolnshire, Eng., 1598, came with Gov. Endicott to Salem, Mass.,

1628, settled at Lynn, Mass., 1629, drowned in Saugus river, 1648.

FRANCIS, tanner, brother of preceding, b. Eng., 1601, came with his brother to Salem, Mass., afterwards at Lynn, Mass., had the earliest tannery in Massachusetts Bay Colony.

JOHN, inhabitant Ipswich, Mass., 1648.

INGERSOLL

RICHARD, came with Rev. Francis Higginson from Bedfordshire, Eng., to Salem, Mass., 1629, died 1644.

INGHAM

The name from a parish in the hundred of Hopping, County of Norfolk, Eng. A town on low ground, meadow or pasture.

JOHN or JOSEPH married, Saybrook, Conn., 1655.

THOMAS, weaver, at Scituate, Mass., 1640.

INGLES, INGLISH, INGLIS

The name was given in Scotland to distinguish the family of some English settler, the Englishman. In ancient records of the family the name *Anglicus* is often mentioned.

MAUDITT or MAUDETT, fuller, came from Marlborough, Wiltshire, Eng., to Boston, Mass., 1635.

WILLIAM, cordwainer, at Boston, Mass., 1652.

INGOLDSBY

From Saxon Ing-gil-by, the town near the brook in the narrow valley. *Inglesby*, the town of the English or Angles, which was named when the Angles first invaded England. A town in Lincolnshire, Eng.

JOHN, freeman, Boston, Mass., 1642.

INGRAM, INGRAHAM

From Saxon *Engel*, angel and *rein*, purity. Pure as an angel. Randolph, son of Ingeliam, English ancester, 1138.

EDWARD, b. Eng., 1617, came to Salem, Mass., 1635, where he was granted lands 1638.

HENRY, resident Boston, Mass., 1672.

JARED, married Boston, Mass., 1662, removed Swansea, Mass., 1673.

JOHN, b. Eng., 1642, on record first Boston, Mass., removed Hadley, Mass., 1661.

RICHARD, came to N. E. between 1638-42, proprietor Rehoboth, Mass., 1645, removed to Northampton, Mass., 1668.

WILLIAM, cooper, at Boston, Mass., 1653, later Stonington, Conn.

INMAN

EDWARD, glover, resident Providence, R. I., 1646.

IRELAND

A name given to a native of that island. Ireland signifies West-land from Gaelic *Iar*, the west, and the Teutonic *land*.

JOHN, sea captain, admitted to church, Boston, Mass., 1693.

PHILIP, resident Ipswich, Mass., where he died 1692.

SAMUEL, carpenter, b. 1603, came Boston, Mass., 1635, from London, Eng., later settled Wethersfield, Conn.

WILLIAM, at Dorchester, Mass., 1648, removed to what is now Chelsea, Mass., 1654.

IRESON

EDWARD, b. Eng., 1603, came Lynn, Mass., 1635.

RICHARD, Lynn, Mass., 1643.

IRISH

A native of Ireland.

JOHN, came from parish Clisdon, County of Somerset, Eng., to Plymouth, Mass., 1629, at Duxbury, Mass., 1637, removed to Bridgewater, Mass., later Little Compton, R. I.

ISBELL

ROBERT, inhabitant New London, Conn., 1650.

ISLIN

THOMAS, freeman Sudbury, Mass., 1640.

ISSAM, ISHAM

JOHN, married Barnstable, Mass., 1677.

IVES

The name is derived from *Ive* or *Ives*, Gaelic, meaning chief or leader. The English family takes its name from St. Ives, County of Huntingdon, Eng.

JOHN, inhabitant New Haven, Conn., 1669.

JOSEPH, proprietor New Haven, Conn., 1685.

MILES or MICHAEL, Watertown, Mass., 1639, removed Boston, Mass., 1641.

THOMAS, Salem, Mass., 1668.

WILLIAM, b. Eng., 1607, came to N. E., 1635, signed civil compact at New Haven, Conn., 1639, known as Captain William.

IVEY

JAMES, died Braintree, Mass., 1654, no issue.

JOHN, brother of preceding, resident Newbury, Mass., 1643.

WILLIAM, carpenter, brother of preceding, b. Eng., 1607, came Lynn, Mass.,

1635, removed to Boston, Mass., where he died 1652.

IVORY

THOMAS, Lynn, Mass., 1638.

JACKLIN, JACKING

EDMUND, glazier, freeman, Boston, Mass., 1635.

JACKMAN

JAMES, came from Exeter Devonshire, Eng., to Newbury, Mass., before 1648.

JACKSON

The son of Jack or John.

ABRAHAM, apprentice of Secretary Morton, married at Plymouth, Mass., 1657, where he died 1714.

EDMUND, shoemaker, came from Boston, Eng., joined church at Boston, Mass., 1635.

EDWARD, nailer, bapt. St. Dunstans Church, Stepney, Whitechapel parish, London, Eng., 1604, came to Cambridge, Mass., 1643, freeman 1645, purchased land at what is now Newton, 1646, proprietor at Billerica, Mass.

EDWARD, brother of Abraham, lived at Cambridge, Mass., killed 1676, King Philip's war.

HENRY, b. Eng., 1606, came from London, Eng., to Watertown, Mass., 1635, engaged in fishing, freeman Fairfield, Conn., 1669.

JOHN, fisherman, came to N. E., 1635, granted land Salem, Mass., 1637.

JOHN, elder brother Edward, bapt. Stepney, Eng., 1602, settled Cambridge, Mass., 1639.

JOHN, brother Abraham and Henry, b. Eng., 1608, settled Boston, Mass., 1635.

JOHN, freeman, Ipswich, Mass., 1641.

JOHN, married Boston, Mass., 1657.

JOHN, resident Scarborough, Maine, 1663.

JOHN, inhabitant New Haven, Conn., before 1655.

NICHOLAS, Rowley, Mass., 1643.

RICHARD, representative to General Court from Cambridge, Mass., 1637, died aged ninety years leaving no issue.

SAMUEL, came from Plymouth, Mass., joined church Scituate, Mass., 1638.

WALTER, Dover, N. H., 1658.

WILLIAM, Rowley, Mass., 1639, built the first house in what is now Bradford, Mass.

WILLIAM, Saybrook, Conn., 1648.

JACOB, JACOBES

A Hebrew name signifying he that supplants.

BARTHOLOMEW, inhabitant New Haven, Conn., 1668.

GEORGE, resided at what is now Danvers, Mass., 1658; executed for witchcraft, 1692.

NICHOLAS, b. Hanover, County of Suffolk, Eng., came from Hingham, Eng., settled at Watertown, Mass., 1633, freeman Hingham, Mass., 1636.

PETER, resident Hartford, Conn., 1647.

RICHARD, came to Ipswich, Mass., 1634, freeman 1635.

JAFFREY

GEORGE, married Newbury, Mass., 1665, removed Boston, Mass., in 1677 to Newcastle, N. H.

JAGGER

JEREMY, master of trading vessel; early settler Wethersfield, Conn., served Pequot War, 1637, removed 1641, Stamford, Conn.

JAMES

The same as Jacob, see.

CHARLES, married Gloucester, Mass., 1673.

EDMUND, inhabitant Newbury, Mass., before 1670.

ERASMUS, Salem, Mass., 1637, granted land Marblehead, Mass., 1648, died about 1660, no issue.

FRANCIS, came from Hingham, Eng., to Hingham, Mass., 1638, freeman 1643

GAWDY, Charlestown, Mass., 1639, freeman 1642, became inhabitant Boston, Mass., 1657, left no issue.

HUGH, sent over by Mason to Portsmouth, Mass., 1630.

JOSEPH, at Fairfield, Conn., 1674, no male issue.

PHILIP, brother of Francis, came to Hingham, Mass., 1638, died before 1640.

THOMAS, clergyman, b. Lincolnshire, Eng., came to Charlestown, Mass., 1632, removed New Haven, Conn., 1639, returned to Eng., before 1648.

THOMAS, physician, one of founders First Baptist Church, Providence, R. I., 1637.

THOMAS, came from Marlborough, Wiltshire, Eng., 1635, to Dedham, Mass., granted land Salem, Mass., 1638.

JAMESON

The son of James.

ANDREW, one of first members of Scott's Charitable Society, Boston, Mass., 1657.

ROBERT, resident of Watertown, Mass., 1642.

WILLIAM, Casco, Maine, 1685.

JANES, JEANES

The son of Jane.

WILLIAM, preacher, b. County of Essex, Eng., 1610, came to New Haven, Conn., 1643, removed to Northampton, Mass., 1657. Among first settlers Northfield, Mass., returned Northampton, Mass., where he died 1690.

JAQUES

HENRY, carpenter, settled Newbury, Mass., 1640.

JAQUITH

ABRAHAM, admitted member of church Charlestown, Mass., 1643.

JARRATT

JOHN, freeman Rowley, Mass., 1640; no male issue.

JARVIS

The name of French derivation original Gervais. The ancient seat of the family Bretagne, France. The first of the name on record Jean Gervais, 1400.

JOHN, merchant, Boston, Mass., where he died 1648.

JOHN, shipwright, married at Boston, Mass., 1661.

WILLIAM, settled at Norwalk, Conn., removed to Huntington, Long Island, N. Y.

JECOCKES, JECOXE

FRANCIS, resident Stratford, Conn., 1646.

JEFFORD

JOHN, resident Lynn, Mass., 1675.

JEFFREY, JEFFERS

Corrupted from Geoffrey or Godfrey. German from *God* and *fried*, God's peace, or from *gau* and *fried*, joyful peace. This name was borne by the chief of the royal house of Plantagnent.

DAVID, merchant, married Boston, Mass., 1686.

DIGORY, constable Kittery, Maine, 1664.

FRANCIS, resident Falmouth, Maine, 1685.

GEORGE, inhabitant Windsor, Conn., 1669, removed Suffield, Conn., and 1709 to Westerly, R. I.

GEORGE, merchant, came from Scotland to Boston, Mass., 1676, removed Portsmouth, N. H., 1684.

GREGORY, freeman Wells, Maine, 1653.

ROBERT, physician, b. Eng., 1605, came to Charlestown, Mass., 1635, removed to R. I., 1638, a resident of Newport, R. I., 1640.

THOMAS, freeman, Dorchester, Mass., 1634, removed New Haven, Conn., 1638.

WILLIAM, came from County of Sussex, Eng., one earliest settlers in Mass. Bay, before Endicott and Winthrop, freeman Weymouth, Mass., 1630, at Newport, R. I., before 1655.

JEFFTS, JEFFS

HENRY, b. Eng., 1606, proprietor Woburn, Mass., 1640, one first settlers Billerica, Mass., 1654.

JEGGLES

DANIEL, inhabitant Salem, Mass., 1639.

THOMAS, brother of preceding, married Salem, Mass., 1647.

WILLIAM, shipwright, brother of Daniel at Salem, Mass., 1637.

JELLICOE

THOMAS, inhabitant Middletown, Conn., 1684.

JEMPSON, JEMSON

JAMES, inhabitant of Boston, Mass., 1647.

PATRICK, living Dover, N. H., 1659.

JENKINS

From Jenks or John and the patronymic termination ings belonging to, or son of John.

EDWARD, came to Scituate, Mass., 1643.

HENRY, inhabitant N. H. before 1670.

JOEL, freeman Braintree, Mass., 1646, removed Malden, Mass.

JOHN, Plymouth, Mass., 1643, removed Barnstable, Mass., where he married 1653.

LEMUEL, married Malden, Mass., 1671.

OBADIAH, resident Malden, Mass., 1677.

REGINALD, Dorchester, 1630, killed by Indians 1632.

ROBERT, Dover, N. H., 1657, at York, Maine, 1674.

SAMUEL, resident Greenwich, Conn., 1672.

JENKS, JENCKES

The same as Johns; the son of John.

JOSEPH, blacksmith, inventor, cut the dies for the colony's coinage, b. Hammersmith, County of Middlesex, Eng., 1602, built first forge and iron foundry N. E. at Saugus, Mass., 1645.

JOSEPH, b. Eng., 1602, came to N. E. 1643, settled Lynn, Mass., later removed to R. I.

JENNER, JENNE, JENNESS, JENNY

An old form for joiner.

DAVID, settled Charlestown, Mass., resident Boston, Mass., 1685.

FRANCIS, baker, b. Hampton, Eng., 1634, Hampton, N. H., 1671, died Newcastle, N. H., 1716.

JOHN, brewer, came from Norwich, Eng., to Rotterdam, Holland, thence Plymouth, Mass., 1623.

THOMAS, clergyman, Roxbury, Mass., 1634; removed Weymouth, Mass., made a freeman 1636, in 1640 went to Saco, Maine, but soon after returned to Eng. THOMAS, inhabitant Charlestown, Mass., 1658.

JENNINGS

The same as Jenkins, see.

JOHN, living Hartford, Conn., 1639, removed 1641, Southampton, Long Island, N. Y.

JOHN, living Sandwich, Mass., 1667.

JONATHAN, resident Norwich, Conn., 1684.

JOSHUA, b. Eng., 1620, first record, Hartford, Conn., 1647, removed Fairfield, Conn., 1650.

NICHOLAS, b. Eng., 1612, came from Ipswich, Eng., to Hartford, Conn., 1636, afterwards Saybrook, Conn.

RICHARD, clergyman, b. Ipswich, County of Suffolk, Eng., came to N. E., 1636, locating Ipswich, Mass., returned to Eng., 1638.

RICHARD, resident Bridgewater, Mass., 1666, was in N. E. as early as 1635.

RICHARD, came from Barbadoes, West Indies to New London, Conn., 1676.

SAMUEL, freeman Portsmouth, R. I., 1655.

STEPHEN, married Hatfield, Mass., 1677, removed Brookfield, Mass.

THOMAS, freeman Portsmouth, R. I., 1655, was living in the town as early as 1643.

JENNISON

ROBERT, from Colchester, County of Essex, Eng., settled Charlestown, Mass., 1630, removed 1636, Watertown, Mass.

WILLIAM, brother preceding, came to N. E., 1630, freeman Watertown, Mass., 1631, returned Colchester, Eng., 1651.

JEPSON

CHRISTOPHER, inhabitant Dorchester, Mass., 1646.

JOHN, b Eng., 1618-20, at Boston, Mass., 1639.

ROGER, at Saybrook, Conn., removed Middletown, Conn., where he died 1680.

THOMAS, resident Boston, Mass., 1692.

JESSOP, JESSUP

The same as Joseph from the Hebrew signifying increase, addition.

EDWARD, came N. E., before 1649, Stamford, Conn., 1650, removed Newtown, Long Island, N. Y., 1656.

JOHN, Wethersfield, Conn., 1637, removed Stamford, Conn., 1640, thence Greenwich, Conn., finally located Southampton, Long Island, N. Y.

JEWELL

Signifying joy, mirth, precious; a jewel, a precious stone, a name expressive of fondness.

SAMUEL, resident Boston, Mass., 1655.

THOMAS, b. Eng., about 1600, came to N. E., 1635, granted land Braintree, Mass., 1639.

JEWETT

The little Jew, the son of a Jew; from the French word *Jouet,* toy, sport. The family of French Huguenot descent. Henri de Juatt was a knight of the first Crusaders.

JOHN, freeman, Ipswich, Mass., 1676.

JOSEPH, son of Edward J., came to N. E., 1638, locating Dorchester, Mass., thence the following year removed Rowley, Mass., where he was a freeman 1639.

MAXIMILLIAN, brother of preceding, b. Bradford, West Riding, Yorkshire, Eng., 1604, came to N. E., 1638, deacon Rowley, Mass., 1639.

NATHANIEL, freeman Concord, Mass., 1681.

THOMAS, resident Hingham, Mass., 1672.

JILLSON

See Gilson.

JOHNS, JOHNES

EDWARD, son of Richard J., of Somerset, Eng., came to Charlestown, Mass., 1630, resident Boston, Mass., 1637.

JOHNSON

The son of John.

CHARLES, resident New London, Conn.. 1690.

DAVY, came to N. E., 1630, locating Dorchester, Mass.

EDMUND, b. Eng., 1612, came to N. E., 1635, resident Hampton, N. H., 1639.

EDWARD, known as Capt. Edward, author, son of William J., b. parish Hernehill near Canterbury, County of Kent, Eng., 1598, came with Winthrop to N. E., 1630, locating Charlestown, Mass., thence to Salem, Mass., returned to Eng., 1635, came second time 1637 to Charlestown, Mass., one founders of church Woburn, Mass., 1642.

EDWARD, resident Branford, Conn., 1690.

FRANCIS, freeman Salem, Mass., 1631.

ISAAC, resident Charlestown, Mass., 1676.

JAMES, glover, b. Eng., 1607, freeman Boston, Mass., 1636.

JAMES, sent by Mason to Portsmouth, N. H., 1630-31.

JEREMIAH, resident New Haven, Conn., 1662.

JOHN, yeoman, b. Waterham, parish Hernehill Canterbury, County of Kent, Eng., came to N. E. in Winthrop's fleet, 1630. First record among the early settlers, Ipswich, Mass., 1635.

JOHN, resident Newport, R. I., 1638, afterwards Wickford, R. I., 1674.

JOHN, resident Sandwich, Mass., 1643.

JOHN, b. Eng., 1609, came to N. E., 1635, living New Haven, Conn., 1643.

JOHN, b. Eng., 1612, came from London, Eng., to N. E., 1635, freeman Guilford, Conn., 1669.

JOHN, married Rowley, Mass., 1650.

JOHN, Lancaster, Mass., 1654, afterwards Salisbury, Mass., thence Marlboro, Mass.

JOHN, blacksmith, married Charlestown, Mass., 1656, removed 1662, Haverhill, Mass.

JOHN, married Watertown, Mass., 1659, removed Lexington, Mass.

JOHN, married in N. H., 1661.

JOHN, resident Rehoboth, Mass., 1673.

JOHN, Norwich, Conn., 1677.

JOHN, Huguenot refugee, came Rochelle, France, to Oxford, Mass., 1686, killed with three children by Indians, 1696.

JOHN, lighterman, resident Salem, Mass., 1691.

PETER, resident Fairfield, Conn., 1649.

RETURN, took oath of allegiance, Hampton, N. H., 1678.

RICHARD, b. Eng., 1612, settled Charlestown, Mass., 1630, afterwards at Watertown and Lynn, Mass.

ROBERT, came from Kingston-on-Hull, Leicestershire, Eng., one founders New Haven, Conn., 1638.

ROBERT, resident Marblehead, Mass., 1674.

SAMUEL, mariner, resident Boston, Mass., 1653.

SAMUEL, Lynn, Mass., 1664.

SOLOMON, b. Eng., 1615, at Sudbury, Mass., 1638, proprietor 1645, removed Marlboro, Mass., 1653.

STEPHEN, first settled Ipswich, Mass., removed to Andover, Mass., married 1661.

THOMAS, cobbler, admitted inhabitant Hartford, Conn., 1640.

THOMAS, b. Eng., 1610, came to N. E., 1635; was drowned Boston Harbor, 1656.

THOMAS, resident New London, Conn., 1682.

THOMAS, married at Andover, Mass., 1657.

TIMOTHY, resident of Andover, Mass., 1674.

WILLIAM, brother Capt. Edward, b. Hernehill, Canterbury, County of Kent, Eng., 1605, freeman Charlestown, Mass., 1634.

WILLIAM, married Guilford, Conn., 1665.

WILLIAM, resident Stonington, Conn., 1670.

WILLIAM, married at Andover, Mass., 1678.

WINGLE or WINDLE, married at New Haven, Conn., 1664.

ZECHARIAH, resident Charlestown, Mass., 1672.

JOHONNOT

DANIEL, Huguenot, b. Rochelle, France, 1668, living Oxford, Mass., 1686.

JONES

The same as John or Johns. In Hebrew signifies gracious.
In Wales Jones was one of the tribes of Cimbri, that ruled the country when it was free.

ABEL, freeman Northampton, Mass., 1690.

ABRAHAM, resident Hull, Mass., 1657.

ALEXANDER, sent by Mason to Portsmouth, N. H., 1631.

BENJAMIN, inhabitant Malden, Mass., 1681.

CHARLES, b. Eng., 1614, came Dorchester, Mass., 1635.

CORNELIUS, settled Stamford, Conn., where he died 1657.

DAVID, freeman Dorchester, Mass., 1665.

GRIFFIN or GRIFFITH, settled Springfield, Mass., 1646.

HENRY, resident Lynn, Mass., 1642.

HUGH, came Wiscanton parish, Somersetshire, Eng., to Salem, Mass., 1650.

JACOB, died New Haven, Conn., 1675.

JEFFREY, Southold, Long Island, N. Y., 1664, removed Salem, Mass., 1668.

JENKIN, inhabitant Dover, N. H., 1666.

JOHN, clergyman, son of William, of Abergavonny, County of Monmouth,

Eng., came to N. E., 1635, located Concord, Mass.

JOHN, freeman Providence, R. I., 1655, there in 1646.

JOHN, b. Eng., 1615, came from London, Eng., to Portsmouth, N. H., 1635; no issue.

JOHN, b. Eng., 1620, came to N. E., 1635, resident Cambridge, Mass., 1648.

JOHN, resident Boston, Mass., before 1665.

JOHN, resident Charlestown, Mass., 1672.

LEWIS, b. Eng., 1600, came to N. E., 1640, settling Roxbury, Mass., removed Watertown, Mass., 1650.

LEWIS, resident Saybrook, Conn., 1667.

MATTHEW, inhabitant Boston, Mass., 1645.

MORGAN, clergyman, son of John of Bassaley, living near Newport, County of Monmouth, Eng., at Killingworth and Branford, Conn., inhabitant Newtown, Long Island, N. Y., 1680.

RALPH, farmer, settled Plymouth, Mass., before 1643, removed Barnstable, Mass., 1654.

RICE, living Boston, Mass., 1651.

RICHARD, Dorchester, Mass., 1635, where he died 1641.

RICHARD, Farmington, Conn., one first settlers Haddam, Conn., where he died 1670.

ROBERT, Hingham, Mass., 1637, removed Rehoboth, Mass., 1644.

ROBERT, married Salisbury, Mass., 1659.

ROBERT, b. Eng., 1633, resident Amesbury, Mass., 1666.

STEPHEN, freeman Dover, N. H., 1672.

TEAGUE, inhabitant Yarmouth, Mass., 1653.

THOMAS, b. Eng., 1595, came to Dorchester, Mass., 1635, where he died 1667.

THOMAS, Newbury, Mass., 1637, removed Hampton, N. H., 1639, afterwards Kittery, Maine.

THOMAS, tailor, b. Eng., 1602, came from Caversham, Oxfordshire, Eng., to Hingham, Mass., 1638.

THOMAS, butcher, b. Eng., 1612, came from Yarmouth, Eng., to Charlestown, Mass., 1637.

THOMAS, b. Eng., or Wales, 1598, came before 1640 to N. E., first record Gloucester, Mass., 1642, removed New London, Conn., 1651.

THOMAS, resident Taunton, Mass., 1659.

THOMAS, settled Guilford, Conn., 1639, returned to Eng., 1651.

THOMAS, married Boston, Mass., 1654.

THOMAS, inhabitant Springfield, Mass., 1678.

WILLIAM, mason, at Cambridge, Mass., 1635, residing Charlestown, Mass., 1658.

WILLIAM, Portsmouth, N. H., removed to Dover, N. H., 1644.

WILLIAM, lawyer, b. Eng., 1624, came to N. E., 1660, locating New Haven, Conn.

JORDAN, JORDEN

From the Hebrew, the river of Judgment. *Jardain* in Gaelic the western river with respect to the Euphrates. The name is derived from its two springheads *Jor* and *Dan.* The family was seated Dorsetshire, Eng., as early as 1400.

FRANCIS, Ipswich, Mass., 1634.

JAMES, resident of Dedham, Mass., before 1655.

JOHN, signed the covenant Guilford, Conn., 1639.

JOHN, Plymouth, Mass., 1643.

ROBERT, clergyman, came from Worcester, Eng., as early as 1641, established in ministry Richmond Island, near Scarborough, Maine, removed 1675 Portsmouth, N. H., where he died 1679.

STEPHEN, came Ipswich, Mass., 1634, shortly afterwards removed to Newbury, Mass.

JOSSELYN, JOCELYN, JOSLIN

Place name from Jocelin, a town in France. The English family trace their ancestry to Sir Gilbert Jocelyne, who came from Normandy with William the Conqueror.

HENRY, son of Sir Thomas J., County of Kent, Eng., came to Scarborough, Maine, as employee of Mason, patentee, N. H., afterwards engaged under Sir Ferdinand Gorges, became freeman 1658, died Pemaquid, Maine, 1682.

JOHN, brother of preceding, arrived Boston, Mass., 1638, returned Eng., 1672, author "New England" Rarities."

RICHARD, freeman, Saybrook, Conn., 1669.

THOMAS, husbandman, b. Eng., 1592, came N. E., 1635, settling Hingham, Mass., 1637, among grantees Sudbury, Mass., 1640, afterwards removed Lancaster, Mass., where he signed the civil compact, 1654.

JOY

Gladness, exhilaration of spirits; to shout, rejoice.

JACOB, resident Fairfield, Conn., removed Killingworth, Conn., 1673.

THOMAS, house carpenter, resident Boston, Mass., 1638.

WALTER, inhabitant Milford, Conn., 1650.

JOYCE, JESSE, JOSE

The word signifies joyous.

CHRISTOPHER, at Isle of Shoals, N. H., 1651, removed Portsmouth, N. H.

DAVID, goldsmith, married at Boston, Mass., 1698.

JOHN, settled at Lynn, Mass., removed Sandwich, Mass., 1637, thence Yarmouth, Mass., 1643.

WALTER, Marshfield, Mass., 1667.

WILLIAM, at Windsor, Conn., removed Springfield, Mass.; drowned at Enfield Falls, 1645.

JOYLIFFE

JOHN, resident Boston, Mass., 1657, freeman 1673.

JUDD

From Hebrew, *Juda,* praise, confession; and signifies the confessor of God. In Dutch *Jode* or *Jood* meaning Israelite, a Jew: *Jute,* a native of Jutland.

ROGER, freeman Boston, Mass., 1690.

THOMAS, settled Cambridge, Mass., 1634, removed Hartford, Conn., 1636, one of first proprietors Farmington, Conn., 1644, removed Northampton, Mass., 1679.

JUDKIN, JUDKINS

JOB, resident Boston, Mass., 1638.

SAMUEL, married Hingham, Mass., 1667.

THOMAS, Gloucester, Mass., 1651.

JUDSON

A surname of the baptismal class signifying "the son of Jordan" a personal name of great popularity in twelfth century.

SAMUEL, son of Michael of Horton, Yorkshire, Eng., resident Dedham, Mass,. 1646.

WILLIAM, b. Yorkshire, Eng., came to Concord, Mass., 1634, removed Hartford, Conn., 1638, the next year Stratford, Conn., a few years later New Haven, Conn.

KAME

RICHARD, settled at York, Maine, 1670.

KEAYNE

JOHN, came from Southampton, Eng., in 1638 to Hingham, Mass., where he died 1650.

ROBERT, merchant, b. Eng., 1595, a member of the Merchant Taylor Company of London; came to Boston, Mass., 1635, died 1656.

WILLIAM, resident of Boston, Mass., 1656.

KEELER

Occupation name—one who manages barges and vessels.

RALPH, had a lot at Hartford, Conn., 1640; among the first settlers of Norwalk, Conn., where he was made freeman, 1668.

KEELEY

EDWARD, came from London, Eng., 1635, aged 14; a proprietor at New Haven, Conn., 1685.

KEEN, KEAN

The name from the Gaelic word *ceann,* the head, the top, a chief, a commander.

ARTHUR, died at Boston, Mass., 1687.

JOHN, mariner, came from Southampton, Eng., to Boston, Mass., at age of seventeen.

JOSIAH, married at Duxbury, Mass., before 1660.

WILLIAM, granted land at Salem, Mass., 1638.

KEENY, KEENEY

ALEXANDER, freeman at Wethersfield, Conn., 1667, where he died, 1680.

WILLIAM, at Gloucester, Mass., before 1640; removed to New London, Conn., 1651; died 1675.

KEEP

JOHN, at Springfield, Mass., 1660; killed by savages, 1676.

KEESE

JOHN, married at Portsmouth, R. I., 1682.

KEITH

A local name from the parish of Keith, in Banffshire, Scotland. The name is derived from the Gaelic *gaoth,* wind. The old village and kirk are called *Arkeith,* which is a corruption of the Gaelic *ard, gaoth,* signifying high wind. The name may be derived from the Welsh *caeth,* a place surrounded, shut up, inclosed, a deep hollow, a strait. The root of the word is the Welsh *cau,* to close, to shut up. From traditions it is recorded that the family came from Germany in the reign of the Emperor Otho, and from the principality of Hesse, from which they were expelled in some revolution. The first person of the family that old historians notice is Robert De Keith, to whom Malcom II, King of Scotland, gave the barony of Keith in East Lothian as a reward for killing Camus, a Danish general who invaded Scotland. The battle was fought at Barry, seven miles from Dundee, where an obelisk called *Camus' stone* marks the spot of the victory. The

Scottish king dipped his three fingers in the blood of the defeated general, stroked them along the field of Robert De Keith, the Scotch champion's shield, bestowing on him the lorded estates mentioned, also giving him the dignity of Great Marshal of Scotland.

JAMES, first minister of Bridgewater, Mass., b. Aberdeen, Scotland, 1643; came to Mass., 1662; ordained minister 1664; died 1719.

KELLEN, KILLIN, KELLING

JAMES, married, Charleston, Mass., 1679.

KELLOGG

From Cornish British *chelioc* or *kulliag,* a cock, *coileach* in Gaelic and *ceiliog* in Welsh, the C having the sound of K. Other authorities claim the name is from two Gaelic words meaning lake and cemetery. The name dates back in England to the sixteenth century, the earliest records of the family being found in Debden, county of Essex, when Nicholas Kellogg was b. in 1488; taxed in 1525.

DANIEL, son of Martin K., bapt. 1630, at Great Leighs, Eng.; an early settler of Norwalk, Conn., 1655.

JOSEPH, weaver, son of Martin K., fifth generation from Nicholas K., bapt. at Great Lehigh, Eng., 1626. Freeman at Farmington, Conn., 1654; removed to Boston, Mass., 1655, thence 1659 to Roxbury, Mass., and in 1661 to Hudley, Mass.; had the title of lieutenant.

NATHANIEL, settled at Hartford, Conn., 1640; living at Farmington, Conn., 1653, where he died.

KELLOND

THOMAS, merchant, resident of Boston, Mass., 1661.

THOMAS, residing at Boston, Mass., 1687.

KELLY, KELLEY

The words *kill* or *cille* in Gaelic and Celtic denotes a church. In Welsh signification is a grove generally of hazel. The ancient parish of Kelly in Devonshire, Eng., may have taken its name from the family or *vice versa.* It has been the memorial seat of the family from the time of Henry II, and was originally spelt Kelleigh. In Scotland the orthography was slightly changed, the earldom of Kellie deriving its name from a district in Fife anciently called Kellieshire. In Ireland the name of Kelly, O'Kelley, is derived from the Gaelic word *ceallach,* meaning strife of war. It is claimed by Irish antiquarians that the pedigree of the family can be traced backward through sixty-five generations to one Milesuis of Spain.

ABEL, freeman at Salem, Mass., 1641.

BENJAMIN, freeman of Mass., 1669.

DAVID, resident of Boston, Mass., before 1653.

EDWARD, came to Boston, Mass., 1635.

JOHN, came from Newbury, County Berks, Eng., to Newbury, Mass., 1635.

REGINALD, took oath of fidelity at Pemaquid, Maine, 1674.

ROGER, resident of the Isle of Shoals, N. H., 1668.

KELSEY

A town in Lincolnshire, Eng.; *Kelsey* in Cornish British signifies the *dry neck* from *kel,* a neck, and *syck,* dry. Family of Scotch ancestry.

WILLIAM, b. Eng., came to Cambridge, Mass., 1632, removed to Hartford, Conn., thence in 1663 to Killingworth, Conn.

KELTON

THOMAS, resident of Boston, Mass., 1661.

KEMP, KEMPE

In old English, a soldier, one engaged in single combat. The name is derived from the Saxon word to *kemp* or combat, at the present time a foot-ball match in Norfolkshire is called *camping* or *kemping,* also in some parts of Scotland the striving of reapers in the harvest-field is called *kemping.*

EDWARD, blacksmith, settled at Dedham, Mass., before 1638, removed to Wrentham, Mass., 1651, afterwards at Chelmsford, Mass., 1655.

KEMPSTER

From the Dutch *kemper,* to fight or *kamper,* a champion.

DANIEL, freeman at Cambridge, Mass., 1647.

KEMPTHORNE

DANIEL, resident of Cambridge, Mass., before 1653.

KEMPTON

The camp town; place of the army.

EPHRAIM, came to Plymouth colony, 1627, able to bear arms at Scituate, Mass., 1643, died 1645.

MANASSEH, brother of the preceding, one of the "old comers," came to Plymouth, Mass., 1623, one of the first purchasers of Dartmouth, Mass.; died 1663.

KEN

ROBERT, among early settlers of Reading, Mass.

KENDALL

The name derived from the town of Kendal in Westmoreland, Eng., and was so called from the river *Ken,* on which it is situated, and dale: the dale on the river *Ken.* John Kendall, sheriff of Nottingham was killed in 1485 at the battle of Bosworth.

FRANCIS, son of John K., b. England, about 1620, came to Charlestown, Mass., 1640; taxed at Woburn, Mass., 1645.

THOMAS, brother of the preceding, known as Deacon Thomas, came to Lynn, Mass.; freeman in 1648; removed to Reading, Mass., 1652.

KENDRICK, KENRICK

From the Saxon *kennen,* to know, and *ric,* rich, rich in knowledge. The name also derived by other authorities from *cene,* bold, and *rick,* a kingdom, a valiant ruler.

CALEB, resident of Boston, Mass., 1652.

GEORGE, freeman at Scituate, Mass., 1635, removed to Rehoboth, 1645.

JOHN, of Ipswich or Rowley, Mass., married 1657.

THOMAS, married at Rehoboth, Mass., 1681.

KENISON

JOHN, b. Eng., about 1640, at Dover, N. H., 1663.

KENNARD

From Gaelic *ceannard,* a chief, chieftain, a leader, a commander-in-chief, from *ceann,* head, chief, and *ard,* high, lofty.

EDWARD, came from Kent, Eng., about 1660, settled at Portsmouth, N. H.

JOHN, married at Haddam, Conn., 1674.

KENNEDY, CANNADY

From the Gaelic or Celtic words *keanna-ty;* the head of the house or chief of the clan. *Ceannaide* signifies also a shopkeeper, a merchant.

ALEXANDER, resident of Plymouth, Mass., 1678.

DANIEL, settled at Salem, Mass., 1681.

KENNICUT, KINNICUTT

ROGER, married at Malden, Mass., 1661, afterwards in 1677 at Swansey, now Barrington, Mass.

KENNISTON, KINISTON

ALLEN, was at Salem, Mass., 1638; died 1648.

WILLIAM, resident of Dover, N. H., 1646-71.

KENNY, KENNEY, KINNEY

ANDREW, at Malden, Mass., 1690.

HENRY, b. 1624, was first at Roxbury, Mass.; a resident of Salem, Mass., 1653.

JOHN, died at Salem, Mass., 1670.

RICHARD, settler of New Hampshire, 1680.

THOMAS, resident of Gloucester, Mass., 1664.

KENT

The name from the County of Kent, England. The word is derived from *canton,* a corner. England on the northeast stretches itself into a corner. *Cant* in Welsh signifies round, circular.

JAMES, freeman at Newbury, Mass., 1669, settled there as early as 1634.

JOHN, was at Dedham, Mass., 1645, removed to Charlestown, Mass.

JOSEPH, brother of preceding, came to Dedham, Mass., 1645, afterwards resided at Taunton, Mass.

JOSHUA, brother of preceding, was at Dedham, Mass., 1643; returned to England following year; came again to Dedham in 1645, bringing his brother Joseph. He afterwards resided at Block Island, R. I., and Swansea, Mass.

OLIVER, at Dover, N. H., 1648, died 1670.

RICHARD, brother of James, settled at Ipswich, Mass., 1634; removed to Newbury, Mass., 1635.

STEPHEN, brother of preceding, freeman at Newbury, Mass., 1639; removed to Haverhill, Mass., thence to Woodbridge, N. J.

THOMAS, settled at Gloucester, Mass., 1643; afterwards at Suffield, Conn.; died 1658.

WILLIAM, married at Boston, Mass., 1662.

KENYON

From the Welsh *ceinion,* beautiful; *cyndyn* stubborn; *concenn* or *kynan,* strong head, powerful, a leader.

JOHN, b. Eng., 1605, settled at New Shoreman (Block Island) R. I.

KERLEY, CARSLEY

WILLIAM, at Hingham, Mass., 1637, at Sudbury, Mass., 1641; removed to Lancaster, Mass.; made freeman 1647.

KESKEYS

HENRY, resident of Boston, Mass., 1656.

KETCHAM

EDWARD, at Ipswich, Mass., 1635.

KETTLE

From the parish of *Kettle,* in Fifeshire, Scotland.

JOHN, a resident of Gloucester, Mass., before 1658.

RICHARD, butcher, freeman, at Charlestown, Mass., 1635.

ROBERT, brother of John, at Gloucester, Mass., 1653.

KEY, KEYS, KEYES

The name is from the old Roman word *keyus,* signifying warden or keeper.

JOHN, settled before 1657 at Dover, N. H., afterwards removed to Berwick, Maine; killed by Indians, 1690.

ROBERT, settled at Watertown, Mass., 1633; removed to Newbury, Mass., 1643, and to Sudbury, Mass., 1645.

SOLOMON, married at Newbury, Mass., 1653.

KEYSER

From the German, an emperor.

GEORGE, tanner, freeman, Lynn, Mass., 1639; removed to Salem, Mass.

THOMAS, merchant and shipmaster, brother of preceding, at Lynn, Mass., 1638; engaged in the slave trade.

KIBBY, KIBBE, KIBBEE

ARTHUR, fisherman or mariner, at Salem, Mass., where he married 1659.

EDWARD, sawyer, born Exeter, Eng., 1611; settled at Muddy river, Boston, Mass., 1639; died 1661.

HENRY, tailor, freeman, Dorchester, Mass., 1642.

JOSEPH, married Salem, Mass.

WILLIAM, resident of Hull, Mass., 1642.

KIDBY

JOHN, resident of Duxbury, Mass., 1640.

LEWIS, fisherman at Boston, Mass., 1640.

KID, KIDD

"A young goat," also *kid,* from the Saxon *cythan,* to show, discover or make known.

JAMES, took oath of allegiance at Dover, N. H., 1657.

KIDDER

"A dealer in corn, provisions and merchandise; a traveling merchant."

JAMES, son of James K., born East Gunstead, County Sussex, Eng., 1626; settled at Cambridge, Mass., 1649.

STEPHEN, an employee of Mason; at Berwick, Maine, 1633.

THADDEUS, a resident of Marblehead, Mass., 1674.

KILBOURN, KILBORNE

The name derived from the village of Kilburne, County Middlesex, Eng., famous for its fine well of mineral water. *Kil* from the Dutch; *kilde,* Danish, a channel or bed of river, and hence a stream; *bourne* a fountain, a spring well.

GEORGE, son of Thomas K., bapt. Wood Ditton, County Cambridge, Eng., 1612; removed to Roxbury, Mass., 1640.

THOMAS, b. Wood Ditton, County Cambridge, Eng., bapt. 1578; came to Boston, Mass., 1635; afterwards settled Wethersfield, Conn., where he died 1639.

KILBY

CHRISTOPHER, resident of Boston, Mass., 1694.

EDWARD, married at Boston, Mass., 1662.

JOHN, brother of Christopher, resident of Boston, Mass., 1686.

KILCUP

WILLIAM, sieve-maker, resident of Boston, Mass., 1649, few years later at Charlestown, Mass.

KILHAM, KILLIAM, KELHAM

AUSTIN or AUGUSTINE, granted land at Salem, Mass., 1637, afterwards at Dedham, Mass.; freeman at Ipswich, Mass., 1642; member of church, Wenham, Mass., 1655, when he removed to Chelmsford, Mass.

DANIEL, resided at Wenham, Mass.; member of Artillery Company, 1645.

KILTON

ROBERT, came from England to N. E. before 1690 and settled at Providence, R. I.

KIMBALL, KEMBALL

EBENEZER, at Rowley, Mass., 1691.

EPHRAIM, freeman at Wenham, Mass., 1690.

HENRY, b. Eng., 1590, came to Watertown, Mass., 1634.

HENRY, married at Charlestown, Mass., 1656.

JOHN, married at Newbury, Mass., 1665.

JOHN, took oath of fidelity, Amesbury, Mass., 1690.

RICHARD, wheelwright, brother first Henry, bapt. parish of Rattlesden, County Suffolk, Eng., 1595; settled at Watertown, Mass., 1634, removed to Ipswich, Mass., 1638.

THOMAS, merchant, was at Charlestown, Mass., 1653.

KIMBERLEY, KIMBERLY

The name is from the Dutch word *kamper,* a champion, a fighting man, or it may apply to the qualities of a person, a place of a camp or battle, that is *Camper-ley; camberley,* indicates a place among the hills in a narrow valley, from *cum,* a vale, a dell.

THOMAS, settled at Dorchester, Mass., 1635, and removed to New Haven, Conn., 1638-39, afterwards about 1659 became a resident of Stratford, Conn., where he died 1673.

KIME

WILLIAM, at Dover, N. H., 1668-71.

KIMWRIGHT

GEORGE, married at Dorchester, Mass., 1653; removed to Cambridge, Mass., 1664.

KINCADE, KINCAID

From the Gaelic word *ceann*, head, and *cath* or *cad*, battle—the head or front of the battle.

DANIEL, came from Scotland to New Hampshire, 1689.

KIND

ARTHUR, a resident of Boston, Mass., 1646.

KING

The primary sense is a head or leader, Gaelic, *ceann;* Welsh, *cun*, a head, a leader. Saxon *cyng*, and nearly the same in all Teutonic dialects. The King family was seated in the vicinity of Ugborough, England, as early as 1389.

ALEXANDER, was at Wickford, R. I., 1674.

CLEMENT, a resident of Malden, Mass., 1668, later removed to R. I.

DANIEL, merchant, was at Lynn, Mass., 1647.

HEZEKIAH, was living at Weymouth, Mass., 1679.

JAMES, cooper, son of William K., and of the fifth generation from Thomas Kynge, 1538, was born at Ugborough, Eng., 1647, and came to Ipswich, Mass., before 1674, and removed to Suffield, Conn., where he was an original proprieter in 1675.

JOHN, living in Hartford, Conn., 1645; removed to Northampton, Mass.

JOHN, born in Eng., 1600, settled in Weymouth, Mass., before 1655.

MARK, a resident of Charlestown, Mass., 1658.

PETER, a deacon and representative to the legislature, settled at Sudbury, Mass., 1654.

PHILIP, came from England to Weymouth, Mass., 1672.

RALPH, married and resided at Lynn, Mass., 1648.

RICHARD, settled as early as 1635 at Salem, Mass.

SAMUEL, a resident of Plymouth, Mass., 1643.

SAMUEL, was at Weymouth, Mass., in 1659.

THOMAS, b. Eng., 1615, came to N. E., 1634; was at Watertown, Mass., 1640.

THOMAS, b. Shaston, Dorsetshire, Eng., 1600; settled at Sudbury, Mass., 1642.

THOMAS, known as Elder Thomas, son of George K., of Cold Norton, County Essex, Eng., b. 1604; settled at Scituate, Mass., 1635.

WILLIAM, b. Eng., 1608, settled at Salem, Mass., 1635.

WILLIAM, died at Isle of Shoals, 1664.

WILLIAM, resident of Boston, Mass., 1655.

KINGMAN

HENRY, of Welsh descent, was freeman at Weymouth, Mass., 1636.

KINGSBURY

In 1300, Gilbert de Kingsbury was a churchman of Kingsbury, Warwickshire, Eng. The English records mention in 1539 the death of John Kyngesbury of Great Cornaid, Suffolkshire.

HENRY, of the sixth generation from John Kyngesbury, came from Assington, County Suffolk, England, in Winthrop's fleet. He was one of the founders of Ipswich, Mass., 1638.

JOHN, freeman at Watertown, 1636; removed that year to Dedham, Mass.

JOHN, brother of preceding, came to N. E. in Winthrop's fleet and was a resident of Dedham, Mass., 1637.

JOSEPH, brother of Henry and John, came to N. E. at same time and became identified with Dedham, Mass., 1637.

KINGSLEY, KINSLEY

The name is from the Gaelic word *ceannsallach*, authoritative, commanding, ruling. There is an ancient Irish story that Eochardh, a monarch, was defeated by Ena, King of Leinster, at the battle of Cruachan. In this engagement Ena killed Cetmathch, laureate bard to the monarch, although he fled for refuge under the shields of the Leinster troops. For this base deed the ruthless king was stigmatized with the epithet *kinsealach*—that is, the foul and reproachful head, which name descended to his posterity.

JOHN, came from Hampshire, Eng., to Dorchester, Mass., 1635; removed to Rehoboth, Mass., 1648.

JOHN, married at Milton, Mass., before 1676.

SAMUEL, freeman at Billerica, Mass., 1651.

STEPHEN, settled first at Braintree, Mass., where he was a freeman, 1640; removed to Dorchester, Mass., finally to Milton, Mass.

KINGSNORTH, KINGSWORTH

HENRY, signed the covenant for settlement at Guilford, Conn., 1639.

KINSMAN

ROBERT, came from England to Boston, Mass., 1634, granted land at Ipswich, Mass., 1637.

KIRBY

The surname of Danish origin; the first Baron of Kirby was Ivo. Taillebois, who came to England with William the Conquerer. The name of several small towns in England, so called from *kirk*, a church, and *by*, a village or town.

JOHN, bapt. at Rowington, Warwickshire, Eng., 1624, came at age of twelve to Plymouth, Mass.; became a resident of Hartford, Conn., 1645, settled at Cromwell, Conn., 1654.

RICHARD, brother of preceding, came from England 1636; settled at Lynn, Mass.; removed 1637 to Sandwich, Mass., afterwards to Dartmouth, Mass.; he was a Quaker.

WILLIAM, resident of Boston, Mass., 1642; he was the executioner there in 1657-58.

KIRK

From the Teutonic word *kirche* and Gaelic *cearcall*, a circle. The primitive places of worship among the Celts. They were round, a symbol of eternity, and the existence of the Supreme Being, without beginning or end.

HENRY, resident at Dover, N. H., 1665.

ZECHARIAH, living at Boston, Mass., 1686.

KIRKHAM, KIRKMAN

The family seated in the reign of Henry III at Ashcombe under Haldon Hill, afterwards at Blagdon, Eng. The surname is from *kirk*, a church, and *ham*, a village. Kirkham is a small town in England.

THOMAS, was at Wethersfield, Conn., 1648.

KIRMAN

JOHN, a freeman at Lynn, Mass., 1633.

KIRTLAND, KIRKLAND

A corruption of Kirkland, that is, the church land.

NATHANIEL, b. Eng., 1616, came from Sherington near Olney, County Bucks, Eng., to Lynn, Mass., 1635.

PHILIP, shoemaker, brother of preceding; settler at Lynn, Mass., 1635.

KISKEYES, KESKEYS

From the Cornish British, blessed, happy, to bless.

HENRY, married Boston, Mass., 1656.

KITCHELL

ROBERT, was at Guilford, Conn., 1639; the following year removed to New Jersey.

KITCHEN

JOHN, shoemaker, freeman Salem, Mass., 1643.

KITCHERELL, KECHERELL

JOSEPH, was at Charlestown, Mass., 1636.

SAMUEL, resident of Hartford, Conn., before 1646.

KITTREDGE, seaman, granted land at Billerica, Mass., 1660.

KNAPP

From the German word *knappe*, a lad, boy, servant, workman; a squire. The family originated in the province of Saxony, Germany. The English lineage traced to Roher Knapp, of County Sussex, England, 1540.

AARON, came to Plymouth, Mass., 1638; in 1643 removed to Taunton, Mass.

NICHOLAS, b. Eng., came in 1630 to N. E.; settled at Watertown, Mass.; removed 1646 to Stamford, Conn.

ROGER, was at New Haven, Conn., 1643.

WILLIAM, carpenter, b. Eng., 1578, was at Watertown, 1630.

KNEELAND

EDWARD, b. Scotland about 1580, arrived in N. E., 1630.

JOHN, b. Eng., 1632, one of the founders of the Scots' Charitable Society in Boston, 1657.

PHILIP, resident of Lynn, Mass., 1637.

KNELL KNEALE

NICHOLAS, was at Stratford, Conn., 1650.

KNIGHT

A term originally applied to a young man after he was admitted the privilege of bearing arms by a ceremony called knighting, generally conferred by the King.

ALEXANDER, came from Chelmsford, Eng,. to Ipswich, Mass., 1635.

EZEKIEL, granted land at Salem, Mass., 1637, afterwards at Wells, Maine, and Braintree, Mass.

FRANCIS, was at Pemaquid, Maine, 1648.

GEORGE, came from Barrow near Bury St. Edmunds, County Suffolk, Eng., to Hingham, Mass., 1638.

GEORGE, died at Scarborough, Maine, 1671.

GEORGE, resident of Hartford, Conn., 1671.

JOHN, tailor, from Romsey, County Hants, Eng.; came to Newbury, Mass., 1635.

JOHN, maltster, was at Watertown, Mass., 1636; an original proprietor at Sudbury, Mass., 1642; removed Woburn, Mass., 1653.

JOHN, resident of Lynn, Mass., before 1657.

JOHN, freeman at Northampton, Mass., 1676.

JONATHAN, resident of Salem, Mass., 1670.

JOSEPH, freeman at Woburn, Mass., 1652.

MAUTLYN, or MACKLIN, resident of Boston, Mass., 1643.

MICHAEL, married at Woburn, Mass., 1657.

RICHARD, slater, settled at Weymouth, Mass., 1637; recorded as an inhabitant of Boston, Mass., 1642.

RICHARD, merchant, was at Hampton, N. H.; at Portsmouth, N. H., 1643, also at Dover, N. H., 1659, and before 1668 at Boston, Mass.

RICHARD, a resident of Boston, 1652.

RICHARD, carpenter, settled at Newport, R. I., 1648.

RICHARD, bricklayer, resident of Boston, Mass., 1673.

ROBERT, was at Hampton, N. H., 1640; removed to Boston, Mass.

ROBERT, resident of Kittery, Maine, removed to York, Maine.

ROGER, sent over by Mason, 1631, locating at Portsmouth, N. H.

SAMUEL, married at Roxbury, Mass., 1685.

TOBY, resident of Newport, R. I., 1638.

WALTER, b. Eng., 1587, was at Salem, Mass., 1626; living at Duxbury, Mass., 1638.

WILLIAM, mason, granted land at Salem, Mass., 1637.

WILLIAM, granted land at New Meadows, now Topsfield, Mass., 1638.

KNOTT

GEORGE, came from Lynn, Mass., to Sandwich, Mass., 1637.

RICHARD, surgeon, resident of Marblehead, Mass., 1678.

KNOWER

GEORGE, resident of Charlestown, Mass., 1631.

THOMAS, brother of preceding, was at Charlestown, Mass., 1631.

KNOWLES, KNOLL

"The top of a hill." *Knowl* in Cornish British is a promontary, hill or eminence, a projection of a hilly country.

ALEXANDER, freeman of Mass., 1636; removed to Fairfield, Conn.

HENRY, b. Eng., 1609, freeman of Portsmouth, R. I., 1655, having located there 1644; also resided at Warwick, R. I.

JOHN, second minister of Watertown, Mass., b. Lincolnshire, Eng., came to N. E., 1638, settled as pastor at Watertown, Mass., 1640, returned to England, 1651.

JOHN, mariner, settled at Hampton, N. H., before 1660.

RICHARD, b. Eng., 1638, settled at Cambridge, Mass., removed to Hampton, N. H., where he died 1682.

RICHARD, was at Plymouth, Mass., as early as 1639; removed to Eastham, Mass., 1653.

THOMAS, resident of New Haven, Conn., 1645.

KNOWLTON

JOHN, freeman at Ipswich, Mass., 1641.

JONATHAN, was at Malden, Mass., before 1688.

NATHANIEL, freeman of Ipswich, Mass., 1683.

SAMUEL, freeman at Wenham, Mass., 1680.

THOMAS, brother of John, was at Ipswich, Mass., 1648.

WILLIAM, known as Captain William, came from County Kent, Eng., in 1632, died on the voyage, leaving four sons, John, Samuel, Thomas and William.

KNOX

From the Gaelic word *cnoc,* a little hill; figuratively a stout man.

JOHN, resident of Watertown, Mass., before 1686.

LACOCK

LAWRENCE, ship carpenter, was at Boston, Mass., 1644.

LACY

The name derived from a place in France by that name. Sire De Lacy came with William the Conqueror to England. The family afterwards settled in Ireland.

LAWRENCE, resident of Andover, Mass., before 1683.

MORGAN, at Saco, Maine, 1660.

LADD

From the Welsh word *lladd,* to destroy.

DANIEL, son of Nathaniel L., came from Wiltshire, Eng., 1634, to N. E. He was one of the first townsmen in 1639 of Salisbury, Mass., but shortly afterwards became a permanent resident of Haverhill, Mass.

LAHORNE

ROWLAND, at Plymouth, Mass., 1636; in 1649 was a resident of Charlestown, Mass.

LAIGHTON, LEIGHTON

The name is identified with Layton, an old English family seated at Leighton in Shropshire prior to the Conquest. The progenitor mentioned in the Domesday Book is Raenald, an avant of Leston or Leighton. Totitus De Leton is also mentioned in that work.

JOHN, resident of Ipswich, Mass., 1648; may have been a resident of Newport, R. I., ten years previous to this date.

THOMAS, freeman, of Lynn, Mass., 1639, representative 1646-61.

THOMAS, at Saco, Maine, 1645.

THOMAS, b. Eng., 1604, settled at Dover, N. H., 1633, signed Dover Combination, 1640.

WILLIAM, known as Captain William, b. Eng. about 1625; settled Kelleny, Maine, before 1650; killed by Indians near Swanzey, June 24, 1675.

LAKE

From Latin *Lego,* to send, a servant.

HENRY, currier at Salem, Mass., 1649; afterwards at Dorchester, Mass.

JOHN, tailor, freeman at Boston, Mass., 1644.

THOMAS, freeman at Dorchester, Mass., 1641.

THOMAS, merchant, brother of preceding, resident of New Haven, Conn., before 1650.

LAKEMAN

WILLIAM, representative from Isle of Shoals, 1692.

LAKIN

WILLIAM, tradition states, either came from the parish of Ridlengton in the hundreds of Martinsley, County Rutland, or a parish of the same name in the hundreds of Tunstead, County Norfolk; he was a freeman of Groton, Mass., 1670; his grandsons John and William came with him to N. E.

LAMB

The name probably taken from the sign of a lamb at an inn; the Welsh *llamer* signifies to skip; the primitive Gaelic or Celtic *lam* denotes armor, as a dart, a blade, or sword; to *lam,* to disable, injure, maim, from which we have lame and limp.

EDWARD, a resident of Watertown, Mass., 1633.

JOHN, was at New London, Conn., 1664-69.

SAMUEL, freeman at Springfield, Mass., 1690.

THOMAS, merchant, came to N. E., 1630, settled at Roxbury, Mass.

LAMBERT

From the Saxon *lamb* and *beorth,* fair—fair lamb.

EZRA, fisherman at Salem, Mass., before 1689.

FRANCIS, freeman at Rowley, Mass., 1640.

JESSE, married at Milford, Mass., 1680.

JOHN, married at Saybrook, Conn., 1668.

MICHAEL, a resident of Lynn, Mass., 1647.

ROBERT, came from Dartmouth, Devonshire, Eng., one of the founders of Baptist church in Boston, Mass., 1665.

LAMBERTON

GEORGE, merchant, was at New Haven, Conn., 1641; a passenger on the "Phantom Ship" that left New Haven for England and was never heard of.

LAMBSHEAD

THOMAS, resident of Marblehead, Mass., 1666.

LAMPREY

HENRY, cooper, b. Eng., 1616; was first at Boston, Mass.; located about 1660 at Hampton, N. H.

LAMSON

BARNABAS, was at Cambridge, Mass., 1635, died before 1642.

SAMUEL, among the early settlers of Reading, Mass.; a freeman 1677.

THOMAS, died at New Haven, Conn., 1664.

WILLIAM, came from Durham, Eng., in Winthorp's fleet, freeman at Ipswich, Mass., 1637, his name often spelt with a "b." or "p."

LANCASTER

Local name, a town and county of England, the castle or city on the *Loyne* or *Lan* river.

HENRY, b. Eng., 1610, was at Dover, N. H., 1634.

JOSEPH, at Salisbury, Mass., before 1666.

LAND

EDWARD, at Duxbury, Mass., 1666.

LANDER

From the Welsh word *llandir,* glebe lands belonging to a parish or church, or land containing mineral ore.

JOHN, fisherman, at Portsmouth, N. H., or Kittery, Maine, 1639.

THOMAS, b. Eng., 1613, located at Lynn, Mass., 1635, removed to Sandwich, Mass., 1637.

WILLIAM, died at Marshfield, Mass., 1648.

LANDFEAR, LAMPHEAR

From the Gaelic word *lann-feur*, grass land; *lann-fear*, a pike-man; *lann* an inclosure; a house, a church; land, a sword; *feur*, grass; *fear*, a man.

GEORGE, a resident of Westerly, R. I., 1669.

LANDON

From the Cornish British *lan*, an inclosure, and *dun*, a hill or town; Landon, a town in Belgium.

JAMES, member of first Baptist church in Boston, of Charlestown, Mass., 1670.

LANE

From Old Gaelic, *llane* a plain, barren, sandy, level lands. Lane, a narrow way between hedges, a narrow street, an alley.

AMBROSE, shipmaster, was at Portsmouth, N. H.

DANIEL, was at New London, Conn., 1652, one of the grantees of Brookhaven, Long Island, 1666.

EDWARD, merchant, b. Eng., 1620, arrived at Boston, Mass., 1656.

ISAAC, married at Middletown, Conn.. 1669.

JAMES, brother of Edward, carpenter, son of James T. of Portsmouth, Eng., came to N. E., 1656; settled at Malden, Mass., afterwards at Casco Bay, Maine.

JOB, brother of preceding, b. Lancashire, Eng., 1620; was at Rehoboth, Mass., 1644; freeman at Malden, Mass., 1656.

JOHN, resident of Milford, Mass., 1640.

JOHN, cordwainer, at Boston, Mass., 1674.

ROBERT, came from Derbyshire, England, settled at Killingworth, Conn., in 1665 at Stratford, Conn.

SAMSON, came from Teignmouth, Devonshire, England; sent by Mason in 1631 to Portsmouth, N. H.; probably returned to England.

WILLIAM, came from Yorkshire, Eng., 1635, locating at Dorchester, Mass., afterwards at Hartford, Conn.

WILLIAM, cordwainer, resident of Boston, Mass., 1650.

LANESON

JACOB, at Weymouth, Mass., before 1680.

LANG

JOHN, resident of Portsmouth, N. H., 1695.

LANGBURY

GREGORY, took oath of fidelity at Pemaquid, Maine, 1674.

LANGDON

DAVID, at Boston, Mass., before 1685.

GEORGE, at Wethersfield, Conn., 1636, removed to Springfield, Mass.; finally to Northampton, Mass.

JOHN, sailmaker, at Boston, Mass., 1649.

JOHN, joined church at Farmington, Conn., 1653.

JOHN, resident of Boston, Mass., before 1686.

PHILIP, mariner, brother of John of Farmington; came to Boston, Mass., 1675.

TOBIAS, settled at Portsmouth, N. H., 1664.

LANGER

HENRY, at Boston, Mass., 1645.

RICHARD, resident of Hingham, Mass., 1636.

LANGFORD, LANCKFORD

JOHN, freeman at Salem, Mass., 1645.

RICHARD, at Plymouth, Mass., 1632.

LANGHORNE, LONGHORNE

RICHARD, at Rowley, Mass., 1649.

THOMAS, resident of Cambridge, Mass., 1644.

LANGLEY, LONGLEY

From early Anglo-Saxon *lang, leah*, meaning an extended meadow, pasture, or grassy field. The seat of the family was at Langley in the parish of Middleton, and at Agecroft in Lancashire.

ABEL, at Rowley, Mass., 1651.

DANIEL, mariner, resident of Boston, 1689.

JOHN, married at Hingham, Mass., 1666.

RICHARD, settled at Lynn, Mass., 1635.

WILLIAM, son of John L. of Frisby, Lincolnshire, Eng., b. 1614, freeman at Lynn, Mass., 1639, removed to Groton, Mass., 1659.

LANGMEAD, LANGMAID

RICHARD, mariner, died at Boston, Mass., 1660.

WILLIAM, living in New Hampshire before 1675.

LANGSTAFF

HENRY, sent by Mason to Portsmouth, N. H., 1631.

LANGTON, LANCKTON, LANKTON

Local name; the long hill or town, so called from its oblong form.

GEORGE, at Springfield, Mass., 1646.

ROGER, freeman at Ipswich, Mass., 1635.

LANGWORTH

ANDREW, at Newport, R. I., 1656.

LAPHAM

JOHN, married at Malden, Mass., 1671.

JOHN, b. Eng., 1635, married at Providence, R. I., 1673.

THOMAS, a resident of Scituate, Mass., 1635.

LAPTHORNE

STEPHEN, at Scarborough, Maine, 1640.

LARCOM

CORNELIUS, b. Eng., 1653, settled at Beverly, Mass., 1681.

LARGE

JOHN, married at Saybrook, Conn., 1659, at Branford, Conn., 1672.

WILLIAM, at Hingham, Mass., 1635, removed to Cape Cod.

LARGIN

HENRY, resident of Boston, Mass., 1646; no male issue.

LARKHAN,

MORDECAI, at Beverly, Mass., 1681.

THOMAS, at Dover, N. H., 1640; returned to England 1642.

LARKIN, LARKINS

From *lark,* a sweet, shrill musical bird, and *kin,* a child. *Learcean or leargan,* a sloping green, side of a hill near the sea; from Gaelic *lear,* the sea.

EDWARD, living at Charlestown, Mass., 1638.

EDWARD, in list of freeman at Newport, R. I., 1655; removed to Westerly, R. I., 1669.

JOHN, brother of first Edward; at Charlestown, Mass., before 1643.

LARRABEE, LARABEE

GREENFIELD, at Saybrook, Conn., before 1648.

ISAAC, at Falmouth, Maine, 1680, removed to Lynn, Mass.

STEPHEN, b. France, 1630, settled in Malden, Mass., 1655; removed to North Yarmouth, Maine.

WILLIAM, married at Malden, Mass., 1655.

LARY

CORNELIUS, took oath of fidelity at Exeter, N. H., 1677.

LASELL

JOHN, settled at Hingham, Mass., before, 1647.

LASKIN

HUGH, freeman at Salem, Mass., 1639.

LATHAM

The earliest known English ancestor, Sir Oskateel, Latham of Artbury, Eng., in the reign of Edward I.

CARY, at Cambridge, Mass., before 1639, removed to New London, Conn.

ROBERT, brother of preceding, was at Cambridge, Mass.; removed to Marshfield, Mass., 1643, and in 1649 to Plymouth, Mass.

WILLIAM, came as a youth and servant to Governor Carver, in the *Mayflower.* He was at Duxbury, Mass., 1637-39; at Marshfield, Mass., 1643-48, when he returned to England, thence to the Bahamas, where he died of starvation.

LATHROP, LOTHROP

A place name, derived from the parish of Lowthrope, in the East Riding of Yorkshire, England. *Thorp* means village, the word literally being a low village. Walter de Lowthrope was high sheriff of Yorkshire, 1216.

JOHN, b. Elton, Yorkshire, Eng., 1584, the first minister of Scituate; embarked from England to Boston, 1634; the following year in charge of church at Scituate; removed to Barnstable with large portion of his flock, 1639.

MARK, brother of preceding, bapt. Elton, Eng., 1597, was at Salem, Mass., removed to Duxbury, Mass., 1643, and to Bridgewater, Mass., 1656.

THOMAS, freeman, Salem, Mass., 1634; captain of "the Flower of Essex" who at the battle of Bloody Brook lost not only their captain but nearly all of their rank and file. He left no issue.

LATTIMORE, LATIMER

This name was first given to Wrenoc ap Merrick, a learned Welshman, interpreter, which the name signifies between the Welsh and English. The name of his office descended to his posterity.

CHRISTOPHER, a resident of Marblehead, Mass., 1648.

JOHN, at Wethersfield, Conn., 1646.

ROBERT, mariner, at Boston, Mass., and came to New London, Conn., before 1664.

LATTING, LETTEN, LETTIN

RICHARD, at Concord, Mass., before 1641; removed to Fairfield, Conn., thence to Huntington, Long Island.

LAUGHTON

THOMAS, at Boston, Mass., 1660.

LAW

In Scotch the name signifies a hill; *laye* in old French, a hill.

ANDREW, living at Hingham, Mass., 1654.

JOHN, b. Eng., about 1635, settled at Concord, Mass., 1656.

RICHARD, first at Watertown, Mass., at Wethersfield, Conn., 1638, removed to Stamford, Conn.

WILLIAM, at Rowley, Mass., 1643.

LAWES

FRANCIS, weaver, b. Norwich, Eng., arrived at Boston, Mass., 1637.

LAWRENCE

The name from Lawrus, the laurel-tree. The English ancestry is traced to Sir Robert Lawrence of Ashton Hall, Lancashire, England, who accompanied Richard I to the Holy Land, 1191.

DAVID, was in New Hampshire, 1683.

GEORGE, married at Watertown, Mass., 1657.

HENRY, settled at Charlestown, Mass., 1638.

JOHN, bapt. at Wisset, County Suffolk, Eng., 1609, freeman at Watertown, Mass., 1637, removed to Groton, Mass., 1668.

JOHN, at Ipswich, Mass., 1634; one of the patentees of Hempstead, L. I., 1644, and lived there in 1655; removed to New York after it became an English province, and was mayor of the city.

JOHN, living at Muddy River, now Brookline, Mass., before 1657.

JOHN, resident of Wrentham, Mass., 1684.

NICHOLAS, at Charlestown, Mass., 1648.

RICHARD, at Branford, Conn., 1646; removed to Passaic, N. J., 1668.

ROBERT, left England about 1664, settled at Sandwich, Mass; was at Falmouth, Maine, 1680.

THOMAS, married at Hingham, Mass., 1638.

THOMAS, an original settler of Milford, Mass., 1639, died 1648.

THOMAS, at Stamford, Conn., 1670; was a brother of John, and became identified in his late years with politics of New York.

WILLIAM, living at Duxbury, Mass., 1643.

WILLIAM, brother of John and Thomas, came to N. E., 1635, at age of 12; lived first at Ipswich; his second wife married Sir Philip Carteret, Governor of New Jersey.

LAWSON

The son of Law, the familiar abbreviation of Lawrence.

CHRISTOPER, cooper, at Exeter, 1639; removed to Swan Island, in the Kennebeck river, Maine.

DEODATE, minister, son of Rev. Thomas L. of Denton, County Norfolk, Eng., took oath of freeman at Boston, Mass., 1680; called to preach at Salem village, now Danvers, Mass., 1683; was settled as third minister at Scituate, Mass., 1686; dismissed 1698 on account of being absent in England two years.

JAMES, took oath of fidelity at Dartmouth, Mass., 1684.

JOHN, resident of Boston, Mass., 1690.

ROGER, mariner, living at Boston, Mass., 1690.

LAWTON

GEORGE, among the first settlers of Portsmouth, R. I., but admitted an inhabitant of the island of Aquidneck, 1638.

JOHN, died at Suffield, Conn., 1690.

LAY, LEY

EDWARD, at Hartford, Conn., 1640, removed Saybrook, Conn., 1648.

JOHN, brother of preceding, was at Saybrook, Conn., 1648, but on the incorporation of Lyme, Conn., in 1667, became a citizen of that town.

ROBERT, first at Lynn, Mass., 1638; removed to Saybrook, Conn., 1647.

WILLIAM, resident of Boston, Mass., before 1690.

LAZELL

HENRY, at Barnstable, Mass., 1637.

LEACH

The English lineage is traced to John Le Leche, a surgeon to Edward III. The term *leach* is an old synonym for a physician, and is derived from the Teutonic root meaning to heal.

GILES, was at Weymouth, Mass., 1656; removed to Bridgewater, Mass., before 1665.

JOHN, living at Salem, Mass., 1637.

LAWRENCE, brother of preceding, b. Eng., 1589, located at Salem, Mass., 1629.

RICHARD, at Salem, Mass., 1639.

THOMAS, b. Eng., 1652, married at New London, Conn., 1680.

LEADBETTER

A name of a trade, a worker in lead.

HENRY, married at Dorchester, Mass., 1660.

LEADER

GEORGE, at Kittery, Maine, 1652.

RICHARD, superintendent of iron works at Lynn, Mass., 1645; removed to Berwick, Maine, 1650, and 1654 was at Portsmouth, N. H.

THOMAS, resident of Dedham, Mass., 1640; removed to Boston, Mass., 1647.

LEAGER, LEGARE, LEGER

JACOB, tailor, freeman at Boston, Mass., 1641.

LEAMAN

SAMUEL, at Charlestown, Mass.; one of first settlers of Reading, Mass.

LEAR, LEARE

JOHN, at Salem, Mass., 1658.

TOBIAS, married at Portsmouth, N. H., 1665.

LEARNED, LAINED

In the Gaelic *lear* the sea, and *nead* a sheltered place, hence a green sheltered place near the sea; or it may be a name given for scholarship—"John the Learned."

WILLIAM, b. Eng., about 1590, was at Charlestown, Mass., 1632; afterwards at Woburn, Mass., where he died 1646, leaving an only son John.

LEATHE

FRANCIS, shipowner, took oath of allegiance at Topsfield or Rowley, Mass.

LEATHERS

EDWARD, at Dover, N. H., 1665.

LEAVENS

WILLIAM, settled at Roxbury, Mass., 1634.

LEAVENWORTH

A local Welsh name, *llyvngwerth,* the smooth, level farm, castle or court, or the worth or place on the river *Leven.*

THOMAS, b Eng., came to New Haven, Conn., 1664, removed to Woodbury, Conn, where he died 1683.

LEAVER

THOMAS, town clerk, at Rowley, Mass., 1643.

LEAVITT

JOHN, b. Eng., 1610, came from Dorsetshire, settled in Dorchester, Mass., 1630, removed to Hingham, Mass., 1635.

JOHN, resided at Dover or Exeter, N. H., 1645.

THOMAS, settled at Exeter, N. H., 1639, removed to Hampton, N. H., 1644.

LE BARON

FRANCIS, surgeon, b. France, 1668, came to Plymouth, Mass., before 1695.

LE BLONDE

JAMES, a Huguenot, married at Boston, Mass., 1689.

LECHFORD

THOMAS, lawyer, came from London, Eng., to Boston, Mass., but returned to England in 1640.

LECK, LECKE, LEEKE

AMBROSE, at Wickford, R. I., 1674.

LEE, LEA, LEY

From *lee,* a river, a stream; from Welsh *lli* a stream, a pasture, meadow lands not plowed, a common, a sheltered place.

ABRAHAM, a man of some skill in natural science; was at Dover, N. H., 1680; killed by Indians, 1689.

EDWARD, at Hartford, Conn., 1650.

HENRY, came from Cheshire, Eng., to Manchester, Mass., 1650.

JOHN, farmer and soldier, b. Eng., 1598; settled at Ipswich, Mass., 1640.

JOHN, resident of Saco, Maine, 1645.

JOHN, b. County Essex, Eng., 1620; came to N. E. at age of 13; lived at Hartford, Conn.; joined Farmington (Conn.) settlers 1641.

ROBERT, came from London, Eng.; was freeman at Plymouth, Mass., 1637.

SAMUEL, freeman at Malden, Mass., 1671, died 36 years of age, 1676.

THOMAS, brother of Henry and John, came to Ipswich, Mass., 1648, died 1682, aged 82 years.

THOMAS, sailed for N. E., 1641, died on the voyage. His widow married Greenfield Larrabee. The family settled at Saybrook, Conn., afterwards at Lyme, Conn. There was only one son, Lieutenant Thomas L.

WALTER, b. Eng., 1630, freeman, of Conn., 1654; removed to Northampton, Mass., 1656; thence to Westfield, Mass., 1665.

LEEDS

JOHN, mariner, b. Eng., 1641, came from Staplehoe, County Kent, Eng., to New London, Conn., 1674.

JOHN, at Watertown, Mass., about 1680.

RICHARD, b. Eng., 1605, came to Dorchester, Mass., 1637.

JOHN, living at Hingham, Mass., 1647.

THOMAS, married at Duxbury, Mass., 1685, removed to Plympton, Mass., thence to Windham, Conn.

LEEK

PHILIP, took oath of fidelity at New Haven, Conn., 1644.

LEES

HUGH, at Saybrook, Conn., 1648.

LEETE

The present style of the name was adopted by Thomas Leete of Oakington, Eng., in the reign of Queen Elizabeth.

WILLIAM, governor of Conn., son of John L. and in fifth generation from Thomas L. mentioned above. Gov. Leete was born at Dodington, Huntingshire, Eng., 1612-13; signed plantation covenant at Guilford, Conn., 1639; in 1676 removed to Hartford, Conn.

LE FAVOR, FAVOR

JOHN, at Haverhill, Mass., 1641.

PHILLIP, settled at Salisbury, Mass., about 1660.

LEFFINGWELL

LAWRENCE L. lived in County Essex, Eng., 1495.

MICHAEL, at Woburn, Mass., before 1643.

THOMAS, son of Thomas L., known as Lieut. Thomas L.; bapt. White Colne, County Essex, England., 1624; settled at Saybrook, Conn., 1637; in 1659 removed to Norwich, Conn.

LEGAREE

FRANCIS, a Huguenot, goldsmith; resident of Boston, Mass., 1690.

LEGAT, LEGGETT

JOHN, at Hampton, N. H., 1640.

LEGGE, LEGG

An old English surname which is traced to Oswald de Lega de Easthall, who at the time of the Norman Conquest was living at High Legh, County Chester, Eng. Fil Legg is found in the Hundred Rolls, a record antedating the use of surnames.

JOHN, b. Eng., 1612, came to N. E. in Winthrop's fleet, locating at Salem, Mass.; admitted freeman at Marblehead, Mass., 1635.

LEGROVE

NICHOLAS, at Salem, Mass., 1668.

LEIGH, LEGH

A town in England, a pasture or meadow, the same as Ley or Lea.

JOSEPH, resident of Ipswich, Mass., 1651.

LELAND

Laland an island in Denmark, the same as *Leylande,* the ancient manner of spelling the name, and denotes lowlands. In Welsh, *Lle* is a place, and *lan* a church; the latter may signify any kind of inclosure, as *gwinlan, perlan,* an orchard or word applied to gardens, houses, castles or towns.

HOPESTILL, b. Yorkshire, Eng., about 1580, settled at Weymouth, Mass., 1624; died at Medfield, Mass., 1655.

LEMON, LEAMOND, LEMOND

From the French, a corruption of Le Moin, the monk.

JOSEPH, b. Eng., about 1662, came in his youth to Charlestown, Mass.

ROBERT, at Salem, Mass., 1637.

LENNOX, LENOX

From County Lennox, Scotland. The original name was *Leven-ach,* the field on the Leven, which flows through the county, called in Latin *Levinia.* The river was so called from the Welsh word *llyfor,* which signifies a smooth, placid stream; *Leven-ach* for a while spelt and written *Levenax,* and finally *Lennox.* *Arkil,* a Saxon, a baron of Northumberbria, who took refuge from the vengeance of the Norman William under the protection of Malcolm Canmore, appears to have been the founder of the Lennox family.

RALPH, resident of New Haven, Conn., before 1665.

LENTHALL

ROBERT, schoolmaster, came to Weymouth, Mass., 1637, removed to Newport, R. I., 1638; admitted freeman 1640; returned to England 1642.

LENTON

LAWRENCE, at Ipswich, Mass., 1673.

LEONARD

The disposition of a lion; lion-hearted. from *leon,* a lion, and *ard,* Teutonic, nature, disposition. The English family is traced to John Leonard, b. 1479, lived at Knole, County Kent, England.

HENRY, ironmaster, at Lynn, Mass., about 1650.

JAMES, son of Thomas L. of Pontypool, Monmouthshire, Eng., and of seventh generation from John L. mentioned above, came to Providence, R. I., 1645; was afterwards at Lynn and Taunton, Mass.

JOHN, came from Bilston, Staffordshire, Eng; was a proprietor at Springfield, Mass., 1638.

PHILIP, brother of Henry, was at Marshfield, Mass; left no male issue.

RICE, resident of Rehoboth, Mass., 1644.

SOLOMON, b. Monmouthshire, Eng., about 1610; came from Leyden, Holland, to Plymouth, Mass., and was one of early settlers of Duxbury, Mass., removed to Bridgewater, Mass., 1645.

LESTER, LEICESTER

From *Leicester,* a borough town in England. The Saxon word *Leagceaster* from *leag* or *ley,* a field or common, and *cester,* a camp or city, from the Latin *castrum,* a camp of the Roman legion.

ANDREW, an early settler of Gloucester, Mass., freeman 1643, removed to New London, Conn., 1651.

LETTIS, LETTICE

THOMAS, was at Plymouth, Mass., 1638.

WALTER, a resident of Newport, R. I., 1649.

LEVENS, LEAVENS

See Lenox.

JOHN, freeman at Roxbury, Mass., 1634.

LEVERETT

THOMAS, came from Boston, Lincolnshire, Eng., to Boston, Mass., 1633; was ruling elder.

LEVERICH, LOVERIDGE, LEVERIDGE

CALEB, made freeman of Conn., 1664, located at Newtown, L. I.

EBEAZER, brother of preceding, at Newtown, L. I.; left no issue.

HENRY, tailor of Salisbury, Wiltshire, Eng., came to Boston, Mass., 1635.

WILLIAM, came to N. E. 1633; went from Salem, Mass., to Dover, N. H., thence in 1635 to Boston, Mass.; about 1637 to Duxbury, Mass.; finally established at Sandwich, Mass., 1640, from there removed to L. I.

LEVISTON

JOHN, came from Scotland before 1677, settling near North Billerica, Mass.

LEWIS

One of the ancient names of England; in the French *Louis;* Latin *Ludovicus;* Teutonic *Ludwig* or *Leodwig;* from Saxon *leod,* the people, and *wic,* a castle —the safeguard of the people. *Lluaws,* Welsh, signifies a multitude. Original seat of the family in County Kent, Eng.

BENJAMIN, was at New Haven, Conn., in 1669; removed to Wallingford, Conn.; 1675-76 located at Stratford, Conn.

EDMUND, b. Eng., 1595, came from Ipswich, Eng., settled at Watertown, Mass., 1634, removed to Lynn.

FRANCIS, a boatman, at Boston, Mass., 1663.

GEORGE, clothier, b. East Greenwich, Eng.; joined church at Scituate, Mass., 1635, having been previous to this at Plymouth, Mass.; removed 1638 to Barnstable, Mass.

JOHN, at Charlestown, Mass., 1634; one of first settlers of Malden, Mass., 1635.

JOHN, brother of George, came from Tenterden, County Kent, Eng., to Scituate, Mass., 1635; removed to Boston, Mass.

JOHN, at New London, Conn., 1648.

JOHN, a freeman, at Lancaster, Mass., 1665.

JOHN, butcher, living at Boston, Mass., 1659.

JOHN, mariner, resident of Boston, Mass., 1669.

JOHN, living at Westerly, R. I., 1661.

JOHN, settled at Roxbury, Mass., 1640.

JOHN, married at Hingham, Mass., 1682.

JOSEPH, residing at Swansey, Mass., 1672.

PHILIP, at Portsmouth, N. H., 1665; 1672 at Dover, N. H.

ROBERT, b. Eng., 1607, came from Bristol, Eng. to Salem, Mass.; removed to Newbury, where he died, 1644.

THOMAS, at Saco, Maine, before 1630.

THOMAS, resident of Northampton, Mass., 1667.

WALTER, living in Wethersfield, Conn., 1648.

WILLIAM, came to N. E., 1632, locating at Cambridge, Mass.; removed to Hartford, Conn., 1636, thence 1659 to Hadley, Mass.

WILLIAM, freeman, at Roxbury, Mass., 1642; removed to Lancaster, Mass., 1653.

LEY

HENRY, was at Boston, Mass., 1657.

LIBBY, LIBBEY

JOHN, b. Eng. about 1602; came from Broadstairs, in the Isle of Thanet, County Kent, Eng., to N. E. between 1630-35. He went to Maine and was granted land at Scarborough before 1640.

LIGHT

HENRY, was in New Hampshire, where he died, 1677.

JOHN, was at Salisbury, Mass.; removed to N. H., 1676.

LIGHTFOOT

FRANCIS, freeman, at Lynn, Mass., 1636.

JOHN, resident of Boston, Mass., 1653.

WILLIAM, at Marblehead, Mass., 1674.

LILFORD, LILFORTH

FRANCIS, settled at Rowley, Mass., 1643.

THOMAS, brother of preceding, at Rowley, Mass., 1643; removed to Haverhill, Mass., 1654.

LILLIE, LILLY

Llille in Welsh, the place by the river, or stream; from *lli* a stream; *lle* a place; *llu* an army, a troop; *llellu,* the place of the army. In The Cornish-British *lhy* is a troop, a company of horsemen, and *le* or *li* a place.

EDWARD, cooper at Boston, Mass., 1670.

GEORGE, b. Eng., 1638, settled at Reading, Mass., before 1659.

JOHN, at Concord, Mass., about 1660.

JOHN, a resident of Woburn, Mass., 1690.

LUKE, at Marshfield, Mass., 1643.

SAMUEL, merchant, at Boston, Mass., 1686.

LINCOLN

A place name from Lincoln, Eng.; shire-town of Lincolnshire. The name is derived from *lin* in the Gaelic, Welsh and Cornish-British, which signifies a pool, pond, or lake, and *coln,* the ridge or neck of land, so called from its situation, as Lincoln occupies the top and side of a steep hill on the river Witham. The Anglo-Saxon word *lin* and the Roman word *colonia* meaning colony, makes Lincolonia, finally Lincolnshire.

DANIEL, b. Hingham, Eng., 1619, settled 1644 at Hingham, Mass.

ROBERT, laborer, at Boston, Mass., 1646.

SAMUEL, weaver, b. Hingham, Eng., 1619; came to Salem, Mass., 1637; afterwards went to Hingham, Mass.

STEPHEN, came in 1638 from Wymondham, Eng., to Hingham, Mass.

THOMAS, weaver, brother of preceding, b. Wymondham, County Norfolk, Eng., 1603; was at Watertown and Charlestown, Mass., and 1636 settled at Hingham, Mass.

THOMAS, miller, b. Norfolkshire, Eng., 1603; came to Hingham, Mass., 1635; removed to Taunton, Mass., 1652.

THOMAS, cooper, son of Thomas L., came to N. E. 1630; granted land at Hingham, Mass., 1636.

THOMAS, husbandman, brother of Stephen, came from Wymondham, Eng., to Hingham, Mass., 1638.

LINDALL, LYNDALL, LINDALE

From *lin,* a brook or lake, and *dai,* dale.

HENRY, resident of New Haven, Conn., 1646.

JAMES, proprietor of Bridgewater, 1645; at Duxbury, Mass., 1640.

LINDON, LYNDON

AUGUSTINE, mariner, at Boston, Mass., 1652.

LINDSAY, LINDSEY, LINSLEY

A local surname first assumed by the proprietors of the lands and manor of Lindsay, in County Essex, Eng. The eastern part of Lincolnshire was originally called Lindsey, from the place abounding with linden trees.

CHRISTOPHER, original planter at Lynn, Mass., 1630.

JOHN, was at Guilford, Conn., 1650; removed to Branford, Conn., before 1667.

LINES

HENRY, son of John Lyne of Badly, County Northampton, Eng., settled at New Haven, Conn., 1642.

JOHN, fisherman, came from Dartmouth, Devonshire; died at Isle of Shoals, 1675.

RALPH, brother of Henry, settled at New Haven, Conn., 1642; was living at what is now Woodbridge, Conn, 1689.

LING

Teutonic origin, the English word *long,* heath; also a species of long grass; a long, slender fish.

BENJAMIN, was at Charlestown, Mass., 1636; granted lands at New Haven, Conn., 1640.

LINNELL, LYNNELL

ROBERT, b. London, Eng., 1584; settled at Scituate, Mass., 1638; removed to Barnstable, Mass., 1639.

LINTON

From *lin,* a lake or pool, and *ton,* a town; a parish in Roxburgshire, Scot.

RICHARD, at Medford, Mass., 1630; removed to Watertown, Mass., 1638; one of the first settlers of Lancaster, Mass., 1643.

LIPPET, LIPPIT

JOHN, a resident of Providence, R. I., 1630; a signer for agreement for a form of government; freeman at Warwick, R. I., 1655.

LIPPINCOTT

From *Lippe,* a German principality and town on the river Lippe. *Cote,* side or coast. The Saxon word *liban,* and German word *leben,* to abide, to dwell, and *cot,* a cottage.

BARTHOLOMEW, at Dover, N. H., 1658.

RICHARD, a freeman, at Dorchester, Mass., 1640; removed to Boston, Mass., 1644; in 1655 settled in New Jersey; a patentee of the charter at Salisbury, N. J., 1669.

LISCOME, LYSCUM

HUMPHREY, merchant, member of Boston Artillery Co., 1678.

JOHN, resident of Lynn, Mass., before 1693.

NICHOLAS, at Marblehead, Mass., 1663.

LITCHFIELD

From the Saxon *lich,* a dead carcase, and *field,* because a great many suffered martyrdom there in the time of Diocletian. The name of a bishop's see in Staffordshire.

LAWRENCE, was at Boston, Mass., 1640, afterwards at Scituate and Barnstable, Mass.; died at former place 1650.

LITHERLAND, LYTHERLAND

WILLIAM, came to N. E. in Winthrop's fleet, became freeman 1634; removed to Newport, R. I., where he was town clerk.

ZEBULON, resident of Boston, Mass., before 1670.

LITTLE

GEORGE, tailor, came to Newbury, Mass., 1640.

RICHARD, freeman at New Haven, Conn., 1670.

THOMAS, came from Devonshire, Eng., to Plymouth, Mass., 1630, removed to Marshfield, Mass., 1650.

THOMAS, married at Weymouth, Mass., 1657; afterward at Cambridge, Mass.

LITTLEFIELD

DANIEL, at Wells, Maine.

EDMUND, b. Titchfield near Southampton, Eng., 1590; came to N. E., 1637; following year was at Boston, Mass.; removed to Exeler, N. H., and 1645 to Wells, Maine.

FRANCIS, at Woburn, Mass., 1646.

JOHN, at Dedham, Mass., 1650, afterwards at Wrentham, Mass.

THOMAS, at Dover, N. H., 1648, afterwards at Wells, Maine, 1653.

LITTLEHALE

RICHARD, came to Ipswich, Mass., 1634; removed to Newbury and Haverhill, Mass.

LIVEEN

JOHN, came from Barbadoes to New London, Conn., 1677.

LIVERMORE

From the Welsh *lleufer,* a light, and *mawr,* great—the great light. A name given to the first Christian King of Britain, hence called by the Romans Lucius, which has in Latin the same signification.

JOHN, potter, son of Peter L., bapt. Little Thurlow, County Suffolk, Eng., 1604, sailed for N. E. 1634; went to Wethersfield, Conn., and in 1639 to New Haven, but returned to Watertown, Mass., 1650.

THOMAS, at Charlestown, Mass., before 1687.

LIVINGSTON

The founder of the Scotch family in 1124 was a Saxon Thane named Levingus. Livingston is a parish in Linlithgowshire, in West Lothan, Scotland.

JOHN, a member of the Scots Charitable Society, Boston, Mass., 1659.

LLOYD

From the Welsh, meaning gray or brown.

EDWARD, at Charlestown, Mass., before 1682.

JAMES, merchant, came from Bristol, Eng. to Boston, Mass.; at Newport, R. I., 1673.

LOBDELL, LOBDEN

From the Gaelic *lub,* bending, curving; and *dail,* a narrow vale or meadow.

ISAAC, at Hull, Mass., 1658.

JOHN, brother of preceding, married at Hull, Mass., 1659.

NICHOLAS, granted land at Hingham, Mass., 1636.

NICHOLAS, resident of Charlestown, Mass., 1689.

Simon, freeman at Hartford, Conn., 1655; removed to Springfield, Mass., 1666, thence to Milford, Mass., 1671.

LOCKE

JOHN, came from Yorkshire, Eng., settled at Dover, N. H., 1644; became a resident of Hampton, N. H., 1655.

WILLIAM, b. Stepney Parish, London, Eng., 1628; came to N. E. when six years old with Nicholas Davis; married at Charlestown, Mass., 1655; removed to Woburn, Mass.

LOCKWOOD

An ancient English family seated in Stafford, York, Essex and Northampton counties.

EDMUND, came in Winthrop's fleet, settled at Cambridge, Mass.

RICHARD, b. Eng., 1632, was in Maine, 1672.

ROBERT, brother of Edmund, came to Watertown, Mass., 1630; removed to Fairfield, Conn., 1641, later to Norwalk, Conn.

LOFT

RICHARD, maltster, came from Kent, Eng. to Mass., before 1690.

LOGAN

From the Gaelic signifying an inclosed plain or low-lying place. If the residence of a Briton was on a plain, it was called *lann,* from *lagen* or *logen*: if on an eminence, it was termed *dun.*

ALEXANDER, one of the Scots Charitable Society, 1684; residing at Charlestown, Mass.

JACOB, a proprietor at Watertown, Mass., 1642.

LOHAN

WILLIAM, killed by Indians, at Swansey, Mass., 1675, leaving a son Nathaniel, born 1675.

LOKER

JOHN, at Sudbury, Mass., before 1652.

ROBERT, settled at Sudbury, Mass., 1639.

LOLLENDINE

JOHN, original settler at Barnstable, Mass., 1673.

LOMBARD, LUMBART

JOHN, came from England to Cape Cod, 1640; settled at Springfield, Mass., 1646.

THOMAS, came to Dorchester, Mass., 1630, removed to Scituate, Mass., and in 1640 to Barnstable, Mass.

LONG

PHILIP, a resident of Ipswich, Mass., 1648; removed to Boston, Mass.

RICHARD, at Weymouth, Mass., 1635.

RICHARD, resident of Salisbury, Mass., before 1680.

ROBERT, came to Charlestown, Mass., 1635, from Dunstable, County Bedford, Eng.

ROBERT, married at Newbury, Mass., 1647.

SAMUEL, brother of Philip, at Ipswich, Mass., 1648.

THOMAS, a resident of Hartford, Conn., 1665.

THOMAS, living at Roxbury, Mass., 1688.

LONGBOTTOM

JAMES, at Newport, R. I., 1660, and one of the purchasers of what is now Westerly, R. I.

LONGFELLOW

WILLIAM, b. County Hants, Eng., about 1651; came in youth to Newbury, Mass., where he married, 1678.

LONGLEY

RICHARD, came to Lynn, Mass., 1636.

LOOK

THOMAS, came to Lynn, Mass., before 1646.

LOOKER, LUKER

HENRY, member of the Artillery Company, 1640; freeman, Sudbury, Mass., 1643.

JOHN, freeman, Sudbury, Mass., 1646.

MARK, ruling elder of Baptist Church; resident of Newport, R. I., 1644.

LOOMAN, LOMER

STEPHEN, living at New London, Conn., 1687.

LOOMIS, LUMMIS

From Welsh *lom*, bare, naked, exposed; and *maes*, a field, a name of place: the place in the open field. It was first used as a surname in Lancashire, Eng., taken from Lomax, in the parish of Bury, Lancashire, Eng.

EDWARD, b. Eng., 1608, came to N. E. 1635; was at Ipswich, Mass., 1648.

JOSEPH, linen and woolen draper, son of John L., b. Braintree, Eng., 1590, came to Dorchester, Mass., 1638, where he remained a year; removed to Windsor, Conn., where he was granted land 1640.

THOMAS, resident of Salem, Mass., 1668.

LOPER

JAMES, the first person to undertake the catching of whales in Mass.; was located at Nantucket, Mass., 1672.

LORD

The name derived from the Anglo-Saxon *ord,* which comes from *ored,* a governor, with the prefix of the letter L, *le,* denoting the person or place. The Gaelic *ard, ord,* high, lofty, the prime chief, superior. Lord has been derived from *hlaford,* which is compounded of *hlaf,* a loaf, and *ford,* to give; a bread giver.

ABRAHAM, came from Ipswich, Mass., to Kittery, Maine, 1670.

JOHN, was at Kittery, Maine, 1651.

JOHN, died at Watertown, Mass., 1669.

NATHAN or NATHANIEL, came from County Kent, Eng.; purchased land at Kittery, Maine, 1662; removed to South Berwick, Maine.

ROBERT, b. Eng., about 1620; was a freeman at Ipswich, Mass., 1636.

THOMAS, b. Eng., 1585; came from London, Eng., to N. E., 1635, and was one of the early settlers of Hartford, Conn.

WILLIAM, b. Eng., 1590; was at Salem, Mass., 1636, a freeman 1639.

LORING

Name derived from the Prince of Lorraine; the Loraines came to England with William of Normandy.

THOMAS, came from Axminster, Devonshire, Eng., to Dorchester, Mass., 1634; removed following year to Hingham, Mass., and to Hull, Mass., 1646.

LOUD

FRANCIS, of Scotch descent, settled at Sagadahoc, Maine, 1675.

LOVE

From the Danish signifying a lion.

JOHN, a counsellor in N. H., 1692.

THOMAS, married at Boston, Mass., 1652.

LOVEJOY

JOHN, b. Eng., 1622; settled at Andover, Mass., about 1650; made a freeman 1673.

LOVELAND, LOVEMAN

JOHN, died at Hartford, Conn., 1670.

ROBERT, a resident of Boston, Mass.,

1645; removed to New London, Conn., before 1666.

THOMAS, settled at Wethersfield, Conn., before 1670.

LOVEL, LOVELL

The original family name of Lovel was in olden times Percival, so called from a place in Normandy until Asceline, its chief, who flourished in the early part of the twelfth century, acquired from his violent temper the soubriquet of *Lupus* (the wolf); his son William, Earl of Yvery, was nicknamed *Lupellus,* the little wolf, which later was softened into *Lupel,* and at last to Luvel or Lovel.

ALEXANDER, b. Eng., 1619, married at Medfield, Mass., 1649.

DANIEL, resident of Braintree, Mass., 1640.

JAMES, at Weymouth, Mass., before 1665.

JOHN, brother of preceding, died at Weymouth, Mass., 1651.

JOHN, living at Lynn, Mass., 1681.

ROBERT, from Weymouth, England; was a freeman of Mass., 1635; probably resided at Weymouth, Mass.

THOMAS, currier, b. Ireland, 1620; came to Salem, Mass., 1639; was a proprietor at Ipswich, Mass., 1647.

WILLIAM, captain of small coasting vessel, settled at Dorchester, Mass., 1630.

LOVERING

JOHN, from Dedham, County Essex, Eng.; was a freeman at Watertown, Mass., 1636; no issue.

JOHN, at Ipswich, Mass.; at Dover, N. H., 1657.

MARK, resident of Salem, Mass., 1668.

THOMAS, son of William L., of Oldham, County Suffolk, Eng., came to Watertown, Mass., about 1663; left no children.

LOVETT

ALEXANDER, hotel keeper, at Medfield, Mass., 1678.

DANIEL, a resident of Braintree, Mass., 1662.

JOHN, b. Eng., 1610; granted land at Salem, Mass., 1639; dwelt on the Beverly side.

LOVEWELL

JOHN, ensign in Cromwell's army, 1653; settled at Weymouth, Mass., was at Dunstable, Mass., 1690.

LOW, LOWE

The name signifies a hill.

AMBROSE, married at Hingham, Mass., 1688.

ANDREW, resident of New Haven, Conn., 1639.

JOHN, wheelwright, at Boston, Mass., 1637.

JOHN, resident of Sudbury, Mass., 1641.

JOHN, married Hingham, Mass., 1650.

JOHN, resident of Concord, Mass., 1661.

RICHARD, merchant, at Salem, Mass., 1672.

ROBERT, vintner, at Boston, Mass., 1649.

THOMAS, malster, son of Captain John L., a commander of one of the ships of Winthrop's fleet; he came to Ipswich, Mass., 1644.

WILLIAM, a resident of Kittery, Maine, 1662.

LOWDEN

RICHARD, resident of Charlestown, Mass., 1638.

LOWELL

PERCIVAL, merchant, son of Richard L., and of the ninth generation from Walter L. of Yardley, Worcestershire, Eng.

PERCIVAL L., b. Somersetshire, Eng., 1571, came from Bristol, Eng., to Newbury, Mass., 1639.

LUCAR

MARK, freeman, Newport, R. I., 1655.

LUCAS

The same as *Luke,* luminous; *Lucas,* arising to him.

THOMAS, resident of Plymouth, Mass., before 1656.

WILLIAM, married at Middletown, Conn., 1666.

LUCE, LUCY

HENRY, b. Eng. 1640, resident Rehoboth, Mass., 1668.

LUCKIS, LUCKIN

WILLIAM, at Marblehead, Mass., 1648.

LUDDEN

JAMES, a settler of Weymouth, Mass., 1636.

LUDECAS, LEUDECOES

DANIEL resided at Dover, N. H., 1659.

LUDKIN

GEORGE, came from Norwich, Eng. in 1635; one of the first drawers for house lots at Hingham, Mass., removed to Braintree, Mass., where he died, 1648.

WILLIAM, locksmith, brother of preceding, b. Norwich, Eng., 1604; came to Boston, Mass., 1637; removed to New Haven, Conn., 1660.

LUDINGTON

WILLIAM, lived in Charlestown, Mass., in part afterwards became Malden, Mass., 1642.

LUDLOW

From the ancient town of Ludlow in North Wales; *llud* in Welsh signifies whatever connects or keeps together; the same as *caw;* Llud, a prince of the Britons, a commander. The English ancestor in the fifteenth century was William L.

ROGER, came to Dorchester, Mass., 1630, removed 1635 to Windsor, Conn., and to Fairfield, Conn., 1639; went to Virginia, 1654.

LUIN

HENRY, resident of Boston, Mass., 1636.

LUKE

GEORGE, at Charlestown, Mass., 1687.

LUMPKIN, LUMPSKINS

RICHARD, from Boxted, County Essex, Eng., was freeman at Ipswich, Mass., 1638.

WILLIAM, came to N. E. 1637; located at Yarmouth, Mass., 1643.

LUND

THOMAS, early settler and selectman at Dunstable, Mass., 1682.

LUNT

HENRY, came to Ipswich, Mass., 1633, removed to Newbury, Mass., 1635.

LUPTON

THOMAS, early settler at Norwalk, Conn., 1654.

LUSHER

ELEAZER, one of founders of church, Dedham, Mass., 1637.

LUSON, LEUSON

JOHN, freeman at Dedham, Mass., 1639.

LUTHER

From the German word *loth* or *laut,* loud, famed, fortunate; and *er,* honor; fortune and honor. The German *lauter* signifies bright, clear, pure.

JOHN, b. Shrewsbury, Eng., came to Boston, Mass., 1635; one of original purchasers of Taunton, Mass., 1637; at Gloucester, Mass., 1642.

SAMUEL, minister, at Rehoboth, Mass., 1662; ordained 1685, second Baptist minister at Swansey, Mass.

LUX

JOHN, at Saco, Maine, 1664.

WILLIAM, swore allegiance to Mass. at Exeter, N. H., 1657.

LUXFORD

JAMES, resident Cambridge, Mass., 1637.

STEPHEN, living at Haddam, Conn., 1676; no issue.

LYALL, LYSLE, LISLE, LOYAL

FRANCIS, barber surgeon, resident Boston, Mass., 1637; went to England, but returned 1645.

LYDE

ALLEN, married at Portsmouth, N. H., 1661.

EDWARD, resident of Boston, Mass., 1660.

LYFORD

FRANCIS, mariner, at Boston, Mass., 1667; removed to Exeter, N. H., prior to 1680.

JOHN, minister, came to Plymouth, Mass., 1624, afterwards Nantucket and Cape Ann, Mass.; went to Virginia, where he died about 1627.

LYMAN

English ancestry traced to Alfred the Great.

RICHARD, son of Henry L., XXIVth generation from King Alfred, b. High Ongar, County Essex, Eng., 1580, settled Charlestown, Mass., 1631; went with Hooker's colony to Hartford, Conn., 1636.

LYNDE

JOHN, known as Capt. L., was at Malden, Mass., prior 1685.

SIMON, son of Enoch L., b. London, Eng., 1624, resident of Boston, Mass., 1650.

THOMAS, b. Eng. 1593-94, settled at Charlestown, Mass., 1634.

LYNN, LYNNE

HENRY, came to Boston, Mass., 1630; removed to York, Maine, 1640; five years later to Virginia.

LYON

The English family founded by Sir Roger de Leanne, born in France, came to England with William the Conqueror.

GEORGE, freeman, Dorchester, 1669, afterwards at Milton, Mass.

HENRY, came from Glen Lyon, Perthshire, Scotland, to Milford, Mass., 1648, removed Fairfield, Conn., 1652.

JAMES, resident Roxbury, Mass., 1683.

JOHN, at Salem, Mass., 1638; granted land at Marblehead, Mass., 1648.

PETER, freeman Dorchester, Mass., 1649.

RICHARD, brother of James, settled at Fairfield, Conn., 1649.

THOMAS, brother of preceding, at Fairfield, Conn., 1654-70.

WILLIAM, son of William L., bapt. Heston, County Middlesex, Eng., 1620; came to N. E. at age of fourteen with family of Isaac Heath; settled at Roxbury, Mass.

MACARTER, MECARTA

JOHN, married at Salem, Mass., 1675.

MACCALLOM, MAKCALLOM

MALCOLM, one of first members of Scots Charitable Society, Boston, Mass., 1657.

MACCANE

WILLIAM, resident of Wrentham, Mass., before 1670.

MACCARTY

Son of Carrthach, an Irish chieftain, who lived in the eleventh century.

FLORENCE, butcher, one of founders of first society for Episcopalian service in N. E.; lived Boston, Mass., 1686.

THADDEUS, a resident Boston, Mass., before 1683.

MACCLARY, MCCLARY

JOHN, a Scotchman, at Haverhill, Mass., 1655; prisoner from Dunbar or Worcester, sent to N. E. for sale.

MACCOME, MACOMB

ALEXANDER, member of Scots Charitable Society; lived Boston, Mass., 1659.

JAMES, a Scotchman, resident of Westerly, R. I., 1669.

MACCULLOCK, MCCULLOCK, MCCULLOUGH

Son of Cullough. *Cullach* in Gaelic, a boar, figuratively a brave man.

ALEXANDER, member of Scots Charitable Society; living at Boston, Mass., 1684.

THOMAS, member of Scots Charitable Society, living at Boston, Mass., 1684.

MACDANIEL

DENNIS, resident of Boston, Mass., before 1671.

JOHN, married at Boston, Mass., 1658.

MACDOWALL

STURGIS, member of Scots Charitable Society; living at Boston, Mass., 1684.

MACE

"A staff borne as an ensign of office."

WILLIAM, resident Warwick, R. I.

MACGINNIS

Gaelic, the son of Ginnis, *cine* a race, *ois* numerous, *gen* or *gin,* to beget, a numerous clan or race.

DANIEL, married at Woburn, Mass., 1677; removed Billerica, Mass., 1679.

MACK

JOHN, b. Iverness, Scotland, 1653; came to N. E. 1669, settling at Salisbury, Mass.; 1690, removed to Lyme, Conn.

MACKAY

DANIEL, Scotchman, living at Newton, Mass., before 1673.

MACKENTIRE

PHILIP, son of Ebenezer M., of Argyle, Scotland, settled Reading, Mass., 1651.

MACKINTOSH

JOHN, from an ancient Scotch family, settled at Dedham, Mass., before 1659.

MACKLATHLIN, MACKLATHEN

ROBERT, one of Scotch prisoners sent by Cromwell to N. E. to be sold; located at Brookfield, Mass.

MACKMALLEN, MACKMILLION

ALLISTER, b. Scotland, 1631; at Salem, Mass., 1661.

MACKMAN

JAMES, merchant, resident Windsor, Conn., 1690; no issue.

MACOMBER

JOHN, carpenter, from Iverness, Scotland; settled at Taunton, Mass., 1643.

THOMAS, brother of preceding, married at Marshfield, Mass., 1677.

WILLIAM, brother of John and Thomas, first recorded at Dorchester, Mass., 1638; removed Duxbury 1641; afterwards to Marshfield, Mass.

MACOONE, MACKOON

JOHN, married at Cambridge, Mass., 1654.

JOHN, resident of Westerly, R. I., 1669.

MACRANNEY

WILLIAM, married at Springfield, Mass., 1685.

MACUMMORE

JOHN, at Newport, R. I., 1639.

MACWORTH

ARTHUR, early settler at Casco, Maine, 1636; removed Saco, Maine.

MACY

GEORGE, resident Taunton, Mass., 1643.

THOMAS, came from Chilmark, Wiltshire, Eng., to Newbury, Mass., where he was a freeman 1639.

MADDOCKS, MADDOCK, MATTOCKS

The name is derived from a Welsh proper name, same as Madoc, from *mad,* good, the termination *oc* or *og* the same as *y* or *ous* in English; the *og* signifies animation, activity; *oc,* greatness, grandeur; *ox,* quickness, promptitude.

EDMUND, resident Boston, Mass., 1652.

HENRY, swore fealty to Mass. at Saco, Maine, 1653; removed Boston, Mass.

HENRY, married Watertown, Mass., 1662.

JAMES, from Bristol, Eng., to Newbury, Mass., 1642, afterwards at Lynn, Mass.

JOHN, sawyer, brother of preceding, b. Eng., 1592, located first Boston, Mass., afterwards at Lynn and Newbury, Mass.

MADER

ROBERT, freeman, Boston, Mass., 1643.

MADIVER

MICHAEL, at Casco, Maine, before 1658.

MAGOON, MAGOUN

From the Gaelic, a corruption of *mac-*

gorian, which signifies a son of the smith, from *mac,* son, and *gow,* smith.

Henry, at Dover, N. H., 1657; removed Exeter, N. H., 1683.

John, b. Scotland 1625, at Scituate, Mass., 1655; to Hingham, Mass., 1662.

Jonathan, resident Hingham, Mass., 1657.

MAGVARLOW, MACVARLO

Purdy, married at Hingham, Mass., 1667.

MAHOONE

Dorman, resident Boston, Mass., 1646.

MAINE, MAYNE, MAYEN

From French province of that name; *Magne,* great, large, rich, powerful, same as *magnus* in Latin.

Ezekiel, at Stonington, Conn., 1670.

John, at Boston, Mass., 1689; previously, at North Yarmouth, Mass., and York, Maine.

MAJOR

George, from Isle of Jersey to Newbury, Mass., before 1672.

MAKEPEACE

Thomas, b. Eng. 1590, came from Bristol, Eng., to Boston, Mass., 1636, afterwards resided at Dorchester, Mass.

MAKREST

Benoni, married, Salisbury, Mass., 1681.

MALINS

Robert, resident Newport, R. I., 1675.

MALLARD

From Gaelic *meallard,* a high mound, a hill, or eminence, from *meall,* a hill, and *ard,* high.

Thomas, member of Artillery Company at Boston, Mass., 1685, removed to New Hampshire.

MALLORY, MALLERY

A corruption of the French *mallieure;* in Latin *malos,* Leporarius—a name for all hunting the hare.

Peter, signed plantation covenant at New Haven, Conn., 1644.

MALONE, MALOON

A descendant of house of O'Conner, Kings of Connaught; being tonsured in honor of St. John, was called *Maol Eoin*—Bald John, from *maol,* bald or tonsured, and *Eoin,* John, and this was corrupted into Malone.

Hendrick, resident Dover, N. H., 1660.

MALTBY

John, resident New Haven, Conn., before 1676.

William, at Branford, Conn., 1667.

MANCHESTER

A place name.

Thomas, became inhabitant of New Haven, Conn., 1638; was at Portsmouth, R. I., where he was first mentioned 1655.

MANLY, MANLEY

William, at Weymouth, Mass.; freeman at Boston, Mass., 1690.

MANN

In German, a gentleman, or master, the same as *herr,* man. In Welsh, signifies freckled or spotted, also a spot or place. The surname is first mentioned in England in the Doomsday Book in 1086, which records *Willemus filius Manne,* meaning William the son of Man; he appears as a landholder in County Hants. The principal seat of the family was at Bramley, Yorkshire.

Abraham, resident of Providence, R. I., 1676.

Francis, at Providence, R. I., 1673.

James, freeman Newport, R. I., 1653.

John, baker, living Boston, Mass., 1670.

Josiah, soldier under Capt. Turner at Hadley, Mass., 1676.

Nathaniel, brother of preceding, at Boston, Mass., 1670.

Richard, b. Cornwall, Eng., was at Scituate, Mass., 1646; removed to Concord, Mass.

Samuel, resident Dedham, Mass., 1642.

Thomas, at Rehoboth, Mass., 1676.

William, b. Kent, Eng., 1607; proprietor at Cambridge, Mass., 1634.

MANNERING, MANWARING

A corruption of Welsh word *mesnilwarin,* from *meonil* or *maenol,* a farm.

Edward, at Scarborough, Maine, 1663.

Oliver, at New London, Conn., 1683.

Philip, in New Hampshire, 1683.

MANNING

George, shoemaker, original proprietor Sudbury, Mass., 1640; at Boston, Mass., 1653.

Return, married, Hingham, Mass., 1664; was a resident of Boston, Mass.

Richard, at Ipswich, Mass., before 1669.

Thomas, brother of preceding, died at Ipswich, Mass., aged 74.

William, b. Eng., 1592, came from County Essex, Eng., to Roxbury, Mass.; was at Cambridge, Mass., 1634; removed to Boston, Mass., 1664.

MANSFIELD

From a town in Nottinghamshire, Eng., so called from Saxon word *manrian,* traffic and *field,* a place of trade.

ANDREW, from Exeter, Devonshire, Eng., to Boston, Mass., 1636, removed to Lynn, Mass., 1639.

JOHN, at Charlestown, Mass., 1684.

JOHN, freeman at Hingham, Mass., 1684.

RICHARD, son of Sir John Mansfield, mayor of Exeter, Devonshire, Eng., came to Boston, 1634; removed to New Haven, Conn., 1639, where he died, 1655.

THOMAS, was at Lynn, Mass., 1642.

MANTON

SHADRACH, took oath of allegiance at Newport, R. I., 1668.

MARBLE

JOHN, at Boston, Mass., before 1646.
NICHOLAS, at Gloucester, Mass., 1658.

SAMUEL, of Scotch descent, came to N. E. before 1660; married that year at Andover, Mass.

WILLIAM, freeman at Charlestown, Mass., 1654.

MARCH

A boundary, a limit, the boundary lines between England, Scotland and Wales were called "The Marches." Lords Marches were noblemen who anciently inhabited, guarded and secured these marches.

GEORGE, b. Eng. 1622, came to N. E. 1638 as servant to Stephen Kent; freeman at Boston, Mass., 1666.

HUGH, carpenter, brother of preceding, b. Eng. 1618; came to N. E. 1638 as servant to Stephen Kent; afterwards settled at Newbury, Mass.

MARCY

JOHN, b. Ireland, 1662, lived at Woodstock, Conn., 1686.

MARDEN

RICHARD, took oath of fidelity at New Haven, Conn., 1647.

MARGIN

RICHARD, at Dover, N. H., 1659.

MARINER

JAMES, came from Dover, Eng., to Falmouth, Maine, 1686, died at Boston, Mass., 1731, aged 80.

MARION

JOHN, cordwainer, b. Eng. 1620; came to Watertown, Mass., 1640; freeman at Boston, Mass., 1652.

MARK

The same as *marcus,* a field; polite, shining.

PATRICK, resident Charlestown, Mass., 1677.

MARKHAM

DANIEL, b. Plumstead Manor, near Norwich, England, came to Cambridge, Mass., 1655; removed to Middletown, Conn., 1667.

NATHANIEL, freeman, Watertown, Mass., 1682.

WILLIAM, one of first settlers of Hadley, Mass.

MARLO, MARLOW

EDWARD, at Hartford, Conn., 1667.
Thomas, resident Westfield, Mass., 1681.

MARRETT

NICHOLAS, or NICHOLS, was at Salem, Mass., 1636, removed Marblehead, Mass., 1648.

THOMAS, freeman, at Cambridge, Mass., 1636.

MARRIOTT

JOHN, at Marblehead, Mass., 1674.

MARSH

From the Teutonic *maresche,* a morass, a fen, a tract of low, wet land.

ALEXANDER, freeman Braintree, Mass., 1654.

GEORGE, came from Hingham, Eng., to Hingham, Mass., 1635.

JOHN, b. Eng. 1618, came to Cambridge, Mass., 1635; went with Hooker to Hartford, Conn., 1636; removed to Hadley, Mass., 1656.

JOHN, son of John M., came from Brankry, County Essex, England, to Salem, Mass., 1633, where he was a land owner, 1637.

JOHN, resident Charlestown, Mass., 1638.

JONATHAN, at Milford, Mass., 1649; one of first settlers at Norwalk, Conn., 1655.
SAMUEL, resident of New Haven, Conn., before 1648.

MARSHALL

A name of office; master of the house; anciently, one who commands all persons not above princes. Teutonic, *marschalk;* French, *marsechal.*

EDMUND, b. Eng. 1598, came to Salem, Mass., 1636, removed Ipswich, Mass., 1646.

EDWARD, resident of Warwick, R. I., 1658.

EDWARD, early settler of Reading, Mass.

FRANCIS, master mariner, b. Eng. 1605, came to Boston, Mass., 1635.

JOHN, came from Leahorn, County Kent, England, to Duxbury, Mass., about 1631.

JOHN, resident Providence, R. I., 1639.

JOHN, b. Eng. 1621, came to N. E. 1634, with his brother Christopher, a divinity student, who returned to England. John admitted inhabitant of Boston, Mass., 1640.

John, b. Eng. 1632, granted land at Billerica, Mass., 1656.

John, mariner, came from Barnstable, Devonshire, Eng., to Boston, where he died, 1662.

John, resident of Boston, Mass., before 1661.

Noah, died at Northampton, Mass., 1691.

Peter, was at Newbury, Mass., before 1689.

Richard, married, Taunton, Mass., 1676.

Samuel, known as Captain Samuel, settled at Windsor, Conn., 1637.

Samuel, freeman Charlestown, Mass., 1690.

Samuel, was at Boston, Mass., 1681.

Thomas, freeman, at Dorchester, Mass., 1635.

Thomas, shoemaker or ferryman, came from Boston, Eng., to Boston, Mass., 1634.

Thomas, tailor at Boston, Mass., 1643, removed New Haven, Conn.

Thomas, b. Eng. 1613, came from Boston, Eng., to Reading, Mass., 1635.

Thomas, living Salem, Mass., 1657.

Thomas, at Middlesex, Conn., 1669.

Thomas, resident of Andover, Mass., where he died 1708, almost 100 years old.

Thomas, resident of Charlestown, Mass., 1684.

Thomas, residing at Hartford, Conn., 1670.

William, b. Eng. 1595, came to Salem, Mass., 1635.

William, married at Charlestown, Mass., 1666.

MARSHCROFT, MASHCROFT

Daniel, married at Roxbury, Mass., 1665.

MARSHFIELD

Thomas, at Windsor, Conn.; at his death his family removed to Springfield, Mass.

MARSTON

An ancient English family. A Marston of noble lineage was commander of an army corps under William the Conqueror, who granted him large estates in Yorkshire.

John, carpenter, b. Eng. 1617, came from Ormsby, County Norfolk, to N. E. 1637, as a servant of a widow, Mary Moulton, and settled at Salem, Mass.

John, married, Barnstable, Mass., 1657.

John, resident of Andover, Mass., 1667.

Robert, at Hampton, N. H., 1637.

Thomas, Salem, Mass., 1636, removed to Hampton, N. H.

William, brother of preceding, known as Captain William, b. Marston Moor, Eng., 1592; at Salem, Mass., 1637; granted lands at Hampton, N. H., 1640, but returned to Salem, Mass., in a few years.

MARTIN, MARTYN, MARSDEN

This name may be derived from the Latin *martuis,* warlike; from *Mars,* the God of War. In the Gaelic, *mor* is great, and *duin,* a man; *morduin,* a chief, a warrior. The first of the name on record in England was Martin of Tours, who made conquest of Cemmes or Kemeys in County Pembroke, 1077. The roll of Battle Abbey contains the name of Le Sire de S. Martin. The seat of the family was at Somersetshire, England.

Abraham, weaver, at Hingham, Mass., 1635, removed Rehoboth, Mass., 1643.

Ambrose, was at Weymouth, Mass., 1638, removed Concord, Mass., 1639.

Anthony, married at Middletown, Conn., 1661.

Charles, swore allegiance at York, Maine, 1680.

Christopher, *Mayflower* passenger, no issue.

Edward, at Boston, Mass., 1679.

Emanuel, signed petition against imposts, Salem, Mass., 1668.

George, blacksmith, came to N. E. 1639, in employ of Samuel Winsley; was at Salisbury, Mass., 1643; removed to Amesbury, Mass., 1650.

James, b. Eng. 1630, was at Rye, N. H., 1675.

Isaac, at Rehoboth, Mass., 1643.

John, freeman, at Charlestown, Mass., 1638.

John, married, Barnstable, Mass., 1657; removed to Martha's Vineyard.

John, at Swansey, Mass., before 1675.

John, married, Rehoboth, Mass., 1681.

Michael, mariner, Boston, Mass., 1656.

Richard, resident Casco, Maine, 1646.

Richard, merchant, Boston, Mass., 1654.

Richard, settled at Rehoboth, Mass., 1663.

Richard, early settler Portsmouth, N. H.; one of founders first church, 1671.

Robert, brother of third Richard, came from Badecombe, Somersetshire, Eng., in 1635; settled at Weymouth, Mass., where he was admitted freeman 1640; later removed Rehoboth, Mass., finally to Swansey, Mass.; left no issue.

ROBERT, resident New Haven, Conn., 1646.

ROBERT, b. Eng. 1633, was at Marblehead, Mass., 1666.

SAMUEL, was at Wethersfield, Conn., 1646.

SAMUEL, married, Andover, Mass., 1676.

SOLOMON, ship carpenter, b. Eng. 1619, came to Gloucester, Mass., 1635.

THOMAS, freeman Charlestown, Mass., 1639, removed Cambridge, Mass.

THOMAS, mariner, married at Boston, Mass., 1670.

THOMAS, freeman, Marlboro, Mass., 1690.

WILLIAM, early settler at Reading, Mass., 1641.

MARVIN, MARVEN

From Gaelic *morven,* a ridge of very high hills. The English ancestry traced to Reinold or Rynolds.

MARVIN, of Rumsey, England, b. 1541.

MATTHEW, husbandman, bapt. Great Bentley, County Essex, England, in 1600; came to N. E. 1635; an original proprietor at Hartford, Conn., 1638; removed Norwalk, Conn., 1650.

REYNOLD or REGINALD, brother of preceding, son of Edward, grandson of Rynalde, at Hartford, Conn., 1638; 1640 at Farmington, thence to Saybrook and what is now Lyme, Conn.

MASCALL, MASKELL

JOHN, at Salem, Mass., 1651.

ROBERT, servant in family William Pierce 1640; returned to England 1646.

THOMAS, resident of Windsor, Conn., before 1662.

MASON

ARTHUR, married Boston, Mass., 1655.

EDMUND, proprietor at Watertown, Mass., 1642.

EDWARD, one of early settlers of Wethersfield, Conn., 1640; no issue.

ELIAS, at Salem, Mass., 1647.

HENRY, at Scituate, Mass., 1643, removed to Dorchester, Mass.

HUGH, tanner, b. Eng. 1606, came from Ipswich, County Suffolk, Eng., to Watertown, Mass., 1634.

JOHN, known as Major M., b. Eng. 1600 came in Winthrop's fleet; first at Dorchester, Mass.; removed to Windsor, Conn., 1635, thence to Saybrook, Conn., 1647; one of first settlers of Norwich, Conn., 1660; became famous in Pequot War.

JOHN, at Portsmouth, R. I., 1655; at Westerly, R. I., 1669.

JOHN, brother of Hugh, an early settler at Watertown, Mass., died 1678, 73 years.

JOHN, bricklayer, married at Charlestown, Mass., 1659; at Salem, Mass., 1661.

JOHN, resident Concord, Mass., where he died 1667.

JOHN, living at Hartford, Conn., died 1698.

JOHN, merchant, came from London, Eng., to Boston, Mass., 1678.

JOSEPH, resident, Portsmouth, N. H., 1670, left no male issue.

NICHOLAS, at Saybrook, Conn., 1648.

RALPH, joiner, b. Eng. 1600 came from Southwark, Eng., to Boston, Mass., 1635.

ROBERT, at Roxbury, Mass., 1637; removed to Dedham, Mass., where he died 1667.

ROBERT, grandson patentee John Mason, who changed his mother's name Tufton to Mason; lived at Portsmouth, N. H.; counsellor of province 1680.

ROBERT, married, Roxbury, Mass., 1680.

ROGER, proposed as freeman, Hartford, Conn., 1670.

SAMPSON, shoemaker, came Dorchester, Mass., 1651; at Rehoboth, Mass., 1657, and at Swansey, Mass., 1667.

SAMUEL, married at Hingham, Mass., 1670.

THOMAS, at Watertown, Mass., 1637, removed Hartford, Conn., before 1651, thence to Northampton, Mass., 1656.

MASSEY, MASSIE

From town and lordship of Massey, near Bayeux, Normandy.

JEFFREY, one of first members of church at Salem, Mass.; freeman 1634.

MASTERS

JOHN, came in Winthrop's fleet, freeman at Cambridge, Mass., 1631.

MASTERSON

RICHARD, came to Plymouth, Mass., 1629.

MATHER

From Welsh *madur,* a benevolent man; *meduer,* a reaper. *Mattair* in Gaelic is a mother; in Anglo-Saxon, *math* means honor, reverence.

RICHARD, minister, son of Thomas M.; grandson John M., b. Lowton, parish of Winwick, Lancashire, Eng., 1598, came to Boston, Mass., 1635, settled at Dorchester, Mass., 1636.

MATSON, MATTESON

The son of Matthew

HENRY, b. Denmark, 1646, came to East

Greenwich, R. I., where he was a land owner 1678.

THOMAS, gunsmith, came to Boston, Mass., 1630, removed to Braintree, Mass., 1636.

MATTHEWS

From Hebrew, "the gift of the Lord."

FRANCIS, sent over by Mason to Portsmouth, N. H., 1631; was at Exeter, N. H., 1639; removed Dover, N. H., 1647.

HUGH, married, Newbury, Mass., 1683.

JAMES, at Charlestown, Mass., 1634; removed to Yarmouth, Mass., before 1639.

JOHN, freeman Roxbury, Mass., 1642.

JOHN, at Rehoboth, Mass.; removed to Springfield, Mass., 1644.

JOHN, tailor, at Boston, Mass., 1645.

JOHN, married at Charlestown, Mass., 1659.

JOHN, resident of Marlboro, Mass., 1681.

MATTHEWSON

JAMES, settled at Providence, R. I., 1658.

MATTOCKS

DAVID, freeman at Braintree, Mass., 1650.

JAMES, cooper, came from Bristol, Eng., to Boston, Mass., before 1635.

RICHARD, married at New Haven, Conn., 1669.

MATTOON

HERBERT, at Kittery, Maine, 1652.

PHILIP, early settler at Springfield, Mass.; resident of Deerfield, Mass., 1686.

MAUDE

DANIEL, minister, came from Bristol, Eng., to Boston, Mass., 1635; first minister at Dover, N. H.; left no issue.

MAUDSLEY, MOSELEY

The name is found in the Doomsday Book as Moleslie, which signifies a retired hamlet. It is derived from the Saxon words *meos,* moss; and *ley;* field.

HENRY, b. Eng. 1611, came to Braintree, Mass., 1635.

JOHN, freeman Dorchester, Mass., 1639.

MAULE, MAULD

THOMAS, shopkeeper, a Quaker, settled at Salem, Mass., 1669.

MAVERICK

ANTIPAS, resident of Isle of Shoals, 1647.

ELIAS, freeman, Charlestown, Mass., 1633, afterwards at Winnesemet, now Chelsea, Mass.

JOHN, came from Plymouth, Eng., to Dorchester, Mass., 1630.

Moses, brother of Elias, freeman at Salem, Mass., 1634, living on Marblehead side.

SAMUEL, b. Eng. 1602; at Noodles Island in Boston Harbor as early as 1628, where he built a fort with four small pieces of artillery. He was a King's Commissioner, 1665.

MAWNEY

MOSES, a Huguenot, came from France 1685, settled at East Greenwich, R. I.

MAWRY, MOREY, MOWRY

ROGER, freeman Salem, Mass., 1631.

MAXFIELD

CLEMENT, came Dorchester, Mass., 1658; previously resident of Taunton, Mass.

JAMES, cordwainer, Boston, Mass., 1675.

JOHN, at Salisbury, Mass., 1652, at Gloucester, 1679.

MAXSON, MAGGSON

RICHARD, blacksmith, at Newport, R. I., 1638.

MAXWELL

One Macchus in the eleventh century obtained lands on the Tweed, in Scotland, from Prince David, to which he gave the name *Macchus-ville,* since corrupted to Maxwell. Maxwell is *Macsual* in Gaelic, from *Mac,* son, and *sual,* small, little.

ALEXANDER, came Wenham, Mass., 1690.

JAMES, member Scots Charitable Society, 1684.

JOHN, freeman at Andover, Mass., 1669.

MAY

Name probably given to a child born that month. May in Saxon is a daisy, a flower; Gaelic *mai* or *maith,* good, pleasant, fruitful. In Welsh, *mai,* the earth, the producer; *ma,* mother, tender, kind.

JOHN, b. Mayfield, County Sussex, Eng., 1590, settled at Roxbury, Mass., 1640.

JONATHAN, married Hingham, Mass., 1686.

MAYER

HENRY, butcher, Boston, Mass., 1686.

ROBERT, resident Boston, Mass., 1683.

THOMAS, from County of Norfolk, Eng., to Hingham, Mass., 1638.

MAYFIELD

JOHN, married at Lynn, Mass., before 1666.

MAYHEW

ROBERT, son of William Mahew of Goldynglane, St. Giles, Cripplegate, Eng.; received a grant of tenement in Manor of Talmage's, parish of Brockley, County Suffolk, Eng., 1399-1400.

JOHN, mariner, from Devonshire, Eng., married at New London, Conn., 1676.

ROBERT PARKHURST, mercer, 14th generation from William M.; came Boston, Mass., 1631, settled at Watertown, Mass., removed to Martha's Vineyard 1645.

THOMAS, merchant, b. Tisbury, Eng., 1591-92, settled Watertown, Mass., 1633; removed to Martha's Vineyard 1647; died Edgartown, Mass., 1682. Robert mentioned above may have been his son, as Thomas married for his first wife a Parkhurst.

MAYNARD

JOHN, at Cambridge, Mass., 1634, removed Hartford, Conn., before 1646.

JOHN, resident Duxbury, Mass., 1640.

JOHN, b. Cambridge, Eng., 1610, was at Cambridge, Mass., 1634; original proprietor at Sudbury, Mass., 1640, one of petitioners at Marlboro, 1656.

JOHN, carpenter, Boston or Dorchester, Mass., 1648.

WILLIAM, came from Hampshire, Eng., to New London, Conn., where he married, 1678.

MAYO

The name of a country and town in Ireland, from *moi* or *moy,* Gaelic, a plain, *moy* a river, and *ai* a region or territory,—the region or tract on the river Moy.

JOHN, minister, came to Boston, Mass., 1638; removed to Eastham, Mass., 1646; returned Boston, where he was first minister of North Church, 1655, dismissed 1673, when he went to Barnstable, Eastham and Yarmouth, Mass.

JOHN, came in youth, with Robert Gamblin, Jr., from Rawling, County Kent, to Roxbury, Mass., 1632.

McDONALD, McDONELL

The most powerful family of the Highlands of Scotland, styled "King of the Isles." Somerled, Thane of Argyle, flourished about 1140; was ancestor of all the McDonalds. The clan's name is derived from Donald, his grandson.

JOHN, resident Boston, Mass., 1657.

McDOUGALL

The son of Dougall, that is the black stranger, the foreigner or native of the Lowlands.

ALLISTER, resident of Boston, Mass., 1658.

McEWEN, McCANE

ROBERT, tailor, Scotchman, resident of Stratford, Conn., 1685.

McINTIRE, McINTYRE

From Gaelic, the son of Kintyre;—a promontory or headland, from *cean,* head, and *tir,* land; also the son of a carpenter.

PHILIP, b. Argyle, Scotland, 1648, resident Reading, Mass., 1666.

McKENNEY

JOHN, resident Scarborough, Maine, 1668.

MEACHAM

JEREMIAH, fuller, at Salem, Mass, 1660.

MEAD

A meadow, a tract of low land; the sense is, extended or flat, depressed land. The family of Norman descent. Hervey de Piato, ancestor in 1200.

GABRIEL, b. Eng. 1587, freeman Dorchester, Mass., 1638.

JAMES, resident Wrentham, Mass., before 1694.

JOSEPH, at Stamford, Conn., 1657, freeman Greenwich, Conn., 1662.

NICHOLAS, resident Charlestown, Mass., 1680.

RICHARD, freeman Roxbury, Mass., 1665.

WILLIAM, brother of Gabriel, came from Eng. 1635, settled at Wethersfield, Conn., 1641, removed to Stamford, Conn.

WILLIAM, brother of Richard, died at Roxbury, Mass., 1683.

MEADER

JOHN, came from Durham, Eng., 1650, to Boston, Mass.; resident of Dover, N. H., 1653.

MEAKINS, MEEKINS

JOHN, freeman Hartford, Conn., 1669.

MEANE, MEANS

JOHN, resident Cambridge, Mass., 1638.

MEARS

ROBERT, tailor, b. Eng. 1592, came from London, Eng., to Boston, Mass., 1635.

MEASURE, MASUER

WILLIAM, married New London, Conn., 1664.

MECOCK, MEACOCK, MAYCOCK

THOMAS, at Milford, Mass., 1658; removed Guilford, Conn., 1667.

MEDBURY

JOHN, inhabitant of Swansey, Mass., before 1682.

MEEK

Mild of temper, soft, gentle; *Mac* in Gaelic, a son.

RICHARD, at Marblehead, Mass., 1668.

MEEKER

ROBERT, married at New Haven, Conn., 1651, removed Fairfield, Conn., before 1670.

WILLIAM, living at New Haven, Conn., 1657.

MEIGS

VINCENT, b. Eng. 1583, came from Devonshire or Dorsetshire, Eng., to N. E., 1637; was at New Haven, Conn., 1644; settled at Guilford, Conn., 1644.

MELCHER

EDWARD, at Portsmouth, N. H., 1684.

MELLIN, MELLEN, MELYEN

ISAAC, of Dutch descent, was at New Haven, Conn., 1657, removed 1664 to Virginia.

JACOB, leather seller, brother of preceding, took oath of fidelity at New Haven, Conn., 1655.

RICHARD, freeman Weymouth, Mass., 1639, removed Charlestown, Mass., before 1642.

SAMUEL, brother of Isaac, died at Fairfield, Conn., before 1660.

MELLOWS, MELLHOUSE

ABRAHAM, freeman Charlestown, Mass., 1634, where he died 1639.

OLIVER, freeman, Boston, Mass., 1634, removed Braintree, Mass., where he died 1638.

MELVILLE

DANIEL, merchant, Barnstable, Mass., 1691, removed Eastham, Mass.

MELVIN

The name was originally Esmaleville or Malavilla, from a baron of Pays de Caux, Normandy, France, and in records in the Doomsday book, 1086. It is a corruption of Melville.

JOHN, tailor, Charlestown, Mass., prior to 1676.

MENDAM, MENDALL, MENDON

ROBERT, hotel keeper, Duxbury, Mass., 1638, removed Kittery, Maine, before 1647.

WILLIAM, resident Braintree, Mass., 1667.

MEPHAM, MAPHAM, MIPHAM

JOHN, at Guilford, Conn., 1639.

MERCER

One who deals in silks and woolen goods.

THOMAS, died at Boston, Mass., 1699.

MERCHANT, MARCHANT

JOHN, settled Braintree, Mass., 1639, proprietor at Woburn, Mass., 1642, removed Yarmouth, Mass., 1648.

WILLIAM, resident Watertown, Mass., 1639.

MEREDITH, AMEREDITH

The family is of British origin; old chronicles relate that the first settlement of the family was situated on the Welsh shore, where the sea washed in with great impetuosity and noise, from which it is added they took the name of *Meredyth* or *Ameredith; Maredydd,* Welsh, the animated one.

JOHN, resident Kittery, Maine, 1670.

MERIAM

Originally spelt Merryham; *ham* means home or house, and literal signification of the name is merry house or happy home.

GEORGE, freeman Concord, Mass., 1641.

JOHN, freeman Boston, Mass., 1647.

JOSEPH, clothmaker and merchant, son of William M., of Kent, Eng., b. 1600, settled at Concord, Mass., 1638.

ROBERT, brother of preceding, freeman at Concord, Mass., 1639.

SAMUEL, resident at Charlestown, Mass., 1691.

WILLIAM, of Hudlow, County Kent, Eng., freeman at Concord, Mass., 1645; shortly afterwards removed to Lynn, Mass.

MERLAN

JOHN, resident Hampton, N. H., 1649.

MERRICK, MYRICK

Descended from Meyrick or Llewellyn in reign of Henry VIII.

JAMES, at Marblehead, Mass., 1668.

JOHN, died Hingham, Mass., 1647.

THOMAS, b. Wales 1620, was at Hartford, Conn., 1638, removed to Springfield, Mass.

WILLIAM, farmer, brother of preceding, b. Wales 1603, was at Charlestown, Mass., 1636; at Duxbury, Mass., 1640, one of original proprietors of Bridgewater, Mass., later removed to Eastham, Mass.

MERRILL, MERLE, MERRELLS

The family originally was domiciled in province of Aisne, France, where the name is perpetuated by the village of Merle. The family was knighted both in France and England. The French signification of the name is a blackbird.

JEREMIAH, resident of Boston, Mass., prior to 1652.

JOHN, original settler of Newbury, Mass.; freeman 1640.

NATHANIEL, brother of preceding, b. Wiltshire, Eng., 1610, came in 1635 to Newbury, Mass.

THOMAS, at Hartford, Conn., about 1646.

MERRIMAN

The English ancestor, Theophilus M.

NATHANIEL, known as Captain Nathaniel M., b. Tenderton, County Kent, Eng., 1613; settled New Haven, Conn., 1663; one of original settlers Wallingford, Conn., 1670.

MERRITT

EZEKIEL, at Newport, R. I., 1639.

HENRY, b. Eng. about 1590, settled at Scituate, Mass., where he was joined by his wife and children, 1637.

JAMES, resident of Boston, Mass., 1655.

JOHN, brother of Henry, at Scituate, Mass., prior to 1643.

NICHOLAS, at Marblehead, Mass., 1648.

THOMAS, settled at Rye, N. Y., 1673.

WILLIAM, constable at Duxbury, Mass., 1647.

MERROW, MERO

HENRY, married Woburn, Mass., 1660.

MERRY

CORNELIUS, Irish descent, granted land at Northampton, Mass., 1663.

CORNELIUS, resident Hartford, Conn., before 1695.

JOHN, resident of Boston, Mass., 1663.

JOSEPH, at Haverhill, Mass., 1640; removed Hampton, N. H., thence Edgartown, Mass.; died 1710, tradition says 103 years old.

WALTER, shipwright, at Boston, Mass., as early as 1633.

MERRYFIELD

HENRY, resident Dorchester, Mass., 1641.

MERSERVE

The name is derived from the French *vert merservye,* ill-treated.

CLEMENT, came from Isle of Jersey, Eng., a taxpayer at Portsmouth, N. H., 1673; later removed to Newington, N. H.

MERWIN

MILES, b. Wales 1623, came to Milford, Conn., 1645.

MESSER

EDWARD, inhabitant New Hampshire, 1689.

MESSINGER, MASSENGER

A corruption of the French *messager,* a messenger or bearer of dispatches.

ANDREW, at Hartford, Conn., 1639, at Norwalk, Conn., 1672, and New Haven, Conn., 1687.

EDWARD, resident Windsor, Conn., before 1650.

HENRY, joiner, came to Boston, Mass., 1640.

METCALF, MEDCALF

In the Welsh, *medd* signifies a vale, a meadow, and *caf,* a cell, a chancel, a church, *ie* the church in the vale; English ancestor, Adam de Medikalf 1278.

BRIAN METCALF is mentioned in Middleham Rolls 1465-66.

JOSEPH, freeman, Ipswich, Mass., 1635.

MICHAEL, weaver and tapestry maker, son of Rev. Leonard M., and sixth generation from Brian M., b. Tatterford, County Norfolk, Eng., 1586, came to N. E., 1637, settled at Dedham, Mass.

STEPHEN, brickmaker, at New Haven, Conn., 1639.

METHUP

DANIEL, at Watertown, Mass., 1664.

MEW

ELLIS, took oath of fidelity at New Haven, Conn., 1669.

MICO

JOHN, merchant, at Boston, Mass., 1689.

MIDDLEBROOK

They were among the earlier Teutonic tribes, who crossed the North Sea and colonized the British Isles. They settled in Lincolnshire, Nottinghamshire, and Yorkshire.

JOSEPH, b. Eng. about 1610 came to Concord, Mass., 1635; settled at Fairfield, Conn., 1644.

MIDDLECOTT

RICHARD, son of Edward M., came from Warminster, County Wilts, Eng., to Boston, Mass., before 1674.

MIDDLETON

From a small town in Dorsetshire, England; the middle town.

JAMES, Dover, N. H., 1658, removed to Maine, 1665.

WILLIAM, Boston, Mass., about 1670.

MIGHILL

THOMAS, at Roxbury, Mass., 1637, removed to Rowley, Mass., where he was a freeman 1640.

MILBOURNE

From *miln,* a mill, and *borne* or *bourne,* a brook, *i. e.* the mill brook.

WILLIAM, minister at Saco, Maine, 1680.

MILBURY, MILLBURY

HENRY, at York, Maine, 1680.

MILDMAY

Derived from the Saxon *mild,* soft or tender; and *dema,* a judge; and was given to one of the early ancestors of the family from his tempering the severity of the law with mercy. Among early ancestors of the family was Sir Walter M., in reign of Queen Elizabeth.

WILLIAM, son of Sir Henry M., County Essex, was student at Harvard College 1647.

MILES or MYLES

JOHN, b. Eng. 1618, came to N. E. 1635; freeman at Concord, Mass., 1639.

JOHN, minister, b. Wales, 1621; first

Baptist clergyman at Boston, Mass.; at Weymouth, Mass., 1663, and Swansey, Mass., 1683.

JOSEPH, submitted to jurisdiction of Mass. at Kittery, Maine, 1652.

RICHARD, one of founders of Milford, Conn., 1639, resident New Haven, Conn., 1643.

RICHARD, Boston, Mass., 1664.

SAMUEL, freeman Dedham, Mass., 1645.

MILK, MILKE

JOHN, authorized chimney sweep at Salem, Mass., 1663.

MILLARD

JOHN, tanner, Rehoboth, Mass., 1643.

THOMAS, granted land at Mount Wollaston, Mass., 1639.

MILLER.

From Gaelic *meillear,* having large lips; *malair,* a merchant; *maille,* armor; and *fear,* a man; a man in armor, a soldier. The name appears in parish records of County Sussex, Eng., as early as 1300.

ANDREW, early settler Dover, N. H., where he was representative 1674-76.

EPHRAIM, resident of Kittery, Maine, before 1690.

JOHN, son of Robert M., grandson of John M., was proprietor Rehoboth, Mass., 1643.

JOHN, first settler Wethersfield, Conn., 1636, removed Stamford, Conn.

JOHN, from Maidstone, County Kent, Eng., settled at Lynn, Mass.; was at Salem, Mass., removed to East Hampton, L. I., 1649.

JOHN, b. Eng. 1632, came from London, Eng., and was at Yarmouth, Mass.

JOHN, freeman Springfield, Mass., 1690.

JOSEPH, b. Eng. 1620, came from London, Eng., 1635, was at Newbury, Mass., and Dover, N. H.

JOSEPH, freeman Marlboro, Mass., 1685.

NICHOLAS, able to bear arms at Plymouth, Mass., 1665.

PAUL, at Boston, Mass., before 1692; no male issue.

RICHARD, granted land, Charlestown, Mass., 1637; no male issue.

SAMUEL, freeman Springfield, Mass., 1690.

SYDRACH, cooper, Salem, Mass., 1629.

THOMAS, resident Rowley, Mass., 1646.

THOMAS, planter, Boston, Mass., before 1668.

THOMAS, married Springfield, Mass., 1649.

THOMAS, carpenter, b. Eng. 1610, came from Birmingham, Eng., to Dorchester, Mass., 1635; removed to Rowley, Mass., and in 1653, Middletown, Conn.

WILLIAM, planter, Ipswich, Mass., 1638, original settler Northampton, Mass., 1654.

MILLERD, MILLARD

BENJAMIN, resident Rehoboth, Mass., 1690.

JOSEPH, living at Rehoboth, Mass., 1690.

ROBERT, at Rehoboth, Mass., 1690.

SAMUEL, residing at Rehoboth, Mass., 1690.

THOMAS, mariner, selectman Gloucester, Mass., 1642; removed to Newbury, Mass., that year.

MILLETT, MYLLETT

RICHARD, came in Winthrop's fleet to N. E.; freeman 1633.

THOMAS, b. Eng. 1605, came to Dorchester, Mass., 1635.

MILLIKEN

The name of Saxon-Norman origin; in 1273 John Mullkyn came from Low Countries to England and was at Suffolk, England. The family is of Scotch ancestry.

ANDREW, at Scarboro, Maine, 1651.

ARTHUR, brother of preceding, resident of Scarboro, Maine, 1651.

HUGH, brother of preceding, b. Eng. 1640, at Boston, Mass., 1681.

MILLING

SIMON, resident of Watertown, Mass., before 1686.

MILLINGTON

JOHN, married at Windsor, Conn., 1668, removed Suffield, Conn.

MILLS

Gaelic, *milidh,* a soldier, the *d* being silent; living near a mill.

BENJAMIN, resident Dedham, Mass., 1677.

EDWARD, inhabitant Boston, Mass., 1645.

JOHN, freeman, Boston, Mass., 1630, removed Braintree, Mass.; town clerk 1653.

JOHN, resident of Scarborough, Maine.

JOSEPH, planter, Kittery, Maine, 1647.

PETER, tailor, came from Amsterdam, Holland, named Van Molyn, corrupted in English to Mills; settled at Windsor, Conn.

RICHARD, at Stratford, Conn., 1653; Stamford, Conn.; removed Westchester, N. Y., 1663.

ROBERT, brother of Joseph, died Kittery, Maine, 1647.

SAMUEL, married Windsor, Conn., 1639.

SAMUEL, came from Lancashire, Eng., to Weymouth, Mass., before 1640; settled Dedham, Mass., 1644.

SIMON, Windsor, Conn., 1639.

THOMAS, freeman Wells, Maine, 1653.

MILTON

From Saxon *miln,* and *ton,* or the middle town; a place name from town of Milton, County Kent, Eng.

GEORGE, resident of New London, Conn., 1663.

MINAID

THOMAS, resident of Hingham, Mass., 1636.

MINGAY

JEFFERY, freeman at Hampton, N. H., 1640.

MINOR, MINER

Henry M., a soldier under Edward III, and granted coat-of-arms.

THOMAS, son of William M., of Chew Magna, County Somerset, Eng.; of tenth generation from Henry M. One of founders of a church at Charlestown, Mass., 1632; removed New London, Conn., 1645, to Stonington, Conn., 1683.

MINORD

JAMES, resident of Boston, Mass., 1645.

MINOT

Thomas M., of Saffron Walden, County Essex, England, was Archbishop of Dublin, 1363.

GEORGE, son of Thomas M., seven generations from Thomas M., b. Saffron Walden, County Essex, Eng., 1594, freeman at Dorchester, Mass., 1634.

JOHN, died at Boston, Mass., 1659.

MINTER

TOBIAS, came from Newfoundland to New London, Conn., 1672.

TRISTAM, died New London, Conn., before 1674.

MIRIAM

JOHN, selectman Boston, Mass., 1691.

MIRICK, MYRICK

JAMES, son of Rev. William M. b. Eng. 1612, at Newbury, Mass., 1656.

JOHN, brother of preceding, b. 1614, freeman at Charlestown, Mass., 1641.

THOMAS, brother of preceding, b. 1620, was in N. E., 1645.

WILLIAM, was at Charlestown, Mass., 1636, became proprietor at Eastham, and Duxbury, Mass.

MITCHELL

From the Saxon *muchel,* big; a corruption of Michael. An ancient Scottish family that later settled at Halifax, Yorkshire, England.

ANDREW, resident Charlestown, Mass., before 1688.

EXPERIENCE, came to Plymouth, Mass., 1623, removed to Duxbury, Mass., 1631; late in life to Bridgewater, Mass., where he died 1680.

GEORGE, carpenter, Boston, Mass., 1644.

JOHN, resident Hartford, Conn., 1660.

MATTHEW, b. South Outram, Parish Halifax, Yorkshire, Eng., 1590. Arrived Boston, Mass., 1635, removed Concord, Mass., 1636, thence to Springfield, Mass., Saybrook, Conn., and in 1637 Wethersfield, Conn., finally, 1640 to Stamford, Conn.

RICHARD, b. Isle of Wight, Eng., 1686, located at Newport, R. I.

THOMAS, at New Haven, Conn., 1652.

THOMAS, resident Boston, Mass., 1664.

THOMAS, at Block Island, R. I., 1684.

WILLIAM, married at Newbury, Mass., 1648.

WILLIAM, died Charlestown, Mass., 1678.

MITCHELSON, MICHELSON

EDWARD, Cambridge, Mass., 1636, marshal-general of colony, 1654.

WILLIAM, married at Cambridge, Mass., 1654.

MITTEN

MICHAEL, Falmouth, Maine, 1637.

MIX, MEEKS

From *mixe,* an ancient territory of France.

THOMAS, resident of New Haven, Conn., 1643.

WILLIAM, brother of preceding, at New Haven, Conn., before 1650.

MIXER, MIXTER

ISAAC, b. Eng. 1603, came to Ipswich, Mass., 1634.

MOREES

HENRY, householder at Salem, Mass., 1676.

MOKUM, MOKEY

ROBERT, Ipswich, Mass., 1639, resident Boston, Mass., 1668.

MONK

From Welsh *mon,* sole, separate, alone; Gaelic *monach,* a man who retires from the ordinary concerns of the world and devotes himself to religion.

CHRISTOPHER, Boston, Mass., about 1675.

GEORGE, vintner, at sign of the Blue Anchor, Boston, Mass., about 1675.

MONROE

From *Monadh* or *Mont Roe* from the mount on the river Roe in Ireland, whence the family came. *Moine Roe,* a mossy place on the Roe. *Munroe,* from, of or about the Roe. The river is sometimes written *Munree.*

THOMAS, b. 1660-65, married at Taunton, Mass., 1698.

MONTAQUE, MOUNTAGUE

From French *DeMont Aigue,* from sharp and steep mountain.

GRIFFIN, at Brookline, Mass., 1635, at Cape Porpoise, Maine, 1653.

RICHARD, son of Peter M., of parish of Burnham, County Bucks, Eng., b. Eng. about 1614; at Welles, Maine, 1646, removed to Boston, Mass., and 1651 to Wethersfield, Conn.

MOODIC

THOMAS, member of Scots Charitable Society, Boston, Mass., 1684.

MOODY

A name given for the disposition; *Mevidwy* in Welsh signifies an anchorite, a recluse, hermit, a monk; Welsh ancestry.

ELEAZER, freeman Boston, Mass., 1690.

JOHN, son of George M., of Moulton, County Suffolk, Eng., came to Roxbury, Mass., 1633, removed to Hartford, Conn.; proprietor 1639.

WILLIAM, blacksmith, came from Ipswich, Eng., to Ipswich, Mass., 1634; among first settlers of Newbury, Mass., 1635.

MOON, MOONE

A corruption of *Mohan,* or it may be a local name from the island Anglesey, or *Mona,* so called from the Welsh word *Mwyn,* mines, from its stone quarries and mines; others derive the name from *mon* or *mona,* alone, separated. *Mwyn* Welsh affable pleasant.

ROBERT, tailor, Boston, Mass., 1645.

MOORE or MORE, MOOERS

From Gaelic, *Mor* great chief, tall, mighty, proud; *moar,* a collector of manorial rents in Isle of Man. *Moore* from *Moor*—John o' the Moor. Thomas de More was one of survivers of battle of Hastings.

ABRAHAM, married Andover, Mass., 1687.

ANDREW, resident of Windsor, Conn., 1671; at Poquonock, Conn., granted land what is now Granby, 1680.

CALEB, at Salem, Mass., 1668.

EDMUND, b. Eng. 1614, came from Southampton, Eng., to Boston, Mass., 1638; found as early as 1640 in records of Newbury, Mass.

ENOCH, resident of Charlestown, Mass., 1675.

FRANCIS, freeman at Cambridge, Mass., 1639.

GEORGE, at Lynn, Mass., 1659.

GOLDIN, freeman, Cambridge, Mass., 1636; at Lexington, Mass., 1642; removed to Billerica, Mass.; no male issue.

ISAAC, came from Farmington, Conn., one of first settlers of Norwalk, Conn., before 1645.

JAMES, brother of George, married Lynn, Mass., 1657.

JAMES, "a Scottish man," one of founders of Scots Charitable Society, Boston, Mass.; married there, 1657.

JEREMY, came to Hingham, Mass., 1638, from Wymondham, County Norfolk, Eng.; removed to Boston, Mass., 1643.

JOHN, came from Dorchester, Eng., to Dorchester, Mass., 1630, removed to Windsor, Conn., 1635, later to Simsbury, Conn.

JOHN, freeman at Roxbury, Mass., 1632.

JOHN, freeman at Cambridge, Mass., 1636.

JOHN, received as inhabitant of Newport, R. I., 1638, at Warwick, R. I., 1655.

JOHN, resident of Lynn, Mass., 1641.

JOHN, living at Braintree, Mass., 1643.

JOHN, b. Eng. 1611, settled at Sudbury, Mass., 1640, later removed to Lancaster, Mass.

JOHN, brewer, resident of Boston, Mass., 1673.

JOHN, married at Lynn, Mass., 1673.

JOHN, freeman at Lynn, Mass., 1691.

JOHN, fisherman, at Kittery, Maine, 1667.

JONATHAN, of Scotch ancestry, living at Exeter, N. H., 1650.

JOSEPH, married at Sudbury, Mass.

MATHEW, married at Newbury, Mass., 1662.

MILES, at Milford, Conn., 1646, removed 1657 to New London, Conn.

RICHARD, came as servant in *Mayflower,* afterwards at Scituate, Mass.

RICHARD, b. Eng. 1615, came to N. E. 1635, granted land at Salem, Mass., 1638.

RICHARD, granted land in 1647 at Cape Porpoise, now Kennebunk, Maine, and at Scarborough, Maine, 1667.

RICHARD, at Lynn, Mass., before 1661.

ROBERT, tailor, at Boston, Mass., 1651, removed next year.

ROBERT, resident of Boston, Mass., 1686.

SAMUEL, freeman at Salem, Mass., 1632.

SAMUEL, resident of Boston, Mass., 1670.

SAMUEL, at Lynn, Mass., 1676.

SAMUEL, married at Newbury, Mass., 1653.

THOMAS, came to Dorchester, Mass., 1630, removed to Windsor, Conn., 1635, afterwards to Southold, L. I.

THOMAS, sent by Mason to Portsmouth, N. H., 1631.

THOMAS, son of Thomas M., b. Eng. 1615-16, came to Salem, Mass., 1653.

THOMAS, mariner, married at Cambridge, Mass., 1653.

WILLIAM, at Salem, Mass., 1639, at Ipswich, Mass., 1665.

WILLIAM, York, Maine, 1652.

WILLIAM, Westerly, R. I., 1669, at Norwich, Conn., 1677.

WILLIAM, resident of Amesbury, Mass., 1670.

MOREHOUSE, MOOREHOUSE

JONATHAN, married at Fairfield, Conn., before 1684.

THOMAS, at Wethersfield, Conn., 1640, removed to Stamford, Conn., 1641; at Fairfield, Conn., 1653.

MOREY

BENJAMIN, at Wickford, R. I., 1674.

GEORGE, b. Eng. 1612, came to N. E. 1635, died Duxbury, Mass., 1640.

FRANCIS, Salem, Mass., 1686.

JONATHAN, married at Plymouth, Mass., 1659.

JOSEPH, Wickford, R. I., 1674.

NATHANIEL, married at Providence, R. I., 1666.

ROGER, came from Salem, Mass., to Providence, R. I., 1649.

THOMAS, married at Roxbury, Mass., 1673.

MORFIELD, MOOREFIELD

JOHN, came from Hingham, Eng., to Hingham, Mass., 1638.

MORGAN

From Celtic origin, *mor,* the sea, and *gan,* born i. e., born near the sea. The name was in common use before the Norman Conquest.

FRANCIS, at Kittery, Maine, 1664.

JAMES, b. Wales, 1607, married at Roxbury, Mass., 1640, removed to New London, Conn., before 1657.

JAMES, resident of Boston, Mass., before 1676.

JOSEPH, married at Lynn, Mass., 1669.

MILES, brother of James, b. Landaff, Glamorganshire, Wales, 1615, came to Boston, Mass., 1636, removed to Springfield, Mass., 1643.

OWEN, married at New Haven, Conn., 1650, afterwards at Norwalk, Conn.

RICHARD, came from Wales to Portsmouth, N. H., before 1658, removed to Brentwood, near Exeter, N. H., 1659.

ROBERT, was at Saco, Maine, 1636, and Kennebec, Maine, 1665.

ROBERT, b. Wales, 1601; was at Salem, Mass., as early as 1636.

ROGER, died at Charlestown, Mass., 1675.

SAMUEL, resident at Marblehead, Mass., 1674.

WILLIAM, at Amesbury, Mass., 1677, removed to N. H.

MORLEY

A place name from Morlaix, in Brittany, France, derived from the Welsh or British word *mor,* the sea, and *ley,* a valley.

JOHN, freeman at Braintree, Mass., 1645, removed to Charlestown, Mass., 1658.

MORRILL, MORRELL, MORREL

The name is of French origin, identical with Merrill, "having yellow hair."

ABRAHAM, planter, millwright and iron founder, came to Cambridge, Mass., 1632, original proprietor of Salisbury, Mass., 1642.

ISAAC, brother of preceding, b. Eng. 1588, came Roxbury, Mass., 1632.

JEREMIAH, resident of Boston, Mass., 1652.

JOHN, b. Eng. 1640, settled at Eliot, Maine, 1666.

RICHARD, inhabitant New Hampshire, 1640.

MORRIS

From Welsh *mawr,* and *rys,* a hero, a warrior, a brave man; *maith,* the great, the warlike, same as *mavors.*

DANIEL, at Hampton, N. H., 1640.

DORMAN, at Boston, Mass., before 1672; removed to Conn.

EDMUND, carpenter, came from parish Kington Magna, near Shaftesbury, Dorsetshire, Eng., to Roxbury, Mass.

EDWARD, b. Waltham, County Sussex, Eng., 1630; recorded at Roxbury, Mass., 1652; removed to Woodstock, Conn.

JOHN, resident of Hartford, Conn., 1640.

RICE, resident of Charlestown, Mass., 1634.

RICHARD, came to N. E. in Winthrop's fleet, freeman 1631 at Boston, Mass.; at Roxbury, Mass.; went 1638 to Exeter, N. H.; freeman, Portsmouth, R. I., 1655.

ROBERT, resident of Rehoboth, Mass., 1640.

THOMAS, signer of Plantation Covenant at New Haven, Conn., 1639.

THOMAS, at Casco, Maine, 1652; following year, Dover, N. H.

WILLIAM, Charlestown, Mass., 1658; removed Wethersfield, Conn., before 1669.

MORRISON

Of Scotch ancestry. The origin of the name is probably, the son of Mary Moore, or Maurice, and as originally written in the Saxon was *Mooressom*.

ANDREW, resident of New Haven, Conn., 1690.

DANIEL, b. 1668, settled Newbury, Mass., before 1690.

MORSE

Contraction of Morris; *Mors,* the name of a large island in Denmark, a marsh.

ANTHONY, shoemaker, b. Eng. 1606, came from Marlborough, Wiltshire, England, and was freeman Boston, Mass., 1636.

CHRISTOPHER, mariner, at Boston, Mass., 1662.

EZRA, was at Dedham, Mass., 1639.

FRANCIS, resident of Boston, Mass., 1667.

JOHN, at Charlestown, Mass., 1637, removed next year to Ipswich, Mass.

JOHN, tailor, at Boston, Mass., where he married 1652.

JOSEPH, b. Eng. 1587, came from County Suffolk, Eng., to Ipswich, Mass.; proprietor 1637.

ROBERT, brother of Anthony, at Boston, Mass., 1644; lived at Rowley, Mass., removed to N. J.

SAMUEL, son of Rev. Thomas M., of Foxearth, County Essex, Eng., b. 1585; came to Watertown, Mass., 1635, was at Dedham, Mass., 1636, and Medford, Mass., 1640.

WILLIAM, shoemaker, brother of Anthony, came from Marlborough, Wiltshire, Eng., to Boston, Mass.; settled 1635 at Newbury, Mass.

MORTIMER, MORTIMORE, MALTIMORE

One of ancient names of England traced to Roger DeMortimer, a relative of WILLIAM the Conqueror. He was at battle of Hastings, and became Baron of Wigmore, Castle Herefordshire.

EDWARD, merchant, at Boston, Mass., 1674.

RICHARD, brother of preceding, resident of Boston, Mass., 1664.

THOMAS, constable at New London, Conn., 1680.

MORTON

From parish Morton, in Nithsdale, Dumfriesshire, Scotland. From Gaelic *mor,* big, great; and *dun* or *ton*, a hill. The earliest records of the family is in Dauphine, France, where the Comtes and Marquieses Morton de Chabrillon occupied many important positions. In Battle Abbey Roll and Doomesday Book appears the name of Robert, Comte de Mortain, half-brother of William the Conqueror, who became founder of the English family.

CHARLES, son of Rev. Nicholas M., descended of ancient family of Nottinghamshire, b. Cornwall, Eng., 1626; came to Boston, Mass., 1686; chosen first vice-president of Harvard College.

GEORGE, merchant, b. Austerfield, Yorkshire, Eng., 1585, came to Plymouth, Mass., 1623, died following year.

JOHN, resident of Boston, Mass., 1649.

JOHN, at Salem, Mass., 1668.

RICHARD, blacksmith, freeman at Hartford, Conn., 1669, removed to Hatfield, Mass., 1670.

THOMAS, brother of George, came to Plymouth, Mass., 1623; one of original purchasers of Dartmouth, Mass., 1652.

THOMAS, came to Plymouth, Mass., 1621, soon returned to England.

THOMAS, pettifogger, came from London, Eng., settled plantation of Merry Mount, 1622, sent back to England 1628.

WILLIAM, one of first settlers of New London, Conn., 1646.

WILLIAM, freeman at Windsor, Conn., 1646.

MOSELEY, see Maudsley

MOSES

HENRY, married at Salem, Mass., 1659.

JAMES, of Scotch descent, b. Eng. about 1615, settled at Portsmouth, N. H., 1639.

JOHN, married at Windsor, Conn., 1647.

JOHN, shipwright, Welsh descent, came to Plymouth, Mass., 1632.

MOSHER, MORSHER, MOSIER

ARTHUR, resident Boston, Mass., 1678.

HUGH, came to Boston, Mass., 1632, settled at Salem, Mass., removed to Newport, R. I., 1661, afterwards at Westerly, R. I.

MOSMAN

JAMES, of Scotch ancestry, b. Eng. 1626, was at Wrentham, Mass., 1667; removed to Roxbury, Mass., 1679.

MOSS

JOHN, b. Eng. 1604, signed original compact New Haven, Conn., 1639.

JOHN, married Woburn, Mass., 1686.

JOSEPH, at Portsmouth, N. H., 1665.

MOTT

French word signifying a round artificial hill.

ADAM, tailor, b. Eng. 1596, admitted freeman Roxbury, Mass., 1636; later at Hingham, Mass.; at Portsmouth, R. I., 1638.

NATHANIEL, able to bear arms at Scituate, Mass., 1643; removed Braintree, Mass., 1656.

MOULD

HUGH, shipbuilder, at Barnstable, Mass.; married New London, Conn., 1662.

SAMUEL, resident of Charlestown, Mass., 1689.

MOULDER

EDWARD, merchant, Quaker, Boston, Mass., 1671.

MOULTHROP, MOULTROP

MATTHEW, resident of New Haven, Conn., 1639.

MOULTON

Place name from small town in Devonshire, England. First of name in England was Sir Thomas de Moulton, who came with William the Conqueror, and was rewarded with great tracts of lands in Lincolnshire, for bravery at the battle of Hastings.

JACOB, at Charlestown, Mass., 1663.

JAMES, joined church at Salem, Mass., 1637, was at Wenham, Mass., 1667.

JOHN, husbandman, came from Ormsby near Great Yarmouth, County Norfolk; b. 1599, came to Newbury, Mass., 1637, removed to Hampton, N. H., 1639.

JOHN, resident of Salem, Mass., before 1692.

ROBERT, shipbuilder, came to Salem, Mass., 1629, freeman Charlestown, Mass., 1631, returned to Salem, Mass., 1637.

ROBERT, married at Salem, Mass., 1672.

THOMAS, brother of first Robert, lived on Malden side of Charlestown, Mass., 1631.

THOMAS, b. Eng. about 1614, came to Newbury, Mass., 1637, removed to Hampton, N. H., 1639, afterwards to York, Maine, 1654.

WILLIAM, brother of preceding, b. Ormsby, County Norfolk, Eng., about 1617; came to N. E. 1637, located at Hampton, N. H., 1639.

MOUNTAIN

A name of place.

RICHARD, joined church at Boston, Mass., 1646.

MOUNTFORT, MUNFORD, MUMFORD

BENJAMIN, merchant, b. Eng. 1645, came from London, Eng., to Boston, Mass., 1675.

EBENEZER, resident of Boston, Mass., 1676.

EDMUND, tailor, at Boston, Mass., 1664.

HENRY, brother of preceding, at Boston, Mass., before 1688.

John, took oath of allegiance at Providence, R. I., 1671.

WILLIAM, mason, Boston, Mass., 1671.

MOUNTJOY, MUNJOY

A name adopted by one of the crusaders from a place near Jerusalem. It was from *Mount-Joye* the pilgrims first viewed that city, and it is described as a "full fair place and a delicyous." Some religious houses in England had their *Mountjoys*, a name given to eminences where the first view of the sacred edifice was obtained. This name is still retained in a division of the Hundred of Battel, not far from the remains of the majestic pile reared by William the Conqueror. Boyer defines *Mont-Joie* as a heap of stones made by a French army as monument of victory.

BENJAMIN, mariner, died at Salem, Mass., 1659.

GEORGE, master marine, brother of preceding, son of John of Abbotsham, near Biddeford, Devonshire, Eng., freeman at Boston, Mass., 1647, removed to Casco, Maine, 1659.

WALTER, at Marblehead, Mass., 1668, afterwards Salem, Mass., 1672.

MOUSALL

JOHN, freeman at Charlestown, Mass., 1634, removed to Woburn, Mass.

RALPH, brother of preceding, one of founders of church at Charlestown, Mass., 1630.

MOUSSETT

THOMAS, a Huguenot at Boston, Mass., 1687, removed to Braintree, Mass.

MOWER

RICHARD, mariner, b. Eng. 1615, came to N. E. 1635; was at Salem, Mass., 1638.

MOWRY

JOHN, b. Eng. 1616, came from London, Eng., to N. E. 1635; was at Providence, R. I., 1676.

NATHANIEL, b. Eng. about 1644, an early settler at Smithfield, R. I.

ROGER, first at Plymouth, Mass.; made freeman 1631, soon after removed to Salem, Mass.; 1643 to Providence, R. I.

MOXON

The son of Maggie or Margaret.

GEORGE, from Yorkshire, Eng., first minister at Springfield, Mass., 1637, coming there from Dorchester, Mass.

MOYSE

JOSEPH, resident of Salisbury, Mass., 1655.

MUDGE

JERVIS, at Wethersfield, Conn., 1643.

THOMAS, brother of preceding, b. Devonshire, Eng., 1624, was at Malden, Mass., 1657.

MUDGET, MUDGETT

THOMAS, shipwright, at Lynn, Mass., became resident of Salisbury, Mass., 1665.

MULLERY

JOHN, at Boston, Mass., 1672.

MULLIGAN, MULLEGIN, MULLEKIN

From Gaelic *mullechean,* the top or summit, a height.

HUGH, member of Scots Charitable Society, Boston, Mass., 1684.

ROBERT, brother of preceding, at Rowley, Mass., 1688.

MULLINER

THOMAS, at New Haven, Conn., 1640, granted land at Branford, Conn., 1646.

MULLINS, MOLINES

From French *DeMoulin,* from the mill.

WILLIAM, *Mayflower* passenger, died 1621.

WILLIAM, married at Boston, Mass., 1656.

MUMFORD

Name the same as Montford, from Latin *De Monte Forte,* that is, from strong or fortified hill or mountain.

EDMUND, married at Boston, Mass., 1663.

STEPHEN, minister, came from London, Eng., to Newport, R. I., 1664, first preacher of Seventh Day Baptists in R. I.

THOMAS, b. Eng. 1625, came to Newport, R. I., 1655 removed Portsmouth, R. I.

MUN, MUNN

A familiar abbreviation of Edmund.

BENJAMIN, at Hartford, Conn., 1637, removed to Springfield, Mass., 1649.

DANIEL, resident of Milford, Conn., before 1666.

SAMUEL, wheelwright, living at Woodbury, Conn., 1680.

MUNDAY, MONDAY

Derived from Abbey of Mondaye, in Dukedom of Normandy.

WILLIAM, came to N. E. 1634, early settler at Salisbury, Mass.

MUNDEN

ABRAHAM, married at Springfield, Mass., 1644.

MUNGER

NICHOLAS, married at Guilford, Conn., 1659.

MUNNINGS, MULLINGS

EDMUND, b. Eng. 1595, came to Dorchester, Mass., 1635; returned England 1658.

GEORGE, b. Eng. 1597, came from Ipswich, County Suffolk, Eng., to Watertown, Mass., 1634; original proprietor of Sudbury, Mass.; resident of Boston, Mass., 1645.

MUNROE, MUNRO, MONROE

WILLIAM, b. Scotland 1625, came from London, Eng., to Lexington, Mass., 1651.

MUNSELL

A local name from *Monsall,* a dale of Derbyshire, Eng., or a person originally from *Mansle,* France.

THOMAS, b. Eng. about 1650, on record at New London, Conn., 1681.

MUNSON, MONSON

RICHARD, sea captain, of Scotch descent, at Portsmouth, N. H., 1661.

THOMAS, b. Eng. 1612; at Hartford, Conn., 1637, removed to New Haven, Conn.

MUNT, MOUNT

THOMAS, mason, at Boston, Mass., 1635.

MURDOCK

ROBERT, b. Scotland, about 1665; settled Plymouth, Mass., 1688, resident of Roxbury, Mass., 1692.

MURPHY

BYRON, Irishman, resident of Boston, Mass., 1661.

MURRAY, MURRY, MORAY

De Moravia, a family of warlike people called *Moravii,* who came from Germany to Scotland and affixed their own nomenclature to district now called the shire of *Moray.* The root of the name in both Moravian or Gaelic signifies the great water, from *mor,* great, and *an* or *av,* water.

JAMES, was at Dover, N. H., 1658.

JONATHAN, came to Conn., 1680.

MUSGRAVE, MUSGROVE

The King's falconer, from the Saxon *meus,* the place where the hawks were kept; and *grave,* keeper.

JABEZ, at Concord, Mass., 1649; a resident of Newbury, Mass., 1680.

MUSSELWHITE

JOHN, laborer, came from Longford, near Salisbury, Wiltshire, Eng., to N. E. 1635; freeman at Ipswich, Mass., 1639.

MUSSEY, MUZZEY

ESTHER, widow, settled at Cambridge, Mass., 1633; married, 1635, William Rusco or Resure.

JOHN, at Ipswich, Mass., 1635, removed to Salisbury, Mass., where he died 1690.

ROBERT, one of first settlers at Ipswich, Mass., 1644.

THOMAS, inhabitant of Maine, 1663-81.

MUSSILLOWAY

DANIEL, Irishman, at Newbury, Mass., 1665.

MYCALL

JAMES, married, at Braintree, Mass., 1657.

MYGATE, MYGATT

JOSEPH, freeman, Cambridge, Mass., 1635, removed next year to Hartford, Conn.

MYLAM, MILAM

HUMPHREY, cooper, resident of Boston, Mass., 1648.

MYLES

JOHN, from Swansea, Wales, joined church at Rehoboth, Mass., 1663, removed to Swansea, Mass., 1667.

MYRICK, see Mirick

NALY

RICHARD, disfranchised as Quaker, Kittery, Maine, 1669.

NANEY, NANNY

ROBERT, merchant, b. Eng. 1613, first at Dover, N. H., 1635, afterwards Saco, Maine; resident Boston, Mass., 1652.

NARRAMORE

RICHARD, shipmaster, in Mass. 1687.

THOMAS, fisherman, Dorchester, Mass., 1664, removed Boston, Mass., 1681.

NASH

Supposed to be corruption of *atten-ash,* at the Ash; Naish, a place near Bristol, England. In Gaelic, *naisg,* made fast bound, protected; probably an old fortress or watch-tower.

EDWARD, at Norwalk, Conn., 1654.

GREGORY, came to Charlestown, Mass., 1630, died following year.

ISAAC, at Dover, N. H., 1657, removed York, Maine, where he died 1662.

JAMES, settled at Weymouth, Mass., 1638.

JOHN, at Newbury, Mass., 1652; Salisbury, Mass., 1660.

JOHN, cooper, married at Dorchester, Mass., 1667.

JOSEPH, at Weymouth, Mass., 1674, removed Boston, Mass., 1678.

JOSHUA, married, Boston, Mass., 1659.

SAMUEL, b. Eng. 1593; at Plymouth, Mass., 1632, removing to Duxbury, Mass., 1643.

THOMAS, came to N. E. 1637; at New Haven, Conn., 1640.

NASON

JOSEPH, at Dover, N. H., 1671.

RICHARD, son of John N., b. Stratford-on-Avon, Eng.; bapt. 1606; at Kittery, Maine, 1639.

NAYLOR

A maker of nails.

EDWARD, merchant, came to Boston, Mass., 1665.

NAZITER

MICHAEL, at Saco, Maine, 1666.

NEAL

In Cornish British, signifies power, might; that is, the powerful, or mighty. *Neul* or *nial* in the Gaelic signifies a cloud or hue, figuratively, a dark complexion.

ANDREW, taverner, at Boston, Mass., before 1664.

EDWARD, at Weymouth, Mass., 1662, removed to Westfield, Mass.

FRANCIS, married at Falmouth, Maine, before 1693.

HENRY, at Braintree, Mass., 1640.

JOHN, freeman, Salem, Mass., 1642.

WALTER, came to Portsmouth, N. H., as governor of Gorges and Mason patent; returned to England 1633.

NEEDHAM

A local surname from *Needham,* a market town in County Suffolk, Eng., the village of cattle. From Saxon *neat,* Danish *nod,* a herd, and *ham,* a village. In another sense it may denote the clean, fair town.

ANTHONY, b. Eng. 1628, married at Salem, Mass., 1655.

EDMUND, at Lynn, Mass., 1639; one of grantees of Southampton, L. I., 1640, died at Lynn, Mass., 1677.

JOHN, at Boston, Mass., 1679.

NICHOLAS, signer original compact at Exeter, N. H., 1638.

WILLIAM, at Newport, R. I., 1638; freeman Braintree, Mass., 1648; no male issue.

NEFF

From French *naif,* artless, candid; *nef*

a water-mill; the nave of a church.

WILLIAM, at Newbury, Mass., removed Haverhill, Mass., where he married, 1665.

NEGUS, NEGOS

BENJAMIN, shopkeeper, Boston, Mass., before 1640.

ISAAC, cooper, Taunton, Mass., 1675.

JABEZ, carpenter, freeman, Boston, Mass., 1691.

JONATHAN, at Lynn, Mass., 1630; freeman Boston, Mass., 1634.

NEIGHBORS, NABORS

JAMES, cooper, Boston, Mass., before 1657; at Huntington, L. I., where he died.

NELSON

The name of Scandenavian origin and derived from *Nierson,* meaning son of Niles, and in Scotch form meant the son of *Neil.*

JOHN, son of William N. and nephew of Sir Thomas Temple, captain of Artillery Company, Boston, Mass., 1680.

MATTHEW, resident Portsmouth, N. H., 1684.

THOMAS, came from Yorkshire, Eng., was one of founders of Rowley, Mass., 1638; returned to England, where he died 1643.

WILLIAM, married at Plymouth, Mass., 1640.

NEST

JOSEPH, at New London, Conn., 1678.

NETHERLAND

WILLIAM, freeman Boston, Mass., 1635.

NETTLETON

SAMUEL, came to Milford, Conn., 1639, settled at Branford, Conn.; died Fairfield, Conn., 1655.

NEVERS

RICHARD, at Woburn, Mass., before 1689.

NEVISON

NEVIN, from Gaelic *naomh,* holy, sacred, consecrated. The Welsh *nef,* heaven; *nefanedig,* heaven born; *nefddawn,* heaven-gifted. Nevison the son of Nevin.

JOHN, son Rev. Roger N., came from East Horsley, County Surrey, Eng., to N. E. 1668; at Watertown, Mass., 1670.

NEWBERRY, NEWBURY

A place in Berkshire, England, raised out of the ruins of an old town called Spingham. In Saxon, Newtown. The earliest known lineage is *Torf,* Seigneur de Torville, born A. D. 920.

RICHARD, freeman Weymouth, Mass., 1645, removed Malden, Mass., 1660.

THOMAS, Bapt. Eng. 1594; lived at Marshwood, Dorsetshire, Eng., came to Dorchester, Mass., 1630, died 1635.

WALTER, married, Newport, R. I., 1675.

NEWBY

GEORGE, at Boston, Mass., before 1680.

NEWCOMB

Surname of Saxon origin, and comes from *New,* with its modern significance, and *combe,* a low situation, a vale between two hills. The English family traced to Hugh Newcome of Saltfleetly, County Lincoln, Eng., reign of Richard II.

ANDREW, shipmaster, mariner, married at Boston, Mass., 1664.

FRANCIS, b. St. Albans, Hertfordshire, Eng., 1605, came to Boston, Mass., 1635, settled at Braintree, Mass., 1638, later removed to what is now Quincy, Mass.

NEWCOMEN

ELIAS, constable Isle of Shoals, N. H., 1650.

NEWELL

JOHANNIS DE NOVA AUIA, otherwise John de Newehall, built a manor house in County Norfolk, England.

ABRAHAM, b. Eng. 1584, came from Ipswich, Eng., to Roxbury, Mass., 1634.

ANDREW, merchant at Charlestown, Mass., before 1684.

JOHN, married, Charlestown, Mass., 1665.

JOSEPH, resident Charlestown, Mass., bebefore 1681.

THOMAS, b. Hertfordshire, Eng.; at Hartford, Conn.; original settler Farmington, Conn., 1640.

NEWGROVE

JOHN, at Dover, N. H., 1648.

NEWHALL

Same derivation as Newell.

ANTHONY, at Lynn, Mass., 1636, died there 1657.

JOSEPH, freeman Lynn, Mass., 1690.

THOMAS, brother of Andrew, came to Lynn, Mass., 1630.

THOMAS, resident Malden, Mass., before 1687.

NEWLAND

ANTHONY, resident Salisbury, Mass., 1650, removed Taunton, Mass.

HENRY, resident Taunton, Mass., 1666.

JEREMIAH, at Taunton, Mass., 1657.

WILLIAM, at Lynn, Mass., before 1637; removed Sandwich, Mass., that year.

NEWMAN

DANIEL, at Stamford, Conn., 1670.

FRANCIS, governor of New Haven Colony, at New Haven, Conn., 1638.

JOHN, came to New England 1634, settled at Ipswich, Mass., at Wenham, Mass., 1690.

SAMUEL, minister, son of Richard N. b. Banbury, Oxfordshire, Eng., bapt., 1602, came to N. E. 1636; was year and half at Dorchester, Mass.; five years at Weymouth, Mass., and nineteen years at Rehoboth, Mass.; died 1663.

THOMAS, came N. E. 1634, at Ipswich, Mass., 1639.

NEWMARCH

JOHN, at Ipswich, Mass., 1638, and Rowley, Mass., 1645, returning to Ipswich 1648.

NEWPORT

RICHARD, resident of Boston, Mass., 1668.

NEWTON

Local, the name of several small towns in England—the new town.

ANTHONY, at Dorchester, Mass., and Braintree, Mass., 1640, settled Lancaster, Mass., 1652.

JOHN, freeman Dorchester, Mass., 1632.

RICHARD, b. Eng. 1601, settled Sudbury, Mass., 1640, removed to Marlboro, now Southboro, Mass., 1647.

ROGER, son of Samuel, first minister, Farmington, Conn., b. Eng. 1620; at Hartford, Conn., 1636; was second minister at Milford, Conn., 1660.

THOMAS, one of first five settlers of Fairfield, Conn.; removed Newtown, L. I.

THOMAS, b. 1661; came from New Hampshire to Boston, Mass., 1688.

NICHOLS

The name is baptismal, signifying the son of Nicholas; found in Hundred Rolls as early as 1273.

ADAM, on record at New Haven, Conn., 1645; removed Hartford, Conn., 1655, and to Hadley, Mass., 1661; freeman Boston, Mass., 1670.

ALLEN, married, Barnstable, Mass., 1670.

CYPRIAN, came from Witham, County Essex, Eng., freeman at Hartford, Conn., 1669.

FRANCIS, b. Eng. 1600, one of first seventeen settlers Stratford, Conn.; 1639, removed to province of New York.

HUGH, married at Salem, Mass., 1694.

JAMES, married at Malden, Mass., 1660.

JOHN, at Greenwich, R. I., 1687.

MORDECAI, mariner, married at Boston, Mass., 1652.

NICHOLAS, took oath of allegiance at Andover, Mass., 1678.

RANDOLPH, resident Charlestown, Mass., before 1643.

RICHARD, settled at Ipswich, Mass., where admitted freeman 1648; removed to Reading, Mass.

ROBERT, married at Watertown, Mass., 1644, granted land at Casco Bay, Maine.

ROBERT, at Saybrook, Conn., 1664-73.

THOMAS, at Hingham, Mass., 1637, removed to Scituate, Mass.

THOMAS, at Sandwich, Mass., 1643.

THOMAS, married, Malden, Mass., 1655, removed Salisbury, Mass.

THOMAS, settled at Newport, R. I., before 1642.

THOMAS, resident Amesbury, Mass., 1665.

WALTER, freeman Charlestown, Mass., 1638.

WILLIAM, at Salem, Mass., 1638, granted land and removed New London, Conn., 1655.

WILLIAM, proprietor Topsfield, Mass., 1652, where he died 1694, aged upwards of 100 years.

NICHOLSON

EDMUND, inhabitant Marblehead, Mass., 1648.

JAMES, died Charlestown, Mass., 1668.

JOHN, resident Falmouth, Maine, 1675.

ROBERT, at Falmouth, Maine, 1675.

WILLIAM, b. Norwich, Eng., 1604, came to Mass. 1637, lived at Boston, Watertown, Plymouth, Mass., removed Yarmouth, Mass., 1643.

NICK, NEEK

CHRISTOPHER, at Marblehead, Mass., 1668.

JOHN, married at Lynn, Mass., 1676.

WILLIAM, brother of preceding, at Marblehead, Mass., 1674.

NICKERSON

WILLIAM, weaver from Norwich, Eng., b. Eng. 1604, came first to Watertown, Mass., 1637, removed to Boston, Mass., soon after.

WILLIAM, married, Eastham, Mass., 1691.

NICHOLSON

ROBERT, at Scarborough, Maine, before 1676.

NIGHTINGALE

BENJAMIN, at Braintree, Mass., 1689.

WILLIAM, b. Eng. 1637, settled at Braintree, Mass., 1660.

NILES

JOHN, b. Wales, 1603, came to Dorchester, Mass., 1634; removed Braintree, Mass., 1636, freeman there 1647.

JONATHAN, freeman Hull, Mass., 1680.

NIMS

The French name DeNismes is of Huguenot origin.

GODFREY, on record Northampton, Mass., 1667; removed to Deerfield, Mass., 1684.

NIXON

JOHN, inhabitant, R. I., 1663.

MATTHEW, at Salem, Mass., 1639.

NOAKES, NOKES

A corruption of *atten oak* "at the oak"; *en* was added to *at* when the following word began with a vowel as "John Atten Ash"—John Nash, that is, John at the Ash. Mr. John Nokes is a celebrated personage in legal matters, as well as his constant antagonist Mr. John Styles (John at the Style). The names are so common that Jack Noakes and Tom Styles designate the rabble.

ROBERT, resident Boston, Mass., 1667.

NOBLE

Great, elevated, dignified.

THOMAS, b. Eng. 1632, came to Boston, Mass., 1652, settled Springfield, Mass., 1653, removed Westfield, Mass., 1669.

NOCK

THOMAS, at Dover, N. H., 1655.

NODDLE

WILLIAM, came in Winthrop's fleet; drowned 1632.

NORCROSS

JEREMIAH, b. London, Eng., before 1600; came to Watertown, Mass., 1638; returned England 1646, leaving sons Nathaniel and Richard in N. E.

NORCUT, NORCOTT

Local name, the north-cot; as Eastcott and Westcott.

DANIEL, at Boston, Mass., before 1635.

WILLIAM, married at Marshfield, Mass., 1664.

NORDEN

NATHANIEL, freeman Marblehead, Mass., 1690.

SAMUEL, shoemaker, brother of preceding; at Boston, Mass., 1651.

NORMAN

A native of Normandy, a northman. The inhabitants of Sweden, Denmark, and Norway were anciently so called.

HUGH, married Plymouth, Mass., 1639, removed Yarmouth, Mass., before 1643.

JOHN, at Salem, Mass., 1631.

RICHARD, brother of preceding, came from Dorchester, Eng., to N. E., 1626, and later settled at Salem, Mass.

THOMAS, living at Boston, Mass., 1674, removed Topsfield, Mass., where he was made freeman 1681.

NORRIS

Norroy, or North-King; a title given in England to the third King-at-arms. *Norrie* the French for a foster-child.

EDWARD, minister, b. Eng. 1589, came to N. E. 1639, fourth minister at Salem, Mass., where he died 1659.

NICHOLAS, b. Eng. about 1641, came at age of fourteen to N. E.; was at Hampden, N. H., 1663, afterwards at Exeter, N. H.

OLIVER, at Sandwich, Mass., 1691.

NORTH

JOHN, born Eng. 1615 came to Boston, Mass., 1635, one of first settlers of Farmington, Conn.

RICHARD, one of first proprietors Salisbury, Mass., 1640; removed Salem, Mass., before 1649.

THOMAS, at New Haven, Conn., 1644.

THOMAS, took oath of allegiance, Hadley, Mass., 1678.

NORTHAM

A local name, the north house or village—*north-ham.*

JAMES, settled at Concord, Mass., 1640, removed to Wethersfield, Conn., 1644, to Hartford, Conn., 1655, where he died before 1662.

NORTHCUT

WILLIAM, at Yarmouth, Mass., 1643.

NORTHEND

EZEKIEL, b. Eng. about 1622, inhabitant Rowley, Mass., 1645.

JOHN, one of first settlers Wethersfield, Conn., removed Stamford, Conn.

NORTHEY

JOHN, b. England about 1607; at Marblehead, Mass., 1648; became a Quaker.

NORTHROP, NORTHUP, NORTHOP

A place in England; the North *thorp* or village.

JOSEPH, came from Yorkshire, Eng., settled at New Haven, Conn., 1638; removed Milford, Conn., where he died 1669.

STEPHEN, at Providence, R. I., 1645, freeman, Kingstown, R. I., 1658.

NORTON

From Norton, a town in Yorkshire, England. The North-town. The name of French origin; ancestry traced to Le-Signeur de Norville, who came to England with William the Conqueror. The ancient seat of the family was at Sharpenboro, now a mere hamlet, in Bedfordshire, England.

FRANCIS, steward, sent by Mason to Portsmouth, N. H., 1631, removed to Charlestown, Mass., 1637.

FRANCIS, one of first settlers Wethersfield, Conn.; at Milford, Conn., 1660, thence removed New Haven, Conn., 1662, where he was drowned 1667.

GEORGE, carpenter, came with Higgison from London, Eng., to Salem, Mass., 1629, removed Gloucester, Mass., 1641.

HENRY, at York, Maine, 1652, returned England 1657.

JAMES, resident New Haven, Conn., 1640.

JOHN, came Charlestown, Mass., 1629; removed York, Maine, leaving there 1633.

JOHN, eminent divine, son of William N., of Bishop Stortford, County Herts, Eng., came to N. E. 1635, ordained Ipswich, Mass., 1636.

JOHN, carpenter, b. Eng. 1637, at Salem, Mass., 1660.

JOHN, b. London, Eng., 1622, on record at Branford, Conn., 1646; removed Hartford, Conn., 1659; afterwards to Farmington, Conn.

JOSEPH, b. Eng. about 1640, married at Salisbury, Mass., 1662.

NICHOLAS, b. Eng. 1610, one of pioneers of Weymouth, Mass., 1639; removed to Martha's Vineyard.

RICHARD, cooper at Boston, Mass., 1648.

THOMAS, miller, a signer of first compact at Guilford, Conn., 1639.

THOMAS, resident of Salem, Mass., 1654.

WILLIAM, brother of Rev. John N., b. Eng. 1610, came from London, Eng., settled at Ipswich, Mass., 1635.

NORWICH

From city and seaport of Norwich, County Norfolk, England. The North-harbor, from *North,* and *Wick,* a harbor or port.

JOHN, freeman Hingham, Mass., 1640.

NORWOOD

FRANCIS, married at Gloucester, Mass., 1663.

NOSEWORTHY

ROBERT, mariner Boston, Mass., 1675.

NOTT

From Saxon *hnott,* smooth, round, a nut. The name may have come from wearing the hair short and smooth.

JOHN, at Wethersfield, Conn., 1640.

NOWELL, NORWELL

From French word *Noll,* Christmas; a name given to a child born at that time. They came to England with William the Conqueror. Robert Nowell, bishop of the Orkneys in 12th century.

GEORGE, blacksmith, resident Boston, Mass., 1662.

INCREASE, secretary of Mass. Bay Colony; b. Sheldon, Eng., 1593, came in Winthrop's fleet 1630, settled at Charlestown, Mass.

PHILIP, mariner at Salem, Mass., drowned 1675.

ROBERT, married at Salem, Mass., 1668.

THOMAS, early settler Windsor, Conn.; no issue.

NOYES, NOYCE, NOISE

Noy an abbreviation for Noah. In Cornish British, *noi,* a nephew, and *noys,* night. The English family descended from William des Noyers, a military commander under William the Conqueror, the name being finally corrupted to Noyes.

JAMES, minister, son of Rev. William N., b. Choulderton, County Wilts, 1608; second minister, Newbury, Mass., 1635.

JOHN, freeman Boston, Mass., 1676.

JOSEPH, at Salisbury, Mass., 1640.

JOSEPH, married at Charlestown, Mass., 1656.

NICHOLAS, brother of Rev. James N., born about 1616, came to N. E. 1634, freeman Newbury, Mass., 1637.

PETER, at Sudbury, Mass., 1639.

RICHARD, resident Newbury, Mass., 1647.

NUDD

THOMAS, son of Roger N., grandson of John N., b. Ormsby, Eng., 1629, came with stepfather Henry Dow, who settled at Hampton, N. H., 1643.

NURSE, NOURSE

FRANCIS, b. Eng. 1618, settled Salem, Mass., 1639.

JOHN, brother of preceding, married at Salem, Mass., 1672.

SAMUEL, brother of preceding, married, Salem, Mass., 1677.

NUTE

JAMES, sent by Mason to Dover, N. H., 1631.

NUTT

MILES, freeman Watertown, Mass., 1637.

NUTTER

HATEVIL, b. Eng. 1603, one of founders of Dover, N. H., 1633.

NUTTING

JOHN, married Woburn, Mass., 1650; removed to Groton, Mass.; at Chelmsford, Mass., 1655.

NYE

The familiar abbreviation of Isaac among the Dutch. The Danish *noie,* exact, precise, nice; *ny,* new, recently produced. Love Nye the Danish ancestor

1316; Randolph Nye settled in Sussex, England, 1527.

Benjamin, b. Bidlenden, County Kent, Eng., 1620, came to Lynn, Mass., 1635, removed to Sandwich, Mass., 1637.

OAKES

From a dwelling near the oaktrees.

Edward, freeman Cambridge, Mass., 1642.

George, resident Lynn, Mass., 1654.

Nathaniel, b. Wales, 1645, at Dorchester, Mass., 1660-65; at Marlboro, Mass., 1686.

Samuel, freeman Boston, Mass., 1690.

Thomas, brother Edward, freeman Cambridge, Mass., 1642.

OAKMAN

Samuel, at Scarborough, Maine, 1657.

OBER, ORBEAR

Richard, at Salem, Mass., 1668, removed Beverly, Mass., 1679.

Thomas, at Watertown, Mass., 1649.

OCKINGTON, OKINGTON

William, resident Boston, Mass., 1669.

ODELL, ODLE

The family is of ancient English ancestry, in later years located at Bedfordshire, England.

Reginald, resident Boston, Mass., 1687.

William, came to Concord, Mass., 1639, removed Southampton, L. I., 1642, soon afterwards Fairfield, Conn.

ODIORNE

John, b. Eng. about 1627, came to Portsmouth, N. H., 1650.

ODLIN, ODLYN, originally AUDLEY

John, cutler or armorer, b. Eng. 1602, early settler, Boston, Mass.; disfranchised as an antinomian 1637; died 1685.

OFFITT (sometimes spelt Affitt)

Thomas, at Roxbury, Mass., 1632, freeman 1633, removed Springfield, Mass., 1635, and 1639 Milford, Conn., later resident of Stamford, Conn.

OFFLEY

David, member Artillery Company, Boston, Mass., 1638, removed Plymouth, Mass., 1643; returned Boston, Mass.

Thomas, collector of port, Salem, Mass., 1686-89.

OFIELD

Thomas, mariner, resident Boston, Mass., 1669.

OGDEN

From Saxon *ock*,-oak tree, and *den* valley; the oak vale or shady valley. *Ogduine* in Gaelic signified a young man, from *og,* young, and *duine,* a man. Ogdyn in Welsh has the same signification.

John, was at Stamford, Conn., 1641, patentee Hempstead, L. I., 1644, resided at Southampton, L. I., 1656. Went to Elizabethtown, N. J., 1662.

Richard, brother of preceding, came to N. E. 1641, was at Fairfield and Stamford, Conn., 1667.

OGLEBY

James, at Scarborough, Maine, 1676.

OKEY

John, resident Boston, Mass., 1686.

OLCOTT

Thomas, merchant, original proprietor Hartford, Conn., 1636, died there 1654-55.

OLD, OLDS

The origin of the name is undoubtedly found in the nickname "The Old." The early ancestor of the English family that is known by the records was Roger Wold, a thane of Yolthrope, Yorkshire, where he lived on his estate, 1189-99. In sixteenth century, name became Olde.

Robert, son of John, and of fifteenth generation from Roger Wold, was b. Sherborne, Dorsetshire, Eng., 1645; is recorded at Windsor, Conn., 1667, and was granted, under the title of Dr. Ould in 1670, fifty acres of land at Suffield, Conn., being one of first five proprietors of town.

OLDAGE, OLDIGE, OLDRIDGE

Richard, at Dorchester, Mass., went to Windsor, Conn., before 1640; no male issue.

OLDEN

John, inhabitant Boston, Mass., 1668.

OLDHAM

John, Indian trader, came to Plymouth, Mass., 1623, removed Nantasket and Cape Ann, Mass.; freeman Watertown, Mass., 1631.

Thomas, brother of preceding, came to N. E. 1635; was at Duxbury, Mass., 1643, afterwards at Scituate, Mass.

OLIN

A name of French origin from Olinville, near Rouen, France.

John, came from Wales, to West Greenwich, R. I., 1678.

OLIVER

So named from the olive-tree, an emblem of peace.

David, took oath of allegiance at Pemaquid, Maine, 1674.

John, at Boston, Mass., 1632, freeman Newbury, Mass., 1640.

JOHN, member of first church at Boston, Mass., 1683.

JOSEPH, at Scarborough, Maine, 1676.

RICHARD, at Salem, Mass., 1668; at Monhegan, Maine, 1674.

THOMAS, son of John O., grandson of Thomas of Bristol, Eng., b. 1568, one of founders of First Church of Boston, 1632.

THOMAS, calendar, b. England 1601, came from Norwich, Eng., to Salem, Mass., 1637.

THOMAS, inhabitant Fairfield, Conn., 1660-70.

OLMSTEAD

A place or town by the green oaks, from *holm*, an oak, and *stead*, a place. *Holme*, low lands on a river, an island.

JAMES, freeman Cambridge, Mass., 1632, removed to Hartford, Conn., 1636.

JOHN, surgeon, nephew of the preceding, at Hartford, Conn., 1640; removed Saybrook, Conn., and 1660 Norwalk, Conn.; no issue.

RICHARD, nephew of James, original proprietor at Hartford, Conn.

OLNEY

THOMAS, shoemaker, b. St. Albans, Hertfordshire, Eng., 1600, came to Salem, Mass., 1635; to Providence, R. I., 1638.

ONGE

FRANCIS, came from Bristol, England, to Watertown, Mass., 1631; died in a few years.

ONION

JOHN, at Braintree, Mass., 1640.

ROBERT, b. Eng. 1609, came to Roxbury, Mass., 1635.

ONTHANK, UNTHANK

CHRISTOPHER, freeman Warwick, R. I., 1655.

ORCHARD

An inclosure of fruit-trees *Orcheard*, a Gaelic word meaning a goldsmith.

ROBERT, merchant, Boston, Mass., 1668.

ORCUTT

WILLIAM, at Weymouth, Mass., 1664, removed Scituate, Mass., 1669, afterwards to Bridgewater, Mass.

ORDWAY

ABNER, inhabitant Watertown, Mass., 1643, afterwards Wenham, Mass., and 1659-60 at Rowley, Mass.

JAMES, brother of preceding, b. Wales, 1620; at Dover, N. H.; removed to Newbury, Mass., where he married, 1648.

SAMUEL, inhabitant Newbury, Mass., 1680.

ORME, ORMES

From French, signifying an elm-tree.

JOHN, inhabitant Salem, Mass., 1656.

RICHARD, resident Boston, Mass., 1682.

ORMSBY, ORMSBEE

From *orme*, an elm, and *by*, a town; name of place surrounded by elms.

EDWARD, son of Ann O. (a widow); at Boston, Mass., 1634, removed Dedham, Mass., 1639.

RICHARD, b. Eng. 1608, recorded at Saco, Maine, 1641; removed Salisbury, Mass.

ORRIS, ORIS, ORRICE

GEORGE, blacksmith, b. Eng. 1614, came to Boston, Mass., 1635.

ORTON

THOMAS, married, Windsor, Conn., 1641.

THOMAS, at Charlestown, Mass., 1642.

ORVIS, ORVICE

Urfhas in the Gaelic signified fair offspring. *Arvos*, Cornish British, a place on or near an entrenchment, from *ar* and *foss*.

GEORGE, married at Farmington, Conn., 1652.

OSBORN, OSBURN

From Saxon *hus*, a home, and *bearne*, a child; a family-child, an adopted child.

CHRISTOPHER, at Duxbury, Mass., 1638.

JAMES, married Springfield, Mass., 1646.

JEREMIAH, tanner, at New Haven, Conn., 1642.

JOHN, inhabitant Braintree, Mass., 1641.

JOHN, living at Weymouth, Mass., 1640.

JOHN, married at Windsor, Conn., 1645.

JOHN, resident Boston, Mass., 1670.

NICHOLAS, took oath of fidelity, Pemaquid, Maine, 1674.

RICHARD, brother of Jeremiah, one of first settlers Hingham, Mass., 1635; removed New Haven, Conn., before 1640, thence to Fairfield, Conn., 1653.

THOMAS, freeman Charlestown, Mass., 1648.

THOMAS, brother of Richard, at New Haven, Conn., 1639; removed East Hampton, L. I., 1650.

WILLIAM, merchant, of a Yorkshire family, came to Salem, Mass., 1630; removed Dorchester, Mass., 1642, afterwards Braintree, Mass., finally to Providence, R. I.

WILLIAM, inhabitant Braintree, Mass., 1650.

WILLIAM, died at New Haven, Conn., 1662.

OSGOOD

From the Saxon *os,* and a root word implicative of Deity.

Christopher, b. Eng. about 1600, settled at Ipswich, Mass., 1633-34.

JOHN, brother of preceding, b. Wherwill, Hampshire, Eng., 1595, settled Ipswich, Mass., removed to Newbury, Mass., where made freeman 1639, and before 1645 to Andover, Mass.

WILLIAM, carpenter and millwright, brother of preceding, b. Eng. 1605, proprietor at Salisbury, Mass., 1640.

OSLAND

HUMPHREY, married at Newton, Mass., 1667.

OTIS

From Greek *ωτος,* the genitive singular *ους,* the ear, a name given for quick hearing.

JOHN, son of Richard O., b. Glastonbury, County Somerset, Eng., 1581; settled Hingham, Mass., 1635; removed Weymouth, Mass., 1653.

RICHARD, son of Stephen O., an elder brother of preceding, b. Glastonbury, Eng., was at Boston, Mass., 1655, removed to Dover, N. H., 1656.

OTLEY

ABRAHAM, inhabitant Lynn, Mass., 1641.

ADAM, brother of preceding, at Lynn, Mass., 1641.

OTWAY

JOHN, owned land Lynn, Mass., 1657.

WILLIAM, at Taunton, Mass., 1654.

OVERMAN

THOMAS, freeman, Boston, Mass., 1671.

OVIAT, OVIETT

THOMAS, at Milford, Conn., 1665.

OWEN

From Celtic, signifying the good offspring. *Oen,* Welsh, and Gaelic *uam,* a lamb.

JOHN, b. Wales 1634, settled at Windsor, Conn., 1645.

SAMUEL, innkeeper, b. Wales, 1651, married at Springfield, Mass., 1681, removed to Brookfield, Mass., 1688.

THOMAS, member Artillery Company, Boston, Mass., 1639.

TIMOTHY, died Marblehead, Mass., 1670.

WILLIAM, freeman Braintree, Mass., 1657.

OXENBRIDGE

JOHN, doctor and minister, son of Daniel O., b. Daventry, Northamptonshire, Eng., 1606, came to Boston, Mass., 1669.

OXMAN

WILLIAM, b. Eng. 1633, at Salem, Mass., 1668.

PACEY, PACYE

NICHOLAS, was at Salem, Mass., 1639.

PACKARD

SAMUEL, came from Wymondham, County Norfolk, Eng., to Weymouth, Mass., and was at Hingham, Mass., 1638, and 1660 removed to Bridgewater, Mass.

PACKER

GEORGE, at Portsmouth, R. I., 1655.

JOHN, resident of New London, Conn., 1655.

THOMAS, living at Salem, Mass., before 1685.

THOMAS, physician, came from London, Eng., to Portsmouth, N. H., 1686.

PADDLEFORD, PADDLEFOOT

JONATHAN, married at Cambridge, Mass., 1652.

PADDOCK

From the Old English, a meadow, croft or field; an enclosure in a park.

ROBERT, settled at Plymouth, Mass., 1634; a proprietor 1638.

PADDY

WILLIAM, skinner, came from Southampton, Eng., to Boston, Mass., 1635. He was of the guild of skinners of London and a liveryman of the metropolis.

PADNER

EZEKIEL, inhabitant of Boston, Mass., 1668.

PAGE, PAIGE

A name given to youths between seven and fourteen years of age while receiving their education for Knighthood. English ancestor, John de Pagham 1151.

ABRAHAM, tailor, came from Great Baddow, County Essex, Eng., to Boston, Mass., 1654.

ANTHONY, was at Dover, N. H., 1662-66.

BENJAMIN, married at Haverhill, Mass., 1666.

CORNELIUS, brother of the preceding, resident Haverhill, Mass., 1677.

EDWARD, cooper, inhabitant Boston, Mass., before 1653.

GEORGE, married at Saco, Maine, 1653.

GEORGE, at Branford, Conn., 1667.

HENRY, freeman, Hampton, N. H., 1666.

ISAAC, married at Boston, Mass., 1653.

JOHN, b. Eng., 1586, came in Winthrop's fleet from Dedham, County Essex, Eng., settled Watertown, Mass.

JOHN, freeman, Dedham, Mass., 1640.

JOHN, was at Hingham, Mass., and signed petition to General Court 1645, removed to Haverhill, Mass., 1652. Afterwards at Saybrook, Conn., 1684.

JOSEPH, married, Haverhill, Mass., 1669.

NATHANIEL, was at Roxbury, Mass., 1685, removed Billerica, Mass., 1688, original purchaser at Spencer and Lancaster, Mass.

NICHOLS, brother of the preceding, came from Plymouth, Devonshire, Eng., to Boston, Mass., 1637.

ONESIPHORUS, married at Salisbury, Mass., 1664.

ROBERT, b. Ormsby, County Norfolk, Eng., 1604, came to Salem, Mass., 1637.

THOMAS, tailor, b. Eng. 1607, came to Boston, Mass., from parish of all Saints Staynings, Marklane, London, Eng.; was at Saco, Maine, 1636, probably removed to Casco, Maine.

PAINE

The name originated from the Latin word *pagamus,* the intercedent of which was *paugus* or village. Some authorities claim it is from French *paon,* a peacock, also from *payne,* a pagan, unbaptized; a rustic.

ANTHONY, received as inhabitant at Portsmouth, R. I., 1638.

EDWARD, at Lynn, Mass., 1637; Charlestown, Mass., 1638, removed to Exeter or Dover, N. H., 1643, returned to England, 1649.

JAMES, at Newport, R. I., 1660.

JOHN, died at Middletown, Conn., 1681.

MOSES, freeman, Braintree, Mass., 1641.

PHILIP, married, New Haven, Conn., 1679.

ROBERT, treasurer of Essex County, Mass., b. County Suffolk, Eng., 1601, freeman Ipswich, Mass., 1641.

SAMUEL, resident Boston, Mass., 1670.

STEPHEN, came from Great Ellingham, County Norfolk, Eng., to Hingham, Mass., 1638, removed Rehoboth, Mass., 1645.

STEPHEN, married, Dedham, Mass., 1652.

STEPHEN, freeman at Charlestown, or Malden, Mass., 1665.

THOMAS, weaver, b. Eng. 1587, came from Wrentham, County Suffolk, Eng., to Salem, Mass., 1637.

THOMAS, came to Plymouth, Mass., freeman Yarmouth, Mass., 1639, first deputy to the General Court from that town.

THOMAS, married, Boston, Mass., 1659.

THOMAS, swore allegiance York, Maine, 1680.

THOMAS, captain of a privateer, resident of Newport, R. I., 1683.

TOBIAS, came from Jamaica to Boston, Mass., where he married 1665.

WILLIAM, b. Eng. 1598, came from London, Eng., to Watertown, Mass., 1635, removed to Ipswich, Mass., died at Boston, Mass., 1660.

WILLIAM, shoemaker, b. Eng. 1620, came to Salem, Mass., 1635.

PAINTER

THOMAS, came to Hingham, Mass., 1637, and in 1644 to Providence, R. I., thence in 1655 to Newport, R. I. One of first settlers of Westerly, R. I., 1669.

WILLIAM, sea captain and merchant, died Charlestown, Mass., 1666.

PALFREY, PALFRY, PALFRAY

JOHN, came with his mother, who married George Willis, to Cambridge, Mass., where he married 1664.

PETER, was at Salem, Mass., 1626, freeman 1630, removed to Reading, Mass., about 1639.

PALGRAVE, PALSGRAVE

RICHARD, physician, came from Stepney, County Middlesex, Eng., to N. E. in Winthrop's fleet, settled at Charlestown, Mass.

PALMER

A pilgrim so called from the palm branch which he constantly carried as a pledge of his having been to the Holy Land.

ABRAHAM, merchant, came Salem, Mass., 1628, founder first church Charlestown, Mass., 1630.

EDWARD, was at Boston, Mass., 1639, removed to Hampton, N. H.

EPHRAIM, at Greenwich, R. I., 1672.

GEORGE, wine cooper, member artillery company, Boston, Mass., 1641, among freemen Warwick, R. I., 1655.

HENRY, freeman Newbury, Mass., 1642, removed Haverhill, Mass., Representative from that town 1667.

HENRY, at Wethersfield, Conn., 1642.

HENRY, took oath of fidelity at Pemaquid, Maine, 1674.

JOHN, mariner, b. Eng. about 1600, came to Hingham, Mass., 1635, removed Scituate, Mass., 1639.

JOHN, b. England 1610, came from Ipswich, Eng., to Charlestown, Mass., 1639.

JOHN, at Portsmouth, N. H., 1650, removed Hampton, N. H.

JOHN, carpenter, freeman Boston, Mass., 1640, removed Rowley, Mass., 1647.

JOHN, brother of Henry, was at Wethersfield, Conn., afterwards Fairfield, Conn., freeman of Conn., 1657.

JOHN, at Pemaquid, Maine, before 1674.

JOHN, married at Scarborough, Maine, 1676, removed to Boston, Mass., 1680.

JOHN, resident Falmouth, Maine, 1689.

MICHAEL, an original signer of the plantation covenant Branford, Conn., 1667.

NICHOLAS, early settler of Windsor, Conn., 1637.

RICHARD, married Salem, Mass., 1672.

SAMUEL, married Rehoboth, Mass., 1681.

SAMUEL, freeman Rowley, Mass., 1684, afterwards at Salem, Mass.

THOMAS, resident Rowley, Mass., 1643.

THOMAS, merchant, one of the founders Brattle Street Church, Boston, Mass.

TIMOTHY, living at Suffield, Conn., 1676.

WALTER, brother of Abraham, came from Nottinghamshire, Eng., to Charlestown, Mass., 1629, removed Rehoboth, Mass., 1646, and to Stonington, Conn., 1653.

WILLIAM, came to Plymouth, Mass., 1621, removed Duxbury, Mass., 1627.

WILLIAM, landowner at Great Ormsby, County Norfolk, Eng., came to Watertown, Mass., 1636, removed to Newbury, Mass., 1637, and to Hampton, N. H., 1638.

PALMERLY, PARMELEE

JOHN, b. Eng. 1615, came to N. E. 1635, at Guilford, Conn., 1639, New Haven, Conn., 1659.

PALMES

EDWARD, known as major, merchant at New Haven, Conn., 1659, removed next year New London, Conn.

WILLIAM, married Salem, Mass.

PALMETER

NATHANIEL, at Killingworth, Conn., 1667.

PANTRY, PANTREE

WILLIAM, came to Cambridge, Mass., 1634, one of original proprietors, Hartford, Conn., 1636.

PAPILLANS, PAPILLON

PETER, sea captain, resided at Boston, Mass., 1679.

PARD

SAMUEL, inhabitant Boston, Mass., 1671.

PARDEE

GEORGE, tailor and schoolmaster, of French Huguenot ancestry, b. Eng. 1619, came to New Haven, Conn., 1638.

PARDON

WILLIAM, freeman of Mass., 1645.

PARENTS

JOHN, settled Haddam, Conn., 1662.

PARIS, PARRIS

CHRISTOPHER, inhabitant Boston, Mass., 1649.

JOHN, married, Braintree, Mass., 1664.

SAMUEL, minister, son of Thomas P. of London, Eng., freeman Boston, Mass., 1638, minister at Salem, Mass., now Danvers, Mass., 1689, afterwards at Stow, Watertown, Concord and Dunstable, Mass.

SAMUEL, resident Boston, Mass., 1681.

THOMAS, brother of the preceding, was at Boston, Mass., 1686.

PARISH

THOMAS, physician, b. Eng. 1613, came to Cambridge, Mass., 1635, returned to Eng.

PARK, PARKE, PARKS

A piece of ground inclosed and stocked with deer and other beasts of chase.

EDWARD, at Guilford, Conn., 1685.

JACOB, was at Concord, Mass., 1657, afterwards at Rowley, Mass.

RICHARD, was proprietor at Cambridge, Mass., now Lexington, Mass., 1636.

ROBERT, b. Preston, Eng., 1580, came to Boston, Mass., 1630, settled at Wethersfield, Conn., 1639, removed New London, Conn., 1649, and 1658 to Stonington, Conn.

PARKER

The name is derived from the Latin word *parcarius,* meaning parkkeeper or shepherd.

ABRAHAM, b. Marlborough, Wiltshire, Eng., about 1612, married at Woburn, Mass., 1644, removed Chelmsford, Mass., 1653.

AZRIKAM, mariner, at Boston, Mass., 1662.

BASIL, recorder of the Province, was at York, Maine, 1649, died in 1651.

EDMUND, married Roxbury, Mass., 1647.

EDWARD, settled at New Haven, Conn., 1644.

ELISHA, married Barnstable, Mass., 1657.

GEORGE, carpenter, b. Eng. 1612, came to N. E. 1635, at Portsmouth, N. H., 1638.

JACOB, resident Chelmsford, Mass., 1654.

JACOB, married Roxbury, Mass., 1687.

JAMES, minister and merchant, came to Dorchester, Mass., 1630, removed to Weymouth, Mass., where he was representative 1639-43, thence to Portsmouth, N. H., finally to Barbadoes, died Boston, Mass., 1666.

JAMES, b. Eng. 1618, came to N. E. 1640, taxpayer Woburn, Mass., 1645, a grantee of Billerica, Mass., 1654, removed Chelmsford, Mass., 1658, and to Groton, Mass., 1660.

JOHN, carpenter, came from Marlborough, Wiltshire, Eng., to Boston, Mass., 1635, afterwards at Muddy River now Brookline, Mass.

JOHN, at Saco, Maine, 1636, purchased Parker's Island, now Georgetown, Maine, 1650.

JOHN, inhabitant Hingham, Mass., 1636, afterwards removed Taunton, Mass.

JOHN, shoemaker, was at Boston, Mass., 1644.

JOHN, at Woburn, Mass., 1653, removed to Billerica, Mass., where he was the first town clerk.

JOHN, freeman Cambridge, Mass., 1654.

JOHN, freeman York, Maine, 1652.

JOHN, freeman Newport, R. I., 1655.

JOSEPH, tanner, owner of corn mill, b. Eng., 1614, came from Rumsey, Hants, Eng., in 1638, to Newbury, Mass., removed Andover, Mass., 1645.

JOSEPH, married at Chelmsford, Mass., 1655.

MATTHEW, died Boston, Mass., 1652.

NATHAN, baker, brother of first Joseph, b. Eng. 1618, came to Newbury, Mass., 1638, removed Andover, Mass., 1645.

NICHOLAS, came to Roxbury, Mass., 1633.

RALPH, was at Gloucester, Mass., 1647, removed New London, Conn., 1651.

RICHARD, merchant, at Boston, Mass., 1638.

ROBERT, butcher, came from Wiolpit near Bury St. Edmunds, County Suffolk, Eng., to Boston, Mass., 1634.

ROBERT, married Barnstable, Mass., 1657.

SAMUEL, at Hingham, Mass., 1638, owned land in Weymouth, Mass., 1682.

SAMUEL, married Dedham, Mass., 1657.

THOMAS, minister, only son Rev. Robert, b. Eng. 1595, came to Newbury, Mass., 1634, preached Ipswich, Mass., a year; returned Newbury, Mass., where he died a bachelor 1677.

THOMAS, b. Eng. 1605, settled Lynn, Mass., 1635, made freeman 1637, removed in that year Reading, Mass.

WILLIAM, original proprietor Hartford, Conn., 1636, removed Saybrook, Conn.

WILLIAM, b. Eng. 1600, elder brother of John of Taunton, Mass., at Taunton, Mass., 1643.

WILLIAM, at Watertown, Mass., 1640.

WILLIAM, married at Scituate, Mass., 1639.

PARKHURST, PARKIS

GEORGE, came from Ipswich, County Suffolk, Eng., 1635, freeman Watertown, Mass., 1643, removed Boston, Mass., 1645.

PARKINSON

WILLIAM, at Dover, N. H., 1684.

PARKMAN

Derivation same as Parker.

ELIAS, mariner, settled at Dorchester, Mass., 1633, freeman 1635, removed to Windsor, Conn., finally to Boston, Mass., 1648.

PARMENTER, PARMITER

Trade name signifying tailor. In the Hundred Rolls, spelt in Latin *William Parmuntauas.*

BENJAMIN, granted land at Salem, Mass., 1637.

JAMES, at Hull, Mass., 1669.

JOHN, of French Huguenot descent, b. Eng. 1588, settled Roxbury, Mass., removed to Watertown, Mass., 1638, one of first proprietors of Sudbury, Mass., 1639.

JOHN, housewright, resident Boston, Mass., 1667.

ROBERT, freeman Braintree, Mass., 1650.

PARNELL

From the Italian word *Petronilla,* pretty stone. A wanton, immodest girl.

JOHN, resident Dover, N. H., 1666-68.

THOMAS, swore fidelity to Mass. at Pemaquid, Maine.

PARR

ABEL, freeman Boston, Mass., 1641.

SAMUEL, resident, Salem, Mass., 1665.

PARRIS

THOMAS, came to L. I., N. Y., 1663, later removed to Boston, Mass., afterwards to Pembroke, Mass.

PARROTT, PAROTE, PARRETT

From *Peraidd,* Wales, the sweet or delicious river now the *Dee.*

FRANCIS, freeman Rowley, Mass., 1640; town clerk fourteen years.

JOHN, b. Eng. 1675, settled Stratford, Conn., 1700.

PARSONS

The first founder of this family was probably a clerical character. The word is derived from the Latin *Persona,* the person who takes care of the souls of his parishioners. Walter Parsons lived at Mulso, Ireland, 1290.

BENJAMIN, came from Torrington, Devonshire, Eng., with his elder brother Cornet Joseph P. to Boston, Mass., 1635, removed Springfield, Mass., 1639.

GEORGE, a resident Boston, Mass., 1667.

Hugh, married Springfield, Mass., 1645.

Jeffrey, born Ashprington, Devonshire, Eng., 1631, settled at Gloucester, Mass., 1654.

Joseph, known as Cornet Joseph, elder brother of Benjamin, b. Eng. 1613, settled at Boston, Mass., 1635, removed to Springfield, Mass., 1645, Northampton, Mass., 1655.

Joseph, resident Boston, Mass., 1685.

Mark, living Kennebeck, Maine, 1665.

Philip, one first settlers Enfield, Conn.

Richard, freeman Windsor, Conn., 1640.

Robert, freeman Lynn, Mass., 1639.

Thomas, soldier Pequot War, 1637, resided Windsor, Conn.

William, joiner, came from Southampton, Eng., 1635, to Boston, Mass.

PARTRIDGE.

Alexander, came to Boston, Mass., 1645; removed R. I., living Newport, 1655.

George, brother Rev. Ralph, resident Duxbury, Mass., 1636, proprietor Bridgewater, Mass., 1645, original proprietor Middleboro, Mass., 1662.

John, brother William, b. Navesbock, Eng., 1620, married Medford, Mass., 1655, later removed Dedham, Mass.

Nathaniel, tailor, freeman Boston, Mass., 1643.

Oliver, member of church, Dorchester, Mass., 1636.

Ralph, first minister Duxbury, Mass., came from Sutton, County Kent, Eng., to Boston, Mass., 1636.

William, son of John P. of Olney, County of Bucks, Eng., freeman Salisbury, Mass., 1639.

William, came from Berwick on Tweed, Eng., married Hartford, Conn., 1644.

William, at Medfield, Mass., 1649, freeman 1653.

PASCO

Hugh, resident Salem, Mass., 1668.

John, at Dorchester, Mass., 1685.

PASMORE, PASMER, PASMERE

Bartholomew, resident Boston, Mass., 1641.

James, located Concord, Mass., 1642.

Richard, at Ipswich, Mass., 1674.

William, living Boston, Mass., 1674.

PATCH

Edmund, farmer, bapt. 1597, son of Nicholas P. of the Parish Petherton, Somerset, Eng.; settled Salem, Mass., 1637, one founders of Beverly, Mass.

James, living on Beverly side, Salem, Mass., 1646.

John, brother of preceding, freeman Beverly side, Salem, Mass., 1678.

Nicholas, brother of Edmund, granted land Salem, Mass., 1639, one founders of Church Beverly, Mass., 1667.

William, at Scituate, Mass., 1640.

PATCHIN, PATCHING

Joseph, married Roxbury, Mass., 1642, removed Fairfield, Conn., 1666.

PATEFIELD, PEATFIELD

John, resident Charlestown, Mass., 1654.

PATESHALL, PATTESHALL, PADDESHALL

Edmund, swore fidelity to Mass.; Pemaquid, Maine, 1674.

Richard, resident Boston, Mass., 1665.

Richard, mariner, lived Boston, Mass., died Pemaquid, Maine, 1701.

Robert, merchant, Boston, Mass., 1652, magistrate temporary, County Devonshire, Maine, killed by Indians, Pemaquid, Maine, 1689.

PATIE, PATTEE, PETTY, PATTY

Sir William Pattee, English ancestor.

Peter, b. Lansdowne, Eng., 1648, settled at Virginia 1669, located Haverhill, Mass., 1676-77.

PATRICK

From the Latin *Patricius,* noble, a senator, the name of the tutelary saint of Ireland.

Daniel, came in Winthrop's fleet, freeman Watertown, Mass., 1631, removed to Conn., killed at Stamford, Conn., 1643.

William, resident Hartford, Conn., 1645.

PATTEN

Richard P., English ancestor, living near Chelmsford, County Essex, Eng., 1119.

Nathaniel, at Dorchester, Mass., 1640, left no issue.

Thomas, resident Salem, Mass., 1643.

Thomas, son of John, came from Bristol, Eng., to Boston, Mass., to settle his brother Nathaniel's estate 1675, returned to Eng.

William, settled Cambridge, Mass., 1636.

PATTERSON, PATTISON

Scotch ancestry, the son of Patrick.

Andrew, came from Hamilton, Scotland, to Perth Amboy, N. J., finally to Stratford, Conn.

Edward, b. Eng. 1602, at New Haven, Conn., 1639.

Edward, carpenter, at Rehoboth, Mass., 1643, removed Hingham, Mass., 1652, finally to Dover, N. H., 1657.

JAMES, came from London, Eng., 1651, one of the followers in Scotland of Charles II, received land Billerica, Mass., freeman 1680.

PETER, married Saybrook, Conn., 1678.

WILLIAM, merchant, at Boston, Mass., 1665.

PATTON

WILLIAM, first mentioned Cambridge, Mass., 1635.

PAUL

Signifies little, small, Latin *Paulus.*

BENJAMIN, at New Haven, Conn., 1639.

DANIEL, shipbuilder, brother of preceding, came from Ipswich, Eng., to Ipswich, Mass., 1640, removed Kittery, Maine, 1648.

JOHN, married Malden, Mass., 1657.

RICHARD, soldier, came Boston, Mass., 1636, a proprietor Taunton, Mass., 1667.

SAMUEL, married Dorchester, Mass., 1667.

STEPHEN, at Kittery, Maine, 1682.

WILLIAM, manufacturer, weaver, b. Scotland 1624, settled Taunton, Mass., 1643.

PAYSON

EDWARD, b. County Norfolk, Eng., freeman Roxbury, Mass., 1640.

GILES, b. Eng. 1609, brother of preceding, came from County Essex, Eng.; freeman Roxbury, Mass., 1637, removed Dorchester, Mass.

PAYTON

BEZALIEL, mariner, married at Boston, Mass., 1642.

ROBERT, at Lynn, Mass., 1639.

PEABODY, PAYBODY, PABODIE

The name is said to have originated in the year 61 during the reign of Nero. Queen Boadicea was located at Icena, Britain. She opposed the Romans in their invasion of the country and with her son Boadie, took refuge in the craggy heights of Wales. *Boadie* among the Cambri or Britons signifies a man or a great man, and *Pea* signifies a large hill, a mountain from which Boadie came to be called Peabodie or the *Mountain Man* which became the name of the tribe. In some branches of the family *Boadie* became anglicized to Mann, and *Pea* to hill.

JOHN, came to N. E. with his sons Francis and William 1635, settled at Plymouth, Mass., removed Duxbury, Mass., one of the original proprietors Bridgewater, Mass.

WILLIAM, at Little Compton, R. I., where he died in his 80th year 1744; his descendants spelt their name Pabodie.

PEACH

JOHN, b. 1612, was at Salem, or Marblehead, Mass., 1648-79.

PEACHE, PEACHY

THOMAS, Charlestown, Mass., 1678.

PEACOCK

Taken from the name of the well-known fowl; pea contracted from Latin *pavo,* Saxon *pawa,* French *paon;* a name given for fondness of display

JOHN, at New Haven, Conn., 1638, removed next year Milford, Conn., removed Stratford, Conn., 1650, where he died 1670.

RICHARD, glazier, freeman Roxbury, Mass., 1639.

WILLIAM, came as youth of 12 years in 1635 to N. E., resident Roxbury, Mass., 1652.

PEAK

CHRISTOPHER, freeman Roxbury, Mass., 1635.

JOHN, inhabitant Stratford, Conn., 1650.

WILLIAM, married Scituate, Mass., 1650, where he settled 1643.

WILLIAM, resident New London, Conn., 1660.

PEAKEN

JOHN, died New Haven, Conn., 1658.

PEALE

DANIEL, inhabitant Marblehead, Mass., 1651.

PEARCE, see Pierce

PEARSON, see Pierson

PEASE

The name is of German origin, the form being *Pies* or *Pees,* and authorities give its derivation from the pea-plant.

HENRY, came to Boston in Winthrop's fleet 1630, died 1648.

JOHN, b. Eng. 1607, came from Great Baddow, County Essex, England, to Salem, Mass., 1634; granted land Martha's Vineyard 1646, proprietor Norwich, Conn., 1659.

ROBERT, brother of preceding, son of Robert P. came with his brother to Boston, Mass., 1634, settled at Salem, Mass., 1637.

SAMUEL, commander of ship against pirates, was at Boston, Mass.; mortally wounded in Martha's Vineyard Sound 1689.

PEASLEE

JOSEPH, lay preacher and farmer, freeman Newbury, Mass., 1642, later removed Haverhill 1645, and made freeman what is now Amesbury, Mass., 1656.

PEAT

JOHN, husbandman, b. 1597, came from Duffield parish, Derbyshire, Eng., settled in Strafford, Conn., where he died 1678.

PECK

An English family of antiquity, the name being from medieval English word *pek* "the hul of the pek" meaning the hill of the peak in Derbyshire, another form of the name is *Peak*. The family first known in Hesden and Wakefield, Yorkshire; afterwards removed to Beecles, County Suffolk. The first authentic records mention John del Pek at London 1273.

HENRY, inhabitant New Haven, Conn., 1638.

JOSEPH, son of Robert P., XXI generation from John del Pek, bapt. 1587, came from Beecles, County Suffolk, to Hingham, Mass., 1638, removed Rehoboth, Mass., 1645.

JOSEPH, brother of Henry, settled New Haven, Conn., 1643, removed Milford, Conn., 1649.

PAUL, b. County Essex, Eng., 1608, came to Boston, Mass., 1635, the following year removed Hartford, Conn.

RICHARD, b. Eng. 1602, came from London, Eng., to Boston, Mass., 1635, afterwards Rehoboth, Mass.

ROBERT, minister, brother of Joseph, came from Hingham, County Norfolk, Eng., to Hingham, Mass., 1638.

THOMAS, shipwright, at Boston, Mass., 1652.

WILLIAM, merchant, b. Eng. 1601, resident of New Haven, Conn., 1639.

PECKER

JAMES, b. Eng. 1622, inhabitant Charlestown, Mass., 1658, removed Haverhill, Mass., 1663, afterwards Boston, Mass., 1682.

PECKHAM, PECKUM

JOHN, first on record Newport, R. I., 1638.

PEDRICK

JOHN, early settler Marblehead, Mass., first record 1674.

PEEK

GEORGE, at Marblehead, Mass., 1674.

PELHAM

From the lordship of Pelham in Hertfordshire, Eng., either from *pede,* a tower, castle; or from *pool,* a small lake, and *ham,* a village.

HERBERT, lawyer, came from Lincolnshire, Eng., to Cambridge, Mass., 1638, granted land Salisbury, Mass., 1644, first treasurer Harvard College 1643, returned to England 1649. No male issue; his daughter Penelope married Governor Josiah Winslow.

JOHN, brother of preceding, b. Eng. 1615, came from London, Eng., 1635, to Boston, Mass.

WILLIAM, brother of preceding, freeman Boston, Mass., 1630, afterwards Sudbury, Mass.; returned to England.

PELL

In the Welsh signifies far off, at a distance.

JOSEPH, butcher, freeman Lynn, Mass., 1639, died Boston, Mass., 1650.

THOMAS, tailor, b. Eng. 1613, came to New Haven, Conn., 1635, removed Fairfield, Conn., where he was made freeman 1662.

WILLIAM, tallow chandler, freeman Boston, Mass., 1635.

PELLETT, PELLATE

From the French *pelletier,* a furrier, or skinner.

THOMAS, farmer, settled Concord, Mass.. 1660.

PELT

JOHN, b. Duffield parish, Eng., 1597, settled Stratford, Conn., 1635, where he died 1678.

PELTON

This was a commonplace name before the Norman Conquest. William The Conqueror according to the Domesday Book 1086, granted Peldon or Pelton Manor to William the Deacon; later the family took the name from the manor. The Pelton family lived in Northamptonshire, Wiltshire, Somersetshire and Buckshire.

JOHN, engaged in fishing business, came to Boston, Mass., 1630, removed Dorchester, Mass., 1635.

PEMBER

THOMAS, resided New London, Conn., 1686.

PEMBERTON

JAMES, came in Winthrop's fleet, freeman Charlestown, Mass., 1630.

JAMES, freeman Newbury, Mass., 1646, removed Boston, Mass., 1652.

JOHN, freeman Boston, Mass., 1634, removed Newbury, Mass.

PEMBROKE

ELKANAH, one founders Brattle street Church, Boston, Mass., was at Dedham, Mass., 1643.

PENDALL

WILLIAM, shipwright, New London, Conn., 1676.

PENDLETON

The summit of a hill, from Gaelic *pendle,* the summit, and *dun,* a hill. *Pendalton,* the town at the head of the valley.

BRYAN or BRIAN, freeman Watertown, Mass., 1634, removed Sudbury, Mass., 1638, thence to Ipswich, Mass.; 1676 was at Portsmouth, N. H.

CALEB, resident Westerly, R. I., 1679.

PENFIELD

SAMUEL, married Lynn, Mass., 1650.

THOMAS, at Rehoboth, Mass., 1681.

WILLIAM, inhabitant Middletown, Conn., 1663.

PENGILLY

JOHN, freeman Ipswich, Mass., 1678, removed to Suffield, Conn., 1679.

PENHALLOW

SAMUEL, chief justice Supreme Court, b. St. Mabyn near Bodmin in Cornwall, Eng., 1665, arrived Charlestown, Mass., 1686; married Portsmouth, N H., 1687.

PENLEY

SAMSON, living Falmouth, Maine, 1658.

PENN

From the Cornish British, the top of a hill, the head.

JAMES, came with Winthrop 1630, freeman Boston, Mass., 1630.

WILLIAM, passenger in Winthrop's fleet 1630, settled Braintree, Mass., in his later life resided Boston, Mass.

PENNELL

WALTER, freeman Saco, Maine, 1653.

PENNIMAN, PENNYMAN

From the Welsh *Pen-y-mon,* the top of the mountain.

JAMES, b. Eng. 1600, came Boston, Mass., 1631, removed Braintree, Mass., 1638.

PENNINGTON

Derived from the manor of Pennington, in Lancashire, England, anciently written *Penitone,* in the Domesday Book *Pennegetum.*

EPHRAIM, settled New Haven, Conn., 1643.

PENNY, PINNY

The top of a mountain or hill. A mountain in Spain is called by the inhabitants *La Penna* "de los Enamorados" or the Lovers' Rock. The word has the same meaning as the English *pinnacle.*

HENRY, secretary Province of New Hampshire 1683.

ROBERT, granted land Salem, Mass., 1638.

THOMAS, at Gloucester, Mass., 1652.

PENOYER, PENNYER

ROBERT, b. Eng. 1614, came Boston, Mass., 1635, afterwards Stamford, Conn.

PENTICUS

JOHN, inhabitant Charlestown, Mass., 1638.

PENWELL

WALTER, died Saco, Maine, 1683.

PEPPER

FRANCIS, at Springfield, Mass., 1645, no issue.

RICHARD, b. Eng. 1607, came from Ipswich, Eng., to Roxbury, Mass., 1634; no issue.

ROBERT, brother of preceding, married Roxbury, Mass., 1643.

PEPPERELL

WILLIAM, fisherman, came from Devonshire, Eng., to Isle of Shoals, N. H., 1634, removed to Kittery, Maine, 1680. Father of Sir William Pepperell.

PEPYS

RICHARD, came from Cottenham, Cambridgeshire, to Boston, Mass., 1642.

PERCIVAL

JAMES, at Sandwich, Mass., 1675, removed to East Haddam, Conn., 1706.

PERCY, PEERCE, PRECEY, PERCIE

The ancestry of this family is traced to Manfield, a Danish chieftain; one who assisted in the subjugation of Normandy 912. RICHARD, was standard bearer of Richard III at Battle of Bosworth 1485 and founded Pearce Hall in Yorkshire, England. The renowned family of *Percy* of Northumberland, Eng., derived their name from Percy Forest in the Province of Maen, Normandy, whence they came with William the Conqueror to England; one bearing the name was commander of his fleet. The name signifies a stony place from *pierre.* It may signify a hunting place, from *pirren,* Teutonic, to hunt; *percer,* French, to penetrate, to force one's way.

JOHN, married Gloucester, Mass., 1673.

MARMADUKE, tailor, came from Sandwich, County Kent, Eng., to Salem, Mass., 1637.

RICHARD, son of Richard P., XXIst generation from Manfied, b. Eng. 1615. On record Portsmouth, R. I., 1654.

ROBERT, inhabitant New London, Conn., 1678.

PERHAM, PERAM

ABRAHAM, resident Rehoboth, Mass., 1679.

JOHN, inhabitant Rehoboth, Mass., 1643, removed Chelmsford, Mass., 1664.

PERIGO

ROBERT, at Saybrook, Conn., 1665.

PERIT

BENJAMIN, resident Stratford, Conn., 1669.

PERKINS

From *Peir* or *Peter* and the patronymic or diminutive termination *ins*—little Peter or the son of Peter. Pierre de Morlaix sometimes written Peter Morley alias Perkins was high steward of the estates of Sir Hugo Despencer 1380-81. The family was seated at Upton, County Berks, Eng.

ABRAHAM, b. Eng. 1611, settled Hampton, N. H., 1640.

EDMUND, married Boston, Mass., 1678.

ISAAC, brother of Abraham, XI generation from Pierre de Morlaix, bapt. Hillmorton, Warwickshire, Eng., 1611. Came to N. E. 1630-34, located Ipswich, Massachusetts 1637, removed Hampton, N. H., 1638.

JOHN, b. Newent Gloucestershire, Eng., 1590, came with Roger Williams to Boston, Mass., 1631, removed Ipswich, Mass., 1633.

JOHN, resident New Haven, Conn., 1688.

JONATHAN, inhabitant Norwalk, Conn., 1671-77.

LUKE, living Charlestown, Mass., 1666.

THOMAS, born Eng. about 1600, was at Dover, N. H., 1665.

WILLIAM, minister, son William P. a merchant tailor of London, Eng., b. Eng. 1607, came Boston, Mass., 1632, removed Weymouth, Mass., 1643, preached Gloucester, Mass., 1651-55, second minister Topsfield, Mass.

WILLIAM, took oath of allegiance Dover, N. H., 1662.

PERLEY

ALLAN or ALLEN, b. Wales 1608, came from London, Eng., to Ipswich, Mass., 1635.

PERRIN, PERRAN, PERING

HENRY, at Newport, R. I., 1656, removed to Long Island.

JOHN, b. Eng. 1614, settled Braintree, Mass., 1635, removed Rehoboth, Mass.

PERRY, PURY

If not synonymous with Parry, it is from the French word *Pierre,* a stone signifying a stony place abounding in rocks.

ANTHONY, Welsh descent, resident Rehoboth, Mass., 1658-78.

ARTHUR, tailor, resident Boston, Mass., 1638.

EDWARD, Quaker, b. Devonshire, Eng., about 1630, came to Plymouth, Mass., settled at Sandwich, Mass., where he married 1653.

EZRA, brother of preceding, b. Eng. 1625, married Sandwich, Mass., 1652.

FRANCIS, wheelwright, b. Eng. about 1608, came Salem, Mass., 1631.

ISAAC, freeman Boston, Mass., 1631.

JOHN, brother of preceding, came to Roxbury, Mass., 1632.

JOHN, resident Taunton, Mass., 1643.

JOHN, proprietor New Haven, 1685.

JOHN, son Rev. John P., Farnborough, Eng., b. 1613, settled Watertown, Mass., 1666.

JOSEPH, resident Rehoboth, Mass., 1651.

NATHANIEL, married Rehoboth, Mass., 1683.

RICHARD, first record New Haven, Conn., 1640-47.

THOMAS, inhabitant Ipswich, Mass., 1648.

THOMAS, married Scituate, Mass., 1643.

WILLIAM, brother of preceding, at Scituate, Mass., 1638, removed Watertown, Mass., 1640.

PETERS

ANDREW, distiller, married Boston, Mass., 1659, removed Ipswich, Mass., 1665, thence Andover, Mass.

HUGH, fourth minister Salem, Mass., b. parish of St. Ewe, town Fowey, Cornwall, 1599, came to N. E. 1635.

THOMAS, minister, brother of preceding, came to N. E. 1644, to Saybrook, Conn., afterwards New London, Conn.

PETERSON

CORNELIUS, inhabitant Boston, Mass., 1685.

JOHN, resided Duxbury, Mass., 1670.

PETTEE

JOSEPH, located Weymouth, Mass., 1681.

PETTELL

ANTHONY, fisherman, came from Isle of Guernsey, Eng., to Marblehead, Mass., 1653.

PETTENGELL, PATTENGGELL

RICHARD, came from Staffordshire, Eng., to Salem, Mass., freeman 1641, was at Wenham, Mass., finally located Newbury, Mass.

PETTIBONE

JOHN, Welsh descent, freeman Windsor, Conn., 1658, one first settlers Simsbury, Conn., 1669-70.

PETTIFORD, PETFORD, PITTFORD

PETER, at Salem, Mass., 1641, removed Marblehead, Mass., 1648.

PETTIT, PETTES

GILBERT, at Salem, Mass., 1668.

JOHN, living Roxbury, Mass., 1639, removed to Stamford, Conn., or L. I.

THOMAS, at Exeter, N. H., 1639, signed original covenant 1647.

PETTY

JOHN, was at Windsor, Conn., afterwards Springfield, Mass., married at Boston, Mass., 1662.

PETER, resident Haverhill, Mass., 1680.

PETTYGOOD

PETER, at Marblehead, Mass., 1641.

RICHARD, resident Ipswich, Mass., 1641.

PEVERLY

JOHN, sent over by Mason to Portsmouth, N. H., 1631.

PHELPS

The name may come from the Danish *Hvalp*: Swedish *Valp*, a whelp. Ancient family of Tewksbury, Gloucestershire, Eng.; the earliest English ancestor there on record is James Phelps 1520.

CHRISTOPHER, married Salem, Mass., 1658.

EDWARD, resident Newbury, Mass., removed Andover, Mass.

GEORGE, b. Tewsbury, Eng., about 1606. came to Dorchester, Mass., 1630, freeman 1635, removed Windsor, Conn., about this date.

HENRY, brother of Edward, came Salem, Mass., 1634.

JOHN, resident Charlestown, Mass., 1659.

WILLIAM, bapt. Tewksbury, Eng., 1599, landed Hull, Mass., 1630, settled Dorchester, Mass. One of the original settlers Windsor, Conn., 1636.

PHENIX, PHOENIX

ALEXANDER, Scotch ancestry, at Wickford, R. I., 1652.

PHETTEPHACE

Family traced to Fetteplace, the Norman who came to England with William the Conqueror.

PHILIP, inhabitant Portsmouth, R. I., 1681.

PHILBRICK, PHILBROOK

ROBERT, Ipswich, Mass., 1637.

THOMAS, shipmaster, came from Lincolnshire to Watertown, Mass., 1636, removed Hampton, N. H., 1651.

PHILIP, PHILLIPS

The name signifies in Greek a lover of horses, being the combination of two words *Philos* and *Hippos*.

ANDREW, resident Charlestown, Mass., 1657.

BENJAMIN, married Marshfield, Mass., 1682.

CHARLES, resident Lynn, Mass., 1656.

GEORGE, son of Christopher P. of Rainham, St. Martins near Rougham in Hundred of Gallow, County Norfolk, Eng., first minister Watertown, Mass., b. Norfolk, Eng., 1593, came to N. E. in Winthrop's fleet, died 1644.

GEORGE, freeman Dorchester, Mass., 1631, removed Windsor, Conn., 1636.

HENRY, butcher, freeman Dedham, Mass., 1639, removed Boston, Mass.

JOHN, died Portsmouth, N. H., 1642.

JOHN, baker, came N. E. 1630, settled Dorchester, Mass., removed Boston, Mass., 1650.

JOHN, came Plymouth, Mass., 1630, purchased land Duxbury, Mass., 1639, removed to Marshfield, Mass.

JOHN, inhabitant Wenham, Mass., 1647.

JOHN, native of Wales, b. 1607, was at Casco, Maine, 1642, removed Kittery, Maine, where he was living 1684.

JOHN, master mariner, brother of Henry, married at Charlestown, Mass., 1655.

JOSEPH, inhabitant Boston, 1684.

MARTIN, living Medfield, Mass., 1664.

MICHAEL, settled Newport, R. I., where he was living 1668.

NICHOLAS, butcher, brother of Henry, settled Dedham, Mass., 1636, removed in later life to Weymouth, Mass.

NICHOLAS, married, Boston, Mass., 1651.

SAMUEL, married, Taunton, Mass., 1676.

SAMUEL, bookseller, resident Boston, Mass., 1681.

THOMAS, took oath of fidelity, Pemaquid, Maine, 1674.

WALTER, b. Eng. 1619, was at Wiscasset, Maine, 1661, resident Salem, 1689.

WILLIAM, among first purchasers Taunton, Mass., 1637.

WILLIAM, inhabitant Hartford, Conn., 1639.

WILLIAM, freeman Charlestown, Mass., 1640.

WILLIAM, mariner, resident Boston, Mass., 1650.

ZACHARIAH, member artillery company Boston, Mass., 1660.

PHILPOT

THOMAS, saltmaker, resident Boston, Mass., 1642.

PHINNEY, FINNEY, FENNYE

ISAAC, resident Medfield, Mass., 1657.

JOHN, came Plymouth, Mass., 1638, removed Barnstable, Mass., 1650.

ROBERT, brother of preceding, resident Plymouth, Mass., 1650.

PHIPPEN, FIPPEN, FITZPEN

DAVID, came from Weymouth or Melcombe Regis, Dorsetshire, England, to Hingham, Mass., 1635.

PHIPS, PHIPPS

JAMES, gunsmith, founded Phippsburg, Maine, near mouth Kennebec river before 1649, father Sir William Phipps.

SOLOMON, carpenter, at Charlestown, Mass., 1641.

PICKARD, PICKETT

JOHN, admitted church Salem, Mass., 1649, afterwards removed Rowley, Mass.

PICKERAM, PICKRAM

GEORGE, came Watertown, Mass., with his father John P., who died 1630; member of church 1646.

PICKERING

A market town of North Yorkshire, Eng. In the reign of Edward VI, Gilbert Pickering purchased the manor of Tichmersh.

JOHN, carpenter, b. Eng. 1615, came from Newgate, in Coventry, Warwickshire, Eng., to Ipswich, Mass., 1634, removed Salem, Mass., 1637.

JOHN, was at Cambridge, Mass., 1630, removed Portsmouth, N. H., 1633.

PICKETT, PIGGOTT

From the French *Riote,* pitted with small-pox, spotted in the face.

CHRISTOPHER, married in what is now Brookline, Mass., 1647.

JOHN, came Salem, Mass., 1648, removed two years later Rowley, Mass., in 1660 to Stratford, Conn.

JOHN, married New London, Conn., before 1656.

PICKLES

JONAS, married Scituate, Mass., 1657.

PICKMAN

BENJAMIN, son Nathaniel P. of Bristol, Eng., bapt. Lewen's Mead, Bristol, Eng., 1645, married Salem, Mass., 1667.

NATHANIEL, came from Bristol, Eng., Salem, Mass., 1654.

PICKTON

THOMAS, granted land on Beverly side Salem, Mass., 1639.

PICKWORTH

AMARIAH, resident Salem, Mass.

JOHN, came to Plymouth, Mass., 1631, at Salem, Mass., 1637, granted land New London, Conn., 1651, but forfeited it for non-residence.

PIDCOCK, PIDCOKE

GEORGE, married Scituate, Mass., 1640.

PIERCE, PEIRCE, PEARCE

The same as Percy, which see. Two brothers William and Serio de Percy came to England with William the Conqueror. The male issue became extinct in the reign of Henry II when the female descendant, Agnes de Perci, married Josceline, son of Duke Louvain with agreement he was to assume the name of Percy.

ABRAHAM, shared in divide of cattle Plymouth, Mass., 1629, removed Duxbury, Mass., 1643, one purchasers of Bridgewater, Mass., 1645.

AZERIKAM or AZIAKIM, came from Rehoboth or Swanzey, Mass., to Warwick, R. I.

DANIEL, b. Eng. 1611, blacksmith, came from Ipswich, County Suffolk, Eng., to Watertown, Mass., 1634, removed Newbury, Mass., 1638.

EDWARD, weaver, b. Norwich, County Norfolk, 1588, settled Watertown, Mass., 1638.

GEORGE, smith, married at Boston, Mass., before 1660.

GEORGE, married, Portsmouth, R. I., 1687.

GILES, inhabitant Greenwich, R. I., 1687.

JOHN, b. Norwich, County of Norfolk, Eng., 1585, settled Watertown, Mass., 1637, projected the settlement Sudbury and Lancaster, Mass.; died 1661.

JOHN, resident Boston, Mass., 1643.

JOHN, husbandman, freeman Gloucester, Mass., 1651.

JOHN, resident Charlestown, Mass., 1652, removed Kittery, Maine.

JOHN, mariner, married Boston, Mass., 1654.

JOHN, resident Boston, Mass., 1660.

JOHN, bricklayer, resident Boston, Mass., 1670.

JOHN, married Springfield, Mass., 1677.

JOHN, took oath of allegiance York, Maine, 1681.

JOHN, b. Eng. 1632, settled Portsmouth, R. I., freeman 1666.

MARMADUKE, came from Sandwich, County Kent, Eng., to Salem, Mass., 1637.

MICHAEL, known as Captain, b. Eng. 1615, settled Hingham, Mass., 1645, removed Scituate, Mass.

NEHEMIAH, cooper, member of artillery company Boston, Mass., 1671.

RICHARD, b. Eng. 1590, resident Portsmouth, R. I., 1654.

RICHARD, printer, came from Bristol, Eng., to Boston, Mass., 1632.

ROBERT, brother John the mariner, freeman Dorchester, Mass., 1642.

ROBERT, married at Charlestown, Mass., 1657.

SAMUEL, resident Malden, Mass., before 1656, removed Charlestown, Mass.

THOMAS, b. Eng. 1583-84, freeman Charlestown, Mass., 1635, proprietor Woburn, Mass., 1643.

THOMAS, resident Gloucester, Mass., before 1668.

WILLIAM, came Boston, Mass., 1633, freeman 1634, died 1661.

WILLIAM, resident Barnstable, Mass., 1643.

WILLIAM, mariner, resident Boston, Mass., 1653, died 1669.

WILLIAM, resident Falmouth, Maine, 1680.

WILLIAM, married Suffield, Conn., 1688.

PIERPONT

Name of Norman origin, antedating the Norman Conquest. The Castle of Pierrepont took its name in the time of Charlemagne, from a strong bridge to replace a ferry on an estate located in Picardy in the diocese of Laon, France. The first of whom there is an authentic record: Sir Hugh de Pierpont 980 A. D. and Robert de Pierpont came to England with William the Conqueror to whom the family is traced. *De Petra Ponte* from the French signifies from the stone bridge, in Latin, *De Petra Ponte.*

JAMES, came to N. E. with his two sons, John and Robert, settled Roxbury, Mass., removed Ipswich, Mass.

ROBERT, brother of preceding, resident Ipswich, Mass., 1648.

PIERSON, PEARSON, PERSON

From the French Pierre and son, antedating this from the Danish Peterson.

ABRAHAM, minister, b. Yorkshire, Eng., 1613, came Boston, Mass., 1640, minister Lynn, Mass., same year, settled Southampton, L. I., thence 1647 went to Branford, Conn., removed 1667 Newark, N. J.

BARTHOLOMEW, resident of Watertown, Mass., 1639.

GEORGE, resident Reading, Mass., where he died 1679.

HENRY, settled Lynn, Mass., 1640, removed L. I.

HUGH, resident Watertown, Mass., 1649.

JOHN, died Middletown, Conn., 1677.

JOHN, known as Deacon, settled Rowley, Mass., 1647; set up the earliest fulling-mill in America.

JOHN, b. Yorkshire, Eng., 1615, was at Lynn., Mass., 1639, removed Reading, Mass., 1644.

STEPHEN, resident Derby, Conn., 1679.

THOMAS, at Branford, Conn., 1668, removed Newark, N. J.

PIGG, PIDGE, PIGGE

ROBERT, New Haven, Conn., 1644, died there 1660.

THOMAS, brother of preceding, freeman Roxbury, Mass., 1634.

PIGDEN

THOMAS, resident Lynn, Mass., 1647.

PIKE

Sir Richard Pike, English ancestor.

GEORGE, resident Marblehead, Mass., 1668.

JAMES, Charlestown, Mass., 1647, removed Reading, Mass.

JOHN, came from Langford, Eng., to Ipswich, Mass., 1635, removed Salisbury, Mass., where he died 1654.

JOHN, came from Bridgewater, Somersetshire, Eng., to Newbury, Mass., 1636.

JOSEPH, resident Charlestown, Mass., 1683.

RICHARD, at Newbury, Mass., 1655, settled Falmouth, Maine, 1675.

PILE

WILLIAM, Salisbury, Mass., 1659, removed Nantucket, Mass., thence Dover, N. H.

PILING, PILLEN

JOHN, fisherman, Kittery, Maine 1639, afterwards Dover, N. H., 1653.

PILLSBURY

WILLIAM, inhabitant Boston, Mass., 1640, removed Newbury, Mass., 1651.

PIMORE

THOMAS, proprietor New Haven, Conn., 1685.

PINCKNEY, PINKNEY

PHILIP, Fairfield, Conn., 1650, removed East Chester, N. Y., 1665.

PINDAR, PINDER, PINTER

HENRY, b. Eng., 1580, came to N. E., 1635, at Ipswich, Mass., 1641.

SAMUEL, resident Ipswich, Mass., 1683.

PINGREE

Name of French origin, probably taken into England by a Huguenot refugee; signifies green pine.

AARON, resident Ipswich, Mass., 1648.

MOSES, saltmaker, brother of the preceding, b. Eng., 1610, known as deacon, resident Ipswich, Mass., 1642, died 1695.

PINION

NICHOLAS, at Lynn, Mass., 1647, removed New Haven, Conn., before 1667.

PINKHAM

In its ancient form, the word was *Pyncombe* from *Pyn*, a pine, and *Combe*, a hollow or ridge, a place where sturdy trees grow.

RICHARD, came to N. E., 1633, settled Dover, N. H., 1640.

PINNEY, PYNNY

HUMPHREY, son of John P., b. Somersetshire, Eng., settled Dorchester, Mass., 1630, removed Windsor, Conn., 1635.

THOMAS, freeman, Gloucester, Mass., 1672.

PINSON, PINCHIN, PINCIN

ANDREW, b. Eng., 1623, came Wethersfield, Conn., about 1665, where he died 1697.

EDMUND, married at Cambridge, Mass., 1665.

THOMAS, inhabitant of Scituate, Mass., 1636.

PIPER

NATHANIEL, b. Dartmouth, Devonshire, Eng., about 1630, came to Ipswich, Mass., 1665.

RICHARD, living Haddam, Conn., 1669.

PIPON

JOHN, master of ship, at Salem, Mass., 1673.

PITCHER

ANDREW, settled Dorchester, Mass., 1634, freeman 1641.

PITKIN

WILLIAM, attorney, b. Eng., 1635, came Hartford, Conn., 1659.

PITMAN, PITNAM

EZEKIEL, inhabitant New Hampshire, 1683.

JOHN, living in that part of Salem now Danvers, Mass., 1690.

JONATHAN, married, Stratford, Conn., 1681.

NATHANIEL, granted land Salem, Mass., 1639.

THOMAS, resident Marblehead, Mass., 1648.

WILLIAM, married, Boston, Mass., 1653, removed Dover, N. H.

PITNEY

JAMES, at Ipswich, Mass., 1639, removed Marshfield, Mass., 1643, and Boston, Mass., 1652.

PITT

WILLIAM, came Plymouth, Mass., 1621, not present at division of cattle 1627; at Marblehead, Mass., 1674.

PITTEE, PITTY, PITTEY

JOSEPH, freeman Ipswich, Mass., 1680.

WILLIAM, early settler Weymouth, Mass.

PITTICE

JOHN, at Ipswich, Mass., 1648.

PITTS

EDMUND, weaver, came from Hingham, Eng., to Hingham, Mass., freeman, 1640.

PETER, settled at Taunton, Mass., before 1643.

SAMUEL, married, Taunton, Mass., 1680.

WILLIAM, came from Hingham, Eng., to Hingham, Mass., 1638, at Marblehead, Mass., 1654.

PITTUMS, PITTONS

JOHN, resident Boston, Mass., before 1678.

PIXLEY

WILLIAM, married, Hadley, Mass., 1663.

PLACE, PLAISE

ENOCH, b. Eng., 1631, married, Dorchester, Mass., 1657, removed Kingston, R. I., 1663.

PETER, b. Eng., 1615, came from London, Eng., to Boston, Mass., 1635, freeman 1646.

WILLIAM, blackmith, granted land Salem, Mass., 1637.

PLAISTED, PLAYSTEAD

JOHN, inhabitant, New Hampshire, 1679; chief justice, 1716.

ROGER, brother of preceding, known by the title of Captain, went from Boston, Mass., to Kittery, Maine, 1654.

PLATT

ABEL, at Rowley, Mass., 1678.

ISAAC, at Huntington, L. I., admitted freeman Conn., 1664.

JAMES, at Rowley, Mass., 1691.

JOHN, freeman Norwalk, Conn., 1691.

JONAS, at Rowley, Mass., 1691.

RICHARD, bapt. Bovington, Eng., 1603, settled at New Haven, Conn., 1638, granted lands Milford, Conn., 1646, chosen deacon 1669, died 1684-85.

THOMAS, butcher, resident Boston, Mass., 1669.

PLUMB, PLUM

The name of Norman-French origin; family traced to Robertus Plumme appears in 1180 in the Great Roll of Normandy accompanied by that of Robert Plome. In Hertfordshire, Eng., there is a record of James Plume in 1240.

GEORGE, came from Taworth, county Essex, Eng., to New London, Conn., before 1654.

JOHN, shipowner, son of Robert, bapt.

Great Yeldham, Eng., 1594, removed from Dorchester, Mass., to Wethersfield, Conn., 1635, thence 1644, Branford, Conn., where he died.

JOHN, mariner, son George, grandson of George, great grandson of John P., a native of Terling, county Essex, where he was b. about 1510. John, the American emigrant b. Topperfield, county Essex, Eng., 1634, came to Hartford, Conn., 1663, and to New London, Conn., 1678.

ROBERT, married, Milford, Conn., 1639.

PLUMLY, PLUMLEY, PLUMLEIGH

ALEXANDER, settled at Boston, Mass., granted land Braintree, Mass., 1639.

PLUMMER

FRANCIS, linen weaver, came from Woolwich, Eng., settled Boston, Mass., 1633, freeman 1634, removed Newbury, Mass., 1635.

SAMUEL, son of John P., b. Eng., 1619, freeman Newbury, Mass., 1641, died 1702.

PLYMPTON, PLIMPTON

An ancient English name; it was applied to a monastery established by West Saxon kings. In 1086 the village of Plimpton existed in the parish of Spofforth in the West Riding of Yorkshire. Gilbert and Nigel P. were born in the Manor of Plimpton 1184. The word is of Cornish-British extraction from *Plym* a river, and *ton* a town. The town situated on the river Plym in Devonshire, Eng. The family is traced in England through twenty generations.

HENRY, died Boston, Mass., 1653.

JOHN, b. county Cambridge, Eng., 1620, settled Roxbury, Mass., 1641, at Dedham, Mass., 1643, removed Medfield, Mass., 1652, one of the proprietors of Deerfield, Mass., 1673.

ROBERT, resident New London, Conn., 1681.

THOMAS, was at Sudbury, Mass., 1643.

POCHER

GEORGE, died Braintree, Mass., 1639.

POD

DANIEL, was at Ipswich, Mass., 1642.

POLAND

SAMUEL, b. Eng., 1623, settled Ipswich, Mass., 1648.

POLLARD

A tree having its top cut off: a fish; *Poularde,* a fat chicken; *Pol,* Dutch, a loose or lewd man, and *ard,* disposition; *Poule-ard* chicken-hearted.

GEORGE, was at Salem, Mass., before 1646.

THOMAS, son of William, b. Coventry, Warwickshire, Eng., about 1670, came to America 1690, was at Billerica, Mass., 1692.

WILLIAM, innholder, resident Boston, Mass., before 1644.

POLLY or POLLEY

From Poilley, in the province of Orleans, France, whence the family originally came.

GEORGE, married, Woburn, Mass., 1649.

JOHN, brother of the preceding, resident Roxbury, Mass., 1650.

POMEROY, POMROY, PUMMERY, PUMRY

From French *Pomme-roi,* a kind of apple, the royal apple, king's apple or king of apples; a name probably given to a gardener for his skill in raising them, or a name of a place where such apples were raised. Radolphus (Ralf or Ralph) de Pomeroy came to England with William the Conqueror.

ELTWEED, bapt. Eng. 1585, came Dorchester, Mass., 1630, removed Windsor, Conn., 1636, thence Northampton, Mass., 1672.

THOMAS, at Portsmouth, N. H., before 1679.

POMFRET

WILLIAM, town clerk Dover, N. H., 1640.

POND

DANIEL, on record at Dedham, Mass., 1652.

ROBERT, died at Dorchester, Mass., 1637; no male issue.

SAMUEL, married, Windsor, Conn., 1642.

PONDER

JOHN, married, Westfield, Mass., 1668.

PONTON, PONTING

RICHARD, husbandman, resident Boston, Mass., 1649, removed Hartford, Conn., 1662.

PONTUS

WILLIAM, at Plymouth, Mass., 1633.

POOLE, POOL, POLE

A small collection of water in a hollow place supplied by a spring; a small lake. "John at the Pool" became "John Pool." A town in Dorsetshire, Eng. Sir William Poole an English ancestor.

EDWARD, came from Weymouth, Eng., to Weymouth, Mass., 1635, removed Newport, R. I., 1638.

JOHN, came to N. E. 1633, located Cambridge, Mass., proprietor Lynn, Mass., 1638; became founder of Reading, Mass.

JOHN, carpenter, married, Beverly 1692, where he died 1716.

RICHARD, a bachelor, died New London, Conn., 1662.

SAMUEL, merchant, resident Boston, Mass., 1642.

WILLIAM, came Dorchester, Mass., 1630, removed Taunton, Mass., 1637; brother of Elizabeth, patron saint of Taunton, Mass.

POOR, POORE

DANIEL, b. Eng. 1624, came N. E. 1638; eleventh settler Andover, Mass., 1644.

JOHN, elder brother of the preceding, emigrated from Wiltshire, Eng. At Lynn and Ipswich, Mass., 1635; one early settlers Newbury, Mass.

JOHN, mariner, married, Hampton, N. H., 1661.

NICHOLAS, resident Lynn, Mass., 1637.

SAMUEL, brother of Daniel and John, b. Eng. 1620, settled Newbury, Mass., 1638.

POPE

From Greek and Latin *Popa,* a priest.

EPHRAIM, died Boston, Mass., 1677.

JOHN, shoemaker, came from county Sussex, Eng., to Dorchester, Mass., 1633.

JOHN, at Springfield, Mass., 1678, removed Windsor, Conn., 1683, where he died that year unmarried.

JOSEPH, son Robert P. of Yorkshire, Eng., came to Salem, Mass., before 1636.

THOMAS, b. Eng. 1608, settled at Plymouth, Mass., 1631.

THOMAS, brother first John, was at Dorchester, Mass., before 1670.

THOMAS, resident Suffield, Conn., 1687.

WALTER, at Charlestown, Mass., 1634, died before 1641, leaving no male issue.

PORTAGE

GEORGE, merchant Boston, Mass., before 1685.

PORTER

Ancient English family descended from William de la Grande, who came with William the Conqueror to England and acquired lands near Kenilworth in Warwickshire. Ralph or Roger La Grande was Keeper of the Doors "Grant Porteur" at court of Henry I.

ABEL, resident Boston, Mass., before 1641.

DANIEL, surgeon, settled Farmington, Conn., before 1644.

EDWARD, came Roxbury, Mass., 1636.

ISRAEL, freeman Hadley, Mass., 1684.

JOHN, came to N. E. 1630, settled Dorchester, Mass., removed Windsor, Conn., 1635, where he died 1648.

JOHN, tanner, b. Eng. 1595, came from Dorchester, Eng., to Boston, Mass., removed Dorchester, Mass., 1635, afterwards Hingham, Mass., in 1644 to what is now Danvers, Mass.

JONATHAN, granted land Salem, Mass., 1637.

JONATHAN, resident Salem, Mass., 1636, a sergeant 1647, removed Huntington, L. I., before 1660.

NATHANIEL, freeman 1637, living Salem, Mass., 1638.

RICHARD, came from Weymouth, Eng., to Weymouth, Mass., 1635.

ROBERT, one first settlers Farmington, Conn., married 1644.

ROGER, husbandman, b. Eng. 1583; came from Long Sutton, county Hants, Eng., 1638, to Watertown, Mass.

SAMUEL, died Salem, Mass., 1659.

STEPHEN, freeman Andover, Mass., 1691.

THOMAS, married, Hartford, Mass., 1644, removed Farmington, Conn.

PORTIS, PORTORIS

ROBERT, resident Boston, Mass., 1645.

PORTMORT, PORMONT, PURMONT

PHILEMON, freeman Boston, Mass., 1635; first grammar school master; removed Exeter, N. H., 1638.

POST

The name of German origin. Herien Von Post 1030.

JOHN, married, Woburn, Mass., 1650.

RICHARD, blacksmith, among first settlers New London, Conn., from where he removed 1651-2.

STEPHEN, came from Gravesend, Eng., to Boston, Mass., 1633, at Cambridge, Mass., 1634, removed Hartford, Conn., 1636, inhabitant Saybrook, Conn., 1649.

POTTER

One who makes earthen vessels.

ABEL, b. Eng. 1638, proprietor Dartmouth, Mass., 1667, removed Warwick, R. I.

ANTHONY, b. Eng. 1628, settled Ipswich, Mass., 1648.

GEORGE, died Portsmouth, R. I., 1638.

HUMFREY, married, Salem, Mass., 1656; no male issue.

INDIGO or INIGO, married Charlestown, Mass., 1663.

JOHN, at New Haven, Conn., 1639.

LUKE, freeman Concord, Mass., 1639.

MATTHIAS, at Braintree, Mass., 1661.

NATHANIEL, admitted as an inhabitant of Island of Aquineck, R. I., 1639.

NICHOLAS, bricklayer, settled Lynn, Mass., 1651, removed Salem, Mass., 1660.

ROBERT, freeman Lynn, Mass., 1634, removed Newport, R. I., 1638, two years later to Warwick, R. I.

VINCENT, b. Eng. 1614, came to Boston, Mass., 1635, returned to England 1639.

WILLIAM, b. Eng. 1608, came to Watertown, Mass., 1635, removed New Haven 1643.

WILLIAM, b. Eng. 1610, came to Braintree, Mass., 1635, a freeman 1640, removed Roxbury, Mass.

WILLIAM, resident New Haven, Conn., 1641.

POTTS

RICHARD, at Kennebeck, Maine, before 1676.

THOMAS, resident Dover, N. H., before 1690.

POULTON, POULTER

From the town of Poulton in Lancashire, Eng., also a place near Marlborough in Wiltshire, so called from *pool,* a small lake, and *ton,* a town.

JOHN, came from Raleigh in county Essex, Eng., to Billerica, Mass., 1658.

POUT, POAT

WILLIAM, at Marblehead, Mass., 1668-74.

POWELL

A contraction of the Welsh *Ap Howell,* the son of Howell. It may also be deduced from *Paul,* of which it was a former orthography.

JOHN, resident Charlestown, Mass., before 1669.

MICHAEL, at Dedham, Mass., 1639, removed Boston, Mass., 1647.

RALPH, married Marshfield, Mass., 1676.

ROBERT, took oath of fidelity Exeter, N. H., 1677.

ROWLAND, at Gloucester, Mass., 1657.

THOMAS, resident New Haven, Conn., 1641, removed L. I.

THOMAS, inhabitant Saco, Maine,, 1670.

THOMAS, married, Windsor, Conn., 1676.

WILLIAM, resident Charlestown, Mass., 1636.

WILLIAM, inhabitant Taunton, Mass., 1643.

POWERS

From the old Norman name *Le Poer,* borne by an officer under William the Conqueror, after, in the roll of services in the Battle Abbey. The name may come from the Welsh *Powyr,* a descendant of Leod, who was the father of *Mandebrog.* Richard le Poer was high sheriff of Gloucestershire 1187.

JOHN, at Charlestown, Mass., 1643.

NICHOLAS, early settler Providence, R. I., where he died 1657.

WALTER, b. Eng. 1639, arrived Salem, Mass., 1654, settled in what is now Littleton, Mass., 1661.

POWNING, POUNDING

HENRY, freeman Boston, Mass., 1644.

POWSLAND, POWSLEY, POWLAND

JAMES, married, Salem, Mass., 1670.

RICHARD, at Falmouth, Maine, 1674-90.

PRANCE

PHILIP, master mariner, at Salem, Mass., 1689.

PRATT

From the Latin *Pratum,* a meadow. *Prat* in the Dutch signifies proud, arrogant, cunning. John Pratt or de Pratellis or de Prates, held the manor of Parrickborne (Merlin Bridge and Pelham Hundred 1200).

ABRAHAM, surgeon, came in Winthrop's fleet, settled at Charlestown 1631, where he died 1645.

EPHRAIM, resident Weymouth, Mass., before 1698.

JOHN, surgeon, son of Rev. William P., bapt., Stevenage, Eng., 1584, came to Cambridge, Mass., where he was a freeman 1634, removed Hartford, Conn., 1637; drowned off the coast of Spain 1644, left no issue.

JOHN, resident Hingham, Mass., removed Weymouth, Mass., 1646.

JOHN, carpenter, b. Malden, Eng., about 1615, came to Malden, Mass., 1635, removed Hartford, Conn., 1636.

JOHN, resident Kingston, R. I., before 1664.

JOHN, freeman at Dorchester, Mass., 1643, where he had resided since 1634.

JOSEPH, resident Weymouth, Mass., before 1664.

JOSHUA, came to Plymouth, Mass., 1623, one of the purchasers, Dartmouth, Mass., 1652.

JOSHUA, resident Medfield, Mass., 1649.

MATTHEW, b. Eng. 1600, freeman Weymouth, Mass., 1640, removed Rehoboth, Mass.

MICAH, resident Weymouth, Mass., before 1691.

PETER, married, Lyme, Conn., 1679.

PHINEAS, joiner, brother of first Joshua, son of Henry P., b. Eng. 1590, came to Weymouth, Mass., 1622, removed Plymouth, Mass., 1623, a resident Charlestown, Mass., 1648.

RICHARD, son of John P. of Malden, County Essex, where he was bapt. 1615, came to Charlestown, Mass., about 1640.

SAMUEL, carpenter, freeman Weymouth, Mass., 1666.

SAMUEL, resident Wickford, R. I., 1674.

THOMAS, freeman Watertown, Mass., 1647, settled Framingham, Mass., 1679.

THOMAS, resident Weymouth, Mass., 1659.

THOMAS, living Malden, Mass., before 1661.

WILLIAM, brother of John the carpenter, had the rank of lieutenant; came to Cambridge, Mass., 1633, removed Hartford, Conn., 1636, finally Saybrook, Conn., 1645.

WILLIAM, freeman Weymouth, Mass., 1651.

PRAY

Original spelling of the name Pie, which indicates French origin.

ELISHA, swore allegiance Providence, R. I., 1682.

JOHN, married, Braintree, Mass., 1657.

JOHN, swore allegiance Providence, R. I., 1671.

QUINTON, b. Eng. 1595, came Lynn, Mass., 1645, removed Braintree, Mass., thence Providence, R. I., swore allegiance to King James 1668.

RICHARD, brother of preceding, resident Lynn, Mass., 1645.

WILLIAM, swore allegiance at Providence, R. I., 1682.

PREBLE

ABRAHAM, settled Scituate, Mass., 1636, removed York, Maine, 1642.

PRENCE

THOMAS, governor Plymouth Colony, son Thomas of Lechlade, Gloucestershire, Eng., came to Plymouth, Mass., 1621, removed Duxbury, Mass., 1635, thence Eastham, Mass., 1645.

PRENTICE, PRENTISS

An ancient surname as early as 1318; Thomas Prentiz is recorded in English history.

HENRY, planter, member of church Cambridge, Mass., 1636, original proprietor Salisbury, Mass., freeman 1650.

THOMAS, b. Eng. 1621, came Cambridge, Mass., 1648, known as Captain, commander of Mounted troops in King Philip's War.

VALENTINE, came from Nazing, County Essex, Eng., to N. E. 1631, settled Roxbury, Mass., 1633.

PRESBURY

JOHN, buried Sandwich, Mass., 1648.

JOHN, constable, Saco, Maine, 1670.

PRESCOTT

The name of Welsh origin from *Prys,* a coppice, and *cwt,* a cottage. In Saxon the contraction of two words, priest and cottage, signifying priest cottage or priest's house. Also known Prescott, a small town in England.

JAMES, son of James P., and the fifth generation from James P. of Standish, Lincolnshire, England, came from Digby in that county to Hampton, N. H., 1665.

JOHN, blacksmith, came from Sowerby in the parish of Halifax, Yorkshire, Eng., to Watertown, Mass., 1640, removed Lancaster, Mass.

PETER, freeman, Salem, Mass., 1682.

PRESSIE, PRESSY

JOHN, b. Eng. 1638, came to New England 1650, taxed at Salisbury, Mass., 1659. Removed Amesbury, Mass., 1664.

PRESTON

Ancient North Britain family. Name assumed at the time of Malcolm, King of Scots, Leophus de Preston 1046. A town in Lancashire, Eng. The town in the coppice, or the bushy hill, from *Prys* and *ton,* also *Preston;* the town where brass is manufactured, from *Pres,* brass, Welsh.

JOHN, married, Boston, Mass., 1661.

JOHN, resident Andover, Mass., before 1691.

ROGER, tanner, b. Eng. 1614, came to N. E. 1635, first appears on records Ipswich, Mass., 1639, removed Salem, Mass., 1657.

SAMUEL, married, Andover, Mass., 1672.

THOMAS, settled in what is now Danvers, Mass., 1669.

WILLIAM, son of William, grandson of George P. of Valley Field, Eng., came from Yorkshire, Eng., settled New Haven, Conn., 1635.

PRETIOUS, PRETIOSE

CHARLES, blacksmith, married, Boston, Mass., 1653.

PRICE

From the Welsh, a corruption of *Ap Rice,* the son of Rice.

DAVID, freeman Dorchester, Mass., 1636.

RICHARD, member Artillery Company Boston, Mass., 1658.

RICHARD, freeman Boston, Mass., 1664.

ROBERT, resident Northampton, Mass., 1678, removed Deerfield, Mass.

WALTER, merchant from Bristol, Eng., settled Salem, Mass., 1641.

WILLIAM, married, Watertown, Mass., 1657.

PRICHARD, PRITCHARD

From Welsh, a corruption of *Ap Richard,* the son of Richard.

HUGH, of Bioughton, Denbighshire, Wales, at Gloucester, Mass., 1641-45, removed Roxbury, Mass.

RICHARD, at Yarmouth, Mass., 1643, admitted church Charlestown, Mass., 1660.

ROGER, at Springfield, Mass., 1643, freeman 1648, removed Milford, Conn., 1653, thence to New Haven, Conn., where he died 1671.

WILLIAM, at Lynn, Mass., 1645, removed Ipswich, Mass., 1648, one first settlers Brookfield, Mass.

PRIDE

JOHN, brickmaker, at Salem, 1637; had a grant of land 1641 and died 1647.

PRIEST

DEGORY, Mayflower passenger, died 1621.

JAMES, freeman Weymouth, Mass., 1643.

JOHN, at Weymouth, Mass., 1657.

JOHN, married, Salem, Mass., 1673.

JOHN, resident, Woburn, Mass., 1679.

PRIME

JAMES, inhabitant Milford, Conn., 1654.

MARK, at Rowley, Mass., 1643.

PRINCE

JOHN, son of Rev. John P. of East Shefford, County of Berks, b. Eng. 1610, freeman Watertown, Mass., 1635, removed to what is now Hull, Mass., 1638.

NATHANIEL, resident Salem, Mass., 1664.

RICHARD, tailor, freeman, Salem, Mass., 1642.

ROBERT, brother of the preceding, granted land Salem, Mass., 1649.

THOMAS, at Gloucester, Mass., 1649.

WILLIAM, resident Dover, N. H., 1671.

PRINDLE

A croft or small field, Scotch descent.

JOHN, resident Milford, Conn., 1645.

WILLIAM, living New Haven, Conn., 1653.

PRINGRYDAY, PRIMIDAYES, PRIMRIDES

EDMUND, married, Springfield, Mass., 1666, killed by Indians, 1675; no issue.

PRIOR, PRYOR

EDWARD, inhabitant Kennebeck, Maine, 1665.

HUMPHREY, married, Windsor, Conn., 1663.

MATTHEW, granted land Salem, Mass., 1638, removed Brookhaven, Long Island, where he was living 1665.

THOMAS, came from London, Eng., to Scituate, Mass., 1634, where he died 1639.

PROCTOR

Name derived from the Latin *procurator,* meaning one who acts for another, *ie* a proxy. The family was originally seated in Yorkshire, but at beginning of the sixteenth century was established at Shawdon.

GEORGE, freeman Dorchester, Mass., 1637.

RICHARD, at Yarmouth, Mass., 1643.

RICHARD, freeman Boston, Mass., 1690.

ROBERT, freeman Concord, Mass., 1643, one of the founders Chelmsford, Mass., 1653.

PROUTY

RICHARD, settled Scituate, Mass., 1667.

PROVINDER

JOHN, took oath of fidelity Charlestown, Mass., 1674.

PRUDDEN

JAMES, inhabitant Milford, Conn., 1639, died 1648.

PETER, minister, brother of the preceding, b. Eng. 1600, came Boston, Mass., 1638, settled over church at Milford, Conn., where he died 1656.

PUDEATER

JACOB, married, Salem, Mass., 1666.

PUDINGTON, PUDDINGTON

GEORGE, at York, Maine, 1640.

ROBERT, inhabitant Portsmouth, N. H., 1640, removed Newtown, L. I.

PUDNEY

JOHN, married, Salem, Mass., 1662.

PUFFER, POFFER

The family is of German origin.

GEORGE, died Braintree, Mass., 1639.

JAMES, married, Braintree, Mass., 1655.

MATTHEW or MATTHIAS, brother of the preceding, at Braintree, Mass.; became one of first settlers Mendon, Mass., afterwards lived Wrentham, Mass.

PULLING, PULLIN

English ancestor Richard Pullume 1600.
ABRAHAM, settled Boston, Mass.

PULLMAN

JASPER, took oath of allegiance York, Maine, 1681.

PULSIFER

Of French Huguenot descent; the nearest resemblance to the name in French is *Pulosevits.*

BENEDICT, inhabitant Ipswich, Mass., 1664, died 1673.

PUNCHAID

WILLIAM, came from Isle of Jersey, Eng., married, Salem, Mass., 1669.

PUNDERSON, PONDERSON

JOHN, came from Yorkshire, Eng., to Boston, Mass., 1637, removed New Haven, Conn., 1639.

PURCHASE

ABRAHAM, inhabitant Salem, Mass., 1680.

JOHN, resident Hartford, Conn., 1639.

JOHN, at Boston, Mass., before 1652.

OLIVER, b. Eng. 1613, freeman Dorchester, Mass., 1636, removed Taunton, Mass., where he was enrolled in militia 1643, removed Lynn, Mass., 1653.

THOMAS, brother of preceding, in Maine 1628, commissioner Saco Maine, 1636, removed Lynn, Mass., 1675.

PURPLE

EDWARD, married, Haddam, Conn., 1674.

PURRINGTON, PURINTON

GEORGE, settled York, Maine, 1640.

JOHN, clerk of the writs, Kennebunk, Maine, 1668.

ROBERT, freeman Portsmouth, N. H., 1672.

PURRYER

WILLIAM, b. Eng. 1599, came from Olney, County Bucks, Eng., to Ipswich, Mass., 1635, removed Southold, L. I.; freeman Conn. 1662.

PUTNAM

The name derived from the Flemish word *putte*, a well, plural *puttern*, and *ham* signifying a house or town. There is also English village called Pattenham. The English ancestor was Simon de Pattenham 1199.

JOHN, yeoman, son of Nicholas P. of Penne, Eng., XVI generation from Simon de P. John, b. Aston Abbotts, county Bucks, England, 1580, came Salem, Mass., 1630.

PUTNEY

JOHN, married Salem, Mass., 1662.

PYGAN, PYGON, PIGGIN, PIGGON

ALEXANDER, innholder, came from Norwich, county Norfolk, Eng., to New London, Conn., 1667, removed Saybrook, Conn., 1679, returned New London, Conn., 1685, where died 1701.

PYNCHON, PINCHEON

WILLIAM, b. Springfield, county Essex, Eng., 1590, came Winthrop's fleet 1630, settled Roxbury, Mass.; founded Springfield, Mass., 1636.

PYNE

THOMAS, freeman Mass., 1635.

QUARLES

WILLIAM, b. Eng. 1647, at Salisbury, Mass., 1665, removed Ipswich, Mass., 1678.

QUELCH

BENJAMIN, resident Boston, Mass., 1694.

QUICK

NATHANIEL, died New Hampshire, 1677.

WILLIAM, mariner, resident Charlestown, Mass., 1636, freeman Newport, Rhode Island, 1638.

QUILTER

MARK, resident Ipswich, Mass., 1637.

QUIMBY, QUINBY

JOHN, at Stratford, Conn., 1654, removed Westchester, N. Y., 1664.

ROBERT, ship carpenter, inhabitant Amesbury, Mass., before 1657, removed Salisbury, Mass., 1663.

QUINCY

The name derived from town in Normandy, also appears in the Roll of Battle Abbey. Baron Saher de Quince signer of the Magna Charter.

EDMUND, son of Edmund Q. of Wigsthrope, county Northampton, baptized 1602, came to N. E. 1628, returned England; arrived second time 1633, became inhabitant Boston, Mass., removed to what is now Quincy, Mass., 1635.

QUING, QUIN

From *Quin*, a village in Clare county, Ireland.

ARTHUR, resident Boston, Mass., 1677.

RABUN, RABONE, RAWBONE

GEORGE, inhabitant Exeter, N. H., 1639.

RADDEN, RADDIN

THADDEUS, at Marblehead, Mass., 1674.

RAGLAND

JOHN, died Boston, Mass., 1690.

RAINES, RAYNES

FRANCIS, freeman York, Maine, 1652.

RAINBOROW

WILLIAM, member artillery company 1639, removed Watertown, Mass., 1640.

RAINSFORD, RANSFORD

EDWARD, came Winthrop's fleet 1630, freeman Boston, Mass., 1637, died 1680.

EDWARD, fisherman, b. Eng. 1609, came Boston, Mass., 1635.

RAM

GEORGE, b. Eng. 1610, came N. E. 1635.

RAMACKE

CHRISTIAN, member grand jury Kittery, Maine, 1659.

RAMSDELL, RAMSDEN

A Saxon word signifying the winding valley or the extremity of the valley.
DANIEL, inhabitant Plymouth, Mass., 1665.

JOHN, at Lynn, Mass., 1630.

JOSEPH, b. Eng. about 1620, on record Plymouth, Mass., 1641.

RAND

In the Anglo Saxon, Dutch, Danish and German languages the word *ram* signifys a border, margin or edge. It first appeared as a surname in 1475, when Rands of Rands Grange, a small *township* near Bedale, Yorkshire, Eng., is mentioned.

FRANCIS, sent over by Mason to Portsmouth, N. H., 1631, at Exeter, N. H., 1657.

HENRY, married, Stow, Mass., 1682.

JAMES, came to Plymouth, Mass., 1623.

JOHN, mariner, lived Braintree, Mass., 1657.

JOHN, freeman, Dover, N. H., 1672.

ROBERT, came to N. E. 1635, admitted freeman that year Charlestown, Mass., in that year, lived at Lyme, Conn., where he died 1639-40.

ROBERT, inhabitant Lynn, Mass., 1649.

RANDALL

From Saxon *ran* fair, and *ulph* help.

ANTHONY, physician at Salem, Mass., 1688.

JOHN, resident Watertown, Mass., before 1659.

JOHN, settled Westerly, R. I., 1667, removed Stonington, Conn., 1670, died 1684.

PHILIP, freeman Dorchester, Mass., 1634.

RICHARD, fisherman at Scituate, Mass., 1640, settled Saco, Maine, afterwards Dover, N. H.

ROBERT, came from Wendover, Buckshire, Eng., freeman Weymouth, Mass., 1647.

STEPHEN, brother first John, married, Weymouth, Mass., 1653.

THOMAS, fisherman, married, Marblehead, Mass., before 1665.

WILLIAM, living Marshfield, Mass., 1637, removed Scituate, Mass., 1640.

WILLIAM, at Newbury, Mass., before 1649.

RANGER

EDMUND, stationer, freeman Boston, Mass., 1671.

RANKIN

If the name is of Danish origin it came from *Rank*, right, upright, erect. If it is Gaelic it would be derived from *Roinn*, a promontory, share or division, and *Ceann* head, the head of the promontory, a name of place. *Rankin* in Dutch signifies pranks, tricks.

ANDREW, resident York, Maine, died before 1678.

JOHN, lived Roxbury, Mass., 1653.

RANNEY

From *Renaix, Reinow* or *Renais*, a town of Switzerland. *René* from Latin *renatus* renewed, born again, regenerated.

THOMAS, came from Scotland 1659, located Hartford, Conn., removed Middletown, Connecticut.

RANSOM, RANSOME

The price paid for redemption from captivity or punishment.

MATTHEW, married Saybrook, Conn., 1683.

ROBERT, on record Plymouth, Mass., 1654.

RAPER

THOMAS, resident Boston, Mass., 1685.

RASHLEY

HENRY, died Boston, Mass., before 1657.

THOMAS, brother of preceding admitted church Boston, Mass., 1640, removed Gloucester, Mass., 1641; became a minister, returned to England, 1652.

RASOR

RICHARD, married, Boston, Mass., 1660.

RATCHELL, RACHELL

ROBERT, married, Boston, Mass., 1652.

RATCLIFF, RATCLIFFE

JOHN, resident Boston, Mass., 1664.

PHILIP, at Marblehead, Mass., before 1630, banished from the colony 1631.

ROBERT, came to Plymouth, Mass., 1623.

ROBERT, minister, first Episcopal minister settled in N. E. 1686, returned England 1689.

WILLIAM, married, Stamford, Conn., 1659, removed Greenwich, Conn., 1669.

RATHBON, RATHBONE

From the Saxon, signifying an early gift.

JOHN, son of Richard R., b. Eng. 1610, resident Roxbury, Mass., 1660, one of original purchasers of Block Island, R. I., 1678.

RATSTOCK

JOSHUA, resident Boston, Mass., 1687.

RAVENSCROFT

ANTHONY, at Westerly, R. I., 1661.

SAMUEL, member artillery company, Boston, Mass., 1679.

RAWLINS, RAWLINGS, ROLLINS

From *Raoul*, French for Ralph, and the patronymic termination *ings*;—Ralph's son; English ancestry traced to Roger Rawlin, Lord of a manor in County of Norfolk, England, 1634.

JAMES, freeman Newbury, Mass., 1634, resident Dover, N. H., 1636.

JASPER, freeman Roxbury, Mass., 1633, removed Wethersfield, Conn., 1635, later Windsor, Conn., returned Roxbury, Mass., 1646, removed Boston, Mass., 1654.

John, resident Boston, Mass., 1686.

Nicholas, married, Newbury, Mass., 1678.

Richard, plasterer, at Boston, Mass., 1638, freeman 1643.

Robert, swore allegiance Amesbury, Mass., 1677.

Thomas, brother Jasper, resident Roxbury, Mass., 1630, removed Winthrop, Mass., 1639, thence Scituate, Mass., later to Boston, Mass.

Thomas, granted land Dorchester, Mass., where he died 1693, aged 70 years.

RAWLINSON, ROWLANDSON

The son of Rawlings.

Thomas, freeman Ipswich, Mass., 1638.

RAWSON

The Christian name of Ralph was in the early English spelt Rawf, then son was suffixed, the consonant f being dropped, the surname therefore became Rawson.

Edward, grandson of Edward R. b. Gillingham, Dorsetshire, Eng., 1615, came Newbury, Mass., 1637, removed Boston, Mass., 1650.

RAY, REA

This name may have several origins. *Ruadh* and *Reagh,* Gaelic, swarthy, red, sandy complexioned. *Re,* the moon. *Ray,* a beam of light, luster. *Re,* from *ruo,* to rush, applied to a stream, rapids, whence the river *Reay* in Caithness, Scotland. *Rea,* Cornish British, wonderful, strange. *Rhe,* Welsh, a run, *Rhedu,* to run. Rhae, Welsh, a battle, the place of battle; a chain. The family is of Scotch descent but settled in Derbyshire, Gloucestershire, Lincolnshire and elsewhere in England.

Caleb, resident Boston, Mass., 1683.

Daniel, brother of preceding, came from county Suffolk, Eng., to Plymouth, Mass., 1630, removed Salem, Mass., 1631.

James, married, Hingham, Mass., 1682.

Richard, at Warwick, R. I., 1656.

Simon, brother of Caleb and Daniel, came from Braintree, county Essex, Eng., to Braintree, Mass., where he died 1641.

RAYMOND

From Teutonic *rein,* pure, and *mund,* mouth, pure mouth; one who abstains from wanton discourses. *Raymund,* German, quiet, peace.

John, at Beverly, Mass., 1670, died 87th year, 1703.

Richard, brother of preceding, freeman, Salem, Mass., 1634, removed to Norwalk, Conn., thence to Saybrook, Conn., 1664, where he died 1692.

Thomas, freeman Salem, Mass., 1690.

William, known as Captain, brother of John and Richard, located Beverly, Mass., about 1652.

RAYN, RAYNES

Francis, selectman York, Maine, 1649.

Joseph, attorney general at Portsmouth, N. H., 1685.

RAYNER, REYNER

From Raner, a leader of the Danes, who invaded Britain; a pirate, a robber, a term given to a warrior.

Henry, married, Boston, Mass., 1662.

Humphrey, b. Gildersome in the West Riding of Yorkshire, Eng., freeman Rowley, Mass., 1642.

John, minister, brother of the preceding, b. Gildersome, Eng., at Plymouth, Mass., 1635, removed Dover, N. H., 1653, where he died 1669.

John, resident Rowley, Mass., 1691.

Samuel, inhabitant Watertown, Mass., 1654.

Samuel, living Charlestown, Mass., 1687.

Thurston, b. Eng. 1594, came from Ipswich, county Suffolk, England, to Watertown, Mass., 1634, removed Wethersfield, Conn., 1636, to Stamford, Conn., 1641, afterwards Southampton, L. I.

RAYNGER

Edmund, resident Boston, Mass., 1672.

READ, REED, READE

From Saxon *Rede,* advice, counsel, help, or from the fenny plant, a reed. Brianus de Rede was living in 1139, at Morpeth on the Wessback river in the north of England.

Arthur, inhabitant Stratford, Conn., 1676.

Benjamin, fit to bear arms, Duxbury, Mass., 1643.

Edward, at Marblehead, Mass., 1674.

Esdras, proprietor, Boston, Mass., 1638, same year removed Salem, Mass., later Wenham, Mass., and 1655 to Chelmsford, Mass.

Israel, inhabitant Woburn, Mass., 1670.

John, son of William R., b. Eng. 1598, came to N. E. 1630, settled Dorchester, Mass., removed Weymouth, Mass., 1637, became resident Rehoboth, Mass., 1643.

John, married Scituate, Mass., 1662.

John, b. Cornwall, Eng., settled Providence, R. I., removed Norwalk, Conn., 1687.

Joseph, resident Boston, Mass., 1671, freeman Lynn, Mass., 1681.

Josiah, freeman Lynn, Mass., 1681.

JOSIAH, at New London, Conn., 1662, removed Norwich, Conn., married, Marshfield, Mass., 1666.

OBADIAH, married Boston, Mass., 1664.

PHILIP, resident Weymouth, Mass., 1640.

PHILIP, physician at Lynn, Mass., 1669, removed Concord, Mass., where he died 1696.

RICHARD, resident Marblehead, Mass., 1674.

RICHARD, inhabitant Boston, Mass., 1687.

ROBERT, at Exeter, N. H., 1638, one first settlers Hampton, N. H., finally removed Boston, Mass.

SAMUEL, brother first Richard, resident Marblehead, Mass., 1674.

THOMAS, came Winthrop's fleet, settled Salem, Mass., 1630, freeman 1634.

THOMAS, at Milford, Conn., 1646, removed Newtown, L. I., 1656.

THOMAS, freeman Sudbury, Mass., 1656.

WILLIAM, resident Boston, Mass., before 1659, afterwards Marblehead and Charlestown, Mass. Died at sea 1667.

WILLIAM, born Mardstone, Eng., 1587, freeman Weymouth, Mass., 1635.

WILLIAM, b. Eng. 1587, settled Dorchester, Mass., 1635, removed Rehoboth, afterwards Woburn, Mass.

WILLIAM, brother first John, resident Boston, Mass., 1646.

WILLIAM, resident Boston, Mass., 1665.

READER

JOHN, granted land Springfield, Mass., 1636, removed New Haven, Conn., 1643, thence Stratford, Conn., 1650, later Newtown, L. I., 1656.

REAPE

SAMUEL, married, Newport, R. I., before 1669.

THOMAS, married, Boston, Mass., 1660.

WILLIAM, b. Eng. 1628, resident Newport, R. I., 1664, where he died 1670.

RECORD

The same as *Rikerd* or *Richard*, of which it is a corruption, liberal-hearted; rich in disposition.

JOHN, soldier in King Philip's War, married, Hingham, Mass., 1677, lived at Weymouth, Mass.

REDDING, RIDDAN, READING

JOHN, married Sandwich, Mass., 1676.

JOSEPH, came to Boston, Mass., in Winthrop's fleet, freeman Cambridge, Mass., 1634, removed Ipswich, Mass., 1637.

MILES, cooper, brother of preceding, came in Winthrop's fleet, freeman, Boston, Mass., 1634, proprietor Billerica, Mass., 1665.

THADDEUS, resident Lynn, Mass., 1660, removed Marblehead, Mass., 1674.

THOMAS, freeman Saco, Maine, 1653.

REDDOCK

HENRY, resident Providence, R. I., 1645-55, living Warwick, R. I., 1661.

JOHN, proprietor Sudbury, Mass., 1640.

REDFIELD, REDFIN

WILLIAM, tanner, proprietor Cambridge, Mass., 1639, removed New London, Conn., 1646.

REDIAT, RIDIAT, RADGATE

JOHN, freeman Sudbury, Mass., 1645.

REDINGTON

ABRAHAM, at Rowley, Mass., 1667, afterwards at Topsfield or Boxford, Mass.; no issue.

DANIEL, freeman Topsfield, Mass., 1685.

THOMAS, freeman Boxford, Mass., 1690.

REDKNAP, REDNAPE

JOSEPH, wine-cooper, came from London, Eng., to Lynn, Mass., freeman 1634.

REDMAN

JOHN, blacksmith, early settler Hampton, N. H., 1642, where he resided 1685.

ROBERT, was at Dorchester, Mass., died Milton, Mass., 1678.

REDWAY, REDWEY, READAWAY, REDDAWAY

JOHN, resident Rehoboth, Mass., 1646.

REEVE, REEVES

From *Reeve*, a bailiff, provost, or steward.

JOHN, b. Eng. 1616, came to N. E. 1635, removed Windsor, Conn., 1636, granted land Salem, Mass., 1643.

ROBERT, resident Hartford, Conn., 1663.

THOMAS, came Roxbury, Mass., 1638, freeman 1644, removed Springfield, Mass., 1646.

THOMAS, freeman, Conn., 1662, resided Southampton, L. I., 1673.

WILLIAM, brother of John, b. Eng. 1613, came to N. E. 1635, living at Salem, Mass., 1668.

REITH

RICHARD, married, Lynn, Mass., 1665, at Marblehead, Mass., 1675.

RELPH, RALPH, RELF

THOMAS, married, Warwick, R. I., 1655; previous to this at Guilford, Conn.

REMICK

CHRISTIAN, b. Eng. or Holland 1631, freeman Kittery, Maine, 1652.

REMINGTON, RIMMINGTON

A place name from Remmington, a township in the parish of Gisburn, West Riding, Yorkshire, England.

JOHN, came from Yorkshire, Eng., to Newbury, Mass., 1637, later removed Rowley, Mass., and about 1662 to Roxbury, Mass.

JOHN, resident Haverhill and Andover, Mass., before 1661.

THOMAS, freeman Rowley, Mass., 1672, removed Windsor, Conn., 1675, thence to Suffield, Conn., 1677.

THOMAS, married, Hingham, Mass., 1688, removed Roxbury, Mass.

RENDALL

JAMES, married, Portsmouth, N. H., 1686.

REVELL

THOMAS, merchant, resident New London, Conn., 1662-66.

REW

EDWARD, resident Newport, R. I., 1638, removed Taunton, Mass., 1643.

REX

WILLIAM, proprietor Watertown, Mass., 1642, afterwards living Boston, Mass.

REYNOLDS, RENOLD, RENOLDS

From Saxon *rhein*, pure, and *hold*, the old English for love, *ie* sincere or pure love. It may also signify strong or firm hold.

HENRY, granted land Salem, Mass., 1642, removed Lynn, Mass., 1647.

JAMES, at Plymouth, Mass., removed to R. I., settling before 1674 at Warwick.

JOHN, b. Eng. about 1612, settled Watertown, Mass., 1634, removed Wethersfield, Conn., 1636, thence Stamford, Conn., 1641, freeman Greenwich, Conn., 1669.

JOHN, at Isle of Shoals, N. H., 1647.

JOHN, at Saybrook, Conn., one first settlers, Norwich, Conn., 1659.

JOHN, carpenter, resident Weymouth, Mass., 1660.

JONATHAN, brother first John, representative from Stamford, Conn., 1667 and 1673.

ROBERT, shoemaker, came from Aylesford, Eng., to Boston, Mass., 1632, freeman 1634, removed Wethersfield, Conn., 1636.

THOMAS, on tax list New London, Conn., 1666.

WILLIAM, married, Duxbury, Mass., 1636.

WILLIAM, weaver, settled Providence, R. I., 1637, signed agreement of government 1640, removed North Kingston, R. I.

WILLIAM, admitted church member at Salem, Mass., 1640.

RHODES, ROADS, RHOADS

From the island of Rhodes in the Mediterranean Sea; Rhodes, a town in Guienne, France.

HENRY, iron monger, b. Eng. 1608, located Lynn, Mass., 1641.

JEREMIAH, swore allegiance Providence, R. I., 1671.

JOHN, resident Salem, Mass., 1678.

JOHN, freeman Lynn, Mass., 1684, previous at Marblehead, Mass., 1673.

RICHARD, at Salem, Mass., 1669.

THEOPHILUS, freeman Boston, Mass., 1683.

WALTER, swore allegiance Providence, R. I., 1668.

WILLIAM, resident Block Island, R. I., 1678.

ZACHARY, b. Eng. 1602-3, inhabitant Rehoboth, Mass., 1643, removed Providence, R. I., 1657.

RICE, ROISE

Another form of *Rys*, Welsh, to rush, a rushing, figuratively, a hero, a brave, impetuous man.

EDMUND, known as deacon, b. Barkhamstead, county of Herts, Eng., 1594, settled in Sudbury, Mass., 1638, removed Marlboro, Mass., 1660.

JOHN, resident Boston, Mass., 1669.

JOHN, b. Eng. 1646, of Welsh descent, came to N. E. 1661; married Warwick, R. I., 1674.

JONATHAN, married Norwich, Conn., 1661.

MICHAEL, freeman, New London, Conn., 1663.

NATHANIEL, freeman New London, Conn., 1669.

NICHOLAS, resident Boston, Mass., 1672.

PHILIP, tailor, united with church, Boston, Mass., 1640.

RICHARD, at Cambridge, Mass., 1635, removed Concord, Mass., 1636.

ROBERT, freeman Boston, Mass., 1634, removed New London, Conn., before 1657 from Stratford, Conn.

SAMUEL, inhabitant New London, Conn., 1669.

TIMOTHY, freeman Concord, Mass., 1690.

RICH

Wealthy, opulent, anciently, great, noble, powerful. Family of ancient English origin. Edmund Rich, Archbishop of Canterbury, 1236.

OBADIAH, resident Salem, Mass., 1669.

RICHARD, mariner, first record Dover, N. H., 1671.

RICHARDS

Derivation same as Record (see). A Welsh patronymic. Sir Richard Richards inherited manor at Caerynwick, Marionette county, Wales.

EDWARD, came to N. E. 1632, married, Dedham, Mass., 1638.

EDWARD, joiner, b. Eng. 1621, resident Lynn, Mass., 1633, where he died 1690.

JAMES, inhabitant Weymouth, Mass., 1684.

JOHN, in Plymouth Colony 1637, removed New London, Conn., 1658.

JOHN, at Westfield, Mass., before 1686.

JUSTINIAN, inhabitant New Hampshire 1689.

NATHANIEL, came to N. E. 1632, settled Cambridge, Mass., removed Hartford, Conn., 1636, thence Norwalk, Conn., 1652.

NATHANIEL, brother of Edward, inhabitant Dedham, Mass., 1642.

RICHARD, resident Salem, Mass., 1667, died 1678.

THOMAS, came Dorchester, Mass., 1630, removed Weymouth, Mass., freeman 1640; died 1650.

THOMAS, inhabitant Hartford, Conn., 1639, where he died soon after.

THOMAS, freeman Boston, Mass., 1645.

WILLIAM, first recorded Plymouth, Mass., 1633, removed Scituate, Mass., 1637, afterwards Weymouth, Mass.

RICHARDSON, RICHESON

The son of Richard.

AMOS, merchant Boston, Mass., 1640, one of the purchasers of the Narragansett land, settled at Westerly, R. I.

EDWARD, b. Eng. 1617, settled Newbury, Mass., 1640.

EZEKIEL, came from Bradford, Yorkshire, Eng., to Charlestown, Mass., 1630, removed Watertown, Mass., 1635, died Woburn, Mass., 1647.

GEORGE, b. Eng. 1595, came Watertown, Mass., 1635.

ISAAC, married, Woburn, Mass., 1667.

JAMES, brother of Ezekiel, was at Woburn, Mass., removed Chelmsford, Mass., 1659.

JOHN, brother of George, granted land Watertown, Mass., 1637, removed Exeter, N. H. 1642.

JOSHUA, married, Newbury, Mass., 1679.

NATHANIEL, freeman Woburn, Mass., 1690.

RICHARD, resident Boston, Mass., 1654.

SAMUEL, brother of Ezekiel, son of Thomas R. of West Mills, Hertfordshire, Eng., b. 1610, freeman Charlestown, Mass., 1638, removed Woburn, Mass., 1640.

THOMAS, brother of preceding, b. West Mills, Hertfordshire, Eng., 1608; was at Charlestown, Mass., 1636, freeman 1638, one original settler Woburn, Mass., 1640.

THOMAS, b. Eng. 1637, settled Farmington, Conn., removed Waterbury, Conn., about 1679.

WILLIAM, b. Eng. about 1620, came Newbury, Mass., 1640, where he married 1654.

WILLIAM, resident Newport, R. I., 1638.

RICHBELL, RIZBELL

JOHN, merchant Charlestown, Mass., 1648, removed Oyster Bay, L. I., before 1662.

RICHELLS, RITCHELL, RICHAL

SIGISMUND, resident Wethersfield, Conn., 1661, afterwards at Branford, Conn.

RICHMOND

From Saxon *ric*, rich, and *mund*, mouth—rich mouth; figuratively, eloquent. Roaldus de Richmond, English ancestor 1060.

JOHN, bapt. Crichlade, Wiltshire, Eng., 1597, settled Saco, Maine, 1635, one first purchasers Taunton, Mass., 1637, living in R. I. 1655, died Taunton, Mass., 1664.

RICKARD, RICKER, RICKET

GEORGE, resident Dover, N. H., 1670.

GILES, b. Eng. 1579, freeman Plymouth, Mass., 1637.

MATURIN, brother George, resident Dover, N. H., 1670.

THOMAS, inhabitant Scituate, Mass.

THOMAS, resident Salem, Mass., 1670.

RICKETSON

WILLIAM, resident Dartmouth, Mass., 1681.

RIDDAN, RIDDAINE

THADDEUS, merchant, freeman Lynn, Mass., 1672.

RIDER, RYDER

BENJAMIN, married Yarmouth, Mass., 1670.

JAMES, resident Cambridge, Mass., 1651.

PHINEAS, inhabitant Falmouth, Maine, 1658.

SAMUEL, b. Eng. about 1601, married Yarmouth, Mass., 1643.

THOMAS, caulker, resident Boston, Mass., 1634.

THOMAS, freeman Watertown, Mass., 1690, removed Framingham, Mass.

WILLIAM, b. Eng. 1650, married Watertown, Mass., 1674, removed Sherborn, Mass., 1675.

RIDGE

JOHN, died Newbury, Mass., 1666.

RIDGEWAY, RIDGAWAY

JOHN, living Malden, Mass., 1670.

RIGBY

EDWARD, at Lancaster, Mass., 1654.

JOHN, freeman Dorchester, Mass., 1637, died 1647.

RIGGS

From the Danish *rig,* wealthy, rich; or the name may be local denoting a steep elevation, a range of hills, or the upper part of such a range.

EDWARD, came Roxbury, Mass., 1632, freeman, 1634.

STEPHEN, inhabitant Marblehead, Mass., 1674.

THOMAS, townclerk, Gloucester, Mass., fifty-one years; married 1658.

RILEY

HENRY, inhabitant Rowley, Mass., where he died 1710, aged eighty-two years.

JOHN, came from Stepney, Eng., to Plymouth, Mass., 1621, was landholder Wethersfield, Conn., 1643.

RINDGE

DANIEL, living Roxbury, Mass., 1639, removed Ipswich, Mass., 1648.

JARVIS, freeman Salisbury, Mass., 1690.

RING

From the Dutch, a canton, a district of an ecclesiastical congregation.

ANDREW, b. Eng. 1616, came to Plymouth, Mass., with his mother, 1629, made freeman 1646, one of the first settlers Middleboro, Mass.

JOHN, carpenter, settled Salisbury, Mass., 1638.

JOHN, married, Ipswich, Mass, 1664.

ROBERT, brother first John, came to N. E. 1638, one first settlers Salisbury, Mass.

THOMAS, at Salem, Mass., 1637, removed Exeter, N. H., where he died 1667.

RIPLEY

A market-town in Yorkshire, England, from Saxon *ryhan,* to divide or separate, and *ley,* uncultivated lands, a pasture.

WILLIAM, came from Hingham, County Norfolk, Eng., to Hingham, Mass., 1638.

RISCRAFT

RICHARD, took oath of allegiance, Northampton, Mass., 1679.

RISDEN

ROBERT, mariner, resident, Boston, Mass., 1654.

RISHWORTH

EDWARD, inhabitant Exeter, N. H., 1643.

RISING

JAMES, married, Boston, Mass., 1657, admitted to church Salem, Mass., 1662, removed Windsor, Conn., 1665, thence Suffield, Conn., 1679, where he died 1688.

RISLEY, RISLA, RYSLEY, RISSLY

RICHARD, settled Cambridge, Mass., 1633, removed Hartford, Conn., 1636.

RITH, RIETH

RICHARD, resident Marblehead, Mass., 1675.

RIX

THOMAS, barber surgeon, b. Canninghatt, Eng., 1622, settled Salem, Mass., 1649.

THOMAS, married, Wethersfield, Conn., 1690.

WILLIAM, weaver, resident Boston, Mass., 1645, died 1657.

ROACH

THOMAS, married New London, Conn., 1651.

ROANES, ROANE

WILLIAM, at York, Maine, 1672.

ROATH

ROBERT, settled Norwich, Conn., 1660-65.

ROBBINS

BENJAMIN, married Wallingford, Conn., 1687.

JOHN, son of John R., b. Hedingworth, Eng., resident Wethersfield, Conn., 1638.

NICHOLAS, living Duxbury, Mass., 1638, died 1650.

RICHARD, resident Charlestown, Mass., 1639, removed Boston, Mass., later Cambridge, Mass.

ROBERT, inhabitant Concord, Mass., 1678.

SAMUEL, died Salisbury, Mass., 1665.

THOMAS, b. Eng. 1620; at Salem, Mass., as late as 1675.

THOMAS, resident of Duxbury, Mass., 1643, removed Salem, Mass., 1650.

WILLIAM, settled Reading, Mass., 1680, died Boston, Mass., 1693.

ROBERTS

From the Saxon *rod,* counsel, and *bert* or *bericht,* bright or famous, famous in council.

DAVID, married Woburn, Mass., 1678.

GEORGE, living Exeter, N. H., 1677.

GILES, brother of David, inhabitant Scarborough, Maine.

Hugh, tanner, married Gloucester, Mass.,

1649, removed New London, Conn., 1652, finally Newark, N. J.

JOHN, Welsh descent, came Roxbury, Mass., 1636, freeman 1639, died 1651; no male issue.

JOHN, resident Marblehead, Mass., 1668.

JOHN, freeman Boston, Mass., 1671.

JOHN, killed by Indians, Northampton, Mass., 1675.

JOHN, soldier, Roxbury, Mass.; killed by Indians, Sudbury, Mass., 1676.

JOHN, married, Hartford, Conn., removed Newtown, L. I., 1684.

JOHN, married, Gloucester, Mass., 1678.

JOHN, resident Boston, Mass., 1686.

JOSEPH, sent by Mason, Portsmouth, N. H., 1632.

ROBERT, living Boston, Mass., 1640, at Ipswich, Mass., 1648, died 1663.

SIMON, married, Boston, Mass., 1654.

THOMAS, settled Dover, N. H., 1623.

THOMAS, married, Duxbury, Mass., 1640.

THOMAS, freeman Providence, R. I., 1655.

WILLIAM, resident Dover N. H. 1645. Killed by Indians 1675. No male issue.

WILLIAM, resident Charlestown, Mass., 1648, removed New Haven, Conn.

WILLIAM, married, Hingham, Mass., 1667.

ROBIE, ROBY

From Danish *ro,* rest, repose, and *by,* a town. The peaceful town. The family, originally from Castle Donnington, Leicestershire, Eng., can be traced to John Robie who died 1515.

ANDREW, married, Hartford, Conn., 1691.

HENRY, b. Eng. 1618, settled Dorchester, Mass., 1639, removed Exeter, N. H., 1640, to Hampton, N. H., 1650.

RICHARD, resident Marblehead, Mass., 1674.

ROBINSON, ROBERTSON

It is claimed the Robinsons were Saxon Thanes before William the Conqueror.

ABRAHAM, resident Gloucester, Mass., 1642.

EDWARD, freeman Newport, R. I., 1655.

FRANCIS, resident Saco, Maine, 1643.

FRANCIS, freeman Boston, Mass., 1671.

GEORGE, resident Rehoboth, Mass., 1646-77.

GEORGE, married, Boston, Mass., 1657.

GEORGE, resident Swanzey, Mass., 1680.

GEORGE, resident Watertown, Mass., 1684.

ISAAC, son of Rev. John R., b. Eng. 1610, came to N. E. in Winthrop's fleet, taxed Plymouth, Mass., 1634, freeman Scituate, Mass., 1636, removed Barnstable, Mass., 1639.

JACOB, married, New Haven, Conn., 1690.

JAMES, married, Dorchester, Mass., 1664.

JAMES, living Scarborough, Maine, 1666.

JOHN, resident Salem, Mass., 1639.

JOHN, living New London, Conn., 1646-49.

JOHN, wheelwright, at Ipswich, Mass., 1640.

JOHN, at Haverhill, Mass., removed Exeter, N. H., 1657.

JOSEPH, married, Andover, Mass., 1671.

NATHANIEL, resident Boston, Mass., 1655, removed Cambridge, Mass., freeman there 1673.

NICHOLAS, b. Eng. 1605, came to N. E. 1635.

RICHARD, freeman Charlestown, Mass., 1641.

ROBERT, married, Newbury, Mass., 1664.

ROWLAND, b. near Long Bluff, county Cumberland, Eng., 1654, settled Kingston, R. I., 1675.

SAMUEL, died Hartford, Conn., 1683.

STEPHEN, inhabitant Exeter, N. H., 1689.

STEPHEN, resident Dover, N. H., 1662.

THOMAS, resident Boston, Mass., before 1662.

THOMAS, came from Guilford, Eng., 1666, removed Hartford, Conn., 1684.

THOMAS, at Scituate, Mass., before 1640.

THOMAS, living Boston, Mass., 1646.

THOMAS, at Salisbury, Mass., 1652.

THOMAS, resident New London, Conn., 1665-66.

THOMAS, residing Roxbury, Mass., about 1640.

THOMAS, cordwainer, will probated Boston, Mass., 1700.

WILLIAM, resident Braintree, Mass., 1662.

WILLIAM, living Dorchester, Mass., 1636, freeman 1642, died 1668.

WILLIAM, tailor, settled Salem, Mass., before 1642, at Newton, Mass., 1678, later removed Cambridge and Watertown, Mass.

WILLIAM, on record Concord, Mass., 1671, removed to what is now Newton, Mass., 1673.

WILLIAM, resident Lynn, Mass., 1683.

ROCK

JOSEPH, resident Boston, Mass., 1652.

ROCKETT, ROCKWOOD

JOHN, at Dorchester, Mass., 1633.

JOSEPH, married Rehoboth, Mass., 1681.

NICHOLAS, lived in what is now Medfield, Mass., 1640, removed Braintree, Mass.

RICHARD, brother of John, living Dorchester, Mass.; 1635 removed Weymouth, Mass.

ROCKWELL

ABRAHAM, at Windsor, Conn., 1640; no issue.

JOHN, settled Dorchester, Mass. One first settlers Windsor, Conn., where he died 1662.

JONATHAN, resident Norwalk, Conn., 1687-94.

WILLIAM, b. Eng. 1595, came Dorchester, Mass., 1630, removed Windsor, Conn., 1636.

RODMAN

Ancient English surname, the English ancestor John Rodman.

THOMAS, surgeon, Quaker, resident Newport, R. I., 1682.

ROE, ROWE

From Gaelic, signifying red-haired; the Norman. French, *Rou,* Rufus.

ANTHONY, resident Falmouth, Maine, 1663-83.

EDWARD, swore allegiance Exeter, N. H., 1677.

ELIAS, married, Charlestown, Mass., 1656.

HUGH, first lived Weymouth, Mass., resident Hartford, Conn., 1661, at Suffield, Conn., before 1678, where he died 1689.

JOHN, b. Ireland 1628, settled Lynn, Mass., 1655, removed Easthampton, L. I.

JOHN, resident Gloucester, Mass., 1651.

MARK, resident York, Maine, 1666.

MATTHEW, living New Haven, Conn., 1651.

NICHOLAS, lawyer, living Portsmouth, N. H., 1640.

RICHARD, brother of Elias, lived Charlestown, Mass.; perished at sea 1666.

RICHARD, resident Dover, N. H., 1650.

THOMAS, resident Hampton, N. H., 1678.

ROGERS

The name is derived from the Teutonic *Rhu,* rest, quiet, peace, and *gard,* a keeper; or *Rhu-geren,* one desirous of rest; *Rodgarus,* all counsel or strong counsel. The English descent is traced to Sir John Fitz Roger.

DAVID, resident Braintree, Mass., 1641.

ELEZER, minister, son of Richard R. of Weathersfield, county Essex, Eng., came to N. E. 1638, first minister, Rowley, Mass.

HENRY, took oath of allegiance Springfield, Mass., 1678.

JAMES, b. Eng. 1615, settled New London, Conn., 1635, acquired land Stratford, Conn., removed Milford, Conn., 1652, finally returned New London, Conn.

JAMES, freeman Newport, R.. I., 1640.

JEREMIAH, married, Dorchester, Mass., 1660.

JOHN, came Plymouth, Mass., 1631, removed Duxbury, Mass., 1634.

JOHN, freeman Watertown, Mass., 1637.

JOHN, married, Weymouth, Mass., 1639, removed Scituate, Mass., 1644.

JOHN, baker, freeman, Watertown, Mass., 1639, removed Billerica, Mass.

JOHN, at Dedham, Mass., 1636, afterwards Watertown, Mass.

JOHN, resident Branford, Conn., 1662, removed Huntington, L. I.

JOHN, married Duxbury, Mass., 1666.

JOHN, died Boston, Mass., 1670.

JOHN, glazier, resident Salem, Mass., 1681.

JOHN, representative Bristol, R. I., 1689.

JONATHAN, resident Westerly, R. I., before 1680.

NATHANIEL, minister, son Rev. John R. of Dedham, county Essex, Eng., b. Haverhill, Eng., 1598. Arrived Boston, Mass., 1636, settled Ipswich, Mass., 1638.

RICHARD, resident Dover, N. H., 1642.

ROBERT, b. Eng. 1625, became resident Newbury, Mass., 1651.

SIMON, shoemaker, b. Eng. 1615, came from London, Eng., to N. Eng., 1635; lived first Concord, Mass., removed Boston, Mass., 1642.

THOMAS, Mayflower passenger.

THOMAS, freeman Watertown, Mass., 1637.

THOMAS, resident Saco, Maine, 1652.

WILLIAM, merchant, Boston, Mass., 1667.

WILLIAM, living Charlestown, Mass., 1678.

WILLIAM, died Nantucket, Mass., 1673.

WILLIAM, b. Eng. 1600, resident Wethersfield, Conn., 1637-40, living Hempstead, L. I., 1649-56.

ROLFE

DANIEL, son of Robert R.; resided Ipswich, Mass., died Salem, Mass., 1654.

HENRY, b. Eng. 1590, came from Wiltshire, Eng., to Newbury, Mass., before 1642.

JOHN, husbandman, brother of preceding, b. Eng. 1588, came from Melchit Park,

Wiltshire, Eng., to Newbury. Mass., 1638, one of the proprietors Nantucket, Mass., 1663, died 1664.

ROLLO

ALEXANDER, early proprietor East Haddam, Conn., removed Middletown, Conn., where he died 1709.

ROLLOCK

ROBERT, died Sandwich, Mass., 1669.

RONALLS

JOHN, resident Wickford, R. I., 1674.

JOSIAH, brother preceding, at Wickford, R. I., 1674.

SAMUEL, brother of preceding, living Wickford, R. I., 1674.

ROOD

THOMAS, resident Norwich, Conn., 1649.

ROOKER

WILLIAM, took oath of allegiance Hadley, Mass., 1679.

ROOME, ROME

JOHN, came from Bristol, Eng., to Portsmouth, N. H., 1638.

ROOT

A place lying low, the base, foot or bottom of a mountain, the lower part of land.

JOHN, came from Badby, Northamptonshire, Eng., settled Farmington, Conn., where he died 1684.

JOSIAH, came from county Kent, Eng., to Salem, Mass., 1635.

RALPH, b. Eng. 1585, came Boston, Mass., 1635.

RICHARD, member church Salem, Mass., 1636, afterwards at Lynn, Mass., removed Fairfield, Conn.

ROBERT, resident Newport, R. I., 1639.

THOMAS, weaver, son John R. of Badby, Eng., b. 1605; came Salem, Mass., 1637, removed Hartford, Conn., soon after, to Northampton, Mass., 1654; died 1694.

THOMAS, mariner, died Boston, Mass., 1683.

ROPER

A common English name; the progenitor was of Norman descent known as *Musard,* which was Latinized as *Hasculpus.* A grandson of the progenitor, assumed the title of *De Rubra Spatha,* which after being corrupted into *Rospeare, Rousper Rooper,* finally became *Roper.*

JOHN, b. New Buckingham, county Norfolk, Eng., 1588, settled Dedham, Mass., 1637.

JOHN, resident Charlestown, Mass., 1647-58, removed Lancaster, Mass.; killed by Indians, 1676.

WALTER, resident Hampton, N. H., 1639, removed Ipswich, Mass., before 1666.

ROPES

GEORGE, resident Salem, Mass., 1637.

JAMES, living Boston, Mass., 1680.

SAMUEL, brother of George, at Salem, Mass., 1668.

WILLIAM, brother of preceding, married Salem, Mass., 1676.

ROSE

GEORGE, one founders of church, Braintree, Mass., 1639, freeman Concord, Mass., 1640, died 1649.

GEORGE, resident New Haven, Conn., 1662.

JOHN, came Watertown, Mass., 1636, removed Branford, Conn.

RICHARD, inhabitant Salem, Mass., 1668.

ROBERT, b. Eng. 1594, came from Ipswich, county Suffolk, Eng., to Watertown, Mass., 1634, removed Wethersfield, Conn., 1639, thence Stratford, Conn., before 1648.

ROGER, mariner, married Watertown, Mass., 1661.

THOMAS, living Scituate, Mass., before 1660.

THOMAS, married New London, Conn., before 1683.

ROSS

From the Gaelic, a shire of Scotland, *Ros,* a peninsula, an isthmus, a promontory. *Rhos* in Welsh is a moor, a bog. *Ros* in Cornish British is a mountain, a meadow, a common; *Rose* and *Rosh* signifies a valley or dale between hills.

ALEXANDER, inhabitant New Hampshire 1688.

GEORGE, b. Scotland 1635, settled New Haven, Conn., where he married 1659.

GEORGE, early settler Concord, Mass., where he died 1649.

JAMES, b. Eng. about 1635, resident Sudbury, Mass., 1656.

JAMES, married Falmouth, Maine, 1657

JOHN, married, Cambridge, Mass., 1659.

JOHN, resident Ipswich, Mass., 1664.

KILLECRISS may be Gilchrist, resident Ipswich, Mass., 1678.

THOMAS, married, Cambridge, Mass., 1659.

ROSSETER, ROCESTER

EDWARDS, assistant in Winthrop's council, came to N. E. 1630, located Dorchester, Mass., but died same year, leaving only son in America, Dr. Bryan R., who removed Windsor, Conn., 1636, removed Guilford, Conn., 1652.

HUGH, granted land Taunton, Mass., 1637.

ROSWELL, ROSEWELL

Rosveldt, the rose-field; *Rosville*, the town on the heath or promontory.

WILLIAM, merchant, inhabitant Charlestown, Mass., 1658, became resident Branford, Conn., removed New Haven, Conn., 1668.

ROTHERFORD, RUDDERFORD, RUTHERFORD

From the lands of Rutherford on the river Tweed, in parish, Maxton, Roxburghshire, Scotland. The name derived from Welsh *Ruther*, rushing, swift and *fford*, a ford or way.

HENRY, living New Haven, Conn., 1643.

ROUNDS

A descriptive surname; seat of the English family in counties of Kent and Oxford, England.

MARK, gunsmith, on record, Sandwich, Mass., 1681, afterwards Portland, Maine, 1716.

PHILIP, mentioned in New England Archives 1678.

ROUNDY, ROUNDEE, ROUNDAY

PHILIP, married, Salem, Mass., 1671.

ROUNSEVILLE

PHILIP, b. Honiton, Eng., settled Freetown, Mass., 1680.

ROUS, ROUSE, ROWSE

From French, signifying, red, red-haired, same as Rufus.

ALEXANDER, at Cambridge, Mass., removed Groton, Mass., 1672.

EDWARD, resident Gloucester, Mass., 1651.

FAITHFUL, freeman Charlestown, Mass., 1641.

JOHN, married, Duxbury, Mass., before 1640, removed Marshfield, Mass., where he died 1684.

SIMON, representative Little Compton, R. I., 1690.

WILLIAM, goldsmith, Boston, Mass., 1676; died 1705, aged 65.

ROWDEN

JOHN, resident Salem, Mass., 1652-68.

ROWELL

From river *Rouel* in the Netherlands. Jacob at Amesbury, Mass., 1699.

NATHANIEL, resident Salisbury, Mass., 1650.

PHILIP, living Amesbury, Mass., 1677.

THOMAS, settled Salem, Mass., 1649, removed Salisbury, Mass., 1650, resident Ipswich, Mass., 1652-58, died Andover, Mass., 1643.

THOMAS, worsted comber, resident Boston, Mass., 1658.

Valentine, carpenter, married Salisbury, Mass., 1643.

ROWLAND

HENRY, resident Fairfield, Conn., 1650-70, died 1690.

RICHARD, inhabitant Salem, Mass., 1648, at Marblehead, Mass., 1673.

SAMUEL, resident Stratford, Conn.

ROWLE

RICHARD, inhabitant Newbury, Mass., 1678.

ROBERT, at Marblehead, Mass., 1668.

ROWLEY

From Saxon; *row*, sweet or pleasant, and *ley*, a field.

HENRY, at Plymouth, Mass., 1632, removed Scituate, Mass., 1634, removed Barnstable, Mass., 1639.

MOSES, brother of preceding, married Barnstable, Mass., 1652.

THOMAS, married, Windsor, Conn., 1669, removed Simsbury, Conn., 1682.

ROWTON

RICHARD, b. Eng. 1599, came to N. E. 1635.

ROY

From Gaelic *Ruadh, Roe, Roy*, red-haired, also *Roye*, a town in England. *Roi*, French King, hence LeRoy.

JOHN, resident Charlestown, Mass., before 1670.

ROYAL, RYALL

ISAAC, carpenter, married, Dorchester, Mass., before 1668.

JOSEPH, resident Charlestown, Mass., before 1683.

WILLIAM, cleaver of timber, at Salem, Mass., 1629, removed Casco, Maine, 1636.

RUCK

SAMUEL, freeman Boston, Mass., 1683.

THOMAS, resident Charlestown, Mass., 1638, removed Salem, Mass., 1640.

THOMAS, innholder, at Boston, Mass., 1651.

RUDD

JOHN, resident Norwich, Conn., at Preston, Conn., 1686.

JONATHAN, settled New Haven, Conn., 1640, removed Saybrook, Conn., 1646, freeman Hartford, Conn., 1651.

RUDDOCK, RUDDYK

JOHN, freeman Salisbury, Mass., 1640.

RUEL

JOHN, married Saco, Maine, 1668.

RUGG

JOHN, swore allegiance Maine 1665.

JOHN, resident Lancaster, Mass., 1654.

RUGGLES

A town in France on the Eure. Thomas R., English ancestor 1547.

JEFFREY, came from Sudbury, county Suffolk, Eng., in Winthrop's fleet, died 1630.

JOHN, freeman Boston, Mass., 1632.

JOHN, shoemaker, b. Eng. 1591, came from Nazing, county Essex, Eng., to Roxbury, Mass., 1635.

THOMAS, son of Nicholas, great grandson Thomas R., brother of preceding, b. Sudbury, county Suffolk, Eng., 1594, came Roxbury, Mass., 1637.

RUMBALL

DANIEL, blacksmith, resident Salem, Mass., 1644.

THOMAS, b. Eng. 1613, at Boston, Mass., 1635, settled Stratford, Conn.

RUMRILL, RUMERELL, RUMMERELL

SIMON, married Enfield, Conn., 1692, where he had resided since 1672.

RUMSEY, RUMSIE

ROBERT, inhabitant Fairfield, Conn., before 1670.

RUNDLE

WILLIAM, at Greenwich, Conn., 1672.

RUNDLET, RUNLET, RANLET

CHARLES, settled Exeter, N. H., 1675.

RUSCO, RESKIE, RESKOE, RESCUE

WILLIAM, b. Eng. 1594, came Cambridge, Mass., 1635, original proprietor Hartford, Conn., 1636.

RUSH

JASPER, freeman Dorchester, Mass., 1644.

RUSS

A Russian so called in Holland.

JOHN, at Newbury, Mass., 1635.

RUSSELL

From the French signifying red-haired, somewhat reddish; carrot-color. The ancestry of the family has been traced to Sigurd Hring Turstain, King of Sweden 735. In thirteenth generation from Turstain, William Bertrand was with his son Hugh at the battle of Hastings. The latter inherited the castle of Rozel in England, was corrupted in the twelfth century to Russell.

GEORGE, b. Eng. 1616, came from Hawkhurst, county Kent, Eng., settled Hingham, Mass., 1636, removed Scituate, Mass., 1646.

GEORGE, youngest son William, fifth Earl of Bedford, admitted freeman, Boston, Mass., 1680, returned England 1683.

HENRY, resident Weymouth, Mass., 1639; no male issue.

HENRY, b. Eng. 1610, at Ipswich, Mass., 1665.

JAMES, resident New Haven, Conn., before 1643.

JOHN, b. Eng. 1597, freeman Cambridge, Mass., 1636, removed Wethersfield, Conn., 1649, thence Hadley, Mass., 1659; died 1680.

JOHN, shoemaker, resident Charlestown, Mass., 1640, one first settlers Woburn, Mass., where he became freeman 1644.

JOHN, resident Marshfield, Mass., 1643-51.

JOHN, living New Haven, Conn., 1664.

JOHN, representative Dartmouth, Mass., 1665-83.

JONATHAN, brother of preceding, took oath of allegiance Dartmouth, Mass., 1684.

RALPH, came from Pontipool, County Monmouth, Eng., to Taunton, Mass., one first settlers Dartmouth, Mass.

RALPH, married, New Haven, Conn., 1663.

RICHARD, b. Eng. 1611, son of Paul R., came from Hertfordshire, Eng., to Charlestown, Mass., 1641.

ROBERT, b. Eng. 1630, of Scotch descent, married, Andover, Mass., 1659, died 1710.

THOMAS, b. Eng. 1641, freeman Charlestown, Mass., 1676, died in that year.

THOMAS, Marblehead, 1674.

WILLIAM, carpenter, resident Cambridge, Mass., 1645.

WILLIAM, mason, married, Boston, Mass., 1653.

RUST

Ancient surname of England, also found in Germany, derived from the French *LeRous*, signifying a ruddy or russet complexion. It may have come from Holland or Low Dutch dialect, signifying repose or rest. Hugh Rust was living in England 1312.

EDWARD, resident Dedham, Mass., 1665.

HENRY, glover, came from Hingham, County Norfolk, Eng., to Hingham, Mass., 1633, removed Boston, Mass., 1651.

ISRAEL, married, Northampton, Mass., 1669.

NATHANIEL, freeman Ipswich, Mass., 1674.

NICHOLAS took oath of allegiance Springfield, Mass., 1678.

RUTTER

JOHN, b. Eng. 1616, came to Sudbury, Mass., 1638.

RUTTY

EDWARD, resident Milford, Conn., 1677, removed Killingworth, Conn., 1678.

SABIN

William, signed compact, Rehoboth, Mass., 1643.

SABLE, SABLES

John, inhabitant of Hartford, Conn., 1639.

SACKET, SACKETT

John, married at New Haven, Conn., 1652.

Simon, brother of the preceding, came from Bristol, Eng., to Cambridge, Mass., 1638, his widow became the wife of William Bloomfield and removed to Hartford, Conn.

SADD

John, tanner, came from Earl's Colne, county of Essex, Eng., to Hartford, Conn., before 1674.

SADLER

Abial, soldier in the colonial service at Gloucester, Mass., 1689.

Anthony, shoemaker, came from Southampton, Eng., to Newbury, Mass., 1638, removed to Salisbury, Mass., and was drowned Feb. 23, 1651.

John, freeman at Gloucester, Mass., 1642.

John, resident on the Glastonbury side of Wethersfield, Conn., 1643.

Richard, town clerk, came from Worcester, Eng., 1636, to Lynn, Mass.; returned to Eng. 1641.

SAFFERY

Solomon, mathematician, engaged in running line between Mass. and Conn., 1642.

SAFFIN, SAFFYN

John, lawyer, selectman at Scituate, Mass., 1653, freeman at Boston, Mass., 1671, removed to Bristol, R. I., 1690; judge of Supreme Court of Mass., 1701.

SAFFORD

A corruption of Seaford, a town in the county of Sussex, Eng.

Thomas, b. County of Suffolk, Eng., settled at Ipswich, Mass., 1641.

SAGE

David, b. Wales, 1639, came to N. E. 1650, one of early settlers of Middletown, Conn., 1652.

SALE, SEALE, SAILE

Sahl or *saal,* in German signifies a hall or court. French, *salle.* The name, however, may be local and derived from the river Sale in France, or Saal, a river in Bavaria.

Edward, b. Eng. 1611, came from London, Eng., to Salem, Mass., 1635, reremoved Rehoboth, Mass., 1644.

Obadiah, freeman, Boston, Mass., 1681.

SALISBURY, SARISBURY

A Saxon word, a city and capital of Wiltshire, Eng. The old town of Salisbury anciently stood upon a hill where there was no water, therefore the name sometimes written Salusbury, signifies a town of health, a dry town.

John, came Boston 1630-40, taxpayer Suffolk county, Mass., 1689.

Nicholas, b. Eng. 1637, on record Salisbury, Mass., 1685.

William, b. Danbigshire Waters, 1622, came Dorchester, Mass., 1648, settled Milton, Mass., 1664, removed Swansea, Mass., 1671.

SALLOWS

Benjamin, Salem, Mass., 1637.

Michael, resident Salem, Mass., 1635.

SALLS

Samuel, married, Lynn, Mass., 1663.

SALLY, SALLEE

Manes, admitted to church Charlestown, Mass., 1647.

SALMON, SALMONDS, SAMMON

Clement, married, Boston, Mass., 1660.

Daniel, at Lynn, Mass., 1630, served in Pequot's War.

George, resident Salem, Mass., 1668.

John, at New Haven, Conn., 1682.

John, died Newport, R. I., 1676.

Samuel, prosecuted as Quaker, Salem, Mass., 1660.

Thomas, inhabitant Northampton, Mass., 1659.

William, took oath of allegiance, Amesbury, Mass., 1677.

SALTER

A name of a trade; one who sells salt.

Charles, resident Boston, Mass., 1685.

Eneas, mason, Boston, Mass., 1673.

Henry, residing Charlestown, Mass., 1656.

Matthew, at Marblehead, Mass., 1674.

Sampson, fisherman, came from Caversham, county of Oxford, Eng., to Newport, R. I., 1639.

Theophilus, at Ipswich, Mass., 1648, removed Salem, Mass., 1654.

Walter, at Boston, Mass., 1658, shortly afterwards settled on Long Island.

William, shoemaker, Boston, Mass., 1634, freeman, 1636.

SALTONSTALL

Richard, a Knight, son of Samuel S. and nephew of Sir Richard S., came from Halifax in the West Riding, county of York, in Winthrop's fleet, settled at Watertown, Mass.; returned to England 1631.

SAMFIELD

AUSTIN, at Fairfield, Conn., 1658, died 1661.

SAMPSON

ABRAHAM, at Duxbury, Mass., 1638, original proprietor Bridgewater, Mass., 1645.

HENRY, brother of the preceding, *Mayflower* passenger in the family of his uncle Edward Tilley; freeman Duxbury, Mass., 1635.

JAMES, at Dartmouth, Mass., 1686.

JOHN, merchant at Boston, Mass., removed Beverly, Mass., 1671.

JOHN, married, New London, Conn., 1672.

ROBERT, came to Boston, Mass., 1630, was a cousin of Gov. Winthrop and son of John S. of the parish of Kersey, county of Suffolk, Eng. The family was ancient in the ranks of Knight and resided at Sampson's Hall. He was a member of the artillery company 1639, and returned to England soon afterwards.

ROGER, inhabitant Ipswich, Mass., 1654.

SAMS, SAMMES

Constantine, resident Boston, Mass., 1678.

JOHN, at Roxbury, Mass., 1640, returned to Eng. and was a successful preacher at Coggeshall, county of Essex.

RALPH, tailor, located Dorchester, Mass., removed Boston, Mass., 1659.

THOMAS, granted land Salem, Mass., 1638, living Marblehead, Mass., 1648.

SAMUEL

JOHN, married at Boston, Mass., 1652.

SAMWAYS, SAMOIS, SAMWIS

RICHARD, at Windsor, Conn., 1640.

SANBORN, SAMBORNE

The name is derived from the Anglo-Saxon words *sand* and *bum* (a stream). It is, however, a place name from Sambourne in Wiltshire, Eng. The name is mentioned in England as early as 1194, spelled *DeSandbourne;* the lineage is traced to Nicholas Sambourne of Wiltshire, 1320.

JOHN, son of William, of Brimpton, Berkshire, Eng., b. Eng., 1620, was brought by his grandfather, Rev. Stephen Bachiler, to Boston, Mass., 1632. He settled Hampton, N. H., 1640, and was known as Lieut. John.

STEPHEN, youngest brother of the preceding, settled at Hampton, N. H., returned to England with his grandfather.

WILLIAM, brother of the preceding, b. Eng., 1622, settled Hampton, N. H., 1639.

SANBROOKE

THOMAS, will probated 1650.

SAND, SANDS, SANDES, SANDYS

From a Danish word meaning sense, wit, or from *Sand, Sandy,* a Scottish abbreviation of Alexander.

HENRY, early settler Boston, Mass., was at Rowley, Mass., 1639.

JAMES, b. Reading, Berkshire, Eng., 1622, settled Taunton, Mass., 1658, removed before 1673 to Block Island now New Shoreham, R. I.

JOHN, married Boston, Mass., 1653.

SANDERSON

EDWARD, b. Eng. 1615, came from Norfolk, Eng., to N. E. 1638, for a short time at Watertown and Cambridge, Mass., became in that year one of the first settlers of Hampton, N. H.

ROBERT, brother of the preceding, one of first settlers at Hampton, N. H., 1638.

SANDON

ARTHUR, licensed to keep an inn, Salem, Mass., 1639.

SANFORD, SAMFORD, SANDFORD

From Sanford, a place in Westmoreland, Eng., the sand-ford. Thomas de Sanford, a follower of William the Conquerer, founded the Shopshire clan.

ANDREW, at Hartford, Conn., 1651, removed Milford, Conn., 1667.

JAMES, married, Boston, 1656.

JOHN, freeman Boston, Mass., 1632, resided Portsmouth, R. I., 1647.

JOHN, resident Boston, Mass., 1654.

NATHANIEL, resident Hartford, Conn., 1653, where he died 1687.

RICHARD, laborer Boston, 1640.

THOMAS, son of Ezekiel S., grandson Thomas S., a tradesman of Essex, Eng., b. 1607, came to Boston, 1631, landholder Dorchester, 1634, settled Hartford, Conn., 1639, one of the original settlers, Milford, Conn.

ZACHARY, settled at Hartford, Conn., was at Saybrook, Conn., 1651.

SANGER

RICHARD was at Hingham, Mass., 1636.

RICHARD, blacksmith, came from Dunhead, county of Wilts, Eng., as a servant of Edmond Goodenow; at Sudbury, Mass., 1646; removed Watertown, Mass., 1649.

SANKEYS

ROBERT, b. Eng. 1605, came from London, Eng., to Saco, Maine, 1635.

SANSOM

RICHARD, tailor, b. Eng. 1607, came to Nantucket, Mass., 1635.

SARGENT, SEARGEANT, SERGEANT

Name from a military title.

EDWARD, resident Newbury, Mass., 1684.

JOHN, Saco, Maine, 1680.

JONATHAN, resident Branford, Conn., 1646.

PETER, merchant, came from London, Eng., to Boston, Mass., 1667.

STEPHEN, resident Boston, Mass., 1670.

WILLIAM came from near Bath, Eng., to Ipswich, Mass., 1633; one of the first settlers of Newbury, Mass., 1635; with Rev. Stephen Bachiler, began Hampton, N. H., plantation 1638, removed Salisbury, Mass., and in 1655 helped in the settlement of Amesbury, Mass.

WILLIAM, preacher, b. Northampton, Eng., 1602, came to Charlestown, Mass., 1638, preached Malden, Mass., 1648-50, removed Barnstable, Mass, 1656.

WILLIAM, granted land Gloucester, Mass., 1649.

WILLIAM, called second, b. Bristol, Eng.; at Gloucester, Mass., 1678.

SAULE

THOMAS, resident of New Haven, Conn., 1639.

SAUNDERS, SANDERS

CHRISTOPHER, resident Windsor, Conn., 1671.

DANIEL, died Cambridge, Mass., 1640.

EDWARD, at Portsmouth, N. H., 1639.

GEORGE, brother of Christopher, freeman Windsor, Conn., 1667.

JAMES, took oath of allegiance, Haverhill, Mass., 1677.

JOHN, came N. E. 1638, at Newbury, Mass., 1642, an original grantee Salisbury, Mass., returned to England, 1655.

JOHN, son of the preceding, came to N. E. 1635, locating Hampton, N. H., before 1643, removed Wells, Maine, 1645.

JOHN, member of the church, Salem, Mass., 1637.

JOHN, at Billerica, Mass., 1679.

JOSEPH, inhabitant Dover, N. H., killed by the Indians 1689.

MARTIN, currier, b. Eng. 1595, came Boston, Mass., 1635, innkeeper Braintree, Mass., 1639, freeman 1640.

ROBERT, at Cambridge, Mass., 1636, removed Boston, Mass., 1639, thence to Dorchester, Mass.

TOBIAS, Scotch ancestry, came to Taunton, Mass., 1643, freeman Newport, R. I., 1655, removed Westerly, R. I., 1669.

WILLIAM, carpenter, among original settlers of Hampton, N. H., 1638.

SAUNDERSON

EDWARD, married Watertown, Mass., 1645.

ROBERT, freeman Hampton, N. H., 1639.

SAVAGE

EDWARD, at Dorchester, Mass., 1664.

JOHN, freeman, Middletown, Conn., 1654.

JOHN, married Rehoboth, Mass., 1668.

JOHN, resident Nantucket, Mass., 1672.

JOHN, constable Chatham, Mass., 1681.

THOMAS, tailor, son of William S., a blacksmith of Taunton, county of Somerset, Eng., where the name prevails in the parish register to the reign of Queen Elizabeth, b. Eng. 1608, arrived Boston, Mass., 1635, on account of religious principles went to Providence, R. I., 1638, but returned the following year to Boston, Mass., afterwards resided at Hingham and Andover, Mass.

SAVIL, SAVEL, SAVILLE

EDWARD, resident Weymouth, Mass., 1640.

WILLIAM, at Braintree, Mass., 1640.

SAVORY, SAVARY

ROBERT, married Newbury, Mass., 1656.

THOMAS, resident Plymouth, Mass., 1643.

THOMAS took oath of allegiance, Ipswich, Mass., 1634, removed Newport, R. I., 1639, thence Sandwich, Mass.

WILLIAM, brother of the preceding, at Ipswich, Mass., 1634.

SAWDY

JOHN, cordwainer, at Boston, Mass., 1654.

SAWIN

JOHN, son of Robert S., of Boxford, county of Suffolk, Eng., brought by his mother, a widow, to Watertown, Mass., 1641, made freeman 1651, died September 2, 1690.

SAWTELL, SARTELLE, SAUTELL

RICHARD, freeman Watertown, Mass., 1635, removed Groton, Mass., 1662, where he died August 21, 1691.

THOMAS, brother of the preceding, freeman at Boston, Mass., 1649. No issue.

SAWYER

EDMUND, at Ipswich, Mass., 1636, removed York, Maine, before 1661.

EDWARD, son of John S., a farmer of Lincolnshire, Eng., came to N. E. 1636 settled at Ipswich, Mass., removed Rowley, Mass.

HENRY, Haverhill, Mass., 1646, the next year Hampton, N. H., and York, Maine 1676.

JAMES, at Ipswich, Mass., 1669, removed Gloucester, Mass., 1677.

JOHN, married, Marshfield, Mass., 1666.

ROBERT, Hampton, N. H., 1640.

THOMAS, brother of Edward, b. Eng. 1616, came to N. E. 1636, settled Rowley, Mass., 1639, one of the first settlers Lancaster, Mass., 1647.

WILLIAM, brother of the preceding, b. Eng. 1613, at Salem, Mass., 1640, at Wenham, Mass., 1645, finally removed Newbury, Mass.

SAXTON, SEXTON

An under office of the church, a place named from *Sax-town*, a town of the Saxons.

GEORGE, resident Westfield, Mass., 1667.

GILES came to Boston or Charlestown, Mass., 1630.

JOSEPH, married, Stoughton, Conn.

PETER, preacher, from Yorkshire, Eng., at Scituate, Mass., 1640, returned to England where he died October 1, 1651.

RICHARD, married, Windsor, Conn., 1646.

THOMAS, miller, resident Boston, Mass., 1645.

SAYER, SAYERS, SAYRE

THOMAS, at Lynn, Mass., 1635, became one of the purchasers of Southampton, L. I., 1640.

SAYLE, SAYLES

JOHN, b. Eng. 1633, freeman Providence, R. I., 1655.

SAYWARD, SAYWORD

Edmund, at Ipswich, Mass., 1635.

HENRY, at Hampton, N. H., 1646, removed Portsmouth, N. H., 1650, afterwards York, Maine, 1664.

RICHARD, resident of New Hampshire, 1662.

SAYWELL

ROBERT, b. Eng. 1605, came Boston, Mass., 1635.

SCADDING

WILLIAM, Taunton, Mass., 1638.

SCADLOCK

WILLIAM, freeman, Saco, Maine, 1653, died 1662.

SCALES

JOHN, at Rowley, Mass., 1648.

SCAMMON, SCAMMAN, SCAMMOND

WILLIAM, at Boston, Mass., 1640.

SCAMP

ROBERT, married Gloucester, Mass., 1661.

SCANT

WILLIAM, married Braintree, Mass., 1654.

SCARBOROUGH, SCARBARROW

A Saxon word from the seaport and borough, Scarborough in Yorkshire, England, from *scear*, a sharp rock or hill and *burgh*, a town or fort on or by the sharp-peaked rocks.

JOHN, freeman Boston, Mass., 1640.

SCARLET

BENJAMIN, b. Eng. 1624, bound as an apprentice to Capt. Endicott, of Salem, Mass., 1635.

JOHN, at Springfield, Mass., 1640, removed Boston 1650.

SAMUEL, master of a schooner, brother of preceding, freeman and constable, Boston, 1672.

SCATE

JOHN, at Boston, Mass., 1659.

SCATHE, SKEATH

JOHN, cordwainer, Hingham, Mass., 1647, later at Boston, Mass.

SCHRICK

PAULUS, Dutchman, Hartford, Conn., 1635.

SCOFIELD, SCOVIL, SKOFIELD

ARTHUR, proprietor Middletown, Conn., 1671.

DANIEL, grandson Sir Cuthbert S., of Scofield, Manor, England, b. Rochdale, Lancashire, Eng., came Ipswich, Mass., 1639, removed Stamford, Conn., 1641, where he died 1670.

EDWARD, resident Haddam, Conn.

JOHN, married, Farmington, Conn., 1666, removed Waterbury, Conn., thence Haddam, Conn., where he died 1712.

JOHN, married, Middletown, Conn., 1698.

RICHARD, b. Eng. 1626, came Ipswich, Mass., 1648, removed Stamford, Conn., 1650, where he died 1671.

WILLIAM, settled Haddam, Conn., after 1668.

SCOLLEY, SCHOLLEY

JOHN, b. 1641, lived at Charlestown, Mass., at Malden, Mass., 1674.

SCOON, SCONE

JOHN, married, Westfield, Mass., before 1676.

SCOTCHFORD

JOHN, town clerk, Concord, Mass., where he died June 10, 1696. No issue.

SCOTT

Most authorities claim the name is derived from Scota, a daughter of Pharoah, King of Egypt, drowned in the Red Sea. A native of Scotland, the original word in Ossian is *Scuta*, which signified restless wanderer, hence the propriety of the name *Scuite* or Scot.

BENJAMIN, b. Eng., settled Braintree, 1643, removed to Cambridge, Mass., 1644, to Rowley, Mass., before 1652, where he died 1671.

EDMUND, Farmington, Conn., 1649, original proprietor Waterbury, Conn., where he died 1691.

JOHN, freeman Mass. 1639.

JOHN, freeman Mass. 1643.

JOHN, servant at Salem, Mass., 1648, removed Providence, R. I.

JOHN, b. Eng. 1607, at Charlestown, Mass., 1658, where he died Jan. 25, 1682.

JOHN, married, Springfield, Mass., 1659, removed Suffield, Conn., before 1683.

JOHN, married, Roxbury, Mass., 1672.

RICHARD, shoemaker, b. Eng. 1607, joined church, Boston, Mass., 1634, removed to Ipswich, Mass., in that year, removed Providence, R. I., 1637, converted to Quakerism, first Quaker resident Providence, R. I.

ROBERT, came in Winthrop's fleet, settled Boston, Mass., where he died Feb., 1654.

ROBERT, inhabitant, Ipswich, Mass., 1638.

ROGER, at Lynn, Mass., 1642.

THOMAS, b. Eng. 1594, came Ipswich, Mass., 1634.

THOMAS, at Hartford, Conn., 1637, was killed careless by John Ewe, Nov. 6, 1643, leaving one son who left no issue.

WILLIAM, at Hadley, now Hatfield, Mass., 1668.

SCOTTOW, SCOTTAWAY

Joshua, b. Eng. 1615, merchant, brought by his mother, a widow, to Boston, 1634, captain and magistrate at Scarborough, Maine, 1676, died Jan. 20, 1698.

THOMAS, joiner, elder brother of the preceding, joined church Boston, Mass., 1641. Will probated Dec. 18, 1661.

SCRANTON

From the Dutch *schrantsen,* to tear, seize or break, so named perhaps from his warlike propensities.

DENNIS, resident New Haven, Conn., 1660.

JOHN, farmer, came from Guilford, Eng. to Boston, Mass., 1637, two years later was one of the founders Guilford, Conn.

SCRIBNER

BENJAMIN, married, Norwalk, Conn., 1680.

JOHN, came from Kent, Eng., before 1652 to Hampton, N. H., afterwards at Dover and Exeter, N. H.

SCRIPTURE

SAMUEL, b. Eng. 1650, settled Groton, Mass., before 1675.

SCRIVEN, SCRIEVEN

JOHN, died Dover, N. H., Oct. 2, 1675.

WILLIAM, at Kittery, Maine, 1680.

SCROOP

ADRIAN, at Hartford, Conn., 1665.

SCROUGS

THOMAS, freeman Salem, Mass., 1635.

SCUDDER

JAMES, at Woburn, Mass., before 1647.

JOHN, b. Eng. 1624, came N. E. 1635, was at Charlestown, Mass., 1639, and Salem, Mass., 1640, removed to Southold, L. I., 1654.

JOHN, at Barnstable, Mass., 1640.

THOMAS, granted land Salem, Mass., 1648.

SCULLARD, SKULLARD

SAMUEL, at Newbury, Mass., 1637, removed next year Hampton, N. H., returned to Newbury.

SEABROOK

ROBERT, at Stratford, Conn., before 1668.

SEABURY

JOHN, resident Boston, Mass., before 1642.

SEAGER, SEEGER, SEGER

HENRY, married Newton, Mass., 1671.

RICHARD, at Hartford, Conn., 1650.

SEAILES

JAMES, freeman Rowley, Mass., 1684.

SEALIS, SELLICE

RICHARD, at Scituate, Mass., 1635.

SEAMAN

A sailor that follows the sea.

CALEB, at New Haven, Conn., 1646.

JOHN, inhabitant Wethersfield, Conn., removed to Stamford, Conn., 1641.

THOMAS, lived at Swansea, Mass., 1687.

SEARCH

JOHN, weaver, admitted inhabitant Boston, Mass., 1641.

SEARLE, SEARLES

ANDREW, settled Ipswich, Mass., removed Kittery, Maine, 1668, thence to Rowley, Mass., where he died Nov. 7, 1670.

DANIEL, a gentleman of large estate, on record, Boston, Mass., 1666.

EDWARD, living at Warwick, R. I., 1679.

EPHRAIM, freeman Boston, Mass., 1672.

JOHN, married, Springfield, Mass., 1639.

JOHN, married, Boston, Mass., 1661, removed Stonington, Conn., 1670.

RICHARD, at Providence, R. I., 1638.

ROBERT, b. Dorchester, Eng., 1640, settled at Dorchester, Mass., 1660.

SEARS

DANIEL, mariner, resident Boston, Mass., 1652.

JOHN, at Charlestown, Mass., 1639, freeman Woburn, Mass., 1641. No issue.

RICHARD, came to N. E. 1630, identified Marblehead, Mass., 1637, one of the founders Yarmouth, Mass., 1639.

SEAVER

A Gaelic word, *saibher,* rich; *Sever,* a town in France.

ROBERT, b. Eng. 1608, came to N. E. 1634, settled in Roxbury, Mass.

SEAVERNS, SEAVERN

JOHN, tailor, resident Boston, Mass., before 1642.

SAMUEL, married, Charlestown, Mass., 1666.

SEAVY, SEAVEY

WILLIAM, b. Eng. 1600, sent over by Mason to Portsmouth, N. H., 1631, at Rye, N. H., 1657; died 1671, leaving large property.

SEBORN, SIBBORNE, SEBORNE

JOHN, resident Boston, Mass., 1644.

SECCOMB

RICHARD, inhabitant Lynn, Mass., 1660.

SEDGWICK

A town or harbor abounding with sedge, *wick.*

ROBERT, b. Eng. 1611, came N. E. 1635, at Charlestown, Mass., 1636, founder of artillery company, became major general, sent by Cromwell to Jamaica, where he died May 25, 1656.

SEELEY

JOHN, at Isle of Shoals, N. H., 1647, removed Newbury, Mass.

ROBERT, came in Winthrop's fleet, settled at Watertown, Mass., removed Wethersfield, Conn., 1635, joined New Haven Colony 1638, among the founders Fairfield, Stamford, Conn., Huntington, L. I., and Elizabeth, N. J.

WILLIAM, brother of John, at Isle of Shoals, N. H., 1656.

SELDEN, SELDON

THOMAS, freeman Hartford, Conn., 1640.

SELLAN, SELLEN

THOMAS, inhabitant Ipswich, Mass., 1633, removed Braintree, Mass., 1638.

SELLOCK, SELLICK, SILLECK

DAVID, soap boiler, at Boston, Mass., before 1638.

SELMAN

JOHN, took oath of fidelity Pemaquid, Maine, 1674.

SEMOND

WILLIAM, inhabitant Boston, Mass., 1640.

SENDALL

SAMUEL, at Newbury, Mass., later Boston, Mass., 1651.

SENDEN

SAMUEL, living at Marblehead, Mass., 1668.

SENSION, SENTION, ST. JOHN

MATTHEW or MATTHIAS, settled Dorchester, Mass., 1631, removed Windsor, Conn., 1640, one first settlers Norwalk, Conn., 1654.

NICHOLAS, younger brother of preceding, b. Eng. 1622, came N. E. 1635, to Wethersfield, Conn., 1640.

SENTER

Name originated in Normandy.

JOHN, inhabitant Boston, Mass., 1650.

SESSIONS

ALEXANDER, b. Wantage, Berkshire, Eng., 1645, freeman Andover, Mass., 1677.

SEVERANCE, SEVERNS

A river rising in the mountains, Plynlimmon, in Wales.

JOHN, victualler and vinter, resident Ipswich and Boston, Mass., original proprietor Salisbury, Mass., 1637.

SEWALL, SEWELL

Probably from *sea* and *wall,* a structure of stone or other materials intended for defense or security against the sea. The name may have various significations in Gaelic; *suil* is a willow; *suail,* small, inconsiderable. *Su,* south and *wold, wald, wild, well,* an uncultivated place, a wood, a plain, a lawn, hills without wood, as *Suwold, Suwall, Suwell.* John de Sewede, accompanied Edward the Black Prince into Aquitaine. The English ancestry traced to William Shewall or Sewall, living in Coventry, Warwickshire, England, in 1540.

EDWARD, died Exeter, N. H., 1684.

HENRY, son of Henry, third generation, from William, mentioned above, bapt. 1576, came Ipswich 1634, removed following year Newbury, Mass., died Rowley, Mass., 1657.

SEWARD

High admiral, who kept the sea against pirates; from *sea* and *ward,* a keeper.

EDWARD, at Ipswich, Mass., 1637, returned to England 1643.

GEORGE, at Guilford, Conn., 1651, signed the original covenant Branford, Conn., 1668, removed Newark, N. J.

RICHARD died Portsmouth, N. H., 1663.

ROBERT, brother of preceding, Exeter, N. H., 1639.

ROGER, mariner, Boston, Mass., 1655.

SHACKFORD

WILLIAM, house-carpenter, b. Eng. 1640, settled Dover, N. H., 1662, at Portsmouth, N. H., 1669.

SHADDUCK, CHADDOCK, SCHADECK

The name of a lordship in Germany.

ELIAS, married, Windsor, Conn., before 1692; no male issue.

SHAFLIN

MICHAEL, tailor, came from Salisbury, Wiltshire, Eng., to N. E. 1635, granted land Salem, Mass., 1637.

SHALER, SHALLOR, SHALLER

MICHAEL, freeman Boston, Mass., 1690.

THOMAS, freeman, Haddam, Conn., 1671. removed Killingsworth, Conn., 1677, returned to Haddam, Conn.

SHANNON

A Gaelic name from the Shannon river in Ireland. From *sen*, gentle, and *abhain*, a river, the tranquil river.

NATHANIEL, b. Londonderry, Ulster county, 1665; resident Boston, Mass., 1687.

RICHARD, married, Portsmouth, N. H., 1689.

SHAPLEIGH

ALEXANDER, shipbuilder and merchant, came from Kingsweare, Devonshire, Eng., to Kittery Point, Maine, 1635; returned to England 1650, where he soon died.

SHARP, SHARPE

CHARLES, in New Hampshire, 1684.

JOHN, at Dover, N. H., 1663.

JOHN, inhabitant Westerly, R. I., 1668.

JOHN, merchant Cambridge, Mass., before 1699.

RICHARD, freeman Boston, Mass., 1674, where he died August 5, 1677.

ROBERT, b. Eng. 1615 came to N. E. 1635, located Dorchester, Mass., removed to Muddy river, (Brookline) Mass., 1650.

THOMAS, came to Boston, Mass., in Winthrop's fleet, soon after embarked for England.

SHARSWOOD

GEORGE, at New London, Conn., 1666.

SHATSWELL, SHOTSWELL, SATCHWELL

JOHN, at Ipswich, Mass., 1633; will probated March 30, 1647.

SHATTUCK

WILLIAM, b. Eng. 1621-22, proprietor at Watertown, Mass., 1642.

SHAW

From the Scotch, a plain surrounded by trees or an open space between woods.

ABRAHAM, b. Halifax, Yorkshire, Eng., settled at Watertown, Mass., 1636, removed Dedham, Mass., 1638, two years later to Cambridge, Mass.

ANDREW, at Salem, Mass., 1691.

ANTHONY, married, Boston, Mass., 1653, removed Portsmouth, R. I.

EDWARD, at Duxbury, Mass., 1632.

JOHN, at Plymouth, Mass., 1632, one of the purchasers Dartmouth, Mass., 1652.

JOHN, tailor, Malden, Mass., before 1667.

JOHN, resident Rehoboth, Mass., before 1680, formerly at Weymouth, Mass.

JOSEPH, cooper, married, Boston, Mass., 1653.

JOSEPH, married, Charlestown,, Mass., 1664.

ROGER, at Cambridge, Mass., 1636, removed Hampton, N. H., 1639.

THOMAS, resident Hingham, Mass., 1637, removed Barnstable, Mass., before 1643.

THOMAS, inhabitant Charlestown, Mass., before 1645.

WILLIAM, servant at Salem, Mass., 1657.

SHAWSON

GEORGE, at Duxbury, Mass., 1638, removed Sandwich, Mass., 1640.

SHEAFFE

EDMUND, came from Cranbrook, County of Kent, Eng., to Boston, Mass., before 1650.

JACOB, cousin of the preceding, b. Cranbrook, County of Kent, Eng., 1616, son of Edmund; came to Boston, Mass., with his mother, removed Guilford, Conn.; died March 22, 1659.

SAMPSON, merchant Boston, Mass., 1672.

WILLIAM, married, Charlestown, Mass., 1672.

SHEARER

THOMAS, tailor, married, Boston, Mass., 1659.

SHEARS, SHEERES

JEREMIAH, died York, Maine, 1664.

SAMUEL, married, Dedham, Mass., 1658.

WILLIAM, at Boston, Mass., 1657.

SHEATHER

JOHN, Guilford, Conn., 1650.

SHED, SHEDD

DANIEL, settled Boston, Mass., 1640, removed Billerica, Mass., 1659.

SHEFFIELD

EDMUND, married, Roxbury, Mass., 1641.

ICHABOD, at Dover, N. H., 1658, removed Portsmouth, R. I., 1661.

JOSEPH, brother of the preceding, at Portsmouth, R. I., 1643, where he died 1655.

THOMAS, mariner, resident Boston, Mass., 1663.

WILLIAM, mariner, inhabitant Boston, Mass., 1653.

WILLIAM, at Dover, N. H., 1658, removed Hingham, Mass., 1675, afterwards to Sherborn, Mass., where he died Dec. 6, 1700.

SHELDON, SHELDEN

A Cornish British name from *schell,* a spring, and *dene,* a small valley, the spring in the valley. Also a place name from Sheldon in the parish of Bakewell, Derbyshire, Eng., parishes of this name in Derbyshire and Warwickshire.

GODFREY, b. Eng. 1599, came to N. E. 1660, settled Scarborough where he died 1671.

ISAAC, son of Isaac S., b. Eng. 1627, came Windsor, Conn., 1651, settled Northampton, Mass., 1655.

JOHN, married, Billerica, Mass., 1659.

JOHN, b. Eng. 1630, came to N. E. 1650-60, settled Providence, R. I., 1675.

NICHOLAS, married, Providence, R. I., 1682.

TIMOTHY, swore allegiance Providence, R. I., 1682.

WILLIAM, at Billerica 1659.

SHELLEY, SHERLEY, SHIRLEY

Derived from Shelley, a local town in the counties of Essex, Suffolk and York, Eng.; from *schell,* a spring, and *ley,* a field.

ROBERT, came Boston, Mass., 1632, removed Barnstable, Mass., 1640.

SHELLSTONE

ROBERT, resident Boston, Mass., 1678.

SHELTON

DANIEL, merchant, b. Deptford, Yorkshire, Eng., settled Stratford, Conn., 1686.

SHEPARD, SHEPPARD, SHEPHERD

ANDREW, merchant, died Boston, Mass., 1676.

EDWARD, freeman Cambridge, Mass., 1643.

FRANCIS, at Charlestown, Mass., 1677.

GEORGE, freeman Providence, R. I., 1646.

JOHN, b. Eng., 1599, brother of Edward, settled Braintree, Mass., 1635.

JOHN, married, Cambridge, Mass., 1649.

JOHN, representative from Lynn, Mass., 1689.

JOHN, resident Rowley, Mass., 1691.

JOHN, freeman Concord, Mass., 1690.

RALPH, b. Eng. 1606, came from Stepney, Eng., to Charlstown, Mass., 1635, the following year removed Dedham, Mass., afterwards lived Rehoboth, Weymouth, Concord, finally Malden, Mass.

SAMUEL, b. Eng. 1613, freeman Cambridge, Mass., 1636, returned England before 1658.

SAMUEL, took oath of allegiance Haverhill, Mass., 1677.

SOLOMON, freeman Salisbury, Mass., 1690.

THOMAS, preacher, son of William S., b. Towcester, county of Northampton, Eng., Nov. 5, 1605, came to N. E. 1634, settled Cambridge, Mass., where he died Aug. 25 or 28, 1649.

SHEPARDSON

DANIEL, blacksmith, at Charlestown, Mass., 1632.

SHEPLEY, SHIPLEY

JOHN, granted land Salem, Mass., 1637.

SHEPWAY, SHIPWAY

JOHN, at Portsmouth, N. H., before 1662.

SHERBURNE

The first on record in England, Richard Sherburn, b. 1380, d. 1449.

GEORGE, resident Portsmouth, N. H., 1650.

HENRY, settled Portsmouth, N. H., 1632.

JOHN, brother of preceding, son of Joseph Augustus, of Oldham, Eng., b. Hampshire, Eng., 1615, at Portsmouth, N. H., 1643.

WILLIAM, at Portsmouth, N. H., 1644.

SHERIN

ROBERT, b. Eng., 1602, came to Watertown, Mass., 1634, afterwards at Ipswich, Mass.

SHERLOCK

JAMES, appointed sheriff of Suffolk county, Mass., by Andros, resided at Portsmouth, N. H., 1687.

SHERMAN

The origin of the name is German and is an occupation surname, one who used to shear or dress cloth, a *shearman.* The early family seat of the family was in the county of Suffolk, Eng., where the name is found as early as 1420, the English lineage can be traced to Thomas Sherman, born 1420.

EDMUND, settled Watertown, Mass., 1632, original proprietor Wethersfield, Conn., 1636, freeman New Haven, Conn., 1640, where he died 1641.

JOHN, clergyman, son of the preceding, b. Dedham, county of Essex, Eng., Dec. 26,1613, came Boston, Mass., 1634, removed Watertown, Mass., soon after to Wethersfield, Conn., and 1643, Milford, Conn., died Sudbury, Mass., Aug. 8, 1685.

JOHN, cousin preceding, b. Dedham, county of Essex, Eng., freeman Watertown, Mass., 1637.

JOSEPH, resident Wethersfield, Conn., 1639, removed Stamford, Conn., 1641.

PELEG, married, Portsmouth, N. H., 1657.

PHILIP, son of Samuel S., seventh generation of Thomas S., mentioned above, b. Dedham, Eng., Feb. 5, 1610, came to Roxbury, Mass., 1634, removed to R. I. 1636, settled Portsmouth, R. I., became a Quaker, died Dec. 12, 1655.

RICHARD, merchant, Boston, Mass., will probated July 31, 1660.

SAMUEL, at Ipswich, Mass., 1636.

SAMUEL, husbandman, brother of Philip, resided Boston, Mass., before 1637.

SAMUEL, brother of Rev. John, at Wethersfield, Conn., 1640, removed Stamford, Conn.

THOMAS, at Ipswich, Mass., 1638.

WILLIAM, came from Northampton, Eng., to Plymouth, Mass., 1629, settled Duxbury, Mass., 1630, removed Marshfield, Mass., 1643.

SHERRITT, SHARRATT, SHERROT

HUGH, freeman Ipswich, Mass., 1635, removed Haverhill, Mass., before 1647, where he died Sept., 1678.

SHERWIN

EBENZER, settled Roxford, Mass., 1690.

JOHN, b. Eng., 1644, married, Ipswich, Mass., 1667.

SHERWOOD

From the Saxon *sher, scir,* clear, and *wood,* a clearing in the woods, or the cleared woods. It may, however, be derived from *shire,* the Saxon word *scire* and the German word *schier* meaning to divide, a portion or division of land of which divisions there are forty in England, twelve in Wales, and twenty-four in Scotland.

GEORGE, died New London, Conn., May 1, 1674.

MATTHEW, freeman, Fairfield, Conn., 1664.

STEPHEN, freeman Greenwich, Conn., 1664.

THOMAS, b. Sherwood Forest, Nottinghamshire, Eng., 1585, came to N. E. 1634, settled Wethersfield, Conn., 1643, at Stratford, Conn., 1645, removed Fairfield, Conn.

SHESTELL, SHESTEN

THOMAS, lighterman, householder, Boston, Mass., 1695.

SHETHER, SHEATHER

JOHN, at Guilford, Conn., 1650, removed Killingworth, Conn., 1669.

SHILLINGSWORTH

THOMAS, freeman Plymouth, Mass., 1644.

SHINE

THOMAS, took oath of fidelity, Malden, Mass., 1674.

SHIPMAN

A trade name shipman equivalent to sailor. It is, however, an ancient English family and is a place name. There are several branches of the family, one at Welby, Herefordshire, one in the County of Kent, another Sarington, Nottinghamshire.

EDWARD, it is stated came from England to Saybrook, Conn., 1639, if so he must have been in his childhood, freeman 1667, died Sept. 15, 1697.

SHIPPEN

EDWARD, b. Eng., 1639, came to Boston, Mass., member of artillery company, 1669, removed Newport, R. I., 1688, to Philadelphia, Pa., 1693, and was first mayor under the charter of 1701.

SHIPPEY, SHEPPY, SHIPPIE

THOMAS, Charlestown, Mass., 1637.

SHOOTER

PETER, died, Braintree, Mass., July 15, 1655, no male issue.

SHORE, SHORES, SHOREY

JEREMY, pioneer Kittery, Maine, 1649.

SAMPSON, tailor, freeman Boston, Mass., 1642.

SAMUEL, Kittery, Maine, 1685.

SHORT

LUKE, came from Dartmouth, Devonshire, Eng., to Marblehead, Mass., about 1690.

SHORTHOSE, SHORTHUS

ROBERT, residing Charlestown, Mass., 1634.

SHORTRIDGE, SHORTRIGGS

RICHARD, freeman Portsmouth, N. H., 1672.

SHOTTEN, SHATTON

GEORGE, came with his mother Margery S. to Boston, Mass., 1638, removed Rowley, Mass., 1640, finally Taunton, Mass.

Sampson, freeman Newport, R. I., 1638, later disfranchised. No male issue.

SHREVE, SHERIVE

Thomas, Plymouth, Mass., 1643.

SHRIMPTON

Epaphras, son of Edward, London, Eng., resident Boston, Mass., 1687.

Henry, brazier, came from Bednal Green, County Middlesex, Eng., admitted church Boston, Mass., 1639.

Jonathan, elder brother of the preceding, resident Boston, Mass., 1648, died 1673.

Robert, resident Boston, Mass., 1648.

SHUMWAY

Peter, French Huguenot descent, settled Oxford, Mass., 1660.

SHURTLIFF, SHIRTLEY

From Saxon word *Sceort,* short, and cliff, a short cliff, separated, cut off.

William, carpenter, Plymouth, Mass., 1634, removed Marshfield, Mass.

SHUTE

Enoch, Weymouth, Mass., 1636.

Richard, mariner, Milford, Mass., 1642, removed Pemaquid, Maine, before 1651.

Richard, married, Milford, Mass., 1656, removed East Chester, N. Y.

Robert, brother first Richard. Will probated Boston, Mass., March 24, 1651, unmarried.

William, married, Boston, Mass., 1659.

SHUTER, SHOOTER

Peter, died Braintree, Mass., 1654.

SIBLEY, SEBLEY, SYBLEY

John, came Salem, Mass., 1629, freeman 1635, removed Manchester, Mass., 1640.
Richard, resident Salem, Mass., 1656.

SIGOURNEY, SIGOURNAY

Andrew, b. 1639 of French Huguenot descent at Oxford, Mass., 1686, removed Boston, Mass., where he died April 16, 1727.

SIGSWORTH

George, resident Boston, Mass., before 1679.

SIKES, SYCKES, SYKES

Name designates a small spring well.

Richard, freeman Springfield, Mass., 1640.

SILL, SYLL, SCILL

John, inhabitant Cambridge, Mass., 1637.

SILLIMAN

Daniel, resident Fairfield, Conn., 1658.

SILLIVANT, SELEVANT

Daniel, New Haven, Conn., 1654.

SILSBEE, SILSBY

Henry, b. Eng., about 1618, settled Salem, Mass., 1639, removed Ipswich, Mass., 1647, to Lynn, Mass., 1658; will probated Dec. 16, 1700.

SILVER

Thomas, Ipswich, Mass., 1637, removed Newbury, Mass., 1649.

SILVESTER, SYLVESTER

Nathaniel, purchased Shelter Island, Long Island, 1651.

Richard, came to N. E. in Winthrop's fleet, freeman, Weymouth, Mass., 1636, removed to Scituate, Mass., 1642, where he died 1663.

Thomas, died Watertown, Mass., Nov. 27, 1696.

SIMMONS, SIMONDS, SYMONDSON

A corruption of Simeon or Simon, the son of Sim; some authorities claim the name is of Dutch origin.

John, b. Eng., 1615, proprietor Salem, Mass., 1636.

John, b. 1640, resident Rowley, Mass., 1671, removed Haverhill, Mass., 1678.

John, resident Taunton, Mass., 1679.

Michael, paid tax, Dover, N. H., 1665.

Moses, one of the first comers, b. Leyden, Holland, came Plymouth, Mass., 1621, settled Duxbury, Mass., original proprietor Dartmouth, Bridgewater and Middleboro but did not remove to any of those places.

Richard, resident Salem, Mass., 1668.

Samuel, settled Ipswich, Mass., 1637.

Samuel, at Haverhill, Mass., 1669.

Samuel, killed by accident, Newbury, Mass., June 18, 1682.

Thomas, innkeeper, sold property Braintree, Mass., 1640.

William, died Boston, Mass., about 1642.

William, settled Concord, Mass., 1639, removed Woburn, Mass., 1644.

William, Haverhill, Mass., 1657.

SIMPKINS

Nicholas, tailor, Boston, Mass., 1634, removed Yarmouth, Mass., 1638, returns Boston, Mass., before 1649.

Vincent, married Stamford, Conn., 1641.

SIMPSON, SIMSON, SYMSON

Alexander, brickmaker, Scotch descent, resident Boston, Mass., 1659.

Francis, Quaker, lived Salem, or Marblehead, Mass., 1648.

Henry, settled York, Maine, 1638, died before 1655.

John, b. Eng., 1605, settled Watertown, Mass., 1635, died June, 1643.

PETER, died Milford, Mass., 1685.

THOMAS, resident Salisbury, Mass., 1664.

SINCLAIR, ST. CLAIR, SINKLER

A corruption of St. Clair and that from St. Clara from the Latin *cearus,* pure, renowned, illustrious. The family is traced back to Rogenwald, Earle of Maerle of Norway, a favorite of King Harold 888, A. D. His son Rollo became the first duke of Normandy by marriage 912 to the daughter of Charles the Simple of France, receiving as a concession the St. Clair castle in the province of Normandy. The surname St. Clere was adopted by his great grandson, Malger, who was great uncle to William the Conqueror, and his three sons were among the followers of that monarch when he fought the Battle of Hastings, William the youngest son known by the sobriquet "The Seemly St. Clair," disagreed with his uncle and formed an alliance with Malcolm III of Scotland and was defeated at the battle on the Tweed and lost his life. He was the ancestor of the American family of St. Clair.

JOHN, son of Henry S. of Brownstone and Lybster, England, and of the XXIII generation from Rogenwald Sinclair, b. Eng., 1630, and was at Exeter, N. H., 1658, his name appearing on the records spelt Sinkler, which in the early part of the nineteeenth century became St. Clair.

SINGLETARY, SINGLETERY

RICHARD, Salem, Mass., 1637, freeman Newbury, Mass., 1638, at Haverhill, Mass., 1652, died October 25, 1687, and it is claimed age 102 years.

SINNET, SENNOT, SENNITT

WALKER, resident Boston, Mass., 1647.

SISSON

A place name derived from *Sissonne,* a town in France.

GEORGE, married, Portsmouth, R. I., 1667.

JAMES, brother of the preceding, resident Dartmouth, Mass., 1684.

RICHARD, b. Eng., 1608, freeman Portsmouth, R. I., 1653.

SIVERNS

JOHN, resident Lynn, Mass., 1684.

SKEEL, SKEELS

JOHN, resident of Stamford, Conn., 1670.

SKEETH

WILLIAM, died Charlestown or Woburn, Mass., 1672.

SKELLING

THOMAS, granted land, Salem, Mass., 1643, removed Gloucester, Mass.

SKELTON

In Saxon the hill of separation in boundary, derived from Anglo-Saxon *sakling,* a hut, and the British word *ton,* originally of Danish derivation. The English family dates back to the Skeltons of Armathwaite Castle, county of Cumberland in the reign of Edward I. John de Skelton was Knight of the shire, 1318. Adam de Skelton was English ancestor, 1330.

BENJAMIN, on record, Salem, Mass., 1639.

NATHANIEL, resident Salem, Mass., 1648.

SAMUEL, clergyman, b. Eng., 1584, came from Lincoln, Eng., to Salem, Mass., 1629, where he died August 2, 1634.

SKERRY

FRANCIS, freeman, Salem, Mass., 1637.

HENRY, cordwainer, brother of the preceding, b. Eng., 1606, came from Yarmouth, county of Lincoln; freeman, Salem, Mass., 1638.

SKIDMORE, SKIDMER, SCUDMORE

From Cornish British *scudh* or *scuth,* the shoulder, and *mor* big, large, broad shoulders; *scheidmuur,* a Dutch word signifying a partition or division, wall.

JAMES, resident Boston, Mass., 1636.

JOHN, inhabitant, Cambridge, Mass., 1641.

RICHARD, resident Cambridge, Mass., 1641.

THOMAS, married, Cambridge, Mass., 1642, settled Lancaster, Mass., afterwards New London, Conn., removed Huntington, L. I., 1672.

SKIFF

JAMES, settled Plymouth, Mass., 1636, removed to Lynn, Mass., 1637, and to Sandwich, Mass., 1643.

STEPHEN, representative from Sandwich, Mass., 1676.

SKILLING, SKILLIN, SKILLINGS

THOMAS, Gloucester, Mass., 1642, removed Falmouth, Maine, 1665.

SKILLINGER, STILLINGER

JACOB, a Dutchman at New London, Conn., 1661.

SKINNER

A name signifying dealer in skins and hides.

EDWARD, died Cambridge, Mass., 1639-41.

FRANCIS, commander of the fort at Pemaquid, Maine, 1683.

JOHN, came from Braintree, county of Essex to Hartford, Conn., 1636.

JOSEPH, married, Windsor, Conn., 1666.

THOMAS, b. Eng., 1617, came from Chichester, county of Sussex, Eng., living Malden, Mass., 1645.

THOMAS, baker, freeman, Boston, Mass., 1673.

WALTER, resident, Salem, Mass., 1680.

SKOULING

ROBERT, came from Hingham, Eng., to Hingham, Mass., 1638.

SLACK

A valley or small shadow dell.

WILLIAM, resident Weymouth, Mass., 1690.

SLADE

Ancient English family known as de la Slades and is derived from *slade,* signifying a small strip of green sward in a woodland. The name appears in English records as early as 1300 in the writs of Parliament where Nicholas de la Slade is mentioned.

EDWARD, native of Wales, freeman, R. I., 1658.

WILLIAM, son of Edward S., Somersetshire, Eng., of Welsh descent; freeman, Newport, R. I., 1659.

SLAPUM

PETER, selectman, Fairfield, Conn., 1669.

SLATER

JOHN, died, Marblehead, Mass., 1665.

JOHN, came from Wales to Lynn, Mass., 1680, removed to Connecticut at Willimantic, Mansfield, Ashford and Willington, after 1716.

SLAUGHTER

JOHN, freeman, Simsbury, Conn., 1674.

SLAWSON, SLASON, SLOSSON

GEORGE, at Lynn, Mass., 1637, removed Sandwich, Mass., 1643, thence Stamford, Conn., 1644, where he died Feb. 17, 1695.

THOMAS, granted land Stamford, Conn., 1641.

SLEEPER

Name derived from the Dutch; a cartman or one who carries goods on sledge.

AARON, took oath of Allegiance, Hampton, N. H., 1678.

THOMAS, b. Eng., 1616, settled Hampton, N. H., 1638.

SLEY, SLYE

CHRISTOPHER, died Boston, Mass., Nov. 25, 1697.

ROBERT, resident Conn., 1649.

SLOCUM, SLOCOME

ANTHONY, b. Eng., 1590-91, on record Taunton, Mass., 1637, early settler, Dartmouth, Mass.

GILES, brother of preceding, freeman Portsmouth, R. I., 1655.

SLOMAN, SLUMAN, SLOWMAN

SIMON, resident Newbury, Mass., before 1691.

THOMAS, married Norwich, Conn., 1668.

SLOPER

RICHARD, b. Eng., Nov., 1630, at Dover, N. H., 1657, later Portsmouth, N. H., where he died 1716.

SLOUGH, SLOW, SLOFF

JOHN, resident Newport, R. I., 1639.

WILLIAM, resident New Haven, Conn., 1644, removed Milford, Conn., 1645.

SLOWE

THOMAS, freeman, Providence, R. I., 1655.

SMALL

A description name from the statue of a person.

EDWARD, at Piscataqua, Maine, 1632, removed Kittery, Maine, 1640, at Dover, N. H., 1647.

JOHN, at Plymouth, Mass., 1632, removed Eastham, Mass., 1642.

JOHN, came to N. E. 1635, resident Salem, Mass., 1643, removed R. I., 1658.

JOHN, resident Braintree, Mass., removed Mendon, Mass., 1662.

THOMAS, resident Salem, Mass., 1670.

SMALLEY, SMOLLETT

BENJAMIN, surgeon, came from Dumbarton, Scotland, to Plymouth, Mass., 1687, removed to Connecticut.

JAMES, freeman, Concord, Mass., 1690.

JOHN, resident Plymouth, Mass., 1632, removed Eastham, Mass., 1642.

SMALLIDGE, SMALLEDGE

WILLIAM, inhabitant Ipswich, Mass., 1650.

SMART

CHARLES, Marblehead, Mass., 1668.

JOHN, came from county of Norfolk, Eng., to Hingham, Mass., 1635.

SMEAD, SMEED, SMED

RICHARD, at Windsor, Conn., 1672.

WILLIAM, married Dorchester, Mass., 1658.

SMEDLEY, SMEADLY, SMEEDLY

BAPTIST, b. Eng., 1607, came from the parish of Odell, Bedfordshire, Eng., to Concord, Mass., 1636, where he died Aug. 16, 1675.

JOHN, elder brother of preceding, freeman, Concord, Mass., 1644.

SMITH

The most common of all surnames as it was applied to artificers in wood as well as metal, in fact to all mechanical workers, hence its great frequency. Among the Highlands of Scotland the smith ranked third in dignity to the chief from his skill in fabricating military weapons and his dexterity in teaching the use of them. In Wales there were three sciences which a tenant could not teach his son without the consent of his lord, *Scholarship, Bardism* and *Smithcraft*. The latter was one of the liberal sciences and the term was more comprehensive; different branches of knowledge were united in the profession which are now practiced separately, such as raising the ore, converting it into metal, etc.

ABIEZER or ABRAHAM, freeman, Charlestown, Mass., 1677.

ABRAHAM, householder, Charlestown, Mass., 1658.

ABRAHAM, married, Middletown, Conn., 1678.

ABRAHAM, on record, Cambridge, Mass., 1676.

ARTHUR, resident Hartford, Conn., 1640.

ARTHUR, inhabitant Hartford, Conn., 1684.

ASAHEL, at Dedham, Mass., 1642.

BATHOLOMEW, resident Dover, N. H., 1640.

BENJAMIN, one of the first hundred admitted Providence, R. I., 1645.

BENJAMIN, b. Eng., 1612, freeman Lynn, Mass., 1641.

BENJAMIN, living Boston, Mass., 1650.

BENJAMIN, came to Providence, R. I., 1660.

BENJAMIN, resident Salisbury, Mass., 1685.

CHRISTOPHER, freeman, Dedham, Mass., 1643.

CHRISTOPHER, resident Providence, R. I., 1655.

DANIEL, died Watertown, Mass., July 14, 1660.

DANIEL, resident, Rehoboth, Mass., 1650.

DANIEL, householder, Charlestown, Mass., 1678.

DELIVERANCE, resident, Dartmouth, Mass., 1686.

EDWARD, inhabitant Weymouth, Mass., before 1642, removed Rehoboth, Mass., freeman, Newport, R. I., 1655.

EDWARD, took oath of allegiance, Providence, R. I., 1668.

EDWARD, resident Boston, Mass., 1655.

EDWARD, freeman, New London, Conn., 1669.

EDWARD, married Exeter, N. H., 1669.

ELIEZER, resident Dartmouth, Mass., 1686.

ELISHA, at Warwick or Newport, R. I., 1677.

FRANCIS, freeman, Watertown, Mass., 1637.

FRANCIS, cardmaker, freeman, Roxbury, Mass., 1631.

FRANCIS, freeman, Hingham, Mass., 1635, removed Taunton, Mass.

GEORGE, granted land Salem, Mass., 1635, removed Ipswich, Mass., 1648.

GEORGE, b. Hertfordshire, Eng., freeman, New Haven, Conn., 1639-47.

GEORGE, tailor, came from Salisbury, Eng., to N. E. 1635, removed Dover, N. H., 1645.

GILES, resident Hartford, Conn., 1639, removed Fairfield, Conn., 1651, where he died 1669.

HENRY, first minister Wethersfield, Conn., b. near Norfolk, Eng., 1588, came in Winthrop's fleet, settled Dorchester, Mass., removed to Wethersfield, Conn., 1635, removed Springfield, Mass., 1636.

HENRY, of Harpham Hall, near Hingham, Eng., came to N. E., 1638, settling at Hingham, Mass., removed Rehoboth, Mass., 1643, where he died 1649.

HENRY, husbandman, b. Eng., 1607, came from New Buckenham, county of Norfolk, to Dedham, Mass., 1637, among the first settlers Medfield, Mass.

HENRY, resident Boston, Mass., 1652.

HENRY, inhabitant Rowley, Mass., 1656.

HENRY, b. Eng., 1619, settled Stamford, Conn., 1641, died 1687.

HENRY, married, Cambridge, Mass., 1673.

HEZEKIAH, resident Dartmouth, Mass., 1686.

HUGH, freeman, Rowley, Mass., 1642.

ISRAEL, carpenter, Boston, Mass., 1672.

JAMES, granted land Gloucester, Mass., 1642, removed to Salem, Mass., 1648, where he died 1661.

JAMES, shipmaster, admitted church Boston, Mass., 1644.

JAMES, died Rehoboth, Mass., 1653.

JAMES, located Weymouth, Mass., before 1639.

JAMES, resident Danvers, Mass., 1692.

JEREMIAH, married Eastham, Mass., 1678

JOHN, came from Devonshire, Eng., to Dorchester, Mass., 1630.

JOHN, b. Eng., 1595, at Salem, Mass., 1631, removed Providence, R. I., 1635, later to Warwick, R. I.

JOHN, freeman, Watertown, Mass., 1636.

JOHN, one of first purchasers Taunton, Mass., 1637.

JOHN, at Plymouth, Mass., 1643, one first settlers Eastham, Mass.

JOHN, freeman, Weymouth, Mass., 1637.

JOHN, tailor, admitted church Boston, Mass., 1639, will probated June 13, 1674.

JOHN, miller, resident Newport, R. I., 1639.

JOHN, joined the church Barnstable, Mass., 1640.

JOHN, resident Lynn, Mass., removed Reading, Mass.

JOHN, inhabitant Sudbury, Mass., 1647.

JOHN, blacksmith at Guilford, Conn., 1643.

JOHN, ship carpenter, at Charlestown, Mass., before 1656.

JOHN, surveyor, called John the Mason, settled Providence, R. I., lived Warwick, R. I., 1657.

JOHN, resident Dedham, Mass., 1644.

JOHN, located Milford, Conn., 1640, one ten owners, of Derby, Conn.

JOHN, settled Hampton, N. H., 1644.

JOHN, came to Dorchester, Mass., 1635.

JOHN, freeman, Hingham, Mass., 1647.

JOHN, called Jamaica John, died Providence, R. I., about 1685.

JOHN, resident Taunton, Mass., 1663.

JOHN, tailor, living Salem, Mass., 1659.

JOHN, Mason, inhabitant Salem, Mass., 1671.

JOHN, called Nailor Smith, resided Boston, Mass., 1653, removed New London, Conn., 1658, died Oct. 4, 1670.

JOHN, resident, Dedham, Mass., 1661.

JOHN, married, Eastham, Mass., 1667.

JOHN, married, Eastham, Mass., 1668.

JOHN, mason, living Boston, Mass., 1678.

JOHN, tailor, took oath of allegiance, Hampton, N. H., 1678.

JOHN, cooper, took oath of allegiance, Hampton, N. H., 1678.

JOHN, bricklayer, married Boston, Mass., 1671.

JOHN, mason, householder, Charlestown, Mass., 1678.

JOHN, resident, Newport, R. I., 1678.

JOHN, living Dartmouth, Mass., 1686.

JOHN, tanner, resident Cambridge or Newton, Mass., before 1676.

JOHN, living Gloucester, Mass., 1689.

JOHN, married Salem, Mass., 1689.

JONATHAN, took oath of allegiance, Exeter, N. H., 1677.

JOSEPH, freeman, Wethersfield, Conn., 1657.

JOSEPH, brother of Christopher, married Hartford, Conn., 1656.

JOSEPH, resident Norwalk, Conn., 1675.

JOSEPH, took oath of allegiance, Hampton, N. H., 1678.

JOSEPH, proprietor New Haven, Conn., 1685.

JOSEPH, resident Dartmouth, Mass., 1686.

JOSEPH, married Barnstable, Mass., 1689.

JOSEPH, minister, married Middletown, Conn., 1698.

JOSHUA, resident Weymouth, Mass., 1668.

JOSIAH, living Taunton, Mass., 1687.

LESTER, b. Eng., 1632, came Boston, Mass., 1656.

Martin, took oath of allegiance, Northampton, Mass., 1679.

MATTHEW, cordwainer, came from Sandwich, county of Kent, Eng., to Charlestown, Mass., 1637.

MATTHEW, swore oath of fidelity Watertown, Mass., 1652.

MICHAEL, living in Malden side of Charlestown, Mass., 1644.

MORRIS, married Gloucester, Mass., 1681.

NATHANIEL, householder, Charlestown, Mass., 1658.

NATHANIEL, married Haverhill, Mass., 1663.

NATHANIEL, living Weymouth, Mass., 1679.

NATHANIEL, took oath of allegiance, Hampton, N. H., 1678.

NATHANIEL, married Hartford, Conn., 1686.

NEHEMIAH, weaver, b. Eng., about 1605, shepherd New Haven, Conn., 1644, removed New London, 1660, thence to Norwich, Conn., 1669, died 1686, known as Shepperd Smith.

NICHOLAS, married Milford, Conn., 1664.

PELATIAH, freeman, Malden, Mass., 1680.

RALPH, clergyman, came to N. E. 1629, resided Manchester, Salem, Mass., New London, Conn., early settler Eastham, Mass., died Boston, Mass., March 1, 1661.

RALPH, came from Hingham, county of Norfolk, England, to Hingham, Mass., 1635, removed Eastham, Mass.

RICHARD, came from Gloucestershire, Eng., one first purchasers Taunton, Mass., 1638, removed Providence, R. I.

RICHARD, b. Eng., 1617, first record Wethersfield, Conn., 1649.

RICHARD, son Richard of Shropham, county of Norfolk, Eng., came to Ipswich, Mass., 1642.

RICHARD, resident New London, Conn., 1652, removed Wethersfield, Conn.

RICHARD, swore fidelity Watertown, Mass., 1652, removed Lancaster, Mass., 1654.

RICHARD, b. Eng., 1613, came Boston, Mass., 1656.

RICHARD, freeman, Lyme, Conn., 1671.

RICHARD, married Salisbury, Mass., 1666.

RICHARD, married New London, Conn., 1670.

RICHARD, living Falmouth, Maine, 1684, removed Marblehead, Mass., 1689, later Gloucester, Mass.

ROBERT, wine cooper, resident, Boston, Mass., 1637; returned to England.

ROBERT, tailor, settled Exeter, N. H., 1639, removed Hampton, N. H., 1657, settled Boxford, Mass., 1661.

ROBERT, resident Ipswich, Mass., 1648.

Robert, mariner, married Boston, Mass., 1662.

ROBERT, b. Eng., 1611, resident Hampton, N. H., 1657, died 1706.

ROBERT, married Charlestown, Mass., 1687.

ROWLAND, inhabitant Marblehead, Mass., 1648.

SAMUEL, died Lynn, Mass., 1642.

SAMUEL, b. Eng., 1602, came from Ipswich., Eng., to N. E. 1634, settled Watertown, Mass., removed Wethersfield, Conn., 1638, and to Hadley, Mass., 1659.

SAMUEL, granted land Salem, Mass., 1637, died Wenham, Mass., 1642.

SAMUEL, married Boston, Mass., 1659.

SAMUEL, married Eastham, Mass., 1665.

SAMUEL, resident Taunton, Mass., 1662.

SAMUEL, freeman, Fairfield, Conn., 1670.

SAMUEL, living Medfield, Mass., 1670.

SAMUEL, proprietor at Ipswich, Mass., 1678.

SAMUEL, freeman, Reading, Mass., 1691.

SAMUEL, on record Haverhill, Mass., 1683.

SHUBAEL, married Sandwich, Mass., 1678.

SIMON, brother first Christopher, settled Wethersfield, Conn., 1644, one original settlers Haddam, Conn.

STEPHEN, married Roxbury, Mass., 1666.

THOMAS, resident Saco, Maine, 1640.

THOMAS, granted land Salem, Mass., 1639.

THOMAS, weaver, came from Rumsey, county of Hants, England to Newbury, Mass., 1635.

THOMAS, resident Ipswich, Mass., 1641.

THOMAS, inhabitant Gloucester, Mass., 1643.

THOMAS, builder, resident Boston, Mass., 1671.

THOMAS, mariner, married Boston, Mass., before 1656.

THOMAS, blacksmith, married Branford, Conn., 1656, removed Guilford, Conn., 1659.

THOMAS, at Roxbury, Mass., 1660.

THOMAS, married Providence, R. I., 1661.

THOMAS, one first settlers Haddam, Conn., where he died 1674.

THOMAS, resident Newbury, Mass., 1668.

THOMAS, butcher, living Charlestown, Mass., 1664.

THOMAS, residing Suffield, Conn., 1685.

THOMAS, living Sandwich, Mass., 1688.

WALTER, married, Milford, Conn., 1677, where he died 1709.

WILLIAM, freeman, Weymouth, Mass., 1635, removed Rehoboth, Mass., 1643.

WILLIAM, admitted inhabitant Charlestown, Mass., 1638.

WILLIAM, b. Eng., 1589, constable, Falmouth, Maine, 1636, died unmarried in March, 1676.

WILLIAM, married Lynn, Mass., 1666.

WILLIAM, freeman, Boston, Mass., 1662.

WILLIAM, brother first Christopher, settled Wethersfield, Conn., 1644.

SNAWSELL

ABRAHAM, residing Marblehead, Mass., 1672.

THOMAS, merchant at Boston, Mass., 1652.

SNELL

From Dutch word, *snel,* agile, swift, nimble.

CHRISTOPHER, taxed Dover, N. H., 1671.

JOHN, resident Boston, Mass., 1669.

THOMAS, largest land holder Bridgewater, Mass., 1671.

SNELLING

JOHN, son Thomas S. of Plympton, St. Mary, Devonshire, Eng., at Saco, Maine, 1653, removed Boston, Mass., 1657, where he died 1672.

NICHOLAS, married Gloucester, Mass., 1662.

WILLIAM, physician, brother of John, located Newbury, Mass., 1651, removed Boston, Mass., 1654.

SNOOKE

JAMES, came from Fifehead Magdalen, near Shaflesbury, Dorsetshire, Eng., will probated Weymouth, Mass., July 19, 1656.

SNOW

From Dutch word *snoo,* cunning, subtle, crafty, sly.

ANTHONY, resident Plymouth, Mass., 1638, removed Marshfield, Mass., 1643.

James, resident Woburn, Mass., 1674.

JOHN, brother of the preceding living Woburn, Mass., 1668.

JOSEPH, brother preceding identified with Eastham, Mass., 1671.

JOSIAH, married Marshfield, Mass., 1669.

NICHOLAS, first comer, Plymouth, Mass., 1623, removed Eastham, Mass., 1654.

RICHARD, living Woburn, Mass., 1645.

STEPHEN, married Eastham, Mass., 1663.

THOMAS, barber, resident Boston, Mass., 1636.

WILLIAM, b. Eng., 1617, came Plymouth, Mass., 1635, removed Bridgewater, Mass., 1682.

SOLART, SALART

JOHN, at Wenham, Mass., 1656.

JOSEPH, brother of the preceding, resident Ipswich, Mass.

SOLEY, SOLLY

JOHN, living Charlestown, Mass., 1686.

MANUS, resident Charlestown, Mass., 1646.

MATTHEW, brother of John, at Charlestown, Mass., 1681.

SOLLENDEN, SALINDINE

JOHN, married Barnstable, Mass., 1679.

SOMER, SOMERS, SOMES

Gaelic and Welsh, *so swl,* or *sal, soil,* and *mer,* a lake, water, the sea. ie alluvial land.

JOHN at Marshfield, Mass., 1686.

MORRIS, resident Gloucester, Mass., 1642.

SOMERBY

ANTHONY, school master, son of Richard, grandson of Henry of Little Bytham, Lincolnshire, Eng., bapt. 1610, came to N. E. 1639, freeman Newbury, Mass., 1642, died July, 1686.

HENRY, brother of the preceding, bapt. 1612, freeman Newbury, Mass., 1642.

SOPER

JOSEPH, married Boston, Mass., 1656.

SOULE, SOLE, SOUL

A small territory in France, between Bearn and the Lower Navarre.

GEORGE, "Mayflower" passenger, removed Duxbury, 1638.

SOUTHCOATE, SOUTHCOT

RICHARD, freeman, Dorchester, Mass., 1630, returned Eng. the following year.

SOUTHER, SOUTER, SOWTHER

JOHN, married Boston, Mass., 1661.

JOSEPH, resident Boston, Mass., 1657.

NATHANIEL, clerk of the court at Plymouth, Mass., 1636, removed Boston, Mass., 1649.

SOUTHMEAD, SOUTHMAYD

WILLIAM, mariner, shipwright, married Gloucester, Mass., 1642, removed Pomfret, Conn., where he died in 1649.

SOUTHWELL

A place name, a town in Nottinghamshire, Eng. The southwell or plain.

WILLIAM, married Northampton, Mass., 1687.

SOUTHWICK

LAWRENCE, glassblower, settled Salem, Mass., 1639, was banished as a Quaker, took refuge Shelter Island, L. I., 1659, where he died the following year.

SOUTHWORTH

CONSTANT, son of Constant S.; his widowed mother married Gov. Bradford, b. Leyden, Holland, 1615, freeman, Plymouth, Mass., 1637.

THOMAS, brother of the preceding, b. 1616, died Plymouth, Mass., Dec. 8, 1669.

SOWDEN

THOMAS, living Marblehead, Mass., 1674.

SOWELL

THOMAS, died Boston, Mass., Dec. 7, 1654.

SPARHAWK, SPARROWHAWK

JOHN, died Cambridge, Mass., Sept. 21, 1644.

NATHANIEL, innkeeper, brother of the preceding, b. Dedham, county Essex, Eng., 1598, freeman, Cambridge, Mass., 1639. He died June 28, 1647.

SPARK, SPARKS

EDWARD, servant, b. Eng., 1613, came Saco, Maine, 1635.

JOHN, married Boston, Mass., 1661.

SPARRELL

CHRISTOPHER, freeman, Wells, Maine, 1653.

SPARROW

RICHARD, settled Plymouth, Mass., 1632, removed Eastham, Mass., 1653.

SPAULDING, SPALDING

A place name from Spalding in Lincolnshire, Eng. *Spalding,* a ravine, from the German *spalte.*

EDWARD, settled Braintree, Mass., 1634,

removed Wenham, Mass., 1645, thence to Chelmsford, Mass., where he died Feb. 26, 1670.

SPAULE, SPOWELL, SPAUL

THOMAS, resident Boston, Mass., 1644.

WILLIAM, resident Boston, Mass., 1652.

SPEAR

GEORGE, freeman, Braintree, Mass., 1644.

SPENCER, SPENSER

The name is derived from the Norman French.

The common ancestor of the English family assume the name *LeDespenser,* Latin *dispensator,* from being steward to the household of William the Conqueror. The family seat founded at the time of the Conquest was at Stratford, Eng.; the kitchen was in the early days known as *spence.*

ABRAHAM, married Boston, Mass., 1677.

JARED, son of Michael S., bapt. Stratford, Eng., 1576, came to Cambridge, Mass., 1632, with his five sons, of whom John returned to England. Thomas, known as Sergeant Thomas, and William removed Hartford, Conn., 1636. Michael located Haddam, where his father joined him, 1662.

JOHN, brother of the preceding, took oath of allegiance, Ipswich, Mass., 1634.

MICHAEL, brother of Jared, at Cambridge, Mass., 1634, removed Lynn, Mass., 1637.

ROGER, mariner, at Saco, Maine, 1652, removed Charlestown, Mass., 1653.

STEPHEN, resident Boston, Mass., 1661.

THOMAS, sent by Mason to N. E. 1630, at Kittery, Maine, 1652, living Saco, Maine, 1654.

THOMAS, brother of Jared, freeman, Cambridge, Mass., 1634.

THOMAS, living Concord, Mass., 1666.

WILLIAM, brother Jared, freeman Cambridge, Mass., 1634, removed Hartford, Conn., 1639, died 1640.

SPENNING, SPINNING, SPINAGE

HUMPHREY, living New Haven, Conn., 1639, died Sept. 29, 1656.

SPERRY

RICHARD, freeman, New Haven, Conn., 1644.

SPICER

A name of a trade, a grocer.

PETER, living New London, Conn., 1666, removed Norwich, Conn., where he died 1695-96.

SPICK, SPECK

JARED, resident Windsor, Conn.

SPIGHT

JAMES, living Charlestown, Mass., 1647.

SPINKE, SPINK

Name of a bird, a finch.

ROBERT, freeman, Newport, R. I., 1655, removed Wickford, R. I., 1674.

SPINNEY

THOMAS, settled Kittery, Maine, 1659, died Aug. 31, 1701.

SPOFFORD, SPAFFORD

The name appears in the Doomsday Book in 1066, originating from *spa* a spring, and ford, constructed into Spaford. The family traced their origin from Yorkshire, where there is a small town bearing the name Spafforth.

JOHN, b. Eng., 1612, one of the founders Rowley, Mass., 1638, removed Georgetown, Mass., 1668.

SPOONER

THOMAS, freeman, Salem, Mass., 1637, died 1664.

WILLIAM, brother of the preceding, came from Colchester, Eng., to Plymouth, Mass., 1637, removed Dartmouth, Mass., 1660.

SPOWELL

THOMAS, living Boston, Mass., 1656.

SPRAGUE

The origin of the name is Dutch from *spraak,* speech, language figuratively eloquent. Another origin is the Norse word *spreek,* signifying lively, active, nimble in the mere physical sense. Sir Edward Spragge was Knighted by Charles I for gallant conduct in an engagement with a Dutch fleet.

FRANCIS, resident Plymouth, Mass., 1623, one of original purchasers of Dartmouth, Mass.

RALPH, son of Edward S. of Upway, Dorsetshire, Eng., b. Eng. 1603, came to Salem, Mass., 1628, removed Charlestown, Mass., 1629, afterwards lived on the Malden side.

RICHARD, brother of the preceding, b. Eng., 1605, freeman Charlestown, Mass., 1631, died Nov. 25, 1668.

WILLIAM, youngest brother of the preceding, b. Eng., 1609, settled in Charlestown, Mass., 1629, removed Hingham, Mass., 1636.

SPRING

JOHN, planter, b. Eng., 1589, came from Ipswich, county of Suffolk, Eng., to Watertown, Mass., 1634.

SPRINGFIELD

EMANUEL, married Boston, Mass., 1655.

SPROAT

ROBERT, married Scituate, Mass., 1660.

SPURR, SPOURE, SPORE

JOHN, joined church Boston, Mass., 1638.

ROBERT, at Dorchester, Mass., 1654.

SQUIRE, SQUIER

GEORGE, at Concord, Mass., 1642, removed Fairfield, Conn., 1634, where he died 1691.

JOHN, freeman Boston, Mass., 1686, removed Reading, Mass.

THOMAS, probably came in Winthrop's fleet to Boston, Mass., removed Charlestown, Mass., 1632.

STACKHOUSE

RICHARD, at Salem, Mass., 1638, removed to Beverly side.

STACY, STACIE, STACEY

The name is a form of the Latin *Statius* from *sto,* to stand, stationed, standing still, fixed.

HENRY, at Marblehead, Mass., 1648, removed Salem, Mass., 1677.

HUGH, came Plymouth, Mass., 1621, removed Dedham, Mass., 1640.

JOHN, brother of Henry, at Lynn or Marblehead, Mass., 1641.

RICHARD, died Taunton, Mass., Dec. 7, 1687.

SAMUEL, at Salem, Mass., 1678.

SIMON, at Ipswich, Mass., 1641, where he died Oct. 27, 1699.

WILLIAM, freeman, Salem, Mass., 1680.

STAFFORD

THOMAS, b. Warwickshire, Eng., 1605, admitted inhabitant Newport, R. I., 1638, removed to Warwick, R. I., where he died 1677.

STAGPOLE

JAMES, granted land Dover, N. H., 1694.

STAINES

An old word for stones, a market town in Middlesex, England.

RICHARD, sailmaker at Boston, Mass., 1654.

STAIRES, STAIR

A Gaelic word, signifying stepping stones in a river, a path made over a bog.

THOMAS, resident Windsor, Conn., 1644.

STALLION

EDWARD, resident New London, Conn., 1650.

STAMFORD

THOMAS, at Scarborough or Saco, Maine, swore fidelity to Massachusetts, 1658.

STANBURY, STANBERRY, STANBOROUGH

JOSIAH, Lynn, Mass., 1639, removed Southampton, L. I., where he died 1659.

STANCLIFFE

JAMES, Middletown, Conn., 1686, where he died Oct. 3, 1712.

STANDISH

MILES or MYLES, "Mayflower" passenger, removed Duxbury, Mass., where he died Oct. 3, 1656.

THOMAS, b. Eng., 1612, Wethersfield, Conn., 1636, where he died 1692.

STANDLAKE

DANIEL, resident Scituate, Mass., 1636, where he died in May, 1638.

STANFORD, STANIFORD

JOHN, married Ipswich, Mass., 1680.

ROBERT, Scituate, Mass., 1670, removed Marshfield, Mass., 1680.

THOMAS, living Charlestown, Mass., 1688.

STANHOPE

A place name from Stanhope in the bishopric of Durham, Eng.; from *stan,* stone, and *hope,* the side of a hill, or low ground amid hills.

The first English record of the name is Walter de Stanhope of the county of Durham.

JONATHAN, b. Eng., 1632, married Charlestown, Mass., 1656, removed Sudbury, Mass., where he died Oct. 25, 1702.

STANIELL, STANIARD, STONIARD

ANTHONY, glover, came to N. E. 1635, at Exeter, N. H., 1644.

STANLEY, STANDLEY

A place name from a market town in Gloucestershire, England. The place of a tin mill; *stan,* tin, from the Welsh *ystaen,* and *ley* from the Saxon *stan,* a stone, and *ley*-the stoney place.

CHRISTOPHER, b. Eng., 1603, came to Boston, Mass., 1635, where he died 1646.

GEORGE, married Beverly, Mass., 1680.

JOHN, embarked for N. E. 1634, died on the voyage.

JOHN, only son of the preceding, b. Eng., 1624, came with his uncle Thomas S. to Hartford, Conn., 1636, removed Farmington, Conn.

MATTHEW, b. Eng., 1638, resident Lynn, Mass., 1646, removed Topsfield, Mass., 1664, died Nov. 14, 1712.

THOMAS, brother of first John, freeman, Lynn, Mass., 1635; removed Hartford, Conn., 1636, settled Farmington, Conn., 1650, known as Capt. Stanley.

TIMOTHY, brother of the preceding, freeman, Cambridge, Mass., 1634, removed Hartford, Conn., 1635.

STANNARD, STANARD

JOSEPH, early settler Hartford, Conn., settled at Haddam, Conn., 1667.

STANTON

From *stan,* a stone, and *ton,* a hill or town.

ROBERT, admitted inhabitant Newport, R. I., 1639.

THOMAS, b. Eng., 1615, came to Virginia, 1635, one of original proprietors Hartford, Conn., settled Stonington, Conn., 1658, died 1678.

STANWOOD, STAINWOOD

PHILIP, a resident Gloucester, Mass., 1652.

STANYAN, STANIAN, STANION

ANTHONY, freeman, Exeter, N. H., 1644, afterwards at Hampton, N. H. and Boston, Mass.

STAPLES

Name derived from the village of Estaples, France, also it is claimed that it was adopted for the invention of an iron staple or the maker of it.

ABRAHAM, Dorchester, Mass., 1658, removed Weymouth, Mass., 1660, thence Mendon, Mass., where he was made freeman 1673.

JEFFREY, resident Weymouth, Mass., 1640.

JOHN, b. Eng., 1610, appears as early inhabitant Weymouth, Mass., 1636.

PETER, granted land Kittery, Maine, 1671.

SAMUEL, married Braintree, Mass., 1652.

THOMAS, Fairfield, Conn., 1645.

THOMAS, brother of Peter, Kittery, Maine, 1671.

STAPLETON

SAMUEL, resident Newport, R. I., 1679.

STAR, STARR

Name from the German, stiff, rigid, inflexible.

COMFORT, surgeon, b. Ashford, county of Kent, Eng., settled Cambridge, Mass., 1634, settled Duxbury, Mass., 1638, removed Boston, Mass., where he died Jan. 2, 1660.

SAMUEL, married New London, Conn., 1663.

THOMAS, brother of Comfort, came from Canterbury, county of Kent, to Boston, Mass., 1635.

WILLIAM, died Lynn, Mass., 1666.

STARBOARD, STARBIRD

THOMAS, married Dover, N. H., 1688.

STARBUCK

EDWARD, b. Eng., 1604, came from Derbyshire, Eng., to Dover, N. H., 1635, removed Nantucket, Mass., 1660, where he died 1690-91.

STARK, STARKE, START

From Anglo Saxon *stare,* German *Starck,* strong, firm, confirmed to the utmost degree.

AARON, of Scotch descent, settled Hartford, Conn., 1639, removed Windsor, Conn., 1643, finally to New London, Conn.

ROBERT, died Concord, Mass., 1646.

WILLIAM, resident Lynn, Mass., 1641.

STARKEY

Strong of body, from *Stark.*

GEORGE, at Lynn or Malden, Mass., 1646.

JOHN, clothier and weaver, b. Eng., 1638, came from Standish, Lancashire, Eng., to Boston, Mass., 1667, afterwards resided Charlestown and Malden, Mass.

ROBERT, at Concord, Mass., 1646.

STARKWEATHER

ROBERT, located Roxbury, Mass., 1640, removed Ipswich, Mass., 1651.

STARLING

EDWARD, freeman, York, Maine, 1655.

STEARNS, STERN

From Danish *Stierne,* a Star. Severe in look, harsh, bold.

CHARLES, freeman Watertown, Mass., 1646.

ISAAC, b. Nayland, Suffolkshire, Eng., freeman, Watertown, Mass., 1631, came in Winthrop's fleet, died June 19, 1671.

NATHANIEL, freeman, Dedham, Mass., 1649.

STEBBINS, STEBBIN, STEBBING

A place name from Stebbings, originally *Stubing,* a town in county of Essex, Eng., so called from *stub,* Saxon, *styobe.* Latin *stipes,* the stump of a tree, and *ing,* a field or meadow.

EDWARD, freeman, Cambridge, Mass., 1634, removed Hartford, Conn., 1635.

JOHN, proprietor Watertown, Mass., 1644, removed New London, Conn., 1645.

JOHN, baker, freeman, Roxbury, Mass., 1647.

MARTIN, brewer, brother first John, married Roxbury, Mass., 1639, removed Boston, Mass., 1645.

ROWLAND, b. Stebbing, county of Essex, Eng., 1594, settled Roxbury, Mass., 1634, removed Springfield, Mass., 1635, later Northampton, Mass., where he died Dec. 14, 1671.

STEDMAN, STUDMAN

AUGUSTINE, Newbury, Mass., 1678.

GEORGE, married Charlestown, Mass., 1674.

ISAAC, merchant, b. Eng., 1605, located Scituate, Mass., 1635, removed Boston, Mass., 1650, died 1678.

JOHN, b. Eng., 1601, came Cambridge, Mass., 1638, died Dec. 16, 1693.

JOHN, resident Hartford, Conn., 1651, freeman Wethersfield, Conn., 1654, died Nov. 24, 1678.

ROBERT, freeman Cambridge, Mass., 1639.

THOMAS, New London, Conn., 1649.

THOMAS, living Muddy Creek now Brookline, Mass., married before 1671.

STEDWELL, STUDWELL, STEADWELL

JOSEPH, at Greenwich, Conn., 1697.

THOMAS, died Stamford, Conn., 1670.

STEELE

A name given to a person who was inflexible, hard, firm or enduring.

GEORGE, proprietor Cambridge, Mass., 1632, removed Hartford, Conn., 1635.

HENRY, resident Cambridge, Mass., 1632.

JOHN, brother of George, came from Braintree, Eng., to Dorchester, Mass., 1630, removed to Cambridge, Mass., 1632, and to Hartford, Conn., 1635, thence Farmington, Conn., 1645.

NICHOLAS, resident Taunton, Mass., 1654.

STEERE

JOHN, living Providence, R. I., 1645.

RICHARD, resident New London, Conn., 1690.

STENT, STINT

ELEAZER, resident New Haven, Conn., 1645.

STEPHENSON

ANDREW, living Cambridge, Mass., 1640.

JOHN, shoemaker, inhabitant Boston, Mass., 1643.

MARMADUKE, Quaker, resident Boston, Mass., 1659.

THOMAS, living Dover, N. H., before 1641.

STEPNEY

FRANCIS, dancing master, living Boston, Mass., 1686.

STERLING, STIRLING

A place name from the city of Stirling, England, the Gaelic name of which is *Strila,* supposed to signify the place of strife, from *Stri-thralla.*
The earliest known progenitor was Walter de Sturielying, born about 1100; he was mentioned in the charter granted by King David I of Scotland.

WILLIAM, ship carpenter and miller, Scotch descent, b. near London, Eng., 1637, resident Salem, Mass., 1660, removed Rowley, Mass., settled Haverhill, Mass., 1697, removed Lyme, Conn.

STETSON, STITSON, STUTSON

In Danish, *stedson,* a stepson.
JOHN, died York, Maine, 1673.

ROBERT, b. Eng., 1613, granted land Scituate, Mass., 1634.

VINCENT, living Milford, Conn., 1646, removed Marblehead, Mass., 1674, returned Milford.

WILLIAM, freeman, Charlestown, Mass., 1632.

STEVENS, STEPHENS

From the Greek, signifying a cross.

CYPRIAN, b. London, Eng., 1644-45, arrived Boston, Mass., 1660, married Chelsea, Mass., 1672, finally settled Lancaster, Mass.

EDWARD, resident Marshfield, Mass., 1665.

EDWARD, married Boston, Mass., 1700.

ERASMUS, innkeeper, living Boston, Mass., 1671.

FRANCIS, resident Rehoboth, Mass., 1675.

GEORGE, cooper, died Boston, Mass., 1655.

HENRY, stone mason, b. Eng., 1611, inhabitant Boston, Mass., 1635.

HENRY, servant, Lynn, Mass., 1634.

HENRY, resident Stonington, Conn., 1668.

HENRY, proprietor, New Haven, Conn., 1685.

JOHN, b. Eng., 1609, came from Caversham, county of Oxford, Eng., settled Newbury, Mass., 1637, later removed Andover, Mass., 1645.

JOHN, freeman Salisbury, Mass., 1641.

JOHN, at Guilford, Conn., 1650, where he died Oct. 2, 1669.

JOHN, resident Chelmsford, Mass., 1679.

JOHN, b. Eng., 1611, settled Salisbury, Mass., 1640.

JOSEPH, resident Braintree, Mass., 1677.

JOSEPH, freeman, Mendon, Mass., 1673.

RICHARD, resident Taunton, Mass., 1670.

ROBERT, living Braintree, Mass., 1641.

THOMAS, son of Thomas S., brother of Cyprian, freeman, b. London, Eng., 1623, came to N. E. 1635, freeman Sudbury, Mass., 1665.

THOMAS, resident Stamford, Conn., 1641.

THOMAS, baker, living Boston, Mass., 1670.

THOMAS, mariner, living Boston, Mass., before 1672.

THOMAS, married Newbury, Mass., 1672.

THOMAS, took oath of allegiance, Casco, Maine, 1665.

THOMAS, at Westerly, R. I., 1680.

WILLIAM, shipbuilder, came Boston, Mass., 1632, removed Salem, Mass., 1636, and Gloucester, Mass., 1642.

WILLIAM, brother of first John, b. Eng., 1617, freeman Salem, Mass., 1642, where he died May 10, 1653.

WILLIAM, married Charlestown, Mass., 1673.

STEVENSON

JAMES, married Reading, Mass., 1661.

STEWART, STEWARD, STUART

Walter, the son of Fleance, and grandson of Banquo, was created by Malcom III. Lord High Steward of Scotland, from which office his family afterwards took and retained the name of Stewart, and from them descended the royal family of *Stuart.*

ALEXANDER, shipwright, on record Charlestown, Mass., 1675, removed Marlboro, 1688.

DANIEL, Barnstable, Mass., before 1665.

DUNCAN, shipwright, brother of Alexander, Newbury, Mass., 1659, removed Rowley, Mass., 1669.

JAMES, came Plymouth, Mass., 1621, must have removed before 1627.

JAMES, resident Weymouth, Mass., 1669.

JOHN, married Springfield, Mass., 1650.

ROBERT, at Milford, Conn., removed Norwalk, Conn., 1660.

WILLIAM, died Lynn, Mass., 1664.

STICKNEY, STICKNEE

The family of Saxon origin; John de Stickney, ancestor 1331.

WILLIAM, bapt. Frampton Church, Eng., 1592, came from Hull, county of York, Eng., to Boston, Mass., 1637, removed Rowley, Mass., 1639, where he died Jan. 25, 1665.

STILEMAN, STYLEMAN, STILLMAN

ELIAS, settler at Salem, Mass., 1629, died 1662.

GEORGE, merchant tailor, b. Steeple Ashton, Eng., 1654, settled Hadley, Mass., removed Wethersfield, Conn.

STILES, STYLES

Ancient Anglo-Saxon family, name derived from Stighele, meaning at the stile or steps or rising path and was first applied to dwellings thus situated.

FRANCIS, carpenter, son of Thomas S. of Ampthill, county of Bedford, Eng., b. 1601, located Dorchester, Mass., 1635, removed Windsor, Conn., 1636, removed Saybrook, Conn., 1647.

HENRY, carpenter, eldest brother of the preceding, bapt. Millbrook, Bedfordshire, Eng., 1593, settled Dorchester, Mass., 1635, removed Windsor, Conn., 1636, died Oct. 3, 1651.

JOHN, brother of the preceding, bapt. Millbrook, Eng., 1595, first lived Dorchester, Mass., 1635, removed Windsor, Conn., where he died June, 1662.

ROBERT, married Boxford, Mass., 1660.

STILLWELL, STILWELL

JASPER, one first planters Guilford, Conn., 1640, where he died 1690.

STILSON

VINCENT, resident Milford, Mass., 1646, where he died 1690.

STIMPSON, STIMSON

ANDREW, came from Newcastle on the Tyme, Eng., 1637, admitted freeman Cambridge, Mass., 1643.

GEORGE, of Welsh descent, resident Ipswich, Mass., 1668.

JOHN, joined church Charlestown, Mass., 1685.

JONATHAN, married Watertown, Mass., 1673.

STOCKBRIDGE

JOHN, wheelwright, b. Eng., 1608, settled Scituate, Mass., 1635, removed Boston, Mass., 1656, where he died Oct. 13, 1657.

JOHN, swore fidelity Haverhill, Mass., 1677.

STOCKER

DANIEL, married Lynn, Mass., 1672.

EBENEZER, married Lynn, Mass., 1674.

SAMUEL, married Lynn, Mass., 1666.

THOMAS, resident Chelsea and Lynn, Mass., 1651-72.

STOCKIN, STOCKEN, STOCKING

The name appears in Doomesday Book as Stocking with an ending ham, the latter being the old Saxon *heim,* or *home,* indicating Stockingham. The original seat of the family was in the county of Suffolk, Eng.

GEORGE, b. county of Suffolk, Eng., 1582, came to N. E. 1633, settled Cambridge, Mass., one of the original founders Hartford, Conn.

STOCKMAN

JOHN, married Salisbury, Mass., 1671.

STOCKWELL

QUINTIN or QUINTON, tax payer, Dorchester, Mass., 1663, removed Hatfield, Mass., 1672, proprietor Deerfield, Mass., 1673, removed Branford, Conn., 1679.

WILLIAM, b. Eng., 1650, was at Ipswich and Salem, Mass.

STODDARD, STODDER

By tradition the first of the name came with William the Conqueror to England as a standard bearer to Viscompte De-Pulesdon, a noble Norman, and was anciently written De La Standard, corrupted to *Stodard* or *Stodart.* William Stoddard a Knight, was also with William the Conqueror.

ANTHONY, linen draper, resident Boston, Mass., 1639, recorder of Boston, for nineteen years. died March 16, 1687.

JOHN, b. Eng., 1612, lived New London, Conn., 1652.

JOHN, settled Hingham, Mass., 1638, died Nov. 28, 1661.

JOHN, married Wethersfield, Conn., 1642.

STOKES

A parish in Buckinghamshire, also town in Suffolk, and Gloucestershire, Eng. The name signifies, a place, settlement, *Stuge,* Danish, a ravine.

HENRY, took oath of fidelity Permaquid, Maine, 1674.

STONARD, STONNARD, STONHARD

JOHN, resident Roxbury, Mass., 1645.

STONE

A town in England was anciently given to an individual near a place called Stone. "Will at the Stone."

ELIAS, resident Charlestown, Mass., 1687.

GREGORY, son of David S., grandson Simon S., bapt. Bromley, county of Essex, England, 1592, settled Watertown, Mass., 1635, removed Cambridge, Mass., 1637, died Nov. 30, 1672.

HUGH, married Andover, Mass., 1667.

HUGH, b. Eng., 1638, freeman, R. I., 1678, resided Providence and Warwick, R. I.

JOHN, ferryman, granted land Salem, Mass., 1636, one founders Beverly, Mass.

JOHN, b. Hertfordshire, Eng., 1610, original proprietor Hartford, Conn., 1636, removed Guilford, Conn., 1639, where he signed the Plantation Contract.

JOHN, resident Boston, Mass., 1659.

JOHN, living Hull, Mass.; will probated 1664.

JOHN, early settler Groton, Mass., 1676.

SAMUEL, clergyman, brother of Gregory, b. Hertford, county of Herts, Eng., came to N. E., 1633, settled Cambridge, Mass., removed Hartford, Conn., 1635, chaplain to Capt. Mason's troops, Pequot War, died July 20, 1663.

SAMUEL, freeman, Concord, Mass., 1682.

SIMON, husbandman, elder brother of Gregory, b. county of Essex, Eng., 1585, freeman, Watertown, Mass., 1636, died Sept., 1665.

WILLIAM, brother second John, signed covenant, Guilford, Conn., 1639, died Nov., 1683.

STORER

An occupation surname signifying the storer or one who stored goods, also an official title in the feudal household.

AUGUSTUS, son of Rev. Thomas S., vicar of Bilsby, Eng., where he was born, came from Alford, Lincolnshire, Eng., to Dover, N. H., 1634, also at Exeter, N. H. and Boston, Mass., died before 1643.

RICHARD, came with his mother, Elizabeth, wife of Robert Hull to Boston, Mass., 1635.

WILLIAM, an early settler in Maine.

STORES, STORRS

From the Danish *storre,* greater, larger, stout, strong; in Teutonic means great, in the sense of rule, power, authority. The earliest mention of the English records is Rogeries de Stores of Beckfontes, 1278. William Storrs to whom the American family is traced lived in Nottinghamshire.

SAMUEL, son of Thomas S., fifth generation from William S., bapt. Sutton, Nottinghamshire, 1640, came to Barnstable, 1663, removed Mansfield, Conn., 1698, where he died April 30, 1719.

STORKE

JOHN, married Rowley, Mass., 1660.

SAMUEL, resident Lynn, Mass., 1677.

STORY

ANDREW, living Ipswich, Mass., 1639.

AUGUSTUS or AUGUSTINE, Exeter, N. H., 1639.

GEORGE, merchant, resident Boston, Mass., 1642.

ROWLAND, shipwright, at Boston, Mass., 1673.

SAMUEL, living Ipswich, Mass., 1691.

WILLIAM, carpenter, b. Eng., 1614, came from Norwich, county of Norfolk, Eng., to N. E., 1637, settled Ipswich, Mass., 1642.

WILLIAM, taxed Dover, N. H., 1656.

STOUGHTON

The name derived from *Stoche* or *Stoke,* a place in Surrey, England, and *tun,* a word signifying inclosure. In the reign of Stephen I, 1135-54, Godwin de Stockton lived at Stockton, Surrey, Eng. Another English ancestor was Henry de Stoughton.

ISRAEL, freeman, Dorchester, Mass., 1632, commander of Massachusetts forces in the Pequot War, died London, Eng., 1644.

NICHOLAS, married Taunton, Mass., 1674.

THOMAS, brother Israel, son of Rev. Thomas S., freeman Dorchester, Mass., 1630, removed Windsor, Conn., 1639, died Sept., 1684.

WILLIAM, settled Dorchester, Mass., selectman 1671, judge of court of oyer and terminer, 1692.

STOVER, STOVARD

SILVESTER, resident York, Maine, 1652.

STOWE, STOW

A fixed place or mansion; a town, a garrison.

JOHN, came from Hawkhurst, county of Kent, Eng., to Roxbury, Mass., 1634.

STOWELL

SAMUEL, weaver, b. Eng., 1620, proprietor, Hingham, Mass., 1647.

STOWERS, STOWER

JOHN, came from Parham, county of Suffolk, Eng., to Watertown, Mass., 1634, removed Newport, R. I.

NICHOLAS, one of eleven settlers at Charlestown, Mass., 1629, removed Salem, Mass.

STRAIGHT, STRAITE

THOMAS, resident Watertown, Mass., 1644.

STRAINE, STRAINER

A town in the north of Scotland written Strane.

RICHARD, brewer, inhabitant Boston, Mass., 1647, returned to England before 1659.

STRANGE

GEORGE, freeman, Dorchester, Mass., 1634, removed Hingham, Mass., 1639.

JOHN, living Boston, Mass., 1651.

LOT, Portsmouth, R. I., 1689.

STRANGUAGE, STRANGEWAYS

WILLIAM, mariner, Boston, Mass., 1651.

STRATTON, STRETTON

A Cornish British word. The hill full of springs.

BARTHOLOMEW, living Boston, Mass., 1659.

CALEB, mariner, inhabitant Boston, Mass., 1661.

ELEAZER, resident Andover, Mass., died March 15, 1689.

JOHN, Scarborough, Maine, 1633, removed Salem, Mass., 1637, later Easthampton, L. I.

JOHN, b. Eng., 1606, at Salem, Mass., 1631.

JOHN, b. Eng., 1642, at Watertown, Mass., before 1668.

SAMUEL, b. Kent, Eng., 1592, settled Watertown, Mass., 1647, died Dec. 20, 1672.

STREAME, STREME, STERTE

JOHN, b. Eng., 1621, came with his uncle, Zechariah Whitman, to Boston, Mass., 1635, removed Milford, Conn., 1646.

THOMAS, brother of the preceding, resident of Weymouth, Mass.

STREET

FRANCIS, purchaser Taunton, Mass., 1637, died 1665; no male issue.

NICHOLAS, teacher and clergyman, son of Nicholas S., grandson of Nicholas S. and great grandson of Richard S., a clothier of England, whose will was proven Sept. 30, 1592, was bapt. Bridgewater, Eng., 1603, came from Taunton, Eng., to Taunton, Mass., 1637, removed New Haven, Conn., 1645, died there April 22, 1674.

STEPHEN, freeman of Massachusetts, 1644, lived either at Concord or Sudbury, Mass.

STREETER

SAMUEL, at Edgartown, Mass., 1663, where he was drowned Nov. 19, 1669.

STEPHEN, b. Kent, Eng., came to N. E., 1639, on record Gloucester, Mass., 1642, removed Charlestown, Mass., 1644.

STRICKLAND

The name derived from *Strick-land* or *Stirkland,* that is the pasture ground of young cattle called stirks or steers in the parish of Moreland, county of Westmoreland, England, where the family once had considerable possessions.

JOHN, came Mass., 1630, removed Hempstead, L. I.

PETER, resident New London, Conn., 1670.

STRIKER

JOSEPH, married Salem, Mass., 1673.

STRONG

JOHN, Welsh descent, son of Richard S. of county Cavenarvon, Wales, b. Taunton, Somersetshire, Eng., 1605, settled Dorchester, Mass., 1630; one of first proprietors Hingham, Mass., 1635, removed Taunton, Mass., 1638, at Windsor, Conn., 1649, inhabitant Northampton, Mass., 1661, died April 14, 1699.

STUBBS

JOSHUA, married Watertown, Mass., 1641.

RICHARD, planter, married Hull, Mass., 1659.

STUCKEY

GEORGE, Windsor, Conn., 1640, removed Stamford, Conn., 1657.

STUDLEY

The family originally from the counties of Kent and York, Eng.

JOHN, Gloucester, Mass., 1651, removed Boston, Mass., 1659.

STUKELEY

THOMAS, freeman, Suffield, Conn., 1681.

STURGIS, STURGES

In English history William de Turges held grants of land from Edward I. His estate included the village of Turges, was situated in the county of Northampton where many generations of the family lived. The village of Turges was afterwards known as Northfield. The English family is traced to Roger Sturges who lived at Clipson, county of Northampton, Eng., and whose will was executed 1530.

EDWARD, son of Philip S., sixth generation from Roger S., mentioned above, b. Hannington, Eng., resident Charlestown, Mass., 1634, removed to Yarmouth, Mass., 1639.

JOHN, b. Eng., 1627, freeman, Fairfield, Conn., 1668.

JOHN, resident R. I., 1672.

PHILIP, born Hannington, Eng., came to N. E., 1634, settled Sandwich, Mass.

SAMUEL, married Barnstable, Mass., 1697.

THOMAS, resident Yarmouth, Mass., 1681.

STURTEVANT, STURDEVANT

SAMUEL, Dutch ancestry, b. Rochester, Eng., came to Plymouth, Mass., 1641, died 1669.

WILLIAM, resident Norwalk, Conn., 1676.

SUMMERS

The name is derived from Saxon *Sumer,* Celtic or Gaelic *samh,* sun. *Summer,* one who casts up an account. The name may be a corruption of *Summer.*

HENRY, married Woburn, Mass., 1660.

JOHN, resident Duxbury, Mass., before 1680.

SUMNER

One whose duty consists in citing delinquents to the ecclesiastical courts, an apparitor, literally a *summoner.*

THOMAS, resident, Rowley, Mass., 1643.

WILLIAM, only child of Roger S., a husbandman of Bicester, Oxfordshire, Eng., where he was b. 1605, settled Dorchester, Mass., 1636, died March, 1692.

SUNDERLAND, SUNDERLINE, SYNDERLAND

A seaport town in the county of Durham, Eng. Land separated, divided, parted.

JOHN, parchment maker, b. Eng., 1618, admitted church Boston, Mass., 1643, removed Eastham, Mass., where he died Dec. 26, 1703.

SUSSELL

RICHARD, freeman, Portsmouth, R. I., 1653.

SUTHERLAND

MATTHEW, resident, R. I., 1639.

SUTLIFFE

ABRAHAM, living Scituate, Mass., 1640.

THOMAS, resident Branford, Conn., 1668.

SUTTON

A town in Devonshire, Eng., the south town.

BARTHOLOMEW, resident Boston, Mass., 1667.

DANIEL, living Boston, Mass., 1667.

GEORGE, married Scituate, Mass., 1641.

JOHN, came from Attleburg, county of Norfolk, Eng., to Hingham, Mass., 1638.

LAMBERT, freeman, Woburn, Mass., 1644, earlier at Charlestown, Mass., died Nov. 27, 1649.

RICHARD, householder, Charlestown, Mass., 1677.

RICHARD, living Andover, Mass., 1664.

SIMON, residing Scituate, Mass., 1647.

WILLIAM, married Eastham, Mass., 1666.

SWADDON

PHILIP, Watertown, Mass., 1630, removed Kittery, Maine, 1640.

SWADOCK

JOHN, took oath of allegiance, Haverhill, Mass., 1685.

SWAIN, SWAYNE, SWAINE

From the Danish, *swan.* Swan, a youth, a servant, a herdsman.

RICHARD, b. Eng., 1601, came N. E., 1635, settled Rowley, Mass., 1639, removed Hampton, N. H., in that year, settled Nantucket, Mass., 1663, where he died April 14, 1682.

WILLIAM, b. Eng., 1585, freeman, Watertown, Mass., 1636, removed Wethersfield, Conn., 1639 and to Branford, Conn., 1644.

SWALLOW

AMBROSE, resident Chelmsford, Mass., 1692.

SWAN, SWANN

The family is descended from a Dane of noble ancestry who early settled in the south-eastern part of England. The family have possessed landed properties in counties of Kent and Derby, since the time of William the Conqueror. John Swan of Southfleet, was Baron of the borough of Sandwich, reign of Henry VI.

HENRY, freeman, Salem, Mass., 1639.

JOHN, b. Eng., 1621, came N. E., 1640, freeman, Cambridge, Mass., 1668, died June 5, 1708.

RICHARD, b. Eng., 1600, settled Boston, Mass., 1638, removed Rowley, Mass., 1639.

ROBERT, resident Haverhill, Mass., 1646.

THOMAS, physician, resident Boston, and Roxbury, Mass., 1655, died February, 1688.

SWARTON

JOHN, Beverly, Mass., 1672.

SWASEY, SWAZEY, SWAYSY

JOSEPH, settled Salem, Mass., 1668.

SWEET, SWAITE, SWEETE

Swede a native of Sweden, Swit of Switzerland.

HENRY, married Swansea, Mass., 1687.

JAMES, son of Isaac S. at Salem, Mass., 1631, freeman Warwick, R. I., 1655.

JOHN, shipwright, freeman, Boston, Mass., 1640.

JOHN, shoemaker, died Charlestown, Mass., 1695.

JOHN, brother of James, freeman, Warwick, R. I., 1655.

JOHN, resident Wickford, R. I.

JOHN, settled Salem, Mass., before 1637, removed Providence, R. I.

SWEETMAN, SWETMAN, SWETNAM

THOMAS, freeman, Cambridge, Mass., 1638.

SWEETSER, SWITZER

SAMUEL, resident, Malden, Mass., 1701.

SETH, b. Tring, Hertfordshire, Eng., 1606, came Charlestown, Mass., 1637, died May 21 or 24, 1662.

SWETT

JOHN, b. Eng., 1590, came from Isle of Guernsey in the English Channel to Salem, Mass., 1636, freeman Newbury, Mass., 1642.

SWIFT

A name given for swiftness in moving. It may however come from Swift, a river in England.

THOMAS, son of Robert S. of Rotterham, Yorkshire, Eng., b. Eng., 1600, freeman Dorchester, Mass., 1635, died May 4, 1675.

WILLIAM, b. Bocking, county of Suffolk, Eng., came to N. E., 1630, proprietor Watertown, Mass., 1636, removed Sudbury, Mass., finally to Sandwich, Mass., where he died Jan., 1644.

SWILLAWAY, SWILLOWAY

HENRY, resident, Malden, Mass., 1666.

SWINERTON, SWANNERTON

JOB, came from Straffordshire, Eng., to Salem, Mass., where he joined the church, 1639, removed Danvers, Mass., died April 11, 1689.

SWYDEN, SWINDEN

WILLIAM, b. Eng., 1615, came Ipswich, Mass., 1635.

SYKES

RICHARD, freeman, Dorchester, Mass., 1640.

SYMMES

JOHN, swore allegiance to Massachusetts at Scarborough, Maine, 1658.

ZECARIAH, clérgyman, son of Rev. William S., b. Canterbury, county of Kent, Eng., 1599, came Boston, Mass., 1634, removed Charlestown, Mass., died Jan. 28, 1672.

SYMONDS

HENRY, freeman, Boston, Mass., 1643, died Sept., 1643.

JAMES, married Woburn, Mass., 1685.

JOHN, b. Eng., 1616, freeman, Salem, Mass., 1637.

JOHN, resident Braintree, Mass., 1640.

JOHN, sent by Mason to Portsmouth, N. H., 1631, removed Kittery, Maine, 1650.

JOSEPH, married Hartford, Conn.

MARK, b. Eng., 1585, freeman Ipswich, Mass., 1638, died April 28, 1659.

SAMUEL, came from Yeldham, county of Essex, Eng., freeman Ipswich, Mass., 1638, deputy governor of Mass., 1673, in which office he died Oct. 12, 1678.

THOMAS, resident Braintree, Mass., 1638.

WILLIAM, settled Ipswich, Mass., 1635.

WILLIAM, resident Concord, Mass., 1636.

WILLIAM, married Woburn, Mass., 1644, died June 7, 1672.

TABOR, TABER

Tabur or *Tobar,* Gaelic; a spring-well, water, a river. *Tabor,* a city in Bohemia which the Hussites fortified and made the seat of their war for twenty years; on this account they were called *Taborites.* The family probably derive their name from this city.

PHILIP, b. Eng., 1605, freeman at Watertown, Mass., 1634, removed Yarmouth, Mass., 1639, thence to New London, Conn., 1651, freeman Portsmouth, R. I., 1656, later resided at Providence, Newport and Tiverton, R. I.

TAFT

The name in Ireland spelt *Taaffe.* Sir William T. was a Knight of Protestant faith in 1610.

ROBERT, housewright, b. Ireland, 1640; first at Braintree, Mass., 1678, afterwards Bristol, R. I., lated was prominent in the organization of the town of Mendon, Mass.

TAINER, TAINNER

JOSIAH, at Marblehead, Mass., 1674.

TAINTOR, TYANTOR, TAINTER

The name is derived from the French word *teinturer,* a dyer. The family has been represented in England since the Norman Conquest, the name Le Tainturer being found in the records as early as 1222. Charles, shipowner and merchant, came from Wales and settled at Wethersfield, Conn., 1643, removed Fairfield, Conn., 1647, lost at sea on a coast voyage, 1654.

JOSEPH, b. 1613, came Watertown, Mass., 1638, died Feb. 20, 1690.

MICHAEL, younger brother of Charles, freeman, Branford, Conn., 1668, representative 1670-72.

TALBOT

It was in 1035 that Hugh Talebot granted a charter to Tunite du Mont, Rouen, Normandy; Le Sire Talebot, a Norman Knight, came to England with William the Conqueror. John Talbot was created in 1442 the first Earl of Shrewsbury. The name signifies a mastiff.

CHRISTOPHER, turner, Boston, 1686.

JAMES, resident Boston, Mass., 1663.

JARED or GARRETT, married Taunton, Mass., 1664.

MOSES, at Plymouth, Mass., afterwards at Kennebeck, Maine, where he was killed in April, 1634.

PETER, son of George T. of Blackburn, Eng., came from Carr, Lancashire, England, settled Dorchester, Mass., removed to Chelmsford, Mass., where he died 1704.

WILLIAM, sailmaker, Boston, Mass., 1651.

TALBY, TOLBY

JOHN, resident, Salem, Mass., 1635.

STEPHEN, mariner, Boston, Mass., 1662.

TALCOTT, TAILECOAT, TAYLCOAT

The English family traced to John T. of Colchester, county of Essex, Eng., 1558.

JOHN, son of John T., b. Braintree, county of Essex, Eng., came to Cambridge, Mass., 1632, removed Hartford, Conn., 1636, where he died 1659.

TALLEY, TOLLEY, TAULLEY

RICHARD, b. 1651, resident Dorchester, Mass., where he died Dec. 8, 1717.

THOMAS, brother of the preceding, resident Boston, Mass., 1682.

TALMADGE, TALMAGE

ENOS, married New Haven, Conn., 1682.

ROBERT, resident New Haven, Conn., died before 1685.

THOMAS, came Charlestown, Mass., 1631, freeman Boston, Mass., 1634, removed Lynn, Mass., 1637, and 1640 went to Southampton, L. I.

WILLIAM, brother of the preceding, came in Winthrop's fleet, settled Boston, Mass., freeman, 1643, removed Lynn, Mass.

WILLIAM, carpenter, resided Boston, Mass., in that part known as Muddy river.

TALMAN, TALLMAN

PETER, freeman, Newport, R. I., 1655.

TANKERSLY

GEORGE, resident Boston, Mass., 1673.

TANNER

NICHOLAS, at Swanzey, Mass., 1663, removed Rehoboth, Mass., 1666.

TAPLEY

CLEMENT, freeman Dorchester, Mass., 1640.

GILBERT, innholder, b. Eng., 1634, Dorchester, Mass., 1640, died April 17, 1714.

JOHN, brother of the preceding, resident Salem, Mass., 1660, removed Beverly, Mass.

TAPP

EDMUND, one of the seven pillars that founded the church, New Haven, Conn., 1639; removed Milford, Conn., died 1653.

TAPPAN, TAPEN, TOPPING, TAPPING

A local name from the Welsh; the top of the hanging rock; from *tap*, a hanging rock, and *pen*, top or head.

ABRAHAM, b. Eng., 1608, freeman Newbury, Mass., 1638, died Nov. 5, 1672.

BARTHOLOMEW, freeman Boston, Mass., 1671.

JAMES, resident Milford, Conn., 1662, where he died Aug. 6, 1712.

JOHN, feltmaker or hatter, married Boston, Mass., 1654, died Sept. 14, 1678.

RICHARD, freeman Boston, Mass., 1634.

THOMAS, at Wethersfield, Conn., removed Milford, Conn., 1639; died Branford, Conn., Nov., 1694.

TAPPER

JOHN, resident Boston, Mass., 1688.

TARBELL, TARBOLE, TARBALL

JOHN, freeman, Salem, Mass., 1694.

THOMAS, at Watertown, Mass., 1644, removed Grafton, Mass., 1663, thence Charlestown, Mass., where he married 1676 and died 1681.

TARBOX

JOHN, owner of iron works at Lynn, Mass., 1630, where he died May 26, 1674.

TARE

RICHARD, married Boston, Mass., 1656.

THOMAS, at Portsmouth, N. H., 1655.

TARLTON, TARLETON

HENRY, resident Boston, Mass., 1671.

RICHARD, came from London, Eng., to Newcastle, N. H., 1685, removed Portsmouth, N. H., 1693.

TARNE, TERNEY, TARNEY

MILES, leather-dresser; freeman, Boston, Mass., 1643.

TARR

FERDINANDO, at Braintree, Mass., 1655.

GEORGE, resident Lynn, Mass., before 1662.

JAMES, inhabitant Portsmouth, R. I., 1638.

JOHN, living at Dover, N. H., 1648.

RICHARD, at Marblehead, Mass., 1680, removed Gloucester, Mass., 1690.

TART

EDWARD, servant, name in the will of Nathaniel Tilden, of Scituate, Mass., 1643.

THOMAS, a resident of Scituate, Mass., 1640.

TASKER, TASKET

Name signifies a thrasher.

JOHN, settled Dover, N. H., 1680.

WILLIAM, b. Eng., about 1655, settled Dover, N. H., 1675.

TATENHAM

ELIAS, resident Boston, Mass., 1683.

TATMAN, TOTMAN

JOHN, settled Roxbury, Mass., 1632, freeman, 1638; will dated Sept. 30, 1670.

TAUNTON

MATTHEW, resident Boston, Mass., 1688.

TAY, TOY

HENRY, died at Ipswich, Mass., 1655.

JOHN, trader, died Boston, Mass., 1641.

NATHANIEL, brother of the preceding, married Billerica, Mass., 1677.

WILLIAM, distiller, b. Eng., 1611, granted land Billerica, 1659. Will probated April 12, 1683.

TAYLOR, TAYLOUR, TAILER

A name of trade, and modified to *Tayleure,* the orthography being changed by the bearers to hide what they thought the lowness of its origin.

ABRAHAM at Haverhill, Mass., made his will in 1673.

ABRAHAM, freeman Concord, Mass., 1690.

ANTHONY, feltmaker, b. Eng., 1608, at Hampton, N. H., 1644, removed to Dover, N. H., 1671, died Nov. 4, 1687.

DANIEL, at Saybrook, Conn., 1689.

Edward, resident Providence, R. I., 1655.

EDWARD, freeman, Lynn, Mass., 1648, removed Reading, Mass., 1648, died 1694.

EDWARD, clergyman, b. Sketchley near Hinckley, Leicestershire, Eng., 1642, arrived Boston, Mass., 1668, graduated from Harvard College 1671, and went in that year to Westfield, Mass., died June 29, 1729.

FRANCIS, surveyor, at Dedham, Mass., 1671.

GEORGE, inhabitant Scarborough, Maine, 1636, submitted to Mass. jurisdiction 1658.

GREGORY, freeman Watertown, Mass., 1634, removed Stamford, Conn., where he died Sept. 24, 1657.

HENRY, resident Portsmouth, N. H., 1640; died Boston, Mass., 1649.

HENRY, married Barnstable, Mass., 1650.

HENRY, surgeon; freeman Boston, Mass., 1665.

ISAAC, resident Boston, Mass., 1692.

ISAAC, at Concord, Mass., 1686, removed to Scituate, Mass.

JAMES, married Concord, Mass., 1641.

JAMES, resident Springfield, Mass., 1668.

JAMES, proprietor New Haven, Conn., 1685.

JAMES, inhabitant, Boston, Mass., 1674.

JASPAR, married Barnstable, Mass., 1668.

JOHN, from Haverhill, county of Suffolk, Eng., came to N. E. Winthrop's fleet, freeman, Lynn, Mass., 1630; removed Hartford, Conn., 1640, thence to Windsor, Conn.

JOHN, resident Weymouth, Mass., 1668.

JOHN, freeman, Cambridge, Mass., 1651.

JOHN, took the oath of allegiance, Hampton, N. H., 1678.

JOHN, resident, Charlestown, Mass., 1689.

JONATHAN, residing Springfield, Mass., 1649, died Suffield, Conn., 1683.

JOSEPH, swore allegiance Exeter, N. H., 1677.

JOSEPH, married Boston, Mass., 1686.

NATHANIEL, married Windsor, Conn., 1678.

RICHARD, tailor, brother of the preceding, joined church Boston, Mass., 1642. His will probated Aug. 2, 1673, names no children.

RICHARD, freeman, Charlestown, Mass., 1642, died July 10, 1659, left no male issue.

RICHARD, farmer known as Rock Richard from building his cottage against a rock, married Yarmouth, Mass., 1643, died 1674.

ROBERT, came to Scituate, Mass., freeman, Newport, R. I., 1655.

ROBERT, resident Boston, Mass., 1661.

SAMUEL, innkeeper, b. Eng., 1614, Ipswich, Mass., 1648, died June 29, 1695.

STEPHEN, brother, first John, born Eng., 1618, married Windsor, Conn., 1642; died Dec. 14, 1717.

STEPHEN, resident Boston, Mass., 1668.

THOMAS, settled Watertown, Mass., 1642, removed Reading, Mass., died 1690.

THOMAS, married Norwalk, Conn., 1668, removed Danbury, Conn.

WILLIAM, inhabitant Lynn, Mass., 1642.

WILLIAM, living at Wethersfield, Conn., 1647.

WILLIAM, brother of first James, settled Concord, Mass., 1640, died Dec. 6, 1696.

WILLIAM, merchant at Boston, Mass., 1667.

WILLIAM, brother of the second Isaac, resident Scituate, Mass., 1688.

TEAD, TEED, TIDD

JOHN, b. Eng., 1600, settled Charlestown, Mass., 1637, removed Woburn, Mass., 1640, died April 24, 1657.

JOSHUA, brother of the preceding, b. Eng., 1607; at Charlestown, Mass., 1637, died Sept. 15, 1678.

TELL, TEAL, TEEL

WILLIAM, freeman Malden, Mass., 1690.

TEMPLAR, TEMPLE, TEMPLER

From the Manor of Temple, in Wellesborough, Leicestershire, which name was given by the old Earl of Leicester, one of the Knights Templars, who usually gave the name of Temple to their lands.

ABRAHAM, settled Salem, Mass., 1637.

JOHN, freeman, Boston, Mass., 1671.

RICHARD, at Yarmouth, Mass., able to bear arms, 1643.

RICHARD, at Salem, Mass., 1644, removed Charlestown, Mass., 1646.

ROBERT, at Saco, Maine, before 1670, killed by the Indians, 1676.

THOMAS, English Knight and baronet, came to Boston, Mass., 1657, returned England, where he died March 27, 1674.

TENCH

EDWARD, at New Haven, Conn., 1643.

WILLIAM, a first comer, came to Plymouth, Mass., 1621, died before 1638.

TENNEY, TENNY

DANIEL, married Bradford, Mass., 1680.

JAMES, married Boston, Mass., 1654.

JOHN, elder brother of the preceding, at Rowley, Mass., 1673, removed Scarborough, Maine, before 1690, fled to Gloucester, Mass., on account of Indian hostilities.

MILES, resident Watertown, Mass., 1665.

SAMUEL, married Bradford, Mass., 1690.

THOMAS, b. Eng., about 1614, came from Rowley, Yorkshire, Eng., to Salem, Mass., 1638, settled Rowley, Mass., 1639; afterwards Bradford, Mass.

WILLIAM, brother of the preceding, at Rowley, Mass., 1643.

TERHAN, TURHAN

THOMAS, married Guilford, Conn., 1685.

TERRILL, TURRELL, TIRRELL

A local name signifying The Little Tower; of Anglo-Norman origin, founded at Norman Conquest by Sir Walter Tyrell.

JOHN, died New London, Conn., Feb. 27, 1712.

ROGER, inhabitant of Milford, Conn., 1639.

WILLIAM, married Boston, Mass., 1655, removed Weymouth, Mass.

WILLIAM, tailor at New London, Conn., 1662.

TERRY

JOHN, b. Eng., 1603, came to Dorchester, Mass., 1635, removed Windsor, Conn.

RICHARD, b. Eng., 1618, came from London, Eng., 1635, to N. E., removed Southold, L. I., 1662, and was accepted as freeman of Conn.

ROBERT, brother of the preceding, b. Eng., 1610, came to N. E., 1635.

SAMUEL, b. Barnet, Eng., about 1633, arrived N. E., 1650; at Springfield, Mass., 1654, removed Enfield, Mass., and died 1731.

STEPHEN, brother of John, came Dorchester, Mass., 1630, removed Hartford, Conn., 1637.

THOMAS, b. Eng., 1607, came to N. E. 1635, settled at Braintree, Mass., removed Southold, L. I., 1646, accepted as freeman of Conn., 1662.

TETHERLY

GABRIEL, was in Maine, 1680.

WILLIAM, came from Biddeford, Devonshire, Eng., and was at Boston, Mass., 1664, afterwards went to Maine.

TEW

A Welsh word, signifying a fat or corpulent person.

RICHARD, b. Maidford, Northamptonshire, Eng., came to N. E., 1640, located Portsmouth, R. I., freeman, Newport, R. I., 1654.

TEWKSBURY, TUXBURY

HENRY, b. Eng., about 1635, was married Boston, Mass., 1659, removed to Amesbury, Mass., 1669.

THOMAS, came from county of Gloucester, Eng., and was resident, Manchester by the Sea, Mass., 1680.

THACHER, THATCHER

ANTHONY, clergyman, b. Eng., 1587, came from Salisbury, Wiltshire, Eng., in 1635, to N. E.; taxpayer, Marblehead, Mass., 1637, removed before 1643 to Yarmouth, Mass., died Aug. 22, 1667.

SAMUEL, freeman, Cambridge, Mass., 1642.

THOMAS, clergyman, son Rev. Peter T., b. Salisbury, Wiltshire, Eng., 1620, came with his uncle Anthony, to N. E., arriving Boston, Mass., 1635, settled Ipswich, Mass., removed Boston, Mass., was pastor of Old South Church, 1670.

THARPE

WILLIAM, resident New Haven, Conn., 1647.

THAXTER

THOMAS, linen weaver, came from Hingham, Eng., to Hingham, Mass., 1638.

THAYER

NATHANIEL, resident Taunton, Mass., 1665.

RICHARD, b. Eng., 1601, settled Boston, Mass., 1641.

THOMAS, shoemaker, elder brother of the preceding, b. Thornbury, Eng., 1596, settled at Braintree, Mass., before 1639.

THEALE, THELE, THALE

NICHOLAS, at Watertown, Mass., 1638, removed Stamford, Conn., 1645, where he died Aug. 19, 1658.

THING

The first mention of the name in English history is in 1231, Sir Robert de Twenge, Lord of Kilton Castle, county of Cumberland, Eng.

JOHN, freeman, Boston, Mass., 1680.

JONATHAN, resident Ipswich, Mass., 1641; removed Hampton, N. H., thence Wells, Maine, submitted government of Mass., 1653.

THISTLE, THISSELL

JEFFREY, mariner, came from Abbotsbury, Dorsetshire, Eng., to Marblehead, Mass., 1668, died at sea, 1676.

THOM

JOHN, swore allegiance Exeter, N. H., 1677.

WILLIAM, resident Lynn, Mass., 1638, removed L. I., 1640.

THOMAS

From the Hebrew, signifying a twin.

DAVID, resident Marblehead, Mass., 1648-68, removed Middleboro, Mass., 1668.

EDWARD, agent of Joseph Thompson, a London merchant, at Boston, Mass., 1685.

EVAN, vintner, came from Wales to Boston, Mass., 1640, died Aug. 25, 1661.

FRANCIS, married Boston, Mass., 1665.

GEORGE, at Salem, Mass., 1668.

GEORGE, resident Boston, Mass., 1683.

HUGH, freeman Roxbury, Mass., 1651.

JAMES, resident Salem, Mass., 1646-49.

JOHN, inhabitant New Haven, Conn., 1649.

RICE, b. Eng., 1616, at Kittery, Maine, 1647, removed Boston, Mass., 1654.

ROWLAND, married Springfield, Mass., 1647, removed Hadley, Mass., 1669, and Westfield, Mass., 1670, died Feb. 21, 1698.

WILLIAM, husbandman, b. Eng., 1611, came from Great Comberton, Worcestershire, Eng., to Newbury, Mass., 1637, died March 29, 1677; no issue.

WILLIAM, b. 1573, of Welsh descent, came from Yarmouth, Eng., to Marblehead, Mass., 1637; freeman, 1642, died Aug., 1651.

WILLIAM, resident Newton, Mass., 1687.

THOMPSON, TOMSON, THOMSON, TOMPSON

The name signifies the son of Thomas.

ANTHONY, came New Haven, Conn., 1639, will probated 1648.

ARCHIBALD, at Marblehead, Mass., 1637, drowned in Nov., 1641.

DANIEL, b. 1638, resident Newbury, Mass., 1678.

DAVID, sent out by Gorges to Piscataqua, Maine, 1623, removed 1626 to isle in Boston Harbor, since called by his name; died 1628, leaving infant child, John.

EDMUND, sea captain, son of John T. of Holkham, county of Norfolk, Eng., came from Framingham, county of Suffolk, Eng., to Salem, Mass., 1637, returned England about 1647.

EDWARD, servant of William White, "Mayflower" passenger, died Dec. 4, 1620, before the ship reached Plymouth.

GEORGE, resident Lynn, Mass., 1659.

HENRY, freeman, Cambridge, Mass., 1670.

JAMES, b. Eng., 1593, came in Winthrop's fleet, settled Charlestown, Mass., original settler Woburn, Mass., 1640, died 1682.

JOHN, resident Watertown, Mass., 1634, died 1639.

JOHN, inhabitant, New Haven, Conn., before 1652.

JOHN, came from London, Eng., settled Stratford, Conn., 1640, will probated Aug., 1678.

JOHN, brother of Anthony, married New Haven, Conn., 1651.

JOHN, resident Plymouth, Mass., 1643.

JOHN, inhabitant Barnstable, Mass., 1652.

JOHN, at Wethersfield, Conn., before 1640.

JOHN, mariner, resident New Haven, Conn., 1671.

JOHN, early settler Reading, Mass.

JOHN, married Rehoboth, Mass., 1682.

MAURICE, merchant, engaged fishing trade, Gloucester, Mass., 1631.

ROBERT, resident Boston, Mass., 1639.

SAMUEL, married New Haven, Conn., 1695.

WILLIAM, clergyman, b. Eng., 1599, came

to N. E., 1637, at Kittery, or York, Maine, 1639; same year came to Boston, Mass., resigned from the ministry, died Dec. 10, 1666.

WILLIAM, brother of Anthony, resident New Haven, Conn., 1647.

WILLIAM, b. Eng., 1630, settled Dover, N. H., 1656; removed Kittery, Maine, where he died 1676.

WILLIAM, settled Sudbury, Mass., 1685.

WILLIAM, blacksmith, died Stonington, Conn., 1705.

THORNCOMB

ANDREW, bookseller, resident Boston, Mass., 1685.

THORNDIKE

JOHN, son Rev. George T., rector of Little Carleton, near Lowth, Lincolnshire, Eng., bapt. 1603, came to Boston, Mass., 1632, went to Ipswich, Mass., 1633, returned to England 1668, and died 1670, leaving a son, Paul, as the only male issue.

THORNDON

JOHN, one of the founders of Newport, R. I., 1644.

THORNE, THORN

A town in England; a tree or bush armed with spines or sharp shoots. "Will at the Thorn."

WILLIAM, laborer, Muddy river, Boston, Mass., freeman Lynn, Mass., 1638; removed L. I., 1642.

WILLIAM, from county of Dorset, Eng., married New London, Conn., 1676.

THORNELL

THOMAS, called Captain, died Boston, Mass., March 11, 1660.

THORNICOAST

THOMAS, freeman, Warwick, R. I., 1655.

THORNING

ANTHONY, at Boston, Mass., 1674, came from Barbadoes.

THORNTON

JOHN, freeman Newport, R. I., 1651, removed Providence, R. I., 1670.

PETER, b. Eng., 1615, came to Boston, Mass., 1635.

ROBERT, carpenter, b. Eng., 1624, came from London, Eng., 1635, to Taunton, Mass., removed Boston, Mass., 1657.

THOMAS, tanner, freeman, Dorchester, Mass., 1634, removed Windsor, Conn., 1636.

THOMAS, resident Stratford, Conn., 1651.

THOMAS, clergyman, came Yarmouth, Mass., 1662, removed Boston, Mass., died Feb. 13, 1700.

THORPE

Name signifies a village, the Dutch word *Dorp.*

HENRY, freeman, Watertown, Mass., 1646, died May 21, 1672.

JAMES, resident Dedham, Mass., 1652.

JOHN, carpenter at Duxbury, Mass., 1633.

JOHN, clergyman, undertook to preach Scarborough, Maine, and was silenced by the General Court, 1661.

NATHANIEL, freeman, New Haven, Conn., 1669.

ROBERT, York, Maine, 1660.

SAMUEL, freeman, New Haven, Conn., 1670.

THOMAS, married Ipswich, Mass., 1656.

WILLIAM, b. Eng., 1605, one of the founders of New Haven, Conn., 1638.

THRALL

WILLIAM, b. Eng., 1606, served Pequot War, one first settlers of Windsor, 1636, died Aug. 3, 1678.

THRASHER, THRESHER

One who thrashes grain.

ARTHUR, married Newbury, Mass., 1684.

CHRISTOPHER, resident Taunton, Mass., 1643.

FRANCIS, clothier, resident Milford, Conn., 1686.

THREENEEDLES

BARTHOLOMEW, married Boston, Mass., 1659, will probated April 7, 1702.

THROCKMORTON, THROGMORTON

A corruption of *At Rock-moor-town,* "a town on a rock in a moor," in the vale of Evesham, Fladbury, Warwickshire, England, whence the name was derived.

JOHN, came with Roger Williams, 1630, to N. E., freemen same year.

JOHN, senior, resident Providence, R. I., 1666, removed Monmouth, N. J., where he died before 1687. He and his wife, were excommunicated from the church at Salem, Mass., by Hugh Peters, the same time as Roger Williams.

JOHN, junior, took oath of allegiance, Providence, R. I., 1668.

THROOP

WILLIAM, was representative, from Bristol, R. I., 1691.

THROW

DAVID, took oath of allegiance, Springfield, Mass., 1678.

THURBER

The name is a contraction of Thoreborn of Icelandic origin and was established in England by the Norseman. William Thoreben resided in Oxfordshire, England in 13th century.

JAMES, b. Eng., 1660, at Rehoboth, Mass., 1690.

JOHN, came from Stanton, Lincolnshire, Eng., to Swanzey, Mass., 1669, removed to Rehoboth, Mass., now a part of Barrington, R. I., 1671.

THOMAS, resident Swanzey, Mass., 1682.

THURLO, THURLOUGH, THURLOW

RICHARD, among first settlers Rowley, Mass., 1643, removed Newbury, Mass., 1651, died Nov. 10, 1685.

THURSTON, THIRSTON

The name derived from the hill or town where the Saxon god *Thor* was worshipped by the Anglo-Saxons.

CHARLES, at Plymouth, Mass., 1643.

DANIEL, granted land Newbury, Mass., 1638.

DANIEL, nephew of the preceding, married Newbury, Mass., 1655.

DANIEL, freeman, Medfield, Mass., 1678.

DANIEL, married Rehoboth, Mass., 1681.

EDWARD, Quaker, came to N. E., 1634. Name first appears in records 1647, at Newport, R. I.

JOHN, granted land Salem, Mass., 1638.

JOHN, carpenter, bapt. Eng., 1601, came from Wrentham, county of Suffolk, Eng., to Dedham, Mass., 1637.

JOHN, freeman Newport, R. I., 1655.

RICHARD, mariner at Salem, Mass., 1637, removed Boston, Mass.

THOMAS, b. Eng., 1649, swore allegiance Hampton, N. H., 1678.

THWAITS, THWAITE, THWAYTES

From the Anglo-Saxon *thweotan,* to cut, a piece of ground cleared of wood. In some places in England the word signifies a rivulet; marshy ground; also a meadow.

ALEXANDER, b. Eng., 1615, came Concord, Mass., 1635.

THWING

BENJAMIN, b. Eng., 1619, came as an apprentice to Ralph Hudson to Boston, Mass., 1635, was one of the proprietors Concord, Mass.

WILLIAM, resident Boston, Mass., 1686.

TIBBALS

THOMAS, b. Eng., 1615, came to N. E., 1635, served Pequot War, one first settlers Milford, Conn., 1639, will probated June 1, 1703.

TIBBETS, TYBBOT, TEBBITS

The name has the same signification as Theobald of which it is a curruption. The latter signifies God's power, but in Saxon means powerful or bold over the people. In the Saxon *Psalter, theod* is the same as *gentes,* and the English nation is often called Engla-Theod. Theobald is in the French *Theobaud,* pronounced *Tibbo,* whence Tibbauds or Tibbitts.

HENRY, shoemaker, b. Eng., 1596, came to N. E., 1635, settled Dover, in what is now Rollinsford, N. H., 1643.

HENRY, at Wickford or Westerly, R. I., 1670.

WALTER, freeman, Gloucester, Mass., 1642.

TICKENOR, TICKNOR

MARTIN, took oath of fidelity, New Haven, Conn., 1644.

WILLIAM, at Scituate, Mass., 1646, married Boston, Mass., 1656.

TIFF, TIFT, TEFFE

WILLIAM, freeman, Boston, Mass., 1638.

TIFFANY

The name is a corruption of Theophania, a woman's first name, meaning light-hearted, gay and spirited; other authorities say it is a name of a light silk, an equivalent for taffeta remarkable for its glossy effect and used by painters to trace the outlines of a picture through. A maker or vender of silk.

HUMPHREY, came from Yorkshire, Eng., to N. E., 1660, inhabitant Rehoboth, Mass., 1663, later resident Swansea, Mass., killed by stroke of lightning, July 15, 1685.

TIFT, TEFFT

JOHN, freeman Portsmouth, R. I., 1655, removed Kingstown, R. I., 1674.

SAMUEL, at Wickford, R. I., 1674.

TILDEN, TILTEN

JOHN, at Scituate, Mass., 1643.

NATHANIEL, came from Tenterden, county of Kent, Eng., to Scituate, Mass., 1635.

THOMAS, one of the first comers Plymouth, Mass., 1623, returned to England soon after.

TILESTONE, TILLSTON

THOMAS, b. Eng., 1611, granted land Dorchester, Mass., 1634, died Sept. 11, 1718.

TILL, TYLLS

A local name, a river of England.

JAMES, Scituate, Mass., 1644.

PETER, fisherman and carpenter, living at Boston, Mass.

TILLEY

A town in France.

EDWARD, "Mayflower" passenger, died the first winter at Plymouth, Mass.

HUGH, at Salem, Mass., 1629, as servant to Sir Richard Saltonstall; removed Yarmouth, Mass., 1638, died Jan. 28, 1648.

John, brother of Edward, "Mayflower" passenger, came from Exeter, England, died first winter Plymouth, Mass.; the brothers left no male issue.

Thomas, at Plymouth, Mass., 1643.

William, b. Eng., 1607, settled Boston, Mass., 1635, removed Barnstable, Mass., 1643.

TILLINGHAST

From the German *theilen, Dutch* deelen, to separate, divide, pay over, a dealing house; a place where auctions are held.

Pardon, clergyman, son of Pardon, b. Seven Cliffs, now Eastbourne near Beachy Head, county of Sussex, Eng., 1622, came Providence, R. I., settled as a Baptist minister, 1643, died Jan. 29, 1718.

TILLMAN

One who works a farm.

John, swore allegiance in Maine, 1665.

TILLOTSON

John, b. Yorkshire, Eng., arrived Boston, Mass., 1635, one first settlers Rowley, Mass., removed Newbury, Mass.

TILSON

Edward or Edmund, at Plymouth, Mass., 1643, died Scituate, Mass., 1660.

Ephraim, brother of the preceding, married Plymouth, Mass., 1666.

John, at Rowley, Mass., 1643.

TILTON

Name derived from *Tilt,* a Saxon word signifying a tent, also a place name from a village in England, probably an ancient place of tilling or tents. The family existed prior to the Conquest.

John, resident, Lynn, Mass., before 1640.

William, brother of the preceding, settled Lynn, Mass., 1640.

TIMBERLAKE

Henry, resident Newport, R. I., 1644.

TIMMINS

John, at Scarborough, Maine, 1663.

TINGLEY, TINGLE

Palmer, at Ipswich, Mass., 1639.

Samuel, died Malden, Mass., 1666.

TINKER

John, at Windsor, Conn., 1643, removed Boston, Mass., freeman 1654, one of principal settlers Lancaster, Mass., 1655, removed New London, Conn., 1660.

Thomas, "Mayflower" passenger, died the first winter at Plymouth, Mass.

TINKHAM

Ephraim, b. Eng., about 1606, came from Ashburnham near Plymouth, England, was in the service of John Winthrop in N. E., 1634, received grant of land Duxbury, Mass., 1642, known as Sergeant.

TINNEY

John, at Scarborough, Maine, 1658.

Thomas, came from Rowley, Yorkshire, Eng., to Salem, Mass., 1638, settled Rowley, Mass.

TIPPETT

Henry, resident Wickford, R. I., 1670.

TIPPING, TIPPEN

Bartholomew, inhabitant Exeter, N. H., 1675.

TISDALE

John, b. Eng., 1615-20, settled Duxbury, Mass., 1637, removed Taunton, Mass., 1651.

TITCOMB, TITCOME

William, came from parish of Tidcombe, Wiltshire, Eng., to Newbury, Mass., 1634, where he was one of the original proprietors. He died Sept. 24, 1676.

TITE

Henry, married Boston, Mass., 1655.

TITERTON, TITTERTON, TYTTERTON

Daniel, at Boston, Mass., 1643, removed Stratford, Conn., before 1647; will probated July 6, 1661.

TITUS

Jonathan, resident Rehoboth, Mass., 1680.

Robert, b. St. Catherine's parish, near Stanstead Abbotts, Hertfordshire, Eng., 1600, came from London, Eng., to Boston, Mass., 1635, freeman, Weymouth, Mass., 1643, removed Rehoboth, Mass., 1644.

TOBEY, TOBY, TOBIE

The Welsh for Thomas.

Francis, inhabitant, Mass., 1635.

James, yeoman settled Kittery, Maine, 1669, killed by Indians 1705.

Stephen, married, Portsmouth, N. H., 1688.

Thomas, b. Wales about 1620, settled Sandwich, Mass., 1640.

TODD

Tod, a Scotchword for fox.

Christopher, b. Eng., 1617, came from Pontefract, West Riding, Yorkshire, Eng., to New Haven, Conn., an original settler, 1639, signer of the compact.

John, settled Charlestown, Mass., 1637, removed Rowley, Mass., 1648.

TOLLES

Henry, at Wethersfield, Conn., 1669, removed Saybrook, Conn.

TOLMAN

A collector of toll. In Dutch, *Taalman,* is an interpreter from *Taal,* language, tongue. Constantine Tolmaen, in Cornwall is an ancient place of Druid worship.

Tolmaen is usually applied to a stone that is perforated, from *tol,* a hole, and *maen,* a stone; *twll mwn,* Welsh, a mine, shaft, or pit. The first records of the name in England, when in 825 Sir Thomas Tolman was almoner to Egbert I.

THOMAS, son of Thomas of Salcomb Regis, Devonshire, Eng., b. 1608, settled Dorchester, Mass., 1630, inventory of estate made July, 23, 1690.

TOMLINSON, THOMLINS, THOMLINSON

From Thom or Thomas, and *ing* or *ling,* a child or descendant—the son of Thomas.

BENJAMIN, b. Eng., 1617, settled Lynn, Mass., 1635.

EDWARD, brother of the preceding, came in Winthrop's fleet, freeman, Lynn, Mass., 1631.

HENRY, son of George T., bapt. Derby, Eng., 1606, settled Milford, Conn., 1652.
JOHN, married Boston, Mass., 1660.

ROBERT, resident Milford, Conn., 1648.

THOMAS, freeman, New Haven, Conn., 1644, removed Milford, Conn., 1652, thence to Stratford, Conn.

TIMOTHY, freeman Lynn, Mass., 1633.

TOMPKINS

JOHN, freeman, Salem, Mass., 1642.

JOHN, resident Concord, Mass., 1642.

MICAH or MICHAEL, at Wethersfield, Conn., 1637, removed Milford, Conn., 1639, and to New Jersey, 1666.

NATHANIEL, merchant, settled Fairfield, Conn., 1649, removed East Chester, Westchester county, N. Y., thence to Newport, R. I.

RALPH, freeman, Dorchester, Mass., 1638, removed Salem, Mass., 1647, died 1666.

TONGUE

GEORGE, inhabitant New London, Conn., 1652.

STEPHEN, at Salisbury, Mass., 1687.

TONY

JOHN, one early settlers Reading, Mass., died 1691.

TOOGOOD, TOWGOOD, TWOGOOD

JOHN, servant, Marshfield, Mass., before 1640, removed Springfield, Mass..

TOOKEY, TUKEY

JOB, at Beverly, Mass., 1692, charged with witchcraft.

JOHN, will probated, Charlestown, Mass., March 2, 1668.

TOOLLY, TOLLY, TOOLEY

CHRISTOPHER, resident Killingworth, Conn., 1684.

EDMUND, inhabitant New Haven, Conn., 1644, died April 19, 1685.

THOMAS, freeman, Newport, R. I., 1655.

TOOTHACKER, TOOTHACRE, TOOTHAKER

ROGER, b. Eng., 1612, came to N. E., 1635, died before 1638.

TOPLIFFE

CLEMENT, b. Eng., 1603, freeman, Dorchester, Mass., 1640, died Dec. 24, 1672.

TORREY, TORIE

From the Gaelic *Torr,* a conical hill or mountain, a mound, a grave, tower; piled up, formed into heaps; to heap up, to bury.

JAMES, lieutenant, b. Eng., 1613, married Scituate, Mass., 1640, freeman, 1655.

JOSEPH, lieutenant at Rehoboth, Mass., 1643, removed Newport, R. I., 1654.

PHILIP, brother of James, came from Combe St. Nicholas, Somersetshire, Eng., freeman Roxbury, Mass., 1644.

WILLIAM, captain, son of Philip T., brother of James, b. Eng., 1608, settled Weymouth, Mass., 1540. Will probated July, 1691.

TOTENHAM

HENRY, resident Woburn, Mass., 1646.

TOTMAN

THOMAS, settled Plymouth, Mass., removed Scituate, Mass., 1660.

TOUNG, TONG

GEORGE, innkeeper, New London, Conn., 1656-72.

JAMES, master-mariner, married Boston, Mass., 1654, died the next year.

TOURTELLOT, TOURTELLOTTE

The name is of French origin.

ABRAHAM, Huguenot merchant, b. Bordeaux, France, at Boston, Mass., 1687, resided Roxbury, Mass., removed Newport, R. I., 1697.

GABRIEL, brother of the preceding, died at sea; his descendants removed to Oxford, Mass.

TOUSEY, TOUCEY, TOUSLEY

A local name from the town of Toucey, in the province of Campagne, France.

RICHARD, came from Towsland, Eng., to Wethersfield, Conn., removed Saybrook, Conn., before 1666, died Feb., 1674.

TOUTE

RICHARD, lighterman at Scituate, Mass., 1643, resident Boston, Mass., 1663.

TOUTON

JOHN, a Huguenot, physician of Rochelle, France, resided Rehoboth, Mass., 1675.

TOWER, TOWERS

The name is derived from *tor,* Gaelic and Saxon, French *tour,* and Welsh, *twr,* a heap or pile, applied to conical hills, and to round buildings erected for strength or security.

JOHN, came from Hingham, county of Norfolk, Eng., to Hingham, Mass., freeman 1639, removed Lancaster, Mass., 1654.

WILLIAM, butcher, Boston, Mass., 1668.

TOWLE, TOWEL, TOLL, TOWELL

HENRY, at Wethersfield, Conn., removed Saybrook, Conn., about 1668.

JOHN, resident Sudbury, Mass., 1641.

JOSHUA, married, Hampton, N. H., 1686.

PHILIP, seaman, of Irish ancestry, b. 1616, settled Hampton, N. H., 1657.

ROGER, freeman, Boston, Mass., 1644.

WILLIAM, resident Malden, Mass., 1689.

TOWNE

JACOB, resident Salem, Mass., 1637.

THOMAS, b. 1631, at Lynn, Mass., married Reading, Mass., 1662.

WILLIAM, son of Richard T. of Braceby, Lincolnshire, Eng., came to N. E., 1637, granted land Salem, Mass., 1640, removed Topsfield, Mass., 1651.

WILLIAM, tavern keeper, b. Eng., 1605, freeman Cambridge, Mass., 1637, died April 30, 1685.

TOWNSEND

A local name, one who lived at the end of the town. English ancestry traced to Sir Lodovic de Townshende, a Norman nobleman. Roger Townsend, an ancestor in 1390.

GEORGE, living Reading, Mass.

HENRY, Quaker, came from Norwich, county of Norfolk, Eng., freeman Warwick, R. I., 1655.

JOHN, brother of preceding, freeman Warwick, R. I., 1655, died 1669.

JOHN, brother of George, freeman Reading, Mass., 1678.

JOHN, married Lynn, Mass., 1669.

MARTIN, weaver, b. 1650, married Watertown, Mass., 1668.

RICHARD, brother of Henry and John, freeman Warwick, R. I., 1655.

ROBERT, at Portsmouth, N. H., 1665.

SAMUEL, living Rumney Marsh, Chelsea, Mass., before 1666.

THOMAS, bapt. Eng., 1594, settled Lynn, Mass., 1637, died Dec. 22, 1677.

THOMAS, brother of Samuel, freeman Boston, Mass., 1683.

WILLIAM, admitted church Boston, Mass., 1634, freeman 1636, died before Dec., 1689.

TOWSLY

MICHAEL, married Salisbury, Mass., 1678, removed Suffield, Conn., 1679.

TOWSON

NICHOLAS, on tax list, New London, Conn., 1667.

TOZER, TOSIER, TOZIER

LEONARD, resident Salem, Mass., 1668.

RICHARD, at Boston, Mass., removed Dover, N. H. Mortally wounded by Indian assault on Salmon Falls, N. H., Oct. 16, 1675, died soon afterwards, Kittery, Maine.

TRACY

The surname is taken from the castle and barony of *Tracie* near *vire arrondissement* of Caen, France. There also is a village of the name in the Department of Oise, France. The word may signify a rampant, a terrace. Sire de Tracye was an officer in William the Conqueror's army. Some genealogists claim the family is descended from Ecgbert, a Saxon King, through Alfred the Great, to Sir William De Tracy.

STEPHEN, came to Plymouth, Mass., 1623, removed Duxbury, Mass., 1645.

THOMAS, ship carpenter, known as Lieutenant, son or nephew of Peter T. of the Manor of Stanway, Gloucestershire, Eng., of the 13th generation from Sire de Tracye, b. Tewksbury, Gloucestershire, Eng., 1610, settled Watertown, Mass., 1636, removed Salem, Mass., 1637, hence to Wethersfield, Conn. and went to Saybrook, Conn., 1649, and to Norwich, Conn., 1660.

WILLIAM, at Ipswich, Mass., 1634, removed Newbury, Mass.

TRAFFORD, TRAFTON

Seated at Trafford, Lancashire, Eng., prior to the Norman Conquest, Randolphus de Trafford, 1030.

THOMAS, swore allegiance York Maine, 1681.

TRAIN

From the Gaelic *Treun,* brave, valiant, bold.

JOHN, b. Eng., 1610, came Watertown, Mass., 1635.

THOMAS, mariner, b. Eng., 1634, settled Martha's Vineyard, Mass., 1632-42, died Oct. 15, 1719.

TRARICE, TRERICE

NICHOLAS, sea captain, freeman Charlestown, Mass., 1636.

TRASK

HENRY, resident Salem, Mass., 1634, died 1689.

WILLIAM, known as Captain, b. Eng., 1587-88, one first settlers Salem, Mass., 1626, died 1664-65.

TRAUL, THRALL, TRALL

WILLIAM, settled Wethersfield, Conn., 1636, served in Pequot War.

TRAVERS, TRAVIS

The name is derived from Trevieres in Normandy. Ranulp de Clinchamp in 1138 took the name of Travers. The name appears in England in the Doomesday Book.

DANIEL, carpenter, resident Boston, Mass., 1652.

HENRY or HENRIE came from London, Eng., to Ipswich, Mass., 1634, removed Newbury, Mass., 1635, returned to England, 1648, leaving in N. E., his wife, son and daughter; the son James became resident Gloucester, Mass., 1667.

RICHARD, married Boston, Mass., 1657.

ROBERT, ferryman, Boston, Mass., 1675.

SAMUEL, member of Mather's Church, Boston, Mass., 1670.

TREADWAY, TREDWAY, TREADAWAY

JOSIAH, married Sudbury, Mass., before 1664.

NATHANIEL, weaver, brother of the preceding, at Sudbury, Mass., before 1640, died July 20, 1669.

TREADWELL

EDWARD, Ipswich, Mass., 1638, removed Branford, Conn., 1646, settled Southold, L. I., 1659.

JOHN, at Ipswich, Mass., 1638.

THOMAS, b. Eng., 1605, settled Dorchester, Mass., 1635, removed Ipswich, Mass., 1638.

TREAT

An ancient English family of Somersetshire, Eng., traced to John Treat or Trott of Stapleton, near Taunton, Somersetshire, Eng.

RICHARD, son of Robert T., fifth generation from John T., bapt. Pitminster, Eng., 1584, settled Watertown, Mass., 1635; pioneer settler Wethersfield, Conn., 1637, on the list of freeman of that town, 1669.

TREBY, TREBIE, TRIBBY

JOHN, at Marblehead, Mass., 1668-74.

PETER, at New London, Conn., 1667.

TREE

RICHARD, married Lynn, Mass., 1669.

TREFETHEN

HENRY, Cornish or Welsh descent, served on grand jury, New Hampshire, 1687.

TREFRY, TREFREY, TURFREY, TURFEE

GEORGE, at York, Maine, 1692.

JOHN, resident Boston, Mass., 1689.

TRELAWNEY

From the Cornish British; the open town near the water; from *Tre,* a town, *lawn* open, and *ey,* water.

JOHN, son of Robert T. of Cornwall, Eng., at Kittery, Maine, 1645.

TRESCOTT

THOMAS, mariner, died Dorchester, Mass., 1654.

WILLIAM, brother of the preceding, b. Eng., 1614, freeman Dorchester, Mass., 1643, died Sept. 11, 1699.

TRESLER, TRUSLER

THOMAS, clerk of the market, freeman, Salem, Mass., 1642, died March 5, 1654.

TRESWELL

HENRY, resident of Salisbury, Mass., 1686.

TREVETT, TREVY, TRIVITT

HENRY, at Marblehead, Mass., 1646-74.

TREVORE, TREVOUR

From Cornish British, *Trevear,* the great town.

WILLIAM, "Mayflower" passenger, a hired mariner for the service of the London company, returned to Eng., 1621, but was in N. E. in April, 1650.

TREWORGYE, TRUEWORGIE, TREWORTHY

JAMES, merchant, Welsh or Cornish, descent, son of James T., b. Kingsweare, Eng., at Kittery, Maine, 1636.

JOHN, brother of the preceding, married Newbury, Mass.

NICHOLAS, brother of the preceding, resident of N. E. before 1649.

SAMUEL, died Boston, Mass., 1698.

TRIANS

ANANSIAS, married Saybrook, Conn., 1667.

JOHN, resident Saybrook, Conn., 1667.

TRICK

ELIAS, took oath of allegiance, Pemaquid, Maine, 1674.

TRICKEY, TRICKETT

THOMAS, at Dover, N. H., 1648.

TRILL

THOMAS, resident Hartford, Conn., 1664.

TRIMMINGS

OLIVER, inhabitant, Exeter, N. H., 1644.

TRINER

THOMAS, at Marblehead, Mass., 1674.

TRIPP

There is an amusing anecdote in regard to derivation of this name. Lord Howard's fifth son in explaining to Henry V. how they took the town and castle answered *I tripp'd up the walls.* Saith his majesty "*Tripp* shall be thy name and no longer Howard," and honored him with a scaling-ladder for his coat of arms.

JOHN, settled Portsmouth, R. I., 1638.

TRISTRAM, TRUSTRUM

RALPH, resident Saco, Maine, 1647.

TROOP

WILLIAM, married Barnstable, Mass., 1666.

TROTMAN

JOHN, resident Boston, Mass., 1643, returned England, 1644.

TROTT

BERNARD, merchant Boston, Mass., 1665-75.

JOHN, resident Nantucket, Mass., 1679.

RICHARD, at Wethersfield, Conn., 1642.

SIMON, freeman Wells, Maine, 1653.

THOMAS, freeman Dorchester, Mass., 1644.

TROTTER

From the French word *Trotteur,* a person always on the trot; a rambler.

WILLIAM, married Newbury, Mass., 1652.

TROUT

WILLIAM, took oath of fidelity Pemaquid, Maine, 1674.

TROW

HENRY, freeman Salisbury, Mass., 1676.

TROWBRIDGE

A town in England. The name signifies "through the bridge" perhaps given for some feat of daring or bodily courage. Line traced to Thomas T., 1550.

THOMAS, son of John, grandson of Thomas T., b. Taunton, Somersetshire, Eng., 1610, settled Dorchester, Mass., 1636, removed New Haven, Conn., 1639, returned to Eng., 1641.

TRUANT, TROUANT

MAURICE, at Duxbury, Mass., 1643, removed Marshfield, Mass., died April 21, 1685.

TRUE

From the river *Trieu* in Bretange, France. *Tre* signifies a town.

HENRY, came from Huntsford, Yorkshire, Eng., to Salem, Mass., 1630, removed Salisbury, Mass., 1657.

TRUESDALE, TRUSDELL

RICHARD, butcher, admitted church Boston, Mass., 1634, died 1671; no issue.

SAMUEL, nephew of the preceding, freeman, Cambridge, Mass., 1685.

TRULL

JOHN, b. Eng., 1634, married Billerica, Mass., 1657, died June 15, 1704.

SAMUEL, brother of the preceding, on tax list Billerica, Mass., 1679.

TRUMAN, TREMAN

The surname is of Norman origin. The first known English ancestor Preys Tremayne.

JOHN, b. Nottinghamshire, Eng., first record N. E., New London, Conn., 1666.

TRUMBULL, TRUMBALL, TRUMBELL

DANIEL, at Lynn, Mass., 1647.

JOHN, captain of trading vessel, b. Eng., 1607, came from Newcastle-on-Tyne, Eng., to Cambridge, Mass., 1636.

JOHN, carpenter and school teacher, freeman Roxbury, Mass., 1639, removed Rowley, Mass., 1640.

Ralph, at Marshfield, Mass., 1643.

TRY, TRAY

MICHAEL, freeman Windsor, Conn., 1640, removed Fairfield, Conn. No male issue.

TUBBS

SAMUEL, New London, Conn., 1663.

WILLIAM, married Plymouth, Mass., 1637, one of the proprietors of Bridgewater, Mass.

TUCK, TEWK

ROBERT, innkeeper and tailor, came from Gorleston, county of Suffolk, Eng., to Watertown, Mass., 1636, removed Hampton, N. H., 1638, died Oct. 4, 1664.

THOMAS, b. Eng., 1612, at Salem, Mass., 1637.

THOMAS, resident Charlestown, Mass., 1671.

WILLIAM, proprietor Milford, Conn., before 1675.

TUCKER

HENRY, resident Sandwich, Mass., 1653.

JAMES, inhabitant of Portsmouth or Dover, N. H., 1689.

JOHN, proprietor Watertown, Mass., 1636, removed Hingham, Mass., 1637.

JOHN, resident Boston, Mass., 1655.

JOHN, freeman, Boston, Mass., 1676.

JOHN, married Newbury, Mass., 1670.

MAURICE or MORRIS, cooper, householder Salisbury, Mass., 1659, removed Tiverton, R. I., 1699.

NICHOLAS, died Marblehead, Mass., 1664

RICHARD, b. Eng., 1612, came Casco, Maine, agent Sir Ferdinando Gorges, 1634, removed Portsmouth, N. H., 1665.

ROBERT, son of George of the fourth generation, Willielmus Tucker of Thornley, Devonshire, Eng., b. Kent, Eng., 1604, came Weymouth, Mass., 1635, removed Gloucester, Mass., resident Milton, Mass., 1662.

WILLIAM, died York, Maine, May, 1666.

TUCKERMAN

JOHN, resident Boston, Mass., 1652.

OTHO, inhabitant, Portsmouth, N. H., 1664.

TUCKEY

GEORGE, at Windsor, Conn., 1645.

JOHN, householder Charlestown, Mass., 1658.

TUDOR

The Welsh for *Theodore;* or in old English, pious, as *Tudor Belin,* the pious king.

JOHN, living at Boston, Mass., 1673.

OWEN, inhabitant Windsor, Conn., 1645, died Oct. 30, 1690.

SAMUEL, brother of the preceding, married Windsor, Conn., 1685, died July 6, 1727.

TUFTS

JAMES, came from Hingham, Eng., to Hingham, Mass., 1638.

PETER, b. Eng., 1616-17, came Malden side, Charlestown, Mass., 1650, representative Medford, Mass., 1689, died May 13, 1700.

TULLER

JOHN, married Simsbury, Conn., 1684.

TULLY

JOHN, almanac maker, bapt. Horley, county of Surrey, Eng., 1638, came to N. E. with his mother, 1644, freeman Saybrook, Conn., 1671, died Oct. 5, 1701.

TUPPER

A corruption of part of the motto of the family "Tout perdie."

THOMAS, teacher and preacher, grandson of Robert T. who came from Hesse Cassel, Upper Saxony, Germany, to England; b. Eng., 1578, settled Lynn, Mass., removed Sandwich, Mass., 1637; died March 28, 1676.

TURBAT, TURBUTT

PETER, took oath of allegiance, Wells, Maine, 1653.

TURBEFIELD

HENRY, resident Weymouth, Mass., 1673.

TURELL

DANIEL, blacksmith, came from Instow, Devonshire, Eng., to Boston, Mass., before 1646, died July, 1693.

SAMUEL, resident Boston, Mass., 1657.

WILLIAM, Boston, Mass., 1655.

TURFY, TURFEE

GEORGE, resident Saco, Maine, 1685. Will probated Nov. 17, 1714.

TURNER

The name is of the occupation class. Aylbricht le Turnur, a native of London, Eng., name appears on the Hundred Rolls, 1273.

CHARLES, Salem, Mass., 1643.

DANIEL, living Duxbury, Mass., 1643, removed Hartford or New Haven, Conn.

EDWARD, Milford, Conn., 1651, removed Middletown, Conn., 1665, died April 4, 1717.

ELISHA, married Hingham, Mass., 1687.

EPHRAIM, resident Hartford, Conn., 1691.

HUMPHREY, tanner, b. Eng., about 1593, came from county of Essex, Eng., to Plymouth, Mass., 1628, removed Scituate, Mass., 1633, died 1673.

JAMES, inhabitant, New Haven, Conn., 1649.

JEFFREY, freeman, Dorchester, Mass., 1643, died 1654.

JOHN, "Mayflower" passenger, died in the spring of 1621.

JOHN, merchant, joined church Salem, Mass., 1637, died Barbadoes, 1668.

JOHN, b. Eng., 1620, settled Roxbury, Mass., freeman 1649, one of thirteen original settlers Medfield, Mass.

LAWRENCE, Exeter, N. H., 1650, freeman Newport, R. I., 1657, removed Greenwich, Conn.

MICHAEL, Lynn, Mass., 1637; removed Sandwich, Mass., 1643.

NATHANIEL, came Winthrop's fleet to N. E., freeman Lynn, Mass., 1630, removed New Haven, Conn., 1638, a passenger on the ill-fated ship that sailed for England.

RALPH, resident Scarborough, or Falmouth, Maine, 1663.

RICHARD, resident Boston, Mass., 1638.

ROBERT, innholder, at Boston, Mass., as early as 1633; will probated Aug. 24, 1664.

ROBERT, shoemaker, b. Eng., 1611, came Boston, Mass., 1635.

THOMAS, b. Eng., 1593; came to N. E., 1635, resident Exeter, N. H., 1652.

THOMAS, resident Marblehead, Mass., 1668.

WILLIAM, freeman Dorchester, Mass., 1643, removed Boston, one of the founders of the first Baptist church 1665, captain King Philip's War. Turner Falls, where he defeated the Indians, named for him; the following day he was killed by the Indians.

TURNEY

BENJAMIN, b. Bedfordshire, Eng., settled Concord, Mass., freeman, 1641.

JOSEPH, resident Stamford, Conn., 1687-1701.

TURPIN

THOMAS, fisherman, Isle of Shoals, N. H., removed Portsmouth, N. H., 1645.

WILLIAM, first school-master, Providence, R. I., 1684.

TURVILL

THOMAS, tanner, Newbury, Mass., 1668, died May 22, 1677. No issue.

TUTTLE, TUTTEL, TUTHILL

From the ancient tothills of England, meaning "Hill of God." Locally, a town in Caernarvon, Wales, near the coast. From word Tuthill, signifying a conical hill, the name being given in early times to a number of locations in England. The permanent seat of the family was in Devonshire, Eng. William Totyl was Lord Mayor of Exeter, 1552.

EDWARD, freeman Boston, Mass., 1690.

ELISHA, freeman, Boston, Mass., 1690.

HENRY, came Hingham, Mass., 1637.

JOHN, merchant, b. Eng., 1596, came to Ipswich, Mass., from St. Albans parish, Hertfordshire, Eng., 1635, returned England, 1652, died Carrickfergus, Ireland, Dec. 30, 1656.

JOHN, came from Saxlingham, county of Norfolk, Eng., to Boston, Mass., 1635, removed New Haven, Conn., 1639, thence Southold, L. I., 1641.

JOHN, b. Eng., 1618, came N. E., 1635, settled Dover, N. H., 1640, died 1662.

JOHN, freeman, Boston, Mass., 1690.

JONATHAN, freeman, Boston, Mass., 1690.

RICHARD, husbandman, brother first John, b. Eng., 1593, came to Boston, Mass., 1635.

WILLIAM, husbandman, brother of the preceding, b. Eng., 1609, proprietor Charlestown, Mass., 1636, removed New Haven, Conn., 1639, estate administered June, 1673.

TWELVES, TUELLS, TWELLS

ROBERT, b. Eng., 1614, resident Braintree, Mass., 1645, died March 2, 1691.

TWINING

A Danish word *Twinge,* to force, master, subdue; or a name given for dexterity in archery. *At Wing,* may be abbreviated to Twing.

WILLIAM, freeman, Yarmouth, Mass., 1643, removed Eastham, Mass., 1644, died April 15, 1659.

TWISDEN, TWISDALL, TWISDALE

JOHN, came from County of Kent, Eng., to Scituate, Mass., 1639, resident York, Maine, 1648.

TWISS

DANIEL, son of Dr. William T. of England in N. E., 1656-60.

NATHAN, brother of the preceding, resident N. E., 1650-60.

PETER, first on record Marblehead, Mass., 1680.

WILLIAM, brother of Daniel, living N. E., 1650-60.

TWITCHELL, TWITCHWELL

BENJAMIN, at Dorchester, Mass., grantee Lancaster, Mass., 1654, resident Medfield, Mass., 1663.

JOSEPH, brother of the preceding, resident Dorchester, Mass., 1633, freeman 1643.

TWOMBLY, TWAMBLY

NATHANIEL, resident Dover, N. H., 1658.

RALPH, inhabitant, Dover, N. H., 1658.

TYLER

The name is from the Anglo-Saxon word, *tigele,* a corruption of the Latin *tegula;* title which comes from the verb *tegere,* to cover, hence the tyler, one who bakes clay into tiles. The first English record of the name is Geoffreylc, Tulese, County of Hants, England, 1273.

ABRAHAM, married Haverhill, Mass., 1640, died May 6, 1673.

FRANCIS, drew lot at Branford, Conn., 1679.

GEORGE, brother of preceding, at Branford, Conn., 1674.

JOB, b. Shropshire, Eng., first record Portsmouth, R. I., 1638, removed Andover, Mass., 1640, resident Roxbury, Mass., 1665, thence Mendon, Mass., 1669, returned Roxbury, Mass., located in what is now Boxford, Mass., 1681; will probated 1700.

NATHANIEL, resident Lynn, Mass., 1640.

PETER, brother of Francis, freeman Branford, Conn., 1672.

ROGER, resident Mass., 1650, died New Haven, Conn., 1674.

THOMAS, resident Boston, Mass., 1657.

THOMAS, sea captain, came from Budleigh, Devonshire, Eng., to Boston, Mass., 1685, removed Weymouth, Mass., 1698; on his last voyage captured by a Barbary corsair, fate unknown.

WILLIAM, took oath of fidelity, New Haven, Conn., 1657, removed Wallingford, Conn.

TYLEY, TYLEE

THOMAS, waterman, Boston, Mass., 1664.

TYNG, TING

Among the ancient Celts the place where courts were held, and justice administered was called *Ting,* i. e. to surround; the circle, the temple, or round hill. The Tings at first were only judicial, but in process of time they became legislative. The most remarkable object of this kind is the Tynwald, in the Isle of Man. *Thing* in Saxon, a cause, meeting, a council; German, *ding,* a court. Dutch, *dinger,* a pleader.

EDWARD, merchant, b. Eng., 1600, freeman, Boston, Mass., 1641, died Dec. 28, 1681.

WILLIAM, merchant, brother of preceding, arrived Boston, Mass., 1638, removed Braintree, Mass., representative, 1649-51.

TYSON

The son of *Tys,* an abbreviation among the Dutch of Matthias.

JAMES, Quaker, at Boston, Mass., 1667.

UMPHERVILE, UMBERFIELD, UMFREVILLE

JOHN, resident New Haven, Conn., 1675, proprietor, 1685.

UNDERHILL

A local name. Under the hill.

GEORGE, resident N. H., 1668.

JOHN, known as Captain, b. Warwick, Eng., 1597, came to N. E., 1630, located Boston, Mass., removed Dover, N. H., 1638, finally Queens Co., L. I.; will administered Nov. 4, 1675.

UNDERWOOD

A local name. Under the wood.

HENRY, resident Newport, R. I., 1670.

JAMES, baker, at Salem, Mass., 1654.

JOSEPH, living Hingham, Mass., 1637, removed Watertown, Mass., freeman, 1645.

MARTIN, weaver, b. Eng., 1596, came from Ipswich, county of Suffolk, Eng., to Watertown, Mass., 1634, died Nov. 7, 1672.

THOMAS, brother of Joseph, freeman, Hingham, Mass., 1637, removed Watertown, Mass., selectman, 1656, died 1668.

WILLIAM, married Concord, Mass., before 1640.

UNTHANK

CHRISTOPHER, at Providence, R. I., freeman, Warwick, R. I., 1655.

UPDIKE

GILBERT, resident Newport, R. I., 1664.

UPHAM

The house or town on the height.

JOHN, b. Bicton, Devonshire, Eng., 1598, freeman, Weymouth, Mass., 1635, removed Malden, Mass., 1648, died Feb. 25, 1682.

UPSHALL, UPSALL

NICHOLAS, Dorchester, Mass., 1630, removed Boston, Mass., 1644, died Aug. 20, 1666.

UPSON

STEPHEN, sawyer, b. Eng., 1612, resident Boston, Mass., 1635.

THOMAS, brother of the preceding, settled Hartford, Conn., 1638, removed Farmington, Conn., 1645.

UPTON

The high hill, or the town on the height.

JOHN, blacksmith, settled first Salem, Mass., 1658, removed Reading, Mass.; freeman 1691, died 1699.

URRAN, URAN, URIN

From Cornish British, *urrian* the border, boundary or limit of a country.

JOHN, at Newbury, Mass., 1669, removed New Hampshire, where he married, 1686.

WILLIAM, died New Hampshire, 1664.

USHER

An officer of a court who introduces strangers; the under-master of a school.

HEZEKIAH, printer and bookseller, freeman, Cambridge, Mass., 1639, removed Boston, Mass., 1645, representative for Billerica, Mass., 1671-73, died May 14, 1676.

ROBERT, brother of the preceding, swore fidelity New Haven, Conn., 1644, removed Stamford, Conn., 1647, inventory of estate, Oct. 26, 1669.

USSELL

RICHARD, resident Portsmouth or Newport, R. I., 1653-56.

USSELTON

FRANCIS, married Wenham, Mass., 1657.

UTTLEY.

RICHARD, Ipswich, Mass., 1639.

SAMUEL, married Scituate, Mass., 1648.

UXLEY

HENRY, one first settlers Taunton, Mass., 1637.

VALE, VAIL, VAILL

Low land between hills, a valley.

JAMES, resident Dedham, Mass., 1656.

JEREMIAH, b. Eng., 1618, at Salem, Mass., 1639, removed Gardiner's Island, Boston Harbor, 1651, Southold, L. I., 1659.

VALENTINE

From the Latin *Valentinus,* a name derived from *valens,* able, puissant, brave.

JOHN, freeman, Boston, Mass., 1675.

VALLACK

NICHOLAS, swore fidelity, Pemaquid, Maine, 1674.

VANE

HENRY, son of Sir Henry V. came N. E., 1635, freeman, Boston, Mass., 1635; governor of Mass., 1636, returned England, 1637.

JOHN, granted land Portsmouth, R. I., 1639.

VANGOODENHAUSEN

SAMUEL, Dutch trader, married New Haven, Conn., 1648, removed New York, 1668.

VARLEET, VARLETH, VARLETT

CASPER or JASPER, Dutchman, died Hartford, Conn., 1662.

VARNEY

THOMAS, joined church Boston, Mass., 1664, died Dec. 4, 1692.

WILLIAM, died Ipswich, Mass., 1654.

VARNUM

GEORGE, died Ipswich, Mass., 1649.

VARS

LORD JOHN DE VARS, French nobleman, settled Westerly, R. I., 1677, returned to France for his family, was killed in a duel; his widow and son, Isaac, settled on the R. I. property.

VASSALL

WILLIAM, comptroller of Mass., son of John V., b. Eng., 1593, came in Winthrop's fleet to N. E., returned to England, came second time 1635, settled Roxbury, Mass., removed Scituate, Mass., 1636, finally to Barbados where he died before 1655.

VAUGHAN, VAHAN, VAHEN

From the Welch, the same as *Bychan* or *Vychan,* little, small in stature.

GEORGE, sent by Mason, Portsmouth, N. H., 1631, returned England, 1634.

GEORGE, b. Eng., 1621, married Marshfield, Mass., 1652, settled Scituate, Mass., 1653, removed Middleboro, Mass., 1663, died 1694.

JOHN, b. Eng., about 1615, at Watertown, Mass., 1633, removed Providence, R. I.

JOHN, first record Newport, R. I., 1638, freeman, 1658.

WILLIAM, one founders Baptist church, Newport, R. I., 1644.

WILLIAM, chief justice Supreme Court, married Portsmouth, N. H., 1668, died 1719.

VAULSTONE, VALSTON

THOMAS, at Providence, R. I., 1645, freeman Newport, R. I., 1655.

VEAZEY, VESEY, VEAZIE, VEASEY

Wet or fenny land, near the water, subject to inundation; the same as *Fossey*. Cornish British, *Vosey,* the ditch or fort near the water. Robert de Veci was with William the Conqueror.

GEORGE, b. Eng., 1635, settled Dover, N. H., 1659.

ROBERT, Watertown, Mass., 1636.

WILLIAM, b. Eng., 1616, freeman Braintree, Mass., 1643, died June 16, 1681.

VENNER

THOMAS, wine cooper, freeman Salem, Mass., 1638, removed Boston, Mass., 1645, returned London, Eng., before 1656, executed for raising mob, Jan., 1661.

VENTRIS, VENTERUS, VENTROOS

MOSES, freeman, Farmington, Conn., 1651, died 1697.

WILLIAM, brother of the preceding, b. Eng., 1623, freeman, Farmington, Conn., 1654, removed Haddam, Conn., 1669, died July 2, 1701.

VERE, VEARE, VEIR

EDWARD, died Wethersfield, Conn., 1645.

VERGOOSE, FERGOOSE, GOOSE

ISAAC, b. Eng., 1637, came from near Norwich, county of Norfolk, Eng., to Boston, Mass., 1662, died Nov. 29, 1710.

PETER, brother of the preceding, resident Boston, Mass., 1659, died Dec., 1667.

VERIN, VEREN, VERING

JOHN, married Boston, Mass., 1660.

JOSHUA, roper, came from Salisbury, Wiltshire, Eng., to Salem, Mass., 1635, removed Providence, R. I., 1637, returned to Salem, Mass., 1641.

PHILIP, roper, brother of the preceding, arrived Boston, Mass., 1635, freeman, 1635, imprisoned as a Quaker, 1655.

VERMAES, VERMAYES

MARK, freeman, Salem, Mass., 1639.

VERNON

A place name from Vernon in Normandy.

DANIEL, b. London, Eng., 1643, settled Kingstown, R. I., 1666.

FRANCIS, granted land Medfield, Mass., 1658, removed Boston, Mass., 1663.

VERY

SAMUEL, b. Eng., 1619, came with his mother Bridget to Salem, Mass., 1648.

THOMAS, brother of the preceding, b. Eng., 1626, married Gloucester, Mass., 1650.

VIALL, VILES

JOHN, b. Eng., 1619, inhabitant Boston, Mass., 1639.

VICARS, VICERS, VICARY

In Cornish British *Vicar,* a sovereign lord. Vicar the incumbent of a benefice; one who performs the functions of another.

EDWARD, died New Haven, Conn., 1684.

GEORGE, at Marblehead, Mass., 1637, removed Hull, Mass., 1650.

ROGER, Scarborough, Maine, 1663.

VIGERS, VIGARS

THOMAS, limeburner, b. 1650, at Hartford, Conn., 1685.

VINAL

JOHN, son of Ann, a widow, b. 1636, died Scituate, Mass., Aug. 21, 1698.

STEPHEN, brother of preceding, married Scituate, Mass., 1662.

VINCENT

HUMPHREY, Cambridge, Mass., 1634, removed Ipswich, Mass., before 1638, died Dec. 3, 1664.

JOHN, Lynn, Mass., removed Sandwich, Mass., 1636.

JOHN, resident New Haven, Conn., 1639.

NICHOLAS, b. about 1612, at Manchester, Mass., 1679.

PHILIP, son of Richard V., b. Frisby, near Coningsborough, Yorkshire, Eng., came to N. E., 1637, went to England the following year.

WILLIAM, freeman, Salem, Mass., 1635, removed Marblehead, Mass.

WILLIAM, settled Gloucester, Mass., removed New London, Conn., 1651, removed Providence, R. I., 1666.

VINE

Taken from the plant that bears the grape; a vineyard. "Will of the Vine." "Will Vine."

WILLIAM, resident Charlestown, Mass., 1674.

VINING

JOHN, freeman Weymouth, Mass., 1666.

WILLIAM, resident Portsmouth, N. H., 1683.

VINSON

JOHN, living Weymouth, Mass., 1675.

VINTON

The name is derived from the French word *Vin,* meaning wine compounded with *tenant,* signifying to hold or keep.

EDWARD, died Marblehead, Mass., 1678.

JOHN, b. Eng., 1620, at Lynn, Mass., 1648, died New Haven, Conn., 1663.

VIXEN

ROBERT, inhabitant Eastham, Mass., 1655.

VODEN VORDEN, VOUDEN

JOHN, came from Isle of Jersey, Eng., to Salem, Mass., 1669.

MOSES, brother of the preceding, married Salem, Mass., 1674.

VORE, VOAR

RICHARD, at Dorchester, Mass., 1635, removed Windsor, Conn., before 1640, died Nov. 22, 1683.

VOSE

Vos is a Dutch family name, in Flemish it became DeVos and German Voss.

EBENEZER, b. England, 1636, died Dorchester, Mass., 1716.

ROBERT, b. Garston, county of Lancaster, Eng., 1599, came to Dorchester, Mass., 1640, resided Milton, Mass., 1654.

VOWLES, VOULS, VOWELLS

RICHARD, Fairfield, Conn., 1650-56, removed Greenwich, Conn., freeman, 1662.

VYALL, VIOL, VIALL

JOHN, vintner, resident Boston, Mass., 1639, removed to Swanzey, Mass., died 1686.

WACOMBE, WACKHAM

THOMAS, resident of Portsmouth, N. H., 1684.

WADDELL, WODEL

WILLIAM, at Watertown, Mass., 1643, removed Portsmouth, R. I., 1644, will probated 1692.

WADE

From the Dutch word *weide,* a meadow or pasture.

HENRY, Hingham, Mass., 1652.

JONATHAN, merchant, came from Denver, near Downham Market, Norfolkshire, Eng., 1632, to Charlestown, Mass., freeman 1634, removed Ipswich, Mass., 1636, will probated 1678.

NICHOLAS, brother of the preceding, innkeeper, b. Eng., 1616, settled Scituate, Mass., 1631. Killed in Indian fight at Rehoboth, Mass., 1676.

RICHARD, brother of the preceding, freeman Lynn, Mass., 1637.

ROBERT, Dorchester, Mass., 1635, removed Hartford, Conn., 1640, living at Norwich, Conn., 1669.

SAMUEL, resident Lynn, Mass., 1641.

WILLIAM, married Middletown, Conn., 1658.

WADFIELD

JOHN, living Scituate, Mass., 1643.

WADHAM, WADHAMS

A place name from the old manor of Wadham at Knowston, near South Molton, Devonshire, England.

JOHN, b. Somersetshire, Eng., settled Wethersfield, Conn., 1645-50.

WADFIELD

JOHN, inhabitant, Scituate, Mass., 1643.

WADILOVE

NICHOLAS, at Yarmouth, Mass., 1643.

WADLAND, WALDEN

CRISPIN, shipwright, died Charlestown, Mass., 1671.

WADLEIGH, WADLEY, WADLOW

JOHN, innkeeper at Saco, Maine, 1636, removed Wells, Maine, 1647, died 1671.

WADSWORTH

The name means wood-court, in ancient times courts were held in the woods, hence the name. Also the same as Woodsworth, the farm or place in the woods. The ancient seat of the family Nottinghamshire.

CHRISTOPHER, son of Thomas W., located Duxbury, Mass., 1632, will probated 1677.

TIMOTHY, freeman Boston, Mass., 1690.

WILLIAM, brother of Christopher, b. Eng. about 1600, settled Cambridge, Mass., 1632, removed Hartford, Conn., 1636, where he died about 1676.

WAINWRIGHT

FRANCIS, resident Ipswich, Mass., 1637.

THOMAS, at Wethersfield, Conn., 1643, removed Dorchester, Mass., 1659.

WAITE, WAIT, WAITT, WAYTE

A local name, the same as *Thwaite,* a piece of ground cleared of wood, a meadow.

BENJAMIN, known as Sargeant, b. 1640, at Hatfield, Mass., 1663, killed by Indians at Deerfield, Mass.

GAMALIEL, fisherman, b. Eng., 1598, joined Church Boston, Mass., 1633, lived Long Island, Boston Harbor and died 1685.

GEORGE, resident Providence, R. I., before 1646.

JOHN, b. 1618, known as Capt. John, son of Samuel W. of Wethersfield, Eng., member of Church Charlestown, Mass., 1647, removed Malden, Mass., 1644, died 1693.

JOHN, resident Ipswich, Mass., 1646, died 1665.

JONATHAN, died Northampton, Mass., 1696.

RICHARD, tailor, brother of Gamaliel, b. Eng., 1596, admitted church Boston, Mass., 1634, will probated 1680.

RICHARD, b. Eng., 1608, settled Watertown, Mass., 1637, died 1669.

RICHARD, took oath of allegiance Springfield, Mass., 1678.

SAMUEL, resident Wickford, R. I., 1674.

THOMAS, brother of Gamaliel, b. Eng., 1601, at Portsmouth, R. I., 1639.

WILLIAM, took oath of allegiance Northampton, Mass., 1679.

WAKEFIELD

A market town in West Yorkshire, England, the watch-field.

JOHN, b. Hertfordshire, Eng., came to N. E., 1632, at Salem, Mass., 1637, at Marblehead, Mass., 1638, settled Wells, Maine, 1648 died 1660.

JOHN, b. Eng., 1614-15, at Boston, Mass., removed Edgartown, Mass., 1660.

OBADIAH, freeman, Boston, Mass., 1683.

SAMUEL, at Boston, Mass., before 1675.

WILLIAM, b. Eng., 1618, freeman Hampton, Mass., 1639, removed Newbury, Mass. 1646.

WAKELY WAKLEE, WAKELIN

HENRY, Hartford, Conn., 1660, removed Stratford, Conn., 1668, will dated 1689.

JAMES, Hartford, Conn., 1649, removed Wethersfield, Conn., finally Newport, R. I., 1680.

RICHARD, freeman, Haddam, Conn., 1657, died 1681.

THOMAS, freeman Hingham, Mass., 1636, removed Falmouth, Maine, killed by Indians, 1675.

WAKEMAN, WAKMAN

A title given to the chief magistrate of Rippon in Yorkshire, England, a watchman.

JOHN, son of Francis W. of Bewdley, Worcestershire, Eng., where he was b. about 1598-99. Came to N. E., 1638, removed New Haven, Conn., 1639, treasurer of the colony 1656, died 1661.

SAMUEL, brother of the preceding, came to Roxbury, Mass., 1631, removed Cambridge, Mass., and to Hartford, Conn., 1635. Killed at Bahamas, 1641.

WALBRIDGE

HENRY, came from Dorsetshire, Eng., was at Preston, Conn., 1688.

WALCOT, WALLCOT, WALLCOTT

ABRAHAM, husbandman, settled at Salem 1678, now Danvers, Mass.

JOHN, resident of Watertown, Mass., 1634-35.

JONATHAN, brother of Abraham, married at what is now Danvers, Mass., 1665.

JOSIAH, married at Salem, Mass., 1685.

WILLIAM, at Salem, Mass., 1637, excommunicated at same time as Roger Williams; removed Providence, R. I.

WALDEN

The Saxon and German, designating a wood, a woody place.

EDWARD, died Wenham, Mass., 1679.

WALDO

CORNELIUS, b. Eng., 1624, first record Salem, Mass., 1647, removed Ipswich, Mass., 1654, later, 1665, Chelmsford, Mass., died 1701.

WALDRON, WALDREN, WALROND

From the Saxon word *Wald,* a wood. The English ancestor, Edward Waldron or Walderne, lived at Alcester, Warwickshire.

ALEXANDER, at Dover, N. H., 1664, died 1676, naming in will five brothers, Isaac, William, George, Samuel and Edward.

EDWARD, brother of the preceding, at Ipswich, Mass., 1648, soon afterwards returned to England.

GEORGE, brother of the preceding, at Dover, N. H., 1661, removed Boston, Mass., where he was a resident 1679.

ISAAC, physician, brother of the preceding, at Portsmouth, N. H., 1661, removed York, Maine, 1670, to Boston, Mass., 1676.

JOHN, married Marblehead, Mass., 1673.

JOHN, apprentice to John Heard, Dover, N. H., 1687.

RALPH, at Boston, died Barbadoes, 1653.

RICHARD, bapt. Alcester, Warwickshire, Eng., 1616; at Dover, N. H., 1645; killed by Indians 1689.

WILLIAM, brother of the preceding, son of William W., grandson of George, great-grandson of Edward; bapt. Alcester, Warwickshire, Eng., 1601, freeman, Dover, N. H., 1642.

WILLIAM, gunsmith, brother of Alexander, resident Dover, N. H., 1664-83.

WALES

A native of Wales, a name given by the Anglo-Saxons to the Britons, who originally came from Gaul, which the Saxons pronounced *Wealas, Wales, Welsh* and *Wallia.*

NATHANIEL, shipwright, bapt. Idle, Yorkshire, Eng., 1586-87, came to N. E. 1635, proprietor and freeman, Dorchester, Mass., 1637, removed Boston, Mass., 1654, where he died 1661.

WALFORD

THOMAS, found by the first comers at Charlestown, Mass., and called a smith 1628, removed Portsmouth, N. H., 1631, died 1660.

WALKER

In the north of England and south of Scotland, a fulling-mill is called a walk-mill. This name may signify either a fuller or an officer, whose duty consists in walking or inspecting a certain space of forest ground.

ARCHIBALD, married at Providence, R. I., 1690.

AUGUSTINE *or* AUSTIN, sea-captain and merchant, came from the vicinity of Berwick on the "Tweed," Eng., to Charlestown, Mass., 1638, died Bilboa, Spain, 1653; descendants early settlers Woburn, Mass.

BENJAMIN, one of the founders Brattle Street Church, Boston, Mass.

FRANCIS, at Middleboro, Mass., 1668, removed Duxbury, Mass., 1672.

HENRY, resident Gloucester, Mass., 1647, removed Ipswich, Mass., 1651, died 1693.

ISAAC, merchant, married Boston, Mass., 1644.

ISRAEL, lived Woburn, Mass., 1672.

JAMES, b. Eng., 1619, came to N. E. 1635, at Taunton, Mass., 1643, removed Rehoboth, Mass., 1644, died 1692.

JOHN, freeman Boston, Mass., 1634, removed to R. I., 1637.

JOHN, resident New Haven, Conn., 1639, inventory of his estates taken 1652.

JOHN, married Woburn, Mass., 1672.

JOHN, married Charlestown, Mass., 1674.

JOHN, married Beverly, Mass., before 1686.

JOSEPH, adherent of Massachusetts jurisdiction at Portsmouth, N. H., 1665.

NATHANIEL, a resident of Boston, Mass.

OBADIAH, early settler Reading, Mass.

PHILIP, weaver, brother of James, resident Rehoboth, Mass., 1653-79.

RICHARD, farmer, Captain of the Militia, b. Eng., 1593, settled Lynn, Mass., 1630, removed Reading, Mass., afterwards to Woburn, Mass, died 1687.

RICHARD, shoemaker, b. Eng., 1611, came to N. E. 1635, settled Boston, Mass.

RICHARD, granted land Salem, Mass., 1637.

ROBERT, weaver, b. Eng., 1607, came from Manchester, Lancashire, Eng., to Boston, Mass., admitted to church 1632; a founder of Old South Church; died 1687.

SAMUEL, was at Exeter or Hampton, N. H., 1644.

SAMUEL, married Rehoboth, Mass., before 1654.

SAMUEL, merchant, resident Boston, Mass., 1654.

SHUABEL, town clerk, Rowley, Mass., married Lynn, Mass., 1666; afterwards at Reading and Haverhill, Mass.; died 1689.

THOMAS, brick burner at Boston, Mass., before 1650, died 1659.

THOMAS, schoolteacher, Sudbury 1664, afterwards inn-keeper, will probated 1697.

THOMAS, one of the founders Bristol, R. I. 1687.

WILLIAM, b. Eng., 1620, came from London, Eng., to Hingham, Mass., 1636, settled at Eastham, Mass., where he married 1655.

William, resident of Salem, Mass., 1637.

WALKLEY

HENRY, one first settlers Hartford, Conn., 1637.

WALKUP

GEORGE, married Reading, Mass., 1688.

WALL

"JOHN AT THE WALL"—JOHN WALL.

JAMES, carpenter, sent over by Mason to Portsmouth, 1631, removed Hampton, N. H., 1648, to Exeter, N. H., 1646, returned to Hampton 1654, died soon afterwards.

JOHN, came to N. E. 1630, at Exeter, N. H., 1639, Portsmouth, N. H., 1640.

WALLBRIDGE

HENRY, came from Dorsetshire, Eng., with his brothers William and Stephen to Dedham, Mass., 1685, removed Preston, Conn.

WALLEN, WALLING, WALLINE

RALPH, came to Plymouth, Mass., 1623.

RICHARD, resident Providence, R. I., 1667.

THOMAS, brother of the preceding, b. Eng., about 1630, freeman at Providence, R. I., 1655.

WALLER

A *Gauler* or *Waller*, a foreigner, from the Anglo-Saxon *Waller-went*, foreign men, strangers.

CHRISTOPHER, tray-maker, at Salem, Mass., 1637, granted land 1649, removed Ipswich, Mass., where he died 1676.

JOSEPH, resident Boston, Mass., before 1670, removed Fairfield, Conn., where he died 1672.

MATTHEW, at Salem, Mass., 1637, removed Providence, R. I., on list of freemen 1655, resided at New London, Conn., 1667-74.

THOMAS, shoemaker, Boston, Mass., 1670.

THOMAS, resident Providence, R. I., 1676.

WILLIAM, brother of Matthew, at Salem, Mass., 1637, removed Saybrook, Conn., 1649.

WALLEY

CHRISTOPHER, freeman Concord, Mass., 1682.

JOHN, mariner, freeman Boston, Mass., 1673.

THOMAS, clergyman, b. Eng., 1617, rector of St. Mary's Whitechapel, London, Eng., arrived at Boston, Mass., 1663, where he died 1678.

THOMAS, married Boston, Mass, 1692.

WILLIAM, married Charlestown, Mass., 1684.

WALLINGFORD, WALLINSFORD, WALLINGTON

JOHN, married Dover, N. H., 1687.

NICHOLAS, married Bradford, Mass., 1678. —SON

NICHOLAS, came in boyhood to Newbury, Mass., 1638, as servant of Stephen Kent, admitted freeman 1670; tradition says that he was captured by a Barbary corsair and never returned. —FATHER

WALLIS, WALLACE

The same as *Wales* or *Welch* and formed thus—*Gaulish, Wallish, Wallis* and also *Welsh* or *Welch*, a name given to the Britons by their Danish and Angles invaders because they originally came from Gaul.

JOHN, died Woburn, Mass., 1670.

JOHN, at Scarborough, Maine, 1658, removed Gloucester, Mass., 1678, where he died 1690.

NATHANIEL, brother of the preceding, b. Cornwall, Eng., 1632, removed to Falmouth, Maine, 1658, died 1709.

RALPH, b. Eng., 1595, came to N. E., 1635, settled at Rumney Marsh, now Chelsea, Mass.

RICHARD, at Saybrook, Conn., 1659, removed Norwich, Conn., 1660.

ROBERT, resident Ipswich, Mass., 1659.

THOMAS, freeman of Mass., 1643.

WILLIAM, admitted to the church Charlestown, Mass., 1642.

WARD

A keeper, one who guards or defends. The first one known to assume the name was William de la Ward, who resided in Chester, Eng., 1175.

ANDREW, freeman Watertown, Mass., 1634, removed Wethersfield, Conn., 1635, and to Stamford, Conn., 1641, afterwards to Fairfield, Conn., where he died 1659.

ANDREW, at Wethersfield, Conn., mentioned in his mother's (Joyce W.) will, 1641.

BENJAMIN, ship carpenter, at Boston, Mass., 1639; left no issue.

GEORGE, signed the covenant at New Haven, Conn., 1639, removed Branford, Conn., 1646, and died 1653.

JOHN, physician, lived Boston, Mass., 1652, afterwards at Ipswich, Mass. Will probated 1656; left no issue.

JOHN, son of widow, Joyce W., was at Branford, Conn., finally removed to N. J.

LAWRENCE, brother of George, resident New Haven, Conn., 1639, removed Branford, Conn., 1646, later to Newark, N. J., where he died 1671.

MARMADUKE, freeman, Newport, R. I., 1640.

MILES, known as Captain Miles W., came from Erith, County of Kent, Eng., to Salem, Mass., 1639.

NATHANIEL, clergyman, son of Rev. John W., b. Haverhill, county of Suffolk, Eng., 1570, at Ipswich, Mass., 1634, returned to England before 1647, where he died 1653.

NATHANIEL, original settler Hartford, Conn., 1638, removed Hadley, Mass., 1660, where he died 1664, leaving no issue.

SAMUEL, cooper, b. Eng., 1592, proprietor Hingham, Mass., 1636, removed Charlestown, Mass., 1658, where he died 1682.

SAMUEL, married Branford, Conn., 1658.

SAMUEL, freeman Marblehead, Mass., 1665, had military title of Major and died in Phips' expedition against Quebec, Canada, 1690.

THOMAS, came to N. E., 1630, at Hampton, N. H., 1639.

THOMAS, at Milford, Mass., 1657.

WILLIAM, b. Yorkshire, Eng., 1603, came to Sudbury, Mass., 1639, removed to Marlboro, Mass., 1660, where he died 1687.

WARDALL, WARDHALL, WOODELL, WARDWELL

The name had its origin in medieval institution of "watch and ward."

THOMAS, shoemaker, admitted church Boston, Mass., 1634, removed Exeter, N. H., afterwards Ipswich, Mass., 1648.

WILLIAM, brother of the preceding, resident Boston, Mass., 1634, removed Exeter, N. H., 1637, afterwards resident Ipswich, Mass., but in his later life returned to Boston, Mass.

WILLIAM, at Wells, Maine, 1649.

WARE

A local name. A town in Hertfordshire, Eng., so named from the *wear* in the river Lee at that place.

HENRY, townsman Dorchester, Mass., 1668.

JOSEPH, resident, Salem, Mass., 1682.

ROBERT, settled at Dedham, Mass., 1642, freeman 1647, died 1699.

SAMUEL, freeman Boston, Mass., 1675.

WILLIAM, shoemaker, resident Dorchester, Mass., 1643, removed Boston, Mass., 1652, died 1658.

WARFIELD

JOHN, settled Dedham, Mass., 1642, removed Mendon, Mass., 1685; will dated 1691.

WARHAM

JOHN, clergyman, came from Plymouth, Eng., to Dorchester, Mass., 1630, removed Windsor, Conn., 1635, died 1670.

WILLIAM, married, Newbury, Mass., 1682.

WARLAND

OSCAR, first record marriage at Cambridge, Mass., 1679.

WARNER

The name occurs in the Doomsday Book in the account of the Manors of Warner. The Manor of Pakelsham was granted before 1473 to John Warner of Warner's Hall in Great Waltham.

ANDREW, b. Eng., 1600, settled Cambridge, Mass., 1632, removed Hartford, Conn., 1635, removed Hadley, Mass., where he died 1684.

DANIEL, freeman Ipswich, Mass., 1682.

GABRIEL, resident, Boston, Mass., 1681.

GEORGE, died New Haven, Conn., 1681.

JOHN, Providence, R. I., 1637, lost at sea 1652, leaving no male issue.

JOHN, b. Eng., 1615, came to N. E., 1635, proprietor Hartford, Conn., 1639, removed Farmington, Conn., 1657, patentee Waterbury, Conn., 1673, died 1579.

JOHN, brother of Andrew, married, Middletown, Conn., 1669.

JOHN, married, Ipswich, Mass., 1665.

JOHN, resident Woburn, Mass., before 1684.

JOSEPH, freeman Hadley, Mass., 1673.

RALPH, admitted inhabitant Dorchester, Mass., 1664.

SAMUEL, married, Ipswich, Mass., 1662.

THOMAS, resident Wells, Maine, 1653.

THOMAS, innkeeper, Norwalk, Conn., 1665.

WILLIAM, son of Samuel W., b. Boxsted, county of Essex, Eng., 1590, early settler Ipswich, Mass., 1637.

WARREN

From *Guarenna* or *Varenna,* in the county of Calais in Normandy, whence they came to England with William the Conqueror. The primary sense of the word is to stop, hold, or repel, to guard, keep off. Earl of Warrenne in Normandy, France, 1050, first English ancestor William, first earl of Warren and Surrey, 1066.

ABRAHAM, at Salem, Mass., 1637; at Ipswich, Mass., 1648, where he died 1654.

Arthur, resident Weymouth, Mass., 1638.

Ephraim, resident Boston, Mass., 1685.

James, settled Kittery, Maine, 1656.

John, b. Eng., 1585, came to N. E. in Winthrop's fleet, freeman Watertown, Mass., 1631, will dated 1667.

John, resident Ipswich, Mass., 1654.

John, tobacconist or card-maker, married, Exeter, N. H., 1650, removed Boston, Mass.

John, spinner at Ipswich, Mass., 1670.

Peter, mariner, b. Eng., 1628, purchased land Dorchester, Mass., afterwards Milton, Mass., 1659; died 1704.

Ralph, granted land Salem, Mass., 1638.

Richard, "Mayflower" passenger, merchant at Greenwich, county of Kent, Eng.

Thomas, resident Salem, Mass., 1640.

William, freeman Hartford, Conn., 1658.

William, mariner, married at Boston, Mass., 1690.

WARRINER, WARRENER

William, freeman Springfield, Mass., 1638.

WARWICK, WARRICK

The county town of Warwickshire, England. From the Cornish British *guarth,* a safe-guard, a garrison; and *wick,* Saxon, a port or city. Another authority says *wearing-wick,* from *wear* and *wick,* a harbor.

Henry, resident Saco, Maine, 1636, died about 1673.

WASHBURN, WASHBORNE

From *Wash* which applies to swift moving current, and *burn* or *bourne,* a brook or a small stream. Sir Roger de Washburn of Little Washbourne, Worcestershire, was resident of England in later half of the thirteenth century.

John, founder of the family in America, 12th generation from Sir Roger de W., b. Evesham, Worcestershire, 1597, settled Duxbury, Mass., 1632, original proprietor Bridgewater, Mass., 1645.

William, resident Stratford, Conn., removed Hempstead, L. I.

WASS, WASSE

John, resident Charlestown, Mass., 1645.

Thomas, schoolteacher, swore allegiance Haverhill, Mass., 1677, taught school at Haverhill, Mass., 1660, afterwards Ipswich and Newbury, Mass.; died 1691.

WASSON, WASON

Benjamin, married, Dover, N. H., 1687.

WASTALL, WESTALL, WASSTOLL

John, early settler Wethersfield, Conn., removed Saybrook, Conn., 1669.

WATERBURY

John, hotel-keeper Watertown, Mass., 1646, removed Stamford, Conn., where he died 1658.

William, came in Winthrop's fleet 1630 to Boston, Mass., died soon after on return to England.

WATERHOUSE, WATERUS

A place name from Waterhouse in Staffordshire, Eng., also village in county of Durham, Eng., an ancient family of Lincolnshire who claim their descent from Sir Gilbert Waterhouse of Kirton in the reign of Henry III.

David, resident of Boston, Mass., 1679.

Jacob, living Wethersfield, Conn., 1639, removed New London, Conn., 1645.

Richard, tanner, at Boston, Mass., 1672. settled on Pierce Island, Portsmouth, N. H., before 1688.

Thomas, schoolmaster, b. Eng., 1599, freeman Dorchester, Mass., 1640, died 1679.

WATERMAN

John, arrived Boston, Mass., 1639.

Richard, b. Eng., 1590, came to Salem, Mass., 1629, removed Providence, R. I., 1638, later to Warwick, R. I., 1643, finally removed to Newport, R. I., where he died 1673.

Robert, brother of the preceding, came from Norwich, Eng., to Salem, Mass., 1636; married, Marshfield, Mass., 1638.

Thomas, brother of the preceding at Roxbury, Mass., before 1641, removed Warwick, R. I., 1645, died 1676.

Thomas, freeman Newport, R. I., 1655, removed Wickford, R. I., 1674.

WATERS

A name given to one who navigated the waters or resided near them.

Anthony, town clerk, Hempstead, L. I., 1633.

Bevil, b. Eng., 1633, freeman Hartford, Conn., 1669, died 1730.

Edward, took oath of fidelity New Haven, Conn., 1647, living Westchester, N. Y., 1663.

Jacob, resident Charlestown, Mass., 1682.

John, servant of Gov. Winthrop, came from Neyland, county of Suffolk, Eng., to N. E., 1630.

Joseph, married Boston, Mass., 1655.

Joseph, at New Haven, Conn., 1649, removed Milford, Conn., 1653.

LAWRENCE, resident Watertown, Mass., 1634, removed Lancaster, Mass., 1638.

RICHARD, gunsmith, bapt. St. Botolph Aldersgate, London, Eng., 1604, settled Salem, Mass., 1636; will probated 1677.

RICHARD, freeman Ipswich, Mass., 1639.

SAMPSON, married Boston, Mass., 1666.

SAMUEL, freeman Woburn, Mass., 1684.

STEPHEN, brother of Jacob, resident Charlestown, Mass., 1678.

WILLIAM, swore allegiance to Mass., Pemaquid, Maine, 1674.

WILLIAM, resident Boston, Mass., 1653.

WATHEN, WATHIN

GEORGE, member of church Salem, Mass., 1641.

JOHN, member of church Portsmouth, N. H., 1640.

WATKINS

From *Wat,* and the patronymic termination *kins,* the son of Wat or Walter.

DAVID, resident Stratford, Conn., before 1688.

JOHN, came to Salem, Mass., 1641, died in that year.

JOHN, resident Cambridge, Mass., 1651.

THOMAS, tobacco maker, living Boston, Mass., 1653, freeman 1660, died 1689.

THOMAS, resident Kennebeck, Maine, 1665.

WATSON

The son of Walter.

EDWARD, married, New Haven, Conn., 1653, died 1660.

JOHN, b. Eng., about 1590, came to Roxbury, Mass., 1632, died 1672.

JOHN, b. Eng., 1619, freeman Cambridge, Mass., 1645, died 1711.

JOHN, resident Hartford, Conn., 1644, died before 1656.

JOHN, at Rowley, Mass., 1658, freeman 1672.

JOHN, apprentice, Boston, Mass., 1675.

JOHN, married Salisbury, Mass., 1688.

NATHANIEL, resident New London, Conn., 1647.

PHILIP, formerly at Salisbury, Mass., removed Rowley, Mass., 1678.

ROBERT, married Windsor, Conn., 1646, died 1689.

ROBERT, resident Dover, N. H., 1665.

THOMAS, tailor, admitted church Salem, Mass., 1639, died 1672.

THOMAS, keeper of prison, Boston, Mass., 1674, living Topsfield, Mass., 1684.

WILLIAM, married at Newbury, Mass., 1670.

WATTLES

RICHARD, resident Ipswich, Mass., 1648.

WATTS

HENRY, b. Eng., 1614, settled Scarborough, Maine, 1636.

JAMES, resident Marblehead, Mass., 1668.

JEREMIAH, Salem, Mass., 1678-80.

LAWRENCE, died at New Haven, 1643; left no issue.
no issue.

RICHARD, early settler Hartford, Conn., before 1640.

SAMUEL, swore allegiance Haverhill, Mass., 1677.

SAMUEL, tried as a pirate, Boston, Mass., 1690.

WAY

A road or passage of any kind; a name given to one who resided there. "Will o' the Way."

ELIEZER, resident Hartford, Conn., 1666.

GEORGE, married Saybrook, Conn.

HENRY, b. Eng., 1583, settled Dorchester, Mass., 1630, removed to what is now Chelsea, Mass., 1651, finally to Boston, Mass., 1660, where he died 1667.

RICHARD, resident of Scituate, Mass., 1651.

THOMAS, at Isle of Shoals, N. H., 1649.

WEARE

NATHANIEL, b. Eng., 1635, married Newbury, Mass., 1656, removed Hampton, N. H., 1662, died 1718.

PETER, died Newbury, Mass., 1653, probably father of the preceding.

WEATHERS

JOHN, swore allegiance Hadley, Mass., 1679.

WEAVER

CLEMENT, freeman, Newport, R. I., 1655.

EDMUND, husbandman, b. Eng., 1607, came to N. E., 1635, from London, Eng.

JAMES, brother of preceding, b. Eng., 1612, came to N. E., 1635.

THOMAS, married Boston, Mass., 1674.

WEBB

ADEY or ADDY, resident Plymouth, Mass., 1631; no issue.

BENJAMIN, married Malden, Mass., 1669.

CHRISTOPHER, freeman Braintree, Mass., 1645.

DANIEL, innholder, Salem, Mass., 1689.

GEORGE, resident Dover, N. H., 1642.

HENRY, merchant, came from Salisbury,

county of Wilts, Eng., to Boston, Mass., 1638, died 1660, no male issue.

JOHN, husbandman, came from Marlborough, county of Wilts, Eng., to Boston, Mass., 1634, early settler Chelmsford, Mass., died 1668.

JOHN, brazier, inhabitant Boston, Mass., 1651.

JOHN, resident Northampton, Mass., 1655, died 1670.

JOHN, resident Salem, Mass., 1667.

JOHN, married, Braintree, Mass., 1680.

JONATHAN, died Northampton, Mass., 1694.

JOSEPH, died Stamford, Conn., 1684.

RICHARD, shoemaker, resident Weymouth, Mass., 1640, removed Boston, Mass., 1644, died 1659; no issue.

RICHARD, came from Dorsetshire, Eng., freeman Cambridge, Mass., 1632, removed Hartford, Conn., 1636, to Stamford, Conn., 1655.

RICHARD, brother of third John, swore allegiance Northampton, Mass., 1679.

SAMUEL, brother of fifth John, married, Braintree, Mass., 1686.

STEPHEN, husbandman, brother of first John came to N. E., 1635.

THOMAS, mariner, resident Charlestown, Mass., 1666.

WILLIAM, freeman Roxbury, Mass., 1636, died 1644.

WEBBER

The name is derived from the German word *Weber,* meaning weaver. Webber was the masculine, and Webster the feminine form of the word. The family originally came from Holland and those that bear the surname in New York and New England are generally descended from Wolfret Weber, born Amsterdam, Holland, 1600, who came to New Amsterdam, 1633.

JOHN, resident Boston, Mass., before 1675.

JOSIAS, early settler Reading, Mass.

MICHAEL, b. Scotland 1639, early settler Falmouth, Maine.

RICHARD, inhabitant Portsmouth, N. H., 1688.

THOMAS, mariner, master of the ship "Mayflower;" joined church Boston, Mass., 1644, removed to Kennebeck, Maine, 1649, later to Charlestown, Mass.

WEBSTER

A maker of webs, a weaver.

BENJAMIN, resident of Salem, or Ipswich, Mass., before 1675.

HENRY, resident Boston, Mass., before 1683.

JAMES, brewer, living Boston, Mass., 1659.

JOHN, came from Ipswich, county of Suffolk, Eng., to Ipswich, Mass., 1634, died 1646.

JOHN, b. Glasgow, Scotland, came from Warwickshire, Eng., to N. E., one of original settlers Hartford, Conn., 1636. Governor of Conn., 1656, removed to Hadley, Mass., 1659.

JOHN, brewer, resident Portsmouth, N. H., 1648.

NICHOLAS, married, Stamford, Conn., 1672; will dated 1687.

THOMAS, mariner, admitted church Boston, Mass., 1644.

THOMAS, son of Thomas W., bapt. Ormsby, county of Norfolk, Eng., came with mother, wife of William Godfrey, to Watertown, Mass., 1638, removed with his step-father to Hampton, N. H., 1648.

WEDGE

THOMAS, settled Lancaster, Mass., 1667.

WEDGEWOOD

JOHN, husbandman, settled Ipswich, Mass., 1637, removed Hampton, N. H., 1639.

WEEBON

STEPHEN, died Boston, Mass., 1659.

WEED

JOHN, married Salisbury, Mass., 1650.

JONAS, came from Stamford, county of Northampton, Eng., freeman Watertown, Mass., 1631, removed Wethersfield, Conn., 1635, thence Stamford, Conn., 1642, where he died 1676.

WEEDEN

A local name from *Weedon,* a town in Northamptonshire, Eng., on the river Nen. *Gwid-ton,* the woodyhill.

EDWARD, carpenter, b. Eng., 1613, came from London, Eng., to Boston, Mass., 1635.

JAMES, came Boston, Mass., 1638, removed Portsmouth, R. I., freeman Newport, R. I., 1655, where he died about 1673.

ROBERT, resident Salem, Mass., 1638.

SAMUEL, one of the founders of church, Newport, R. I., 1644.

WILLIAM, brother of the preceding, one of the founders of Baptist Church, Newport, R. I., 1644.

WEEDER, WEEDEN

JAMES, freeman, Newport, R. I., 1655.

WEEKS, WEEKES, WICKES

Ancient English surname; Henry Wyke of Stanton Wake, Somersetshire, Eng., ancestor in the 14th century.

CHRISTOPHER, resident Boston, Mass., before 1695.

FRANCIS, settled Salem, Mass., 1635, the following year removed Providence, R. I.

GEORGE, came to Dorchester, Mass., 1635, freeman 1640.

LEONARD, son of John Wyke, b. Eng., 1635, came from Welles, Somersetshire, Eng.; on record at York, Maine, 1655, the following year removed Portsmouth, N H.

RICHARD, b. Eng., 1670, settled Attleboro, Mass., 1690.

THOMAS, inhabitant Charlestown, Mass., 1636, removed Salem, Mass., 1639.

THOMAS, early settler Wethersfield, Conn., 1640, removed Stamford, Conn., 1641, and to Huntington, L. I., before 1654, there died 1671.

WILLIAM, resident Falmouth, Maine, 1669.

WEIGHT

RICHARD, residing in Boston, Mass., 1655.

WEIGHTMAN, WIGHTMAN

DANIEL, clergyman, b. 1669, pastor Baptist church, Newport, R. I., about fifty years, died 1750.

JOHN, admitted church Charlestown, Mass., 1641.

ROBERT, b. 1671, brother of Daniel, died Newport, R. I., 1728; left no issue.

WEIMOUTH

ROBERT, inhabitant Kittery, Maine, 1652.

WELCH

JAMES, married Swansea, Mass., 1683; will probated 1714.

PHILIP, b. 1638, came from north of Ireland to Ipswich, Mass., 1654; removed Kingston, N. H.

THOMAS, one founders of church, Milford, Conn., 1639, died 1681.

THOMAS, freeman Charlestown, Mass., 1650, died 1680.

WELCOME

WILLIAM, took oath of fidelity Pemaquid, Maine, 1674.

WELD, WELDE

A wood, sometimes written *weald,* the woody part of a country.

DANIEL, town clerk, b. Eng., 1585, freeman Braintree, Mass., 1641, removed Roxbury, Mass., 1651.

JOSEPH, brother of preceding, known as Captain W., b. England 1600, settled Roxbury, Mass., 1636, died 1646.

THOMAS, clergyman, brother of the preceding, settled at Roxbury, Mass., 1632, returned to England 1641, where he died 1661.

WELDEN

A place name from a hamlet in the parish of Hardwicke, county of Bucks; also a parish near Daventry, county of Northampton, bears the name of Welden. The name is also derived from *weald,* woody, a wood, and *den,* a valley.

JAMES, resident Newport, R. I., 1648.

ROBERT, resident Charlestown, Mass., where he died 1631.

WELLER

From the Anglo-Saxon, *wellere,* a hollow or gulf. Probably the same as Waller (which see).

JOHN, swore allegiance Northampton, Mass., 1679.

RICHARD, married Windsor, Conn., 1640.

WELLES, WELLS

A name given to a person who resided there. "John at the Wells"—John Wells. A bishop's see in Somersetshire, so called from the wells or springs there. One of the most powerful houses in Normandy and Provence, France, in the 8th century, when they were known by the name of Vaux; with this surname they accompanied William the Conqueror to England. In the 13th century the English family was known as DeVallibus, and Welles or Wells is a corrupted form of this name.

EDWARD, resident Boston, Mass., 1644.

HUGH, son of Thomas W. of Essex, Eng., b. Eng., 1590, came to N. E., 1635, removed Hartford, Conn., 1636, and to Wethersfield, Conn., 1647; died 1678.

ISAAC, at Scituate, Mass., 1638, removed Barnstable, Mass., 1643.

JAMES, freeman Haddam, Conn., 1669, prior to this, Springfield, Mass., 1650, died 1697.

JOHN, removed from Stratford, Conn., to Hadley, Mass., where he was freeman 1690, died 1692.

JOHN, carpenter, took oath of allegiance Newbury, Mass., 1669.

JOHN, freeman Roxbury, Mass., 1677.

NATHANIEL, b. Eng., 1600, came from Colchester, Eng., to Boston, Mass., 1629, removed to R. I., 1640.

RICHARD, freeman Lynn, Mass., 1639, removed Salisbury, Mass., before 1652, where he died 1672.

ROBERT, known as Deacon, early settler Salisbury, Mass.

THOMAS, brother of Robert, b. Eng., 1605, settled Ipswich, Mass., 1635.

THOMAS, b. Essex, Eng., 1598, came to Boston, Mass., 1635, at Saybrook, Conn., the following year, and Hartford, Conn., 1637, governor of Conn., 1658, died Wethersfield, Conn., 1660.

THOMAS, physician, came Ipswich, Mass., freeman 1647, died 1666.

THOMAS, shipbuilder at New London, Conn., 1648, removed Ipswich, Mass., 1661, removed Westerly, R. I., where he died 1700.

THOMAS, resident Boston, Mass., 1656.

THOMAS, son of Widow Frances, who married for her second husband, Thomas Colman; resident Wethersfield, Conn., before 1652.

THOMAS, brother of Robert, b. Eng., 1605, settled Ipswich, Mass., 1635.

WILLIAM, resident Lynn, Mass., 1641.

WELLINGTON, WILLINGTON

An ancient baronial family of Willington, England, established by William the Conqueror.

ROGER, b. Eng., 1609-10, first record Watertown, Mass., 1636, died 1698.

WELLMAN

THOMAS, b. Eng., 1620, settled Lynn, Mass., 1640.

WILLIAM, married Gloucester, Mass., 1649; will dated 1669.

WELLOW

DANIEL, freeman Cambridge, Mass., 1666.

WELSTEED, WELSTEAD

WILLIAM, inhabitant Charlestown, Mass., 1665.

WELTON

JOHN, living Farmington, Conn., before 1673, died 1726.

WENBOURNE, WINBOURNE, WENBORN

WILLIAM, resident Boston, Mass., 1635, removed Exeter, N. H., 1639, returned Boston, Mass., 1649.

WENDALL, WENDELL

From the Dutch word *Wandelaar*, a walker, hence a traveler. The name may also be from the river Wandle in Surrey, England.

THOMAS, servant at Ipswich, Mass., 1643.

WENSLEY, WINSLEY

EDWARD, represented Salisbury, Mass., in the General Court 1644.

JOHN, mariner, living Boston, Mass., 1664; will dated 1672.

SAMUEL, brother of Edward, freeman Salisbury, Mass., 1639.

WENTOM

EDWARD, resident Kittery, Maine, 1652.

WENTWORTH

The name is of Saxon origin from *guen* or *gwyn*, which signifies white, and *worth*, meaning farm, plain or court, thereby white farm or court taking its style from the soil which is composed of chalk or a whitish clay. The name is also taken from the lordship of Wentworth in Strafford, Yorkshire, Eng., where at the time of the Conqueror lived Reginald or Rynald de Winterwode or Wynterwode. It also is a local origin from the *Worth* farm, a place on the river *Went*, in Northumberland, Eng.

WILLIAM, son of William W. of the XXIst generation from Reginald, mentioned above, was known as elder William W., bapt. Alford, near Lincoln, Lincolnshire, Eng., 1616. Settled Exeter, N. H., his first record being his signature to Rev. John Wheelwright's compact of government 1639; removed Wells, Maine, 1642, to Dover, N. H., 1650, died 1698.

WERMALL, WORMALL

JAMES, settled Scituate, Mass., 1638, living Duxbury, Mass., 1670, died Bridgewater, Mass., 1711.

JOSEPH, inhabitant Scituate, Mass., 1638, removed Duxbury, Mass.

JOSEPH, resident Boston, Mass., 1650.

WESCOTT, WESTCOATT, WESTCOTT

A place name formed by two words *West* and *cot*, the latter signifying a hut or small dwelling place, the same as Eastcott and Southcote; Westmacott in Saxon, a banker, a money lender. Also a place name from parishes in Gloucestershire, Berkshire, and Buckshire, Eng.

DANIEL, inhabitant N. H., 1690.

RICHARD, living Wethersfield, Conn., 1639-44, removed Fairfield, Conn., where he died 1651.

RICHARD, resident Kittery, Maine, 1670.

STUKELEY, b. Eng., 1592, settled Salem, Mass., 1636, removed Providence, R. I., 1637, and to Warwick, R. I., 1648. His is the first name in the grant given by Roger Williams.

WILLIAM, resident Wethersfield, Conn., 1639.

WEST

BENJAMIN, married Enfield, Conn., 1686.

EDWARD, resident Lynn, Mass., 1637.

EDWARD, freeman Medfield, Mass., 1672, removed Sherborn, Mass.

Francis, came from Salisbury, Eng., to Duxbury, Mass., 1643, proprietor Bridgewater, Mass., 1645.

Henry, saddler, freeman Salem, Mass., 1668.

John, resident Ipswich, Mass., 1648.

John, b. Eng., 1624, came to N. E., 1635, settled Saybrook, Conn., 1649.

John, living Saco, Maine, 1640, died 1663.

John, represented Beverly, Mass., in General Court, 1677.

John, freeman Newport, R. I., 1655.

John, secretary of Sir Edmund Andros, resided Boston, Mass., 1687, returned Eng., 1689.

John, at Rowley, Mass., 1691.

Matthew, freeman Lynn, Mass., 1636, removed Newport, R. I., 1646.

Nathaniel, one of founders Baptist church, Newport, R. I., 1644.

Robert, resident Providence, R. I,. 1641.

Samuel, died Salem, Mass., 1685.

Samuel, married Salem, Mass., 1690.

Thomas, b. Eng., 1600, settled Salem, Mass., 1634.

Thomas, freeman Beverly, Mass., 1670.

Thomas, took oath of allegiance Newbury, Mass., 1669.

Thomas, married Wethersfield, Conn., 1677.

Twford, b. Eng., 1616, came from London, Eng., to Boston, Mass., 1635, lived at Rowley, Mass., 1667, Salem, 1677, Ipswich, 1678.

William, married Salem, Mass., 1672.

WESTALL, WESTELL, WESTOLL

A local name, The *West-Hall.*

John, innkeeper, Saybrook, Conn., 1653, died 1683.

WESTBROOK

Job, came from county of Surrey, Eng., to Portsmouth, N. H., before 1690.

John, also from county of Surrey, Eng., at Portsmouth, N. H., 1665.

WESTCAR

John, trader, resident Hadley, Mass., 1665; left no issue.

WESTEAD, WESSTEAD

William, mariner, first on record Charlestown, Mass., at Saybrook, Conn., 1679.

WESTERHOUSEN

William, merchant, took oath of fidelity, New Haven, Conn., 1648.

WESTGATE

Adam, mariner, resident Salem, Mass., 1647-62.

Daniel, freeman Stamford, Conn., 1670.

John, admitted church Boston, Mass., 1640, returned to England before 1647.

WESTLEY

William, settled Hartford, Conn., 1638.

WESTMORELAND

A local name from a county of England, the West-moor-land.

James, resident Boston, Mass., 1652.

WESTON

The west town; derived from a small village in England.

Edmund, b. Eng., 1605, settled Boston, Mass., 1635, granted land Duxbury, Mass., 1640.

Francis, freeman Salem, Mass., 1633, removed Providence, R. I., 1638, later Warwick, R. I.; died 1645, leaving no issue.

John, captain of trading vessel, b. Buckinghamshire, Eng., 1630-31, came to N. E., 1644, locating at Salem, Mass., removed 1653 to that part of Reading now Wakefield, Mass., died 1723.

Matthew, resident Providence, R. I., 1644.

Thomas, merchant, planted colony Weymouth, Mass., 1622, later returned to England.

WESTOVER

Jonas, inhabitant Windsor, Conn., 1649, removed Killingworth, Conn., 1658, became resident Simsbury, Conn., where he died 1709.

WESTWOOD

William, b. Eng., 1606, came from Ipswich, Eng., to Cambridge, Mass., 1632, removed to Hartford, Conn., 1636, left no male issue.

WETHERBEE, WETHERBY

A town in West Yorkshire, Eng.; the wide or extended village; *weider* from the Dutch, a herdsman; *weideri* the place of fattening cattle, and *by,* a village.

John, b. Eng., 1650, settled Marlboro, Mass., 1675, removed Sudbury or Stow, Mass.

WETHERELL, WETHERILL, WITHERELL

John, b. Eng., 1694, freeman Watertown, Mass., 1642, died 1672.

Samuel, resident Scituate, Mass., 1680.

William, schoolmaster and preacher, b. Maidstone, county of Kent, Eng., 1600, came to N. E., 1635, resided Charlestown, Mass., and 1644 at Scituate, Mass., where he was minister of the second church; died 1684.

William, nephew of the preceding, resident Taunton, Mass., 1643.

WETHERIDGE

EDWARD, freeman Boston, Mass., 1644.

WEYMOUTH

JAMES, died Dover, N. H., 1678.

ROBERT, came from Dartmouth, Devonshire, Eng., to Kittery, Maine, in 1652.

TITUS, died Plymouth, Mass., 1656.

WILLIAM, brother of Robert, died New Hampshire, 1654.

WHALE

PHILEMON, freeman Sudbury, Mass., 1646, died 1676.

THEOPHILUS, b. Eng., 1615, settled Kingston, R. I., 1676, died 1719-20.

WHALEY, WHALLEY

Having greenish white eyes; wall-eyed. It is also a name of a village in Lancashire, Eng.

EDWARD, arrived Boston, Mass., 1660.

GEORGE, resident Cambridge, Mass., 1653.

WHAPLES

THOMAS, b. Eng., 1625, living Hartford, Conn., 1664.

WHARFF

NATHANIEL, married Casco, Maine, 1658.

WHARTON

EDWARD, glazier, Salem, Mass., 1655, died 1678.

PHILIP, resident Boston, Mass., 1656.

RICHARD, inhabitant Boston, Mass., 1661.

RICHARD, married Boston, Mass., before 1675.

WHEAT, WHEATE

JOHN, trader at Boston, Mass., 1686.

JOSHUA, b. Eng., 1618, came to Concord, Mass., 1635, returned Eng., 1640.

MOSES, brother of the preceding, b. Eng., 1616, at Concord, Mass., 1635.

WHEATLEY

GABRIEL, died Watertown, Mass., 1637.

JOHN, freeman Braintree, Mass., 1643.

LIONEL, freeman Boston, Mass., 1673.

WHEATON

A village on the river Nen, Northamptonshire, Eng. *Whitton,* Saxon, the white hill. *Whiddon,* Cornish British, white.

CHRISTOPHER, fisherman, Hull, Mass., 1676.

JEREMIAH, resident Rehoboth, Mass., 1676.

ROBERT, came from Swansea, Wales, first settled Salem, Mass. One of the original proprietors Rehoboth, Mass., 1643-46.

SAMUEL, came from Swansea, Wales, resident Swansea, Mass., 1669, afterwards at Rehoboth, Mass., died 1684.

WHEDON, WHEALDON, WHIELDON

A place where mines are worked. *Wheal* is frequently applied to signify a mine, and *dun* or *din,* a hill.

THOMAS, b. Eng., about 1635, took oath of fidelity New Haven, Conn., 1657, removed Branford, Conn., before 1667, died 1691.

WHEELER

A name of a trade.

EPHRAIM, freeman Concord, Mass., 1639, removed Fairfield, Conn., 1644; will dated 1669.

FRANCIS, joined the church Charlestown, Mass., 1645.

FRANCIS, at Salem, Mass., 1646.

GEORGE, b. Eng., 1600, freeman Concord, Mass., 1641.

HENRY, resident Salisbury, Mass., 1659.

ISAAC, living at Charlestown, Mass., 1639.

JOHN, barber, b. Salisbury, Wiltshire, Eng., 1584, came to N. E., 1634, one original proprietors Salisbury, Mass., located at Newbury, Mass., 1652.

JOHN, merchant, New London, Conn., 1667.

JOHN, freeman, Concord, Mass., 1690.

JOSEPH, freeman Concord, Mass., 1640.

MOSES, shipwright, b. Eng., 1598, settled, New Haven, Conn., 1638, removed Stratford, Conn., 1648, died 1698.

OBADIAH, farmer, b. Eng., 1608, settled Concord, Mass., 1638, died 1671.

RICHARD, at Medfield, Mass., 1645, later Lancaster, Mass., killed by Indians 1676.

ROGER, married Boston, Mass., 1659.

THOMAS, tailor, freeman Boston, Mass., 1637, died 1654.

THOMAS, resident Milford, Conn., 1639, removed Derby, Conn., 1664, died 1672.

THOMAS, resident of Lynn or Salem, Mass., 1635.

THOMAS, took oath of fidelity, New Haven, Conn., 1644.

THOMAS, brother of the first John, b. Eng., 1600, removed from Lynn, Mass., to Stonington, Conn., before 1669, died 1685.

THOMAS, b. Bedfordshire, Eng., 1620, signed petition Concord, Mass., 1643, removed Fairfield, Conn., 1644; will probated 1654.

THOMAS, married Concord, Mass., 1657.

TIMOTHY, b. Eng., 1601, freeman Concord, Mass., 1640, died 1687.

WILLIAM, brother of second Thomas,

removed from Concord, Mass., to Stratford, Conn., died 1666.

WILLIAM, freeman, Concord, Mass., 1660.

WILLIAM, married Boston, Mass., 1686.

WHEELOCK

From a village in Cheshire, England.

RALPH, clergyman, b. Shropshire, Eng.; settled Watertown, Mass., 1637, removed Dedham, Mass., 1638, died 1684.

WHEELWRIGHT

JOHN, clergyman, son of Robert W., b. Saleby, Lincolnshire, Eng., 1599, came to Boston, Mass., 1636, removed to Exeter, N. H., 1638, to Wells, Maine, 1641, and to Hampton, N. H., 1647, became resident Salisbury, Mass., in 1658, where he died 1679.

WHELDEN, WHELDING, WHELDON

GABRIEL, will probated Malden, Mass., 1654.

HENRY, at Yarmouth, Mass., 1643.

WHELPLEY

HENRY, at Stratford, Conn., 1645, removed Fairfield, Conn., 1653.

NATHAN, sea captain at New Haven, Conn., 1678, died at sea, 1687.

WHETCOMBE

JAMES, merchant, Boston, Mass., 1669.

WHIDDEN

MICHAEL, b. Eng., about 1650, member of the church, Portsmouth, N. H., 1699.

RICHARD, died Fairfield, Conn., before 1690.

SAMUEL, resident New Hampshire, 1680.

WHIPPLE

JOHN, b. Eng., 1617, freeman Ipswich, Mass., 1640, died 1669.

JOHN, carpenter at Dorchester, Mass., 1632, removed Providence, R. I., 1659, died 1685.

MATTHEW, brother of first John, b. Bocking, county of Essex, Eng., 1605, granted land Ipswich, Mass., 1638, died 1647.

WHIPPO

JAMES, married Boston, Mass., 1692, lived Barnstable, Mass.

WHISTON

HENRY, accepted freeman of Conn., living Huntington, L. I., 1664.

JOHN, resident Scituate, Mass., 1632.

WHITACRE, WHITTACRE, WHITAKER, WHITTAKER

Name of English origin; it appears on the Hundred Rolls as early as 1273. The north part of a graveyard allotted to the poor was called *whittaker,* from *wite,* a penalty, and *acre,*—a place of burial for criminals. A culprit who could not discharge the penalty of *wite* became a "*witetheow*" and was buried in the *whitacre.* Another definition is "the northeast part of a flat or shoal—the middle ground."

ABRAHAM, b. Eng., 1590-95, settled Salem, Mass., 1637, afterwards resided Haverhill, Mass.

JOHN, resident Watertown, Mass., removed Billerica, Mass., at Chelmsford, Mass., 1691.

RICHARD at Rehoboth, Mass., 1668.

WHITCHER

THOMAS, b. Eng., 1622, settled Salisbury, Mass., 1638.

WHITCOMB, WHETCOMB

JAMES, merchant Boston, Mass., 1662.

JOHN, son of Symon W., b. Dorsetshire, Eng., 1588, settled Dorchester, Mass., 1635, removed Scituate, Mass., 1644, afterwards removed Lancaster, Mass., where he died 1662.

WHITE

A name given from the color of the hair or complexion. It may be also local, derived from the Isle of Wight on the coast of Hampshire, England, so-called from the Welsh *gwydd,* wood from its primitive forest.

ANTHONY, b. Eng., 1607, came from Ipswich, county of Suffolk, to Watertown, Mass., afterwards proprietor Sudbury, Mass., died 1686.

BENJAMIN, married Roxbury or Ipswich, Mass., before 1683.

DOMINGO, resident Lynn, Mass., 1668.

EDWARD, b. Eng., 1593, came from Cranbrook, county of Kent, Eng., to Dorchester, Mass., 1635.

EDWARD, freeman Roxbury, Mass., 1647.

ELIAS, resident Marblehead, Mass., 1669-74.

EMANUEL, at Watertown, Mass., 1636, removed Yarmouth, Mass., 1642.

GAWIN, married Scituate, Mass., 1638.

GEORGE, married Rowley, Mass., 1671.

HENRY, took oath of allegiance Hadley, Mass., 1679.

HUMPHREY, at Ipswich, Mass., 1640.

IGNATIUS, married Charlestown, Mass., 1683.

JOHN, b. Eng., 1600, came from Shalford, county of Essex, and settled Cambridge, Mass., 1632, removed Hartford, Conn., 1636, removed Hadley, Mass., 1659, returned Hartford, Conn., where he died 1683.

JOHN, settled Lynn, Mass., 1633, removed Southampton, L. I., 1644, died 1662.

JOHN, son of Robert W., grandson of Robert W., of South Petherton, county of Somerset, Eng., bapt. 1602, settled at Salem, Mass., 1638, returned to Eng., 1648, and came back to Lancaster, Mass., 1653, where he died 1673.

JOHN, resident Watertown, and Cambridge, Mass., 1642.

JOHN, took oath of fidelity Kittery, Maine, 1640.

JOHN, living in what is now Brookline, Mass., before 1654, died 1691-92.

JOHN, resident Charlestown, Mass., 1658.

JOHN, feltmaker at Boston, Mass., 1669.

JOHN, married Taunton, Mass., 1680.

JOHN, freeman Roxbury, Mass., 1677.

JOSEPH, brother of Benjamin, inhabitant Roxbury, Mass., 1684.

JOSIAH, took oath of allegiance Hampton, N. H., 1678.

LAWRENCE, lighterman at Boston, Mass., 1677.

NATHANIEL, freeman Dorchester, Mass., 1643.

NICHOLAS, freeman Dorchester, Mass., 1643.

PAUL, resident Pemaquid, Maine, 1658.

RICHARD, carpenter, b. Eng., 1595, came to N. E. 1635, settled Sudbury, Mass., 1639.

ROBERT, resident Charlestown, Mass., before 1635.

SAMUEL, resident Braintree, Mass., 1689.

THOMAS, known as Capt. Thomas, b. Eng., 1599, freeman Weymouth, Mass., 1636.

THOMAS, freeman Sudbury, Mass., 1640.

THOMAS, died Charlestown, Mass., 1664.

THOMAS, joined the church Charlestown, Mass., 1668.

WILLIAM, woolcarder, came in the "Mayflower," died Plymouth, Mass., 1621, father of Peregrine W.

WILLIAM, b. Eng., 1610, came from London, Eng., to Ipswich, Mass., 1634, freeman Newbury, Mass., 1642, removed Haverhill, Mass., where he died 1690.

WILLIAM, b. Eng., 1610, came from county of Norfolk, Eng., to Ipswich, Mass., 1640, died 1684.

WILLIAM, resident Boston, Mass., 1647; left no male issue.

WILLIAM, b. Eng., 1621, came from London, Eng., to N. E., 1635, freeman Ipswich, Mass., 1671.

WILLIAM, resident Boston, Mass., 1688.

ZECHARIAH, at Salem, Mass., 1669, settled Haverhill, Mass., 1677.

WHITEHAND

GEORGE, joined church Charlestown, Mass., 1633.

WHITEHEAD

ISAAC, resident New Haven, Conn., 1648.

JOHN, married Branford, Conn., 1660.

RICHARD, resident Windsor, Conn., 1640.

SAMUEL, at Cambridge, Mass., 1635, removed Hartford, Conn., 1636, freeman New Haven, Conn., 1669.

WHITEHOUSE

THOMAS, blacksmith, settled Dover, N. H., 1658, died 1707.

WHITFIELD

The white field.

EDWARD, resident Reading, Mass., 1649.

HENRY, clergyman, b. Eng., 1597, one of the founders of the church Guilford, Conn., 1643, returned England, 1650.

JOHN, resident Dorchester, Mass., 1634, removed Windsor, Conn., 1635.

WHITFORD

The white ford.

WALTER, resident Salem, Mass., before 1668.

WHITHAN

HENRY, married Gloucester, Mass., 1665.

WHITING, WHITIN, WHITON

From the Saxon, signifying the white or fair offspring. The Saxon termination *ing,* denoted offspring or child, as *Cuthing,* the child of Cuth, *Dun-ning,* the brown offspring, etc. The name has been used ever since the adoption of surnames. Roger Witen is mentioned in the Doomesday Book in 1085. Allan de Witting, English ancestor, 1119.

GILES, resident Hartford, Conn., 1643.

JAMES, came from Hingham, Eng., to Hingham, Mass., freeman 1660.

NATHANIEL, miller, b. Eng., 1609, granted land Lynn, Mass., 1638, removed Dedham, Mass., 1640.

SAMUEL, clergyman, son of John W., mayor of Boston, Lincolnshire, Eng., where he was born 1597, freeman Lynn, Mass., 1636, died 1679.

WILLIAM, merchant, known as Major W., came from Boxford, county of Sussex, Eng., to Cambridge, Mass., 1633, one of original settlers Hartford, Conn., 1636, died 1647.

WHITLOCK

From the Saxon, signifying fair hair.

JOHN, died Fairfield, Conn., 1658.

WHITMAN

From *wight,* in old English, lively, quick, and *man,* or from Dutch, *wight,* weighty, ponderous, *wight-man,* a stout man, or it may be after all simply *white-man.*

George, settled Kingston, R. I., before 1669, at Wickford, R. I., 1674.

John, b. Eng., 1602, came from Norfolkshire, Eng., settled Dorchester, Mass., freeman Weymouth, Mass., 1639, died 1692.

John, freeman Charlestown, Mass., 1642.

Valentine, resident Providence, R. I., 1652.

Zechariah, brother of first John, b. Eng., 1595, came to N. E., 1635, at Milford, Conn., 1639, removed New Haven, Conn., 1643, died 1666.

WHITMARSH

John, resident Weymouth, Mass., 1655.

Nicholas, brother of the preceding, living Weymouth, Mass., 1661.

Simeon, brother of the preceding, inhabitant Weymouth, Mass., 1669.

WHITMORE, WHITTEMORE, WETMORE

The original family name was de Boterel or Botrel; the first English record is Peter de Boterel, living in Staffordshire in 12th century. The family soon after this took the name of the locality in which they resided, became known as Whitemere, signifying white mere or lake. This spelling was altered and modified until the present form of the name. Sir John de Whytemere was knighted on a battlefield in 1230 for valorous conduct and received a tract of land entitled Whytemere or white meadows. The English ancestry is traced to De Boteral of Staffordshire, Eng., in 1100. His grandson, Ralph, married Avsia de Whitmore, and his grandson John became Sir John de Whitmore.

Francis, son of Nicholas W., XVIIIth generation from De Boteral, b. Hitchen, Hertfordshire, Eng., 1625, resident Boston, Mass., 1630-41, removed Cambridge, Mass., 1648, died 1685.

John, appears at Wethersfield, Conn., 1638, removed Stamford, Conn., 1641, murdered by Indians 1648.

Thomas, b. Hitchen, Hertfordshire, Eng., 1594, settled Charlestown, Mass., 1639.

Thomas, b. Eng., 1615, came to N. E., 1635, settled Wethersfield, Conn., 1639-40, one of first settlers Middletown, Conn., 1649.

WHITNEY

From the Anglo-Saxon word *hwit,* white, and *ey,* water, or ige, an island; the literal signification being white water. The name is of remote English antiquity and the family was founded by Eustace 1085 and styled DeWhitney from the lordship of Whitney which he possessed and is mentioned in the Doomesday Book in that year. Turstin, a Fleming knight, was in the army of William the Conqueror; his great grandson in the twelfth century built a stronghold on the river Wye, where he took up his residence when the name was first taken as a surname. Sir Robert W. was knighted by Queen Mary 1553. It is also a place name from the parish of Whitney in Hertfordshire, England.

Henry, b. Eng. about 1620, first appeared in town records of Southold, L. I., 1649, afterwards lived at Huntington and Jamaica, L. I., and was resident Norwalk, Conn., 1665.

Jeremiah, at Plymouth, Mass., 1643.

John, son of Thomas, grandson of Sir Robert W., bapt. at parish of Isleworth near London, Eng., 1592, settled Watertown, Mass., 1535, died 1673.

WHITON, WHITTON, WHITTEN

James, resident Hingham, Mass., 1648, died 1710.

Thomas, b. Eng., 1599, came to N. E., 1635; where he settled is unknown.

WHITRED, WHITTRIDGE, WITTREDGE

Nathaniel, resident Lynn, Mass., 1637.

William, brother of preceding, b. county of Kent, Eng., 1599, inhabitant Ipswich, Mass., 1637, died 1668.

WHITTEMORE, WHITAMORE

Lawrence, b. Eng., 1572, came from Stanstead Abbey, county of Herts, Eng., freeman Roxbury, Mass., 1637; no issue.

Thomas, died Charlestown, Mass., 1661, was a resident of Reading, Mass.

WHITTEN

Jeremiah, resident New Haven, Conn., 1639, died 1682; no issue.

WHITTIER

Abraham, died Manchester, Mass., 1674.

Thomas, b. Eng., 1620-22, settled Salisbury, Mass., 1638, removed Haverhill, Mass., 1650, died 1696.

WHITTINGHAM

John, son of Baruch W., grandson of William W., the distinguished reformer of Eng., came from Southerton, near Boston, Lincolnshire, England to Ipswich, Mass., 1637, died 1649.

WHITTINGTON

Edward, granted land Andover, Mass., 1673.

WHITTLESEY

The name was first taken by the people living in Whittlesea Fens in the 10th century. William W. the English ancester 1187.

John, tanner and shoemaker, b. Eng., 1623, came in his childhood to Boston, Mass., 1635, married Saybrook, Conn., 1664, died 1704.

WHITWAY

Thomas, hotel keeper, resident of Wethersfield, Conn., removed Branford, Conn., 1646, died 1651.

WHITWELL

Bartholomew, resident Boston, Mass., 1665.

William, innholder at Boston, Mass., before 1653.

WICKENDON, WICKINGTON, WICKENDEN

William, inhabitant Salem, Mass., 1639, removed Providence, R. I., 1640.

WICKHAM, WIKEHAM, WICOM

From the Anglo-Saxon word, *wic,* the winding of a river or port, and *comb,* a valley. A town in Buckinghamshire, England—the sheltered place, house or town.

Daniel, resident Rowley, Mass., 1641.

Richard, at Rowley, Mass., 1661.

Samuel, resident Warwick, R. I., removed Newport, R. I.

Thomas, freeman Wethersfield, Conn., 1658, died 1689.

WICKS

Francis, living Salem, Mass., 1635, removed Providence, R. I., 1637.

John, tanner, b. Eng., 1609, came from Staines, county of Middlesex, Eng., to Plymouth, Mass., 1635, removed to Portsmouth, R. I., 1637, and to Warwick, R. I., 1643; killed by Indians 1675.

Richard, married, Malden, Mass., 1686.

Thomas, died Salem, Mass., 1656.

Thomas, freeman, Huntington, L. I., 1662.

Zachary, swore allegiance to Mass., 1652.

WICKWIRE

John, married, New London, Conn., 1676.

WIDGER

James, took oath of allegiance Pemaquid, Maine, 1674.

WIGGIN

A place name from *Wigan,* a town on the river Douglass, Lancashire, Eng.

Thomas, came from Shrewsbury, England; was one of earliest members of government of New Hampshire, 1631, resided Dover and Hampton, died 1667.

WIGGLESWORTH

Edward, b. Eng., 1604, resident New Haven, Conn., 1638, died 1653.

WIGHT

Israel, resident Boston, Mass., 1664.

Thomas, came from Isle of Wight at Watertown, Mass., 1635, removed Dedham, Mass., 1637, and to Medfield, Mass., 1649, died 1674.

WIGLEY

Edward, at Concord, Mass., 1666.

WILBORE, WILBUR, WILLBORE

A contraction of Wildboar.

Samuel, admitted church Boston, Mass., 1633, one of the corporation that purchased R. I., 1638, removed Taunton, Mass., finally to Boston, Mass., 1645; will probated 1656.

WILBORNE

Michael, married Boston, Mass., 1656.

WILCOCKS, WILCOX

From *will* and *cock,* which signifies little. A "Wilcock," one rather obstinate. The family of Anglo-Saxon origin seated at Bury St. Edmunds, county of Suffolk, before the Norman Conquest, lineage traced to 1200.

Daniel, resident Portsmouth, R. I., 1644, removed to Dartmouth, Mass., finally to Twerton, R. I.

Edward, came Newport, R. I., 1638, one of first settlers to form the civil government.

John, surveyor, inhabitant Hartford, Conn., 1639.

John, resident Dorchester, Mass., 1655.

Joseph, living Killingworth, Conn., 1663.

Stephen, at Stonington, Conn., before 1670.

William, linen weaver, b. St. Albans, Hertfordshire, Eng., 1601, freeman Cambridge, Mass., 1636, removed Stratford, Conn., 1639, later to Hartford, Conn., died 1653.

WILCOME, WELCOME

Richard, keeper of alehouse Isle of Shoals, N. H., 1683.

William, resident Scituate, Mass., 1673, killed in Indian fight, 1676.

WILD, WYLDE, WILDE

Richard, admitted inhabitant Charlestown, Mass., 1636.

William, b. Eng., 1605, came to N. E., 1635, at Rowley, Mass., 1643, resident Ipswich, Mass., 1650-1663.

WILDER

A traveler, foreigner or pilgrim, the same as *Waller*, from the Saxon *Wealh*, a traveler or one who inhabits the forest or grounds uncultivated. Nicholas W., the English ancestor, was a chieftain in the army of the Earl of Richmond at the Battle of Bosworth and landed from France at Milford Haven, England.

EDWARD, came from Plymouth, Eng., with his mother, Martha, a widow. His father, Thomas W., was of Shyslake, Oxfordshire, and proprietor of the Sulham estate in Berkshire, England. Edward was freeman Hingham, Mass., 1644, and died 1690.

THOMAS, brother of the preceding, b. Shiplake, Eng., 1618, proprietor Charlestown, Mass., 1638, removed Lancaster, Mass., 1659, died 1667.

WILDGOOSE

JOHN, took oath of fidelity Pemaquid, Maine, 1674.

WILEY

JOHN, b. Eng. about 1615, settled Reading, Mass., 1640.

WILFORD

GILBERT, resident Ipswich, Mass., 1668, removed Bradford, Mass., 1671.

JOHN, merchant, New Haven, Conn., 1641, removed Branford, Conn., before 1663, died 1678.

JOHN, resident Boston, Mass., 1656.

RICHARD, living Branford, Conn., 1679.

WILKES, WILKS

GEORGE, resident Dorchester, Mass., 1639.
ROBERT, merchant, died Salem, Mass., 1677, no issue.

THOMAS, shipwright, died Salem, Mass., 1662.

WILLIAM, living Boston, Mass., 1633, removed New Haven, Conn., sailed for England 1644, lost at sea.

WILKEY, WILKIE

JOHN, living Boston, Mass., 1653.

WILKINS

From *Wil*, and the patronymic termination *kins*, the son of William. Robert de Winton went from England to Glamorganshire, Wales, 1090.

BRAY, b. 1611, came from Wales to Salem, Mass., 1630, removed Dorchester, Mass., 1641, died 1702.

JOHN, died Salem, Mass., 1672.

JOHN, freeman Boston, Mass., 1673.

RICHARD, bookseller, b. 1624, resident Boston, Mass., 1685, died Milton, Mass., 1704.

THOMAS, married Topsfield, Mass., 1667, no issue.

WILLIAM, resident Gravesend, L. I., 1664.

WILKINSON, WILKESON

The son of Wilkins.
EDWARD, married Milford, Conn., 1672.

HENRY, tallow chandler, b. Eng., 1610, living Ipswich, Mass., 1635.

JOHN, only son of Prudence W., a widow, living Charlestown, Mass., 1635, removed Malden, Mass., where her will was probated 1655; John died 1675.

JOHN, constable Scarborough, Maine, 1640.

JOHN, freeman Connecticut, 1667.

LAWRENCE, b. Lanchester, county of Durham, Eng., came Providence, R. I., before 1646, died 1692.

THOMAS, on the tax list Billerica, Mass., 1679.

WILLARD, WILLERD

One who has a determined disposition; from *will*, choice, command, and *ard*, the Teutonic of *art*, strength, nature, disposition. Richard W. the English ancestor.

GEORGE, son of Richard W., of Horsmonden, county of Kent, Eng., where he was bapt., 1614, came to Scituate, Mass., 1638.

SIMON, Indian trader, brother of the preceding, bapt. Horsmonden, 1605, came to N. E., 1634, settled Cambridge, Mass., one first settlers Concord, Mass., 1636, removed Lancaster, Mass., 1657, bore the military title of Major, died Charlestown, Mass., 1676.

WILLET, WILLETT

Little William, or the son of William. Rev. Thomas W., b. 1510, rector at Bailey, Leicestershire, the English ancestor.

DANIEL, resident Windsor, Conn., 1672, died 1690.

FRANCIS, b. about 1634-35, married Newbury, Mass., 1669.

NATHANIEL, married Hartford, Conn., 1642.

THOMAS, known as Capt. Thomas, grandson of Rev. Thomas W., b. Eng., 1611, came Plymouth, Mass., 1632, settled at Swansea, Mass. On the subjugation of New Amsterdam by the English, he became mayor; he returned Swansea, Mass., where he died 1674.

WILLEY

ALLEN, husbandman, admitted church Boston, Mass., 1634.

ISAAC, resident Boston, Mass., 1640, removed Charlestown, Mass., 1644, and the following year New London, Conn.; died 1685.

THOMAS, living Dover, N. H., 1648.

WILLIAM, WILLIAMS

From the Belgic *Guild-helm,* harnessed with a gilded helmet; or, as others say, from *Welhelm,* the shield or defense of many. The early seat of the family was at Flint, Wales, also in Lincolnshire, England. Sir Robert W., ninth baronet of the house of Williams of Penrhyn, was a lineal descendant from Marchudes of Cyan, Lord of Abergelen in Denbighshire, of one of the fifteen tribes of North Wales, that lived in the time of Roderick the Great, King of Britons about A. D. 849. Howell Williams, Lord of Ribour, was progenitor of the Williams family of Wales.

ALEXANDER, able to bear arms Marshfield, Mass., 1643.

ARTHUR, freeman Windsor, Conn., 1640.

AUGUSTUS, resident Stonington, Conn., 1680.

BELSHAZZAR, died Salisbury, Mass., 1651.

CHARLES, resident Preston, Conn., 1689.

DANIEL, resident Providence, R. I., 1668.

DAVID, at Windsor, Conn., 1662, died 1685, no issue.

EDWARD, resident Scituate, Mass., 1643.

ELEAZER, joined the church Salem, Mass., 1637.

FRANCIS, sent over by Mason to Portsmouth, N. H., 1631, removed Barbadoes, 1645.

FRANCIS, resident Boston, Mass., 1686.

GEORGE, freeman Salem, Mass., 1634.

GREGORY, constable Isle of Shoals,, N. H., 1674.

GRIFFIN, resident Boston, Mass., 1686.

HENRY, at Scarborough, Maine, 1651.

ISAAC, cordwainer at Salem, Mass., 1660.

JAMES, resident Hartford, Conn., 1691, removed Wallingford, Conn., 1700.

JOHN, resident Scituate, Mass., 1643.

JOHN, living Newbury, Mass., 1641.

JOHN, inhabitant Windsor, Conn., 1639.

JOHN, at Salem, Mass., 1664, will probated 1697.

JOHN, butcher at Boston, Mass., 1684.

JOHN, merchant came from Chamberwell, county of Surrey, to Boston, Mass., 1670.

JOHN, married New London, Conn., 1686.

JOSEPH, living Boston, Mass., 1670.

MATTHEW, brickmaker and farmer, first located Watertown, Mass., settled Wethersfield, Conn., 1645.

MATTHEW, taxed Dover, N. H., 1657-68.

NATHANIEL, glover, freeman Boston, Mass., 1640, died 1661.

NICHOLAS, freeman Roxbury, Mass., 1652.

OWEN, freeman Newport, R. I., 1655, removed soon after Norwich, Conn., where he died 1682.

RICHARD, tanner, son of William W., b. Huntingdon, Glamorganshire, Wales, 1599, came to N. E., settled Salem, Mass., 1633. Among first purchasers of Taunton, Mass., 1637.

RICHARD, resident Boston, Mass., 1643.

RICHARD, living Branford, Conn., 1646, removed Fairfield, Conn., 1658.

RICHARD, living Stonington, Conn., 1670.

RICHARD, at Boston, Mass., 1672.

RICHARD, physician, at New Haven, Conn., 1691.

ROBERT, came from Norwich, county of Norfolk, Eng., freeman Roxbury, Mass., 1638, died 1693.

ROBERT, schoolmaster, freeman Providence, R. I., 1655, later Newport, R. I.

ROBERT, resident Boston, Mass., 1672.

ROGER, came to Dorchester, Mass., 1630, removed Windsor, Conn., 1636, returned to Dorchester, Mass., 1649.

ROGER, minister, son of James, brother of second Robert, b. Wales 1599, came to N. E. 1630, settled Salem Mass., removed Providence, R. I., 1635, died 1683.

ROGER, died Milford, Conn., 1656.

SAMUEL, living Yarmouth, Mass., 1643.

SIMON, took oath of allegiance, Hatfield, Mass., 1679.

THOMAS, "Mayflower" passenger, died soon after landing; no issue.

THOMAS, resident Plymouth, Mass., 1635.

THOMAS, ferryman, came to Boston, with Winthrop's fleet.

THOMAS, swore allegiance Saco, Maine, 1636.

THOMAS, made will at Boston, Mass., 1646.

THOMAS, living Rehoboth, Mass., before 1647.

THOMAS, at Eastham, Mass., 1655.

THOMAS, living Wethersfield, Conn., where he died 1693.

THOMAS, b. Eng. 1640, was at Groton, Mass., 1666.

THOMAS, b. 1664, living New London, Conn., 1670, died 1705.

THOMAS, married Newbury, Mass., 1696.

TIMOTHY, able to bear arms Marshfield, Mass., 1643.

WILLIAM, b. Eng. 1597, came from Great Yarmouth, Eng., to Salem, Mass., 1637.

WILLIAM, granted land Dover, N. H., 1653.

WILLIAM, cooper, b. Eng. 1625, settled Hartford, Conn., 1646, freeman 1654, died 1689.

WILLIAM, resident Huntington, L. I., freeman of Conn. 1664.

WILLIAM, resident New London, Conn., 1664.

WILLIAM, married Boston, Mass., 1660, killed in King Philip's War 1676.

WILLIAM, resident Boston, Mass., 1687.

WILLIAM, married Lynn, Mass., 1681.

WILLIAMSON

The son of William.

MICHAEL, b. Eng. 1605, came to Ipswich, Mass., 1635, removed R. I.

PAUL, resident Ipswich, Mass., 1635.

TIMOTHY, freeman Plymouth, Mass., 1647, removed Marshfield, Mass., 1649, died 1676.

WILLIAM, b. Eng. 1605, came to N. E. 1635.

WILLINGTON

ROGER, b. Eng. 1609-10, recorded Watertown, Mass., 1636.

WILLIS

Willy's, the son of Willy, the "s" being added for *son.*

EDWARD, married Boston, Mass., 1668, died 1698.

EXPERIENCE, died Boston, Mass., 1711.

GEORGE, freeman Cambridge, Mass., 1637.

GEORGE, b. Eng. 1602, son of Richard or Timothy W., came from Fenny Compton, Warwickshire, Eng., settled Cambridge, Mass., 1636, removed Hartford, Conn., 1637.

HENRY, resident Boston, Mass., 1653.

JEREMIAH, at Newport, R. I., 1655.

JOHN, freeman Boston, Mass., 1632, died 1634, no issue.

JOHN, married Boston, Mass., 1655.

JOHN, resident Duxbury, Mass., 1640, one first settlers Bridgewater, Mass., 1657.

JOSIAH, mariner, married Boston, Mass., 1675.

JOST or JOIST, surveyor of ordinance and cannonier, of Dutch descent, resident Boston, Mass., 1631, returned to Europe 1632, died at sea.

LAWRENCE, resident Sandwich, Mass., 1643.

MICHAEL, freeman Dorchester, Mass., 1638.

NATHANIEL, schoolmaster, brother of second John, original proprietor Bridgewater, Mass., 1657, died before 1687.

NICHOLAS, mercer from Bury St. Edmunds, county of Suffolk, Eng., freeman Boston, Mass., 1634, died 1650.

RICHARD, married Plymouth, Mass., 1670.

ROBERT, at Boston, Mass., 1643.

ROBERT, inhabitant Rowley, Mass., 1691.

ROWLAND, living Scituate, Mass., 1670.

THOMAS, farmer, settled Lynn, Mass., 1630, removed Sandwich, Mass., 1642.

WILLIAM, married Scituate, Mass., 1638.

WILLISTON, WILLINGSTONE, WILLSTON

JOHN, resident Ipswich, Mass., 1668.

JOSEPH, b. 1667, was resident Springfield, Mass., and of Westfield, Mass., 1691, died 1747.

WILLIX

BELSHAZZAR, married Salisbury, Mass., 1643, died 1651.

WILLOUGHBY

From the lordship of Willoughby in Lincolnshire, Eng., given to a Norman knight, Sir John de Willoughby, by William the Conqueror. The town or habitation by the willows.

FRANCIS, merchant, son of William W. came from Portsmouth Hampshire, Eng., settled Charlestown, Mass., 1638, died 1671.

WILLS

JOSHUA, married Windsor, Conn., 1670, died 1721.

NATHANIEL, resident Ipswich, Mass., 1670.

THOMAS, resident Kittery, Maine, 1670.

WILMORE

GEORGE, living Portsmouth, R. I., 1638.

WILMOT, WILMARTH, WILMOUTH

May be a corruption of *Guillemot,* a name frequent in France, in early times derived from *Guillaume,* William.

BENJAMIN, b. Eng. 1589, took oath of fidelity New Haven, Conn., 1647.

JOHN, freeman Rehoboth, Mass., 1658.

JOHN, died Boston, Mass., 1670.

JONATHAN, married Rehoboth, Mass., 1680.

NICHOLAS, resident Boston, Mass., 1650, will dated 1684.

RALPH, living Charlestown, Mass., 1649.

THOMAS, resident Braintree, Mass., 1649.

WILSHIRE

THOMAS, at Boston, Mass., 1652.

WILSON

The son of William or Will.

ANDREW, resident Boston, Mass., 1690.

ANTHONY, married Fairfield, Conn., 1643, died 1662.

BENJAMIN, among first settlers Taunton, Mass., 1638.

BENJAMIN, mariner, living Charlestown, Mass., 1655, died at sea 1667.

DANIEL, representative from Northampton, Mass., 1665.

EDWARD, miller Boston, also of Roxbury, Mass., died unmarried 1638.

EDWARD, joined church Charlestown, Mass., 1660.

EDWARD, residing Salem, Mass., 1646.

EDWARD, died Fairfield, Conn., 1684.

FRANCIS, married Woburn, Mass., 1683.

GAWIN, b. Scotland 1618, came from Paisley, Scotland, to Kittery, Maine, before 1652.

HENRY, freeman Dedham, Mass., 1641.

JACOB, freeman Braintree, Mass., 1641.

JAMES, residing Woburn, Mass., 1688.

JOHN, clergyman, son of Rev. William W., b. Windsor, Eng., 1588, came in Winthrop's fleet, first minister of the first church in Boston, Mass., died 1667.

JOHN, son of Roger W., b. Scrooby, Nottinghamshire, Eng., settled Woburn, Mass., 1655, died 1687.

JOHN, taxed Dover, N. H., 1666.

JOHN, freeman Billerica, Mass., 1690.

JOSEPH, brother first Benjamin, freeman, Dorchester, Mass., 1638, among early settlers, Taunton, Mass.

JOSEPH, resident Malden, Mass., 1673.

LAMBERT, surgeon, settled Salem, Mass., 1629, soon after returned to England.

MATTHEW, resident New Haven, Conn., 1642.

NATHANIEL, b. Eng. 1622, married Roxbury, Mass., 1645, died 1692.

PAUL, householder Charlestown, Mass., 1677.

PHINEAS, merchant, b. 1628, came from Dublin, Ireland, to Hartford, Conn., 1675, died 1692.

RICHARD, at Boston, Mass., 1639, removed Duxbury, Mass., 1643.

RICHARD, married Boston, Mass., 1654, died the following year; no issue.

ROBERT, early settler Windsor, Conn., removed Farmington, Conn., 1653, died there 1655.

ROBERT, resident Salem, Mass., 1662.

ROBERT, resident Cambridge, Mass., removed Salisbury, Mass.

ROBERT, Scotch descent, first on record, Marlboro, Mass., 1665.

SAMUEL, swore fidelity New Haven, Conn., 1644, removed Fairfield, Conn., 1649.

SAMUEL, married Fairfield, Conn., 1679.

SAMUEL, b. 1622, freeman Portsmouth, N. H. 1655, removed Wickford, R. I., 1674.

SAMUEL, married Woburn, Mass., 1682.

SAMUEL, brother first Joseph, freeman Malden, Mass., 1684.

THEOPHILUS, b. Eng. 1601, settled Ipswich, Mass., 1636, died 1689.

THOMAS, came to Roxbury, Mass., 1633, removed Exeter, N. H., 1637, where his will is dated 1643.

THOMAS, freeman Fairfield, Conn., 1664.

THOMAS, resident Milford, Conn., 1673.

THOMAS, settled Cambridge, Mass., 1635, removed Weston, Mass.

WILLIAM, joiner, son of William W., b. Dunnington, Lincolnshire, Eng., freeman Boston, Mass., 1636, died 1646.

WILLIAM, married Lynn, Mass., 1663.

WILTERTON, WOLTERTON, WINTERTON

GREGORY, tanner, original proprietor Hartford, Conn., 1637, died 1674, no issue.

WILTON

From a town in Wiltshire, England, so called from the river *Willey*, and *ton*, a town.

DAVID, freeman Dorchester, Mass., 1632, removed Windsor, Conn., 1636, and to Northampton, Mass., 1660; no male issue.

NICHOLAS, brother of preceding, married Windsor, Conn., 1656, died 1683.

WINCH

A place in county of Norfolk, England, from Welsh *Ynyis*, an island.

SAMUEL, first record Sudbury, Mass., 1671, married Framingham, Mass., 1674, died 1718.

WINCHCOMBE

From Saxon *Wincel*, a corner, and *comb*, a valley—a valley encompassed on each side with hills.

JOHN, resident Boston, Mass., 1670.

WINCHELL, WINSHALL, WINCHEL

From the Dutch, *winschaal*, a wine-bowl, a wine-shop; from German, *weinsall*, a wine-hall or shop.

ROBERT, at Dorchester, Mass., 1635, removed Windsor, Conn., 1638, died 1668.

WINCHESTER

A city of Hampshire, England, called *Caerwynt* by the Britons, from *Caer*, a city, town or fortified place; and *gwint*, wind, from its being a windy place. The Welsh *gwin* signifies wine, as if called the *"Wine City."* It is also defined as the "White City," from the Welsh *"Caer guenif,"* because it is built upon a chalky soil.

ALEXANDER, came to N. E. 1635, freeman Boston, Mass., 1636, removed Braintree, Mass., 1637, and to Rehoboth, Mass., 1644; died 1647.

JOHN, b. Eng. 1616, came from county of Herts, 1635, located Hingham, Mass., 1636, removed to what is now Brookline, Mass., 1650, died 1694.

WINCOL, WINCALL, WINKLE

HUMPHREY, came from Little Waldingfield, county or Suffolk, Eng., to Cambridge, Mass., 1634.

JOHN, resident Salem, Mass., 1631.

THOMAS, inhabitant Salem, Mass., 1631.

THOMAS, proprietor Watertown, Mass., 1642.

WINDOW

RICHARD, at Gloucester, Mass., 1648, died 1665.

WINDS, WENDES, WINES, WYNES

BARNABAS or BARNEY, freeman, Watertown, Mass., 1635, removed Southold, L. I., 1644.

FAINTNOT, resident Charlestown, Mass., 1635.

WING, WYNGE

A place name from a village in Buckinghamshire, England.

JOHN, settled Sandwich, Mass., 1640.

JOSEPH, freeman Woburn, Mass., 1678.

ROBERT, b. Eng. 1574, came from Ipswich, Eng., to Boston, Mass., 1634.

WINGATE

An English family of great antiquity, settled at Sharpenhoe, parish of Streatley, Bedfordshire, England. The manor of the family in the parish of Ellesborough in Buckinghamshire, in early days was called Wyngate. It was used as a surname in South England and Scotland prior to 1200. The first recorded name of the family was Hemyngde Wingate, lord of the manor 1154-1189.

JOHN, planter, b. Eng. before 1636, granted land Dover, N. H., 1658, died 1687.

WINKLEY

SAMUEL, came from Lancashire, Eng., to Portsmouth, N. H., 1680, later settled Kittery, Maine, finally returned to Portsmouth, N. H.

THOMAS, recorded Cambridge, Mass., before 1638, removed Watertown, Mass., 1642.

WINN, WINNE

The name of Welsh origin from *gwynne*, white; Rhodri ap Gwynedd, Lord of Anglesey, was born about the middle of 12th century. In the tenth generation from him was John Wynne at Meredith of Groydir, county of Caeravon, Wales, who died 1559.

EDWARD, came from Ipswich, Eng., settled Charlestown, Mass., 1638, one first settlers Woburn, Mass., 1641; will probated 1686.

WINNOCK

JOSEPH, resident Scarborough, Maine, 1665.

WINSHIP

Probably the same as Wineshop, Saxon *Win*, German *Wein*, and *Sceapian*, Saxon, to make, furnish; a maker or vender of wine.

EDWARD, son of Lyonel Winship or Wynshoph of Wilton, Ovingham, Northumberland, Eng., b. 1612-13, freeman Cambridge, Mass., 1635, died 1688.

WINSLEAD, WINSLAD, WINSLEED

JOHN, married Malden, Mass., 1652.

WINSLOW

A place name from the town of Winslow in Buckinghamshire, England. Original family seat in Worcestershire, England.

EDWARD, governor, son of Edward W., bapt. Droitwich, Worcestershire, Eng., 1595, "Mayflower" passenger, resident Marshfield, Mass., 1646, died 1654.

GILBERT, brother of the preceding, "Mayflower" passenger, returned to England before 1627, there died before 1650.

JOHN, merchant, brother of the preceding, b. Eng. 1597, came to Plymouth, Mass., 1623, removed Boston, Mass., 1657, died 1674.

JOSIAH, brother of the preceding, bapt. Droitwich, Eng., 1606, arrived Saco, Maine, 1631, removed Scituate, Mass., finally to Marshfield, Mass.; died 1674.

KENELM, joiner and planter, brother of the preceding, bapt. 1599, arrived Plymouth, Mass., 1629, removed Marshfield, Mass., 1641, engaged in the settlement of Yarmouth and other towns in Mass.; died Salem, Mass., 1672.

WINSOR, WINDSOR

The name is a corruption of Saxon word *Wind-shore,* from the shore of the Thames at Windsor, a town in Berkshire, England.

JOHN, resident Boston, Mass., 1667.

JOSEPH, inhabitant Lynn, Mass., 1637, removed Sandwich, Mass., 1643.

ROBERT, turner at Boston, Mass., 1644, died 1679.

WINSTON, WENSTONE

JOHN, resident New Haven, Conn., 1649, died 1697.

WINSWORTH

ROBERT, inhabitant Boston, Mass., 1646.

WINTER

CHRISTOPHER, married Scituate, Mass., removed to what is now Kingston, Mass.

EDWARD, resident Marblehead, Mass., 1668.

JOHN, tanner at Watertown, Mass., 1636; will probated 1662.

JOHN, inhabitant Scarborough, Maine, 1638, died 1645, no male issue.

WINTERTON

From the village of Winterton in the county of Norfolk, England, so called from its cold situation.

THOMAS, resident Providence, R. I., 1657.

WINTHROP

A corruption of Winthrop or *Winethrope,* the wine village, from *win,* wine, and *throp,* a village. ADAM Winthrop the English ancestor 1498.

JOHN, governor, only son of Adam, grandson of Adam, b. Edwardston, county of Suffolk, Eng., 1588, came to N. E. 1630, settled Boston, Mass., died 1649.

WINUS

JOHN, of Dutch descent, married New Haven, Conn., 1664.

WISE

A name given for the quality of wisdom.

HUMPHREY, at Ipswich, Mass., 1639.

JOSEPH, butcher, came to Roxbury, Mass., 1636.

NICHOLAS, freeman of Mass., 1645.

THOMAS, at Saco, Maine, 1636.

WISEMAN

DERIVATION of name same as Wise.

JAMES, resident Braintree, Mass., 1639.

WISWALL

A local name from the town of *Weiswell,* a town in Baden, on the Rhine, Germany.

JOHN, iron manager and general trader, b. Eng. 1602, came to Dorchester, Mass., 1634, removed Boston, Mass., 1655, died 1687.

THOMAS, brother of the preceding, settled Dorchester, Mass., 1634, removed Cambridge, Mass., in that part now known as Newton, Mass., 1654, where he died 1683.

WITCHFIELD

JOHN, freeman, Dorchester, Mass., 1633, removed Windsor, Conn., 1636, died 1678.

WITHAM

THOMAS, died Gloucester, Mass., 1653.

WITHERBEE, WITHERBYE

JOHN, b. county of Suffolk, Eng., about 1650, settled Marlboro, Mass., 1672. One of the founders of Stow, Mass.

WITHERDEN, WYTHERDEN

JOHN, at Scituate, Mass., 1643, removed Boston, Mass., 1650.

WITHEREDGE, WYTHERIDGE

EDWARD, mariner and merchant; joined church Boston, Mass., 1644.

WITHERS

THOMAS, sent by Mason, settled Kittery, Maine, 1631.

WITHINGTON

A contraction of *Wooderington.* From Saxon *wyderian,* to wither; and *dun,* a hill; the withered or dry hill. A place in Northumberland, England, *Weiderington,* the place of pasturing cattle; Dutch, *weide,* a pasture, *weider,* one who takes care of cattle, a herdsman.

HENRY, b. Eng. 1588, one of six founders of church, Dorchester, Mass., 1635, died 1667.

WILLIAM, resident Newport, R. I., 1638.

WITHMAN

JOHN, living Charlestown, Mass., 1641; name sometimes spelt Weightman.

WITT

JOHN, resident Lynn, Mass., 1650, died 1675.

WALTER, freeman Andover, Mass., 1691.

WITTEN

MICHAEL, acknowledged jurisdiction Mass., at Scarborough, Maine, 1658.

WITTER

From the Dutch, a whitener, a fuller, bleacher.

WILLIAM, b. Eng. 1584, settled Lynn, Mass., 1639, died 1659.

WITTONS
PETER, married Boston, Mass., 1652.

WIXAM, WICKSON
ROBERT, at Plymouth, Mass., 1643, removed Eastham, Mass., 1657.

WOLCOTT, WALCOTT, WOOLCOT
The name is of English origin. John Wolcott was the ancestor 1571.

HENRY, b. near Wellington in the southern part of Somersetshire, Eng., about 1578, freeman Dorchester, Mass., 1630, removed Windsor, Conn., 1636, died 1655.

JOHN, resident Salem, Mass., 1635.

JOHN, freeman, Cambridge or Watertown, Mass., 1635.

JOHN, blacksmith, resident New Haven, Conn.

JOSEPH, brother of the preceding, married Suffield, Conn., 1686.

WOLFE, WOOLFE
EDWARD, resident Lyme, Conn., 1671.

PETER, freeman Salem, Mass., 1634, one founders of church Beverly, Mass., 1667, died 1675.

WOLLASTON
JOSIAH, merchant Boston, Mass., 1666.

WOLSEY, WOOLSEY
That is *Wolds-ley,* from *wold,* a wood, a lawn, and sometimes a plain, and *lle,* or *ley,* a place.
GEORGE, resident of N. E. 1653.

WOLTEN
JOHN, came from Plymouth, Eng., 1633, returned England 1654.

WOOD, WOODS
This patronymic was translated from the French *DuBois* and the German *Wald.* It is an ancient surname in Scotland, first called *DuBosco.* The family bore trees in their coat-of-arms.

ANTHONY, married Ipswich, Mass., 1665.
DANIEL, resident Rowley, Mass., freeman Boxford, Mass., 1690.

EDMUND, living Springfield, Mass., 1636, removed Wethersfield, Conn., 1636, thence to Stamford, Conn., 1641, later Hampstead, L. I.

EDWARD, mariner, resident Boston, Mass., 1659.

ELIAS, living Dedham, Mass., 1658.

GEORGE, married Saybrook, Conn., 1660.

HENRY, settled Plymouth, Mass., 1641, removed Yarmouth, Mass., 1645, returned Plymouth, Mass., 1649.

HENRY, resident Concord, Mass., 1651.

HENRY, living Newport, R. I., 1670.

ISAIAH, b. 1627, married 1653, living Ipswich, Mass., 1668.

JEREMIAH, resident Stamford, Conn., 1641.

JOHN, b. Eng., 1610, pin maker, resident Sudbury, Mass., 1641, removed Marlboro, Mass., 1659, died 1678.

JOHN, b. Eng. 1609, resident Lynn, Mass., 1635, removed Salem, Mass., 1646.

JOHN, freeman Dorchester, Mass., 1643.

JOHN, settled Plymouth, Mass., 1636.

JOHN, freeman Newport, R. I., 1655.

JOHN, b. 1620, living Taunton, Mass., 1662.

JOHN, married Ipswich, Mass., 1676.

JONAS, living Springfield, Mass., 1636, removed Wethersfield, Conn., settled Stamford, Conn., 1641, thence Hempstead, L. I.

JOSEPH, married Taunton, Mass., 1680.

JOSIAH, b. Eng. 1629, settled Charlestown, Mass., 1650.

JOSIAH, resident Ipswich, Mass., 1684.

NATHANIEL took oath of fidelity Ipswich, Mass., 1678.

NICHOLAS, freeman Braintree, Mass., 1641, removed Dorchester, Mass., later to Medfield, Mass., 1656; will dated 1670.

NICHOLAS, resident Concord, Mass., 1642.

OBADIAH, baker, brother of the secoud Josiah, living Ipswich, Mass., 1649, died 1694.

RICHARD, member Artillery Company, Boston, Mass., 1642, died 1681.

RICHARD, resident Hingham, Mass., 1659, removed Marblehead, Mass., 1668.

RICHARD, inhabitant Norwalk, Conn., 1694, died at Wallingford, Conn., 1705.

ROBERT, died Dedham, Mass., 1638.

SAMUEL, living Ipswich, Mass., 1643.

SAMUEL, resident Watertown, Mass., 1653, one of early settlers Groton, Mass., 1663, died 1703.

SAMUEL, physician, settled Norwalk, Conn., 1683, removed Danbury, Conn., 1685.

STEPHEN, living Plymouth, Mass., 1643.

THOMAS, carpenter, b. Eng. about 1633, resident Rowley, Mass., 1654.

TRYALL, died Salisbury, Mass., 1678.

WALTER, brother third Henry, living Newport, R. I., 1676.

WILLIAM, author of "New England's Prospect," b. Eng. 1582, came from Matlock, Derbyshire, Eng., to Salem, Mass., 1629, returned to England 1633, settled Concord, Mass., 1638, where he died 1671.

WILLIAM, husbandman, b. Eng. 1608, came to N. E. 1635.

WILLIAM, married Portsmouth, R. I.

WILLIAM, resident Marblehead, Mass., 1668.

WILLIAM, living Stamford, Conn., 1639, removed Newton, L. I., 1640.

WOODBRIDGE

BENJAMIN, son Rev. John W. of Stanton, near Highworth, county of Wilts, Eng., where he was born 1622, came to Newbury or Cambridge, Mass., 1642.

JOHN, clergyman, brother of the preceding, b. Stanton, Wiltshire, Eng., 1613, came to N. E. 1635, settled at Newbury, Mass., one of the founders Andover, Mass., returned England 1647, and to N. E. 1663, locating at Boston, Mass., died 1695.

WOODBURY, WOODBERRY

JOHN, came from Somersetshire, England, first settled on Cape Ann 1624, one first settlers Salem, Mass., 1626, resident Dorchester, Mass., 1628, removed Beverly, Mass., 1630.

JONATHAN, mariner, married Boston, Mass., before 1677.

WILLIAM, brother of the preceding, b. Eng. 1589, granted land Salem, Mass., 1637, died 1677.

WOODCOCK

JOHN, b. Eng. 1615, came from Weymouth, Eng., to N. E. 1635, on tax list Springfield, Mass., 1638, removed Dedham, Mass., 1642, and to Rehoboth before 1673, thence Wrentham, Mass., 1675.

RICHARD, armorer, member of Artillery Company, Boston, Mass., 1658, died 1662.

WILLIAM, died Salem, Mass., 1648.

WOODDAM, WOODAM, WOODHAM

JOHN, bricklayer,resident Ipswich, Mass., 1648.

WOODDY, WOODDEY, WOODY

HENRY, freeman Concord, Mass., 1656, died 1700.

RICHARD, freeman Roxbury, Mass., 1642, died 1658.

WOODEN, WOODING, WOODIN

JOHN, resident Portsmouth, N. H., 1635, removed Hampton, N. H., 1643, thence Haverhill, Mass., 1646.

WILLIAM, married New Haven, Conn., 1643.

WOODFIELD

JOHN, living Scituate, Mass., 1646.

WOODFORD

THOMAS, b. Lincolnshire, Eng., settled Cambridge, Mass., 1632, removed Roxbury, Mass., 1633, and to Hartford, Conn., 1636, finally Northampton, Mass., 1654.

WOODHOUSE, WOODIS, WOODICE

JOHN, died Salem, Mass., 1659.

RICHARD, fisherman, Boston, Mass., 1638.

WOODHULL

WILLIAM, freeman Portsmouth, R. I., 1655.

WOODLAND

EDMUND, resident Salem, Mass., 1673.

JOHN, at Braintree, Mass., 1651, removed Mendon, Mass., 1663.

WOODLEY

WILLIAM, died Marblehead, Mass., 1682.

WOODMAN

The name is first given to those that lived in the forests.

ARCHELAUS, mercer, settled Newbury, Mass., 1635, died 1702, no issue.

EDWARD, brother of the preceding, came from Malford, a parish in Wiltshire, Eng., to Newbury, Mass., 1635.

RICHARD, b. Eng. 1590, freeman Watertown, Mass., 1635, removed Lynn, Mass., 1644, died 1647.

WOODMANSEY

JOHN, merchant Boston, Mass., 1659, died 1685.

ROBERT, schoolmaster at Boston, Mass., 1644, removed Ipswich, Mass., 1655, died 1667.

WOODROP

WILLIAM, clergyman, arrived Boston, Mass., 1674, removed Sherborn, Mass., 1685, returned to England 1687; no issue.

WOODRUFF

Woodrooff, from *wood-reeve*, the governor or keeper of a wood, a forester.

BENJAMIN, resident Salem, Mass., 1660-78.

JOSEPH, brother of the preceding, living Salem, Mass., 1660.

JOSEPH, married Farmington, Conn.

MATTHEW, original proprietor Hartford, Conn., 1636, removed Farmington, Conn., 1640, died 1682.

WOODWARD

Wood-ward, a forest-keeper or officer, who walked with a forest-bill, and took cognizance of all offenses committed. The name LaWodeward appears in the Hundred Rolls, 1273.

DANIEL, married Watertown, Mass., 1689.

EZEKIEL, resident Boston, Mass., 1654.

GEORGE, fishmonger from St. Botolph's

Billingsgate, London, b. Eng. 1600, came to N. E. 1635.

HENRY, physician, b. Eng. 1601, came to N. E. 1635, settled Dorchester, Mass., removed Northampton, Mass., 1659, died 1685.

ISRAEL, married Taunton, Mass., 1670, died 1674.

JOHN, married Taunton, Mass., 1675.

JOHN, freeman, Reading, Mass., 1691.

JOSEPH, resident Providence, R. I., 1676.

NATHANIEL, mathematician and surveyor, resident Boston, Mass., 1630.

PETER, freeman Dedham, Mass., 1642, died 1685.

RALPH, came from Dublin, Ireland, to Hingham, Mass., 1637.

RICHARD, miller, b. Eng. 1590, came from Ipswich, Eng., to Watertown, Mass., 1635, died 1665.

THOMAS, carpenter, Boston, Mass., removed Roxbury, Mass., 1660.

WOODWELL

MATTHEW, brickmaker, first record Salem, Mass., 1661; will probated 1691.

WOODWORTH

The farm or place in the wood.

HENRY, freeman Mass. 1643.

JOHN, resident Taunton, Mass., 1679.

WALTER, came from Kent, Eng., to Scituate, Mass., 1633.

WOOLEN, WOOLLEN

JOHN, resident New Haven, Conn., 1642.

WOOLERY, WOOLSWORTH, WOOLWORTH

RICHARD, weaver, b. 1648, settled Newbury, Mass., 1678.

WOOLEY, WOOLLY, WOLLEY

From *Wold-ley, uncultivated* lands; hills without forests.

EMANUEL, freeman Newport, R. I., 1656.

ROBERT, resident Fairfield, Conn., 1649.

WOOLRIDGE WOOLRYCH

JOHN, resident Dorchester, Mass., 1630, returned to England following year.

MICHAEL, living Fairfield, Conn., 1674.

WOOLSON

THOMAS, came from Wales, settled Cambridge, Mass., 1653, removed Watertown, Mass., 1660, died 1713.

WOOSTER

A corruption of Worcester (which see).

EDWARD, b. Eng. 1622, among first settlers Milford, Conn., 1642, also at Derby, Conn., 1652, died 1689.

WOOTERS, WOUTERS

JOHN, of Dutch descent, resident Branford, Conn., 1667-73.

WORCESTER, WORSTER

A county and city of England, name derived from the Saxon *were,* a forest, and *cester,* a camp or city. Some authorities claim it is from Warcester, the city or castle of strife, from the Saxon *woer,* war, strife, with which the ancient British name *Caerwrangon,* the castle or fort of strife and contention. It was a boundary line for many years between the Britons and Saxons.

WILLIAM, clergyman, the first minister at Salisbury, Mass., 1639, died 1695.

WORDELL, WODELL

WILLIAM, resident Boston, Mass., 1637, removed Portsmouth, R. I., 1643.

WORDEN

ISAAC, b. Eng. 1617, came to N. E. 1635.

JAMES, resident Boston, Mass., 1671.

PETER, came from Clayton, Lancashire, Eng., settled Lynn, Mass.; married Yarmouth, Mass., 1639; died in that year.

SAMUEL, resident Boston, removed Barnstable, Mass., 1684, died before 1698.

WORMALL, WORMELL, WORMWELL

JOSEPH, inhabitant Rowley, Mass., 1640, removed Boston, Mass., 1649, thence Scituate, Mass., where he died 1662.

WORMLEY, WORMELEY

RALPH, resident Dover, N. H., 1684.

WORMSTALL

ARTHUR, swore allegiance Wells, Maine, 1653.

WORMWOOD

HENRY, living Lynn, Mass., 1666.

WILLIAM, resident Kittery, Maine, 1640, living on Isle of Shoals, N. H., 1647.

WORNUM

WILLIAM, resident Boston, Mass., 1646.

WORRALL

JAMES, inhabitant Scituate, Mass., 1638.

WORSLEY

BENJAMIN, a resident of R. I. 1663.

WORTH

From the Saxon; a court, farm, possession, place, field or way; the place valued, sold or granted.

LIONEL, married Salisbury, Mass., 1655.

RICHARD, brother of the preceding, married Newbury, Mass., 1667.

WILLIAM, blacksmith and mariner, b. Devonshire, Eng., 1640, settled Nantucket, Mass., 1665, died 1724.

WORTHERN, WORTHEN, WATHEN

EZEKIEL, married Salisbury, Mass., 1661.

GEORGE, member of the church, Salem, Mass., 1641.

JOHN, settled Salem, Mass., 1641.

WORTHINGTON
NICHOLAS, settled Saybrook, Conn., 1649, freeman Hartford, Conn., 1668, removed Hatfield, Mass., 1677, where he died 1683.

WORTHLIKE
PETER, at Scituate, Mass., 1669.

WORWOOD, WORWARD
RICHARD, died Cambridge, Mass., 1644.

WRIFORD
JOHN, swore allegiance Pemaquid, Maine, 1674.

WRIGHT
English ancestor, John Wright, of Kelvedon Hall, Kelvedon, County of Essex, England.

ABEL, known by the title lieutenant, lived at Springfield, now Westfield, Mass., 1655, died 1725.

ANTHONY, resident Sandwich, Mass., 1643, removed Wethersfield, Conn., before 1658, died 1679; no issue.

BENJAMIN, came from Bolton, Eng., to Guilford, Conn., 1649, removed Killingworth, Conn., where he died 1677.

EDWARD, resident Concord, Mass., 1658, died 1691.

EDWARD, shoemaker, married Boston, Mass., 1657.

EDWARD, bore the military title of captain, resident Sudbury, Mass., 1659, died 1703.

EDWARD, married Scituate, Mass., 1664.

GEORGE, freeman, Braintree, Mass., 1642.

HENRY, freeman Dorchester, Mass., 1635.

ISAAC, came from county of Norfolk, Eng., to Hingham, Mass., 1637, died 1652.

ISAAC, died Lancaster, Mass., 1663.

JOHN, settled Charlestown, Mass., 1640, freeman Woburn, Mass., 1643, died 1688.

JOHN, represented Gloucester, Mass., in General Court 1648.

JOHN, living Newbury, Mass., 1650, died 1658.

JOHN, freeman Watertown, Mass., 1690.

JOSIAH, married Woburn, Mass., 1661.

NICHOLAS, at Lynn, Mass., 1637, removed Sandwich, Mass., 1643.

PETER, brother of the preceding, living Sandwich, Mass., 1638.

RICHARD, resident Lynn, Mass., 1630, removed Boston, Mass., 1636.

RICHARD, first record Plymouth, Mass., 1638.

RICHARD, resident Rehoboth, Mass., 1644.

ROBERT, member artillery company Boston, Mass., 1643.

SAMUEL, b. Eng., 1600, settled Springfield, Mass., 1639, removed Northampton, Mass., 1656; will dated 1663.

THOMAS, settled Watertown, Mass., removed Wethersfield, Conn., 1639.

THOMAS, married Guilford, Conn., 1658.

WALTER, weaver, inhabitant Andover, Mass., 1663.

WILLIAM, came to Plymouth, Mass., 1621, died 1633, no issue.

WILLIAM, died Sandwich, Mass., 1648.

WILLIAM, resident Boston, Mass., 1670.

WROTHAM, WORTHAM
SIMON, freeman Farmington, Conn., 1653, died 1689.

WYARD
JOHN, married Wethersfield, Conn., 1681.

ROBERT, resident Boston, Mass., 1662, of Hartford, Conn., 1666, died 1682.

WYATT, WIAT, WYAT
EDWARD, b. Eng. 1614, freeman Dorchester, Mass., 1645, died 1706.

JAMES, resident Taunton, Mass., 1643.

JOHN, living Ipswich, Mass., 1638, died 1665.

JOHN, sold property Windsor, Conn., 1649, removed Farmington, Conn.

THOMAS, died New Hampshire, 1670.

WYBORNE, WIBORNE, WEYBORNE
THOMAS, came from Tenterden, county of Kent, Eng., to Boston, Mass., 1638, died 1656.

WYER, WIER
EDWARD, married Charlestown, Mass., 1658.

NATHANIEL, at Newbury, Mass., 1637, removed Nantucket, Mass., 1640, died 1681.

PETER, at York, Maine, 1640.

ROBERT, resident Boston, Mass., 1646.

WYETH, WITHE, WYTH
BENJAMIN, at Hampton, N. H., 1644.

HUMPHREY, resident Ipswich, Mass., 1638.

NICHOLAS, b. Eng. 1595, living Cambridge, Mass., 1647, died 1680.

WYLEY, WEYLEY, WILLEY, WYLIE
A form of Willie or William; or wily, artful, sly.

JOHN, b. Eng. 1610, settled Reading, Mass., 1635.

THOMAS, living Dover, N. H., 1648-69.

WYLLIS
GEORGE, governor of Conn., b. Fenny Compton, Warwickshire, Eng., came to N. E. 1638, located Hartford, Conn.

WYMAN, WEYMAN

From the Dutch word *Weiman*, a huntsman, a hunter; one who shoots the game.

FRANCIS, tanner, son of Francis W. of the parish of Westmills, Hertfordshire, Eng., b. 1617, came to N. E., locating at Charlestown, Mass., one of the thirty-two inhabitants of that town who established Woburn, Mass., 1640; died 1699.

JOHN, tanner, brother of the preceding, bapt. West Mills, Hertfordshire, Eng., 1621, came to N. E. 1640, locating Charlestown, Mass., one of the first inhabitants of Woburn, Mass., 1640, died 1684.

JOHN, wheelwright, married Woburn, Mass., 1685.

THOMAS, tailor, resident, Boston, Mass., 1675.

YALE

DAVID, came from Wales, to Boston, Mass., 1637, returned to England 1654.

YARDLEY

JOHN, resident Braintree, Mass., 1688.

YATES

An old word for *Gate*. The same as Gates.

FRANCIS, removed to Stamford, Conn., from Wethersfield, Conn., 1641, afterwards to Westchester, N. Y., where he died 1682.

GEORGE, brother of the preceding, freeman of Conn. 1658.

HENRY, died Guilford, Conn., 1705.

JOHN, resident Duxbury, Mass., 1650.

YEALE

TIMOTHY, married Weymouth, Mass., before 1673.

YELINGS

ROGER, resident Boston, Mass., 1682.

YELL, YEAL

JOHN, married Ipswich, Mass., 1690.

YEO, YOW

THOMAS, married at Boston, Mass., 1654.

YEOMANS

A man free-born, a freeholder; one next in order to the gentry.

EDMUND, resident Charlestown, Mass., 1650, removed Haverhill, Mass., 1666.

EDWARD, settled Charlestown, Mass., before 1650.

YESCUTT

RICHARD, resident Ipswich, Mass.

YORK

A city in England next in esteem to London. The name is derived from *Eure-ric* or *Eouer-ric*, of *Euere*, a wild boar, and *ryc*, a refuge; a retreat from the wild boars which were in the forest of Gautries. The Romans called the city *Eboracum;* it is memorable for the death of two emperors, Severus and Constatius Chlorus, and for the nativity of Constantine the Great.

JAMES, b. Eng. 1614, came to Braintree, Mass., 1635, settled Stonington, Conn., 1660.

RICHARD, resident Dover, N. H., 1648.

SAMUEL, b. 1645, living Gloucester, Mass., 1695, died 1718.

YOUDAEL

PHILIP, at Gloucester, Mass., 1648.

YOUNG

CHRISTOPHER, came from Yarmouth, county of Norfolk, Eng., to Salem, Mass. 1638, died Wenham, Mass., 1647.

EDWARD, fisherman at Boston, Mass., 1691.

GEORGE, married Scituate, Mass., 1660.

HENRY, resident Concord, Mass., 1675.

JOHN, living Salem, Mass., 1638, removed Charlestown, Mass., where he died 1672.

JOHN, resident Plymouth, Mass., 1648, removed Eastham, Mass., where he died 1691.

JOHN, inhabitant Windsor, Conn., 1641, removed Southold, L. I., before 1650.

JOSEPH, resident Salem, Mass., 1638.

JOSEPH, brother of second John, married Eastham, Mass., 1679.

RICHARD, freeman Kittery, Maine, 1652.

ROBERT, took oath of allegiance York, Maine, 1681.

ROWLAND, brother of the preceding, b. Scotland, about 1625, freeman York, Maine, 1652.

YOUNGLOVE

Name given on account of his age and tender affection.

SAMUEL, b. Eng. 1606, came to Ipswich, Mass., 1635, died 1668.

YOUNGMAN

FRANCIS, cordwainer, married Roxbury, Mass., 1685, died 1712.

YOUNGS, YONGS

JOHN, clergyman, b. Eng. 1602, came from St. Margarets, county of Suffolk, Eng. to Salem, Mass., 1637, removed Southold, L. I., 1640.